CHILE

The Arica Desert to Tierra del Fuego

ROYAL CRUISING CLUB
PILOTAGE FOUNDATION

Ian and Maggy Staples
Tony and Coryn Gooch
Drawings by Maggy Staples

Edited by Oz Robinson

Imray Laurie Norie & Wilson Ltd
St Ives Cambridgeshire England

Published by
Imray Laurie Norie & Wilson Ltd
Wych House St Ives Huntingdon
Cambridgeshire PE17 4BT England
☎ +44 (0)1480 462114 *Fax* +44 (0)1480 496109
E-mail ilnw@imray.com.
Website http://www.imray.com

1st edition 1998

ISBN 0 85288 408 7

British Library Cataloguing in Publication Data.
A catalogue record for this book is available from the British Library.

This work, based on surveys over a period of many years, has been corrected from land-based to the ports and harbours of the coast, from contributions by visiting yachtsmen and from official notices.

CAUTION
Every effort has been made to ensure the accuracy of this book. It contains selected information and thus is not definitive and does not include all known information on the subject in hand; this is particularly relevant to the plans, which should not be used for navigation. The RCC Pilotage Foundation believes that this selection represents a useful aid to prudent navigation, but the safety of a vessel depends ultimately on the judgement of the navigator, who should assess all information, published or unpublished.

CORRECTIONS
The RCC Pilotage Foundation would be glad to receive any corrections, information or suggestions which readers may consider would improve the book. Letters should be addressed to the editor, *Chile,* care of the publishers.

CORRECTIONAL SUPPLEMENTS
This pilot book is amended at intervals by the issue of correctional supplements prepared by the RCC Pilotage Foundation. Supplements are supplied free of charge with the books when they are purchased. Additional supplements are also available free from the publishers on receipt of a stamped, addressed A4 envelope and a note of the name of the book for which the supplement is required.

WAYPOINTS
The Pilotage Foundation considers that waypoints should not be included in the text. The reasons are straightforward.

First, the estimation of latitude and longitude may vary by more than a mile between disciplines and there are three disciplines to be considered at any one moment: that used in this volume, that employed on the chart used by the navigator and that programmed into the aid in use. Each discipline may require its own correction and it is unlikely that all three will be the same. Only the first can be known to the author.

Second, waypoints should be chosen in relation to prevailing conditions. Given the inherent inaccuracies of all navigational aids, a waypoint, safe and sensible when visibility is 10 miles, may be dangerous and foolhardy when visibility is 10 metres. The detailed positioning of a ship in relation to the land depends upon interpretation of all information available, including that received by eye, and it does no harm to remind the navigator of this. When conditions are such that no information can be received by eye, encouragement of a false sense of security by adherence to a specified but possibly misleading waypoint is likely to create more problems than it solves.

Positions given in the text and on plans are intended purely as an aid to locating the place in question on the chart.

PLANS
The plans in this guide are not to be used for navigation. They are designed to support the text and should always be used with navigational charts.

All bearings are from seaward and refer to true north. Symbols are based on those used by the British Admiralty – users are referred to *Symbols and Abbreviations (NP 5011).*

Printed in Great Britain by The Bath Press

Contents

Preface, v

Introduction, 1
Organisation and Government, 1
Continental Chile, 1
Geography, 2
Weather, 3
Getting there, 4
Hydrographic information, 5
Lighthouses, 6
RDF beacons, 6
Search and rescue, 6
Security, 6
Money, 6
Supplies and gear, 7
Communications, 7
Transport, 7
Health, 8
Public holidays, 8

Section 1 Arica to Canal Chacao, 9
Section 2 Seno Reloncaví, Golfo de Ancud and Golfo Corcovado, 31
Section 3 Melinka to Laguna San Rafael, 51
Section 4 Canal Darwin to Golfo de Peñas, 74
Section 5 Golfo Peñas to Puerto Simpson, 85
Section 6 Puerto Edén to Canal Sarmiento, 99
Section 7 Canal Sarmiento to Puerto Natales and to Islote Fairway, 113
Section 8 The Straits of Magallan, Tamar to Dungeness, 127
Section 9 Cabo Froward to Brazo Noroeste, 144
Section 10 Brazo Noroeste to Cape Horn, 157
Section 11 The Pacific Islands, 173

Appendix
A. Formalities, 175
B. Weather Forecasts, 177
C. Weather Forecast Areas, 178
D. VHF Coast Radio Stations, 178
E. Direction Finding Stations, 179
F. BBC World Service, 180
G. Cruising in the South, 180
H. Natural History, 181
I. Bibliography, 183
J. Charts, 184
K. Glossary, 186

Index, 189

Preface

The RCC Pilotage Foundation

The Royal Cruising Club Pilotage Foundation was created by members of the RCC to enable them and others to bring their experience of sailing and cruising to a wider public and to encourage the aspiring sailor to cruise further afield with confidence.

The Pilotage Foundation, a registered charity whose object is 'to advance the education of the public in the science and practice of navigation', was established with a generous grant by an American member of the RCC, Dr Fred Ellis, and fulfils its remit by producing and maintaining Pilot Books and Cruising Guides. Present volumes range from the Baltic to the West Indies via West Africa and from Greenland to the Falklands.

The Foundation is extremely grateful and privileged to have been given the copyrights to Pilots written by a number of distinguished authors and yachtsmen, and is charged with the willingly accepted task of keeping the original books up to date. Such authors include Adlard Coles, Robin Brandon and Malcolm Robson. However as opportunity occurs the Foundation has initiated new works of which this Guide to the coast of Chile is the latest.

The Pilotage Foundation is particularly grateful to the Hon. Editor, Oz Robinson, as he has kept at the task of co-ordinating information from many sources over a period of some years, a task which he has tackled with his usual skill and dedication. It was sad that the work of Mariolina and Giorgio Ardizzi could not be incorporated but I hope the Foundation can assist in bringing this considerable volume of pilotage information to the attention of the public in the not too distant future.

W H Batten
Chairman and Director,
The RCC Pilotage Foundation
June 1998

In 1992 the Pilotage Foundation of the Royal Cruising Club (the RCC) realised the increasing interest of yachtsmen in cruising in Chile and began to collect information on the area. Early contributors were members of the RCC and the Ocean Cruising Club of Great Britain, with whom the Pilotage Foundation shares information. They included Hugh Clay, Willy Ker, David Lewis, Laurence Ormerod, Knick and Lynn Pyle, Harry Ross-Skinner, Hal Roth, Bill Tilman, Chris West and his father, Mr West snr. Some of these contributors also assisted Capitán Alberto Mantellero in the preparation of his book, *Una Aventura Navegando Los Canales Del Sur Chile,* which is the prototype of books of this nature on the area. Later a significant addition to our stock of knowledge was the contribution of John and Fay Garey and whilst most of their work has been absorbed into the body of the text, their note on flora and fauna remains in an appendix as it stood. The next major step resulted from a chance meeting with Tony and Coryn Gooch who without comment absorbed the fact of the Foundation's interest in the area, sailed away in *Taonui* for their second cruise from Arica to Cape Horn and later returned a detailed report with plans and including the note on the tandem anchoring system; theirs was a major contribution. During the season of 1997, two other boats, *Ardevora* (Tim and Sophie Trafford) and *Plainsong* (Francis Walker) cruised through the Magallanes and reported on anchorages. But the greatest contribution came from *Teokita* (Ian and Maggy Staples), which in the 1997/98 season set out to cover as many anchorages as possible between Valdivia and Puerto Williams. *Teokita's* crew checked and corrected information which had already been collected and provided information on anchorages not previously recorded. More importantly, plans most helpfully provided by *Taonui* were amplified then re-drawn by Maggy Staples who went on to draw all the other plans which appear in this volume, a very significant work.

Teokita had met *Toupa* (Yves Beauvillen and Marie Goaourit) in Tahiti and *Morgane* (Yves and Florance Monier) in Valdivia. They both produced many anchorage plans. During her travels, *Teokita* met and was helped by others who visited anchorages to verify and draw them. These were notably *Gordian* (Miles Horden), *Parmelia* (Roger Wallace), *Noomi* (Greger and Eva Dahlberg), *Ardevora* (Tim and Sophie Trafford). *Felice* (Hans-Petter Lien), as well as members of the Valdivia Yacht Club, especially *Oscar Prochelle* (Yate Clipper). *Northanger* (Greg Landrein and Keri Pahuk), *Najat* (Keith and Liz Post) and *Pelagic* (Skip Novak and Hamish Laird) also provided useful information. All these contributions greatly helped and are much valued as is the contribution of Katherine Thornhill who read the very first draft. In addition Pedro Llera of Diseño Malla in Valdiva was most helpful in digitising and transmitting the charts by e-mail to Imray.

This work is therefore a compilation of reports, believed reliable, from numerous sources and if the

Editor has failed to single one out, he can only apologise. He points out again, however, that by far the greatest contributions came from *Taonui* and *Teokita* and in particular that the work of Maggy Staples, based on inputs of varying standards of draughtsmanship and often checked in difficult conditions, is a vital contribution. To save time , her drawings were sent to Imrays from Chile via the Internet which contributed to the difference from the usual Imray style of plans.

It is a matter of regret that the Pilotage Foundation came to learn of the excellent work being done by *Saudade III* (Mariolina and Giorgio Ardizzi) in this field too late for it to be fitted into our production schedule. As it is, this guide only mentions some of the hundreds of anchorages that there are in the south. It would take another year or two to collect information about them and to include them all in one volume dealing with the whole of Chile is not practicable; one has to draw a line somewhere. It is to be hoped that the *Saudade* information too will be made available to the yachting fraternity in due course, possibly by means of a supplement to this book.

As ever, much painstaking and detailed work has been done by Imray staff, particularly Julia Knight, Alan Shepherd and Christine Coveney (who spent hours on the Internet). Their contribution towards putting the work together was essential.

This compilation is not, of course, a Pilot but a Guide. The intention of the Pilotage Foundation is to bring it up to date from time to time. In that context, contributions and comments from cruising yachts will be greatly appreciated. They may be sent to the RCC Pilotage Foundation, c/o Messrs Imray, Laurie, Norie & Wilson, Wych House, The Broadway, St Ives, PE17 4BT, England (*e-mail* ilnw@imray.com).

Oz Robinson
Editor
June 1998

Introduction

Organization and Government

The Republic of Chile is headed by an elected President and Congress (seated in Valparaíso though the Administration remains in Santiago). The country is organised into a metropolitan district and twelve other regions each with its own elected government and raising its own taxes; each region is subdivided into provinces.

The rights and wrongs of recent history are not of concern here but it is worth pointing out that though Chile has been turned into a democratic state that works, unlike most other South American countries, the armed forces continue to play a significant part in the life of the country. In the context of this work, the Chilean Navy, referred to as the *Armada,* based at Valparaíso, has absolute authority over every movement of all shipping throughout Chile. The procedures may be tedious at first but the form must be observed. Once a cruise is launched, matters become more relaxed. And let it be said now that all reports mention the unfailing patience, courtesy and helpfulness of the *Armada* in assisting yachts to keep to the rules.

The country

Most of the population of 14 million is of mixed ancestry. Only about 15% live outside towns and some five and a half million live in the metropolitan district of Santiago. Spanish is the common language but there are enclaves where Indian languages are spoken. Knowledge of English is not common, particularly away from population centres. If cruising in Magallanes it is important to have reasonable Spanish to communicate with the *Armada;* take a good Spanish dictionary.

There is religious freedom and though most Chileans are Roman Catholic, Episcopalian and Lutheran congregations are found in areas where foreigners have played a significant role in economic life.

Mining and agriculture are the main economic activities. There is comparatively little mechanical industry; Chile's light industry is competent though limited in scope and geared to the internal market. However, ships are understood. Besides the *Armada*, there is a considerable inshore fishing fleet and some commercial vessels. In the central area of Chile there are a growing number of yachts and cruising in the *canales* of the south is increasingly popular.

Arts and academic life are strong. Music, painting, poetry and prose thrive – Chile numbers two Nobel Prize winners for literature. Primary education is free and obligatory, the literacy rate is high and the education ladder is topped by six universities.

Cruising

The Pilotage Section of this guide works from north to south, so far as that is practicable; in the far south geography dictates that there has to be some doubling back. The section on the Pacific Islands comes at the end. Antarctica is not covered.

This guide is no more than an assemblage of information about ports and harbour from visiting yachtsmen whose work has been made available to the Pilotage Foundation of the Royal Cruising Club and to the Ocean Cruising Club of Great Britain. Further detailed information is available in official publications. Reference has been made to publications of the *Armada* and of the British Hydrographic Office in Taunton. The coastal notes of the first section were largely gleaned from published geographical descriptions.

Continental Chile

The North

This section of 1400M stretches from the border with Peru (18°S) to the Canal Chacao (42°S) which leads to Puerto Montt. It spans first a hot, dry, desert, then from about Quintero southwards, a Mediterranean climate which in turn merges into a temperate, very wet, zone. The coast has long stretches of inhospitable cliff and unapproachable beaches. It is punctuated by commercial harbours, some of which can handle yachts, and numerous anchorages of varying quality. South of Quintero yachting facilities improve. Valdivia (40°S) has good facilities and sheltered sailing in the river. Approximate distances between harbours, often considerable, are given in the text

Chiloé, Chonos and Península Taitao

The middle section is the area east of Isla Chiloé and the Archipiélago de Chonos, between Puerto Montt and the south end of Estero Elefantes at 47°S, some 300M south of Puerto Montt as the crow flies. The last 60M of the southern fjord of this region, Elefantes, is a cul-de-sac. In the north are miles of delightful but rainy cruising, through and round Chiloé and its off-lying islands and the more rugged islands and channels of the Archipiélago de los Chonos with its chain of high mountains. It has few urban intrusions and the whole region, still with some working boats under sail and ox carts in the countryside, deserves some months for exploration. On the coast at the south, Península Taitao leads round to Golfo de Penas, where the first (or last) of more consistently difficult weather may be expected.

The South

Golfo de Penas to Cabo de Hornos is roughly a thousand miles from end to end, discounting wiggles. Civil administration is divided between Regións Magallanes Norte and Magallanes Sur. The two regions are even more sparsely populated than Chonos. Puerto Edén (49°S 74°W) is the first settlement of any size and the next are in the far south, Punta Arenas or Puerto Williams. Puerto Natales, a major tourist town and source of supplies, is 60M off the main route. The route passes through many famous *Canales,* including Magallan and Beagle. Rugged, wet, often extremely windy with *ráfagas* churning the water into flying spume and *rachas* spinning yachts on their anchors (if they hold), the channels are awe inspiring but quite delightful and incredibly scenic in calm conditions. There are numerous anchorages where, with care, a yacht can be perfectly secure.

The routes described do not stray far from the main channels used by commercial shipping which the *Armada* favours and indeed in the far south, it is difficult to obtain permission to move away from them. The Guide first follows the main channel from Canal Messier along to the Magallan Straits and past Cape Froward to Dungeness. Subsequent sections follow the main channel from Cabo Froward to Puerto Williams and beyond. Working southward, departures from the main channel are marked as 'diversion' and the end of the diversion is marked as 'continuation'.

A more detailed introduction to the south is given in Section 5.

The Islands

Of the three Pacific territories, Islas Desventuradas (the Miserable Group of San Félix and San Ambrosio), are not worth visiting. Isla de Pascua (Easter Island) and the Archipiélago de Juan Fernández (which includes San Juan Bautista or Robinson Crusoe island) can be fitted into a stretched passage.

Geography

Continental Chile

Most of Continental Chile is contained between the Andes and the Pacific, between 18°50'S and 55°50'S, from the tropics almost to the roaring forties. In terms of nautical miles, though some 2300M long it is on average only about 97M wide until the far south where the country reaches the Atlantic. The dominant feature is the Cordillera de los Andes, the chain of mountains and volcanoes that runs the length of the country, the crest of which forms one of the boundaries with Argentina. The Andes are highest (7000m and more) in the middle and north of the range. At a short distance off-shore, depths of 7000m have been recorded. The stresses in the system occasionally produce tectonic movements resulting in earthquakes and tsunamis, sometimes catastrophic, as for instance at Valdivia in 1960 when the level of the ground sank 1m and two ships in the river sank.

In the north, the rainless Atacama desert covers the land from Arica on the Peruvian border to Copiapó, some 550M south. It has high daytime temperatures and cold nights. Mining – copper, nitrates, sulphates and salt – is the chief industry. To its south is a zone of semi-desert, still arid but with slight winter rainfall and irrigated agriculture, which then merges with the fertile central valley, the Chilean heartland, between Illapel and Concepción. This valley is protected from the ocean by the Cordillera de la Costa and is the main farming region of the country. Fruit, vegetables and cereals are grown, cattle raised and viticulture is practised in a Mediterranean climate. Temperatures average 28°C in summer and 10°C in winter, when most of the annual 350mm of rain falls. Santiago is situated in this valley.

Between Concepción and Puerto Montt rainfall increases markedly, reaching some 2500mm annually at the southern end. There is an important agricultural and timber industry. However, summers are sufficiently warm and sunny (peaking over 30°C) to attract many tourists to the Lake District, south of Temuco, a beautiful landscape of lakes, rivers, forests and snow-capped volcanoes. One of the world's three temperate rain-forests, *Bosque Valdiviano,* flourishes near Valdivia. It is an incredibly rich and complex assembly of trees and plants, many of them unique to the region.

South of Puerto Montt, the Cordillera de la Costa subsides into Isla Chiloé and the central valley is drowned behind Chiloé and the Archipiélago de Chonos to form one of the finest cruising grounds of the world. Though annual rainfall decreases here to about 2000mm, in winter there may be rain and high winds for days. Despite the rain, Chiloé is a popular place for summer holidays. It has a similarly lush, but subtly different, vegetation to that of Valdivia though much of the forest has been cleared for agriculture which, with tourism and salmon-farming, is the main economic occupation. On the mainland opposite Chonos, the countryside becomes less accessible by road and though the Carretera Austral now winds more than 500M south to Villa O'Higgins, the road has not yet displaced the ferry services of the area.

Beyond Cabo Ráper (47°S) the spine of South America, here re-named Cordillera Patagónica, runs to the shoreline and disintegrates into a myriad of islands, channels and fjords, with spectacular glaciers and mountains. The southernmost regions are cold, rainy and windswept for most of the year but spectacular when the summer sun shines. In Magallanes the scant population is dependent on sheep farming, fishing and, more recently, on oil and gas extraction and tourism.

Moving west to east at any latitude north of Cabo Raper, both terrain and climate are rapidly dominated by the Andes. In the far south, on the east side of the Cordillera Patagónica, there are grasslands, swept by the westerlies, formerly a great sheep farming region.

The Islands

Isla de Pascua is the remnant of now extinct volcanoes. The island is famous for its unique statues, carved by early inhabitants whose ancestry is still in dispute (though a consensus seems to be forming around a Polynesian origin; Thor Heyerdahl's theory of settlement from the South American mainland now seems to be disputed to the extent of being discredited). Though fertile, it has a rugged coastline and the very variable weather which, along with its isolation, is challenging for visiting yachts. Perhaps partly because of the difficulties, the island retains a unique romanticism and mystery, and a it can be rewarding if one is lucky with conditions.

The islands of Archipiélago de Juan Fernández are more attractive and with a slightly greater claim to being a cruising ground, since there are at least two to it. They are warm and humid, with a variety of flora some of which is unique. Facilities are limited and there is no absolutely secure shelter. There has been off-shore seismic activity but nothing on-shore and nothing serious within the last 150 years.

Weather

Systems

The South Pacific High sits within the area bordered roughly by the Equator to the north, Easter Island to the south-west, and the continent of South America to the east. It moves north in winter and south in summer. The fringe of the south-east trades runs along the Chilean coast from about Concepción northwards; to the south the westerlies gain strength. Inshore, the Westerlies may be diverted north or south by the Andes. Winds from an easterly quadrant are rare or short lived on the coast although they may blow 200 or 300M offshore.

The South Pacific High is generally powerful enough to keep the frontal systems which spin off the westerlies of the roaring forties south of Valparaíso. Some systems slip through, however, especially in winter.

A feature of great importance in southern Chile are the *katabatic* winds of the mountains which produce sudden and violent squalls, known as *rachas*.

Rain and temperature

In the north, on the borders with Peru and Bolivia, rainfall is zero, the landscape warm (more than 30°C in summer), stony and deserted. Southwards the hot desert region gives way to a Mediterranean climate with winter rainfall which increases as latitude increases until at Valparaíso it is some 360mm a year. Then quite sharply there is a change to a temperate climate with warm summers, cool winters and much more rain. At Valdivia (40°S) the annual rainfall is 2460mm, varying from less than 100mm per month in summer to around 400mm in midwinter. The inland waters of the cruising grounds from Puerto Montt to Cape Horn are given a little shelter from the heaviest rainfall by the seaward ranges but rain and snowfall is little short of 2000mm a year, less in summer though often falling for days in winter. Temperatures in the far south seldom rise above 20°C in summer – 14°C is a common mid-day temperature – and not far above freezing in winter. Sea temperatures in summer range between 10 and 12°C.

The effect

Sailing down the Long Coast of the north, almost all the natural harbours offer protection from the predominant southerly winds. These winds are weak in the north and there are frequent calms. The southerlies strengthen to the south – a spinnaker or poled-out cruising chute is a useful sail for northbound yachts. By Valparaíso (33°S) they are often strong and there are also strong sea breezes (though winds would be a better word) blowing on-shore. At San Antonio, for example, south of Valparaíso, vessels are advised to enter at night or at daybreak when the SW winds which raise a heavy swell are at their lowest. Along this stretch there is scant protection from the occasional northerly gales. Caldera (27°S) is usually reckoned to be the northern limit of northerly winds.

Around Valdivia the westerlies begin to make themselves known but, as indicated, they tend to be deflected either northwards or southwards by the Andes. South of Puerto Montt, north winds are about as common as south winds, more from the north in winter, more from the south in summer, both with rain on three days out of four.

Beyond Archipiélago de Chonos, the incidence of bad weather increases though rain decreases. The winds are stronger and more from the west and north. There are violent squalls – *rachas* gusting well above F11 are not uncommon, up-rooting poorly moored boats with ease. Bad weather is only alleviated, not eliminated, in the summer. In the far south, winter gales tend to be more frequent but less severe than summer gales.

Forecasts

See appendix B for radio forecasts and weatherfax, appendix C for a map of the forecast areas. Forecasts can be obtained from lighthouses in the south and in some ports a synoptic chart is posted. El Mercurio (a daily paper) publishes a coloured chart based on satellite observations giving an accurate picture of the position of frontal systems.

The sea

The Peru or Humboldt current comes inshore near Cabo Raper and drifts north along the coast in a band some 50 to 150 miles wide at about half a knot. It often slants towards the coast which can be dangerous as it cools the surrounding air and causes fog. Off Cabo Raper the current may drift any way, even east, but the tendency is either north or south. Along the southern coast the west wind drift moves south-east and increases up to 1 knot towards Cabo de Hornos. Between summer and winter, sea temperatures vary from 20 to 15°C in the north and 9 to 5°C in the south. Once or twice a decade, the system is upset by *El Niño,* a mass of warm Pacific surface water. This, when it reaches the coast around Ecuador, pushes south, blocking the lower rungs of the food ladder and causing wide disruption to dependant life as well as upsetting the climate in places as far apart as Australia and Brazil, California and Tierra del Fuego.

Tides are noticeable along the North Coast but tidal ranges are generally less than 1m. South of Puerto Montt, tidal ranges can be as much as 10m and there are strong to very strong (8kt) tidal driven streams in some of the channels. The tide tables *(Tabla de Mareas)* of the Chilean Hydrographic Office (SHOA, or *Servicio Hidrográfico y Oceanográfico de la Armada de Chile)* are essential – see Hydrographic Information below. The SHOA publication is numbered N3009.

Swell is always present on the coast except, strangely, in an area around Cabo Jorge (52°S) where about once a month there appears to be none. Storms in the south produce swell in the north days after it was generated.

Tsunamis (*maremotos*), caused by submarine earthquakes, are of little consequence to a vessel at sea in deep water. Their effect on shore can be serious, like that of a catastrophic tide, low and high. A tsunami warning system is run by New Zealand and the USA. Warnings are issued from Oahu (Hawai'i) and promulgated from Arica, Antofagasta, Coquimbo, Valparaíso, Talcahuano and Puerto Montt.

Getting there

There are essentially four routes by which yachts arrive in Chile:

1. down or across the Atlantic
2. from the North Pacific or Central America
   a. offshore around the South Pacific High or
   b. inshore along the coasts of Ecuador, Peru and Chile
3. across the South Pacific.

Down the Atlantic

The Brazilian coast is renowned as a pleasant and interesting cruising area. South of Brazil there are very few sheltered anchorages. The Argentine coast is very shallow with strong north/south tidal flows. The river mouths are very shallow and treacherous. Caleta Horno (45°03'S 65°42'W) is the only easy anchorage on the coast.

There are two schools of thought about the best strategy. The first is to stay close to the coast along the 50 metre depth line. Here it is said that the wind and waves are lighter. The other is to stay well offshore (150–200 miles) to avoid the bad seas and strong winds that blow off the coast.

The Pacific offshore route

This is the traditional sailing ship route from the north Pacific to southern Chile or the Horn. The theory is to sail close-hauled on a southerly course between 90° and 120°W until the westerlies are encountered around 35° to 40°S, and then run into Valdivia (39°S) or Puerto Montt (41°30'S). Much depends upon the time available for the passage. If coming through Panama in January or February, too late for the cruising season in Chile, some yachts visit the Galápagos, about 900M, and then go on to Tahiti and the Australs before turning towards Valdivia or the Horn; going this way, the distance from the Galápagos to Valdivia is about 8800M. A middle route lies via Gambier, about 7000M and an even shorter route passes by Isla de Pascua, about 4000M, but don't count on being able to land there.

A more direct route is to sail south from Panama to Salinas, Ecuador, about 670 miles, and then make an off-shore loop of about 3100M to Valdivia or crawl down the coast. At first, the winds in the Gulf of Panama are light and variable and thunderstorms are common. It is advisable to stay well off the coast of Colombia, closing the coast around the border with Ecuador. If going off-shore, most of the remainder is close hauled, beating across the south-east trades with a reach or run in to the coast at the end. For a boat that is happy beating in rough conditions, this route may be preferable as it takes less time than the other routes. Unfortunately the high is unstable; the weatherfax from Valparaíso is useful, even if only to tell you why you are still hard on the wind. If you end up in the centre of the high for any length of time the winds will be very light so it is best to leave with full fuel tanks.

The Pacific inshore route

The inshore route is almost all against the prevailing southerly wind and the Humboldt Current. A not untypical passage following the coast from Salinas, Ecuador to Valdivia logged a total of 3,360M, 1,460M under motor and 1,900 under sail.

The Humboldt Current flows up the coasts of Peru and Chile at a rate of 0·5 to 1·5 knots. The prevailing wind is from the south and follows the coast. During the day it is reinforced by the thermal effect of air flowing from over the cold waters of the Humboldt Current onto the warm land. The strength of the thermal wind increases during the summer months. It is often easier to travel at night when the wind is lighter and frequently has an offshore slant.

Dealing with the officials in Peru is time consuming, very frustrating and expensive.

Fortunately there are anchorages where there are no settlements and hence no officials. The Peruvian coast is 1,150M long with few sheltered anchorages, necessitating several overnight legs. In Chile, the anchorages and towns become more frequent. The straight line distance from Arica to Valparaíso is 870M but under sail as much as 1,150M may be logged and the average distance between anchorages rises to about 60M. Although the prevailing winds are decidedly from the south, there are occasional north winds lasting 12 – 24 hours with calms during the night. Though there are fewer anchorages along the 600M from Valparaíso to Valdivia, there is a greater likelihood of west or south-west winds making for easier sailing on a close reach.

This route takes more time than the offshore route but has a number of attractions. The coastal towns in northern Chile are worth visiting. So few yachts travel this coast that the welcome is generous. The anchorages in the Atacama desert are a unique experience. With the availability of anchorages, the inshore route is a great deal easier than the rough offshore passage, particularly for smaller yachts.

Across the South Pacific

The visitors book at the Valdivia Yacht Club periodically records the arrival of a yacht direct from Australia or New Zealand. The weather along the 5000M route from New Zealand is dominated by the depressions which track across the Southern Ocean between 50° and 60°S producing a strong westerly flow up to about 35°S. Gales are most common over winter and their number lessens in November. Tropical cyclones, which generally keep to the western end of the South Pacific, are most likely between January and March and can affect conditions in higher latitudes. With an eye to cruising Patagonia in the Spring, the best choice appears to be to cross in November or December between 40° and 45°S but the decision will be affected by conditions at the time of the start. Places to aim at are Puerto Williams after rounding Cape Horn, Castro via Boca de Guafo, or Valdivia. Puerto Montt via Canal Chacao is possible providing detailed charts and local tidal information are available. Do not attempt to enter the Patagonian canals elsewhere; the landfall is highly complex and there are no ports of entry.

Timing

In elastic terms, the cruising season for the North Coast is September to May and for the south, November to April. Much depends upon the overall plan, for instance whether you are going east or west around south Chile, whether you plan to cross the Pacific after visiting Chile or merely to go North. Even with no knowledge of the plan, some points may be made:

If coming from the north with the intention to cruise Chiloé and Chonos, aim to arrive there early in the season, especially if planning to continue to Patagonia. If approaching Chile from the Atlantic, a later start may be preferable bearing in mind that the passage upwind from Puerto Williams to Puerto Montt might be achieved in a month at a push.

A yacht can be laid-up satisfactorily at Algorrobo, Valdivia and Puerto Montt. In addition each year a number of yachts over-winter in Puerto Williams, tied up alongside the yacht club. The mooring is sheltered and secure. Yachts have been left elsewhere, such as Castro, but at some risk.

Formalities

See Appendix A. When approaching any port listen on Ch16 and, if not called, call the *Capitán del Puerto.*

Cruising or passage making

Before leaving port for any destination, all vessels (including Chilean) must obtain a *zarpe* (a route permit; *zarpar* is to weigh anchor) from the *Armada.* See Appendix A.

Hydrographic information

General

Charts are listed by the nationality of their origin, UK, US or Chile. Small scale charts are listed first, followed by those at a larger scale

Chilean charts have the most detailed information but UK charts are sometimes easier to handle, especially when trying to locate places. The strip maps in this guide which accompany the sketch charts should be helpful in that context. It must be remembered that a sketch chart is a sketch and is not based on a proper survey.

Official information

Chilean, British and US navies swap information and that obtained by one can be expected to appear in another's publication. The Chilean authority is the *Servicio Hidrográfico y Oceanográfico de la Armada* (SHOA). SHOA charts are about the same price as those of the British Hydrographic Office. They are obtainable from their office in Valparaíso, at *capitanías* of other major ports (including Puerto Williams and Punta Arenas), through UK chart agencies (but that takes months) and the Armchair Sailor Bookshop, Newport, Rhode Island which often has the *Atlas Hidrográfico* (see below) in stock.

SHOA produces its own Pilots but the UK Pilots to South America, NP 6 & 7, are comprehensive.

The large scale Chilean charts are a necessary adjunct to this guide if going south of Puerto Montt. SHOA's *Atlas Hidrográfico de Chile* contains all the Chilean charts and is priced at US$120; it represents remarkable value for money. The charts are reduced, beautifully printed and clear but a really good magnifying glass, preferably with an interior light, is necessary. The atlas as a whole is difficult to handle in a seaway but individual sheets can be abstracted for chart work.

Coast lights are not totally reliable. They are

supervised by a branch of the *Armada,* the *Dirección General del Territorio Marítimo,* DIRECTEMAR. A light list *(Libro de Faros y Señales de Niebla)* is issued annually. The UK equivalent is the *Admiralty List of Lights Volume G NP80.* One or the other should be aboard.

A certain amount of tidal information is given in the text based on the UK *Admiralty Tide Tables Vol 3 NP203.* The information is, however, patchy and the tide tables *(N3009 Tabla de Mareas)* produced by SHOA should be obtained.

Warning

Some charts are based upon British Naval surveys of the nineteenth century. Many, but not all, of the old charts have been re-surveyed and re-drawn by SHOA to conform to the database WGS 84. Locations in this text are quoted from various sources and in many cases the database is not known to the Editor. This is particularly important to note in respect of locations south of Puerto Montt where differences of up to two miles have been reported when GPS has been matched against a charted or quoted position. The cause is possibly due to differences between the database of the charts and that used by the GPS receiver which may, or may not, have been WGS 84. The essential point is that the relationship between GPS and a chart can not be relied upon and the ship's position must be checked visually. In the last stages of an approach, the eyeball is more reliable than GPS.

Unofficial information

When cruising south of Puerto Montt, the *Navigator Guide – Una Aventura Navegando los Canales del Sur Chile* by Alberto Mantellero is very helpful and has provided many leads which have been followed up by contributors to this volume.

Lighthouses

The characteristics of lighthouses are included just in case they are needed. In the south, a yacht should be safely moored before dusk; sailing at night is fool-hardy.

RDF Beacons

Although superseded by new techniques, RDF beacons are included as, if working (and often they are not), they remain as back-up to other systems. An estimated range in nautical miles is given for marine radio beacons and the power of the transmitter is given for aero beacons. A list is at Appendix E.

Search and rescue

The Search and Rescue organisation, *Sistema Chileno de Notificación de la Situación de los Buques,* is known as CHILREP. It is run by the *Armada* and commanded by a Vice Admiral. Besides inshore waters and Chilean Antarctica, it covers the Pacific south of 18°12'S and east of 120°00'W to 67°16'W; south of 58°21'S the eastern boundary is 53°00'W. Although, according to CHILREP literature, participation is not obligatory for foreign ships, failure to comply with *zarpe* requirements may initiate a search.

Rescue boats are run by DIRECTEMAR and in the south are stationed at Puerto Montt, Castro, Chacabuco, Puerto Natales, Punta Arenas and Punta Williams.

Security

Chile is one of the safer countries of Latin America. Thefts from yachts are rare and generally owners have not found it necessary to remove deck-stowed working gear whilst in port. It is a matter of judgement whether to lock up if leaving the boat for a few hours. Any club with reasonable facilities tends to be security conscious, often with a 24 hour guard, and many owners employ a *marinero* to keep a boat ship-shape; the system discourages pilfering.

Ashore, the usual centres attract the usual petty criminals – pickpockets at bus terminals and so forth. The port areas of Valparaíso and Puerto Montt have a reputation for petty theft.

On a national plane, the security of the border with Argentina remains a sensitive matter and yachts visiting the Tierra del Fuego area must take particular care to obey the regulations.

Money

The unit is the Peso, indicated by the dollar sign $. Notes are $10.000, $5.000, $2.000, $1.000 and coins $100, $50, $10, $5 & $1. Large denomination notes are difficult to change. It is useful to arrive with a supply of low denomination US dollar notes to trade for pesos, particularly if arriving in Magallanes where banking facilities are very limited.

Take travellers cheques denominated in US dollars. They can be cashed for pesos at large hotels and some supermarkets, also at travel agencies and *casas de cambio* (which may give a better rate than other change agencies). Banks outside Arica, Antofagasta, Santiago and Puerto Montt for some reason will not handle travellers cheques. Some banks in Santiago will cash travellers cheques for US dollars (for instance the American Express Bank). Banking hours are 0900–1400 Monday to Friday.

In certain circumstances, for instance staying in a hotel with a published tariff, it is possible to avoid the 18% IVA if paying by credit card or in US dollars by cash or cheque.

Credit cards are widely used. Identification by passport is usually required. In supermarkets the card and passport should be shown to the management (usually a desk near the entrance) before making a purchase. Cash against Mastercard can be obtained at branches of Fincard (open Monday to Friday 0900–1400hrs, then 1530–1730hrs in the south and 1600–1800hrs in the north), at branches of the Banco de Santiago or against Visa cards at branches of the Banco de Concepción (queues in banks are generally worse than in Fincard).

Supplies and gear

Provisions

In northern and central Chile very good foodstuffs are commonly available. In the Magallanes, there are good supplies in Puerto Natales, Punta Arenas and Ushuaia. Puerto Edén and Puerto Williams have little or nothing to spare. There are excellent wines, many unknown outside Chile, good local spirits (*pisco*, Booths gin manufactured under licence) and some genuine but unknown, and therefore unpopular, Scotch whiskys can be had for prices less than those in the duty free at Gatwick.

Shellfish

Shellfish, particularly mussels and clams, are plentiful in the south. The danger to be aware of is the likelihood of the *marea roja,* the red tide, a bloom of algae discolouring the water. The curse exists up both sides of the American continent to high northern latitudes. The algae produce neurotoxins which are absorbed by bi-valves (e.g. mussels but not other shellfish such as *centollas*). Eating affected bi-valves is invariably fatal; there is no antitoxin. Inquire locally. Algae come and go. If around, news travels fairly fast and on *zarpes* and their shipping broadcasts the *Armada* notes any prohibition of collecting or eating shellfish (though the prohibition may not make the distinction between bi-valves and other shellfish).

Ship's stores

Spares for UK gear are hard to come by and though much can be extemporised take spares for all mechanical and electrical gear. US manufactures are more easily obtained than European. See Appendix A.

Nearly everyone smokes, particularly fishermen. Take cigarettes to trade with.

Special requirements

Apart from heavy weather, cold weather and ocean going gear, the importance of really strong ground tackle cannot be overemphasised when cruising south of Puerto Montt. See Appendix F. Radar can be of great assistance.

Communications

Time

Standard time is UT −4 hours. Summer time, UT −3 hours, operates between early October and early March.

Radio

Important: VHF is mandatory. See appendices for other detail. It is worth asking the *Armada* for their publications on maritime telecommunications services but their information is not always up to date, even in respect of their own schedules.

Telephones

There are eight telephone companies in Chile. Telephone and fax calls may be made, and telephone tokens (*fichas*) bought, from their call offices *(Centros de Llamada)*, open 0800–2300hrs. Phone boxes accept either *fichas* or coin, not both; *fichas* may also be bought at cafés, newsagents etc. which may also allow the use of their phone. Not all phone boxes handle international calls.

Operators at a call office may understand the function of a British Telecommunications card; others on the end of a telephone may not. When making an international call away from a call office, the selected company's access code is first entered, then 00, then the country code. The efficacy of the companies varies with the destination of the call; inquire locally which company is best for the circumstance of the call and for its access code.

The international code for calls to Chile is 56; within Chile, national area codes are preceded by 0.

Mail

Each town and many small villages have a post office, signed as *Correo*. Usual hours are 0830–1230 and 1430–1800 Monday to Friday and 0900–1230 on Saturday. Either buy stamps or have mail franked at the *Franqueo* counter and then post it at the office. Street post boxes *(buzon)* are rare. Airmail to and from Europe or North America takes about 5 days, sea mail ten weeks with luck.

Yacht Clubs will hold mail. It is usually only necessary to name the club and the port if the full address is not known.

Poste restante facilities are available but mail is held for 30 days only (ask for the *lista de correos)*. The envelope will be filed alphabetically under the first letter in the address. The address must start with the surname; do not put an initial or a title first. If staying awhile in Chile, it may be worth renting a post office box *(casilla)*.

Transport

For more detail about public transport see *Guía Turistica del Chile,* available from newspaper kiosks, or an up to date copy of the Lonely Planet or Travel Companion volumes, both titled 'Chile and Easter Island'.

Air

Several companies serve Chile from the East and North. From the West, Chile is served only by Air New Zealand from Auckland and LanChile (or Lan-Chile, Lineas Aereas Nacionales de Chile) from Papeete and Isla de Pascua (heavily booked in January and February).

Within Chile, Lanchile, Ladeco, Nacional and Alta maintain separate and extensive nets serving places and ports north of Chiloé but only Punta Arenas and Puerto Williams in the south. Schedules are published daily in El Mercurio. There are several small lines with light aircraft serving such centres as Puerto Natales and Puerto Williams. There is a small airport tax.

Rail

Except for the line from Arica to La Paz, passenger services do not run north of Valparaíso. Southwards the line runs as far as Temuco. It is very rough and extremely slow. A *Guía Turistica* is available at major stations.

Santiago has an efficient French-built metro.

Buses

Medium and long distance bus services are very good. The best have all mod. con. and sleeper-seats (but do not sit at the back near the heads). *Salón-cama* has 25 seats, *semi-cama* 34 and *salón-ejecutivo* 44. Turbus and Tramaca have a good reputation. Tickets from the central bus terminal found in most towns – book ahead in the high season. Arica – Santiago 28 hours; Santiago – Puerto Montt, 12 hours. Bone shaking micros work local routes, with few formal stopping places and very low fares.

Car hire

There are many car hire firms, expensive and often short of cars at peak holiday times. Prices quoted generally do not include IVA or insurance – be careful about the latter for if the latter is inadequate, a foreign driver involved in an accident may find himself staying in Chile longer than planned. The Automóvil Club de Chile runs an agency with discounts for affiliate members.

Taxis

Taxis have meters (50% extra after 2100hrs and on Sundays) but negotiate fares for out of town and long journeys. Tips not expected unless for some extra service such as baggage handling. All cities have *collectivos*, which have fixed fares little more expensive than bus fares. Like buses, they work between collecting points.

Health

If coming from Panama, Colombia or Bolivia, yellow fever inoculations may be required. Otherwise there are no requirements but typhoid and hepatitis should be considered (inoculations against type B are not available in Chile).

All towns have medical and dental centres. Attention is quick and efficient. Credit cards are often acceptable. Prescription drugs are available over the counter at pharmacies.

In the south, ultra-violet radiation is strong compared to that in low latitudes. Pay particular attention to the prevention and alleviation of sun-burn.

Public Holidays

1 January New Year's Day
March/April Easter
1 May Labour Day
21 May Navy Day
25 May Corpus Christi
29 June St Peter and St Paul
15 August Assumption
11 September National Liberation Day
18 and 19 September Independence Days
12 October Columbus Day
1 November All Saints
8 December Immaculate Conception
25 December Christmas

In addition, there are numerous local religious, folk and cultural festivals. January to March is the main holiday season.

Section 1
Arica to Canal Chacao

Introduction

The characteristics of this coast are hundreds of miles of inhospitable beach and cliff with the few places to land or shelter widely spaced; of a north going sea drift and north going winds, often light to nonexistent in the north and strong in the south. Rainless desert in the north, a Mediterranean climate with winter rains in the middle and a temperate climate in the south with greatly increased rainfall winter and summer and greater intrusion of winds from the north in the winter.

Tides

The following are listed:

a. Mean Spring Range
b. Mean Neap Range
c. The time difference with the standard port, Valparaíso. Variation in the differences between HW and LW is usually zero and never more than 12 minutes.

1·1 Arica

18°28'S 70°19'W

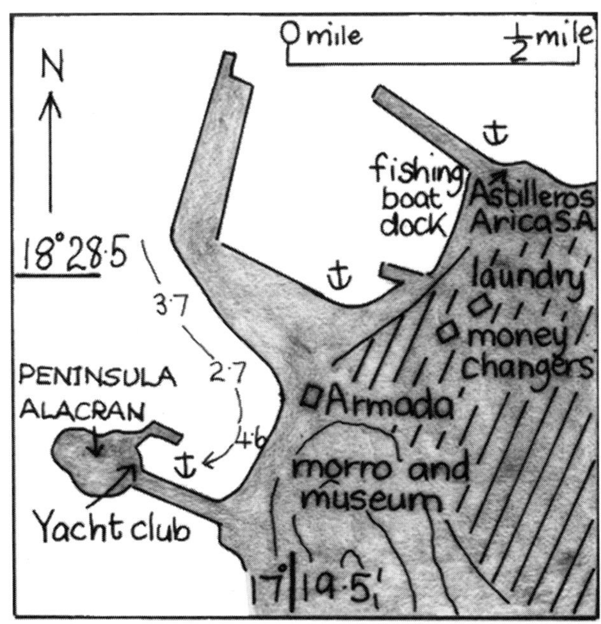

Arica. (Charted positions)

Distances

Callao–570–Arica–70–Pisagua

Charts

UK *3070* US *22221* Chile *110, 101*

Lights

To the north

1987 La Concordia 18°20'·8S 70°21'·5W
Fl.G.5s.41m14M
White tower, orange bands 21m Ra refl.
Aero Fl.R on top Fl.5s on building 1·4M E

Harbour

1986 Molo de Abrigo 18°28'·2S 70°20'·0W 19m14M
Red round concrete tower 12m
1985 North Mole 18°28'·0S 70°19'·3W Fl.G.5s.6m4M
Green round GRP tower 4m F.Y.10m10M on platform 770m ESE
1984 **Peninsula Alacrán NW end 18°28'·9S 70°20'·3W** Fl.15s.22m19M
White GRP tower red band 8m
1983 TV Tower 18°29'·3S 70°19'·6W
Fl.R.2·5s190m20M

To the south

1978 Punta Pichalo 19°35'·5S 70°15'·5W
Fl.12s.54m13M
White GRP tower, red band 4m 309°-vis-221°

RDF beacons

3776 Arica, Chacalluta Airport 18°20'·95S 70°19'·38W
c/s *ARI* 340kHz 1·0kW 24hr
3778 Iquique, Chucumata Airport 20°34'·05S
70°10'·90W c/s *UCU* 368kHz 0·4kW 24hr

Tides

a. 0·9m
b. 0·5m
c. −1hr 03min

Port communications

Port Ch 16 ☎ 23 22 84.
Club de Déportes Náuticos Ch 68 ☎ 22 43 96

General

Arica, pop. about 170,000, rainless and warm (average 24°C in summer, 19°C in winter), sits under the Morro de Arica, a granite headland, scene of a C19 battle with Peru. It is a resort for Bolivians, with surfing, bathing, restaurants, hotels etc. About half Bolivia's foreign trade passes through Arica and it is the terminal for the oil pipeline to Bolivia. The port has a fishing fleet, the town has fish meal plants

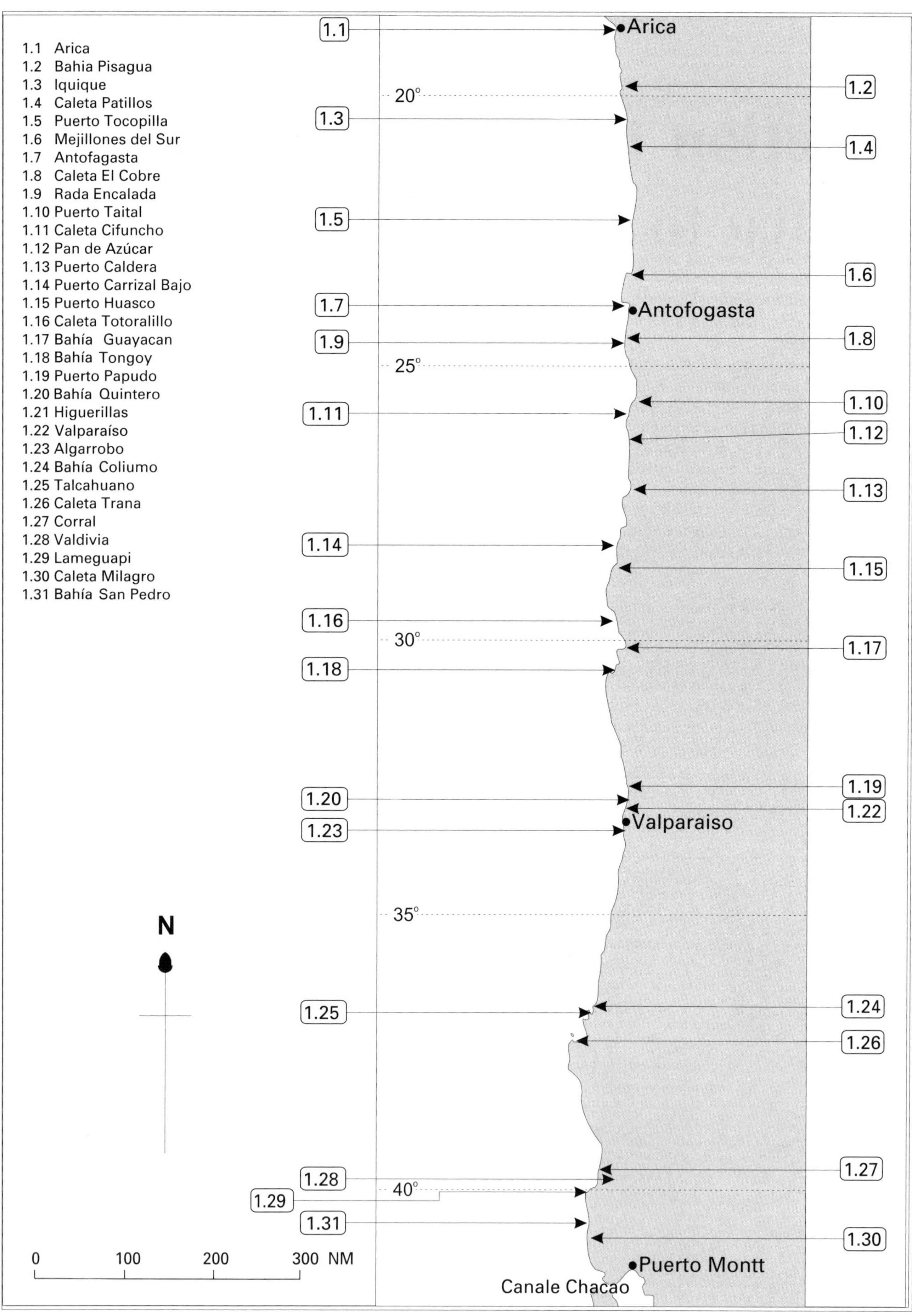
1.1 Arica
1.2 Bahia Pisagua
1.3 Iquique
1.4 Caleta Patillos
1.5 Puerto Tocopilla
1.6 Mejillones del Sur
1.7 Antofagasta
1.8 Caleta El Cobre
1.9 Rada Encalada
1.10 Puerto Taital
1.11 Caleta Cifuncho
1.12 Pan de Azúcar
1.13 Puerto Caldera
1.14 Puerto Carrizal Bajo
1.15 Puerto Huasco
1.16 Caleta Totoralillo
1.17 Bahía Guayacan
1.18 Bahía Tongoy
1.19 Puerto Papudo
1.20 Bahía Quintero
1.21 Higuerillas
1.22 Valparaíso
1.23 Algarrobo
1.24 Bahía Coliumo
1.25 Talcahuano
1.26 Caleta Trana
1.27 Corral
1.28 Valdivia
1.29 Lameguapi
1.30 Caleta Milagro
1.31 Bahía San Pedro
Arica
20°
Antofogasta
25°
30°
Valparaiso
35°
40°
Puerto Montt
Canale Chacao
N
0 100 200 300 NM

and a car assembly plant; it also has a reputation as a transit centre for narcotics.

If the first port of call in Chile, on arrival visit the *policia* for immigration, the *Aduana* for clearance and the *Armada* for a *zarpe*; the Club de Déportes Náutico will help.

Tourism
Day tour Parque Nacional Lauca and Lago Chungará (4600m, cold). Half day: Valle de Azapa. *Local* Catedral San Marco and old Custom House, now Casa de Cultura (Mon–Sat 1000–1300hrs, 1700–2000hrs), both designed by Gustave Eiffel (of the tower); footpath up Morro de Arica, 10 minutes walk from Colón, good views.

Approach
A traffic separation scheme operates in the approach; see charts. The yacht harbour is behind Peninsula Alacrán, not the Molo de Abrigo.

Morro Arica (150m) and Morro Gorda (216m) are conspicuous, the red granite of Morro Arica showing white in the sun. The prevailing wind is SW, strongest in the afternoon, dropping at night, and a land breeze sets in from early morning to about 0900hrs. There may be a 1–2kt set in the roadstead running in either direction parallel to the shore. Swell is common.

Arrival
Arriving in Arica from the north, boats should call the *Armada* on Ch 16 VHF, at least 10 miles out. Instructions will be given for clearance by the *Armada* and other authorities (*Aduana* and *Armada* offices are on the east side of the commercial harbour). Most yachts under 40 feet can then proceed to the yacht club just to the south of the town.

Anchorage
Yacht Club moorings are on the NE side of Peninsula Alacrán (Isla Alacrán is joined to the mainland by a causeway) and protected by a breakwater. The yacht club anchorage is within the breakwater which gives good protection from the prevailing southerly winds. The anchorage is subject to surge which lasts several days when major storms in the south send large swells up the coast of Chile. This occurs most frequently in the winter months. Visiting yachts are tied fore and aft on buoys behind the causeway leading to the club. There is a 24 hour free launch service.

Facilities
Astilleros Arica SA a major boat construction and repair yard for large fishing boats in Arica, have been very helpful to visiting yachts. Maximo Lira 1099, Casilla 202 Arica ☎ 251784 or 225043 *Fax* 251412.
Travel-lift and hard standing at Astilleros Arica.
Fuel from garages in town.
Water from the Club's pontoon (depth 2m); pick up the buoy and secure stern-to.
Fincard; Banco Osorno (VISA); many Casas de Cambio on the corner of 21 Mayo and Colon.
Market at Mercado Central (Sotomayor, between Colón and Baquedano, mornings only) and Terminal Agropecuario (buses marked 'Agro'); supermarket at San Martin and 18 de Septiembre.
Laundries Lavandería Moderna, 18 de Septiembre 457; Americana, Lynch 260 ☎ 231 808.
Club de Déportes Náuticos, excellent facilities – restaurant, showers, swimming area.
British Consulate: Baquedano 351 ☎ 231 960 Casilla 653. Also Consulates of Brazil, Bolivia, Denmark, Italy, Norway, Peru & Spain.

Communications
Air, rail and bus connections to Chile & Bolivia, air, rail and bus connections to Peru, air connections to Ecuador
Car hire Hertz, Budget, American, GP, Viva.
Telephone ENTEL, CTC and VTR, 21 de Mayo 345, 0900–2200. Area Code 80.

Passage

Between Arica and Caleta Chica (19°20'S 70°17'W) the cliffs are broken only by two *quebradas* (ravines), Vitor and Camarones. South of Caleta Chica there are cliffs and beaches. The few bights are either deep and steep-to or rock strewn.

1·2 Bahía Pisagua

19°35'S 70°13'W

Distances
Arica–70–Pisagua–50–Iquique

Charts
UK *3030* US *22205*– Chile *110, 113*

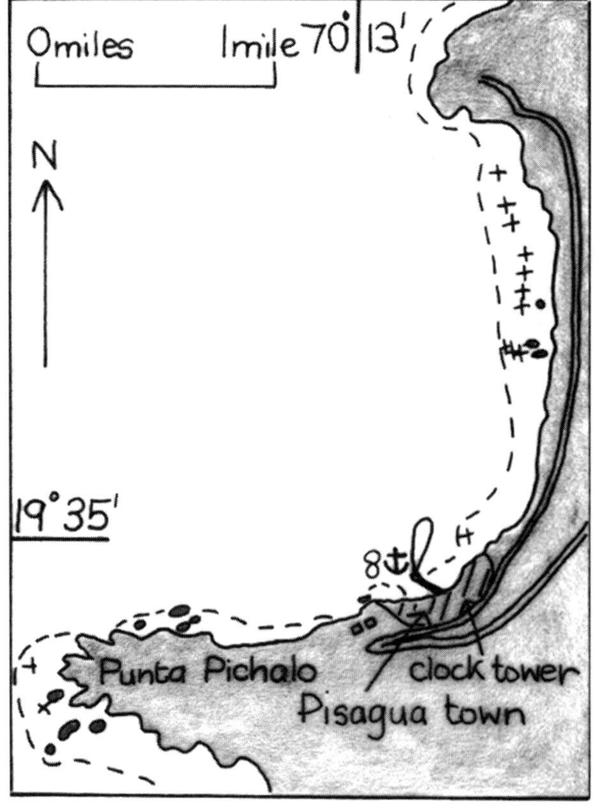

Bahía de Pisagua. (Charted positions)

Lights
To the southwest
1978 Punta Pichalo 19°35'·5S 70°15'·5W
Fl.12s54m13M
White GRP tower, red band 4m

General
Pisagua is the first available shelter south of Arica. It is a reasonable anchorage provided the swell is light. The town was cleared to become a prison in the 1970s. It was rebuilt in the early 1990s. The clock tower (designed by Eiffel) on a prominent mound is a good land-mark. It shows a blue and white light. There is an *Armada* station. Offshore, there may be rafts of petrels, many shearwaters and albatross.

1·3 Iquique
20°12'S 70°09'W

Distances
Pisagua–50–Iquique–35–Caleta Patillos

Charts
UK *3070, 3076* US *22233* Chile *110, 120, 104*

Lights
To the north
1978 Punta Pichalo 19°35'·5S 70°15'·5W
Fl.12s54m13M
White GRP tower, red band 4m
Harbour
1968 **Molo de Abrigo N end 20°11'·8S 70°09'·3W**
Fl.R.10s18m14M
Red ▲ on red conical tower 13m
1969 Espigón de Atraque NE corner 20°12'·0S 70°09'·2W F.G
1969·2 Espigón de Atraque NW corner 20°12'·0S 70°09'·3W F.R
1972 Roca Patilliguaje 20°12'·2S 70°09'·2W
Fl(2+1)G.14s4m3M
Green concrete tower, red band 5m
1974 Muelle de Pasajeros 20°12'·4S 70°09'·2W Ldg Lt 197° *Front* F.R.3M

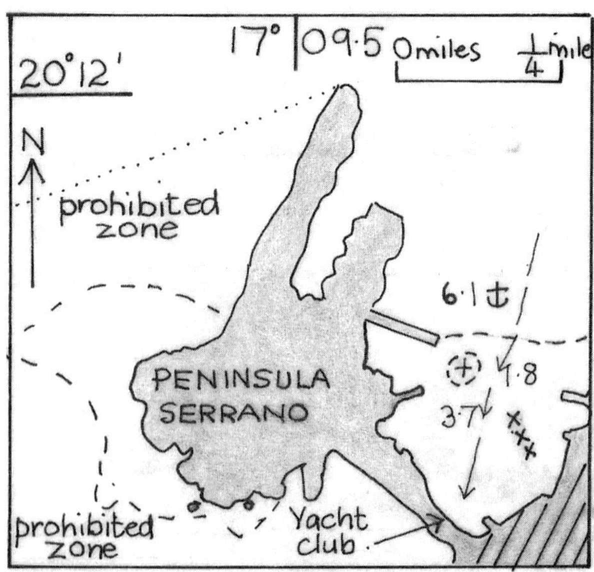

Iquique. (Charted positions)

White ▲, red and white mast 6m
1974·1 20°12'·4S 70°09'·2W *Rear* 43m from front F.R
Black ▼, red and white mast 4m
To the south
1964 Punta Gruesa 20°21'·7S 70°10'·8W
Fl.10s27m 14M
White truncated conical tower 10m 004°-vis-205°
4 masts F.R
1963 Punta Patillos 20°45'·2S 70°11'·9W
Fl.10s40m13M
White round GRP tower red band 4m. 073°-vis-186°, 348°-vis-063°

RDF beacons
3778 Iquique, Chucumata Airport 20°34'·05S 70°10'·90W
c/s *UCU* 368kHz 0·4kW 24hr
3780 Mejillones, Aero 23°06'·35S 70°26'·37W
c/s *MJL* 240kHz 1·0kW 24hr

Tides
a. 0·9
b. 0·5
c. −1hr

Port communications
Port Ch 16, Pilots Ch 08, ☎ 42 28 48/42 34 98.

General
A naval base, oil, commercial and fishing port, Iquique is also the capital of Región 1, Tarapacá, with a population of 140,000. There is an artificial harbour and behind it, an anchorage sheltered from the S and SW. The city has kept much of its late C19 character but with improved facilities for visitors – hotels, restaurants and so forth. It is located on a small coastal plain with beaches; either side the coastline is one of cliffs, up to 800m, interspersed with beaches.

Zona Franca in the suburb Zofri is a duty free zone said to be useful for photographic and electronic goods; there is a limit of US $650 on purchases by tourists.

Tourism
Excursions Rock paintings at the Reserva Nacional Pampa del Tamarugal, 95km; the abandoned nitrate workings at Humberstone.
Local There is a very interesting wooden tower in the main square of Iquique that was built in 1877 and designed by Eiffel. The Naval Museum contains an excellent display of the famous naval battle of 1879 between Chile and Peru that led to the expansion of Chile's border to the north.

Approach
North of Iquique inshore currents are variable and are occasionally strong (4kt).

The port is entered between Punta Piedras, 3M to the north (with rocks and breakers 400m off-shore) and Peninsular Serrano which has a disused light tower, white, 22m high with three 18m radio masts and a wooden tower, 25m, nearby. There is a traffic separation scheme off the immediate entrance.

Anchorage
The Club de Yates is within the port area. The fishing boats anchor in about 7m in the centre of the bay S and E of [1972]Roca Patilliguaje. Further south the bay shallows, and the route to the small yacht club is through depths as little as 2·2m. It is possible to lie bow to the dock in front of the yacht club, but depths at low water can be as little as 1·5m.

Formalities
Call on the *Armada.*

Facilities
Trawler shipyard, engine and other repairs.
800-tonne slipway, mobile cranes.
Fuel from garages
Fincard at Serrano 372 and Zona Franca. Casas de Cambio.
Municipal market Barros Arana Block near Latorre.
Supermarkets etc.
Laundry Bulnes 170, Obispo Labbé 1446.
Club de Yates, Recinto Portuario, restaurant.

Communications
Diego Aracena airport at Chucumata 40km south, internal services to Arica, Antofagasta, Santiago.
Car hire Automóvil Club de Chile, Budget, Hertz, Rent's Procar. Buses to Bolivia and Argentina.
Telephone Area code 57

Passage

Along the coast between Iquique and Antofagasta there are foul grounds and breakers with cliffs and off-shore rocks interspersed with beaches and *caletas.* The chief ports are Tocopilla (22°05'S 70°12'W) and Mejillones del Sur (23°01'S 70°31'W). Tocopilla is a major port in terms of tonnage handled. It has a population of 25,000, a thermal power station supplying electricity to most of N Chile and a mineral port where 80k DWT bulk carriers are advised to take lines out to 'help damp the Pacific swell'; it has a fishing fleet, some hotels and restaurants and a reputation for game fishing. At Mejillones del Sur, away from its explosives and nitrates facilities, an area near the fishing harbour is being developed for holiday makers.

1·4 Caleta Patillos

20°44'·5S 70°11'W

Distances
Iquique – 35 – Patillos – 75 – Tocopilla

Charts
UK *3070* US *22234* Chile *120, 107*

Lights
1963 **Punta Patillos 20°21'·7S 70°10'·8W** Fl.5s40m13M White tower 4m 004°-vis-205° 4 radio masts, red lights

General
Patillos is a good day's run 35 miles south of Iquique. There is reasonable shelter to the north of the pier in 12m. The bottom is rocky but the holding is good. The swell makes in to the bay and

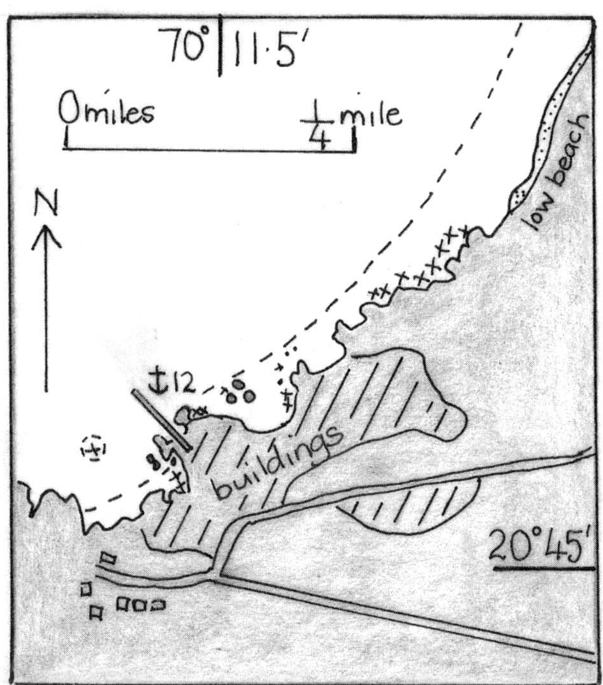

Caleta Patillos. (Charted positions)

a stern anchor may be useful to cut down the rolling. The long pier is used to load salt. There are no officials. The Panamerican Highway is close to the coast at the head of the bay.

1·5 Puerto Tocopilla

22°05'·4S 70°12'·5W

Distances
Patillos–75–Tocopilla–60–Mejillones del Sur

Charts
UK *3077* US *22221* Chile *120, 1300, 131*

Lights
1956 **Punta Algodonales (Islote Blanco) 22°05'·5S 70°13'·0W** Fl.12s23m16M White round GRP tower, red bands 8m 048°-vis-041°

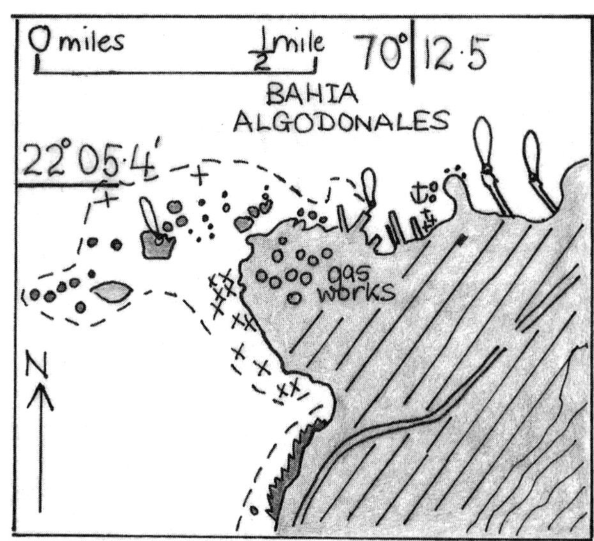

Puerto Tocopilla. (Charted positions)

General

Tocopilla provides good shelter at the end of a long 75 miles beat south from Patillos. It is a dirty industrial port with many piers and cranes and is the seaport for Chuquicamata, the world's largest open pit copper mine, 75 miles to the east. Anchorage is possible in front of the main group of piers.

1·6 Mejillones del Sur

23°05'S 70°28'W

Distances

Tocopilla–60–Mejillones del Sur–30–Antofagasta

Charts

UK *3076* US *22251* Chile *1300, 200, 133*

Lights

1952 Punta Angamos 23°01'·4S 70°30'·9W
Fl.10s108m14M White GRP tower, red band 8m 286°-vis-168°

1953 **Puerto Mejillones del Sur 23°05'·7S 70°27'·1W**
Fl.G.3s19m6M On Harbourmaster's office balcony 038°-vis-326°

General

The town of Mejillones is located on the southern side of a wide bay that provides excellent shelter from the prevailing south and south-west winds. The anchorage is close to the beach in 5m of water, in front of the *Armada* building. The town itself is quite small with limited supplies. Fresh water can be obtained from the *Armada* station. The name of the town may mean something but mussels have not been reported.

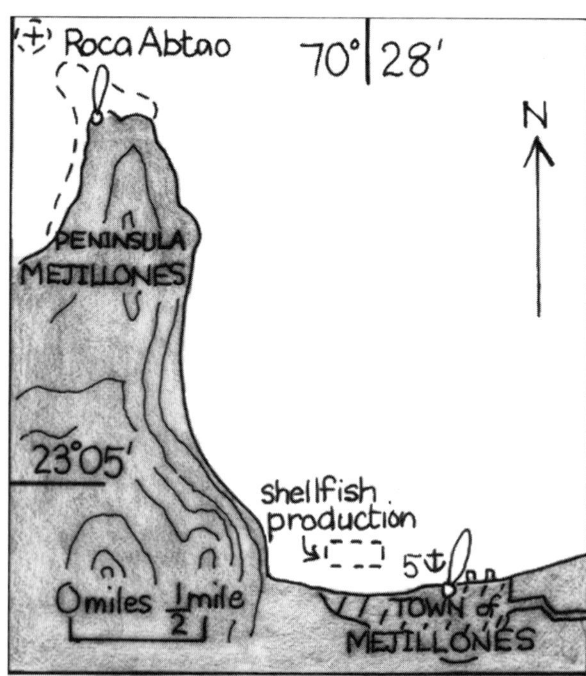

Puerto Mejillones del Sur. (Charted positions)

1·7 Antofagasta

23°39'S 70°24'W

Distances

Mejillones del Sur–30–Antofagasta–215–Caldera

Charts

UK *3071, 3077* US *22222* Chile *200, 212*

Lights

To the north

1952 Punta Angamos 23°01'·4S 70°30'·9W
Fl.10s108m14M
White GRP tower, red band 8m 036°-vis-267°

1948 **Punta Tetas 23°31'·0S 70°37'·8W** Fl.18s33m15M
White GRP tower, red band 8m 286°-vis-168°

Harbour

1946 Molo de Abrigo 23°38'·5S 70°24'·4W
Fl.R.5s17m14M
Red round concrete tower 13m 010°-vis-190°with 5 radio masts with F & Fl red lights within 2M

1947 Mole Este 23°38'·5S 70°24'·3W Fl.G.5s5m8M
Green GRP tower 4m 263°-vis-260°

1947·2 Mole Socopesca 23°38'·3S 70°23'·8W
Fl(4)G.12s4m3M Green framework tower 3m

To the south

1940 Caleta Coloso 23°44'·8S 70°28'·3W
Fl(3)12s35m15M

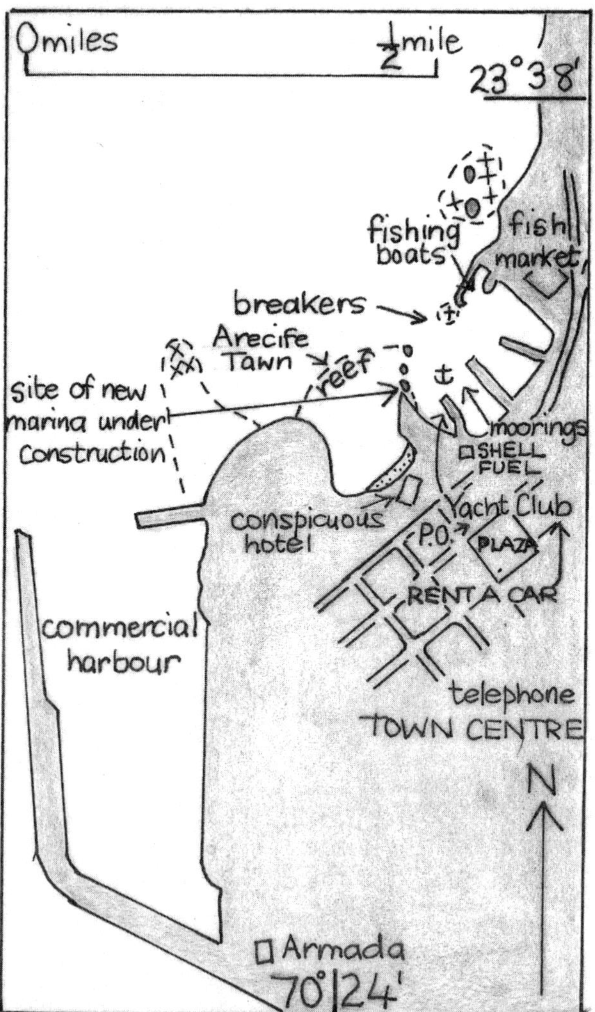

Antofagasta. (Charted positions)

White metal tower, red band 20m occasional Racon 060°-vis-270°

RDF beacons

3778 Iquique, Chucumata Airport 20°34'·05S 70°10'·90W c/s *UCU* 368kHz 0·4kW 24hr

3780 Mejillones, Aero 23°06'·35S 70°26'·37W c/s *MJL* 240kHz 1·0kW 24hr

Tides

a. 0·9m
b. 0·6m
c. −50mins

Port communications

Port Ch **16,** 9, 14 ☎ 26 33 63/26 82 75
Club de Yates Ch 16 ☎ 26 85 83

General

Antofagasta, capital of the Región of Antofagasta, is a somewhat rough town but it is a major commercial centre with a population of 185,000 and has two Universities, good stores, restaurants etc. The port's main activities are handling minerals (particularly copper – train loads are shunted into the port daily along the road outside the yacht club), the Bolivian transit trade and fishing.

Tourism

Numerous organised out of town excursions to the Atacama desert and its towns, mines, geysers, salt pans and resident flamingos. Nearer, bus or hired car excursions to Mejillones, Caleta Coloso or Taltal. In town, the centre is Plaza Colón which has many of the important public buildings

Approach

A large white anchor is inscribed on a hill about 1½ miles E of the 1946Molo de Abrigo which, from the north, may be seen after rounding Punta Tetas. The shore of the Rada de Antofagasta has rocks up to 400m off it.

Entry

The entry to the old harbour, Caleta Pozo del Salitre where the yacht club is situated, is dangerous and certainly should not be attempted at night. The entrance is narrow and lies between Arrecife Tawn (Tawn Reef) and a rock close off 1947·2Molo Socopesca; swell almost always breaks on both sides of the entrance. Within the harbour there are derelict and disused piers and even in good visibility yachts should approach with care. The Club has Mediterranean-style moorings for about 120 yachts up to 3m in draft; on the approach, yachts on the Club moorings will be seen and there is a clear run in on the bearing of these yachts. The moorings are subject to surge in southerly storms. The first week is free.

Anchorage

Fore and aft anchors should be on long scope, over rock, depth 4·2m, and the yacht should lie to face the harbour entrance and the swell, which can be quite large. The Club keeps watch on VHF Ch 16 and will send out a launch to help with anchoring.

Formalities

The *Armada* office is opposite the entrance of the commercial harbour, two miles south of the Club.

Facilities

150-tonne fishing slip; repairs geared to the fishing fleet and garages.

Fuel in cans from the Shell station next door to the Club de Yates.

Water by 400m hose laid by the Club; potable but with a curious backlash of sulphur and chlorine – makes funny tea and coffee.

Banks and *Cambios* including Fincard, Av. Prat 431.

Provisions Municipal market at the corner of Uribe & Matta; 'Las Brisas' supermarket near to Yacht Club.

Laundry Lavandería Pronor on the outskirts will collect and deliver – see the local yellow pages; Laverap, 14 Febrero 1802.

Club de Yates restaurant, showers etc.

Consulates Argentina, Belgium, Bolivia and France.

Communications

Air American, Iberia, Lloyd Aéreo Bolíviano, Lufthansa to N America, Europe and Bolivia. Alta, LanChile, Ladeco & National to Arica, Iquique, Santiago.

Buses to Argentina; organisation of internal services is complex – bus companies have separate booking offices and terminals.

Car hire Avis, Rent-a-Car, Budget, Hertz. Try near the Shell station by the Club de Yates.

Telephone Area code 55 CTC Matta 2625, ENTEL Condel 2142.

Passage

The coast between Antofagasta and Caldera is rocky and steep, often with foul ground off it. There are several possible fair weather anchorages for small boats and a small port, Taltal which has a straightforward approach.

1·8 Caleta El Cobre

24°14'·8S 70°30'·5W

Distances

Antofagasta–35–El Cobre–8–Encalada

Charts

UK *3071* US – Chile *200, 206*

General

Although only 35 miles south of Antofagasta, the passage could be a beat of more than 50 miles and El Cobre may be convenient for a night stop. The holding is good on a sand bottom in 7·5m but the swell can make around the point and the air can be very dusty from the mine just to the south.

1·9 Caleta Blanco

24°22'·1S 70°32'·5W

Distances

El Cobre–8–Encalada–62–Taltal

Charts

UK *3077* US – Chile *200, 205*

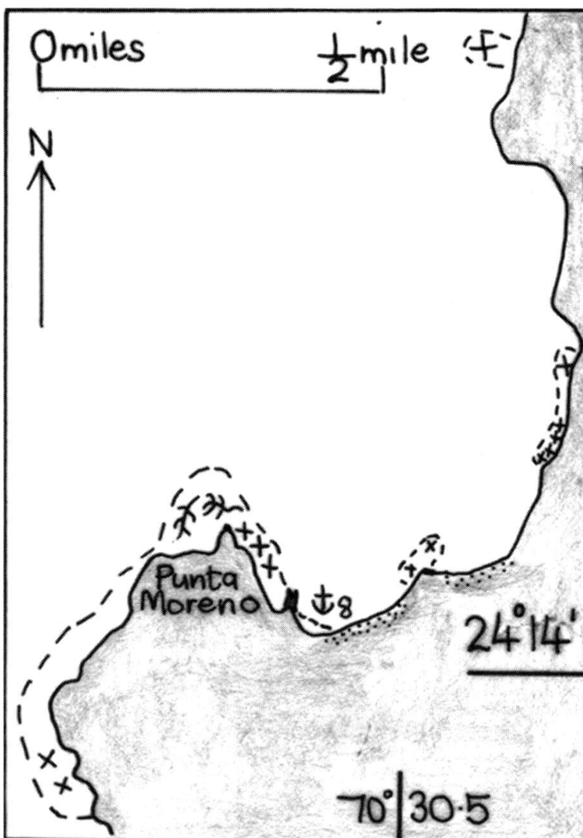

Caleta El Cobre. (Charted positions)

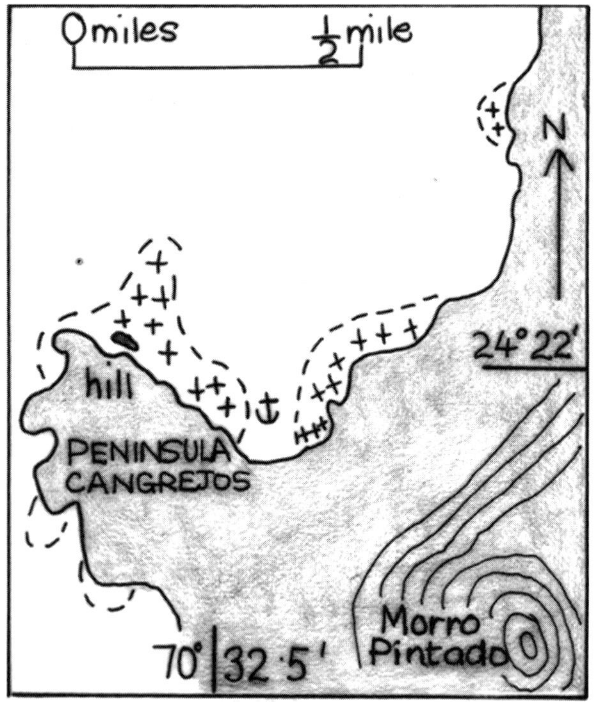

Caleta Blanco Encalada. (Charted positions)

General

Encalada is one of the better anchorages on this part of the coast. The point and the rocks to the north-west stop the swell but a stern anchor may still be useful to cut down rolling. There are a large number of low stone walls built on the hill to the west with no apparent purpose except, possibly, to occupy otherwise idle hands.

1·10 Puerto Taltal

25°24'S 70°29'W

Distances

Encalada–62–Taltal–18 (25 around the headland)–Cifuncho

Charts

UK *3078* US – Chile *200, 207*

General

The anchorage is underneath the hill in the SW corner of the bay amongst the fishing boats. The small town of Taltal is very friendly. Fresh vegetables were readily available. A large statue of the Virgin Mary looks down from the hill in the centre of the town and the view from the top is well worth the climb.

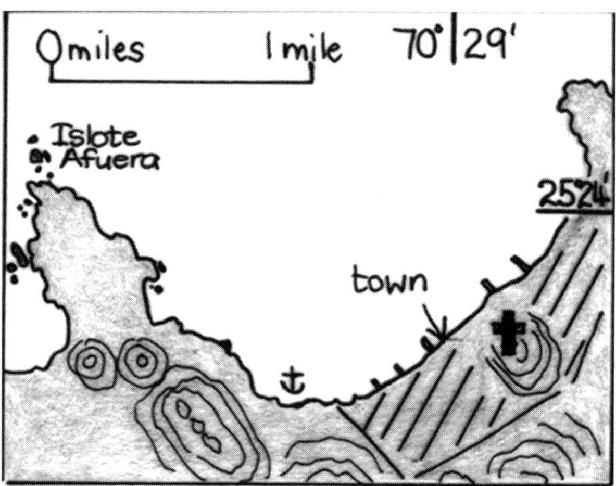

Puerto Taltal. (Charted positions)

1·11 Caleta Cifuncho

25°38'·2S 70°38'·6W

Distances

Tatal–18 (25 around the headland)–Cifuncho–33–Pan de Azúcar

Charts

UK *3071, 3072* US – Chile *200, 206*

Cifuncho provides a sheltered anchorage and some excellent hiking in the dry rocky hills to the east and on the point above the anchorage. It is used by small trawlers. The beach is used by campers.

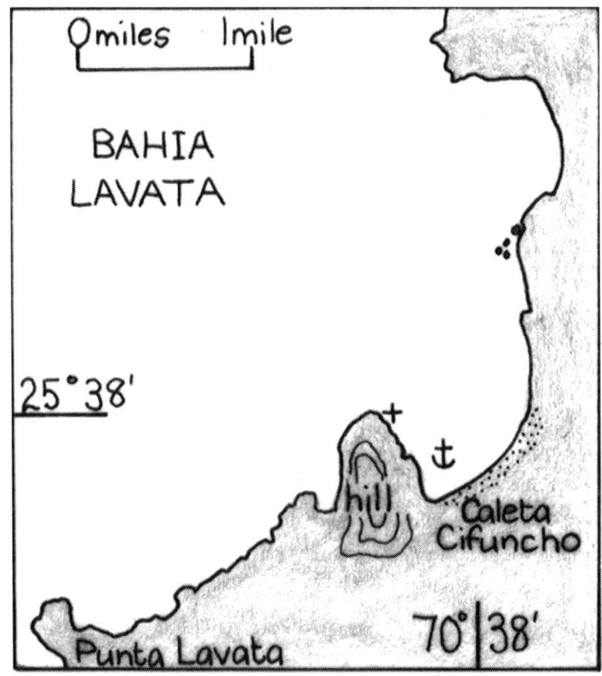

Caleta Cifuncho. (Charted positions)

1·12 Puerto Pan de Azúcar

26°09'S 70°42'W

Distances
Cifuncho–33–Pan de Azúcar–56–Caldera

Charts
UK *3072* US – Chile *200, 206*

General
Pan de Azúcar gives immediate access to the National Park of the same name which is known for its cactii. It is approached by a narrow channel, with shoals either side, behind Isla Pan de Azúcar. Although *NP7* describes Caleta Sur as being more protected, local fishermen consider it dangerous and prefer Caleta Norte, about ½M NE of Punta Rodriguez, with 12m and sand.

1·13 Puerto Caldera

27°04'S 70°49'W

Distances
Pan del Azúcar–56–Caldera–63–Carrizal Bajo

Charts
UK *3078* US *22250, 22252* Chile *300, 311*

Lights
To the north
1936 Punta Achurra 26°17'·9S 70°40'·5W
Fl.15s30m15M
White GRP tower, red bands 8m 330°-vis-150°
Entrance to bay
1924 Punta Caldera 27°03'·0S 70°51'·7W
Fl.12s37m15M
White truncated wooden tower, red bands 18m 020°-vis-278°
1924·5 Punta Calderillo 27°02'·8S 70°49'·4W
Fl(3)9s9m4M

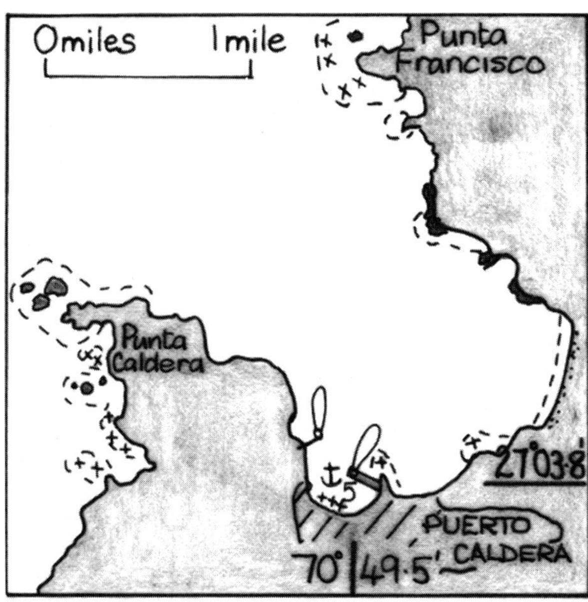

Puerto Caldera. (Charted positions)

White GRP tower red band 3m 325°-vis-128°
Harbour
1925 Mast 27°04'·5S 70°49'·9W Aero Fl.R.13M
1925·6 Ldg Lts 225° *Front* Private 27°03'·3S 70°50'·1W
F.RG.2M Orange ▲ 3m
1925·6 *Rear* 80m from front 27°03'·3S 70°50'·1W
F.RG.2M Orange ▲ 3m
1926 Muelle Fiscal 27°03'·7S 70°50'·2W Fl.G.3s4m7M
Head ■ on green GRP tower 3m
To the south
1923 Punta Caldereta 27°04'·7S 70°52'·2W
Fl.R.5s14m3M
Red GRP tower 3m 069°-vis-305° F.R on jetty 800m SE
1922 Bahía Copiápo 27°20'·6S 70°57'·1W Fl.10s15m5M
Puerto Viejo White GRP Tower, red band 3m 045°-vis-270°
1918 Peninsular Guacolda 28°27'·9S 71°15'·9W
Fl.15s40m19M
White GRP tower, red band 030°-vis-370°

RDF beacons
3782 Caldera 27°04'·48S 70°49'·89W c/s *CLD* 227kHz
1·0kW 24hr

Tides
a. 1·0m
b. 0·6m
c. −35mins

Port communications
Port Ch 16 ☎ 31 55 51

General
A rather spartan anchorage, Caldera is an ore-shipping port with a population of 12,000 and a few shops and restaurants. However it is popular as a holiday resort and accommodation is heavily booked in the season. It is at the northern limit of winds from the north and though exposed to the rare blow from that direction, it has excellent shelter from the prevailing southerly winds.

Immediately to the south are two other bays, Puerto Calderilla and Bahía Inglesa, both of which would provide good shelter in the event of strong southerly winds.

Tourism

Santuario de la Naturaleza, about 15km N past the deserted Playas Ramada and Rodillo, has unusual spherical granite boulders. There is an interesting 50 mile bus trip through the nearby wine-growing country to Copiapo where there is an excellent mineral museum and many old Colonial buildings. The green of the river valley makes a welcome change from the arid Atacama desert.

Approach and anchorage

From the north, leave Punta Francisco (no mark) one mile to port and head south and then south-east to the anchorage. From the south, round Punta Caldera at a distance of about one mile. and then head approximately south-east to the anchorage. A substantial pier, formerly used for ore shipments, with two concrete dolphins on either side of the pierhead, should be left to starboard. On the south-east side of the pier is a small commercial shipyard and next to that the yacht club which has a small floating pontoon for dinghies. Some private moorings are situated off this pontoon and anchorage may be taken among the fishing boats nearby, in about 6m, rock.

Formalities

The *Armada* offices are about half a mile round the bay.

Facilities

Three slips for small craft, limited workshops.
Fuel COPEC station, Edwards & Montt.
Provisions Supermarket Carvallo, between Montt & Ossa Cerda.
Club de Yates bar, cold showers, WC; many members belong to the Hermandad de la Costa.

Communications

Buses, local and national (e.g. 4 services a day to Santiago).
Telephone Area Code 52

Passage

The coast between Caldera and Coquimbo is the usual mix of rock and sandy beaches, often fringed by off-lying rocks and islets. There are several anchorages. One such is at Isla Damas, 29°13'·5S 71°31'·7W, 50M N of Herradura, one of three small uninhabited islands in Bahía Chorros. A reef with a conspicuous rock extends about 400m S from the southern end. A small cove, Caleta Lynch, on the E side of the island has good holding, sand, in 8–10m, sheltered NW-SW-SE. Give a wide berth to the reef that forms the southern limit of this cove.

1·14 Puerto Carrizal Bajo

28°06'S 71°09'·5W

Distances

Caldera–63–Carrizal Bajo–22–Huasco

Charts

UK *3072* US *22250* Chile *300, 304*

General

This shallow river mouth harbour provides a quiet anchorage in south and south-west winds. There is a small village. The bottom is mud with good holding in 3m.

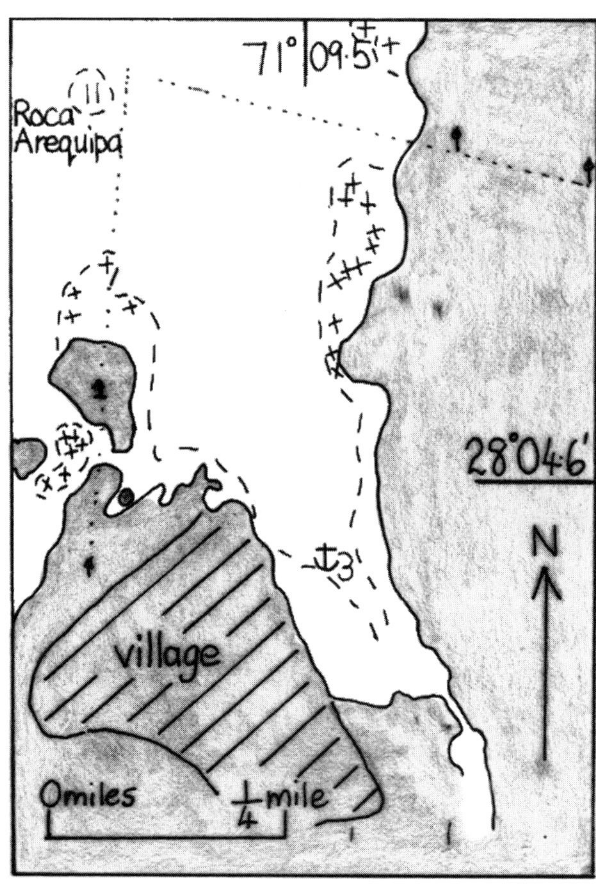

Puerto Carrizal Bajo. (Charted positions)

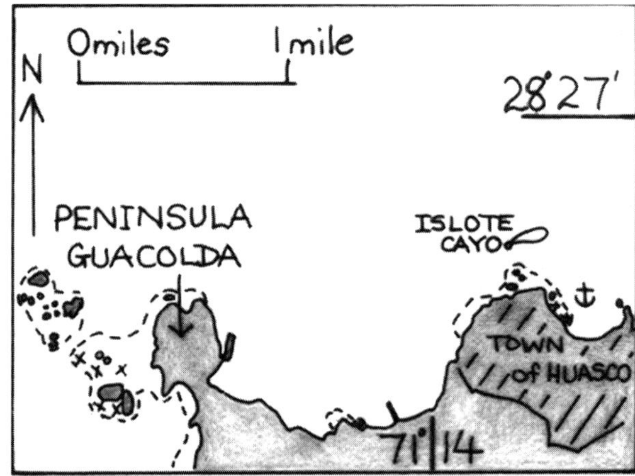

Puerto Huasco. (Charted positions)

1·15 Puerto Huasco

28°27'·8S 71°14'W

Distances

Carrizal Bajo–22–Huasco–75–Totoralillo

Charts

UK *3079* US *22250* Chile *300, 305*

General

Anchor in front of the town in 4–5m. A large number of fishing boats are on buoys and there is a 'free' launch service to the dock. Unfortunately the anchorage is exposed to the swell making around the point. A stern anchor helps.

1·16 Caleta Totoralillo

29°28'·2S 71°20'W

Distances

Huasco–75–Totoralillo–30–Guayacán

Charts

UK *3080* US 22250 Chile *300, 303*

General

Totoralillo is at the southern end of the Atacama desert and the beginning of grasslands and scrubby trees. The anchorage itself is very sheltered in 6m in front of a steep, black stone beach. There are a number of old ruins on shore together with remains of garden plots, protected by well made stone walls and irrigated by laid stone canals. For those who like hiking, the stony hills to the east are very enjoyable.

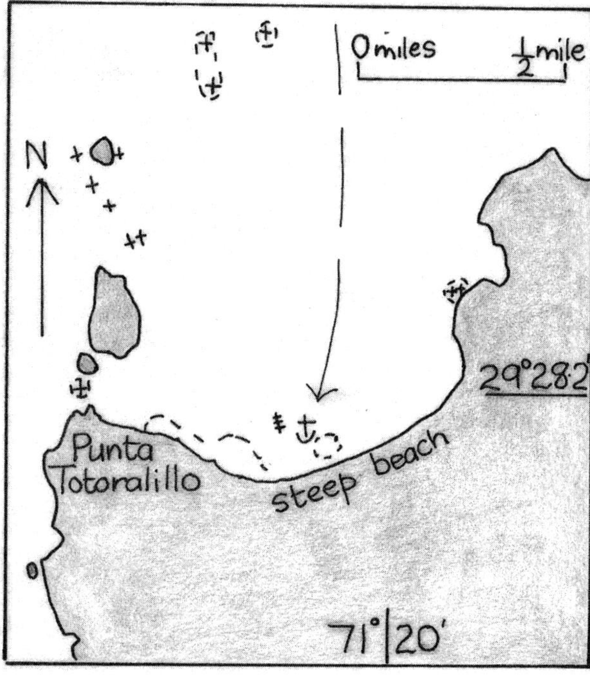

Caleta Totoralillo. (Charted positions)

1·17 Coquimbo – Bahía Herradura de Guayacán

29°59'S 71°21'·5W

Distances

Totoralillo–30–Guayacán–23–Tongoy

Charts

UK *3073, 3080* US *22250, 22282* Chile *300, 400, 401, 411*

Lights

To the north

1918 Peninsular Guacolda 28°27'·9S 71°15'·9W Fl.15s40m19M
White GRP tower, red band 030°-vis-370°

1916 Isla Chañaral 29°01'·8S 71°35'·0W Fl.12s58m13M
White round tower, GRP top, red bands 10m 010°-vis-214°

1904 Islotes Pájaros 29°35'·0S 71°31'·5W Fl(2)10s39m11M
Black tower, red band 162°-vis-158°

1900 **Punta Tortuga 29°56'·0S 71°21'·4W** Fl.13s23m27M
White round metal tower, red band 4m 042°-vis-255°

Entrance

1896·7 Islotes Mewes 29°57'·9S 71°22'·7W Fl(3)G.9s8m3M
Green GRP tower 3m 309°-vis-175°

1896·6 Punta Herradura 29°58'·1S 71°23'·1W Fl.15s19m5M
White GRP tower, red band 3m 101°-vis-103°, 111°-vis-298°

1897 29°58'·9S 71°22'·0W Ldg Lts 140° *Front*

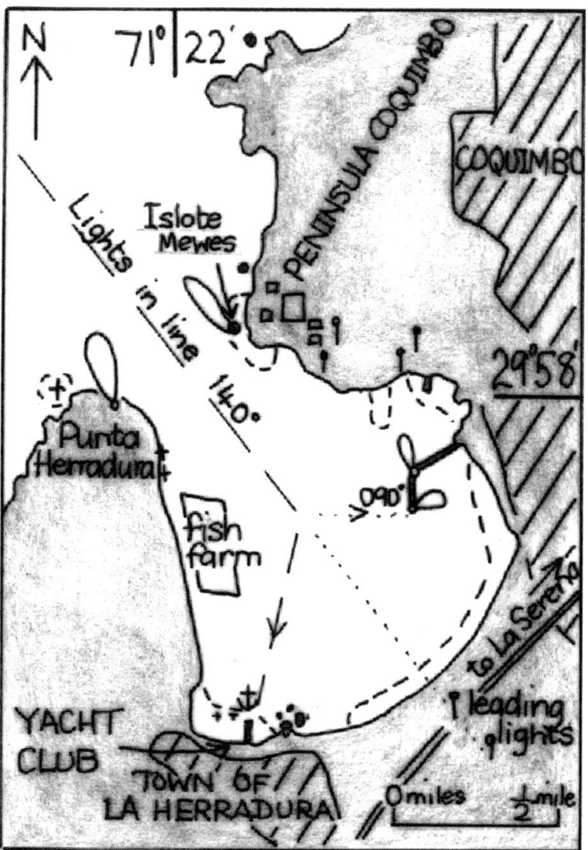

Herradura de Guayacan. (Charted positions).

F.R.17m3M
White ♦, red diagonal stripes, in white ■ 5m
1897·1 29°59'·0S 71°21'·9W *Rear* F.G.32m3M
304m from front White ♦, red diagonal stripes, in white ■ 9m
1898 29°58'·5S 71°21'·8W Ldg Lts 112° *Front* F.R.11m3M
White ♦, red diagonal stripes, in white ■ 9m
1898·1 29°58'·5S 71°21'·8W *Rear* F.G.15m3M
48m from front White ♦, red diagonal stripes, in white ■ 9m

Note There are 6 sets of leading lights within the bay (including those listed above), all with F.G rear and F.R front; two of the sets have one common front light. See plan.

To the south

1896 Punta Laguna de Vaca 30°14'·8S 71°37'·8W
Fl.15s40m16M White GRP tower, red band 4m 039°-vis-265°
1882 Península Los Molles 32°46'·1S 71°32'·0W
Fl.15s91m19M White conical tower, red bands 16m 020°-vis-236·5°

RDF beacons

3782 Caldera 27°04'·48S 70°49'·89W c/s *CLD* 227kHz 1·0kW 24hr

Note Correction dated 22 Feb 96 to *NP7* lists it as off, 1996 *NP282* lists it as on

3784 Punta Tortuga 29°55'·94S 71°21'·56W c/s *TUGA* 322·5kHz 160M 24hr
3786 Tongoy 30°15'·74W 71°29'·43W c/s *TOY* 260kHz 3·0kW 24hr

Tides

a. 1·1m
b. 0·7m
c. −17mins

Port communications

Port (Coquimbo) Ch 16 ☎(51) 31 11 04
Club de Yates ☎ (51) 32 12 80

General

The town of Coquimbo is built on a peninsula looking north over Bahía de Coquimbo and south over Herradura de Guayacán (*herradura* = horseshoe). It has a population of 115,000 and has facilities to match (and regattas in September and February). Coquimbo is now the less important port but is the port authority. Guayacán handles much of the copper and iron ore exported from the region. La Serena (population 120,000), 12km north, is the capital of Región IV, Coquimbo.

Tourism

To the north are La Serena and the Elqui Valley, famous for its production of *pisco*. La Serena is a most interesting city with many old Colonial buildings and churches. There is a long boulevard in the centre of town which contains some magnificent sculptures. It is a university town, and is well known for its pottery. In the centre of town there is a good vegetable, fish and artisan market.

To the south is the Parque Nacional Fray Jorge, with forests dependent upon mist or fog for water (if planning a visit, it is important to check opening times).

Approach

From the north, there are groups of clearly charted but unmarked rocks lying 1M NW of 1900Punta Tortuga which itself is 2½M north of Guayacán; passage is possible between the groups. From the south, 1896Punta Laguna de Vaca has to be passed which is well known for abnormally strong local winds. The bay is invisible until one is off the entrance (note that 1896·6Punta Herradura light cannot be seen from the south).

Entry

On 140° towards leading marks 1897 and 1897·1 between 1896·7Islotes Mewes and 1896·6Punta Herradura. Ignore other leading marks (particularly two sets on 112° which will be crossed in succession). Continue on 140° until the light 1898 on the end of the long pier projecting into the bay bears 090°, then turn to 193° towards the yacht club. This avoids the fish farms on the west side of the bay.

Anchorage

In 4–5m, off the yacht club pier, sand.

Formalities

The office of the *Armada* is in the middle of Coquimbo

Facilities

Private dockyard in Coquimbo, engine repairs possible.
Fuel by can from a garage in Herradura. Fishing craft fuel at the Muelle Mecanizado.
Banks in Coquimbo and La Serena.
Small supermarket, fruit, vegetable and liquor shops in Herradura. Otherwise Coquimbo or La Serena.
Laundry Lavachic self-service, Aldunate 852 Coquimbo.
Water in containers from the yacht club.
Yacht club has a bar, restaurant, and phone. Use of the swimming pool requires an introduction from a member and an entry fee.

Communications

Herradura *Collectivos* and taxis to Coquimbo and La Serena.
Coquimbo national buses.
La Serena national buses (48 a day to Santiago); airport (La Florida) with national flights.
Car hire in La Serena.
☎ Area code 51. Telephone at the yacht club de Yates. CTC, ENTEL in Coquimbo, La Serena.

1·18 Bahía Tongoy

30°17'S 71°37'W

Distances

Guayacán–23–Tongoy–135–Papudo

Charts

UK *3080* US *22275* Chile *400, 401, 403*

General

Tongoy provides excellent shelter from the prevailing southerly winds. The best anchorage is deep into the southwest corner of the wide bay in front of the village. The holding is good on a sandy bottom in 6m. There is also a good anchorage under

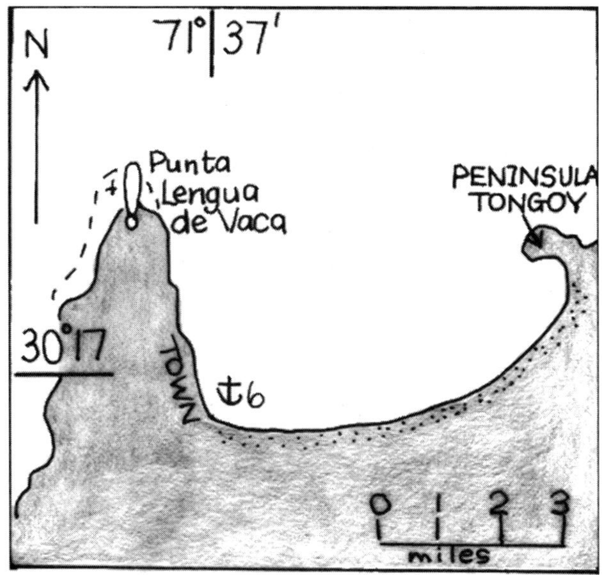

Bahía Tongoy. (Charted positions)

the point in Bahía Guanaquero, ten miles to the north-east of Tongoy.

1·19 Puerto Papudo

32°31'S 71°26'·5W

Distances
Tongoy–135–Papudo–14–Quintero

Charts
UK *3073* US *22293, 22261* Chile *400, 404, 501*

General
In the southern corner of the bay is a small fishing village and many old summer homes with lovely gardens. Anchor off the beach where the colourfully painted fishing boats are drawn up each day. Limited supplies are available in the town in the off-season when the small yacht club is deserted.

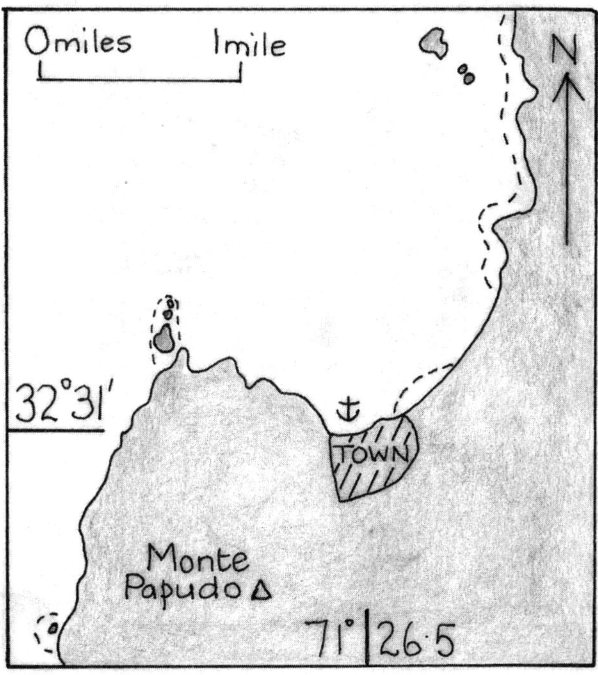

Puerto Papudo. (Charted positions)

1·20 Bahía Quintero

32°46'S 71°31'W

Distances
Papudo–14–Quintero–10–Higuerillas

Charts
UK *1314, 3073* US *22293, 22263* Chile *400, 424, 500*

General
Bahía Quintero is a large open bay surrounded by low-lying land, and is somewhat exposed to the occasional northerly storm. Gas, oil, chemicals and coal are handled commercially. There is an active yacht club inside the peninsular. The yacht club will check visiting yachts in with the *Armada*.

Approach
There is a traffic separation scheme in the approach.

Anchorage
The yacht club has a string of rather closely packed mooring buoys which visitors are welcome to use. Many fishing boats are also moored in this area.

Facilities
The club can haul boats up to about 30ft in length, and there is a storage area on land for the winter storage of members' boats.
The town is an area of summer homes and there are few shops.

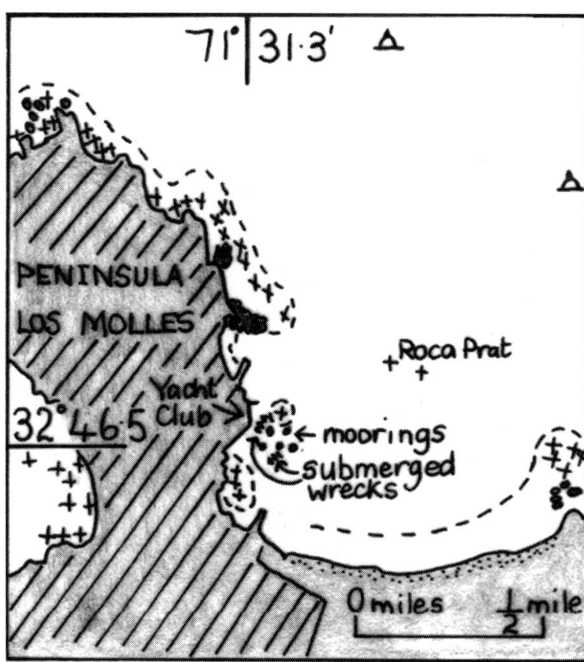

Bahía Qintero

1·21 Higuerillas (Concón, Viña del Mar)

32°56'S 71°34'W

Distances

Quintero–10–Higuerillas–26–Algarrobo

Charts

UK *3073* US *22259, 22293* Chile *400, 426*

Lights

To the north

1882 Península Los Molles 32°46'·1S 71°32'·0W
Fl.15s91m19M
White conical tower, red bands 16m 020°-vis-236·5°

Entrance and harbour

1880 Punta Concón **32°55'·7S 71°33'·1W**
Fl.12s14m18M
White round GRP tower, red band 3m. 352°-vis-234°
Same tower Fl(2)R.6s14m11M
172°-vis-180° over Rocas Concón

1881 Mole de Abrigo 32°56'·0S 71°32'·0W
Fl.R.4s4m6M
White concrete column, red bands 4m

1881·2 32°56'·0S 71°32'·0W Q.Y.5m13M
Brown metal column

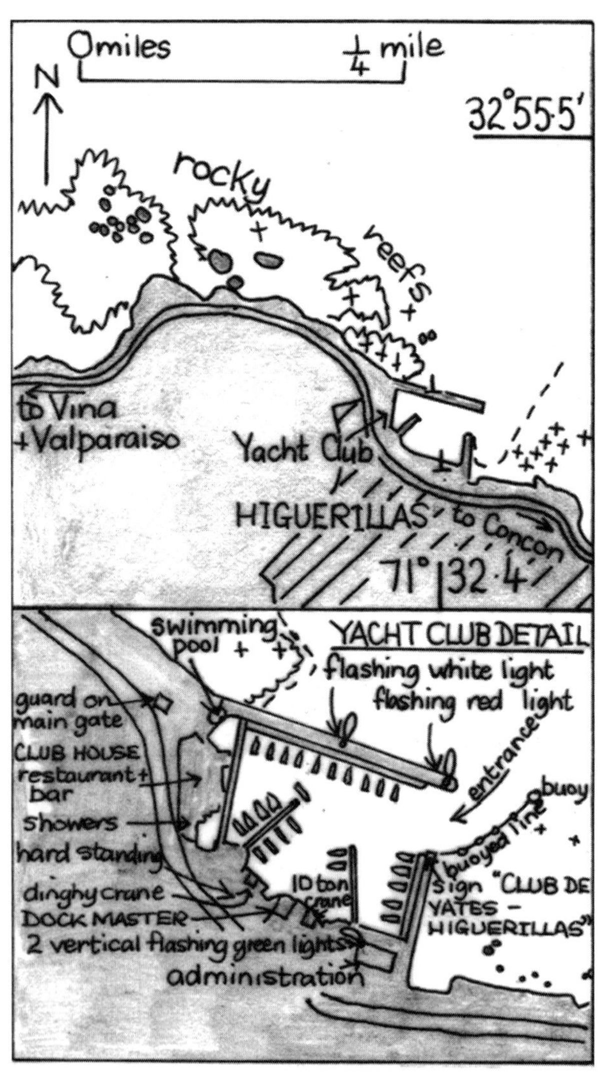

Club de Yates, Vina del Mar. (Charted positions)

1881·4 Caleta Higuerillas 32°56'·0S 71°32'·0W
Q.Y.11m13M Brown metal column

To the south

1874 Punta Angeles 33°01'·2S 71°38'·7W
Fl.10s59m32M
White round metal tower, orange bands 18m. 048·5°-250°

1870 Punta Curaumilla 33°06'·0S 71°45'·0W
Fl.15s83m16M Siren(3)30s
White metal tower, red band, white house 3m. 344°-vis-224°

RDF beacons

3786 Tongoy 30°15'·74S 71°29'·43W c/s *TOY* 260kHz 3·0kW 24hr

3788 Quintero 32°44'·10S 71°29'·68W c/s *ERO* 384kHz 1·0kW 24hrs

3790 Punta Angeles 33°01'·27S 71°39'·17W c/s *VASO* 300kHz 110M 24hrs

Tides

a. 1·1m
b. 0·7m
c. 0mins

Port communications

Club de Yates de Higuerillas Ch 68 ☎ 90 38 39 *Fax* 81 17 69

General

Valparaíso, the port for Santiago, does not cater for yachts and the nearest club, Club de Yates Recreo, though welcoming is on an open roadstead. For visitors, the Club de Yates Viña del Mar (or de Higuerillas) is the nearest haven to the north and Algarrobo the nearest to the south. Higuerillas is a village between Concón and Viña del Mar, itself just to the north of Valparaíso. All the facilities of Viña del Mar (an international resort crammed with hotels and restaurants), Valparaíso and Santiago can be reached easily from Higuerillas.

The area has fog about two days a month in summer, more frequently in winter. Strong southerlies blow in summer in clear weather with a high barometer; the afternoon sea breeze can also be strong.

The yacht harbour provides considerable protection in bad weather but it is not fool-proof, particularly in winter. 2m tides have been experienced and storms can create a surge within the harbour rising and falling 1m within a minute – particular attention must be paid to warps and chafe if a yacht is to be left. Yachts wintering under the north wall have been covered in shingle – most haul out for the off-season. Visitors have been accommodated. If leaving a boat even for a few days, negotiate with the club manager for the services of a *marinero* to care-take; the *marinero* must be given a detailed brief.

Tourism

The delights of the international resort at Viña, the charm of the stairs and lifts of the walkways of Valparaíso, the hassle of the economic centre, Santiago.

Approach

There is a traffic separation scheme off Valparaíso. Strong winds can produce strong currents inshore, sometimes with an onshore set, especially in summer.

From the north pass either side of Rocas Concón, 3½M north of Punta Concón and covered by the red sector of its light; when past, head for Punta Concón. From the south, round Punta Concón about ½M off. The yacht club is just over ½M east of Punta Concón.

Anchorage
In the summer season, there is limited space available along the dock and visiting yachts have to anchor or tie to the yacht club buoy just outside the harbour entrance.

Formalities
On arrival the club manager may examine the ship's papers and report by radio to the *Armada*. It will nevertheless be necessary to call on the *Armada* at the *Gobernación Militar* with papers and passports. If the first port of call, the *Aduana* and *Immigración* (the Maritime Police Office) must be visited for an import licence and a visa (see Appendix A). All are in Valparaíso port or town; obtain the addresses from the Club. It will take more than a day to sort everything out.

Facilities
10-tonne crane, sail repairs, stainless steel welding at the Club. Large DIY store in Viña.
Chandleries in the port area of Valparaíso but quality (even of cordage) doubtful. Better quality at Alfredo Kauer, Frederico Reich 143, Santiago, by the Viña del Mar bus terminal. He also machines brass.
Electronics: agents of European and N American manufacturers are to be found in Valparaíso. Diagnostic skills good but repair skills hampered by, amongst other factors, lack of spares.
Fuel from garage on road to Viña.
Propane bottles can be filled at the large filling station in Concón and in Uruguay St., off the main square in Valparaíso. The yacht club also knows of a place in Viña.
Water on pontoons.
Banks nearest Fincard is in Viña.
Provisions simple shops & fish stalls in Higuerillas; supermarket in Reñaca; sophisticated shops of all types in Viña.
Laundry can be arranged by the Club. Alternatively there are facilities in Reñaca and Viña.
Club de Yates de Higuerillas: very well found. Swimming pool, security guard at gate and night watchman.
British Consul: Errázuriz 730, (Casilla 82-V), Valparaíso ☎ 25 61 17 *Fax* 25 53 65. Also Argentinean, Belgian, Danish, Dutch, German, Japanese, Peruvian, Spanish and Swedish consulates.

Communications
No 9 bus from Concón to Viña via Reñaca every half hour in winter along the coast road, more frequently in summer but the coast road is then crowded with holiday traffic.
No 10 bus from the top of the hill behind the village, in winter more frequent than the No 9, takes the main road which is also served by *collectivos*.
At Viña buses and trains to Valparaíso, buses to Santiago. Airport at Santiago.
Telephone Area code 32

1·22 Valparaíso

33°02'S 71°37'W

Charts
UK *1314* US *22293, 22259* Chile *511*

General
Valparaíso is a major shipping port and a large old town. In the port is the major *Armada* station and on the opposite side of the square is the headquarters of the Chilean Customs. Very few yachts anchor at Valparaíso itself, it is much easier to stop at Higuerillas and travel here by bus. The Valparaíso Yacht Club (Club de Yates Recreo) is located in the bay to the east of the port, but the anchorage is very exposed.

Valparaíso is the headquarters of the *Armada*, and the major training schools are located here and in Viña del Mar. Chilean charts and publications are available from:

Servicio Hidrográfico y Oceanográfico de la Armada, Melgarejo 59, Local 5 Valparaíso ☎ & *Fax* 25 77 31

Passage

The Valparaíso traffic separation scheme runs roughly 350°-vis-170° northeast of Punta Curaumilla and a crossing at right angles (or thereabouts) should present little problem. To the south, the coast is one of headlands and beaches

1·23 Algarrobo

33°21'S 71°41'W

Distances
Higuerillas–26–Algarrobo–130–Coliumo

Charts
UK *3073, 3074* US *22293, 22295* Chile *500, 501, 513*

Lights
To the north
1874 Punta Angeles 33°01'·2S 71°38'·7W
Fl.10s59m32M
White round metal tower, orange bands. 048·5°-vis-250°
1870 Punta Curaumilla 33°06'·0S 71°45'·0W
Fl.15s83m16M Siren(3)30s
White metal tower, red band, white house 3m. 344°-vis-224°
Vicinity
1866 Península Pájaros Niños **33°21'·4S 71°41'·1W**
Fl.R.10s34m7M
Red GRP tower 4m 163°-vis-150°
Same tower Fl.5s33m8M
150°-vis-163° over Los Farallones
1864 Poza Cofradía 33°21'·4S 71°40'·9W
Fl(3)R.9s5m5M
Red round concrete pillar 2m 129°-vis-309°
1863 Cofradía Náutica 33°21'·5S 71°40'·9W

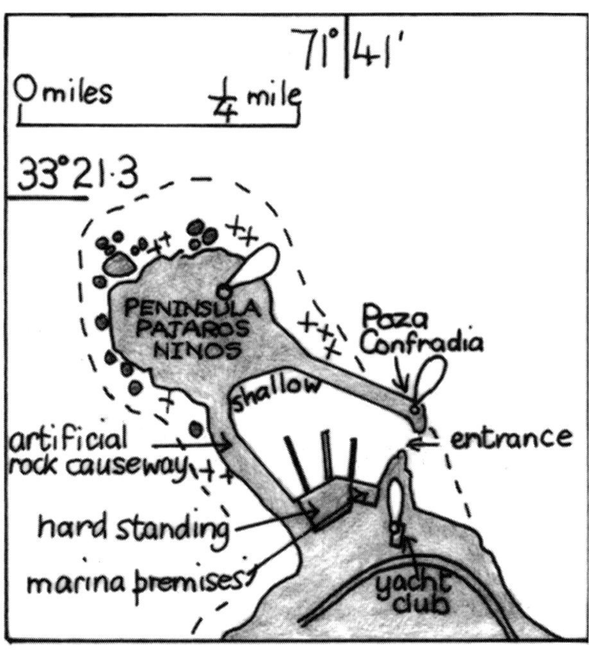

Algarrobo. (Charted positions)

LFl.8s16m11M
Black metal mast 18m 186°-vis-206°

To the south
1857 Punta Panul 33°34'·3S 71°38'·4W
Fl.10s88m20M Siren(2)30s
White round concrete tower, red bands 9m 000°-vis-163°

RDF beacons
3790 Punta Angeles 33°01'·27S 71°39'·17W c/s *VASO* 300kHz 110M 24hrs
3792 Santo Domingo 33°38'·00S 71°38'·00W c/s *SNO* 355kHz 1·0kW 24hrs

Tides
a. 1·1m
b. 0·7m
c. 0mins

Port communications
Ch 16 ☎ 48 11 80

General
The Cofradía Náutica del Pacífico (not to be confused with the Club de Yates) has developed a marina with floating pontoon berths which offers protection in any wind. The marina accommodates over 50 yachts and has an extensive hardstanding served by a travel-lift. It is very expensive but it is the safest place in the area to leave a yacht.

During the season, it would be wise to check availability of berths before arriving. Out of season, there is plenty of room.

Algarrobo is a pleasant, pine-clad watering hole, convenient for weekenders from Santiago, and it has long been a popular centre for yachting regattas. It is only a few miles from Isla Negra, where Pablo Neruda, the famous Nobel Prize-winning poet, constructed his intriguing seaside home, now a museum. However, there are no shops and no buses and it is almost essential to have a car or use taxis to get around.

Approach
The approach is easy in most conditions, although a wide berth should be given to Los Farallones, an unlit but charted group of mainly above-water rocks, lying about a mile Northwest of the harbour (see light 1866).

Facilities
Travel-lift.
Hard standings.
Engine repairs.
Showers and a restaurant.

Passage
Puerto San Antonio is a major port with a reputation for heavy swell between September and March. The rest of the coast is as inhospitable as ever, with inshore currents accelerated by strong winds and often with an on-shore set. Bajo Rappel (31°51'S 72°01'W) has a particularly bad reputation; keep out. The coast between 35°S and 36°30'S is said to be incorrectly charted; keep out.

1·24 Bahía Coliumo
36°32'S 73°56'·7W

Distances
Algarrobo–130–Coliumo–15–Talcahuano

Charts
UK *1319, 3074* US *22290* Chile *500, 600, 611*

General
This is a quiet, picturesque anchorage just inside the headland on the western shore in 6m, in front of the small village.

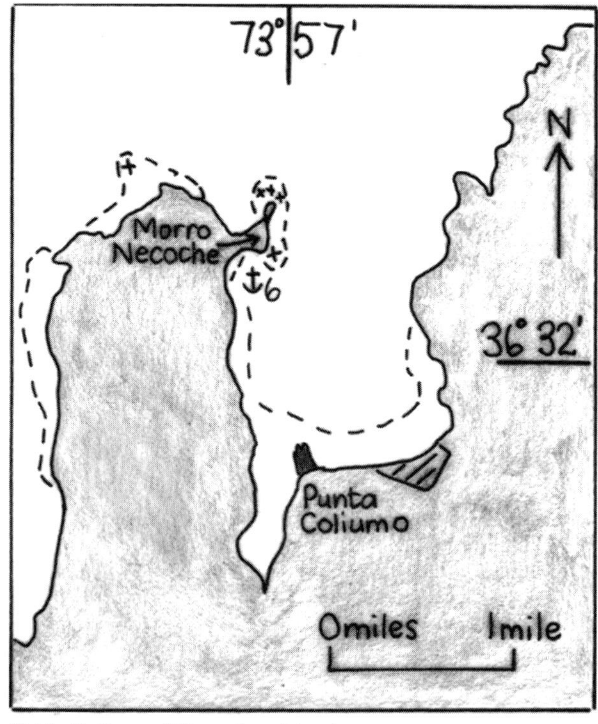

Bahía Coliumo. (Charted positions)

1·25 Talcahuano

36°42'S 73°07'W

Distances

Coliumo–15–Talcahuano–50–Trana

Charts

UK *1319, 3074* US *22290, 22311* Chile *600, 611, 612*

Lights

Approach

1796 Punta Tumbes 36°36'·9S 73°06'·6W
Fl.5s36m18M Siren (3)30s
White round metal tower, red bands 6m 028°-vis-273°

1797 Morro Lobería 36°34'·8S 72°59'·7W Fl.10s79m9M
White GRP tower, red bands 4m 332°-vis-200°

1798 Isla Quiriquina 36°36'·3S 73°02'·9W
Fl.10s89m32M Siren(2)30s
Nr. North end White metal tower, red bands 7m 048°-vis-015°

1802 Punta Arenas 36°38'·3S 73°03'·2W Fl(3)9s7m6M
White metal mast, red bands 6m 192°-vis-035°

Harbour

1814 Banco Belén 36°41'·6S 73°04'·8W
Q(3)10s10m10M
Black GRP tower, yellow band 8m. Ra Rfl.

To the south

1764 Isla Santa Maria 36°59'·2S 73°32'·0W
Fl.15s72m18M
White GRP tower, red bands 8m 006°-vis-344°

RDF beacons

3794 Constitución 35°18'·22S 72°23'·00W c/s *CTN* 340kHz 1·0kW 24hrs

3796 Isla Quiriquina, Punta de Faro 36°36'·56S 73°02'·80W c/s *QINA* 315kHz 160M 24hrs

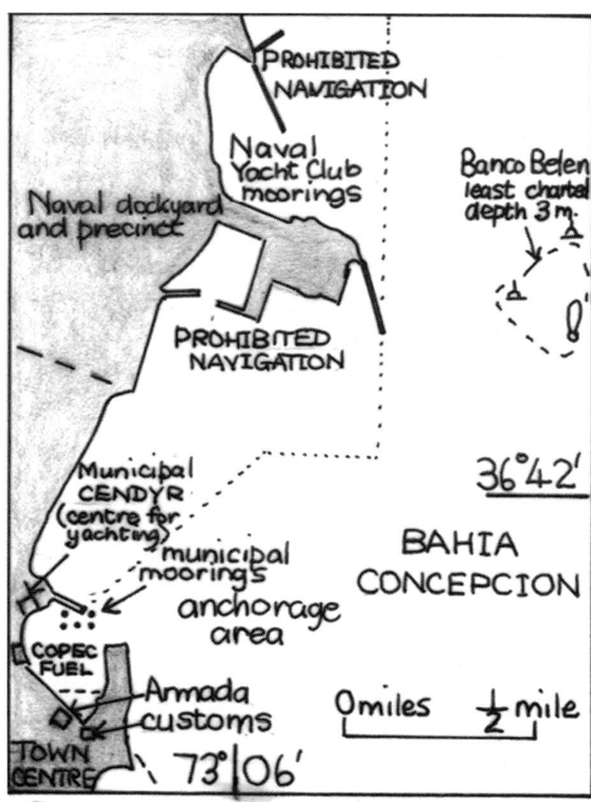

Puerto Talcahuano. (Charted positions)

3798 Concepción 36°50'·50S 73°06'·50W (PA) c/s *CE* 254kHz 1·0kW 24hrs

Tides

a. 1·1m
b. 0·7m
c. +25mins

Port communications

VHF Ch 16 ☎ (41) 54 52 49

General

Talcahuano is a timber and fishing port and a Chilean Naval base. It is on a peninsula on the west side of Bahía de Concepción. The harbour is dirty and reeks from fishmeal processed in nearby factories. Shore facilities are fairly basic (better facilities in Concepción, half an hour by bus) but there is accommodation and there are restaurants. Mainly, however, it offers safe shelter in winds from every direction.

The municipal nautical centre, *Cendyr*, which oversees the moorings, has a helpful staff who will allow the use of their telephone.

Approach

Isla Quiriquina may be passed either side. Cargo vessels are advised to use the east channel, Boca Grande, where there is a traffic separation scheme. The west channel, Boca Chica, has irregular streams which are strong at springs.

Mooring

Pass 1814Banco Belén (3·5m) and pick up one of the municipal buoys at the entrance to the commercial harbour or anchor.

Formalities

Check in on Ch16 and the *Armada* will come and inspect the ship's papers. To check out, a visit to their office is necessary.

Facilities

Repairs; try at the Navy yard (but they are not used to yachts).
Fuel by can from the COPEC station, about half a mile from the *Cendyr* office.
Covered market, basic shops and a supermarket.
Club de Yates – restaurant, lavatories but no washing facilities.

Communications

Bus to Concepción every half hour; eight daily to Santiago, Puerto Montt.
Airfield at Concepción.
Telephone Area code 41 CTC Avenida Colón

Passage

A traffic separation scheme operates at the entrance to Bahía San Vincente, off Punta Guálpen. Most of the coast line north and south of Isla Mocha (which can be passed either side) is sandy beach, usually with heavy swell. South of Punta Nihué (39°18'S 73°14'W) there are rocky headlands interspersed with beaches.

1·26 Caleta Trana

37°09'·5S 73°34'·5W

Distances
Talcahuano–50–Trana–175–Valdivia

Charts
UK *3074, 3075* US *22290, 22312* Chile *600, 604*

Going south, this makes a welcome stop with shelter from the strong southerly winds. The anchorage is tucked in behind the point of Cabo Rumena. It is a small bay with a sandy beach, no officials and one small farm.

Caleta Trana. (Charted positions)

1·27 Bahía Corral

39°53'S 73°24'W

Charts
UK *3075, 3081* US *22335* Chile *623*

General
Bahía Corral is at the entrance to Rio Valdivia. There are two anchorages which may be useful.

The first, Puerto Corral, is on the west coast of Bahía Corral, opposite the entrance to Rio Valdivia. If breaking seas caused by a strong north wind close the river entrance, a boat may wait at Puerto Corral for improved conditions. The best anchorage, close in, will probably be crowded with large fishing boats also taking shelter but a deep water anchorage can be made south of them.

The second, Isla Mancera, gives shelter from westerly winds. The island should be approached by keeping west of the off-lying red buoy north of the island and passing between it and the red buoy directly opposite on the shore of Isla Mancera. Anchor just beyond the small ferry pier in about 3–4m of water. Good holding in mud. The tide runs quite strongly. Mancera is a favourite anchorage for the yacht club and is much visited by day trippers. There is a good restaurant.

1·28 Valdivia

39°48'S 73°15'W

Distances
Trana–175–Valdivia–50–Milagro

Charts
UK *3075, 3081* US *22335* Chile *600, 623, 6271, 6272*

Lights

To the north
1750 Isla Mocha 38°24'·7S 73°53'·5W Fl.12s33m15M
South end White GRP tower, red bands 8m 205°-vis-063°
1744 Morro Bonifacio 39°41'·1S 73°23'·5W Fl.10s42m15M
White concrete tower, orange band 3m 014°-vis-218°

Approach
1726 Morro Gonzalo 39°50'·00S 73°28'·1W Fl(3)15s44m10M
White square tower, red band 4m , hut. 026°-vis-272°
1728 Morro Niebla 39°51'·9S 73°24'·0W Fl.10s50m13M
White GRP tower, red bands 8m 343°-vis-210°
1730 Roca El Conde 39°52'·1S 73°25'·2W Fl.R.5s5m5M
Red framework tower 3m

Entrance to River
1736 Isla Mancera 39°52'·0S 73°23'·6W Fl(3)R.9s6m3M
Red conical GRP pillar 2m 043°-vis-309°
then a host of lights and beacons marking the channel

To the south
1724 Punta Galera 40°00'·0S 73°42'·0W Fl.12s42m15M
White GRP tower, red bands 4m 326°-vis-208°

RDF beacons
3800 Punta Anegadiza, Isla Mocha 38°22'·93S 73°52'·93W c/s *MOCA* 295kHz 110M 24hrs.
3802 Punta Corona, Isla Chiloé 47°47'·10S 73°53'·32W c/s *CONA* 290kHz 110M 24hrs.

Tides

Puerto Corral
a. 1·0m
b. 0·6m
c. +1hr

Valdivia
a. 0·7m
b. 0·3m
c. +2hr 36 min

Port communications
Corral. Ch 16, 13 Irregular
Valdivia. Port Ch 16, 88. Club de Yates Ch 68 (24hrs) ☎ 21 30 21

General
Valdivia lies 10M up the Valdivia River with very good facilities for both yachts and general shopping;

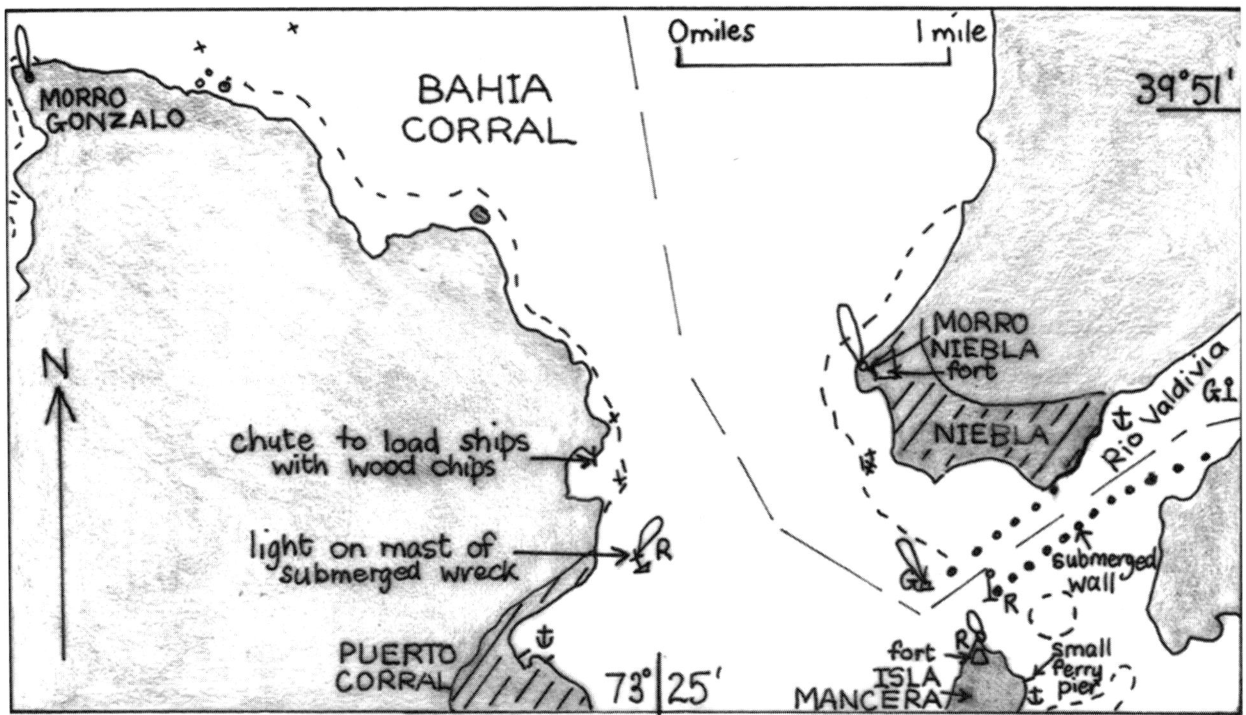

Entrance top Rio Valdivia. (Charted positions)

it is probably the best port in Chile to lay up. There is a small yacht club, with very friendly members and staff but with a crowded basin, about half a mile from the centre of town. The place to berth is at its outstation at La Estancilla, well before the city is reached, on the north side of the river beside Alwoplast (see 'Berthing' and 'Facilities' below). The Club is a very good source of information on the *canales* of the south.

Valdivia is an attractive, cultured university city with a population of 110,000. It has a strong German influence and German is still widely spoken. It is one of the wetter places in Chile, with an average annual rainfall of 2·4 metres; most falls in winter though it rains throughout the year. Temperatures rarely fall below zero and in January can reach 31°C. The combination has resulted in one of the world's three temperate rain forests nearby, the Bosque Valdiviano, which has an extremely rich diversity of species, many of them unique to the area.

The city was devastated by earthquake in 1960 (9 on the Richer scale) which caused a general subsidence of about a metre. Many riparian farms were flooded and the river is now bordered by marshes. Some remains are still visible along the waterfront and two ships wrecked by the accompanying tsunami lie in the approaches, one visible in the river and the other off Corral.

Tourism

From Valdivia it is well worth taking the time to visit the Villarica area and the famous Lake District. There are excellent bus services to points all over Chile. It is for instance a 7hr bus ride to Bariloche in Argentina, South America's major ski resort. A

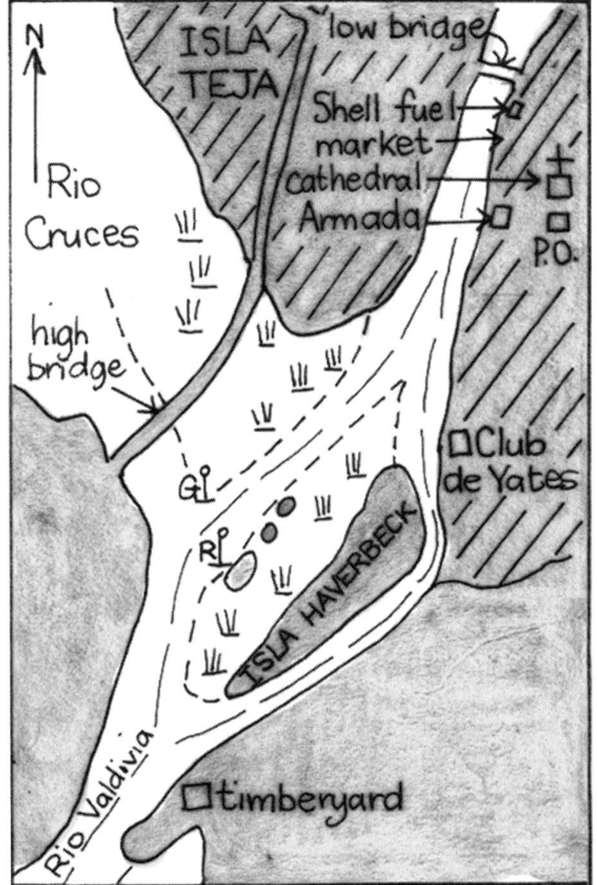

Valdivia Town

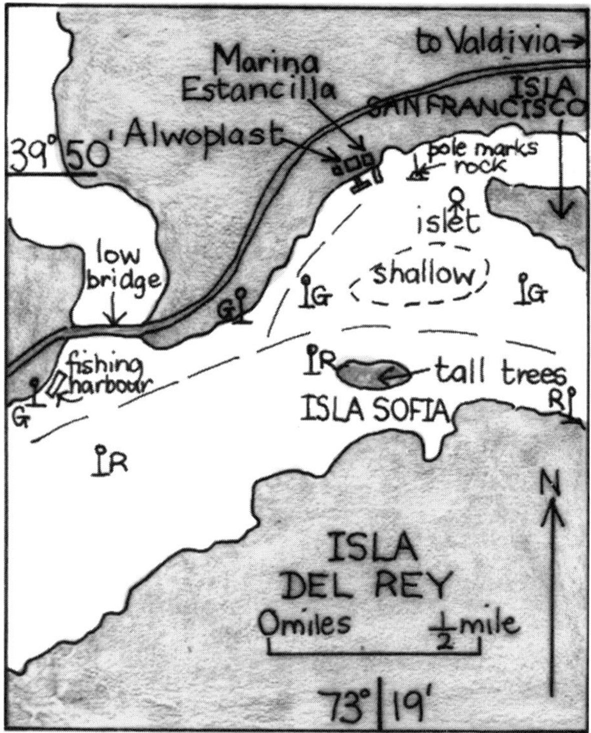

Marinas Estancilla and Alwoplast. (Charted positions)

trip to Bariloche will trigger a new entry into Chile and start the 90 day visitor permit running again (see Formalities, Appendix A).

Closer to hand is the charm of the city, the bird sanctuary Rio Cruces which can be visited by boat (not yours, however) and across the river on Isla Teja the botanic garden, an arboretum and the Museo Austral. Films in English are screened – see the Univ. cinema schedule.

Approach

The Rio Valdivia is tidal. In summer the ebb is unlikely to be critical for most yachts with auxiliary engines; with a favourable wind, the passage can be made under genoa. The channel (3m) is buoyed but there are submerged moles intermittently on both sides of the river from the entrance off Isla Mancera to within two miles of the City. It is advisable to keep in the middle of the fairway.

Call the *Capitán del Puerto* on Ch 88 before entering the river. In strong northerly winds breaking seas north of Isla Mancera may close the entrance. In this condition shelter may be had in Puerto Corral.

Berthing

There are three possibilities.

1. Alwoplast, 4M up the river, a boatyard owned and run by Alec and Dagmar Wopper. Alwoplast will come into view behind the point which has Buoy 13 off it. Pass midway between buoy 13 and buoy 14, where the submerged mole starts again. The Woppers are extremely helpful to visiting yachts and can provide skilled services, particularly in the area of stainless steel work and sail making. Dagmar Wopper is the Lingard agent in Chile.
2. Marina Estancilla, alongside Alwoplast. Make up between the pontoon and the off-lying posts. It may be worth anchoring off the end of the marina pontoon to wait for slack water as the current runs very strongly, particularly on the ebb. The marina has deep water with room for yachts up to 20m.

   There are no services at the marina other than toilets, showers and water but charges are low and the marina is very welcoming, well-sheltered and secure. In 1996 charges were US $4 per day for boats up to 12 metres, US $5 per day 12–15 metres, and US $7 per day over 15 metres. It is one of the few places a yacht may be left in comfort over the winter. Public transport to and from Valdivia is frequent and economical.
3. Club de Yates, 4·5M further up river on the east bank near the town centre. It is very full with members' boats. The railway hoist is able to haul out yachts of up to 24 tons and 16m. It is heavily used by club members so it is worth enquiring about availability. It is usually free at the end of the season in April and May. Members will advise on workshops which can carry out a wide range of repairs.

Formalities

Call the *Capitán del Puerto* on Ch 88 on entering the river. He will arrange to visit the yacht. The *Aduana,* however are in Osorno, a two hour bus ride through beautiful countryside. If entering Chile, the task of clearing customs can be combined with a pleasant day's sightseeing. The bus service is very frequent.

Facilities

All yacht building and repair facilities, bar electronics but including advanced sailmaking, at Alwoplast, 3M downstream between buoys 13 & 14 (39°50'S 73°19'·5W). Travel-lift for light displacement boats; heavy work load – book in advance. Hard standing. Customer berthing. ☎20 32 00 *Fax* 20 32 01.

Good hardware stores (Ferretería Valdivia and Sodimac).

Mauricio Fernando Diaz Flores (Ismael Valdés 460 ☎213 390) is good for repairs to gas stoves, electric drill etc.

Fuel Shell station on quay immediately below the low bridge over Rio Calle Calle.

Propane Julio Toro, 1351 Avenida Pedro Aguirre Cedra, Las Animas (take *collectivo* No 20).

Water at the yacht club, possibly at the Shell station.

Fincard Avenida Picarte 334.

Banks The *cambio* on Calle Carampague, one block from Hotel Pedro de Valdivia (which is by the bridge over the Calle Calle) will change American Express travellers cheques but the rate is not particularly good.

Cambios that on the second floor of the small shopping mall at the corner of Perez Rosales and Camilio Henriquez will change travellers cheques.

Fish & vegetable market on the river close to the *Armada.*

Well stocked supermarkets, shops etc.

Several laundries in town; Lavasol, Camilo Henriques, has same day service at US $1 per kilo.

Club de Yates: secure, quiet, showers, but missing some mod cons. 25-ton 16m slip. Water and showers included but electricity metered and charged separately.
The yacht club marina at La Estancilla has showers, water and electricity (but not for heating) included in the charges.
Consulates German, Italian.

Communications
Local buses from Club to town centre nos. 1, 2 and 3, 35 cents US. From La Estancilla, every half hour 50 cents or a *collectivo*, 75 cents.
National airport at Pichoy 32km north. Buses (26 a day to Osorno, the *Aduana* station and bus junction for Argentina).
Car hire Automóvil Club de Chile, Hertz, First Rent-a-Car and others.
☎ Area code 63. Telefónica del Sur near the town quay.
E mail facility in Calle Libertad near the riverside market, address centro@libertad7.com. Enter the name of the boat or the recipient as the subject.
Post Alex and Dagmar Wopper, Alwoplast Ltda, Casilla 114, Valdivia, will hold mail.

Passage

The distance from Bahía de Corral to the Canal de Chacao is about 120M. The narrows of the Canal are about 10M and it is a further 40M or so on to Puerto Montt.

The prevailing strong SW wind can make this a hard passage, especially as it is against the Humboldt Current. If sailing south in these conditions the passage can take several days. When it is sunny and warm in Valdivia there are almost certainly strong SW winds outside. If it is necessary to depart in these conditions, leave in the late afternoon from Valdivia as the winds generally slacken overnight allowing the yacht to motor-sail in lighter conditions. Several bolt holes can then be used *en route* to shelter from the strong daytime winds. These include Caleta Lameguapi, Caleta Milagro and Bahía San Pedro. It may be better to wait until the winds shift to the north; the passage is then generally easy, taking a day. This shift occurs generally when conditions in Valdivia are wet, chilly and overcast.

Tidal streams in Canal de Chacao are very strong and timing is crucial; there is no slack water and the transit must be made with a fair tide. There are waiting places at both ends of the canal.

1·29 Caleta Lameguapi

40°11'S 73° 43'·5W

Distances
Bahía Corral–26–Caleta Lameguapi–10–Caleta Milagro

Charts
UK *1289* US *22335* Chile *700, 701*

General
If pushed this *caleta* may serve as a short term bolt hole. There are frequently several large fishing boats taking shelter in this bay. They leave at night and resume fishing a few miles off the coast. However, there is plenty of room to anchor in 12–15m close in. The holding is good but some swell enters the bay in strong SW conditions

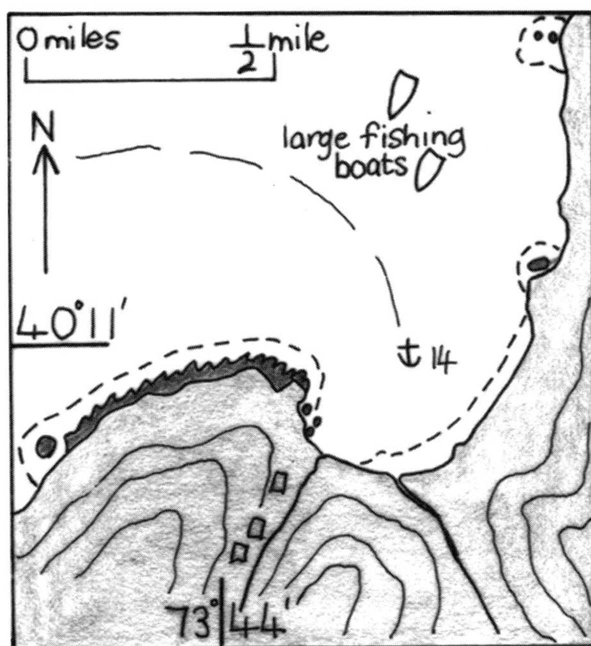

Caleta Lemguapi

1·30 Caleta Milagro

40°20'S 73°45'W

Distances
Valdivia–50–Milagro–35–San Pedro

Charts
UK *1289, 3075* US 22335 Chile *700, 701*

General
The best anchorage is in 4–5m in the south-western corner. The holding is good, but the anchorage is rolly. Caleta Milagra is a more secure anchorage than Caleta Lameguapi.

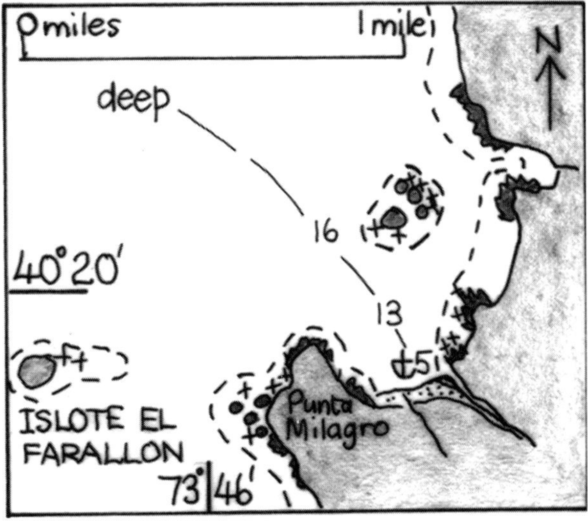

Caleta Milagro. (Charted position)

1·31 Bahía San Pedro

40°56'S 73°53'W

Distances

Milagro–35–San Pedro–55–Puerto Inglés

Charts

UK *1289* US *22335* Chile *700, 701*

General

Bahía San Pedro provides the best anchorage between Valdivia and Canal Chacao if strong SW winds are encountered. Caleta Guayusca provides the most secure anchorage. There is a small village here. Caleta Lliuco looks as though it would provide protection in NW winds. However when winds blow strongly from the N or NW they tend to veer to the west as the low passes over. In these conditions Bahía San Andres becomes a dangerous lee shore. In the 1960s two Armada vessels were wrecked here with loss of lives in these conditions. If a yacht encounters strong northerly winds when travelling towards Valdivia it would be better to turn back to either Caleta Godoy or to Puerto Ingles. In these conditions Puerto Ingles should be approached when the current is on the flood through Canal Chacao.

Caleta Godoy (41°39'S 73°45'W) lies in the north of Bahía Maullin and is protected from the north by Morro Varillasmo. Holding good at 7–10m in sand.

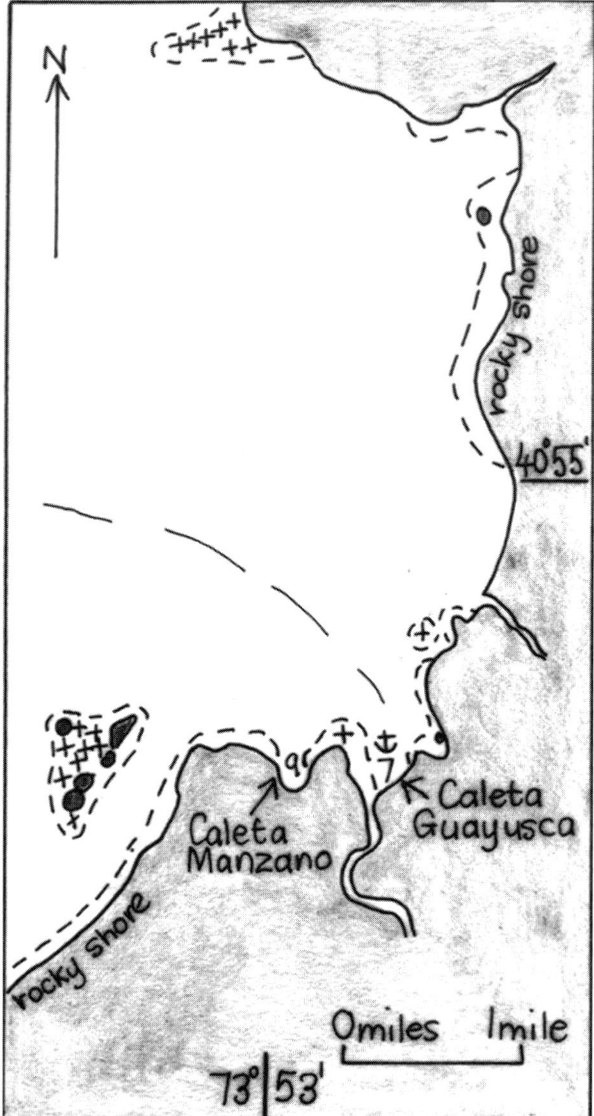

Bahia San Pedro. (Charted positions)

Section 2
Seno Reloncaví, Golfo de Ancud and Golfo Corcovado

General
The area between Puerto Montt and Golfo Elefantes has been described as the best cruising ground in the world. It is spectacular, with numerous isolated anchorages, fascinating country and few developed harbours; this section deals with the northern part of the area. The Guide starts from Canal de Chacao, works clockwise around Seno Reloncaví and then southwards down both sides of Ancud and Corcovado listing anchorages in order of increasing latitude.

Climate
The common winds in the summer are light, S to SW, (mean 5–8kt), cool to warm (mean max. 18°C, mean min. 10°C) with sun and good visibility). When the winds come from the north, a direction associated with passing lows; they may bring warmer weather and rain or overcast conditions. In winter, northerly winds are more frequent. Gale force winds are rare in summer and in winter they tend to exist only for one or two days a month. These general light wind conditions and the sheltered nature of the waters in Seno Reloncavi and the Golfo de Ancud make the sailing quite relaxing, more in the nature of sailing on a large lake than on the open sea. That said, *rachas* do occur and good ground tackle is necessary to cope with them as well as a large tidal range and strong streams – see Appendix F.

Rainfall in the area is high, averaging about 1900mm a year. The highest proportion falls in winter and some places, such as Chacabuco, have the reputation of being wetter.

Salmon farms
Salmon farms, *salmoneras,* have been widely established. Rounding a headland expecting to find convenient shelter for the night, the pens of a *salmonera* are often encountered. However, in most places there is space between the pens, the anchoring buoys and the shoreline for a small craft to anchor with a suitably secure amount of anchor rode paid out. *Salmoneristas* are helpful in making visitors moorings secure – which is in their interest. The pens provide a lee against choppy waves but give little protection from wind or swell. Their detritus promotes the growth of algae on the bottom which can make it more difficult for an anchor to dig in.

Salmon pens have been marked on the sketch plans. However there is continuing investment in fish pens and their positions and numbers change.

Lights and marks
The few lights of passage are not listed; consult the appropriate chart or light list. Channels are well posted with day-marks and beacons. Experience indicates the wisdom of securing well before dark.

Fuel
Fuel is available in Puerto Montt, Castro, Quellon and Aguirre.

Kelp
Kelp can grow in strands 75m long (and therefore in deep channels) and in massive beds. It is a great hindrance to a safe anchorage. It can also break loose and float away, difficult enough to spot by day and impossible to see at night (all the more reason to secure before dark).

2·1 Puerto Inglés
41°47'S 73°52'W

Charts
UK *1289,* 1313 US *22341, 22342* Chile *702, 703*

Port communications
You should report your position to Punta Corona Faro on Peninsula Lacui. The *Faro* will provide tidal and weather information.

General
Located south of the light at Punta Corona, this is an excellent anchorage while waiting for the flood tide before entering Canal Chacao. The holding is good, in sand, 6–7m at low water, just outside the entrance to the lagoon (Estero Chaular). It is also possible to anchor just inside the entrance in 3·5m; here the anchorage is windy in northerlies but the water is calm. Alternatively anchor to the north-east of the salmon pens with the wreck on the stony

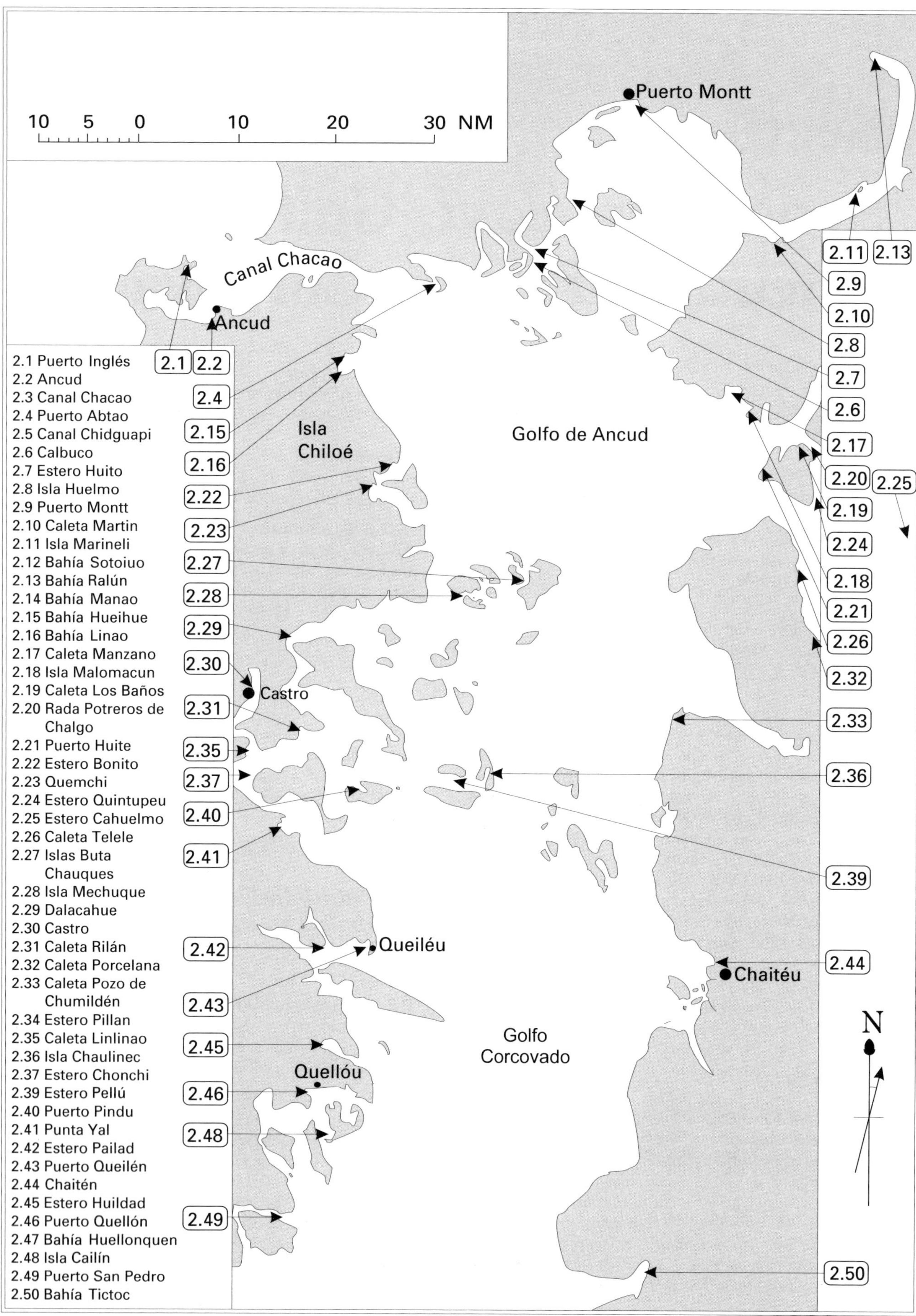

10 5 0 10 20 30 NM
Puerto Montt
Canal Chacao
Ancud
Isla Chiloé
Golfo de Ancud
Castro
Queiléu
Chaitéu
Golfo Corcovado
Quellóu
N
2.1
2.2
2.4
2.15
2.16
2.22
2.23
2.27
2.28
2.29
2.30
2.31
2.35
2.37
2.40
2.41
2.42
2.43
2.45
2.46
2.48
2.49
2.11
2.13
2.9
2.10
2.8
2.7
2.6
2.17
2.20
2.25
2.19
2.24
2.18
2.21
2.26
2.32
2.33
2.36
2.39
2.44
2.50
2.1 Puerto Inglés
2.2 Ancud
2.3 Canal Chacao
2.4 Puerto Abtao
2.5 Canal Chidguapi
2.6 Calbuco
2.7 Estero Huito
2.8 Isla Huelmo
2.9 Puerto Montt
2.10 Caleta Martin
2.11 Isla Marineli
2.12 Bahía Sotoiuo
2.13 Bahía Ralún
2.14 Bahía Manao
2.15 Bahía Hueihue
2.16 Bahía Linao
2.17 Caleta Manzano
2.18 Isla Malomacun
2.19 Caleta Los Baños
2.20 Rada Potreros de Chalgo
2.21 Puerto Huite
2.22 Estero Bonito
2.23 Quemchi
2.24 Estero Quintupeu
2.25 Estero Cahuelmo
2.26 Caleta Telele
2.27 Islas Buta Chauques
2.28 Isla Mechuque
2.29 Dalacahue
2.30 Castro
2.31 Caleta Rilán
2.32 Caleta Porcelana
2.33 Caleta Pozo de Chumildén
2.34 Estero Pillan
2.35 Caleta Linlinao
2.36 Isla Chaulinec
2.37 Estero Chonchi
2.39 Estero Pellú
2.40 Puerto Pindu
2.41 Punta Yal
2.42 Estero Pailad
2.43 Puerto Queilén
2.44 Chaitén
2.45 Estero Huildad
2.46 Puerto Quellón
2.47 Bahía Huellonquen
2.48 Isla Cailín
2.49 Puerto San Pedro
2.50 Bahía Tictoc

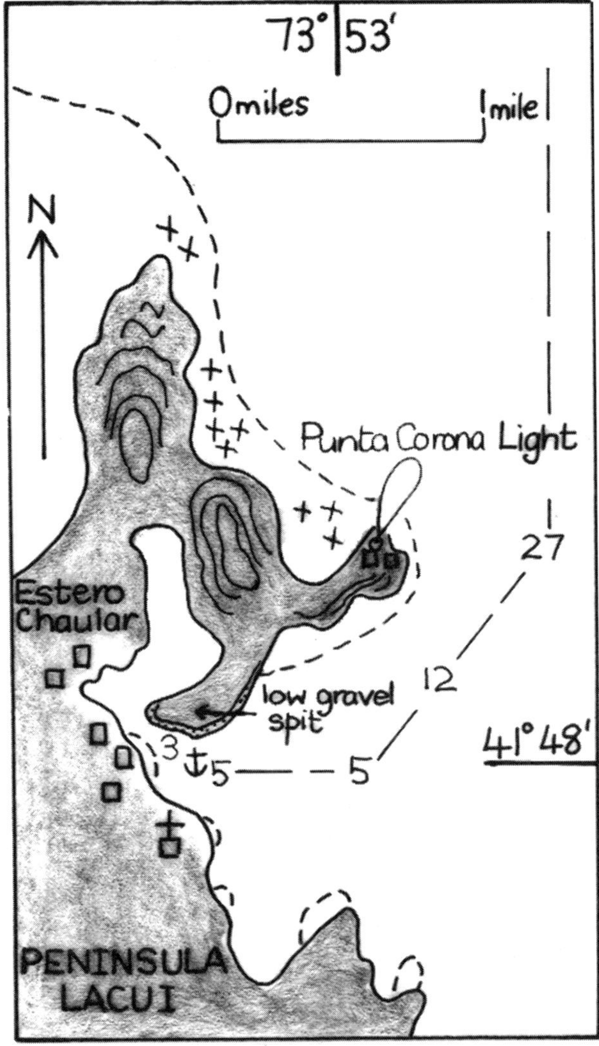

Puerto Ingles

beach bearing 332°. If the wind is too strong from the N, an alternative is Estero Dique, round the corner of Punta Arenas 2·5M west of Ancud.

2·2 Ancud

41°52'S 73°50'W

Charts

UK *1289, 1313* US *22341, 22342* Chile *7210, 703*

General

Ancud is mentioned because yachts should stay away from it. The approach is across shallows which dry and there is virtually no protection from the west. There is no harbour.

2·3 Canal Chacao

Charts

UK *1289, 1313* US *22341, 22342* Chile *700, 7210*

General

Canal Chacao separates Isla Chiloé from the mainland. When approaching, particularly from the west, it is important to establish VHF radio contact with the naval station at the Corona light – call Corona on Ch 16. The station is very helpful and will give conditions in the Canal plus a local weather forecast. The station also transmits local conditions each day, in Spanish, at 0900 and 2100hrs on VHF Ch 14.

When approaching from the north keep 4 miles plus off the west end of Isla Dona Sebastiana as shallow seas to the west of the island can create steep and potentially breaking seas. Turn east through the Canal when on a line 1 mile south of the island.

A useful short cut, especially when coming from Bahía Maullín is to enter the Canal between the East End of Isla Dona Sebastiana and the mainland. Rocks extend out about 1 mile to the east of the island. Even in calm conditions there are overfalls in this gap although in these conditions they are not dangerous.

The passage itself is well marked and wide. It is important to travel to the east on the flood, or to the west on the ebb. There are strong tidal flows along its 15 mile length, with areas of overfalls in the shallow waters at both ends and also in a line extending to the southwest from Peninsula Challahué. In the Canal, the west-going stream begins 1 hour before high water and the east-going stream 1 hour before low water. At springs, the stream may be more than 10kt in the centre and there are tide rips. With wind against tide, very steep and high (5–8m) waves may be encountered, some of which break. It is dangerous for a small craft to enter the channel in these conditions.

There is considerable traffic in the canal, including a ferry service that runs from the mainland to Chacao. Anchorages at the east end of the canal are Manao, Hueihue, Linao and, on the north shore, Abtao.

From Canal Chacao to Puerto Montt and beyond: Seno Reloncaví

2·4 Puerto Abtao

41°48'S 73°21'W

Charts

UK *1289, 1313* US *22341, 22342* Chile *7210, 704, 705*

General

Puerto Abtao is located at the eastern end of Canal Chacao between Isla Abtao and Peninsular Challahué. Favour the side of Isla Abtao when entering from the south through Canal Abtao to avoid the sandbank off the point. Also beware of the numerous salmon pens along the route. There is a prominent church to the east of the village. Good anchorage can be had south of the village between the beach and the salmon pens. Depth is 6m at low water and the holding is good in mud and sand.

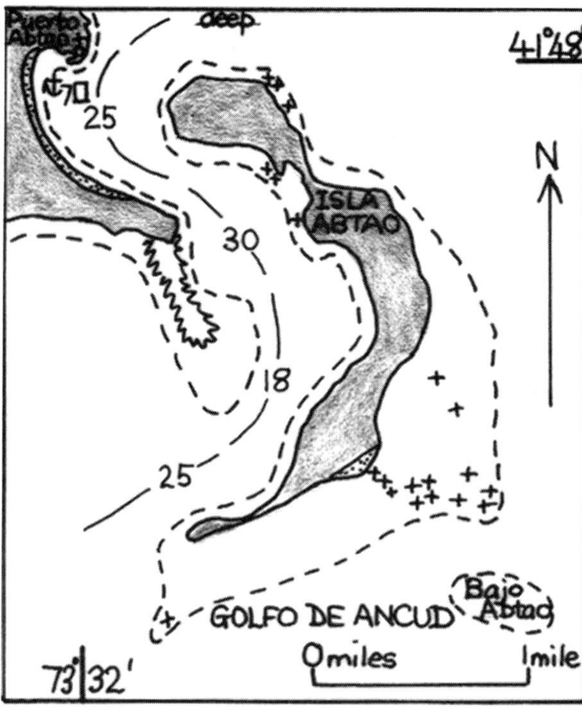

Puerto Abtao. (Charted positions)

2·5 Canal Chidguapi

41°50S 73°07'W

Charts

UK *1289* US *22341* Chile *704, 706*

General

A well-sheltered but deep anchorage on the SW side of the canal between Islas Chidguapi and Puluqui. Anchor in 10–15m (rapidly shoaling bottom) between the W end of the salmon pens and the white beach. Restaurant ashore (booking necessary).

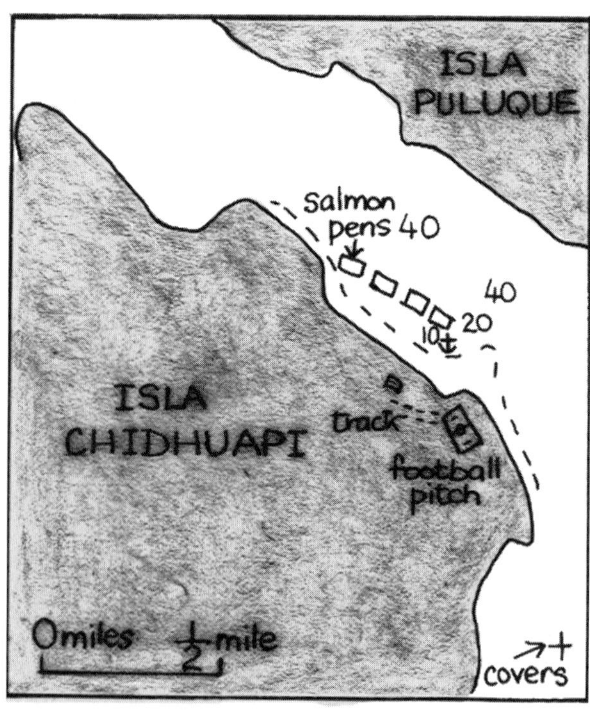

Canal Chidguapi 41°49'·7S 73°05'·4W

2·6 Calbuco

41°47'S 73°08'W

Charts

UK *1313* US *22341* Chile *704, 705, 706*

General

Calbuco is a town perched on top of a hill overlooking the sea and is now linked to the mainland by a causeway. It was a settlement founded by the Spanish in 1604, many decades before Puerto Montt. The town has all the usual facilities and it is a good place from which to visit Puerto Montt by bus.

Anchorages

There are three anchorages.

1. The most secure if the yacht is to be left for some time is to the west of the causeway. The approach is straightforward through Canal Caicaen but keep to the centre to avoid mussel farms on either side. Very good holding in 10–15m.
2. If a yacht wants to collect fuel or visit the town, the best anchorage is to the north of the town, close east of the causeway in about 10m. This is a good overnight anchorage but show an anchor light as a considerable number of fishing boat move in the area – and put the anchor light in the statutory position, the fore-triangle, not at the top of the mast, or it will not be observed, especially when it is raining and the helmsman in steering from within his cuddy. The dinghy can be landed near the causeway by the Copec station which has both clean fuel and water.
3. The third is Surgidero La Vega on the southern side of the northeast corner of the island. Keep to the west shore. Food supplies and fuel (take cans). Open to the south so pick your time and do not stay long.

2·7 Estero Huito

41°45'S 73°10'W

Charts

UK *1313* US *22341* Chile *704, 705* (entrance), *706*

General

Watch for rock off the southern shore; favour the north shore. Delightful and secure anchorage with good holding in sand and rocks. Market one mile up the road. There are many salmon cages.

2·8 Isla Huelmo

41°39'S 73°04'W

Charts

UK *1313* US *22341* Chile *704, 706*

General

A sandspit extends southwest from the southwest point of the island. Go past the *salmoneras* towards a small densely tree'd hill on the mainland and then turn northeast to get behind the sandspit. Charts show the inner pool as drying out; this is not so and there is plenty of water. Anchor either about 100m off-shore (tidal range about 6m) and far enough in for protection from the south or clear of the salmon pens in the inner pool. Anchor with house on Huelmo bearing 133° and cream house on mainland 270°. This is not an excellent anchorage in strong northerlies or southerlies as it is open. It would be better to use Estero Huito.

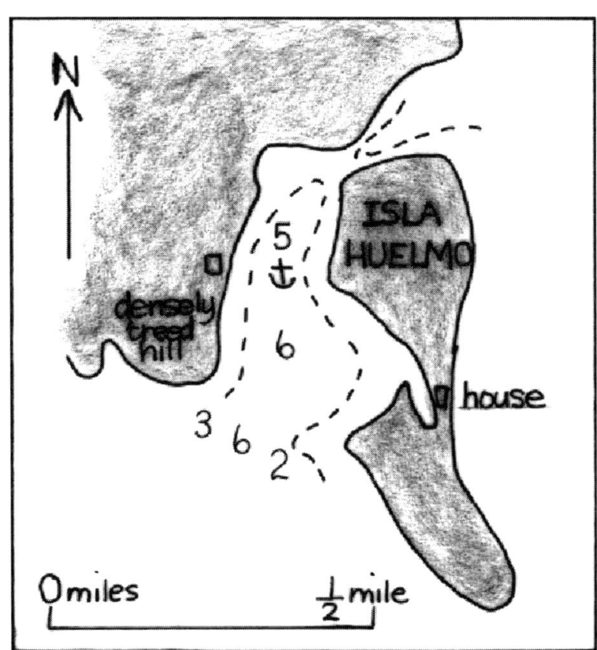

Isla Huelmo 41°39'S 73°04'W

2·9 Puerto Montt

41°29'S 72°57'W

Charts

UK *1289, 1313* US *22341, 22345* Chile *704, 732*

Lights

Harbour

1700 Berthing Jetty, E. End 41°29'1S 72°57'8W

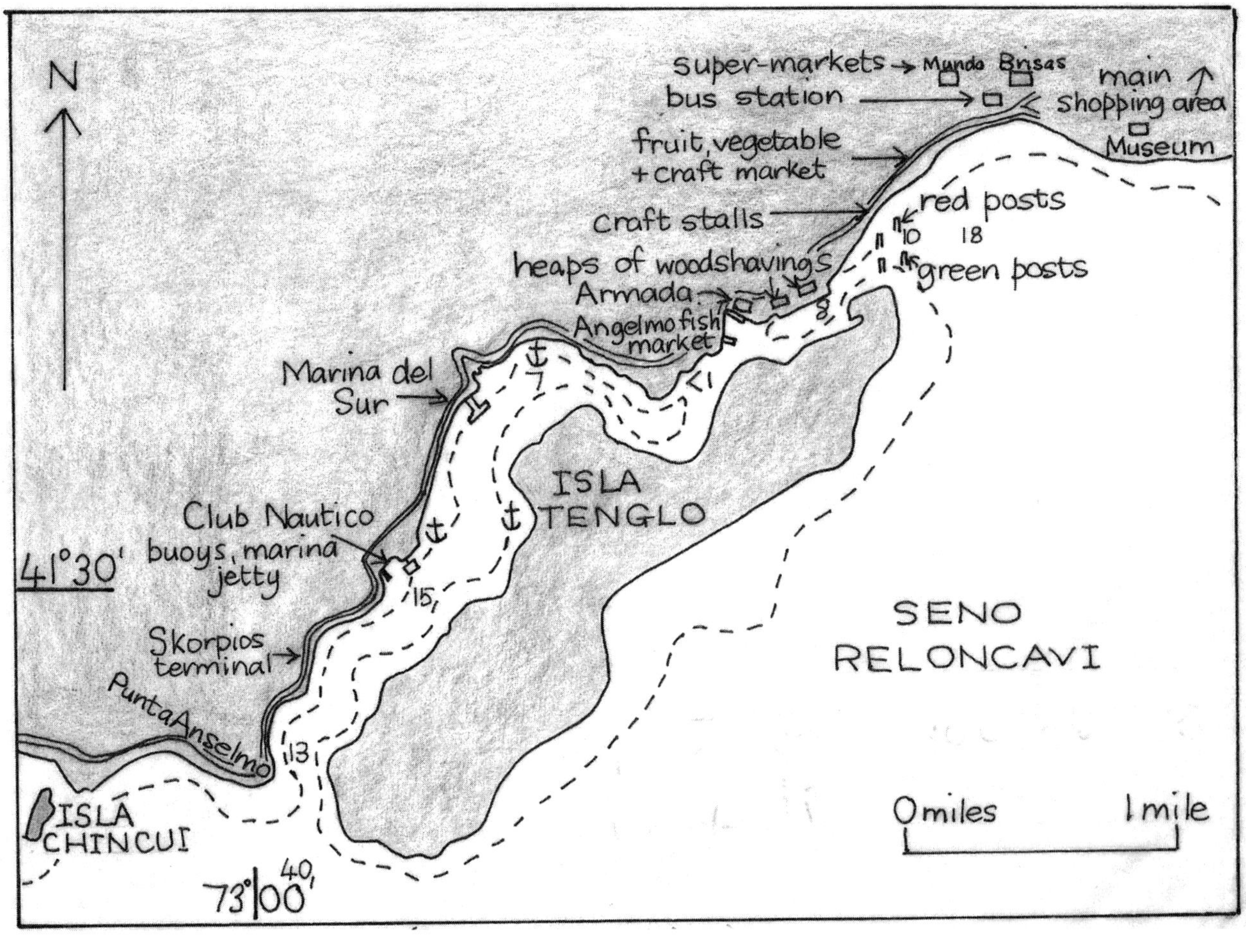

Puerto Montt. (Charted positions)

Fl.R.3s6m4M
White GRP tower, red bands, 4m 217°-vis-272°
Canal Tenglo has lights.

Tides
a. 5·8m
b. 2·3m
c. Standard Port

Port communications
Port Ch16 ☎ 25 23 89
Marina del Sur ☎ 25 91 95

General
Yachts coming in from the Pacific often make Puerto Montt their first port of call. It has good facilities for repairs, maintenance and for restocking the ship. There are two organised places to moor. The first is Marina del Sur at the west end of Canal Tenglo which can accommodate vessels up to 65 feet. The second is to ask for the use of a mooring at Club de Yates, Reloncavi. The latter charges reasonable prices and has a waterboat taxi service. It is also possible to anchor opposite the yacht club and up to the Marina del Sur although there is a lot of boat traffic in this area. Anchoring behind the northern end of Isla Tenglo is prohibited. There is no safe anchorage in front of the town itself.

Puerto Montt is a major tourist centre. Tours to the Lake District start here as do ferries to Castro, Chacabuco, San Rafael and Puerto Natales.

Mooring
Go to Marina del Sur which is most easily approached along the buoyed channel from the southwest end of Isla Tenglo. Frequent buses ($120) and *collectivos* ($120, $150 on Sundays and holidays) to Puerto Montt centre via Angelmó where the *Armada* has its office and where there is a major market.

Formalities
Check with the *Capitán del Puerto* on Ch 16. *Aduana* in town. Staff at Marina del Sur will help.

Facilities
At Marina del Sur

Specialist services such as sail-makers, welders engine fitters and stores such as propane can be arranged by the Marina.
40-tonne platform hoist but much in demand and no hard standing (the boat is left on the platform during repairs).
Drying-out wall (9m tides at Springs).
Diesel and petrol.
Electricity 220V 50 Herz on floats.
Showers and water.
Laundry.
List prices are high but open to negotiation, especially in winter.

In town

Hardware Weitzler on Lota and Perez Rosales.
Money Banco Osorno for Visa (not travellers cheques). Several *cambios*, for instance AFEX on Diego Portales (the sea front) which also takes American Express travellers cheques (Mon–Fri 0900–1900, Saturdays 0900–1300).
Market at Angelmó, the ferry port and naval base halfway between the marina and the centre of town: vegetables, fish, vacuum packed smoked salmon, cheese. There are many good restaurants here.
Supermarkets Las Brisas, opposite bus terminal; Mondial, cheaper. Wymeister for meat.
Laundries (including one at Las Brisas).
Consulates Argentinean, German and Spanish.

Communications
Air Services to Santiago, west coast ports and to Punta Arenas. Buses to Santiago, Chiloé and many other Chilean destinations and to Argentina (for Punta Arenas). Ferry services to Chiloé, Chonos, San Rafael, Puerto Natales.
Car hire Automóvil Club de Chile, Avis, Budget and others.
Telephone Area code 65 ENTEL E. Ramírez 948; Telefónica Sur, Chillán 98.

Diversion Seno Reloncaví

2·10 Isla Manzano – Caleta Martin
41°44'S 72°34'W

Charts
UK *1313* US *22341* Chile *708*

General
A useful spot if the run up to Ralún is disrupted by weather. The anchorage is a fairly small inlet within Caleta Martin on the east side of Punta Chaparano. Enter Caleta Martin until the entrance is seen, behind a small promontory with a rock or islet off it, then take the centre line. Anchor and run a line to the orange-painted concrete block and another line aft. There are many fish cages.

2·11 Isla Marimeli
41°40'·8S 72°26'W

Charts
UK *1313* US *22341* Chile *708*

General
The small bay at the northeast end of this island is one of the most secure and sheltered anchorages in Seno Reloncaví.

2·12 Bahía Sotomo
41°39' 72°23'W

Charts
UK *1313* US *22341* Chile *708*

General
Good shelter can be found by anchoring in 15–18m close-to in the southwest corner of the bay and taking lines ashore. Thermal springs run directly in to the sea nearby and at low water it is possible to take a hot bath.

2·13 Bahía Ralún

41°24'S 72°19'W

Charts

UK *1313* US *22341* Chile *708*

General

Keep to the south shore until Punta Veriles, opposite 1699Cayo Nahuelhuapi (Fl.R.5s3m5M red GRP tower, red band, 3m), has been passed. About 0·75M WSW approx. there may be a large white mooring buoy and a pier ashore. This area offers the only protection against the north wind, a little far from the hotel but worth it. The hotel and restaurant has a good reputation.

From Canal Chacao southwards – Golfo de Ancud

2·14 Bahía Manao

42°52'S 73°32'W

Charts

UK *1313* US *22341* Chile *7210*

General

This is a useful anchorage if waiting for a fair tide through the Canal Chacao or after coming through the Canal from the west late at night. It is open to the east but there is good holding at the head of the bay in about 10m.

2·15 Bahía Hueihue

41°54'S 73°31'W

Charts

UK *1313* US *22341* Chile *710*

General

A small anchorage open to the south with a tidal range of 5–6m. In strong northerly winds there is little shelter and yachts have reported dragging here. If uncomfortable, consider Linao.

Approach

From the south, Punta Lamecura is clear; from the north, Punta Chilén has foul ground SE and Bajo Cholche lies south of Punta Hueihue. Pass about half way between Punta Concura and Punta Hueihue.

Anchorage

Go up near the head of the bay but check depth against swinging room and tidal range. Access to the lagoon, which has good shelter, may be possible at high water; check the approach by dinghy.

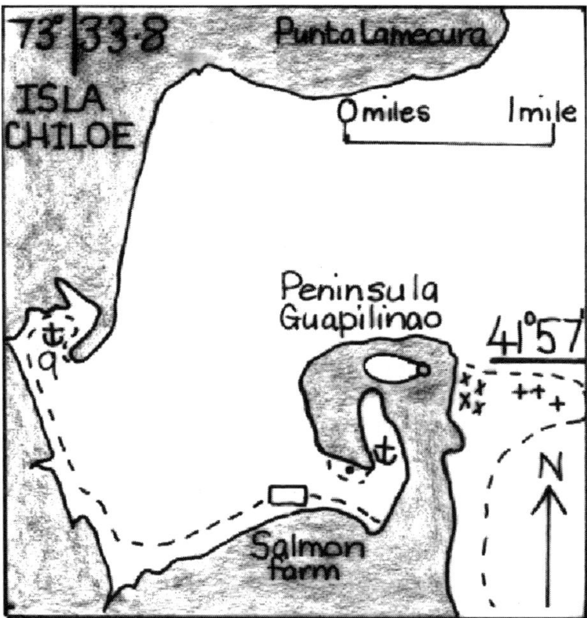

Bahía Linao. (Charted positions)

2·16 Bahía Linao

41°58'S 73°32'W

Charts

UK *1289, 1313* US *22341* Chile *709, 710*

General

Fifteen miles south of the eastern entrance of Canal Chacao, Bahía Linao offers two sheltered anchorages. Reports vary on their quality in bad weather, the anchorage in the eastern hook giving best protection in southerly winds. Unfortunately there is a large oyster farm in the eastern basin that takes up much of the anchoring space. A bow and stern anchor are necessary to hold the boat in position. The basin is quite shallow, 12 feet at the entrance and 6–9 feet north of the oyster farm. A good birding spot.

Beware submerged rocks east of 1664Punta Guapilinao (Fl.G.5s50m5M Green GRP tower 3m 012°-vis-343°). The hamlet at Linao, about a mile away, can supply eggs, bread and beer (in bulk, bring bottles).

2·17 Isla Manzano – Caleta Manzano

42°01'S 72°39'W

Charts

UK *1313* US *22341* Chile *709, 704*

General

For trout fishermen. Isla Manzano lies at the south edge of a drying flat and the *caleta* is on its west side. Enter from the south between the island and the mainland and anchor in a small cove on the mainland side about 500m from the island. Good for south and southwest winds but untenable in northerlies. The trout are in Rio Cisnes; not many, but big. In strong northerlies, Estero Pichicolou has been used successfully as an anchorage.

2·18 Isla Malomacun

42°03'·6S 72°37'·75W

Charts
UK *1313* US *22341* Chile *709, 704*

General
There is a good all-weather anchorage between Malomacun and Isla Toro to the east. Rocky bottom 10m but suitable holding has been found.

Diversion
Canal Hornopiren

General
In settled weather a detour up Canal Hornopiren provides a spectacular route. There are two bays at the north end of Isla Pelada, one in the northwest corner and the other in the northeast corner. Access to both is clear. Anchor in 10–15 with shore lines.

Continuation

2·19 Isla Llancahué - Caleta Los Baños

42°05'S 72°32'W

Charts
UK *1313* US *22341* Chile *709,704*

General
Caleta Los Baños is open to the north but it has running hot water and a hotel. The rock marked at the west entrance of the bay is well offshore and covered at high water (no surf). The river delta, west of the hotel, is shallow. Anchor in 10–15m. A more secure anchorage, although still open to the north, can be found in Caleta Andrade, 1m to the west of Caleta Los Baños. The entrance to this long bay is simple with no dangers. Anchor in 15m silt, good holding. The head of the bay shelves quickly.

2·20 Rada Potreros de Cholgo

42°05'·8S 72°29'·2W

Charts
UK *1313* US *22341* Chile *704,709*

General
The anchorage is between a small unnamed island and Llancahué, ½M NE of Rada Potreros de Cholgo. Coming from the north the island is easily seen. From the south, look out for two houses, one blue, nearest the point below the high hill. A good overnight anchorage except in winds with any easterly component. It would probably be untenable in strong southerlies. There is insufficient room to swing between the small island and Llancahué but a four point tie is possible though small local boats may use the cut. Holding in mud with a few rocky patches.

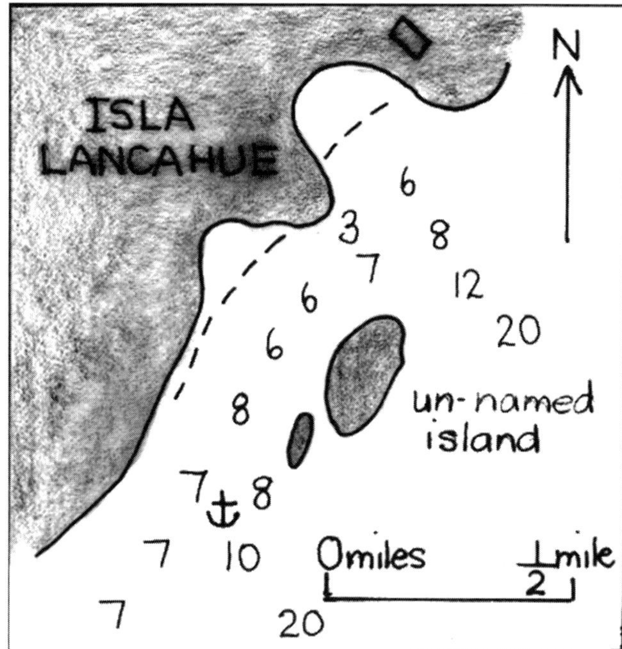

Anchorage in Potreros de Cholgo 42°05'·8S 72°29'·2W GPS

2·21 Isla Llancahué - Estero Bonito

42°08'·5S 72°35'W

Charts
UK *1313* US *22341* Chile *704, 709*

General
The shape of the bay varies with the charts. However it is an enclosed bay offering a very well protected anchorage, good for all winds, on the south side of Isla Llancahué and a useful stop if going south or west. The narrow entrance is hard to spot but a house on the hill is a landmark. Use the small bay to port on entering, anchoring in about 10m. Some rubbish from a fishing camp.

2·22 Puerto Huite

42°07'S 73°26'W

Charts
UK *1313, 1289* US *22341* Chile *704, 709, 710*

Tides
Spring range about 6m

General
The entrance is round the sandspit off Punta Arenas. Favour the eastern side when entering, but be careful rounding the sandspit especially at high water when the head, about 75m off shore, will be covered. The anchorage is deep but provides good protection from all winds. The best place is at the very head of the bay, north of some salmon pens and west of some buildings. There is also good holding

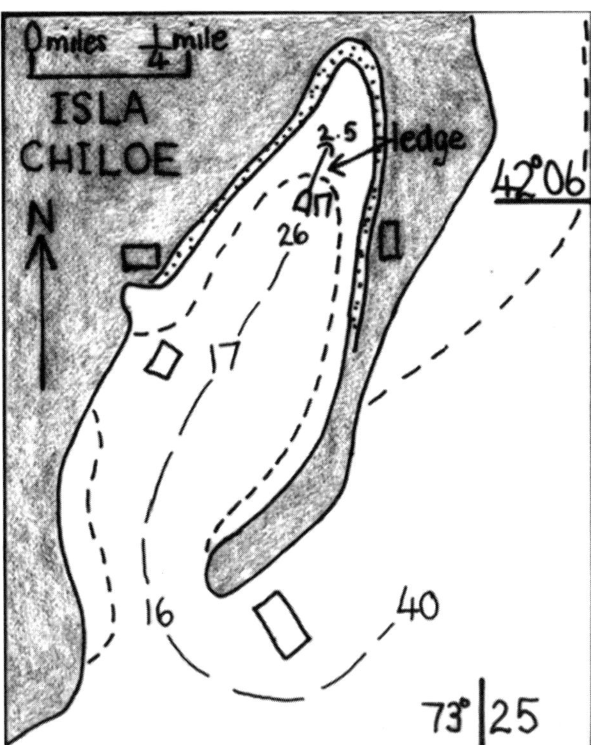

Puerto Huite. (Charted positions)

just inside the sandspit in 15m. Good mussels and clams (but see the warning about the red tide under 'Shellfish' in the introduction). Also a small stream, good for laundry.

2·23 Quemchi

42°08'S 73°29'W

Charts

UK *1313, 3749* US *22341* Chile *710*

General

The anchorage is off the south shore of the village, mud and sand. It is picturesque, with black-necked swans. The village has old wooden buildings (those with red flags outside are butchers), a super market which has accepted dollar travellers cheques, shops, basic restaurants, post and telephone. Bus to Castro and Ancud.

An alternative anchorage, nearer than Huite, is Estero Tubildad, 1·5M north.

2·24 Estero Quintupeu

42°10'S 72°26'W

Chart

UK *1289* US *22341* Chile *709* has the entrance.

General

The entrance is very narrow but once inside, it opens out. Leave a *salmonera* to port. The fjord has deep water (the battleship Dresden hid here for a short while in 1914) but about 3M up, near the head depths fall quickly to a narrow sandspit.

There are two places that have been used as anchorages. The first is a small bay on the south side, with a stream running into it, just after the entrance. Anchor close to the shore in 15m with lines ashore. The second is to go to the head of the bay and anchor in 6–8m on the edge of the sandspit. This requires care as the bottom shelves very quickly and it is very easy to run aground and be left high and dry on the ebb. Estero Quintupeu has been described as spectacular, a dramatic landscape of snow-capped volcanoes and cascades. Beware *rachas.*

2·25 Estero Cahuelmo

42°15'S 72°24'W

Charts

UK *1289* US *22341, 22352* Chile *704*

General

In settled weather Estero Cahuelmo makes a spectacular and peaceful anchorage with the added attraction of thermal pools. The entrance is clear and deep. Proceed towards the head of the *estero.* Well before the end of the fjord it shelves very quickly with depths decreasing from 80m to nothing within a few boat lengths. Anchor just off this sandspit using shorelines. A stream with a waterfall marks the position of the anchorage. At low water it is possible to walk across the sandspit to the thermal pools, which are easily located by a large wooden sign. At high water use a dinghy to cross the sandspit.

2·26 Peninsula Huequi – Caleta Telele

42°17'S 72°31'W

Charts

UK *3749* US *22341, 22352* Chile *709*

General

With shelter from the northwest and some from the north (though the wind may come round the corner of Punta el Cajon), Caleta Telele is on Estero Leptepu, opposite Estero Cahuelmo, and has served well as an overnight anchorage.

2·27 Islas Buta Chauques

42°17'S 73°08'W

Charts

UK *3749* US *22341, 22352* Chile *704, 709*

General

This group lies to the east of Canal Chauques and consists of two islands, Isla Buta Chauques and Isla Aulin. It is a sparsely populated area of attractive sand spits and rolling hills around a substantial lagoon. The approach is more straightforward than suggested by the chart, and there are a number of excellent anchorages.

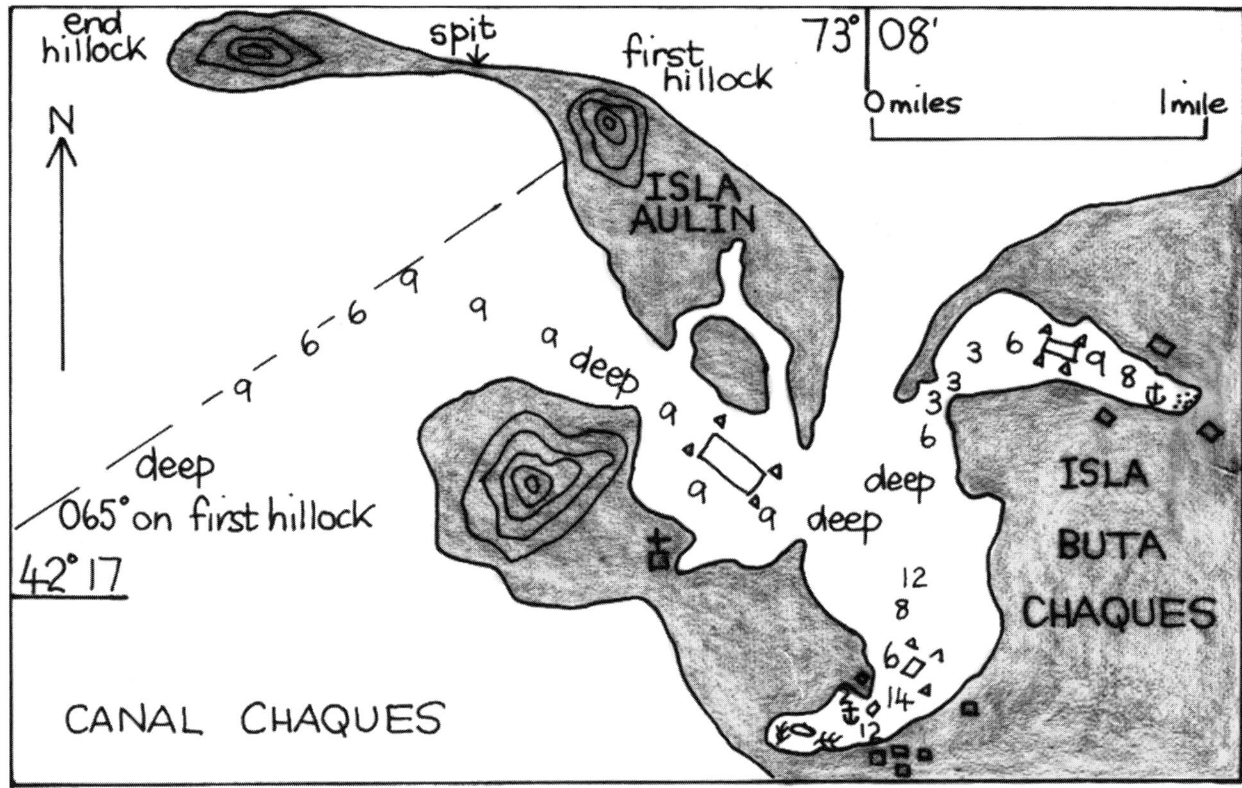

Isla Buta Chauques. (Charted positions)

Approach
Chile chart *609* shows two kelp patches (Boca Del Medio and Boca Pajaros) in the western entrance from Canal Chauques. No kelp was seen in 1998 although the area may be shoal. The approach should be made with caution from the northern part of Canal Chauques using the bearings shown in the diagram. The lagoon itself is relatively free of dangers.

Anchorages
The eastern part of the lagoon divides in two. The northern branch is entered through a narrow channel formed by a sand spit. The channel is clear of obstructions and has a minimum depth of 3m. Anchor at the eastern end of this bay in perfect shelter, 10m mud. Anchorage can be found in the southern branch south of the fish farm in about 10m.

2·28 Isla Mechuque

42°19'S 73°15'W

Charts
UK *3749* US *22341, 22352* Chile *704, 709, 721*

General
The anchorage in front of Mechuque village is very picturesque and well protected from all winds. The fishing village is particularly attractive as the houses are built on stilts (*palafitos*). There has been considerable investment in salmon farming and there are many salmon pens in this group of islands. Smoked salmon can sometimes be purchased – ask in the village. In the event of very strong west winds try the shallow bay to the northeast of the town and anchor on the western side due east of a large *palafito*.

The channel between Isla Mechuque and Isla Añihue to Isla Taucolon is navigable with several well-sheltered anchorages along the way. The passage through the islands is a little difficult to follow when travelling through them. The sketch plan shows the canal with the best route through. There is a spectacular anchorage in the lagoon north of Isla Taucolon. The entrance is straightforward; anchor in 4m just before the final pool. It has good protection except between northeast and southeast. Good views of snow- capped mountains on the mainland.

A pleasant anchorage can also be found in Puerto Voigue though the anchorage on the east side of the sandspit there is full of fish cages.

2·29 Dalcahue

42°23'S 73°40'W

Charts
UK *3749* US *22352* Chile *709, 711*

General
Dalcahue, the place of the three-plank canoes, has a population of 7,000 and many fine old wooden buildings, including one of the oldest wooden churches in Chiloé. It is an interesting place to visit, especially on a Sunday when in addition to the general market, there is a covered craft market with

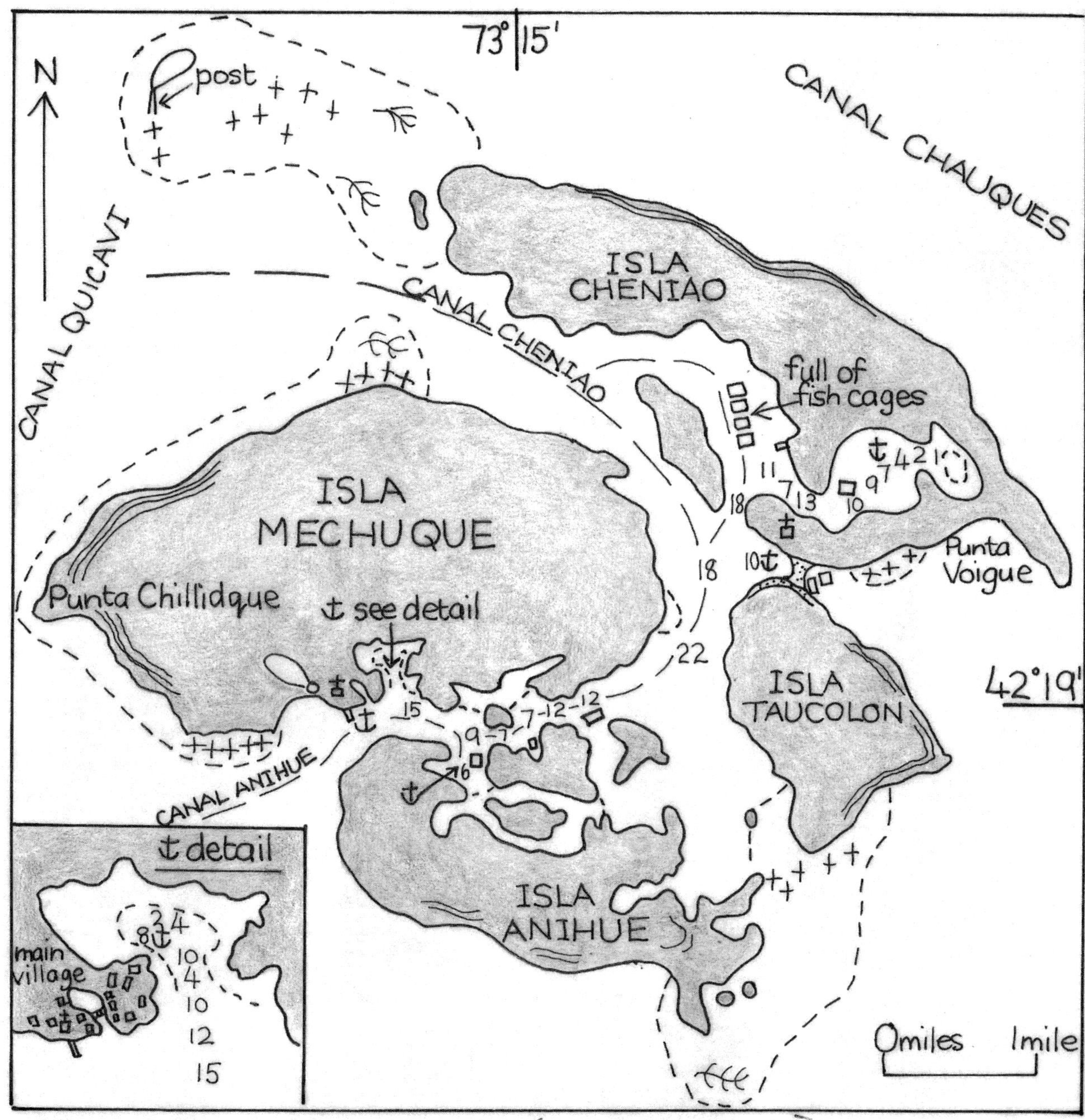

Mechuque group of islands. Showing general location of key anchorages

a vast array of woollen knitted and woven goods – sweaters, ponchos and jackets. There are many small shops and bars.

Anchorage

Anchor in about 10m near the jetty and the covered market. The current runs very strongly past Dalcahue and the anchorage is crowded with local fishing boats. These boats anchor with a long rope rode so when the tide turns it is easy to become tangled up with them. Anchor as clear from the jumble as possible. Alternatively there are several places to go; one is under the power line (43·9m), with a good lee in a strong SW and good holding. Land on the beach or at the ferry ramp.

2·30 Castro

42°28'S 73°46'W

Charts

UK *3749* US *22352* Chile *709, 712*

General

Castro is the capital of Chiloé. It has one of the best timber churches on the island, with a fine interior and twin pink and blue towers. The Church is a national monument but is in fine condition internally; externally, needful repairs are being carried out. The anchorages at Castro are effectively landlocked. A few foreign yachts over-winter, though it can be uncomfortable in a gale when the wind comes either from south or north.

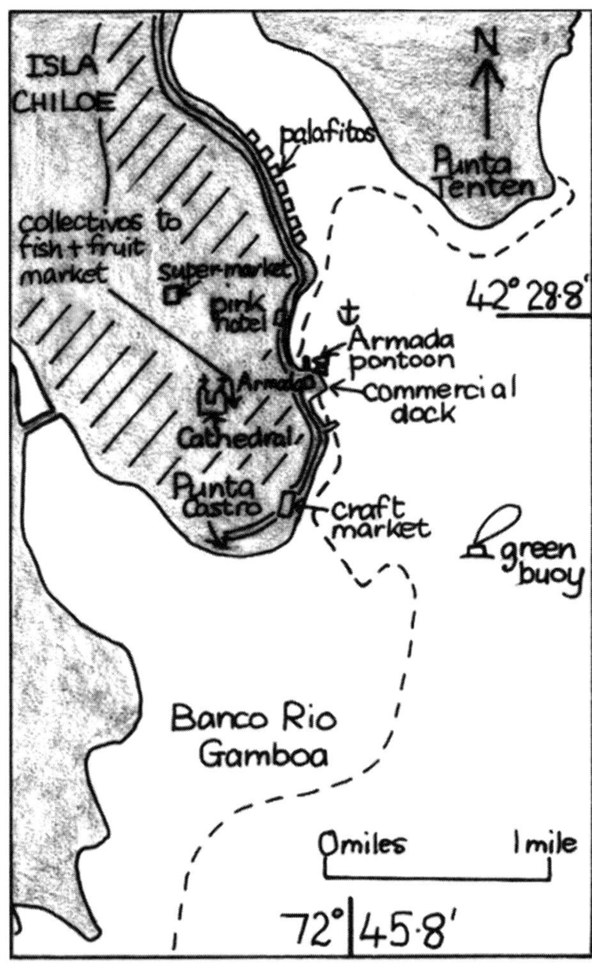

Castro. (GPS positions)

Shoreside facilities are good in terms of shops, modern supermarkets, hotels, restaurants and it is very crowded in the high season. There are good general workshops directly opposite the *Armada* station with a range of light engineering skills, such as repairing exhausts and welding, but little other support for a yacht.

Approach

Straightforward but the Banco de Gamboa immediately south of the town is said to be slowly extending southeast. It is well buoyed with a large green buoy so poses no problem for a yacht.

Anchorage

The anchorage is to the north of the *Armada* station, in 6–14m with reasonable shelter from all except strong southerlies.

Formalities

Check in on Ch16 and visit the *Armada* by using their floating pontoon. The *Armada* is very helpful and if asked will allow a visiting yacht to use their pontoon to tie up the dinghy. This gives total security to the dinghy while ashore.

Facilities

Fishing boats dry out alongside the harbour wall (the tidal range is about 5m).
Diesel at service station on harbour wall (jerry cans required; go at high tide with the dinghy and a length of rope) or from stations elsewhere in Castro. Small open trucks, *fletes*, operate like taxis and are useful in this context.
Propane canisters may be refilled at the home of one of the *collectivo* drivers. Ask another driver or inquire at the *ferretaria* on the corner above the harbour.
Best supermarket (Becker) up San Martin, north of the cathedral. Wide variety of shops in the Plaza de Armas.
The best and most economic place to buy vegetables and fish is at the Feria. Catch a *collectivo* from Avenida San Martin, near the Cathedral.
Small shops (including a butcher selling lamb), fresh fish, vegetable markets on foreshore.
Laundry on the road up to Plaza de Armas.
Several hotels will make available their bathrooms for showers.
Water by container at the service station or from the *Armada*. The *Armada* will also allow a yacht to come up alongside their vessels at the pier to refill by using their long hose. Ask at the office for permission first and warn the Captain of the ship that you will go up alongside.
Handicrafts on the foreshore.
Travellers cheques generally not accepted; Banco del Estado may do so at a poor rate. Try Bilisco, Chacabuco 286 or another at Chacabuco 378 for cash against a credit card. Visa and MasterCard accepted at Becker, hotels etc.

Communications

Through buses to Puerto Montt, Santiago (18hrs) and local buses in Chiloé. A Navimag ferry calls (not on the Montt – Natales route) and other ferries serve the small islands, arriving in Castro in the morning and leaving in the afternoon.
Telephone Area code 65. Phone office at Latorre and San Martin.

2·31 Caleta Rilán

42°32'S 73°38'W

Charts

UK *3749* US *22352* Chile *709*

General

Pass either side of the *salmonera*. The water shoals quickly towards the head of the bay. Very quiet.

2·32 Caleta Porcelana

42°28'S 72°30'W

Charts

UK *3749* US *22352* Chile *709*

General

Caleta Porcelana is a spectacular anchorage in Estero Leptepu, under snow-covered peaks with hot springs nearby. The anchorage 20m off the beach is not easy as it is deep (20m), steep-to and has a rocky bottom. A light tidal current makes a stern line essential. The hot springs are about 800m up the stream, after crossing a log bridge. Vegetables are available at a farm; also (apparently) laundry. The hot springs are very beautiful. There is a charge.

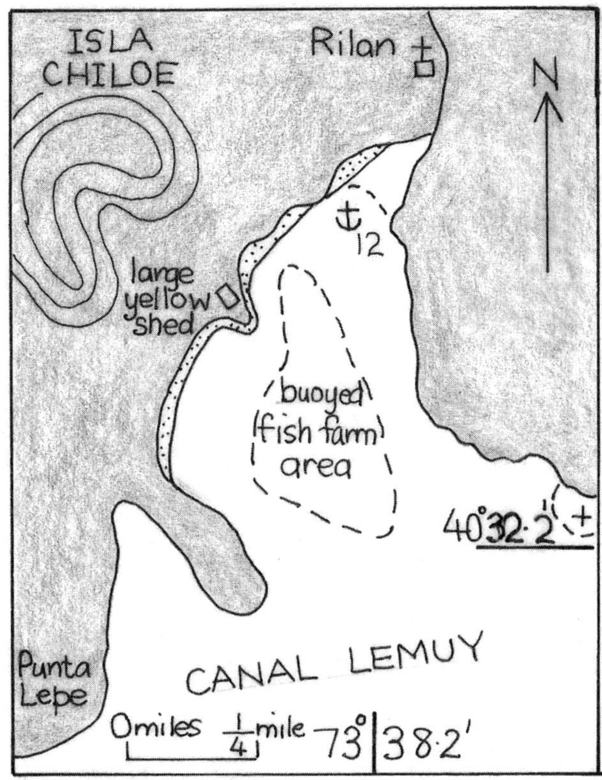

Caleta Rilán. (GPS positions)

The majority of exploration of the Canals by yachtsmen has all taken place in the last 10 – 20 years. However between the two World Wars a small handful of yachtsmen from the Club de Yates, Valdivia, had started to sail among the northern islands and fjords. These included Otto Stolzenbach. In the mid 70's, Justo Schuler, President of the yacht club for many years, and other members of the Club used the log of Otto Stolzenbach to rediscover beautiful places like Caleta Porcelana.

2·33 Caleta Pozo de Chumildén

42°30'·4S 72°48'·9W

Charts
UK *3749* US *22352* Chile *709, 721*

General
A snug anchorage but likely to be uncomfortable in strong northerlies especially at high tide. The inner pool to the southeast of Isla la Leona is small and supports a small fishing fleet. Restricted swinging room may necessitate a stern line to the island, to one of the reefs or a stern anchor.

Approach
Approaching from the north, a red and yellow mark painted on the rocks on the eastern side of the entrance is visible, depending on the light, from 400m. The entrance channel runs SSW between Isla Quemada and Punta Chumildén. Keep to the middle of this channel and then pass with care about 30m from the SW end of Isla Cabras. A submerged

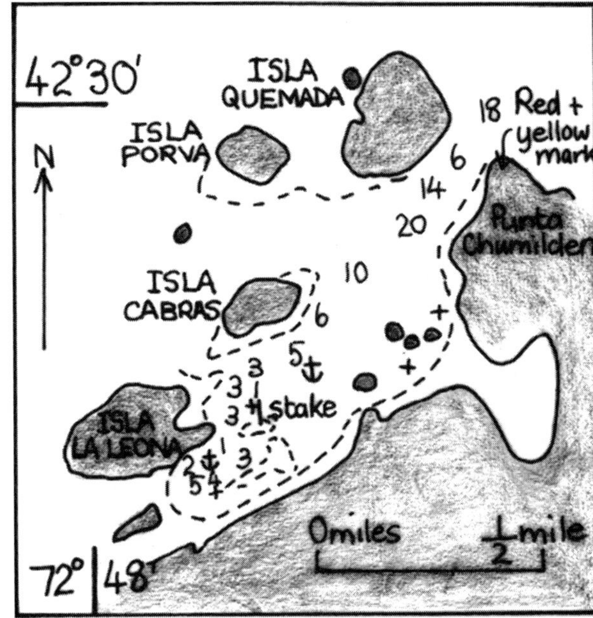

Caleta Pozo de Chumilden 42°30'·4S 72°48'·4W

reef (of rocks) extends N from the rock marked by a stake. Stay on the Isla Cabras and Isla la Leona side of the channel.

Anchorage
The main anchorage is tucked up under Isla la Leona as far as depth permits but beware the reef in the southeast corner of the bay.

2·34 Estero Reñihue – Estero Pillan

42°34'S 72°31'W

Charts
UK *1289* US *22341, 22352* Chile *709*

General
Estero Pillan is a very beautiful and sheltered anchorage at the head of Estero Reñihue. The anchorage can only be entered at high water. When approaching, take care of rocks which can cover at high water and which extend about 100m off the most eastern end of the two Islas Nieves. To stay in adequate depths (5–6m) keep within about 10m of the northern shore. Once inside depths increase quickly. Anchor in about 15–18m on the northern side of the lagoon with lines ashore. Vegetables can be purchased from the farm building and there are small trout in the stream.. There is some salmon farming.

2·35 Caleta Linlinao

42°34'S 73°45'W

Charts
UK *3749* US *22352* Chile *712*

General
Located 6 miles south of Castro, Linlinao provides good shelter, but is a little open to a north wind whistling down Estero Castro. A light on the

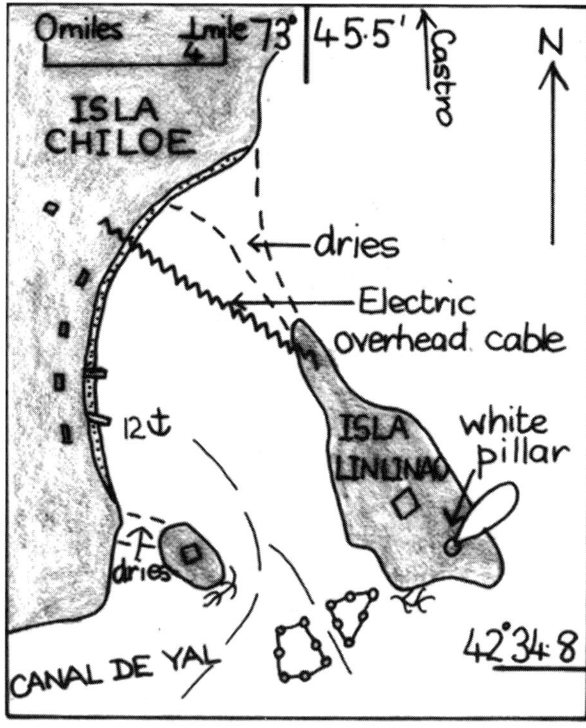

Caleta Linlinao. (GPS positions)

southern end of Isla Linlinao aids in identification. There are several fish pens to be avoided. The best entrance route is along the southern shore. The holding is good in 15m on a mud bottom.

2·36 Isla Chaulinec

42°37'S 73°18'W

Charts
UK *3749* US *22352* Chile *709*

General
There is a rather beautiful, quiet anchorage on the northern side of Isla Chaulinec, in 13m close to the shore in front of a small farm and to the west of the village. There is no protection from west or north winds. The pier in front of the village and the light on shore to the west of the pier are good landmarks.

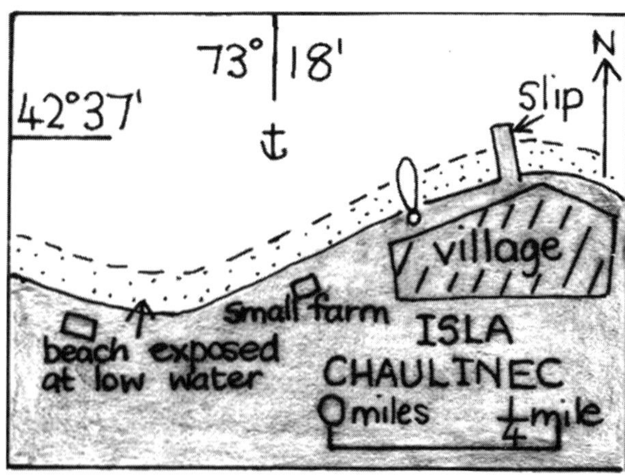

Isla Chaulinec. (Charted position)

In the event of north winds, cross Canal Chaulinec to Caleta Huechun, which lies to the east of the long hook of land at the west end of Isla Alao (42°36'S 73°19'W). Good holding in silt, 6–12m.

2·37 Estero Ichuac

42°37'S 73°44'W

Chart
UK *3749* US *22352* Chile *712*

General
On the east side of Isla Lemuy, opposite Chonchi, Ichuac is open to the west but sheltered from the southwest and has good shelter from the north. Anchor in about 8m at low water, with good holding in mud. This is a very pretty inlet with a small village at the head of the bay.

2·38 Puerto Chonchi

42°37'·6S 73°47'W

Charts
UK *3749* US *22352* Chile *709, 712*

General
Chonchi is a very poor anchorage. It is exposed to the north and the east with an uncomfortable swell developing south of the quay. East of the quay the water deepens very quickly and west of the quay the water shelves and is suitable for small boats only. The quay is very busy with fishing boats. Ask permission to go alongside a fishing boat or anchor just south of the pier in about 10m. A stop at Chonchi would be temporary to reprovision or make a crew change. It is better to cross Canal de Yal to Estero Ichuac.

Canal de Yal

There is an electricity cable across Canal de Yal with 28m of clearance. When rounding Punta Yal, in the southern part of the Canal pass the low-lying Islote Yal on its east side. The Canal is safe, clean and deep.

2·39 Isla Apiao – Estero Pellú

42°37'S 73°13'W

Charts
UK *3749* US *22352* Chile *709, 721*

General
The anchorage in Estero Pellú on Isla Apiao is one of the most delightful and best protected in the islands off Chiloé. The entrance needs care but is straightforward if approached from the south west at half tide. The spring range is 5·5m so at half tide the two large flat rocks, marking the entrance like sentinels, are visible. Leave the western flat-topped rock close to port and then favour the west side of the 40m entrance channel. There is plenty of room

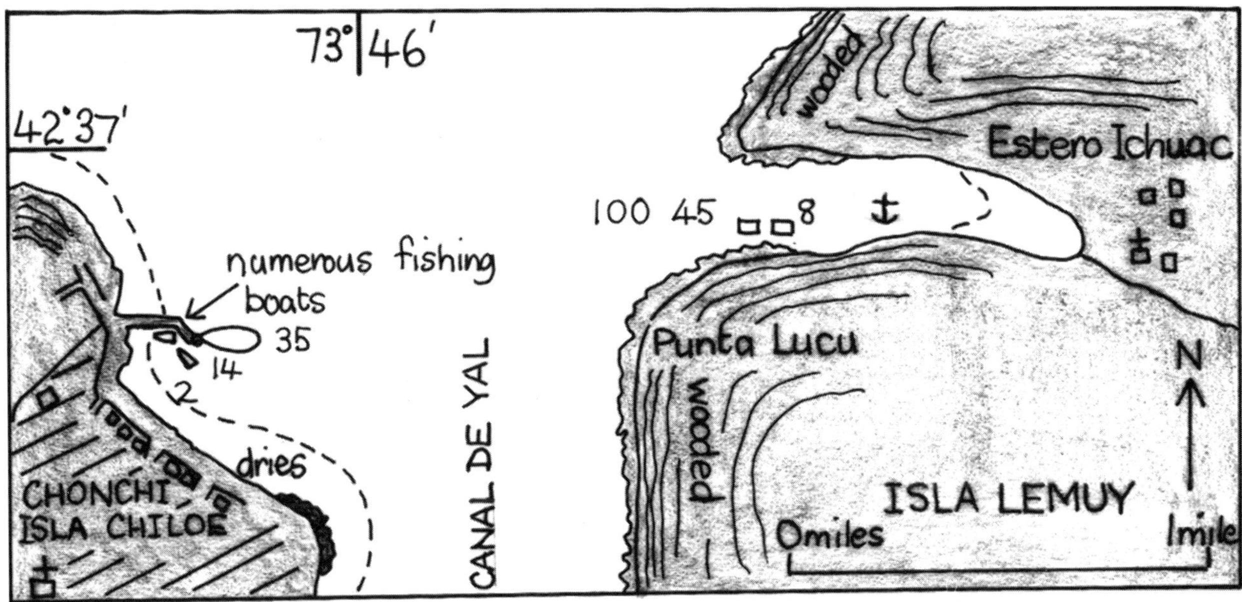

Puerto Chonchi and Estero Ichuac. (Charted positions)

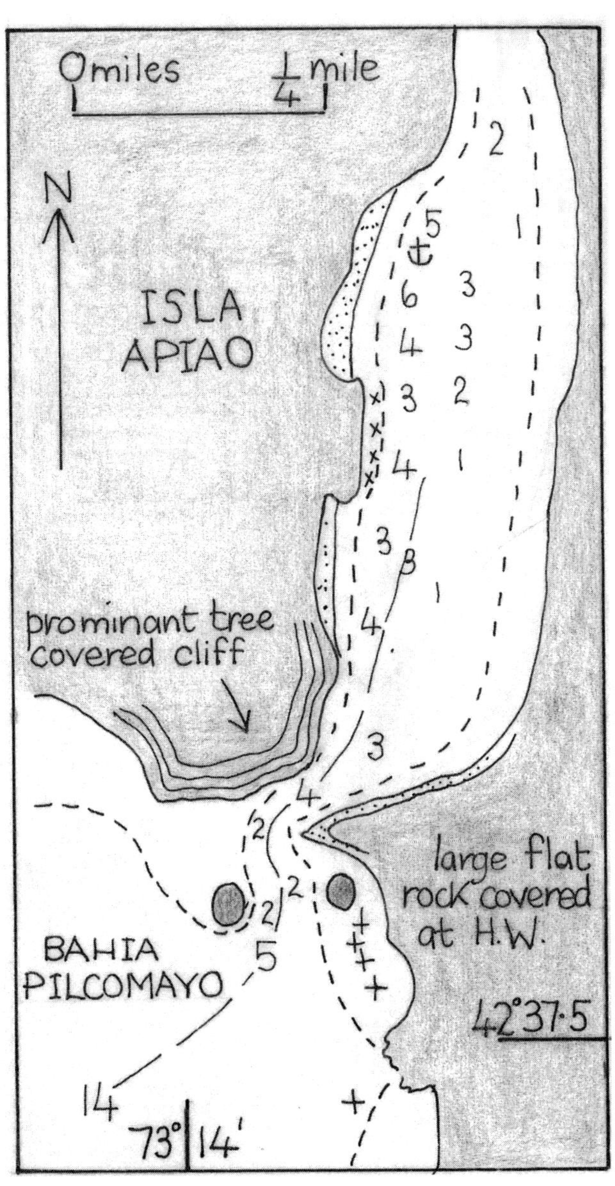

Estero Pellú, Isla Apiao

to anchor in 3–6m inside the Estero; the deeper water is on the west side and it shoals to the north of the second narrows. The best shelter from northerlies is under the bluff of the second narrows. When leaving the west flat rock becomes visible 1–2 hours after high water, providing adequate sign-posting to exit the Estero.

There are no shops but it is possible to buy potatoes, parsley, and other vegetables in season from Luis, who lives on a small holding *(parcela)* on the east side of the Estero.

2·40 Isla Quehui – Puerto Pindo

42°37'S 73°31'W

Charts

UK *3749* US *22352* Chile *709*

General

This is a beautiful anchorage with soft rolling countryside around Estero Pindo. The village of Los Angeles has about 800 inhabitants, several small shops, a pretty wooden church and on a sunny day a pleasant bar to enjoy a beer in its garden.

Approach

Approaching from the west, head for the church; the light structure (1631Puerto Pindo Fl.14s4m5M white GRP tower, red bands 3m) is not visible until a mile off. The entrance looks wide but the deep water is close to the northeast shore.

Anchorage

Anchor off the houses just beyond the ramp or move further to the NE to avoid getting tangled up with local boats. They anchor, using rope, with a lot of scope and therefore swing a long way as the tide turns. The anchorage is well protected in all winds but a modest chop in southeasterlies.

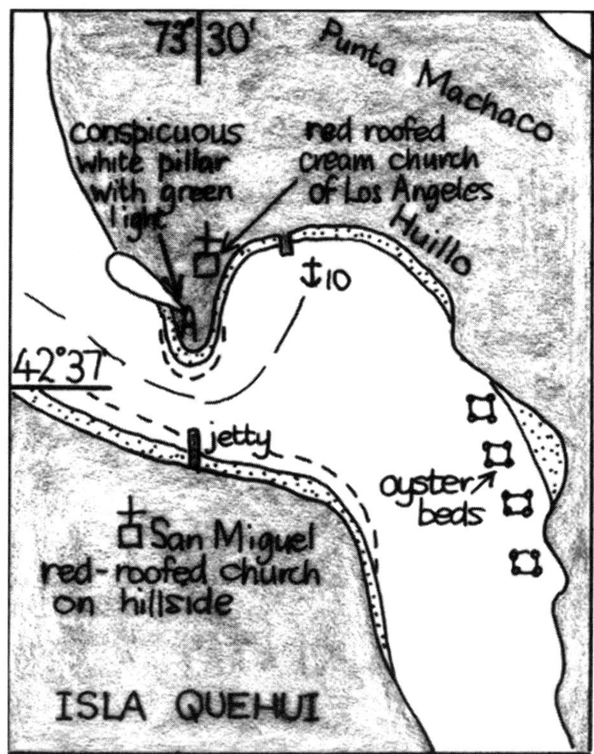

Estero Pindo. (GPS positions)

2·41 Punta Yal

42°40'S 73°40'W

Charts
UK *3749* US *22352* Chile *716*

General
Described as a reasonable all-weather anchorage it is tucked behind Punta Yal and has a *salmonera.* Pleasant walking.

2·42 Estero Pailad

42°52'S 73°36'W

Charts
UK *3749* US *22352* Chile *716*

General
The entrance to this wooded *estero* is easy, wide and deep, past a *salmonera* on the west side. At first the Estero runs between wooded hills, small neat paddocks and low cliffs running by the waterside. After about 1½ miles the Estero begins to open out, where a pretty yellow church becomes visible on the west shore. Anchor here, good holding in about 8–10m.

On the other side of the *estero* from the church is a distinctive blue and yellow farmhouse. Next to this house is an old water-driven flour mill. This no longer works but Hector at the house will be pleased to show the visitor inside the mill *(molino de agua).*

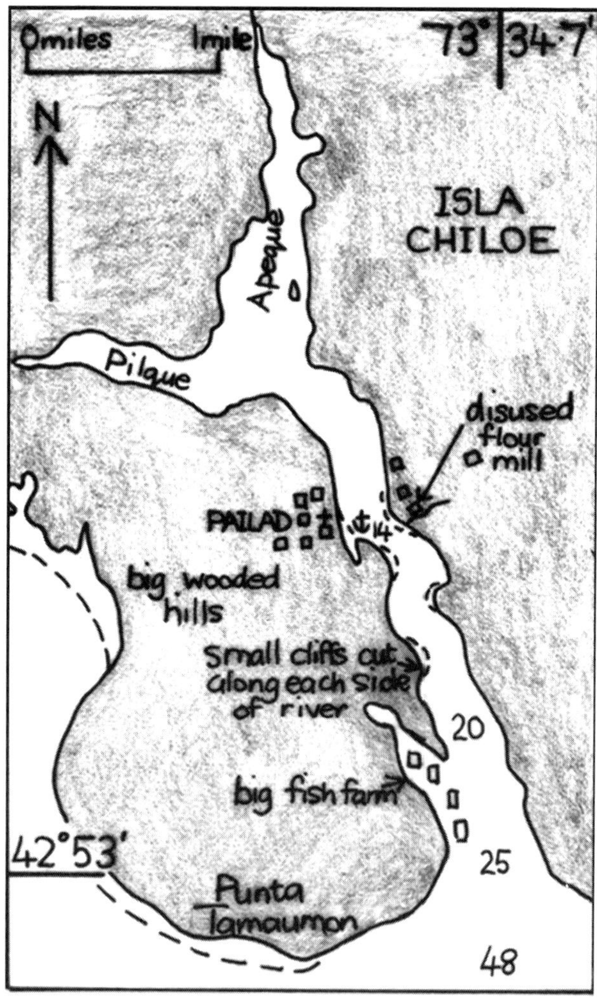

Estero Pailad. (GPS position)

Canal Queilén

The passage through Canal Queilén is straightforward. However where the canal narrows between Punta Yategua and Punta Vilo tidal streams run strongly and can reach 4–5 knots. The stream turns southerly with the ebb.

2·43 Puerto Queilén

42°54'S 73°29'W

Charts
UK *3749* US *22352* Chile *714, 716*

General
Puerto Queilén is a small town with several shops, a small hotel, and hospital. Facilities include telephone, fax and post.

Approach
When approaching from the northeast keep ¾M off Punta Chomio to avoid off-lying shoals. Punta Queilén has a skinny island lying off it to the SW with a tower (4m). The spit continues some distance southwest of the light and is mostly covered at high water

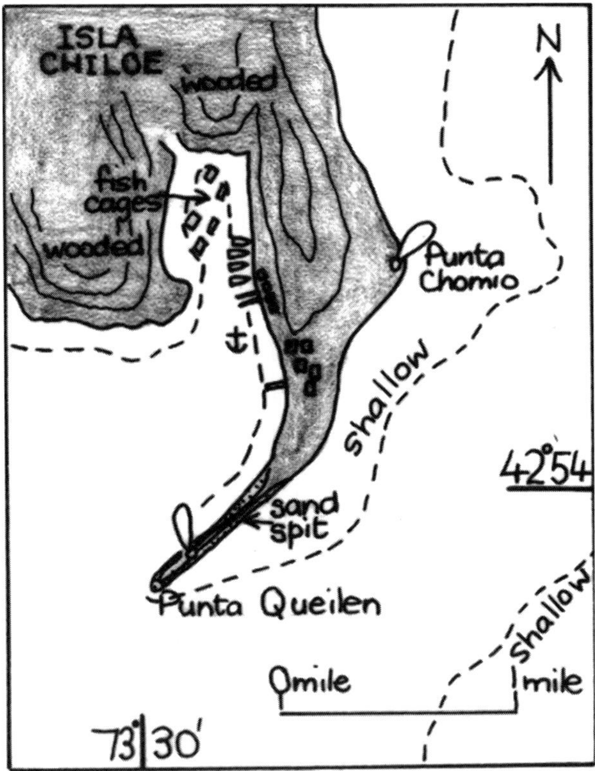

Puerto Queilén. (Charted positions)

Anchorage
Anchor in good holding in 12m west of the town jetty, or a little further south between the two piers. There are a large number of fishing boats at anchor and it is very easy to become tangled up with them. A little exposed in W to SW winds and even in strong north winds there is a chop.

It used to be possible to anchor in Estero Mechai, immediately northwest of Punta Queilén. However this is now crowded with fish cages and anchoring is difficult.

Unless it is necessary to stop at Puerto Queilén to reprovision it is much better to sail an additional 5 miles west and anchor in the peaceful protection of Estero Pailad.

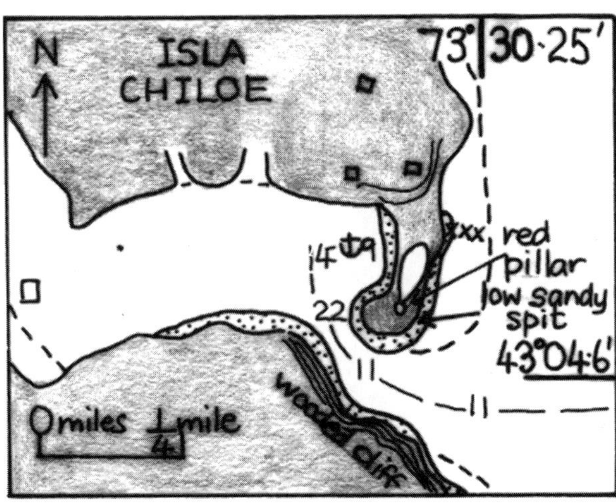

Estero Huildad. (GPS positions)

2·44 Chaitén

42°54'S 72°43'W

Charts
UK *3749* US *22352* Chile *716, 721*

General
Wide-open to the west and southwest, it is not a good anchorage but possible for a short time in good weather if there is a particular reason to call. There are 3 flights daily to Puerto Montt. Provisions and fuel (from service stations) available in town.

2·45 Estero Huildad

43°04'S 73°31'W

Charts
UK *3749* US *22352* Chile *716, 715*

General
The coast east of the entrance is shoal. The entrance has 10m, the tidal range is about 6m. Possibly the best anchorage is behind 1604Huildad lighthouse (8m4M red concrete column 3m) as those further up may be blowy in windy conditions. Good holding in sand, 10m. The north shore has strong currents. When approaching from the north the light is not visible until the yacht is fairly close to the entrance as it is hidden by high land to the northeast of it.

2·46 Puerto Quellón

43°08'S 73°37'W

Charts
UK *3749* US *22352* Chile *715, 716*

General
Puerto Quellón is a busy fishing port of 8000 which also serves cattle farms and the timber industry. It is open to the south. Shore facilities are limited (it has

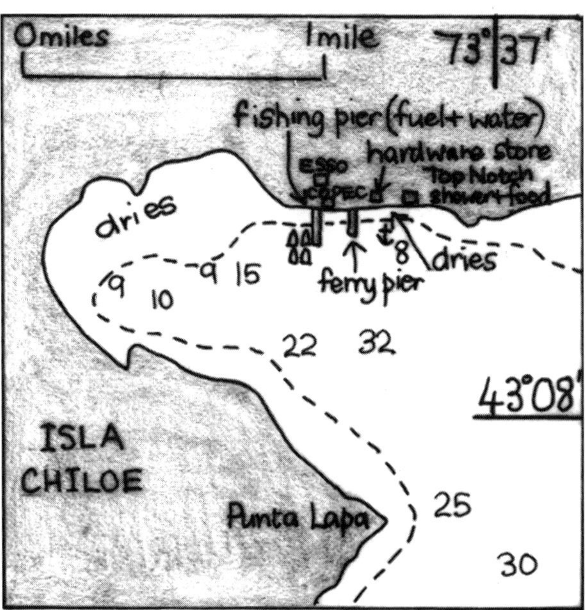

Puerto Quellón. (Charted positions)

a restaurant or two) but it is the last convenient place to get fuel before going south.

Approach

Approach through Canal Laitec and Canal Yelcho is straightforward. However, the shortest route when approaching from or exiting to the north is via Canal Chiguao. With justification the American Chart states that 'extreme caution is to be used when navigating Canal Chiguao'. Access is on a bearing shown on the chart to enter between a sandbank to the south and rocky reef to the north. There is no buoyage to help and the demarcation between deep and shallow water is not easy to see. In addition at springs the east going current runs across Bajo Chiguao at up to 5 knots so it is easy to be set off course. Once inside Canal Chiguao the leading marks, which are low on the shore, help set a course clear of the inner shallows. Going through Canal Yelcho only adds 5 miles to the journey and is infinitely safer.

Anchorage

With the necessity of a dinghy ride in mind, the easiest place to anchor is just east of the main pier. An alternative, protected from the south and with good holding, is 6M west at Punta Carmen, in Estero Yaldad. Anchor here opposite the sawmill but note the stake which may indicate a rock.

Formalities

Check in on Ch 16 and visit the *Capitán del Puerto* opposite the head of the pier.

Facilities

Fuel by can from garages ashore (one fairly close west of the pier).
Water on the western pier.
Fruit and vegetable shop at head of pier.
Some provision shops and butchers.
Change Banco de Estado exacts a US$12 commission on travellers cheques, will not take credit cards but will change US$ cash.

Communications

Buses to Puerto Montt.
Telephone Area Code 657. Office 22 de Mayo and Av. Pedro Montt.

2·47 Bahía Huellonquen

43°10'S 73°31'W

Charts

UK *1289* US *22352* Chile *715, 716*

General

An alternative anchorage to Quellón can be found in Bahía Huellonquen, on the NE corner of Isla Cailin. This is a large bay but is sufficiently enclosed to provide reasonable all-round protection. It is deep so it is necessary to anchor beyond the fish farm cages, fairly close to the beach in 12–14m. The holding is good.

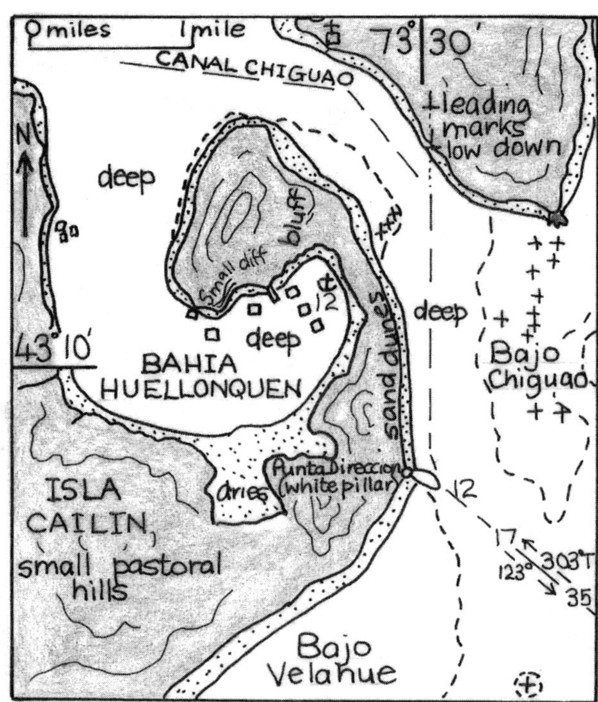

Bahía Huellonquen. (Charted positions)

2·48 Isla Cailín

43°11'S 73°34'W

Charts

UK *1289* US *22352* Chile *715, 716*

General

Situated 5 miles south of the town of Quellón, the long sandy hook on the southwest corner of Isla Cailín provides protection from south and southwest winds. The anchorage can be approached from the north or from the south. Approaching from

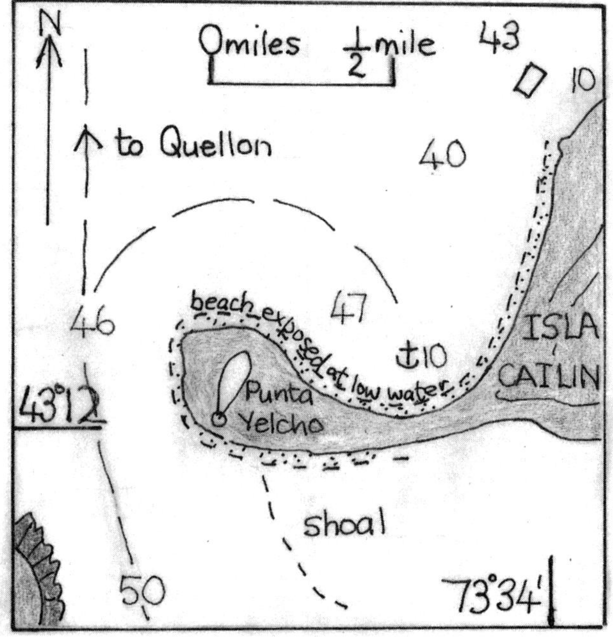

Punta Yelcho, Isla Cailín. (Charted positions)

the south, keep well clear of the shallow water on the southern side of Point Yelcho. The best anchorage is close in to the point, on a sandy bottom with excellent holding. On a clear day, there are spectacular views of the four peaks of Mount Yantele on the mainland.

2·49 Puerto San Pedro

43°19'S 73°41'W

Charts
UK *1289* US *22352, 22360* Chile *714, 715, 716*

Puerto San Pedro is located at the southeastern tip of Isla Chiloé and makes a good stopping place before crossing the open 30 miles to Melinka. There are four anchorages near the entrance of Canal San Pedro.

The first is under the northern shore, near the group of white buildings on the shore. The holding is good in 7–8m on a sand bottom. Take care approaching the shore as it shallows up quickly. It is exposed to south and east winds.

In southerly winds the second anchorage which is behind Isla Observatorio is preferable. Shore lines are required to hold position.

The third anchorage is the one favoured by local fishermen. It is behind the long finger of land, on the south side of the Canal, 2 miles from the entrance. It is surprisingly well sheltered, even in NW wind, with good holding in 10–15m in sand. The entrance is easy and shorelines are not necessary.

The fourth anchorage is tucked into the SW corner behind Islotes Guedancaga. This should be entered at half tide so that the rocks are exposed. Proceed slowly as the rock positions are approximate. This anchorage provides protection from the NW. The anchorage has been used by several yachts. However local fishermen advise using the third anchorage in NW winds.

2·50 Bahía Tictoc

43°37'S 72°54'W

Charts
UK *1288, 1289* US *22352, 22360* Chile *716, 717*

General
Bahía Tictoc provides a first class stopping place when crossing the Golfo de Corcovado and has beautiful surroundings. There are a number of anchorages which should accommodate most weather conditions but the high surrounding hills can produce squalls and it may be necessary to move around to find shelter. Watering is possible. Good fishing.

Approach
The approach from the southwest is the most open, passing southeast of Isla Redonda and the Colocla group.

Anchorages
The anchorages fall into three groups:

Silva Palma and Puerto Tictoc on the north shore of the outer bay. These are both fair weather anchorages.

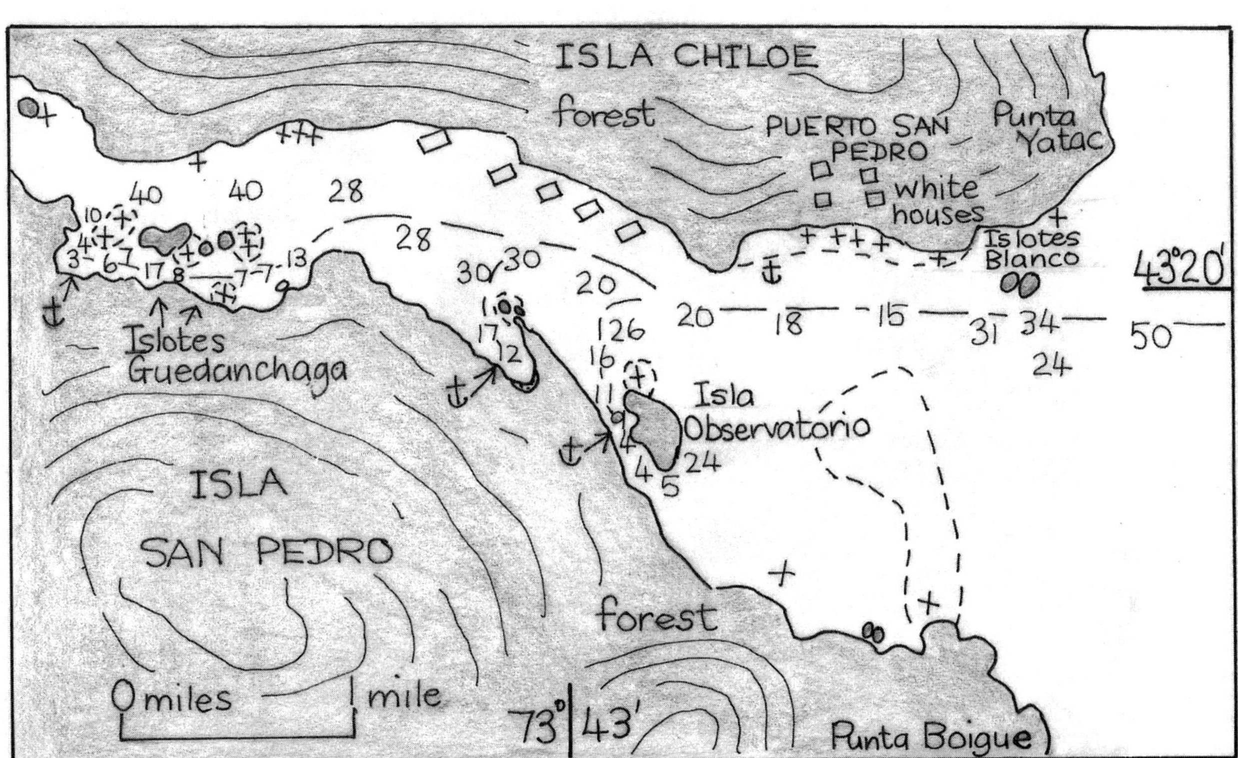

Puerto San Pedro

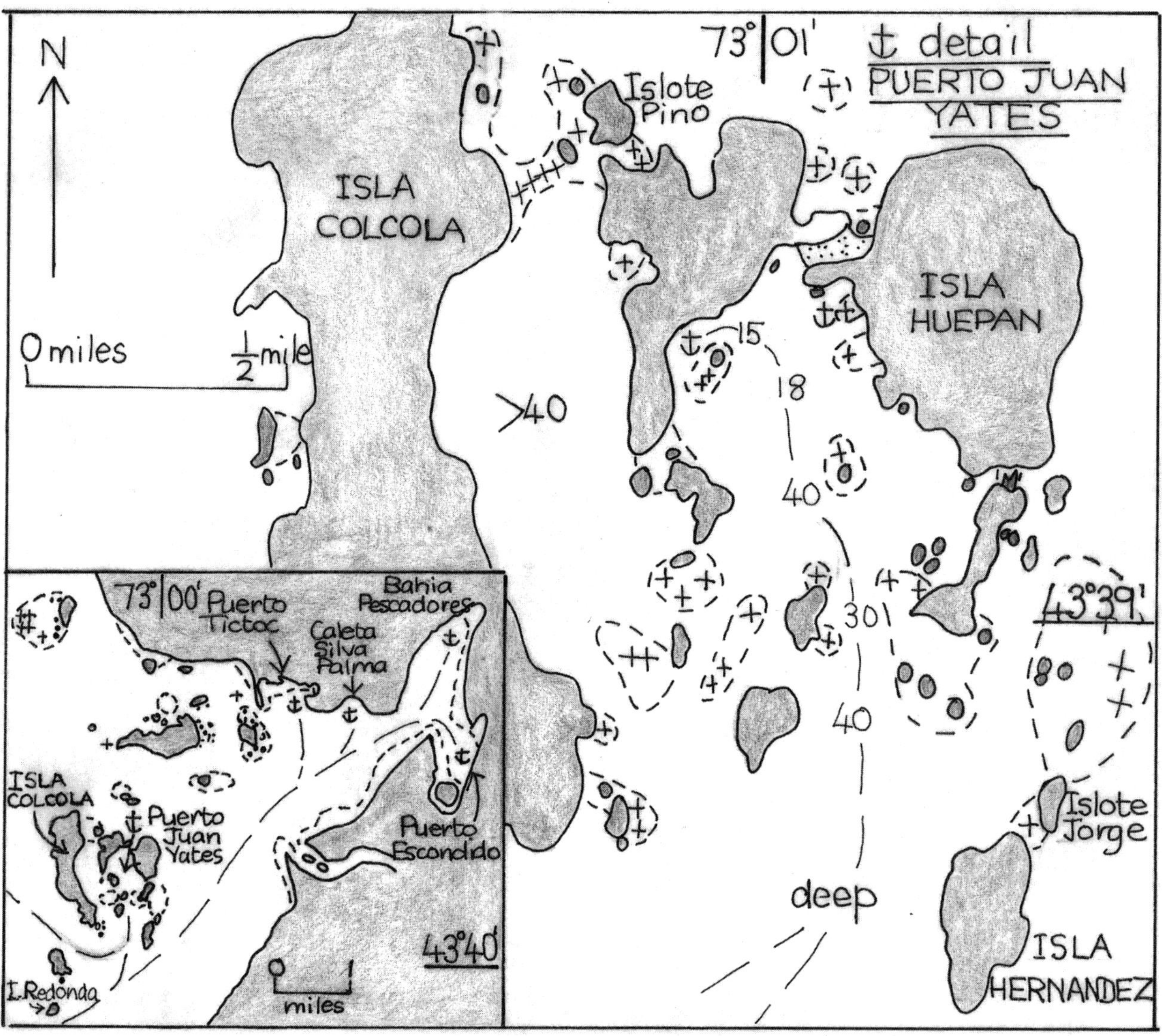

Bahía Tictoc. (Charted positions)

Bahía Pescadores in the northern arm of the inner bay and Puerto Escondido in the southern arm. The very northeastern end of Bahía Pescadores shallows quickly but there is a deep pool on the western edge where it is possible to anchor with lines ashore. In the southern arm, anchor off the fishing settlement, or further south, in appropriate depths. A sand spit marked by stakes extends east in the southern part of this arm.

The third possibility is to anchor among the Isla Colocla group in Puerto Juan Yates, where there are several very secure anchorages well protected from all winds. The access is straightforward. This anchorage saves a 6 mile journey into the inner bay. There is a penguin colony on Islote Pino. Dolphins swim in the anchorage.

Section 3
Melinka to Laguna San Rafael

Chonos is a huge lump of rock, elevated by the forces that built up the Andes, later eroded by ice and water, then submerged and its crevices flooded by the sea. On the east side of this complex, Canal Moraleda leads south to Estero Elefantes which runs behind the Taitao Peninsula and ends at Laguna San Rafael with its glacier. Along the way there are various routes to Canal Darwin and Canal Chacabuco which lead to the Pacific.

1. From the southern end of Chiloé cross the Golfo de Corcovado directly to Puerto Melinka. Then go south along Canals Perez Norte & Sur to join Canal Moraleda east of Isla Melchor. Even in bad weather these canals are well protected and there are many good anchorages *en route*.

   The current flows across the Canal Perez as it floods and ebbs from the Pacific to Canal Moraleda and turns north or south in them depending on the easiest route for the water to flow. On any passage the current can therefore flow in both directions. However the current strengths are generally weak and are not a problem except near Puerto Melinka. In the canals immediately south and east of Puerto Melinka the current flows south strongly for the last half of the flood and the first half of the ebb, and north on the last half of the ebb and the first half of the flood. At the southern end of Perez Sur the flood runs strongly into the Canal from the Moraleda but after several miles the current becomes weak.
2. From the southern end of Golfo Corvocado go directly down Canal Moraleda. In calm weather this is straightforward with good anchorages in Tictoc. In poor weather the strong currents of Canal Moraleda can make conditions very unpleasant and it would be better to rejoin Canal Perez Norte via Canal Pihuel.
3. An alternative is to leave Canal Moraleda by Canal Jacaf, go east about Isla Magdalena (the route is not shown on UK chart *1288*) coming out via Canal Puyuguapi. It is then possible either to rejoin Canal Moraleda or continue south along Canal Ferronave.
4. All routes finish up in Canal Moraleda which runs into Canal Errázuriz. Canal Errázuriz first passes Canal Darwin and then Canal Chacabuco which leads to Canal Pulluche and Boca Wickham.

If you go on to Estero Elefantes and wish afterwards to reach Golfo de Penas, it will be necessary to return at least as far as Canal Chacabuco.

Fuel
Fuel is always available in Chacabuco at mainland prices. It is almost certainly available in Puerto Aguirre from the fuel station on the quay at higher island prices and may be available in Melinka and Puyuguapi.

Charts
There are no large scale US charts covering Estuario Elefantes. The small scale chart is *22370*.

3·1 Guaitecas – Canal Puquitín
43°51'S 73°53'·5W

Charts
UK *1288* US *22360* Chile *716, 718*

General
In the waist of the Guaitecas group. Approach from the southwest between Isla Betecoi and Isla Clotilde or from Puerto Melinka through Canal Lagreze. The route to clear the shoal area between the north point of Isla Clotilde and Isla Ascension passes very close to the former. From this point the passage through Canal Lagreze is straightforward. Continue round the northeast corner of Isla Ascension and the anchorage is in the bay to the north, 10m. A path from the small bay to the west (accessible by dinghy) leads to a beach on Bahía Low.

3·2 Melinka
43°54'S 73°45'W

Charts
UK *1289* US *22360* Chile *716, 718, 801*

General
Puerto Melinka is located on the southeast corner of Isla Ascension, at the northern end of Canal Perez Norte. There is a light just to the east of the town. The tides are much the same as at Tictoc.

Anchorage
The anchorage is in front of the town, 14m with

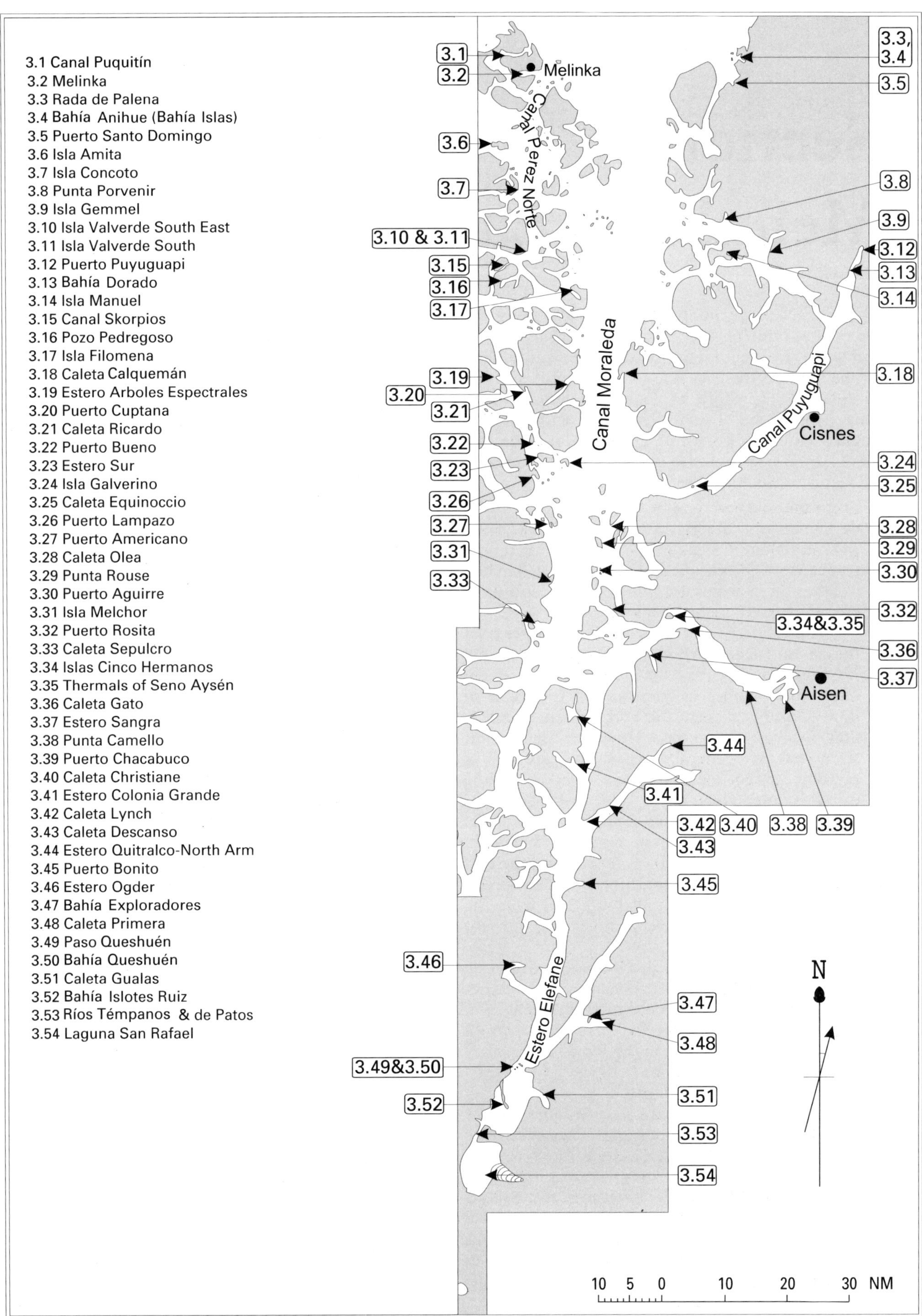
3.1 Canal Puquitín
3.2 Melinka
3.3 Rada de Palena
3.4 Bahía Anihue (Bahía Islas)
3.5 Puerto Santo Domingo
3.6 Isla Amita
3.7 Isla Concoto
3.8 Punta Porvenir
3.9 Isla Gemmel
3.10 Isla Valverde South East
3.11 Isla Valverde South
3.12 Puerto Puyuguapi
3.13 Bahía Dorado
3.14 Isla Manuel
3.15 Canal Skorpios
3.16 Pozo Pedregoso
3.17 Isla Filomena
3.18 Caleta Calquemán
3.19 Estero Arboles Espectrales
3.20 Puerto Cuptana
3.21 Caleta Ricardo
3.22 Puerto Bueno
3.23 Estero Sur
3.24 Isla Galverino
3.25 Caleta Equinoccio
3.26 Puerto Lampazo
3.27 Puerto Americano
3.28 Caleta Olea
3.29 Punta Rouse
3.30 Puerto Aguirre
3.31 Isla Melchor
3.32 Puerto Rosita
3.33 Caleta Sepulcro
3.34 Islas Cinco Hermanos
3.35 Thermals of Seno Aysén
3.36 Caleta Gato
3.37 Estero Sangra
3.38 Punta Camello
3.39 Puerto Chacabuco
3.40 Caleta Christiane
3.41 Estero Colonia Grande
3.42 Caleta Lynch
3.43 Caleta Descanso
3.44 Estero Quitralco-North Arm
3.45 Puerto Bonito
3.46 Estero Ogder
3.47 Bahía Exploradores
3.48 Caleta Primera
3.49 Paso Queshuén
3.50 Bahía Queshuén
3.51 Caleta Gualas
3.52 Bahía Islotes Ruiz
3.53 Ríos Témpanos & de Patos
3.54 Laguna San Rafael
Melinka
Canal Perez Norte
Canal Moraleda
Canal Puyuguapi
Cisnes
Aisen
Estero Elefane
N
10 5 0 10 20 30 NM

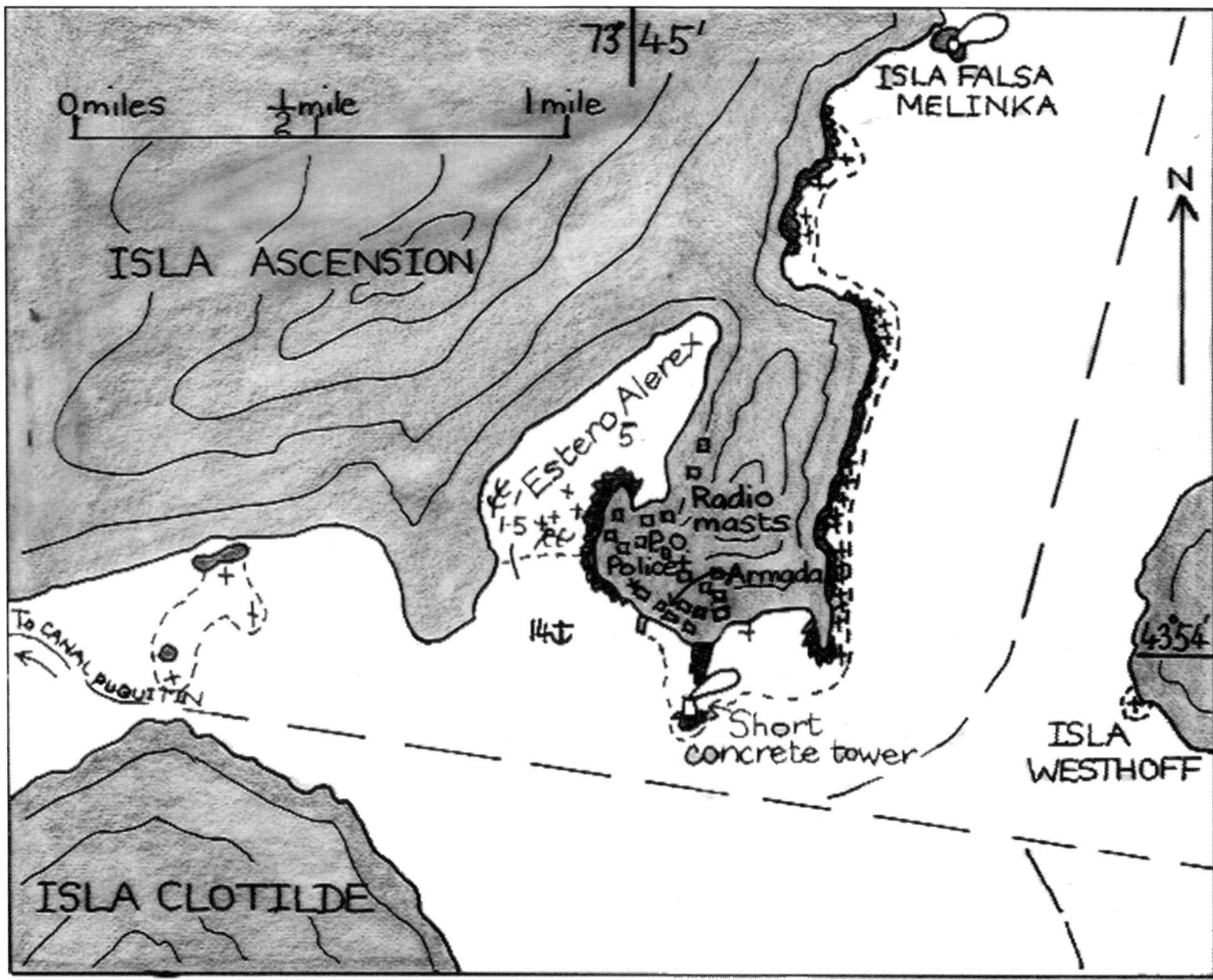

Puerto Melinka

good holding. It is protected from north winds, but exposed to chop from the south.

Formalities

Reported as a good place to renew a *zarpe*. Check with the *Armada* office on arrival, both by radio and by visiting the office. Prior to leaving it is necessary to report the departure time.

Facilities

Emergency repairs are possible.

Water in summer can be a problem as there are no aquifers.

Limited shopping but including a butcher. Freshly smoked fish *(robalo)* at the tin house with a yellow second floor opposite *Perfumeria Chiloé*, near the fishing boat quay.

Communications

Post office and telephone in town. 900m airstrip. TV ashore until the electricity is withdrawn early in the evening.

3·3 Rada de Palena

43°45'·2S 72°56'·0W

Charts

UK *1288* US *22360* Chile *716, 717*

General

The anchorage is in Estero Piti-Palena, behind Isla los Leones, which after a narrow entrance opens out into a bay some 4M long almost totally shut off from the sea. The mouth of Buta-Palena is over the sandbank west of Los Leones and has a bar. This is not navigable by yachts and by dinghy only at high tide and the way through the bar changes continually.

Approach

Tide streams around Peninsula Coca are strong and can cause tide rips. Enter in settled weather on a rising tide to get help from the current. Swell may break on Barra, the sandbank west of Isla los Leones which is reportedly extending northwest. 1586Rada Palena light (Fl.G.5s8m3M Green GRP Tower 3m), (345°-vis-097°) is opposite the entrance to Piti-Palena. Canal Garrao provides a good route by dinghy from Estero Piti-Palena into the Buta-Palena.

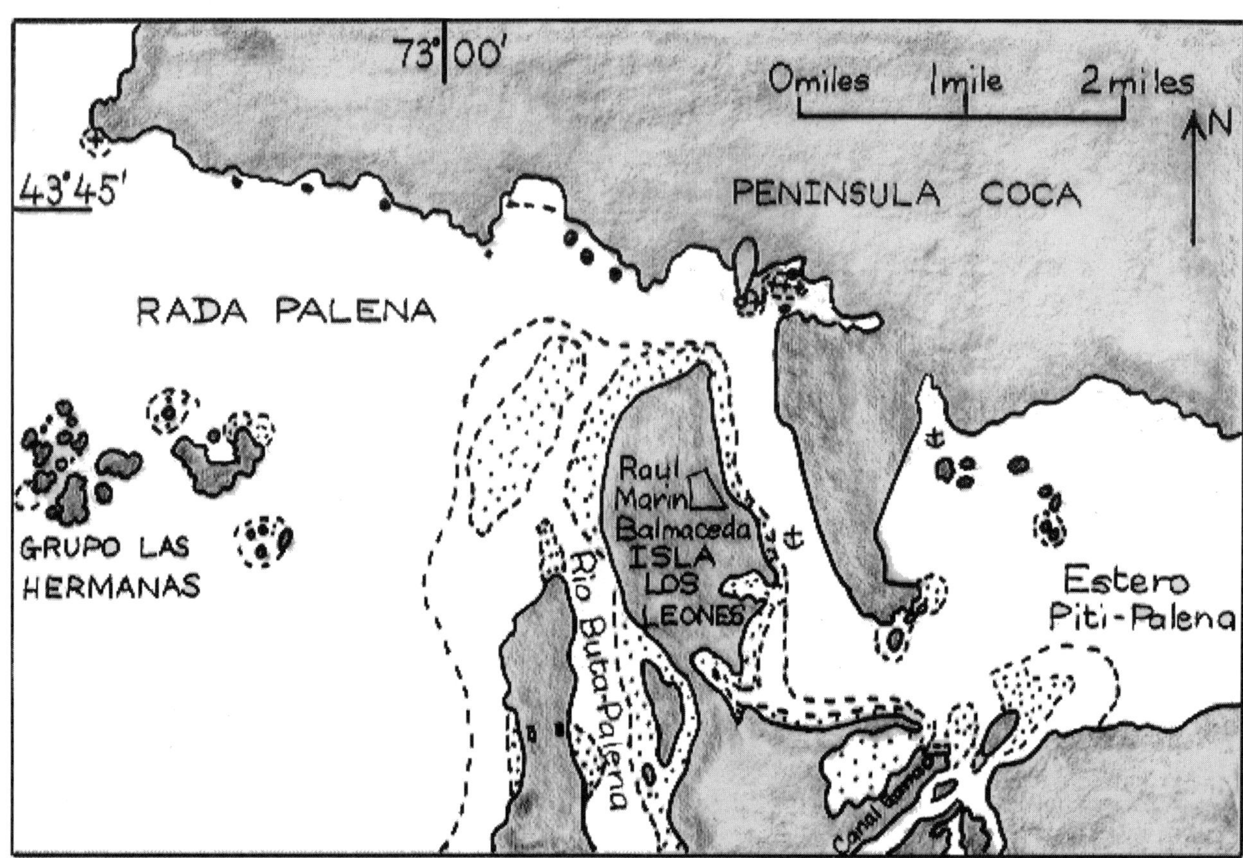

Rada del Palena. (Charted positions)

Anchorage
In the north–south stretch between Los Leones and the mainland, with lines ashore. Not all that good in a northerly. Anchoring is also possible off the village and in the main part of the Estero.

Formalities
The village, Raúl Marin Balmaceda, has an *Armada* presence. The principal *Armada* stations, such as Castro, Puertos Melinka, Aguirre and Chacabuco are manned by navy personal and are known as *Capitanías de Mar.* Raul Marin Balmaceda is an *Alcalde de Mar* and is run by an agent of the navy, in this case the police *(carabineros).*

Facilities
Some supplies in the village.

Communications
Post Office, telephone. 700m airstrip.

3·4 Bahía Anihue (Bahía Islas)

43°52'·3'S 73°02'·4W

Charts
UK *1288* US *22360* Chile *716*

General
The anchorage is first rate, protected from all winds. On the UK and Chilean charts there are no details shown but the access is straightforward as shown on plan 3·4 but needs care. This area is owned by the

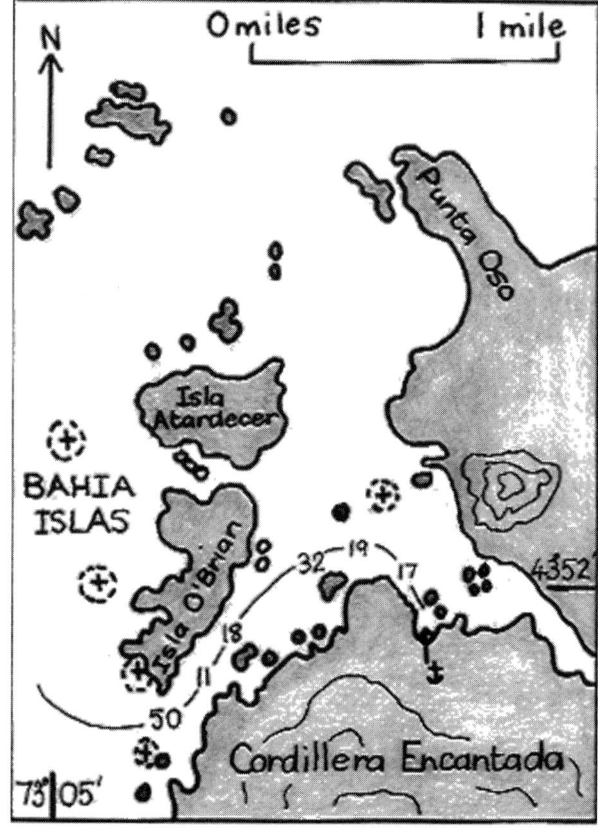

Bahía Anihue. (GPS position)

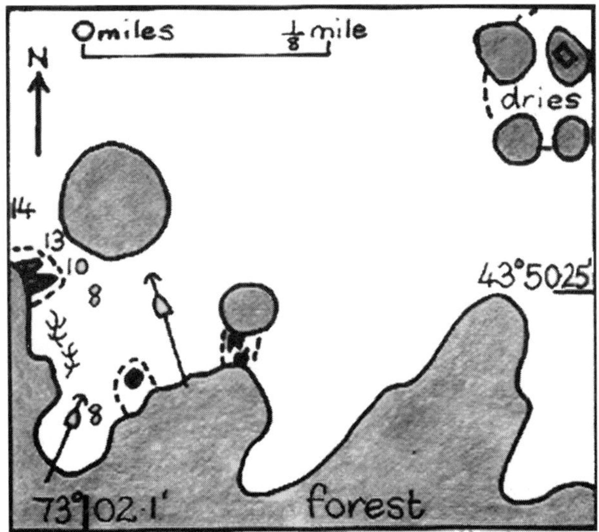

Bahía Anihue (detail). (GPS positions)

American/Chilean family of Juan Carlos Szydlowski who are very helpful and who kindly provided the photographs from which the plan outline was prepared. Call the Szydlowski family on Ch16 (call Anihue, pronounced An Knee Way) to let them know you would like to anchor.

Anchorage
A small secure bay with good holding but use shore line.

3·5 Puerto Santo Domingo

43°57'·5S 73°07'W

Charts
UK *1288* US *22360* Chile *716*

General
Puerto Santo Domingo is an inlet on the mainland bank of Canal Refugio which isolates Isla Refugio. It lies behind a white beach sticking out into the canal to the south of Morro Yelén (Yeli in the UK pilot). Anchor between the point and the lagoon with a line ashore. Good holding. Good in northerlies but a bit exposed in southerlies. Wild strawberries on the beach in January.

Canal Moraleda, Canales Perez Norte and Sur

Charts
UK *1288* US *22360* Chile *803*

General
The more obvious route is down Canal Moraleda. However, the preferred route for yachts is down Canales Perez Norte and Perez Sur which avoid the more exposed conditions in Moraleda. Furthermore, the route is more interesting as it winds through the islands.

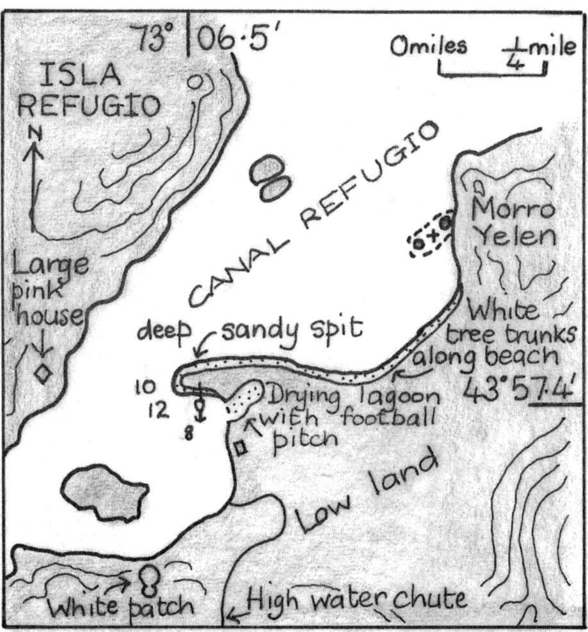

Puerto Santo Domingo. (GPS positions)

3·6 Isla Amita

44°05'S 73°53'W

Charts
UK *1288* US *22360* Chile *803*

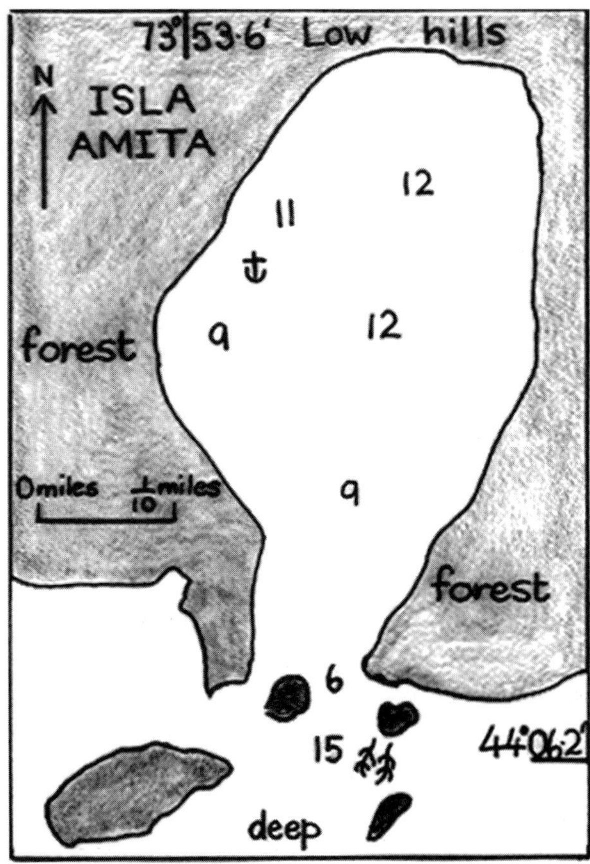

Isla Amita. (GPS positions)

General
The large bay on the south side of Isla Amita may be handy for those using Canal Perez Norte or Canal Tuamapu. The entrance is narrow but well marked by the large islet and three smaller islets lying off the entrance – see plan. The bay is well sheltered, 10–12m, mud.

3·7 Isla Concoto

44°11'·5S 73°48'·5W

Charts
UK *1288* US *22360* Chile *801, 803*

General
A small bay on the east side has been used to give overnight shelter in a strong northerly, 8m good holding.

3·8 Punta Porvenir

44°16'S 73°08'W

Charts
UK *1288* US *22360* Chile *802*

This is an attractive anchorage in the W end of Canal Jacaf. It is a small bay slightly W of Punta Porvenir, north of Isla Wargny and east of the Islas Gala.

The bay can be identified by the beach and waterfall at its head. There are rocks off the west entrance point. The bay is deep and shelves very steeply close to the beach. It provides good shelter, though with some fetch with wind in the S. Anchor in 12–18m, close to the beach.

3·9 Isla Gemmel

44°19'·25S 72°54'·6W

Charts
UK *1288* US *22360* Chile 802

General
Isla Gemmel is on Canal Jacaf, east of Isla Manuel and of the rock in the channel, Roca Robinet, and north of Isla Suárez. The anchorage has good protection from north through west to south but is a bit difficult to find. Once in, anchoring and passing lines is done in flat water even in the heaviest winds. Anchor in 10–12m with lines ashore.

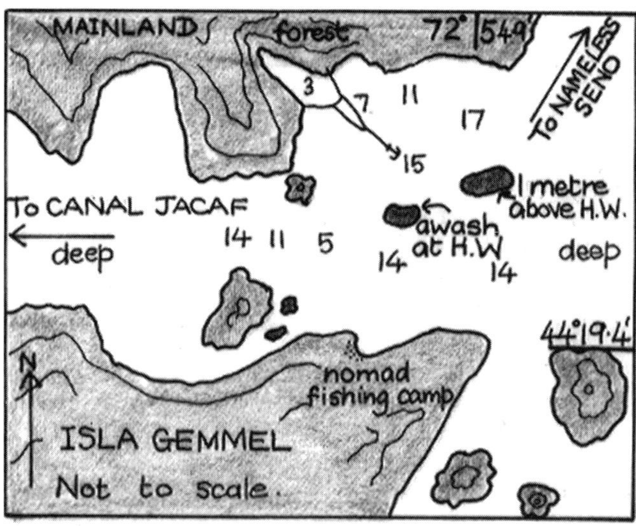

Isla Gemmel. (GPS positions)

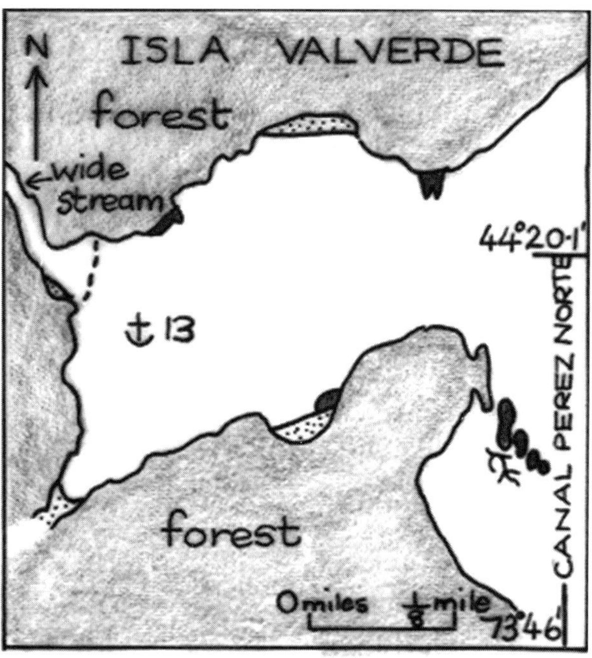

Caleta Tadpole. (GPS positions)

3·10 Isla Valverde – Southeastern Caleta

44°20'S 73°46'W

Charts
UK *1288* US *22360* Chile *801, 803*

General
Located on the southeastern corner of Isla Valverde, this *caleta* unofficially named Tadpole provides excellent shelter from all but east winds. Lines ashore were not necessary. Good holding in 7–15m. The small islet shown on the plan is in fact a peninsular at low water. Approach on a SW heading to avoid rocks along the southern shore.

3·11 Isla Valverde – Southern Estero

44°20'·5S 73°52'·7W (at the southern entrance to the Estero).

Charts
UK *1288* US *22360* Chile *801, 803*

General
Known locally as Estero Picalito, this is an example where the charts are misleading. Isla Valverde is in fact two islands completely separated by a

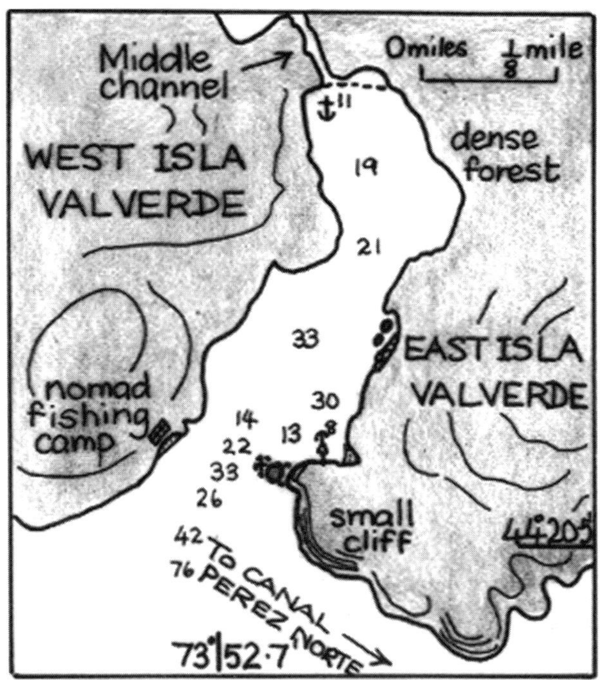

Isla Valverde south. Fishermen's name – Estero Picalito. (GPS positions)

north/south canal. The southern Estero has two good anchorages, which make good stopping places after or before Canal Skorpio. The northern bay is pretty and well-sheltered. It can be reached from Estero Picalito by dinghy or from the north by a channel with minimum depth of 3·5m.

Anchorage
Anchor with shore lines near the entrance of the Estero to the north and east of a small island or at the head of Estero Picalito in 10m, good holding.

3·12 Puerto Puyuguapi

44°20'S 72°34'W

Charts
UK *1288* US *22360* Chile *802*

General
Founded in 1935 by Germans, Puerto Puyuguapi at the head of Seno Ventisquero has about 1000 inhabitants and serves a cattle farming community. Seno Ventisquero (*ventisquero* is glacier) starts at the junction of Canales Jacaf and Puyuguapi, at the northeast corner of Isla Magdalena. The town has a sawmill, a famous carpet factory and a small hospital. Try the pier in the northwest corner with 5m depth or anchor off. Don't stay the night – there is no protection from the southwest; try Bahía Dorada (3·13). Diesel by cans, fresh water and some provisions.

3·13 Bahía Dorada

44°24'·5S 72°38'·8W

Charts
UK *1288* US *22360* Chile *800, 802*

General
Bahía Dorada is on the northwest shore of Seno Ventisquero (see 3·12 Puyuguapi above). The hotel, Hotel Termas, is a five star resort hotel with thermal pools, float planes to fly to the lakes for the fishing and prices to match. The bay is easily entered from the east, north of the two islets which protect it from the Seno but in poor visibility the bay may be difficult to spot as the point to the north is not obvious. Visiting yachts may use all the facilities (including the laundry); the atmosphere is friendly and informal. In 1998 a mooring was 5000 pesos a night, the thermal pools 10,000 pesos a day. Anchoring is difficult because of the depth but a tie-off in the southwest corner should be possible in most conditions. Diesel can be purchased. Launch service to Puyuguapi airfield, 9km south of that town.

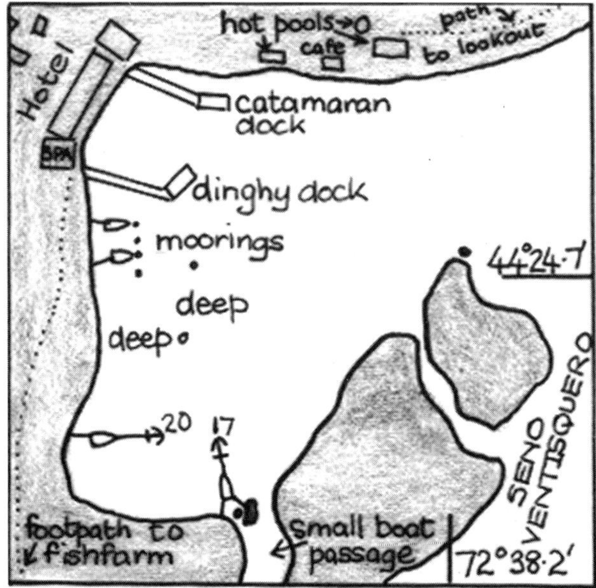

Bahia Dorada (not to scale). (GPS positions)

3·14 Isla Manuel

44°22'·2S 73°07'·1W

Charts
UK *1288* US *22360* Chile *800, 801, 802*

General
A secure anchorage, sheltered from all winds with well-wooded shores providing protection and good tie-off points.

Anchorage in SW. Isla Manuel. (GPS positions)

3·15 Canal Skorpios

44°23'S 73°50'W

Charts

UK *1288* US *22360* Chile *801, 803*

General

This cut between Isla Jéchica and Pen-Davis saves about 5M and is used by the commercial catamaran, *Patagonia Express*, with a draft of 2m. The west arm of Canal Skorpio is foul but the east arm, in pleasant weather, makes a delightful short-cut.

Entering the east arm from the north depths quickly fall from 50 to 18m as the Canal narrows and then to 5–7m as the yacht travels over the first sand bar. Soundings on the plan were taken at half tide and the channel should be taken centrally; the bottom can be clearly seen and there is neither obvious obstruction nor kelp. The Canal quickly widens and deepens and is clear.

At the southern end of the east arm where it joins up with the west arm is another sand bar. This should be taken centrally; the shallow areas are visible as depths fall to 4–6m, again without kelp. Once the bar is passed the Canal quickly deepens to form a wide Canal.

Canal Skorpios

At the southern end of the main Canal depths fall to a minimum of 10–12m until the Canal widens out and Islote Proa is left to starboard.

3·16 Isla Jéchica – Pozo Pedregoso

44°25'·1S 73°51'·5W

Charts

UK *1288* US *22360* Chile *801, 803*

General

Isla Jéchica is almost bisected from the east by a forked *estero*. The entrance and the western arm of this *estero* are deep and free of dangers with clear passage to Pozo Pedregoso at the south west end of this arm. The depths progressively shelve in this Pozo with secure anchorage in about 9m. Good all-

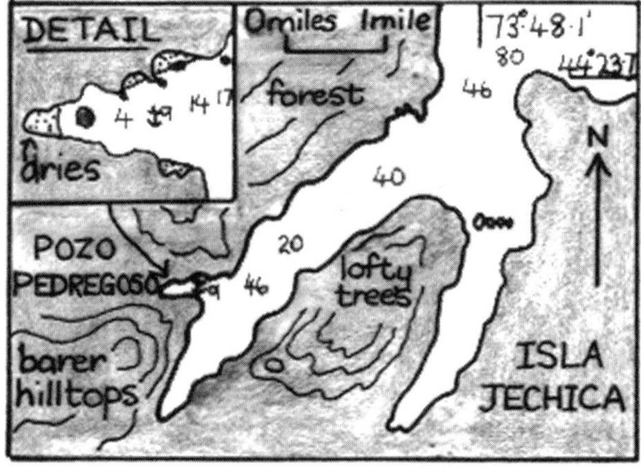

Pozo Pedregoso. (GPS positions)

Flamingos, Atacama *Becky Trafford*

El Niño brought many pelicans to Valdivia fish market in 1998.
Below Sooty sheerwaters (*Sardellas*) fishing for sardines in Bahía Corral *Teokita*

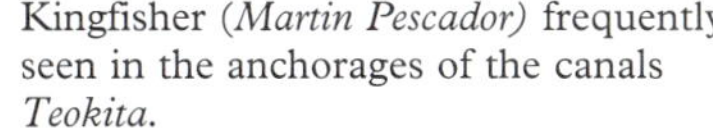

Kingfisher (*Martin Pescador)* frequently seen in the anchorages of the canals *Teokita*.

Palafitos from the anchorage – Castro Chiloé *Teokita*

The church in Pailad from the anchorage – Chiloé *Teokita*

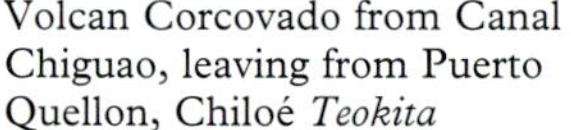

Volcan Corcovado from Canal Chiguao, leaving from Puerto Quellon, Chiloé *Teokita*

Left Looking towards the mainland from Puerto Juan Yates, Bahéa Tic Toc *Teokita*

Above Chacabuco: Ensenada Bahía in the foreground, and Bahía Chacabuco behind

Below Hot springs go into the sea in Seno Aysen – Termas de Puerto Perez *Teokita*

Monte Cono, Bahía San Andres *Teokita*

Caleta Maris Stella, a heap of *cholga* – giant mussel shells where they used to be smoked – now quiet because of the *marea roja Teokita*

Looking out of Caleta Millabu, Isola Clemente in the morning *Teokita*

Right Huge cliffs in Canal Grappler *Teokita*

round shelter and good shellfish (but see the warning in the introduction about the Red Tide, under 'Shellfish' – south of Puerto Melinka the *Armada* state on the yacht *zarpe* that no bivalve shellfish should be eaten because of the high risk of death from Marea Roja).

The southern arm of the main *estero* is cluttered with islets and is foul.

3·17 Isla Filomena

44°28'S 73°35'W

Charts

UK *1288* US *22360* Chile *801, 803*

General

There are five anchorages around Isla Filomena, which is privately owned: two in the northwestern *estero,* two along the south west coast – see plan – and another off the north east coast.

1. Anchorage 1 is likely to be popply in a southwesterly, otherwise good shelter.
2. Enter anchorage 2 at or near low water. A very secure anchorage.
3. Enter anchorage 3 through the narrow northern channel. Holding not tested but a tie off is anyway preferable. An extremely secure and safe anchorage.
4. Anchorage 4: the entrance channel to the lagoon has 3·5m at high water. It is less than 20m wide. All channels into the lagoon are tidal rapids and the anchorage is subject to strong tides. Holding is poor on bare rock (a CQR did not hold but a fisherman's anchor did) and a tie-off is greatly preferable.

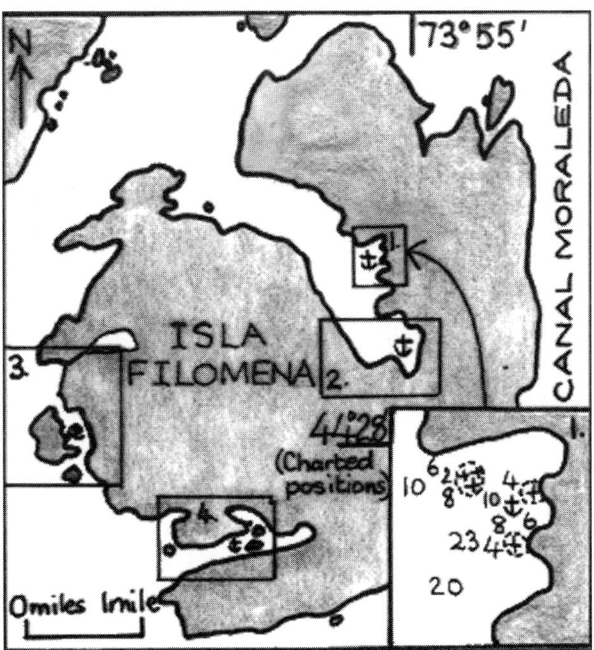

Isla Filomena details 1–4

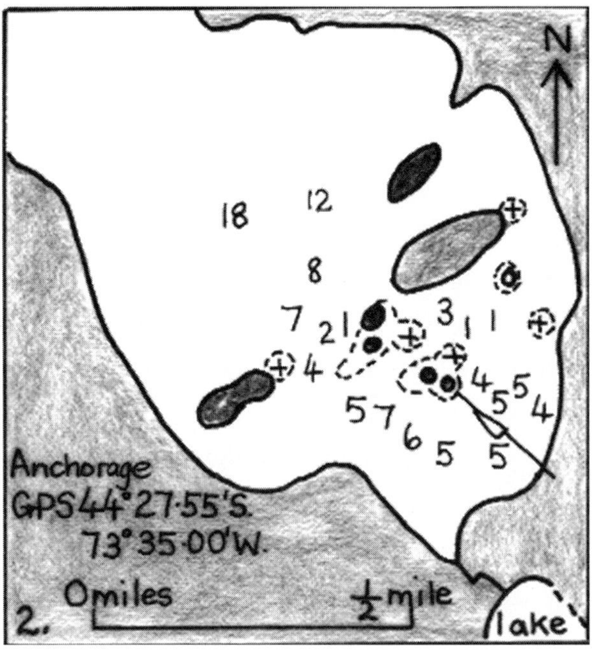

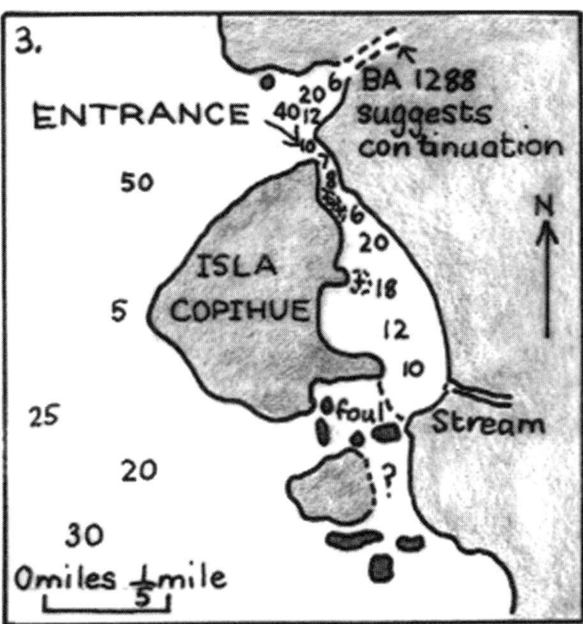

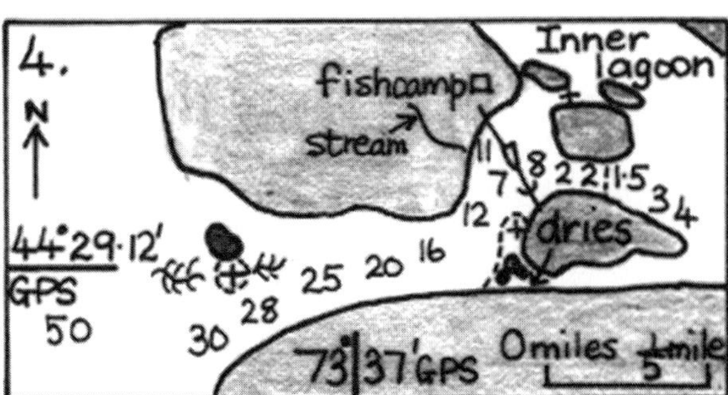

The other small anchorage is between Isla Filomena and the small island just off the NE coast of Filomena, 44°26'S 73°34'W. Tight space and shore lines necessary but perfectly sheltered. Anchor in about 8m.

3·18 Isla Magdalena – Caleta Calquemán

44°39'S 73°27'W

Charts
UK *1288* US *22371* Chile *803, 802*

General
Caleta Calquemán is on the east side of Canal Morelada and 1577·5Punta Calquemán (44°38'·5S 73°27'·4W Fl.5s8m7M White GRP tower Red Bands 4m) is a good landmark to locate the approach. The entrance only opens up when one is close. Hold close to the west shore once abeam of the north end of the island on the east side of the entrance; there is a reef extending north from this island. Anchorage is in the narrow gut in the northwestern-most corner of the *caleta*, in 9–12m with little swinging room (and it may be crowded with fishermen).

It is possible to leave by an inside passage. Steer towards the 'mainland' (which is in fact Isla Magdalena) keeping well north of the reef described above. Once past this island steer somewhat south of east towards the mainland. As you near the mainland a channel opens up to the southwest back into Canal Moraleda. Keep mid-channel.

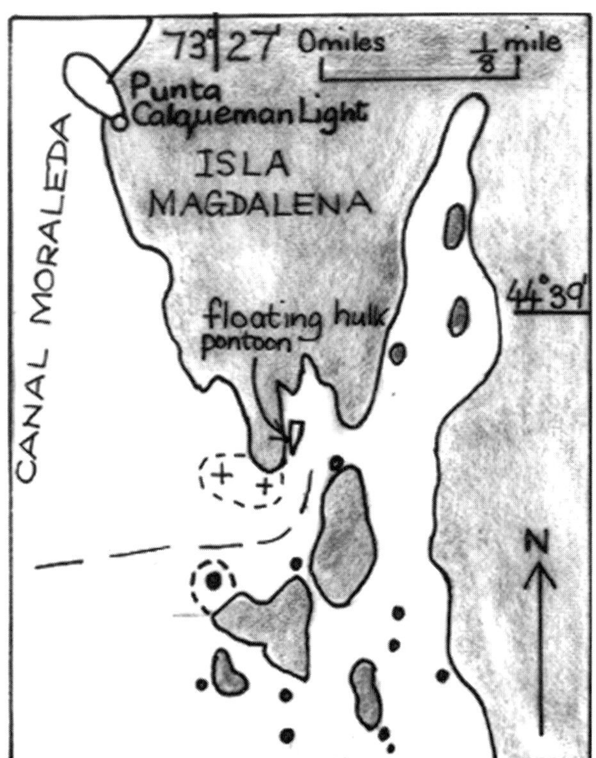

Caleta Calquemán. (Charted positions)

3·19 Isla Benjamin – Estero Arboles Espectrales

44°39'S 73°56'W

Charts
UK *1288* US *22371* Chile *801, 803*

General
Estero Arboles Espectrales is located on the east side of Isla Benjamin which is on the west side of Canal Perez Sur. It provides shelter from all except east winds. It is subject to *rachas*, but the holding is excellent in 6m with a mud bottom. There is a stream at the head of the *caleta* for fresh water. At low water there is a delightful walk for a considerable distance along this stream.

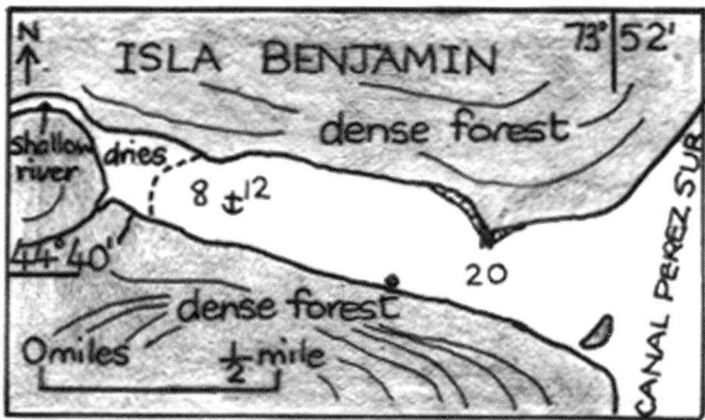

Estero Arboles Espectrales. (GPS positions)

3·20 Isla Cuptana – Puerto Cuptana

44°40'S 73°38'W

Charts
UK *1288* US *22371* Chile *803, 804*

General
Tuck in between the main island and the small islets in about 12m. Enclosed, sheltered and good holding. Fisherman's hut on the shore.

3·21 Caleta Ricardo

44°41'S 73°46'W

Charts
UK *1893* US *22371* Chile *803*

General
Located on the southwestern side of Isla Cuptana, 4½ miles southeast of Isla Benjamin, this unnamed anchorage provides protection from all except south and southeast winds. Stay in the centre when entering. The anchorage is in 7m with good holding. The depth shoals quickly at the head near the streams. A good place to obtain fresh water.

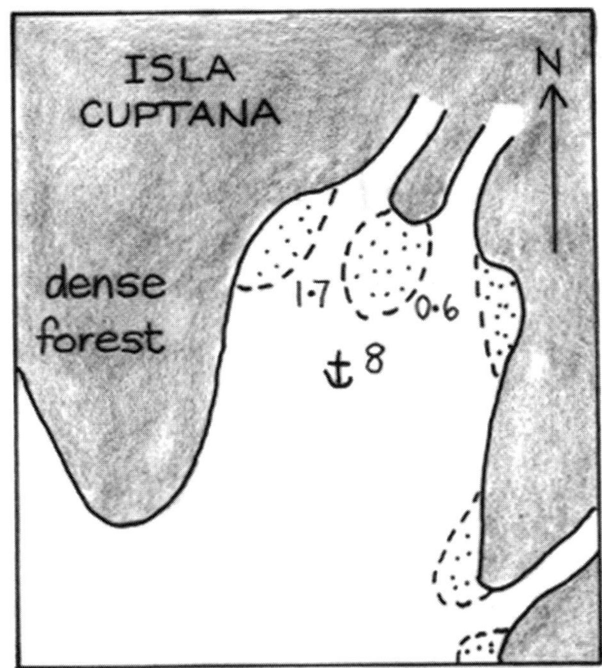

Caleta Ricardo 44°41'S 73°46'W

3·22 Isla Florencia – Puerto Bueno

44°49'·3S 73°45'·25W

Charts
UK *1288* US *22371* Chile *801, 803.*

General
Puerto Bueno is a perfectly sheltered anchorage tucked into the southeast corner of Isla Florencia.

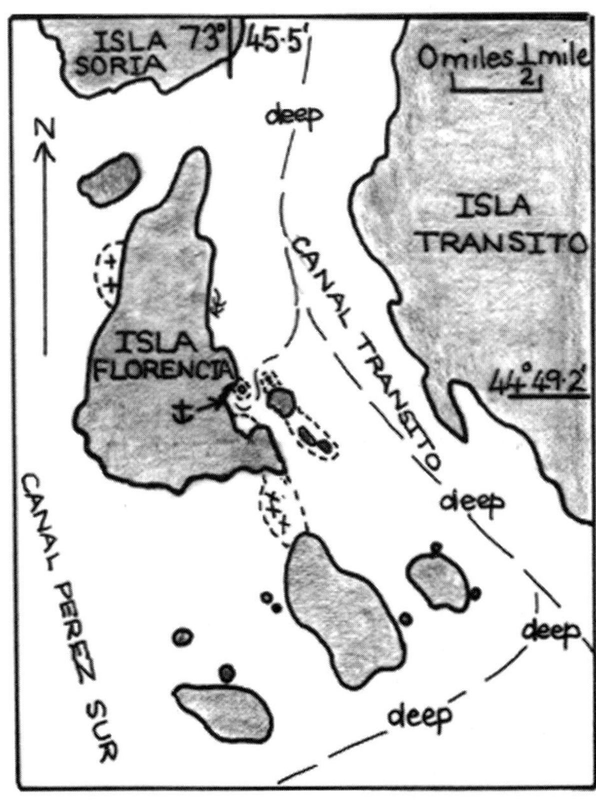

Puerto Bueno. Isla Florencia

Approach from the north or south along Canal Transito (this is deep and clear) or by rounding the northern side of Isla Canal from the west and passing south of Islas Mauricio and Rameses II. This is also clear and deep although the northwest corner of Isla Canal should be given a wide berth.

Approach
Approach the anchorage as shown on the sketch chart. The water remains deep until well into the tiny bay. Although there are rocks and kelp patches, access is straightforward. The anchorage has little swinging room and it is necessary to take a stern line ashore.

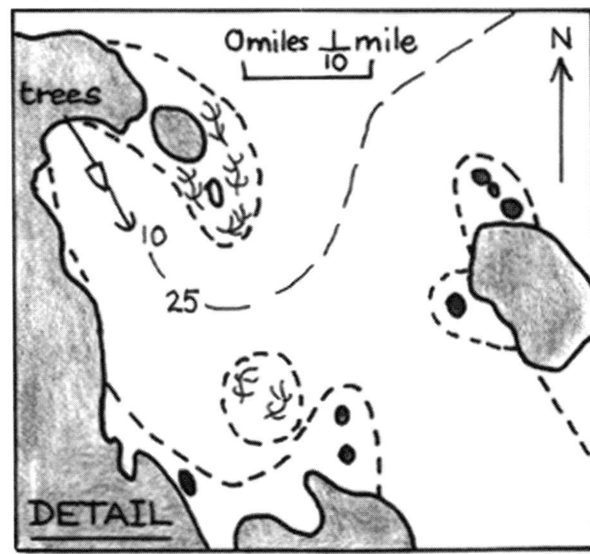

Puerto Bueno detail

3·23 Isla Canal – Estero Sur

44°52'S 73°42'W

Charts
UK *1288* US *22371* Chile *801, 803*

General
When entering or exiting Canal Perez Sur at its junction with Canal Moraleda, Estero Sur (it has no official name) on Isla Canal makes an easy and secure stop-over. It is well protected from all but southern winds and has good holding. A very peaceful place when the wind is blowing outside.

If approaching from the south keep midway between the small island 0·9M to the south and Isla Canal. This small island has a light on its northern side (not listed) with a red banded white tower. The entrance is simple and the *estero* is clean. Anchor in about 10m at the head of the *estero.* There is quite a lot of kelp and weed on the bottom although the anchorage is clear of rocks.

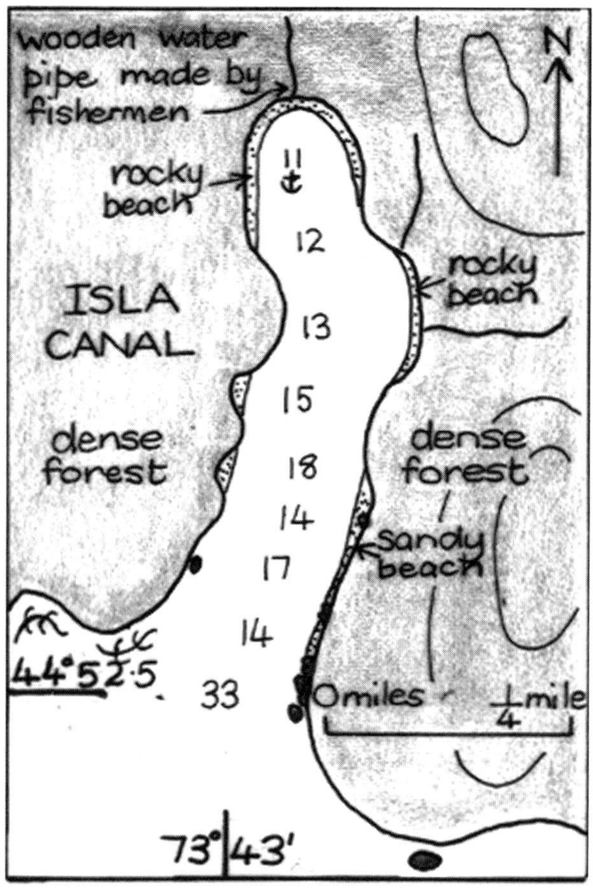

Isla Canal. (GPS positions)

3·24 Isla Galverino

44°54'S 73°41'W

Charts
UK *1288* US *22371* Chile *803*

General
On the east side of the island, the anchorage is well sheltered by tall trees from all winds except from the east. Anchor in about 4m – there is only 2m of water about 60m from the shore. The rocks at the entrance are covered at springs.

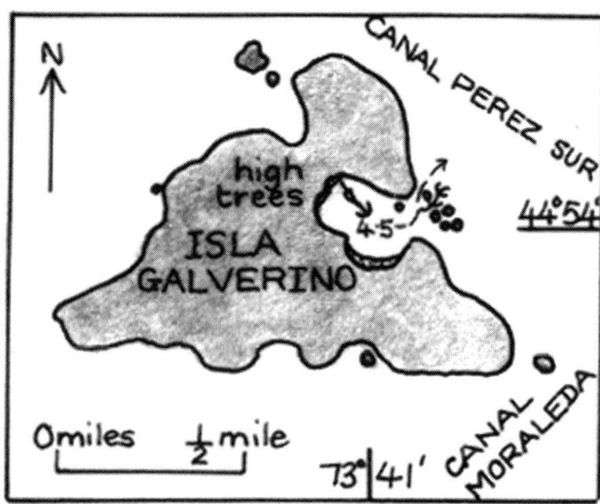

Isla Galverino. (Charted positions)

3·25 Isla Magdalena – Caleta Equinoccio

44°52'·5S 73°03'·5W

Charts
UK *1288* US *22371* Chile *802*

General
Caleta Equinoccio, which has no official name, is an anchorage on Canal Puyuguapi, on the southeast side of Isla Magdalena. It provides a snug stopping place when beating north up Canal Puyuguapi against strong head winds. It is perfectly sheltered against winds from the north with good holding. Anchor in 10m plus at the head of the bay but with minimal swinging room.

Equinoccio is the name of Tony Westcott's yacht. In the 1970s Westcott, in *Equinoccio I*, was one of the first Chileans to explore the northern Canals. This was followed by further exploration in the mid 80s when he sailed a Saga 40, *Equinoccio II*, from the UK to Chile.

3·26 Isla Teresa – Puerto Lampazo

44°54'·3S 73°46'·0W

Charts
UK *1288* US *22371* Chile *801, 803*

General
At the southeast end of Isla Teresa, the inner part of this *caleta* has silted up to about 1m. However, craft drawing less than 3m might close up to the north shore and obtain shelter from the trees. Anchoring out in 10–15m has good holding but very reduced shelter from the north.

3·27 Isla Tangbac – Puerto Americano

45°01'·3S 73°42'W

Charts
UK *1288* US *22371* Chile *801, 804*

General
In the *caleta* between Islas Dar and Tangbac there are two connected anchorages. The outer is open to the southwest and has 18m with a rocky bottom. This would only be satisfactory in calm and settled conditions.

Access to the inner bay, La Darsena ('the inner harbour'), is straightforward using the Chilean chart *804* or the plan. The pass appears to be shoaling with about 3m near low water. However at half tide or higher there is adequate depth and the pass is clear if the path shown is followed. La Darsena is very sheltered and has good holding in mud and sand at the head of the bay. There is a fisherman's camp with two small houses.

Note Chart *804* puts Puerto Americano at the same latitude but 73°37'·5W.

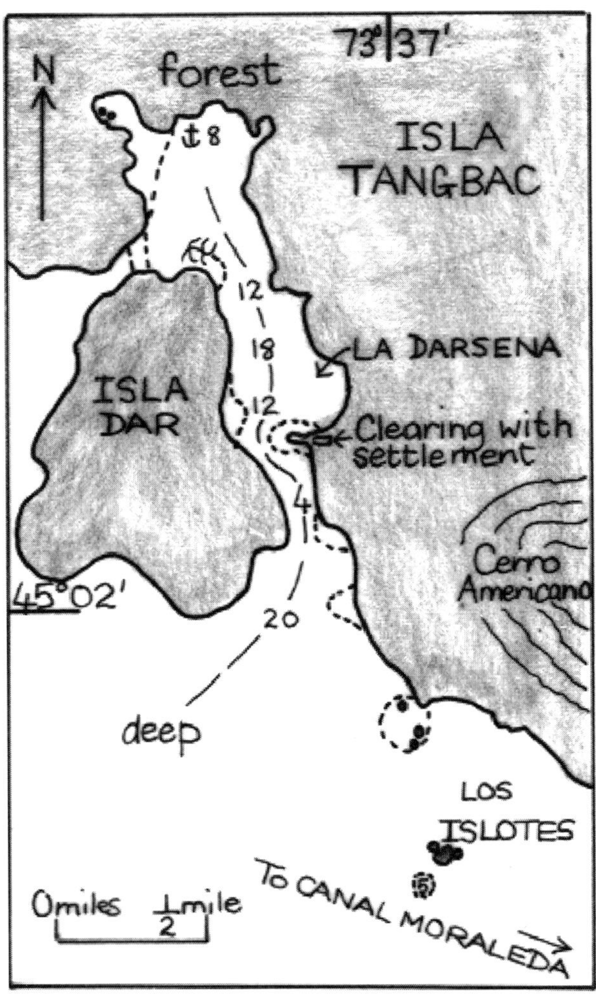

Puerto Americano (Charted positions)

3·28 Isla Orestes – Caleta Olea

45°02'S 73°27'W

Charts

UK *1288* US *22371* Chile *801, 810*

General

This unnamed *caleta* is located on the southeastern corner of Isla Orestes. There is not sufficient room to swing to an anchor, so a line ashore on the southern side is required. It is also reported to be poor holding. The anchorage is very secluded, quiet and well protected, with depths of 6–9m.

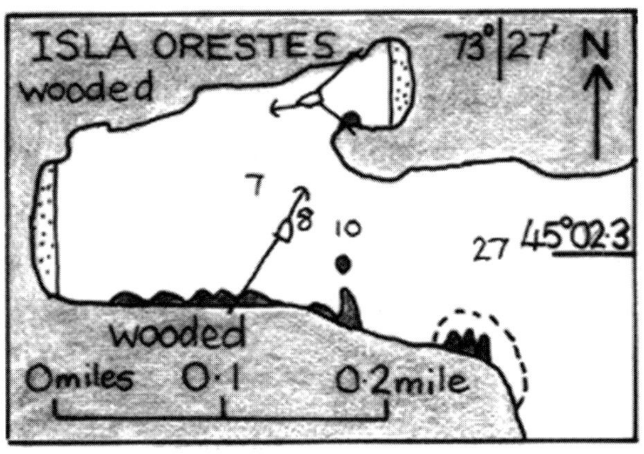

Caleta Olea (Charted positions)

3·29 Isla Larenas – Punta Rouse

45°06'S 73°30'W

Charts

UK 1288 US *22371* Chile *801, 810*

General

A pretty anchorage at the southern end of Isla Larenas sheltered from the north by trees. The holding, in pebbles, has only been tried in mild conditions. Anchor in about 9m; the bottom shelves to 2·5m about 50m from the shore.

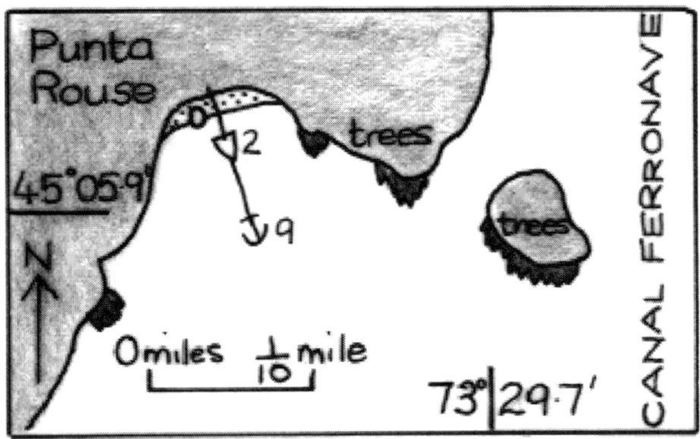

Punta Rouse (Charted positions)

3·30 Isla Las Huichas – Puerto Aguirre

45°09'S 73°31'W

Charts

UK *1288* US *22371* Chile *801, 809, 810*

General

Puerto Aguirre is a small, pretty, fishing village at the south end of Canal Ferronave. Southeast of Puerto Aguirre in Canal Ferronave there is a red daymark and, also, possibly a light on the westernmost of the Islotes Gloria which is not shown on Chilean charts.

It is an official *Armada* post and a yacht calling here must report by radio and personally at the *Armada* office. This office will issue a new *zarpe* and it should be advised the planned time of departure.

Anchorage

If there is space and permission is asked from the *Armada* it is possible to lie alongside the wall for several hours. No charge is made for this. This is particularly useful if picking up fuel.

It is possible to anchor in front of the *Armada* building in 12m. However space is tight and there are a number of buoys congesting this tiny bay. There are two better protected anchorages which are a short dinghy trip, or by foot from Puerto

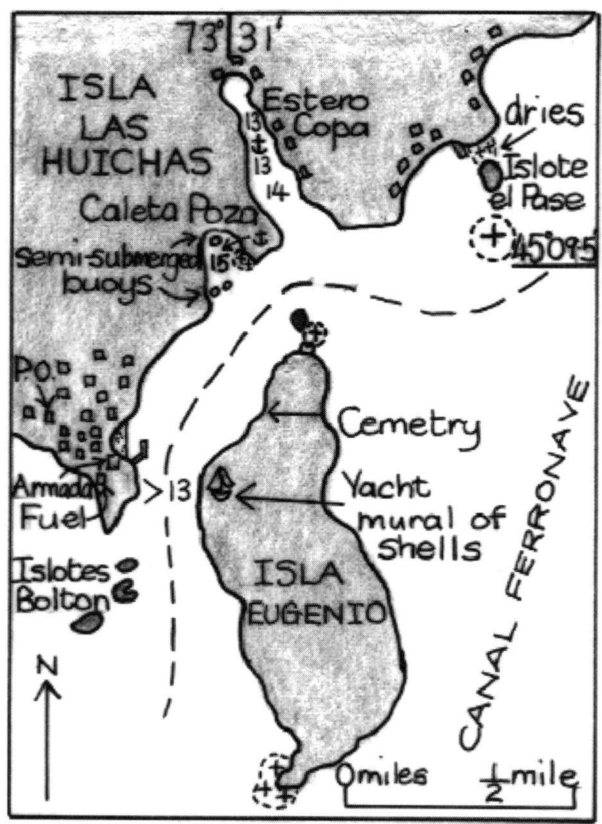

Puerto Aguirre (Charted positions)

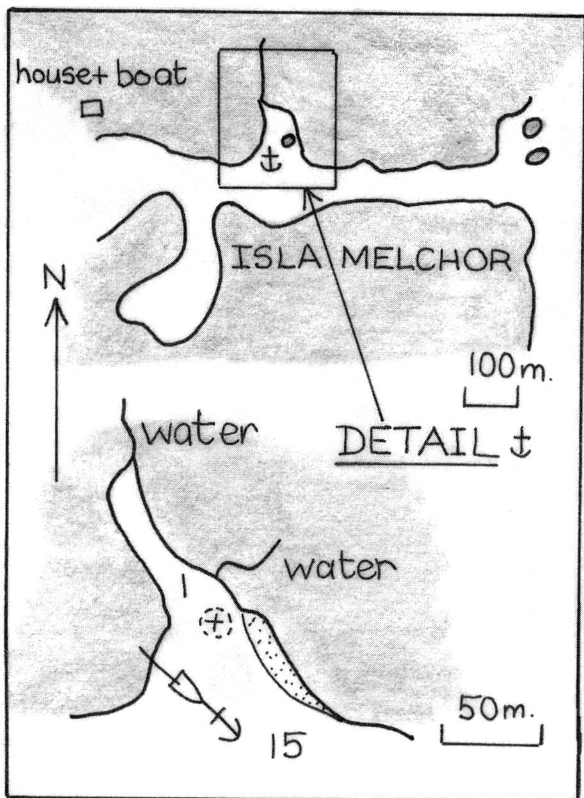

Isla Melchor. (Un-named caleta) 45°11'S 73°42'W

Aguirre. The first, Estero Poza is just to the north of the village and the other, Estero Copa, is a long narrow inlet about ¾ mile to the north. Both have good holding. However in strong northerly winds an uncomfortable swell enters Estero Poza and Estero Copa is more comfortable.

Facilities

- Emergency repairs can be made of a basic kind. There is a hardware store (*ferretería*) and a mechanical workshop (*taller*) and some emergency repairs can be made.
- Diesel is available by can or alongside if a space can be found.
- Basic provisions can be purchased and there is a surprisingly good fruit shop that is well provisioned after the weekly supply ship has called. Prices are reasonable.
- Bars and some restaurants.

Communications

A post office and a Chilexpress office. Small air-strip (mail is handled once a week by air).

3·31 Isla Melchor – Unnamed Estero

45°11'S 73°42'W

Charts

UK *1288* US *22371* Chile *801, 809*

General

A small *caleta* on the north side of the unnamed *estero* running east–west on the east coast of Isla Melchor. Anchor at the entrance to the *caleta*. Holding in sand and pebbles.

3·32 Península Elisa – Puerto Rosita

45°14'S 73°30'W

Charts

UK *1288* US *22371* Chile *810*

General

Puerto Rosita lies 5M south of Puerto Aguirre and is a much more secure and peaceful anchorage than Puerto Aguirre in bad weather. Anchor in the NE bay where the quality of holding is variable or in the main bay with good holding in about 10–12m. The main bay shelves up gently to the head of the bay. There is an excellent stream to replenish water where shown on the plan.

If heading S and W from Rosita beware of the channel between Isla Costa and Punta Alberto on Isla Chaculay which is shoal with minimum depths of 2–3 meters.

3·33 Isla Melchor – Caleta Sepulcro

45°17'S 73°44'W

Charts

UK *1288* US *22371* Chile *801, 841*

General

On the southeast corner of Melchor, inside a big ship anchorage, Puerto Laguna, and northwest of Islas Castillo and Tozzoni. There is a ledge with kelp off Punta Leuquén on the north east side of the

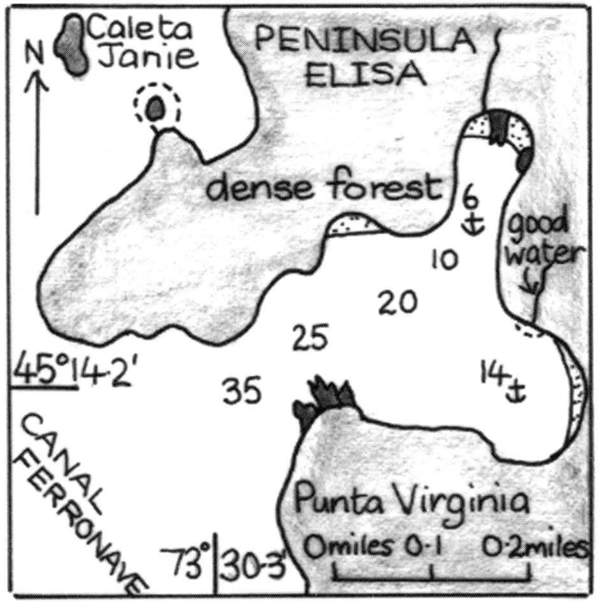

Puerto Rosita. (GPS positions)

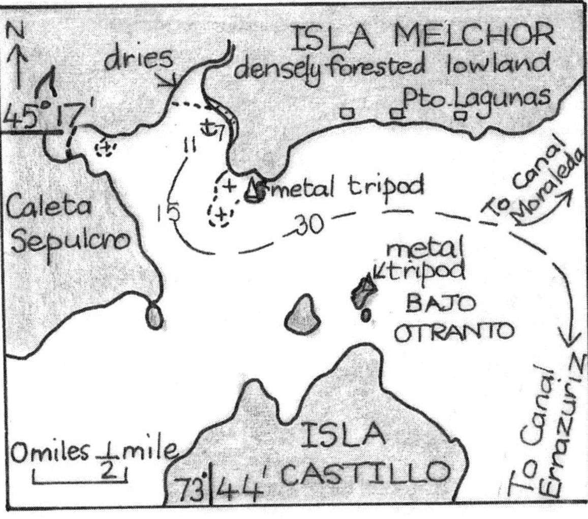

Caleta Sepulcro. (GPS positions)

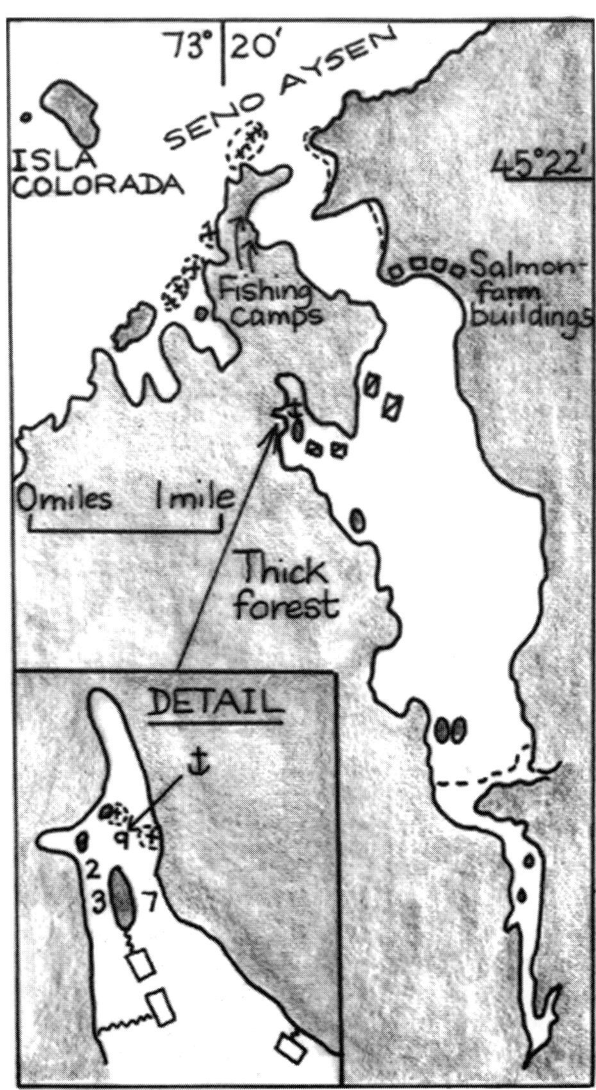

Estero Sangra. (Charted positions)

entrance. Anchor in about 8m at the head of the northeast bay. Excellent holding in sand. Fishermen will sell freshly caught crab *(jaiba)*.

Diversion Seno Aysén

General

Seno Aysén is about 15M long and has its own micro-climate, particularly east of Caleta Gato. It is noted for its whirlwinds *(remolinos)* and williwaws *(rachas)*, so beware. There are several anchorages and two thermal springs, Termas del Chiconal and Punta Tortuga (described as 'stunningly beautiful'). It is easy to be stuck in Chacabuco waiting for fair weather and unless changing crew there, it is probably best avoided. Aysén, 15km further up the just navigable river (2·5m depths, chart *811*), might be reached with local knowledge. Annual rainfall is up to the three metre mark (it is said to rain 366 days in an ordinary year).

3·34 Seno Aysén – Estero Sangra

45°21'S 73°20'W

Charts

UK *1288* US *22371* Chile *809, 8290*

General

This long estuary 1 mile SE of Isla Colorada has no name on the Chilean chart, but is in fact called Estero Sangra. It provides wonderful shelter in most attractive surroundings.

There are many possible anchorage spots in the estuary, according to wind conditions. The two shown on the sketch chart both provide good protection. Beware of lines to the shore from the salmon cages in the bay. The more southerly of the two is completely landlocked and bulletproof. It is difficult to see from the approach as it is very narrow. Favour the E entrance around the islet, keeping mid channel, and the E side within the pool, but not too close to the shore.

3·35 Seno Aysén – Islas Cinco Hermanos

45°15'·5S 73°16'W

Charts

UK *1288* US *22371* Chile *809, 8290*

General

This pretty anchorage lies at the northern end of the most west island in this group. The approach is straightforward from the west passing mid-way between the main island and the small islet to its north. Anchor in 4m in sand with good holding. It is a fair weather anchorage, open to the NW. If the wind shifts NW anchor off Puerto Perez or go to Caleta Gato.

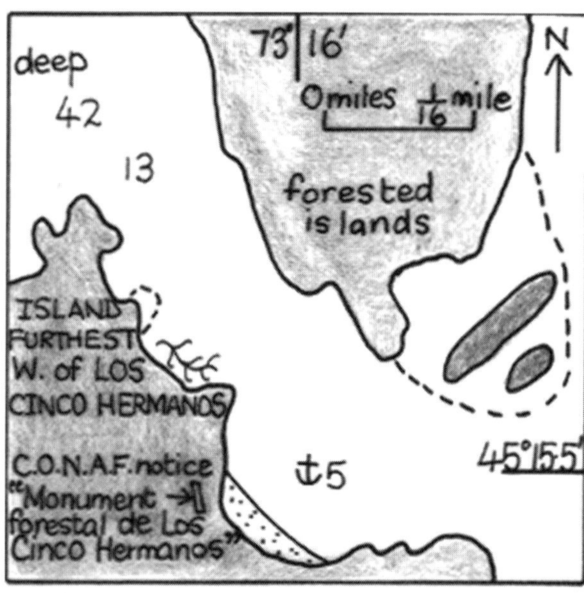

Isla Cinco Hermanos. (GPS positions)

3·36 Thermals of Seno Aysén

There are two thermals that can be visited in good weather.

a. Thermal east of Puerto Perez

This thermal lies northeast of Las Islas Cinco Hermanos in GPS position 45°14'·6S 73°12'W. When approaching the thermal a huge, quarry-like landfall marks the approximate location. The hot spring emerges at sea level and warms the sea in its immediate vicinity. When close the final location of the thermal can be seen by steam rising from the sea. There are no hot inland pools. Anchor very close to the shore in 13m and take a shore-line.

b. Thermal of Chiconal, Punta Tortuga

East of Punta Tortuga lies a large salmon farm with several buildings serving this operation, near a small jetty in the NW corner of the bay. The thermals are several hundred metres behind these buildings. The thermals are private and belong to Pesca Chile. A private yacht will be welcomed to visit the thermals if permission is obtained. This can be done during the week by visiting the salmon farm at Punta Tortuga at a time when they can call their main office in Chacabuco or by visiting the Chacabuco office of Pesca Chile. ☎ (67) 351121. Anchor very near the shore adjacent to the pier in about 14m. The bottom shelves very steeply. Take a stern line to the end of the pier. The staff at the *salmonera* will point out the route to the thermals which lies along a raised wooden boardwalk. This wanders through pretty alpine meadows until 5 small pools are found in ferny dells in the forest. The water in each pool is at a different regulated temperature. It is well worth the effort of reaching these thermals as they are exquisite.

Hot-springs in Seno Aysén. (GPS positions)

3·37 Seno Aysén – Caleta Gato

45°18'S 73°12'W

Charts

UK *1288* US *22371* Chile *809, 8290*

General

This beautiful anchorage is on the southern side of Seno Aysén just east of Punta Angosta. It is an excellent stopping place *en route* to Chacabuco. Anchor in the centre beyond the narrower entrance in about 14m, good holding in mud. Either swing or take shorelines. Do not go too close to the beach at the head of the bay, as it shoals rapidly and the muddy bottom becomes very soft. Good water can be taken from the stream in the southeast corner at the head of the bay. The *caleta* is best shown on UK chart *1288*.

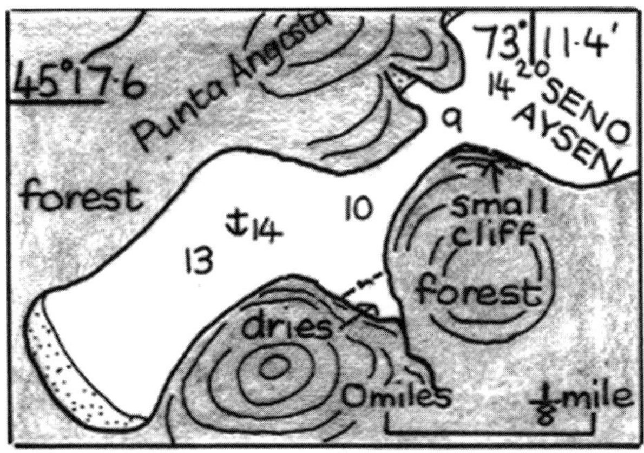

Caleta Gato. (GPS positions)

3·38 Seno Aysén – Punta Camello

45°27'W 72°59'·5S

Charts

UK *1288* US *22371* Chile *809, 8290*

General

This anchorage underneath Punta Camello, on the S. side of Aysén, provides good protection from the west but is subject to *rachas*. The holding is good in 10m of sand at the head of the bay. Beware of the rock in the centre of the entrance. Caleta Dagny, on the west side of Punta Camello, may provide better shelter but has not been tested.

3·39 Seno Aysén – Puerto Chacabuco

45°28'S 72°49'W

Charts

UK *1288* US *22371* Chile *809, 8290, 811, 827.*

General

Bahía Chacabuco is a working port. The main bay is exposed to the winds which are frequently very strong and gust from all directions. It is very wet. Ensenada Baja, behind Península Fontaine, has better protection but even there the gusts are fierce. It is possible to be trapped inside by the weather for several days. Apart from that hazard, Chacabuco is a good place for a crew change via the airfield at Balmaceda which is reached by minibus. The town of Aysén is nearby and has a fair run of shops, banks etc. Further afield, Coihaique provides excellent shopping.

Approach

The approach is straightforward, passing south of Isla Carmen.

Anchorages

Ensenada Baja, to the east around Peninsula Fontaine, is the best place to lie. Detailed sailing directions, to be read in conjunction with plan, are as follows. Enter or leave about an hour before high water:

Approach mid-channel between Isla Transito and Península Fontaine. As the entrance opens up, bear round to starboard and head for a position about two boat lengths off the Fontaine shore. Follow this shore line round, closing to about one boat length off at the eastern end of Fontaine. Depths will drop to 2–3m but keep in to the Fontaine shore to avoid the drying patch off the mainland shore. When a course of about 213° can be made to the southwestern end of the harbour, follow it and anchor beyond the salmon pens in 4–7m.

The holding is not good; boats have dragged, having been happily settled for three or four days. The scenery around is spectacular but the fish-processing plants in Chacabuco cast rather a smelly pall on downwind days.

In Bahía Chacabuco itself, yachts are allowed alongside the jetty subject to shipping movements. This is useful for a quick stop but it is very expensive (2,900 pesos an hour with no discount for a longer stay). It is probably better to go alongside the fishing pier. This is very busy with boats coming and going but a yacht will be allowed to lie temporarily alongside the fishing boats on the outside wall of the fishing jetty. Report to the small office there. This is useful for a crew change or to take on water from a hose that is available there. A small charge may be made for this by the pier master.

There are two possibilities for anchoring in the bay. The first is in the east corner, near the *Armada* and fishing pier, with poor holding and only useful for a short stop. The second is in the southern corner of the bay in front of a collection of agricultural buildings and a large farmhouse with a pale blue roof. Anchor in 10–12m of water, 100–150m north of a small jetty. It would be wise to use 2 anchors in tandem, but the holding is good in silt. The large commercial catamaran, *Patagonia Express*, anchors in this area between its trips to Laguna San Rafael.

Formalities

Check with the *Capitanía del Puerto*. It is necessary to report to the *Armada* by calling Chacabuco radio and by visiting the office, when a new *zarpe* will be issued. Should a visitors visa be nearing its expiry date, it can be renewed in Puerto Aysén.

Facilities

Diesel is available by can at Ensenada Baja.

Water on the piers in Chacabuco but by can at Ensenada Baja.

Provisions available in Aysén; supermarket Don Angelo, Sargento Aldea Block 400 (near Caupolicán). Much better in Coihaique.

Banco de Crédito, Av. Prat, or Banco de Chile (both in Aysén), for Visa.

Laundry (expensive) at Oska, Sgto. Aldea 1221

Communications

Buses every 20 minutes to Aysén and 6 times a day to Coihaique (67km from Aysén), whence buses to the rest of Chile and to Argentina.

Airports at Coihaique and Balmaceda. Navimag ferry services to Puerto Montt.

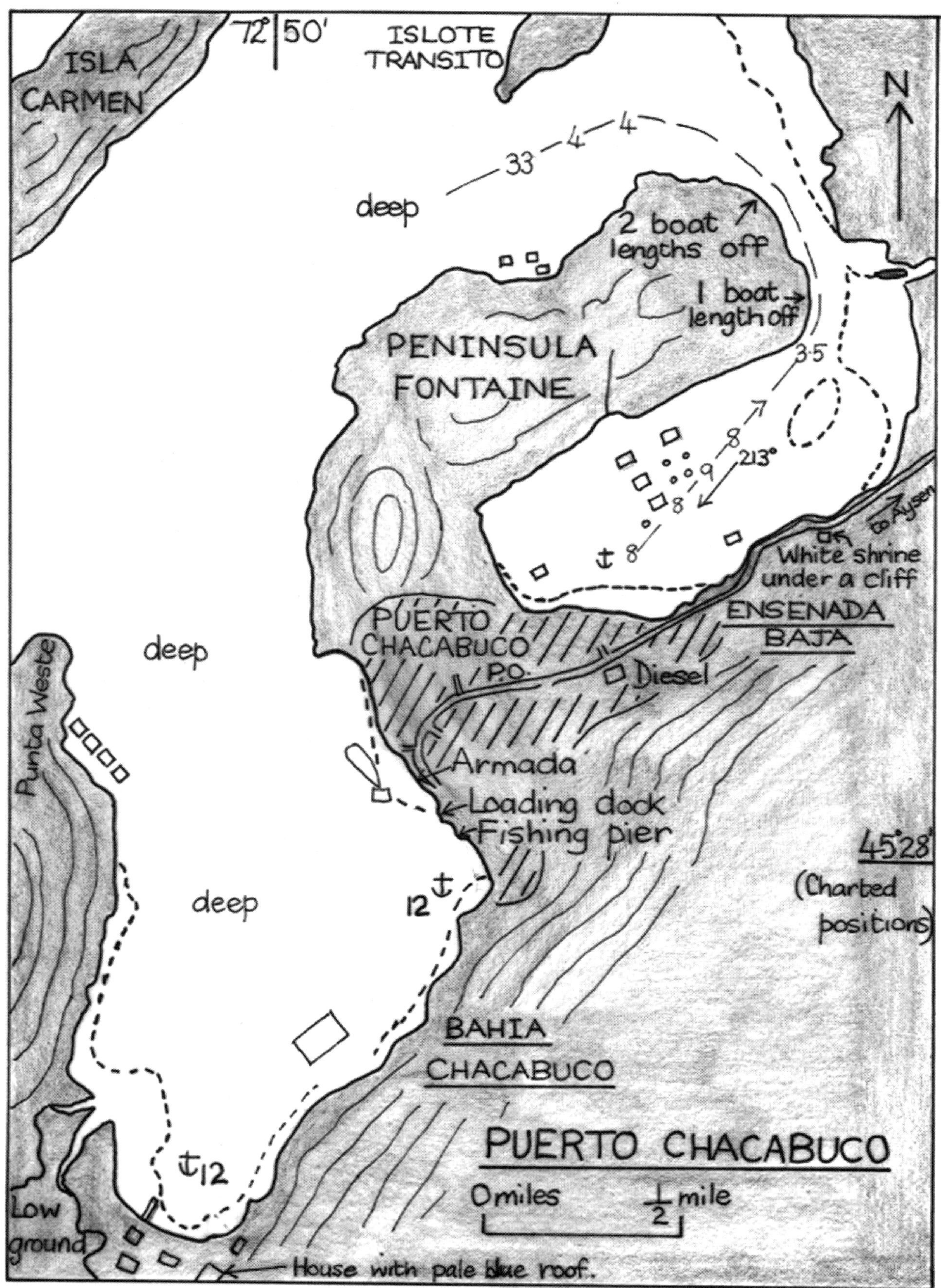

72° 50'
ISLA CARMEN
ISLOTE TRANSITO
N
33
4
4
deep
2 boat lengths off
1 boat length off
PENINSULA FONTAINE
3.5
8
9
213°
8
8
to Aysen
White shrine under a cliff
PUERTO CHACABUCO
ENSENADA BAJA
P.O.
Diesel
deep
Punta Weste
Armada
Loading dock
Fishing pier
45°28'
(Charted positions)
deep
12
BAHIA CHACABUCO
PUERTO CHACABUCO
0 miles
1/2 mile
12
Low ground
House with pale blue roof.

Telephone Area code 67; Companía de Teléfonos de Coihaique at Bernardo O'Higgins, Chacabuco.

Continuation

3·40 Isla Traiguén – Caleta Christiane

45°31'S 73°35'W

Charts
UK *1288* US *22371* Chile *809*

General
Caleta Christiane is the northern-most indentation on the east side of Isla Traiguen with good shelter from north and west. Anchor in about 13m, mud and sand. Fishermen lie parallel to the shore with lines out to the south shore, right at the head of the bay, and an anchor to hold the boat off-shore.

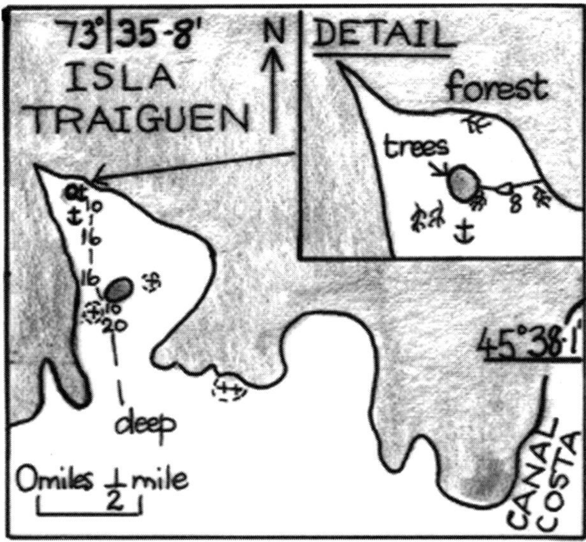

Estero Colonia Grande. (GPS positions)

3·41 Isla Traiguén – Estero Colonia Grande

45°38'·1S 73°35'·8W

Charts
UK *1288* US – Chile *809.*

General
This large Estero is not named on the charts, but is called Estero Colonia Grande by the fishermen from Puerto Chacabuco. It lies third of the way up Canal Costa and is good place to shelter in strong north winds as well as being peaceful and beautiful. The approach is clear of dangers and by passing close to the west of the small island on the plan the rock, that covers, is easily avoided.

3·42 Canal Costa – Caleta Lynch

45°46'·7S 73°34'W

Charts
UK *1288* US *22371* Chile *809*

General
Caleta Lynch, situated just north of Punta Lynch, is a world class anchorage, the best choice along Canal Costa. Enter just north of the central line to the first bay. Entry is simple and deep but the depths become shallower in the southern part of the entrance. The outer entrance should be entered mid-channel to avoid kelp on the southern side. Once inside the outer bay there is immediate shelter from winds blowing strongly in Canal Costa. Hold to the starboard (west) shore on the way in to the inner pool as there is a rock off the east side of the inner entrance. Anchor in the SW corner of the inner pool where there is perfect shelter for several yachts.

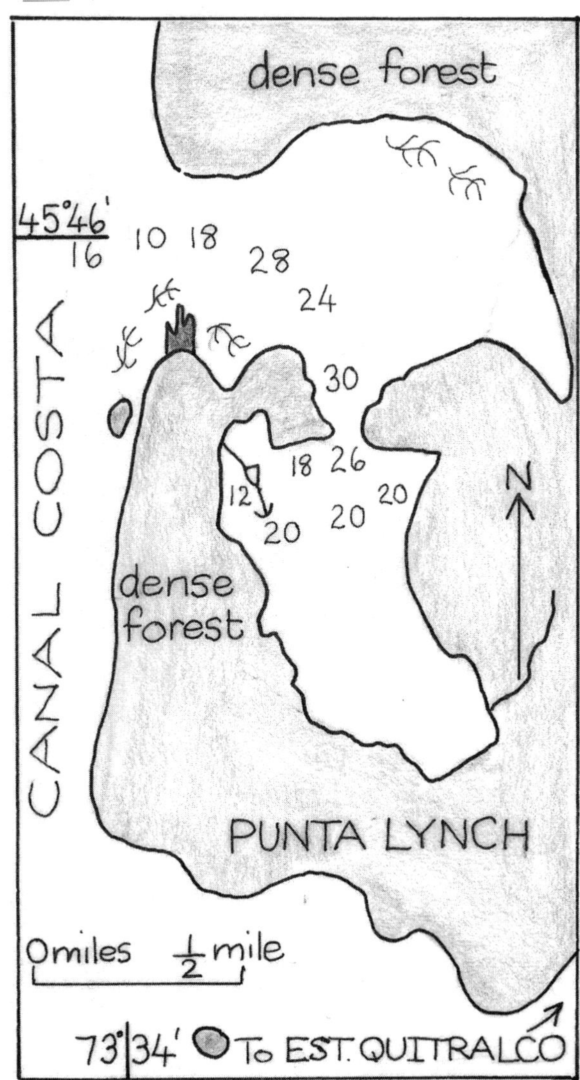

Caleta Lynch. (GPS positions)

Canal Costa

At the south end of Canal Costa there is an uncharted rock 100m WNW of the islet northeast of Isla Raimapu. On the east side of Isla Raimapu just north of 1570·6Raimapu Light there are sea lion and red-legged shag colonies.

Diversion

3·43 Estero Quitralco – Caleta Descanso

45°46'S 73°31'W

Charts
UK *1288* US *22371* Chile *809*

General
This bay, which lies 2 miles NE of Punta Lynch, in Estero Quitralco provides perfect shelter from strong northerly winds. Access is straightforward. Good holding in 6m.

3·44 Estero Quitralco – North Arm

45°35'·5S 73°15'·2W

Charts
UK *1288* US *22371* Chile *809*

General
Estero Quitralco is a huge estuary visited regularly by the commercial passenger ships, *Skorpio 1*, *2* and *3*, which sail from Puerto Montt to Laguna San Rafael. The ships stop at the thermals on the north shore of the main, east, arm of the Estero.

The land at the head of the north arm, extending for many kilometres, is owned by the Westcott family, based in Santiago. Tony Westcott and his brother, Michael have sailed the Canals for years. Contact Tony Westcott via the Valdivia Yacht Club for permission to visit the ranch.

From the anchorage proceed by dinghy at half tide plus up the River Maullín. The countryside opens out into a beautiful level valley surrounded by huge mountains. After about a mile the buildings of the ranch are visible. You will be made welcome. Towing a spinner while travelling up the river will almost certainly catch a large trout or salmon.

Estuario Quitralco. (GPS positions)

Anchorage
Anchor at the head of the arm. The bay is very deep (25m) but shoals very rapidly, almost vertically, where the River Maullín enters the bay. The best anchorage is probably tied off fore and aft in the small bay in the north west corner.

Continuation

3·45 Estuario Elefantes – Puerto Bonito

45°56'·35S 73°34'·25W

Charts
UK *1288* Chile *809, 812*

General
At the northern end of Elefantes and on the east side, it is well sheltered despite its open appearance. There is protection from north and west winds in the north arm of the bay. The bottom is even and mud. There is a sawmill ashore.

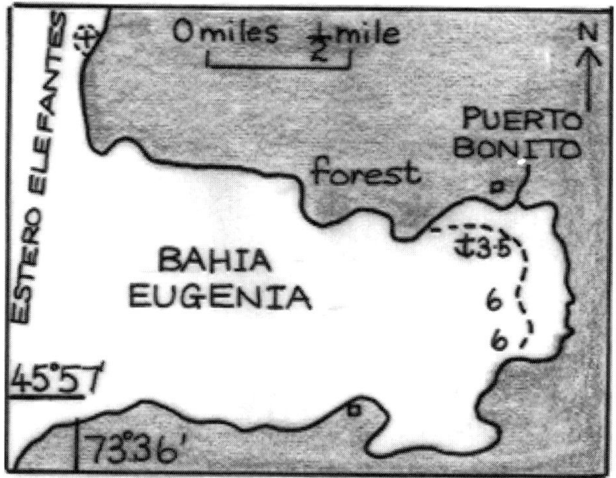

Puerto Bonito. (Charted positions)

3·46 Isla Nalcayec – Estero Odger

46°09'S 73°43'·5W

Charts
UK *1288* Chile *812*

General
Estero Odger is a significant indent on the east side of Isla Nalcayec and is named on Chile *812*. GPS put its position as 46°08'·81S 73°42'·79W. Described as a bullet proof stop-over, two sites are mentioned. One is at the head of the bay anchoring in as shallow water as is suitable, good holding (and an interesting dinghy trip beyond). The other is along the southwest shore, in 8m with lines to the trees, where it is possible to water. There are deep coves inside the entrance on the northeast shore where it is possible to lie up whilst waiting for the tide in Elefantes.

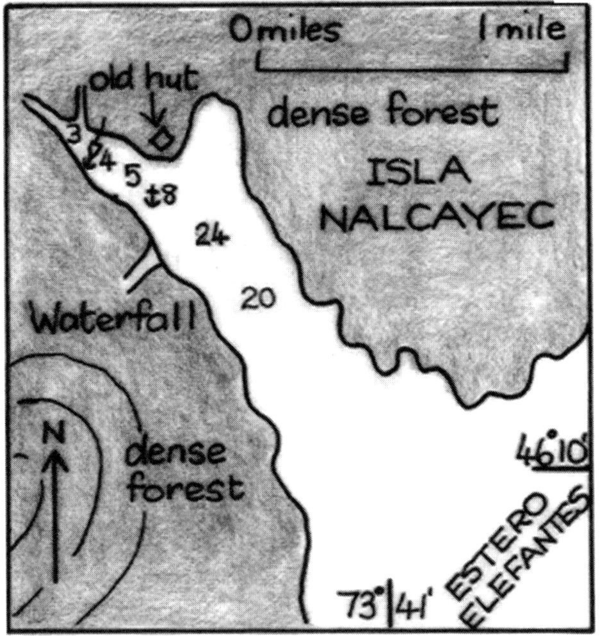

Estero Odger

3·47 Estero Cupquelan – Bahía Exploradores
46°17'·7S 73°31'·5W

Charts
UK *1288* US – Chile *812*

General
Bahía Exploradores is the second, northern, bay on the east side of Estero Cupquelan (Francisco on UK chart *1288*). One of the reasons for anchoring here is to explore the 20M Río Exploradores by dinghy and to catch salmon. However, in the anchorage behind the spit (9m) there is a current which may make the ship lie stern to the wind though otherwise it is described as a good, sheltered, anchorage.

3·48 Estero Cupquelan – Caleta Primera
46°19'·5S 73°36'W

Charts
UK *1288* Chile *812*

General
Caleta Primera is the first bay on the east shore of Estero Cupquelan (Francisco on UK chart *1288*). The entrance is easy, deep and clean. Even in strong northerly winds it is possible to tuck up into the east corner near a prominent stream. In this position the yacht is protected from any swell entering the bay. Holding is excellent in mud but a shore line should be taken to protect the yacht from swinging in case the wind shifts to the south.

This is a spectacular anchorage with vertical waterfalls on the mountains above the anchorage. In addition it is possible to enter by dinghy the second secluded large bay, which lies in a valley surrounded

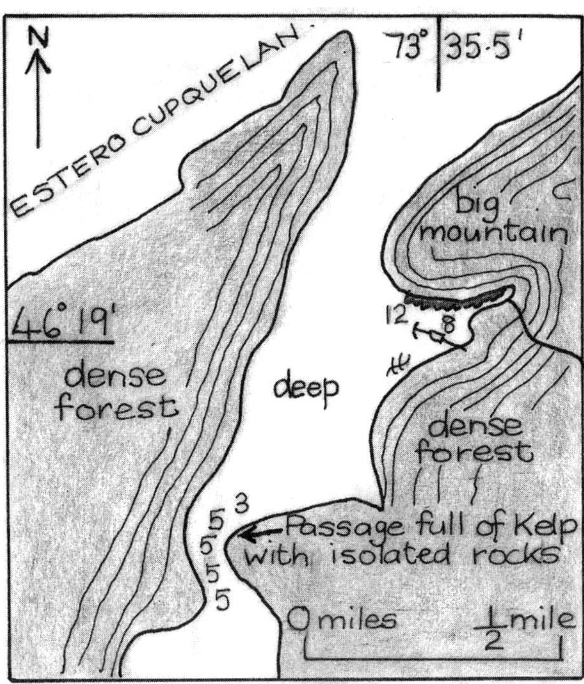

Caleta Primera. (GPS positions)

by tall peaks; it is a fine and sheltered place to explore.

3·49 Paso Quesahuén
46°24'S 73°45'W

Charts
UK *1288* Chile *838*

General
The strait is about 300m wide, the stream reaches 5–7kts at springs and it can be most uncomfortable. Take into account wind and tide conditions and take it around slack water. Approach from the northeast, favour the Isla Leonor side and pass north of 1570·67Islote Pelado (Fl.R.5s6m5M, White GRP tower, red band, 015°-vis-314°). Chile *838* shows a 3·5m patch close east of Leonor; other Chilean charts and UK *1288* do not show this and there is no comment in reports.

3·50 Golfo Elefantes – Bahía Quesahuén
46°24'S 73°47'W

Charts
UK *1288* Chile *838*

General
This bay lies between the mainland and a number of small islets and rocky outcrops just south of Paso Quesahuén. It provides a safe overnight anchorage, or a useful place to wait for a fair tide before tackling the San Rafael Glacier, in an area where there are few alternatives. The area should be approached with caution as it is affected by the strong tidal

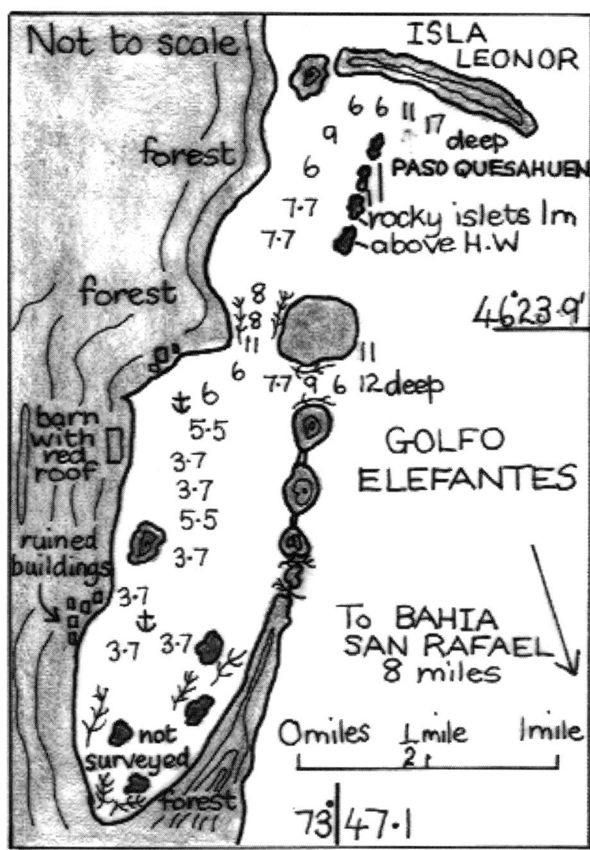

Bahía Quesahuén. (GPS positions)

streams that run in Paso Quesahuén. There are two entrances to the bay: one immediately south of Isla Leonor; the other south of the first prominent islet. Once inside, a yacht can anchor in the northern or southern part of the bay, depending on the wind. Take great care if going south beyond the saw mill and disused pier as there is a reef which dries at half tide about ⅓ of the way from the disused pier to the islet in the centre of the S end of the bay. Holding is good in thick mud. Water is available from a catchment point in a stream just to the left of the house.

3·51 Golfo Elefantes – Caleta Gualas

46°28'·5S 73°45'·5W

Charts
UK *1288* Chile *838*

General
All right in a northerly but useless if the wind comes round to the west. Anchor in 8m behind Punta Huidobro If caught in the *caleta* by a southerly, anchoring is possible off a pebble beach east of Punta García in the southern half of the bay, 8m.

3·52 Golfo Elefantes – Bahía Islotes Ruiz

46°30'·7S 73°51'W

Charts
UK *1288* Chile *838*

General
Lying approximately 1M northwest of Punta Leopardos, this small bay on the west coast of Elefantes may provide a useful anchorage for yachts going to or from Laguna San Rafael. It is easily identified by the three small islets lying off-shore. It can be entered from the north or the east through a narrow channel between the islets and the mainland. Well protected from the south, some shelter from the north is provided by the islets. Holding is good in mud.

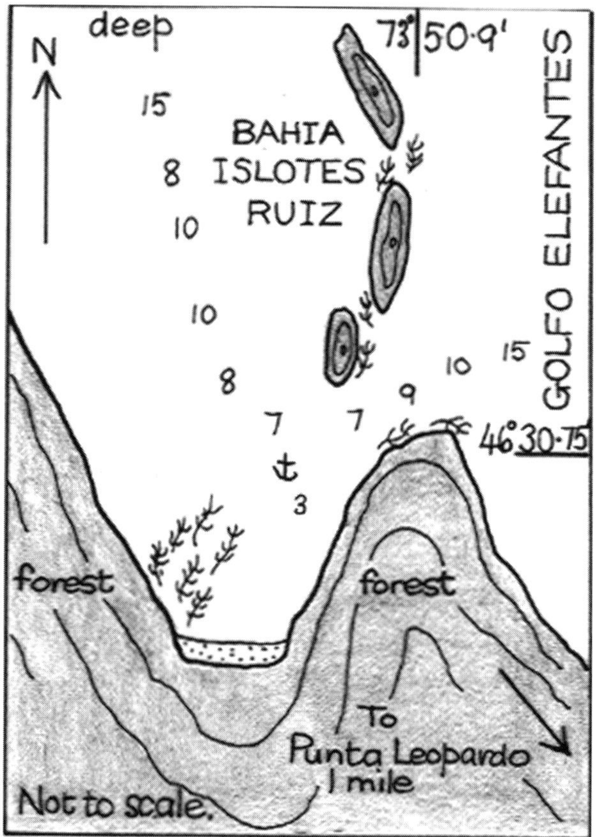

Bahía Islotes Ruiz. (GPS positions)

3·53 Río Témpanos and Río de Patos

46°33'·7S 74°56'·5W

Charts
UK *1288* Chile *838*

Río Témpanos
Río Témpanos comes out on the southwest shore of Bahía San Rafael. Its entrance is deep (18m) but very narrow, between the blobs of islands off Punta Leopardos and 1570·7Bahía San Rafael light (Fl.5s6m5M, White GRP tower, red band, 015°-vis-314°). There is a steep-to spit extending north

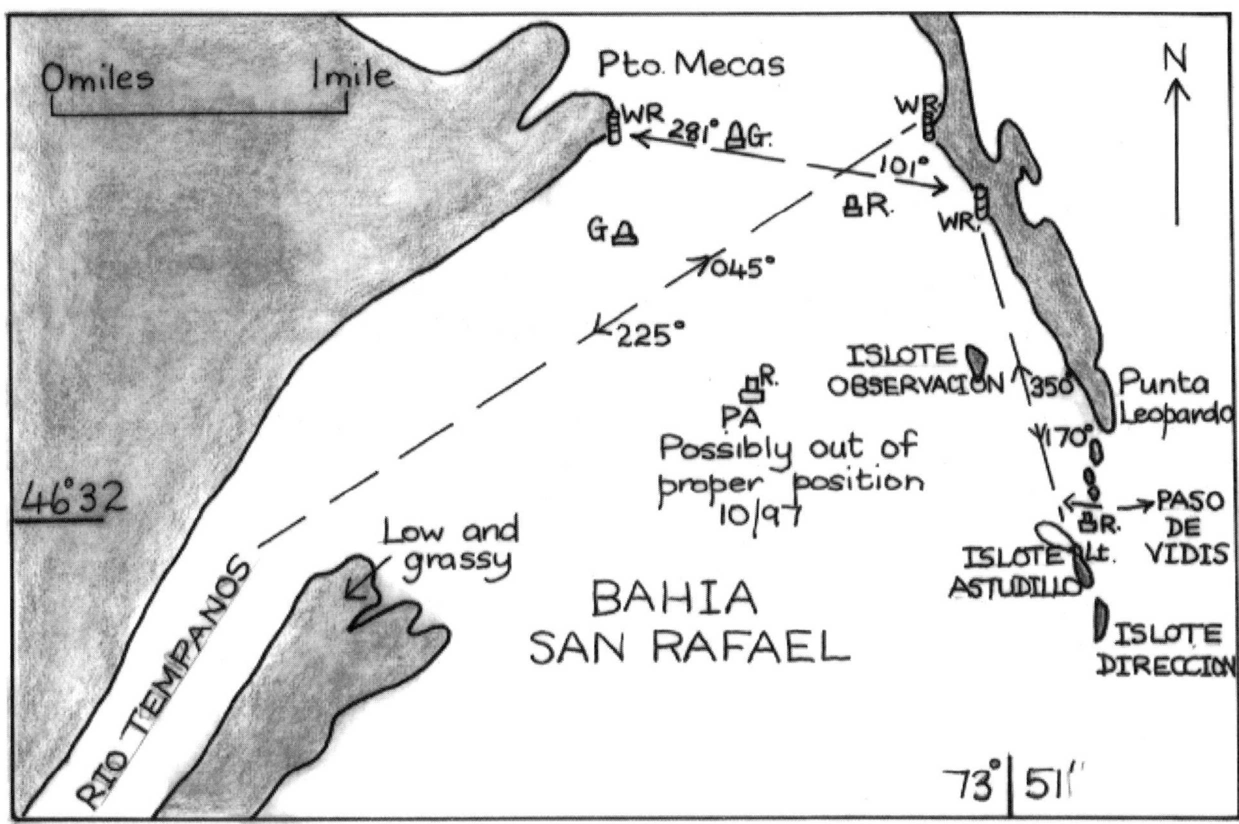

Rio Témpanos. (Charted positions)

from the light and there can be a strong current at the entrance. Enter at the beginning of the flood when the ice is being pushed back. See plan which indicates the marks not yet entered on Chile *838*. Favour the north side. Minimum depth 5·6m over one shoal patch up river.

Río de Patos

Río de Patos is on the west side of Río Témpanos and easily seen when approached from the north. There is plenty of water in the entrance; inside, the depth at first falls to 3m (at low water) but increases to 5m. A little way upstream is a large round pool where the river turns back on itself; anchor in 5m.

3·54 Laguna San Rafael

46°40'S 73°55'W

Charts

UK *1288* Chile *838*

General

The laguna is regularly visited by cruise boats. There is generally plenty of brash ice in the lagoon, along with dolphins, penguins and sea-lions. Río Lucac, which runs within half a mile of the southern shore, joins Río San Tadeo which emerges in Bahía San Quintín, about 15M away on the southern side of Peninsula Taitao.

Approach

Up Río Témpanos – see the approach to Río de Patos.

Anchorage

In settled weather it is possible to anchor within the lagoon. There are many small bays with adequate depth to anchor. However care needs to be taken of floating ice as bergy bits can be sizeable. For example anchor in the northeast bay for a north wind and off the south shore for a south wind. The alternative is to make a day visit to the Laguna and then return to Río de Patos, Bahía Sisquelan or to Caleta Gualas.

Section 4
Canal Darwin to Golfo de Peñas

The exit to the Pacific Ocean

To pass from Rio Témpanos to the Pacific by the approved route it is necessary to return northwards to Paso Tres Cruces, 45°48'S 73°40'W and then turn west. But the adventurous might send the boat the long way round, traverse 15 miles southwest on foot and rejoin it at Bahía San Quintín to continue the journey south.

General

This section deals with links from Canal Errázuriz to the Pacific, the outside passage to Golfo de Peñas and anchorages on the north side of that Gulf.

Charts

There are no large scale US charts south of Peninsula Skyring

Canal Darwin versus Canals Chacabuco and Pulluche

Charts

UK *1288* US *22371* Chile *842, 846*

On a southbound trip, there are two possible routes out from Canal Errázuriz, which is a continuation of Canal Moraleda, to the Pacific Ocean. The northern route is through Canal Darwin, and the southern through Chacabuco and Pulluche. For most yachts the southern route is preferred. There is little shelter at the western end of Canal Darwin, and it is a much longer run to the south to the Puerto Refugio area than if an exit is made through Bahía Anna Pink.

Exiting Canal Pulluche through Boca Wickham and then into Bahía Anna Pink can be very uncomfortable in strong west winds. The state of the sea breaking on Punta Wickham gives a good idea of conditions in Bahía Anna Pink and beyond. Estero Gori looks an obvious anchorage, but the entrance is in fact blocked by foul ground. The seaward approach to Canal Darwin is more straightforward than the approach to Canal Pulluche and may be preferable if coming from the south in poor visibility. Puerto Yates (see below) is a sheltered anchorage 5 miles from the entrance.

4·1 Isla Quemada – Caleta Morgane

45°25'·5S 73°58'·5W

Charts

UK *1288* US *22371* Chile *842*

General

On the south coast of Isla Quemada, Caleta Morgane is a pretty anchorage with a river at its head. Good holding in sand. Beware the rocky shallows.

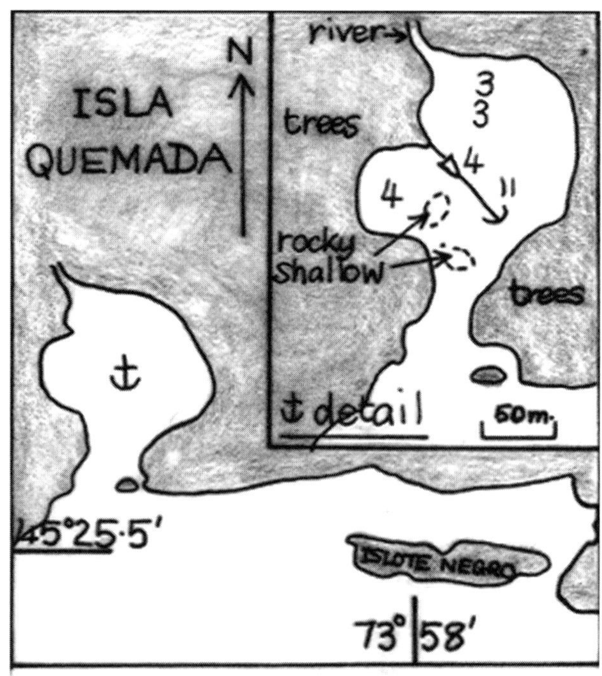

Caleta Morgane. (Charted positions)

4·2 Isla Quemada – Caleta Galvarino

45°24'S 74°01'W

Charts

UK *1288* US *22371* Chile *842*

General

Galvarino is located at the west end of the south coast of Isla Quemada, 10 miles in from the eastern entrance to Canal Darwin. There is a light near the eastern entrance. It is somewhat exposed to the

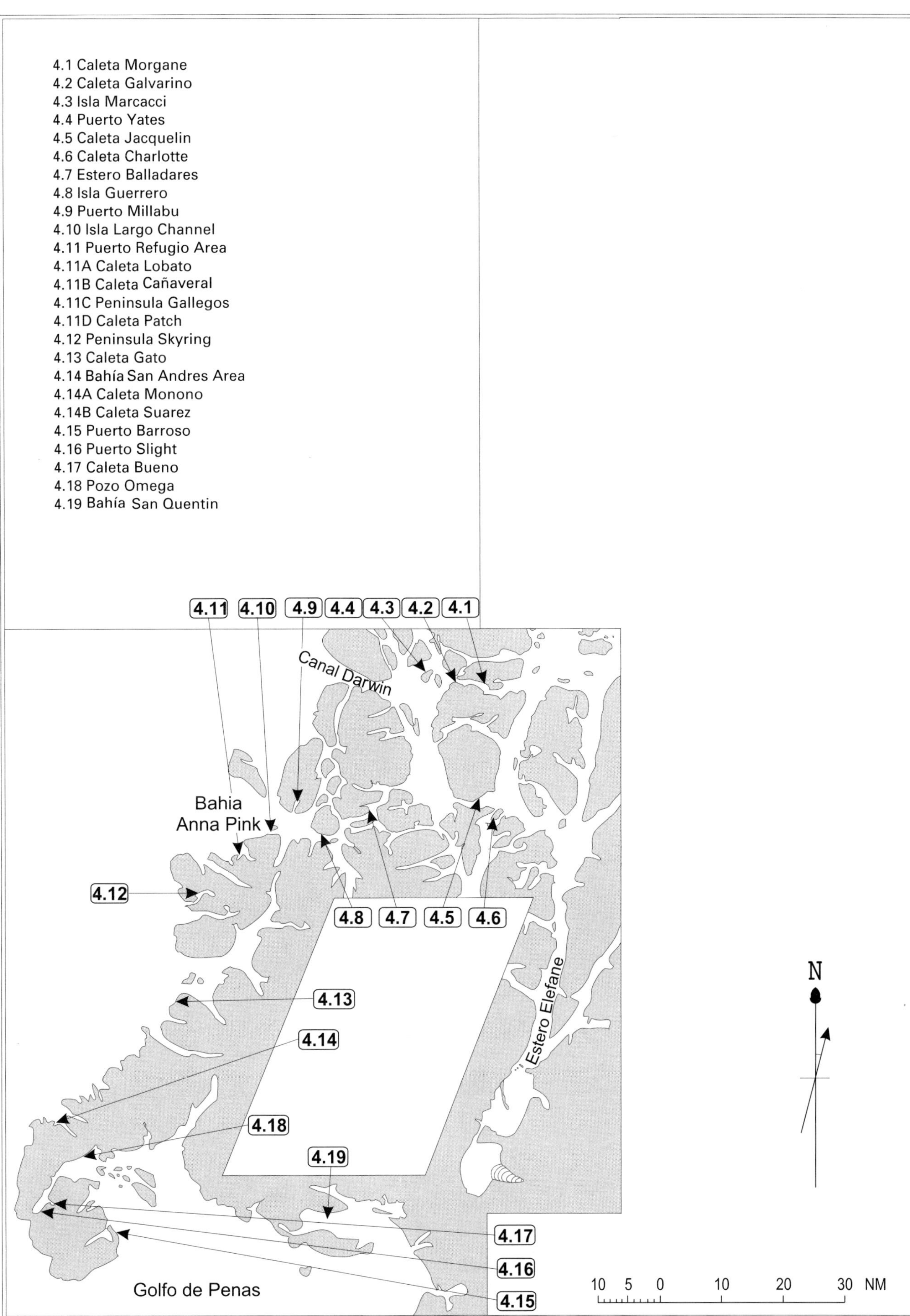
4.1 Caleta Morgane
4.2 Caleta Galvarino
4.3 Isla Marcacci
4.4 Puerto Yates
4.5 Caleta Jacquelin
4.6 Caleta Charlotte
4.7 Estero Balladares
4.8 Isla Guerrero
4.9 Puerto Millabu
4.10 Isla Largo Channel
4.11 Puerto Refugio Area
4.11A Caleta Lobato
4.11B Caleta Cañaveral
4.11C Peninsula Gallegos
4.11D Caleta Patch
4.12 Peninsula Skyring
4.13 Caleta Gato
4.14 Bahía San Andres Area
4.14A Caleta Monono
4.14B Caleta Suarez
4.15 Puerto Barroso
4.16 Puerto Slight
4.17 Caleta Bueno
4.18 Pozo Omega
4.19 Bahía San Quentin
4.11
4.10
4.9
4.4
4.3
4.2
4.1
Canal Darwin
Bahia
Anna Pink
4.12
4.8
4.7
4.5
4.6
4.13
4.14
Estero Elefane
4.18
4.19
4.17
4.16
4.15
Golfo de Penas
N
10 5 0 10 20 30 NM

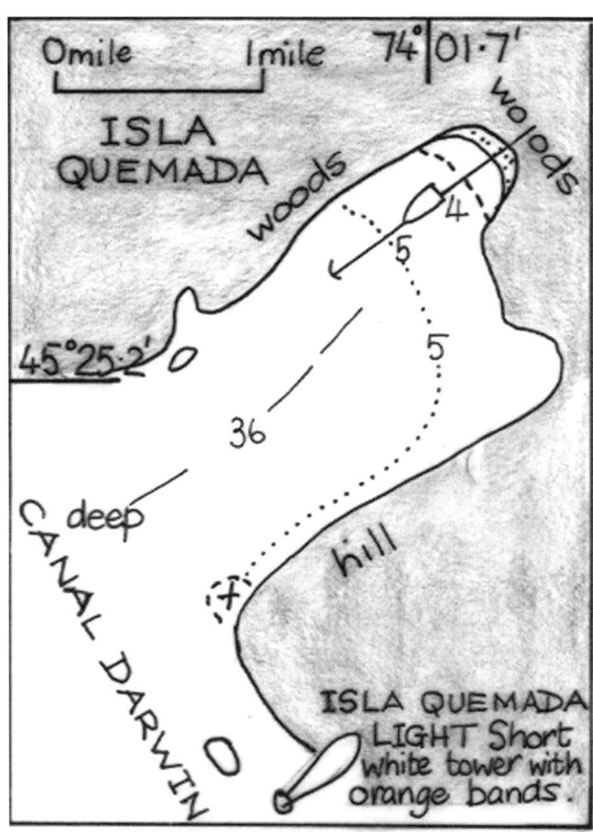

Caleta Galverino. (Charted positions)

south and south west. It is best to anchor as close to the head of the bay as possible with a line ashore. The bottom is sand, but the holding is reported to be only fair.

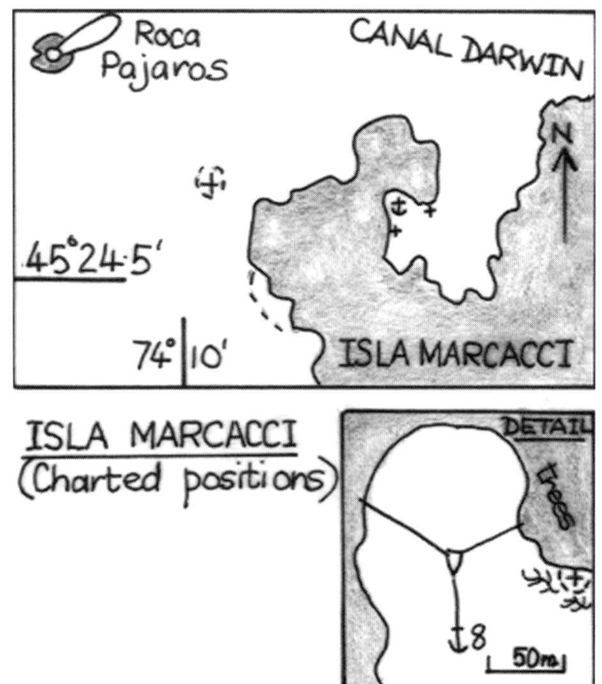

Isla Marcacci. (Charted positions)

4·3 Isla Marcacci

45°24'S 74°09'W

Charts

UK *1288* US *22371* Chile *842*

General

On the northwest corner of Isla Marcacci, well sheltered from all winds. Anchor in about 8m with lines to trees. There are sea lions and otters in the anchorage but plastic rubbish on shore.

4·4 Isla Rivero – Puerto Yates

45°28'S 74°24'W

Charts

UK *1288* US *22371* Chile *840, 841*

General

Puerto Yates is a good place to wait prior to exiting Canal Darwin or a place to rest after a long offshore passage from the south. It is located 3 miles down Canal Williams, on the western side of Isla Rivero. Chart *841* is detailed, the entrance is easy to find, even under radar. The holding is good on a sand bottom in 14m.

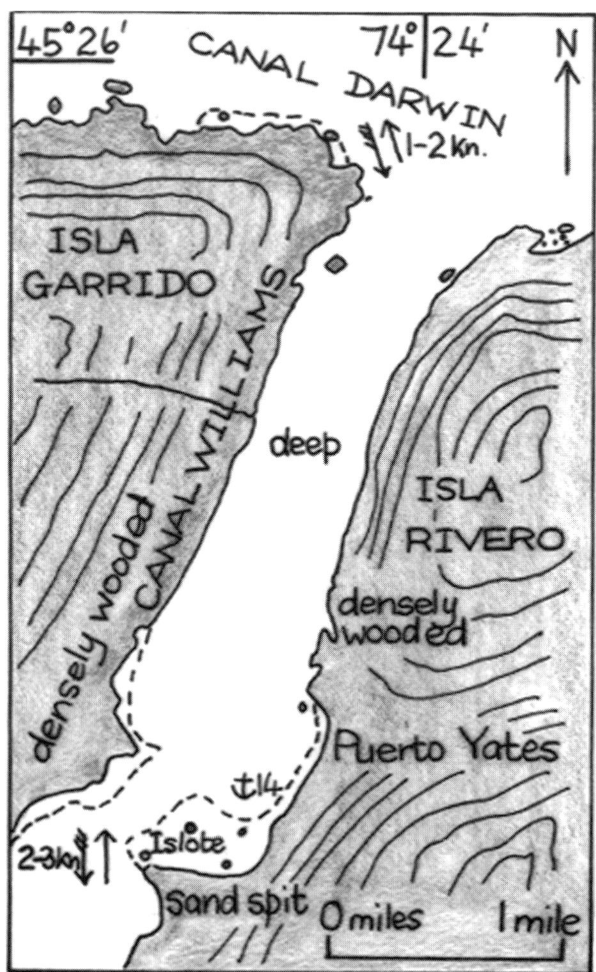

Puerto Yates. (Charted positions)

4·5 Isla Humos – Caleta Jacqueline
45°44'S 73°57'W

Charts
UK *1288* US *22371* Chile *846, 807*

General
Caleta Jacqueline is the unnamed *caleta* shown at the extreme western end of Bahía Harchy, 4M west of Punta Harchy and at the southern mid-point of Isla Humos. The entrance is easily identifiable from E by the pale coloured beach just S of the entrance. Although the bay appears to be open to the E, the shelter is better than it looks because you can tuck around the point to the N. There is considerable kelp in the bay which can be by-passed. Either anchor where shown, 6m, good holding, or go to the waterfall with a line ashore which may be more sheltered. There are often small pieces of pumice on the beaches and in the surrounding waters. Fishermen consider this the most secure anchorage in this sector.

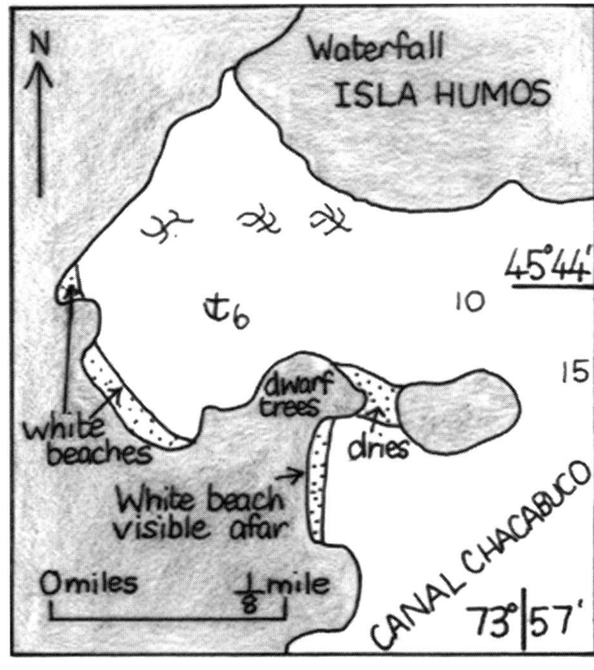

Caleta Jaqueline. (GPS positions)

4·6 Canals Errazuriz & Chacabuco – Caleta Charlotte
45°46'S 73°53'W

Charts
UK *1288* US *22371* Chile *846, 807*

General
This unnamed *caleta* has been nick-named Charlotte after the daughter of Oscar Prochelle, who discovered this anchorage. Approach from the north via the small canal between Isla Fitzroy and Isla Piuco. There is a rock shown on the sketch plan but

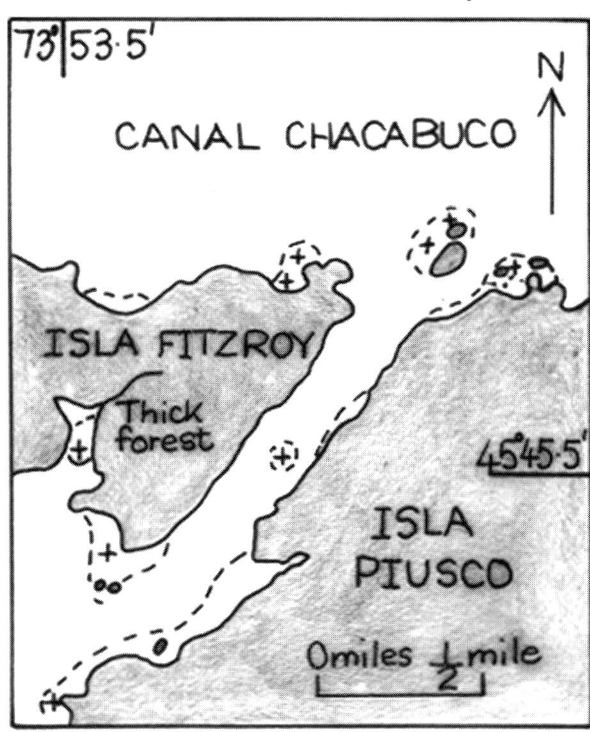

Caleta Charlotte. (Charted positions)

it is well marked by kelp. The rest of the canal is free of dangers. Anchor in the small bay, 6m, sand. The bay is very sheltered even when strong winds are blowing from the north.

4·7 Isla Rivero – Estero Balladares
45°44'S 74°22'W

Charts
UK *1288* US *22371* Chile *807, 840, 846*

General
Estero Balladares is a long fjord off Canal Pulluche. It is very important to move with a favourable tidal current in Canal Pulluche as the flood tide in this area can run up to 4 knots and Balladares is a good place to wait. It provides good shelter and the holding is good in about 10m but is subject to strong *rachas*. Some protection from these can be gained by tucking in behind the headland of Punta Laurel. The two streams on the north side have good drinking water. The western stream has many *Copihue*, the national flower, beside it; Aguada, the eastern stream, was a watering point for ships.

In settled weather it is possible to anchor at the head of Estero Balladares which is very beautiful. Holding in very soft mud in about 7m.

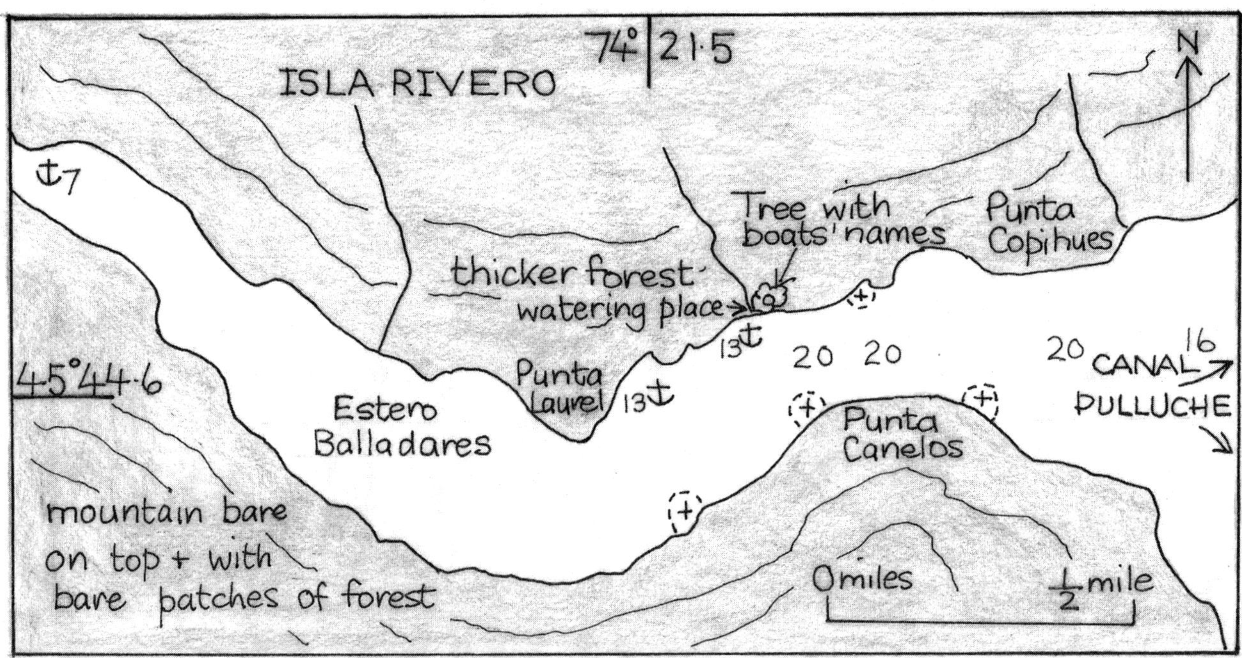

Estero Balladares. (GPS positions)

4·8 Isla Guerrero

45°·48'·9S 74°31'·7W

Charts
UK *1288* US *22371* Chile *8430*

General
On the south coast of Isla Guerrero, about 2·5 miles from of 1563·5Isla Ricardo light (45°49'·4S 74°28'·6W Fl(4)6m4M White GRP tower Red Band 4m) and Punta Wickham bearing 202° approximately 1·5 miles away. Open to the SE but otherwise good shelter. Lines ashore in SW corner. Tide sweeps into the bay on the flood and it is possible that some swell might too if it were rough outside.

4·9 Isla Clemente – Puerto Millabu

45°44'S 74°38'W

Charts
UK *1288* US *22371* Chile *8430, 817*

General
Estero Clemente, the long fjord running into the southern end of Isla Clemente (see chart *817*) provides shelter either in a bay half way up the western side or at the very head of the bay in Puerto Millabu. Isla Clemente is easily identified on the northern side of Bahía Anna Pink as it is an island of large barren mountains dominated by Monte Haddington. Puerto Millabu, at the head of Estero Clemente is a beautiful harbour with sandy beaches and a spectacular waterfall, Cascada Salmón. The bay, a shallow indentation, is in front of some old tent posts below a saddle in the hills. A good place to wait for the weather but subject to *rachas.* Good fishing.

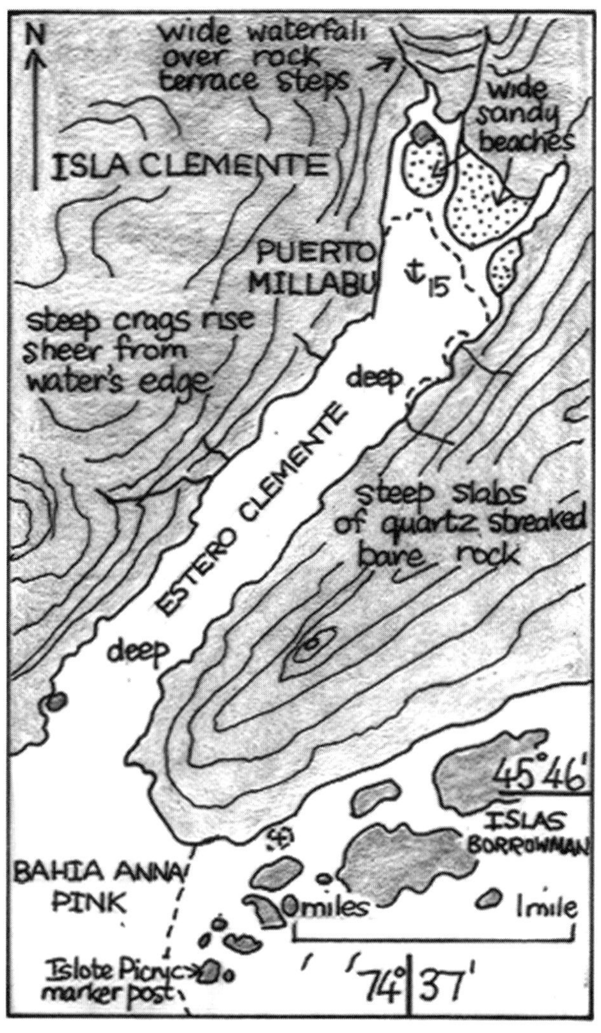

Puerto Millabu. (Charted positions)

Approach
On the east side, the ground south of Punta Salida is shoal with half a dozen small islands. The deep water lies west of southernmost, Isla Picnic, which has a pole beacon.

Anchorage
The holding is good in about 15m at the head of the bay. Anchor on the west side off a small beach with a large off-lying rock. It can be squally so take a line ashore. Watch out for the delta of Río Casma on the northeast side.

Boca Wickham

As mentioned earlier, the state of the sea breaking on Punta Wickham (45°50'S 74°33'W) gives a good idea of conditions in Bahía Anna Pink and beyond.

4·10 Channel between Isla Larga and Península Taitao

45°48'·5S 72°42'W

Charts
UK *1288* US *22371* Chile *840, 8430*

General
The channel between Isla Larga, Isla Dirección and the mainland is regularly used by small *Armada* vessels. It is a good choice for small craft going with the tide as it avoids some of the swell entering Bahía Anna Pink. Care should be taken at the west end of Isla Larga as rocks extend out from the southwest end of the island and from the headland on the mainland opposite. Keep mid-channel to avoid these dangers.

Isla Inchemó

It is about 72M from 1563Isla Inchemó (45°48'·4S 74°59'·2W Fl.12s31m12M White concrete tower 4m 231°-vis-118°) to Cabo Rapér (see below) and a further 20M to the first possible anchorage in the Golfo Tres Montes. From Raper to Isla San Pedro is about 72M. Between Inchémo and Ráper there are the following possible refuges.

4·11 Puerto Refugio Area

45°52'S 74°48'W

Charts
UK *1288* US *22371* Chile *840, 8430, 807*

General
The Puerto Refugio area is a spectacular amphitheatre with big mountains with steep, barren slab faces. Several hard climbs have been made on these slabs, notably by the crew of the British yacht, *Pelagic*. There are four recognised anchorages in this area as shown on the detailed Chilean chart *807.* Puerto Refugio itself does not afford much protection.

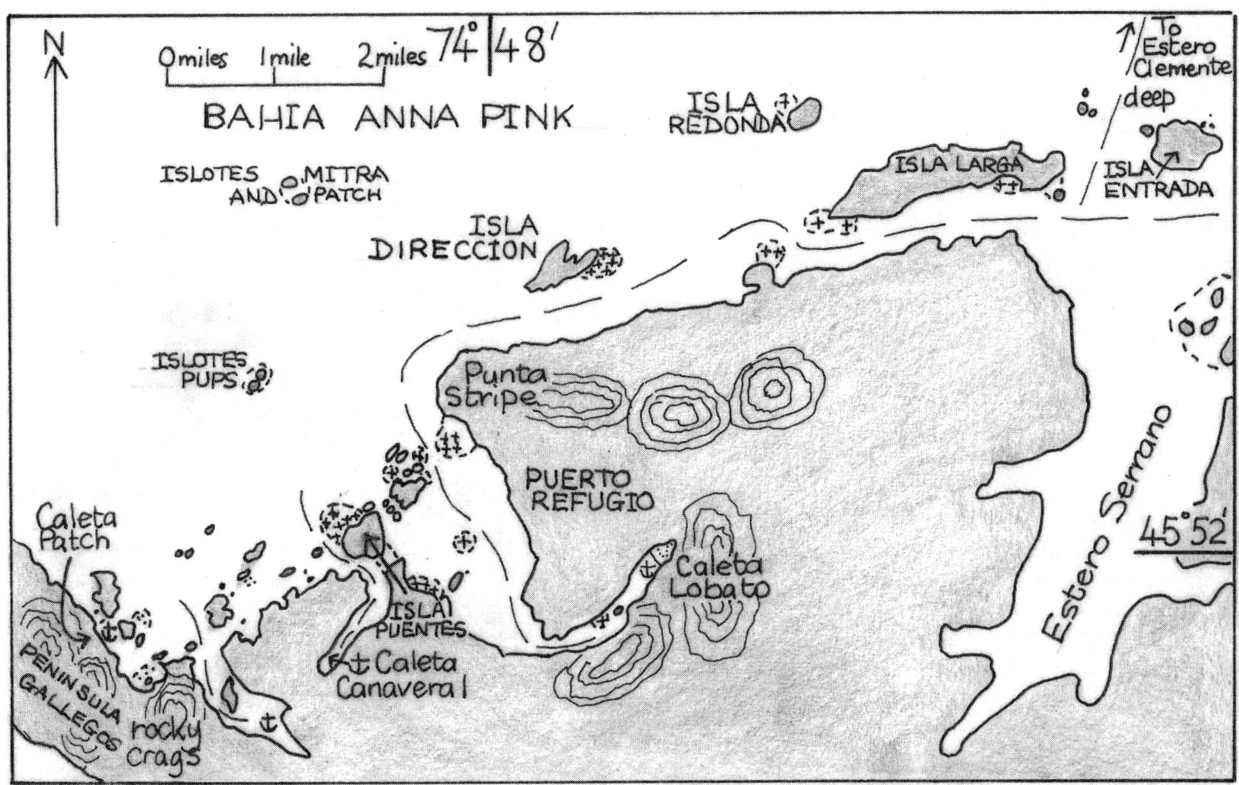

Isla Larga Channel and Puerto Refugio. (Chart positions)

4·11A Caleta Lobato
45°52'S 74°46'W

General
Caleta Lobato runs off to the north east. There is a good anchorage in 12m about half way up the *caleta.* The entrance to Puerto Refugio and then on to Caleta Lobato is between the rocks southwest of Point Stripe and Isla Hyatt. Considerable care has to be taken as there are many rocks and islands in the area.

4·11B Caleta Canaveral
45°53'·1S 74°79'·9W

General
The second anchorage is Caleta Canaveral. This is a long well-protected fjord surrounded with low-lying wooded hills backed by the large mountains of the Puerto Refugio area. It is a first class refuge. The entrance is to the south of Isla Puentes. Approach from the NW keeping clear of the prominent rocks off the northwest end of Isla Puentes. The approach is then midway between these rocks and a prominent separate rock west of Isla Puentes that should be left to starboard. There is good depth all the way into the *caleta* which is approximately 1 mile long. Anchorage is at the head in depths of 12–15m. The holding is rock and thin mud so make sure the anchor is well set and take a line ashore if necessary. The *caleta* is oriented NE/SW, but when the wind is from the W to NW there is still considerable gusting down its length because of the mountains on both sides of the *caleta*.

4·11C Peninsula Gallegos
45°53'·6S 74°50'·8W

General
The third anchorage is at the head of the unnamed *caleta* immediately to the northeast of Peninsular Gallegos. The entrance is to the south of the island in the centre of the *caleta*.

Looking towards Peninsula Gallegos from Caleta Cañaveral

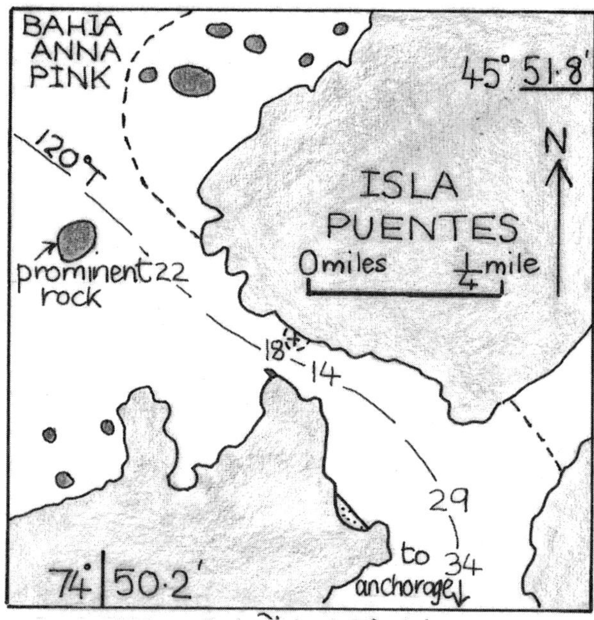

Caleta Canaveral. (GPS positions)

4·11D Caleta Patch
45°53'S 74°52'W

General
The fourth anchorage in the Puerto Refugio area is Caleta Patch. Although recommended by fishermen it is more exposed than the other anchorages.

4·12 Península Skyring – Unnamed Seno
45°57'·6S 74°58'·8W (anchorage)

Charts
UK *1288* Chile *815, 840*

General
This Seno is immediately to the north of Seno Burns and might be considered as the northern arm of that Seno except that its entrance is separate. The entrance is clean although would be subject to swell if a big sea is running.

Once into the northeast reach, steer for the northeast entrance point of the *caleta* which runs back to the west. This point has an islet off it. There is an anchorage in a wooded indentation just to the west of the point with the remains of fishermen's lines around the shore. The bay looks open but is surprisingly sheltered. The bottom is rock so a fisherman anchor might be advisable, along with lines ashore.

There may be other anchorages in the Seno, though the head of the bay which runs back west is reported to be subject to *rachas*.

4·13 Península de Taitao – Caleta Gato

46°17'·5S 75°02'W

Charts
UK *1287, 1288* Chile *815*

General
Although the bay appears on the chart to be open to the west, it offers better shelter than might be supposed because the islands and points at the mouth close if off considerably. Swell does not seems to penetrate and in a strong westerly, the fetch within the bay might be more of a problem than swell from the sea outside. When approaching, the island northwest of the entrance appears to be about one mile further west than shown on chart *815*, at approximately 75°05'·75W by GPS. The southwest entrance point has visible rocks off it with breakers but a mid-channel course is free from dangers. Two anchorages have been tried. Half way up the bay on the north shore there is a point with a small notch behind it with an anchorage in 6m, mud and shingle, with lines ashore. Alternatively anchor near the beach by a stream with lines ashore.

Caleta Gato

4·14 Península de Taitao – Bahía San Andres Area

Charts
UK *1287* Chile *800, 814*

General
Bahía San Andres is a very good place to wait for good weather when crossing the Golfo de Peñas from the north, or to go to after crossing from the south. The Bahía can be approached safely in bad weather and with the help of radar landfall can be made safely, even in thick fog. Once in the shelter of

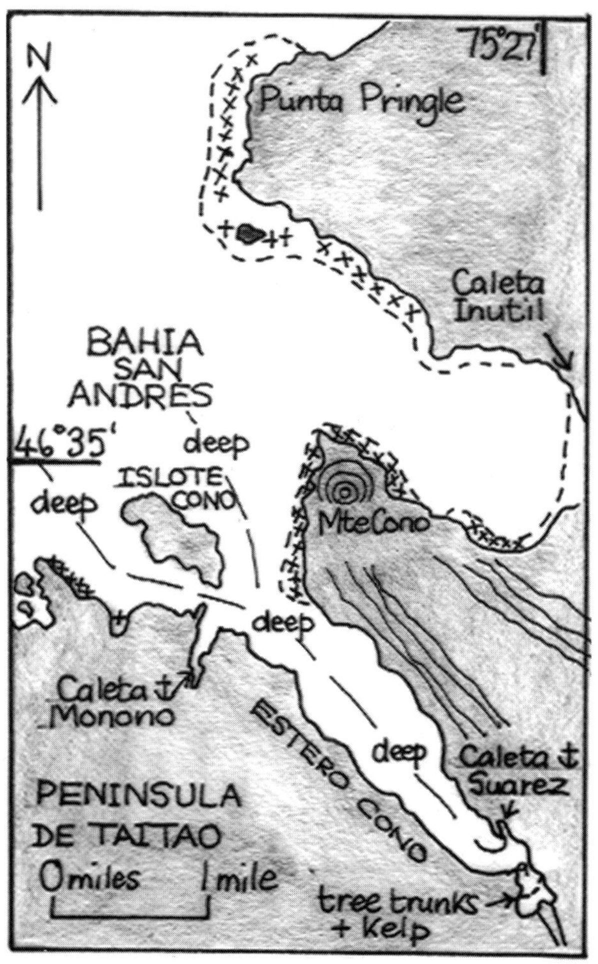

Bahía San Andres. (Charted positions)

Southern approach to Bahía San Andres

the bay there is some shelter and Islote Cono gives shelter to the entrance of both anchorages, both of which are used by local offshore fishermen. They are both really secure in any weather. The most notable feature is Mount Cono at 488 metres, an impressive spike of old volcanic core. (Darwin climbed Mount Cono on his trip through this area.)

4·14A Caleta Monono

46°35'·8S 75°30'·2W

General

This is a narrow north-south oriented *caleta*, the entrance of which is due south of Isla Cono. The Chilean chart *814* does not do it justice. There is considerable depth of at least 8m all the way to the head of the *caleta*, particularly along the western side. However, there is an area of shoaling at the head of the *caleta* and off the stream on the eastern side. A 4-way tie can be had in the 100m wide narrows about halfway down the *caleta*, or anchoring with a line ashore looks possible a little further in on the eastern side just prior to the stream. Fishing boats tie up on the western side against a large prominent flat-topped rock. In strong west- to northwest winds the gusts can be pretty severe through the narrows, but not further down the *caleta*.

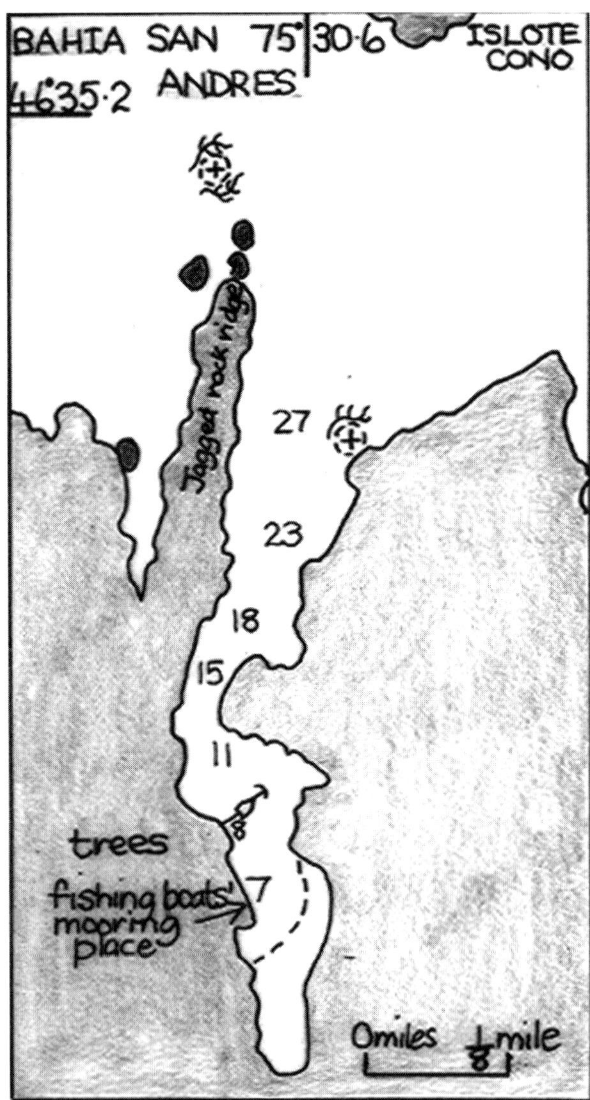

Caleta Monono. (GPS positions)

4·14B Caleta Suárez

46°37'·4S 75°27'W

General

This is a 2·5M *caleta* oriented northwest to southeast. The anchorage is a small bay behind a narrow wooded spit at the southeast end of the Caleta. The approach is easy with deep water right to the edge of the spit. Anchor in about 12m in mud and take stern lines ashore. Protection is perfect from northerly winds and in strong southerly winds extra lines from the bow can be set up. Water from the stream at the head of this bay.

While waiting for good weather it is possible to walk the length of the east shore. Where the *caleta* begins to open out, near a rock pinnacle, there is a large rock pool, good for a swim on a warm day. In addition there is a shallow inner lagoon with a lovely sandy beach at the head of the *caleta*. The whole area is excellent for sea and woodland birds: buff necked ibis, black oyster catchers, ashy-headed and upland geese on the beach and with steamer ducks, blue-eyed shags, and magellanic penguins on the water. The woodland edges reveal the green-backed firecrown, beautiful hummingbirds and flocks of noisy austral blackbirds. The flora at the edge of the forest is reminiscent of an English garden with many familiar species such as hebe, fuchsia, pernettya and gunnera, the giant rhubarb, all growing in wild and natural profusion.

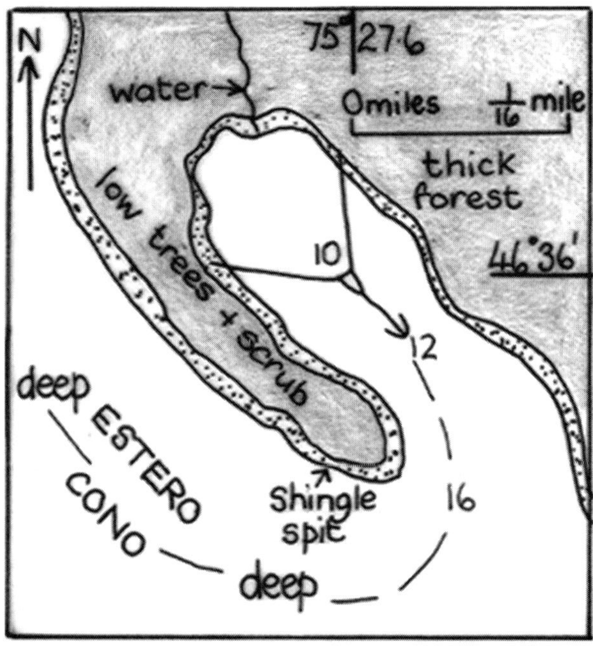

Caleta Suárez. (GPS postions)

Cabo Ráper

1562Cabo Ráper, (46°49'·2S 75°37'·4W Fl.5s60m17M White round concrete tower and building 14m 331°-vis-175°) lies between Bahía San Andres and Puerto Barroso. Ráper should be called on channel 16. They will provide a *pronostico* for the Golfo de Peñas.

Golfo de Tres Montes

The anchorages are listed clockwise from Puerto Barroso.

4·15 Puerto Barroso

46°49'S 75°17'W

Charts
UK *1287* Chile *815, 9110*

General
Puerto Barroso is a good place to stop when travelling south to north if adverse condition are encountered when approaching Peninsula Tres Montes. Anchor in the outer bay with the holding in mud or rock or proceed to the inner bay passing north of Isla Block as shown on the sketch plan. Good holding and well-sheltered.

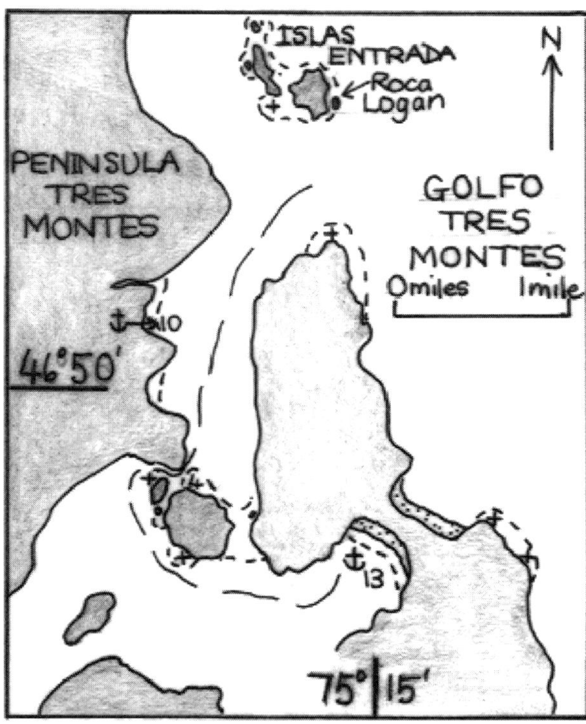

Puerto Barroso. (Charted positions)

4·16 Estero Slight – Puerto Slight

46°48'S 75°34'W

Charts
UK *1287* Chile *815, 9110*

General
Good holding is reported off the pier. The *Armada* maintains a presence here and there are thermal springs at 40°C. About a two and a half mile hike to Cabo Ráper.

4·17 Estero Slight – Caleta Bueno

46°46'·5S 75°30'W

Charts
UK *1287* Chile *815, 9110*

General
A deep inlet with good all-weather properties. Quiet if drawn in close to the shore, stern lines to trees, in the inner northeast arm between the tree side and the gravel fan of the waterfall. The south arm has good holding but may be disturbed by *rachas*.

4·18 Seno Hoppner – Pozo Omega

46°40'S 75°25'·5W

Charts
UK *1287* Chile *9110*

General
Named Omega by Knick Pyle because of its shape, it has good shelter except from the southeast. Favour the east shore on entering. Some protection from the southeast can be obtained by tucking in behind the spit which extends from the west shore at the entrance. Sand and pebble bottom.

Nearby is the barren island Islote Amarillo with a large bird colony, an interesting place to view wild life. A ledge extends 100m from the island on the south east side and the currents can be strong. On the shore line northeast of Amarillo are very hot springs with the possibility of a daytime anchorage, depending on the weather.

4·19 Bahía San Quentín

46°50'S 74°30'W

Charts
UK *1287* Chile *815, 816*

General
The sight of the Andes to the east of Bahía San Quentín has been described as one of the most spectacular views of the region. Four anchorages are mentioned in various pilots but we have no first-hand information about them. These anchorages are Caleta San Tomás (46°52'S 74°25'W), Caleta Barrancos (46°51'S 74°29'W), Puerto Covadonga (46°46'·5S 74°36'W) and Puerto Angamos (46°45'S 74°30'·5W). A fifth, marked on chart *816* off the

northwestern shore of Peninsula Forelius at 46°49'5S 74°36'·6W, has for some reason failed to find favour with visitors. If working north and it has been found advisable to pass through Canal Cheap, one of the Bahía Quentín anchorages will provide respite.

Golfo de Peñas

Charts

UK *1287* Chile *815*

The Gulf of Peñas

General

It is about 67M from Cabo Ráper to Isla San Pedro across the Gulf of Penas which has a reputation for bad weather and deserves considerable respect. The bay is shallow and frequently subjected to cross swells that can kick up a very nasty sea. The most logical timing of a crossing from north to south is to leave Bahía San Andres shortly after the passage of a warm front with the wind veering from the north to northwest though this may be accompanied by rain and poor visibility. But a light southwest wind can give good conditions for a north–south crossing. The trip should be timed so as to arrive at the entrance of the Messier Canal in daylight; though it is five miles wide, there is considerable foul ground to the northwest of San Pedro Light and an error in navigation could be disastrous. If the tide is ebbing out of the Canal, the seas in the entrance can be very confused. The crossing from south to north is usually less of a problem as long as it is timed for a period of west to southwest winds and there is the alternative of Canal Darwin if Bahía Anna Pink looks difficult.

There are a number of anchorages in the immediate area of the entrance of the Messier Canal; Puerto Escondido between Isla Wager and Isla Schroder, Caleta Ideal and Caleta Chica at the southwest corner of Isla Schroder, Puerto Francisco on the eastern side of the entrance in Seno Baker, and Caleta Hale on Isla Orlebar 17 miles south of San Pedro Light. Both Ráper and San Pedro will give forecasts if asked and will also advise on local conditions.

Section 5
Golfo Peñas to Puerto Simpson

Introduction to the South

Restrictions

Strictly speaking, travel in the region is restricted to the canals used by commercial traffic. However, in the canal systems north of Magallan Straits it seems to be recognised that yachts will deviate from the commercial route to explore glaciers. South of Magallan the *Armada* is more sensitive, partially because of its responsibility to aid vessels in distress and therefore the need to know who is where, and partially because of its defence responsibilities. In the Beagle Channel the *Armada* is particular that the anchorages that you intend to use are listed on the *zarpe* and there are certain prohibited anchorages which the *Armada* will not allow on a *zarpe,* though it is understood that in bad weather or an emergency a yacht may use any anchorage along their authorised route. Yachts have been expelled from Chile for using prohibited anchorages without good cause.

That said, there are certain channels, such as Canal Bárbara and Canal Acwalisnan, which are not on the commercial route but are regularly used by fishermen and quite frequently by yachts. It may be possible to use such channels if the *zarpe* is indeterminate about the matter but that is a matter for judgement on the spot. Descriptions are included below, in case they come in handy. One factor in making a decision is that Chilean charts tend not to carry information about depths in such channels and if felt necessary, recourse has to be had to UK or US charts. In 1998, the prohibition on using Canal Gabriel (between Seno Almirantazgo, a *seno* much visited by cruise ships, and Canal Magdalena) was firm.

Reporting

Apart from reporting to lighthouses, call any ship that is met and request her to pass your *PIM* (see Appendix A) to the *Armada.* All ships have a Pilot who usually speaks English. The *Armada* also maintains a number of observation posts in the southern canals which will call passing yachts requesting information about the yacht's name, flag, number of people on board etc. There are posts at Timbales – Canal O'Brien; Punta Yamana – five miles to the east of Olla; Canal Murray – northern entrance; Isla Snipe; Cape Horn. The matter of reporting becomes more serious once the far south is reached. A good station to report your PIM to is Felix Radio, 4146·0kHz USB, between 0700–0800 and 1900–2000hrs; if you have not got HF, use VHF at those times whether or not you think you will be heard – some station may pass your message. Some yachts have found a log of their *PIM* calls helpful when queried by the *Armada* for failing to report.

Anchoring

See appendix F.

Kelp

Kelp is both a blessing and a curse. It grows only on rocks and as such is a useful marker of danger and areas to be avoided both on passage and when anchoring (though the rock to which it is attached may be much deeper than the draft of the boat). It makes for poor holding. A machete is useful for cutting away bundles that come up on the anchor. Rowing through kelp is either difficult or impossible.

The weather

The first characteristic of the weather systems south of the Golfo de Penas is an almost continuous series of depressions that track from the west often moving east–south–east. Linked to them are fresh to strong winds, generally from a west to northwest direction. At 45°S, 20% of the winds are Force 7 or above, whilst below 50°S 30 – 40% of the winds are of this strength in the winter and spring, falling to about 30% in the summer and autumn.

The presence of the high mountains and deep fjords of the Chilean canals, which can cause violent eddies and produce unpredictable squalls or *rachas,* exacerbate these conditions. It is possible to be sailing in pleasant fresh breeze conditions and then encounter a full gale for a period. It is possible to see the wind churn up white water and it is sensible to reef at once. They tend to be stronger than expected. A day of 15 knot winds may well produce 40+knot winds for a period in such a squall. Narrow canals such as Seno Garibaldi can funnel winds

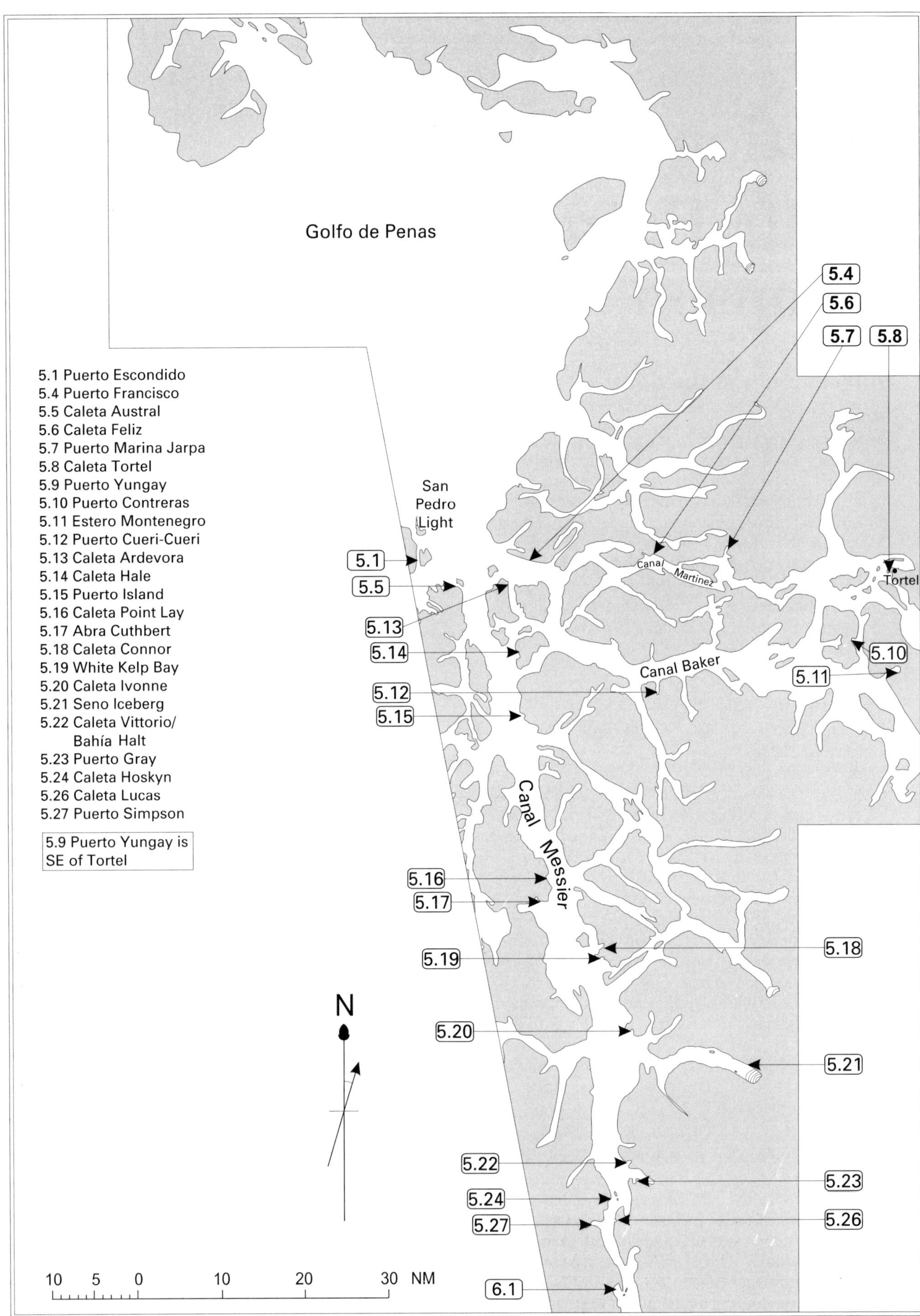
Golfo de Penas
5.1 Puerto Escondido
5.4 Puerto Francisco
5.5 Caleta Austral
5.6 Caleta Feliz
5.7 Puerto Marina Jarpa
5.8 Caleta Tortel
5.9 Puerto Yungay
5.10 Puerto Contreras
5.11 Estero Montenegro
5.12 Puerto Cueri-Cueri
5.13 Caleta Ardevora
5.14 Caleta Hale
5.15 Puerto Island
5.16 Caleta Point Lay
5.17 Abra Cuthbert
5.18 Caleta Connor
5.19 White Kelp Bay
5.20 Caleta Ivonne
5.21 Seno Iceberg
5.22 Caleta Vittorio/
Bahía Halt
5.23 Puerto Gray
5.24 Caleta Hoskyn
5.26 Caleta Lucas
5.27 Puerto Simpson
5.9 Puerto Yungay is SE of Tortel
San Pedro Light
Canal Martinez
Tortel
Canal Baker
Canal Messier
N
10 5 0 10 20 30 NM

down their entire length so that moderate wind conditions elsewhere remain at gale force within such a Seno.

However these conditions do not occur all the time. Sailing in the southern canals is not a continuous battle every day with violent winds. The average wind speeds published in the *British Hydrographic Office South American Pilot Volume II* show that at Cabo Ráper, at the north end of the Golfo de Penas average wind speeds are between 11 and 17 knots and surprisingly at Ushuaia are between 3 and 10 knots. One of the windiest areas is at the western approach to Magallanes, where the average wind speeds are 15 to 18 knots.

These lower than expected averages are as a result of reasonable periods of light winds between lows. On many days it is necessary to motor perhaps with over 50% of journeys being made motoring or motor sailing to make reasonable progress.

Linked with these lows are high levels of precipitation, especially on the western side of the Andes. The annual rainfall can be as high as 4000 mm (15 feet) on the west side of the Archipelago although this falls progressively as the Andes are crossed to reach about 560 mm (just over 2 feet) at Ushuaia. Snow can fall in any month but it is generally occurs between June and October. Even in the summer it is possible to have snow squalls on a bright sunny but cold day.

Average temperatures fall, not unexpectedly, as one heads south. In January average temperatures at the northern end of this region, level with the Golfo de Penas, are 13°C (55°F) whilst at Cabo de Hornos the average is 8°C (46°F). In the winter month of July these averages have fallen 9°C (48°F) and 3°C (37°F) respectively. Perhaps surprisingly, in the light of these low average temperatures, with modern Polartec clothing and the comfort of a boat heater whilst at anchor it is possible to avoid the unpleasantness of being cold for most of the time.

One factor that can change these weather patterns, particularly in the summer months of December to February is the position of the semi-permanent high centred at about 90°W in the Pacific. During the winter months its southern limit retreats north to about 30°S, leaving rain and windy conditions as the prevalent condition all the way to the north of Valdivia. However in the summer this high can extend down to the Golfo de Penas and south for extended periods. Occasionally this high may extend as far south as Cabo de Hornos. When these conditions occur winds tend to be light and sun cream is essential. Without sun cream the strong sun can cause unexpected sunburn. This is as a result of serious depletion of the ozone layer over Patagonia and down to the Antarctic. Temperatures can reach 25° or even a little higher in these conditions.

Fog is rare but squalls and low cloud can reduce visibility to very low levels.

The *Armada* transmits two surface analysis weather faxes daily, one in the morning and one in the evening plus a forecast in the evening. Magallanes radio also issues a verbal forecast on 4146 USB at approximately 1130 local time. Both of these sources of information are useful. However, except when there is a large stationary high sitting over the area the specific interpretation of the weatherfax information is difficult. This becomes increasingly true the further south one travels, particularly in the area of Magallanes south. At the best this information protects the yachtsman from extreme weather. The low systems move and change so quickly that daily predictions and reality rarely coincide. In a day it is possible to have sunny weather, light and gale force winds, squalls and even snow. The weatherfax picture in the morning is already history by the time it is received and the pattern of the lows can have changed markedly a few hours later. Possibly the use of a barograph would give better warning of the rapidly changing systems when pressures changes, both up and down, quickly. In a word the daily weather is one of contrasts. The big plus is that there are many first rate anchorages in which to take shelter if the weather turns unpleasant.

Another factor to reckon with if cruising for an extended period in the far south is that the day rapidly shortens after mid-summer. Around 53°S, in January there are 16 or more hours of daylight. By mid-April it is down to 11 hours and by mid-June, 7 hours. To make the point another way, the distance that can be covered in daylight is about halved between summer and winter.

Three terms: *ráfaga* and *racha* (pronounced 'raka') both mean williwaw, or sudden and violent short-lived squall, usually without precipitation. *Chubasco* is a term used by the *Armada* and in other forecasts and refers to a frontal weather system when winds may increase sharply for a while. They usually bring precipitation.

Administration

Puerto Natales has good shore-side facilities but is well off the main routes. Ushuaia, in Argentina, is a better place to stock up than either Puerto Williams or Punta Arenas. If coming from the Atlantic and aiming at the Beagle Channel, it is worthwhile calling at Ushuaia and then back-tracking to Puerto Williams to enter Chile. If coming from the west, make sure that you clear out of Chile before entering Argentina. Those who are obliged to have a visa for Chile will heed a possible need for a multiple entry visa if calling at Ushuaia.

Fuel

One characteristic of cruising in the south is that in general a very high proportion of the distance is made good under engine. After leaving Chiloé, the next fuel is about 1000 miles away unless a hefty premium is paid at Puerto Eden or a detour made to Chacabuco or Puerto Natales. It is worth carrying as much fuel as possible in cans as the cost of the cans is quickly recovered if set against the cost of fuel in remote places.

The *Empresa Comercial y Agrícola* can supply fuel

at Puerto Edén and Puerto Williams. At Puerto Natales and Punta Arenas there are other sources and Ushuaia is also well supplied. At Puerto Edén, Puerto Williams or other remote places prior notice may be necessary and fuel bought at such sites may be 50% more expensive than that bought in population centres.

Heating
After a cold, windy and wet day a heater provides a great deal of comfort and few boats cruise the area without one. Whilst there may be no problems with a blown heater, such as a Webasto, with other types the back-pressure in the chimney created by *rachas* may well put out the flame and with a drip-feed diesel type, such as a Dickinson or Reflex, fill the cabin with white diesel fumes. Standard chimneys such as the H type do not overcome the problem. One solution is to fit a domestic rotary chimney to the existing chimney pipe. These are available in Valdivia, Puerto Montt and Castro and can be adapted by the shop or by a workshop. The result may not be pleasing aesthetically but it works.

Charts
There are no large scale US charts covering this section. The small scale chart is *22395*.

Golfo de Peñas to Puerto Edén

The entrance to Canal Messier

The entrance is marked by 1558Isla San Pedro light (47°43'·2S 74°53'·5W Fl.1·5.38m16M White GRP tower, black band, 8m. 124°-vis-328° Ch 16 c/s *CBS* Aero RC. Weather forecasts). In this area particularly big discrepancies have been noted between positions as shown on Chilean charts (especially *902*) and on GPS. Navigating by GPS alone is not a safe option; positions must be checked visually.

Four anchorages are noted at the entrance, three on the west side and the fourth, reckoned to be the best, on the east. The first three have good radio communication with San Pedro; communication from the fourth may be hampered by the land.

5·1 Isla Wager – Puerto Escondido

47°45'·4S 74°55'·2W

Charts
UK *1287* Chile *901, 902.*

Between Isla Schröder and Isla Wager. The entrance is very narrow and not to be attempted from the north in poor visibility. 10m, mud, good shelter.

5·2 Isla Schröder – Caleta Ideal

47°46'·8S 74°55'·1W by chart *902*
Average of 5 yachts. GPS 47°45'·5S 74°53'·5W

Charts
UK *1287* Chile *901, 902*

General
Chart *902* shows the approach and entrance well, even if the co-ordinates are hard to reconcile with GPS. It is easy to enter and a good place to end or start a Golfo crossing. It has shelter from the north but is open to the south winds, though fairly well protected from the southwest. The bottom is rocky and although good holding can be obtained this bay would not be a first choice in bad weather. Water from a stream in SW corner.

It is possible to take a dinghy up to the head of the bay and with a short portage pass over into Estero Escondido. 1 mile further north, Laguna Byron can be entered by dinghy through some narrow passes. This Laguna gives the impression of a secret place and is quite delightful. Isla Wager is the island where Wager of Anson's fleet was ship-wrecked in 1741. This is a great adventure story and is well told in two books: *Byron of the Wager* by Peter Shankland – published by Collins 1975 and *The Wager Mutiny* by S W C Pack – published by Alvin Redman Ltd 1964.

5·3 Isla Schröder – Caleta Chica

47°46'·9S 74°54'·2W

Charts
UK *1287* Chile *901, 902*

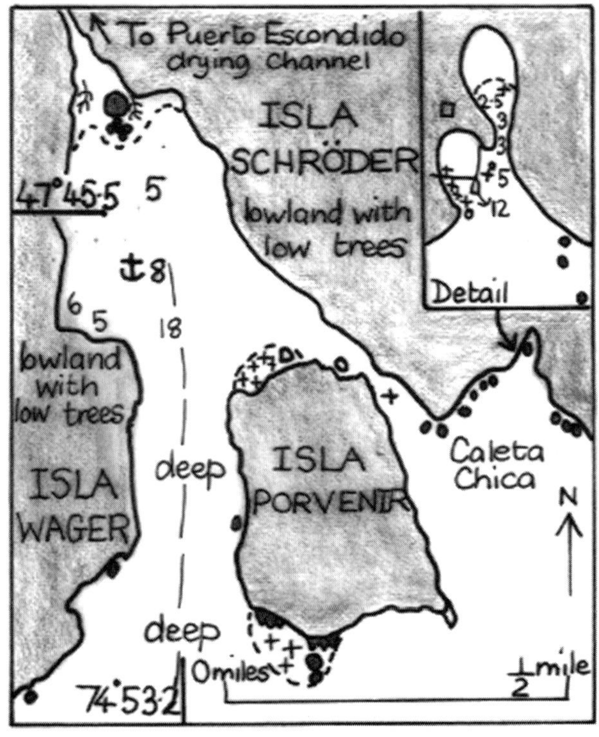

Caletas Ideal and Chica. (GPS positions)

General
Caleta Chica is an open bay. However there is a small nook in the north corner where it is possible to anchor in 12m, abeam of the rocks, and to take lines ashore. There is a lot of kelp. This nook is well protected except from the south-southeast. Good shelter has been obtained here in 50 knot northerly winds, whilst 200m out in the bay there was white water. The yacht can be moored with lines rigged from bow and stern. There is a fisherman's hut on the shore with heaps of mussels (*cholgas*) nearby. Spider crabs and otters have been seen.

Seno Baker

5·4 Península Fresia – Puerto Francisco

47°45'·6S 74°33'·9W

Charts
UK *1287* Chile *901, 918*

General
On the north side of Seno Baker, it is up a narrow channel from the outer bay with two very tight turns.

Approach
The charted position is inaccurate. The entrance is immediately east of a prominent conical shaped hill along the southern shore of Peninsula Fresia. The entrance is unencumbered. The passageway to the inner lagoon is narrow, but deep enough (minimum 3·5m in the first narrows and 4·5m in the second). Vessels up to 20m overall, 5m beam and 3m draft should be able to manage the channel without difficulty. The channel is tree-lined and could do with some trimming. Do not leave on a strong ebb or with a strong following wind, either of which will cause trouble at the corners.

Anchorage
The surrounding land is low and well covered in trees so there is little chance of *rachas*. Inside the basin depths are consistent and the bottom is strong mud. There are a number of small coves around the shore. The best anchorage is in the northwest corner of the inner lagoon with lines ashore. There is another attractive 'lines ashore' position in the bay on the western side between the two narrow cuts. Northwest winds blow strongly across the inner lagoon so the possibilities on the eastern side are rather exposed. Tying in close ashore may be safest but may also bring flying insects.

If in a hurry to moor, shelter can be found tying off to trees in the wide part of the channel but this blocks the fairway and bugs could be a nuisance.

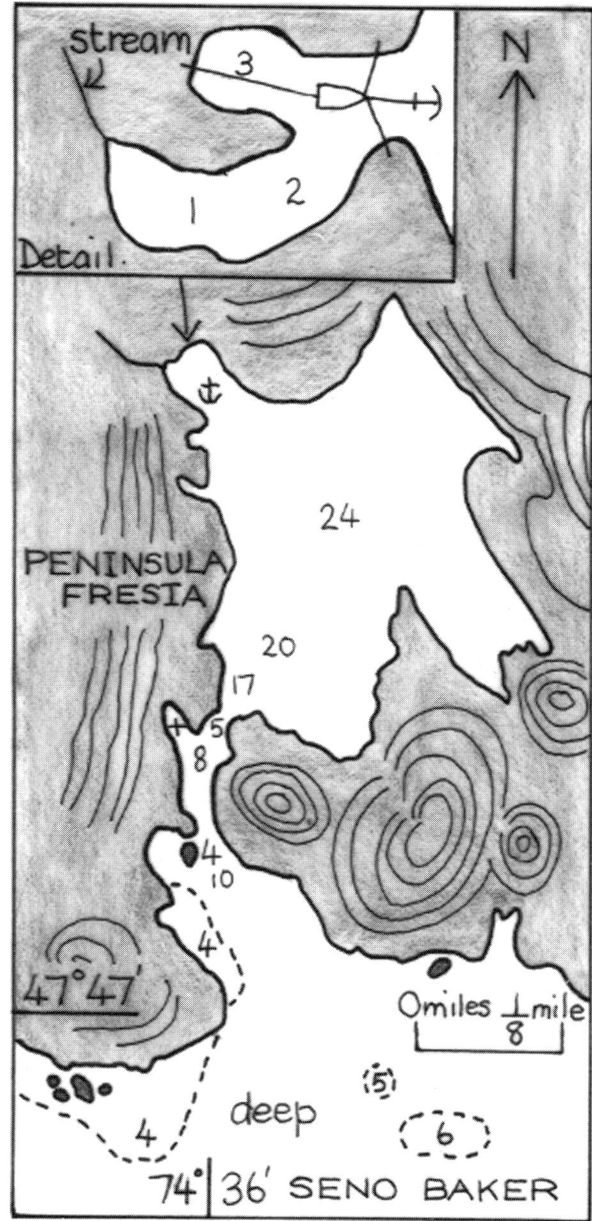

Puerto Francisco. (Charted positions)

5·5 Isla Penguin – Caleta Austral

47°49'S 74°49'·5W

Charts
UK *1287* Chile *901, 902*

The anchorage between Isla Penguin and Isla Juan Stuven provides good shelter from south winds, and is an easy anchorage to make for after crossing the Gulf of Peñas from north to south. Beware that the charts are off by approximately 2 miles from GPS positions in this area. If exiting into Canal Messier through Paso Tate, stay close to the southern shore of Isla Penguin. The pass is full of kelp but with someone on the bow it is possible to wend a way through.

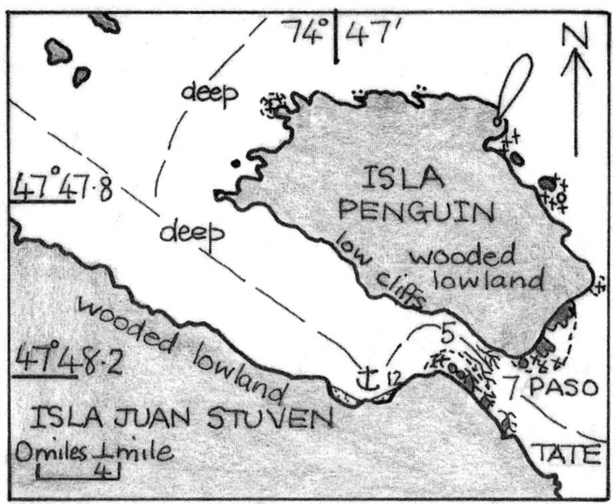

Caleta Austral. (GPS positions)

Diversion Río Baker

Charts
UK *1287* Chile *901*

General
The diversion from Canal Messier through Canal Martinez or Canal Baker is very rarely visited by yachts. However it contains magnificent scenery, good anchorages and today the possibility of making crew changes here. The Carretera Austral (Chile's major project to extend link from Puerto Montt to the southern extreme of the country by a mixture of ferry links and new road, without having to make major detours into Argentina) has now extended as far south as Puerto Yungay on the Rio Bravo. There is a great deal to explore in this area but the following anchorages have been visited.

5·6 Canal Martinez – Caleta Feliz

47°47'S 74°16'·5W

Charts
UK *1287* Chile *901*

General
This unnamed narrow inlet, to the east of Punta Graciela has been described by the crew of yacht *Felice* as one of the most beautiful they have visited and named it Caleta Feliz. The entrance is narrow but clear of dangers. Anchor in about 10m.

5·7 Canal Martinez – Puerto Marina Jarpa

47°48'S 74°03'·5W

Charts
UK *287* Chile *901, 918*

General
On the mainland northeast of Isla Irene, Marina Jarpa is an inlet with a straightforward entrance and waist leading to an inner cove. At the waist, keep to the west as there are rocks off the east shore. In the inner cove, depths about 11m but anchor in 7m near the end with lines to trees.

5·8 Rio Baker – Caleta Tortel

47°50'·5S 73°35'W

Charts
UK *1287* Chile *901, 919*

General
The village of Tortel lies on the west side of Caleta Tortel, near the mouth of the Rio Baker. In recent years investment has been made to develop this small village so that today there is a small airstrip,

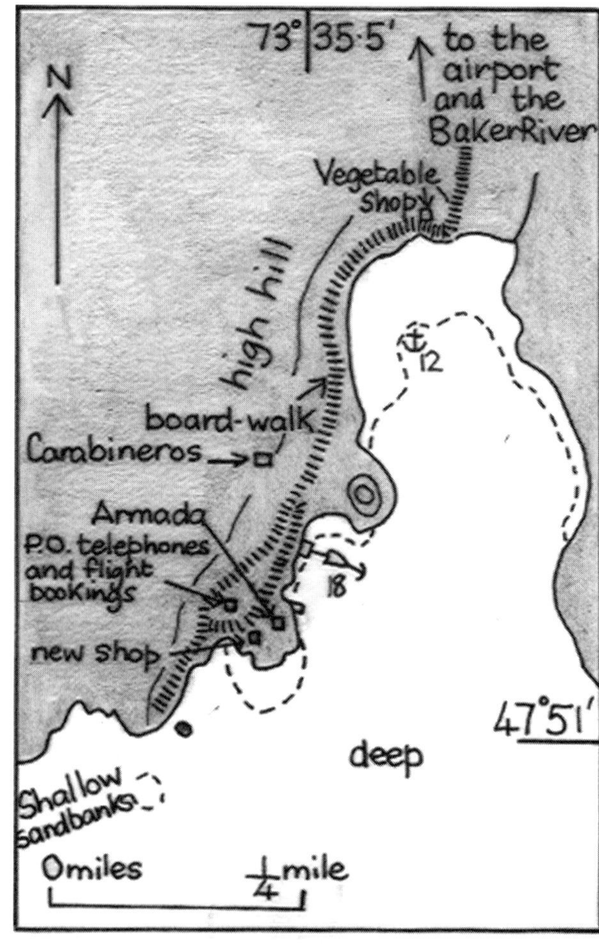

Caleta Tortel. (Charted positions)

Puerto Eden *Teokita*

Looking out of the entrance of Estero Dock – in the morning there was ice right up to the entrance and across Canal Wide *Teokita*

Leaving Caleta Moonlight Shadow looking towards the Cordillera Sarmiento de Gamboa *Teokita*

Caleta Brecknock, Seno Ocasion. *Teokita*

Left Exploring the entrance to Caleta Teokita, Puerto Profundo *Teokita*

Puerto Nutland *Teokita*

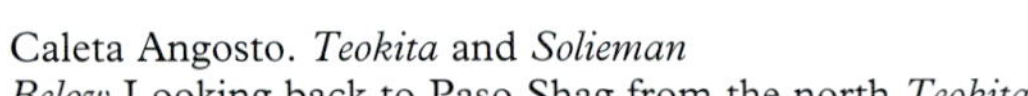

Caleta Angosto. *Teokita* and *Solieman*
Below Looking back to Paso Shag from the north *Teokita*

Looking out from Caleta Cushion, Isla Chair *Teokita*

Caleta Media Dia – Bahía Romanche *Teokita*

Ventiquero Garibaldi *Teokita*

Yacht Club Micalvi, Puerto Williams

Ventisquero Italia – one of many glaciers in the Beagle Channel *Teokita*

Caleta Olla – snug under the shelter of the trees *Teokita*

Pelagic leaving Puerto Williams entrance *Teokita*

new wooden board-walks around the village, post office and telephones.

It is possible to take a dinghy with a powerful outboard up the Rio Baker (the Rio Baker is said to discharge more water into the sea than any other river in Chile), or to take the ferry that goes to La Vagabundos, 15 miles up the river. It is also possible to travel down the Rio Baker from near Cochrane on one of the commercially run 'adventure' zodiacs.

The sketch plan shows two anchorages, the north position is to anchor only and is a convenient distance from the village. The second anchorage is in the central bay by the northern pier, which is used by the *carabineros* launch. Anchor well out in deep water and take a line to the pier. The southern pier is used for loading lumber and is no good for going alongside.

There are few shops and gas can be obtained. Diesel is not available.

Communications

Regular ferry to Los Vagabundos (economic, 4 hours) to link up with the bus service that travels to Cochrane three times a week (Sundays, Tuesdays and Thursdays, 3 hours)

Flights – It is possible to buy a ticket at the post office for the weekly flight on a Wednesday from Tortel to Cochrane. It is also possible to charter a flight but this is expensive.

Post office and telephones.

5·9 Estero Mitchell – Puerto Yungay

47°59·S 73°25'·5W

Charts

UK *1287* Chile *901*

General

Puerto Yungay is at the current southern limit of the Carretera Austral. There is a small military base here and a village is to be developed. The military are helpful and have given assistance with mechanical problems and, if asked, may give individuals a lift along the road to La Vagabundos.

Anchor in an open bay, sheltered from the north in variable depths (4m or more).

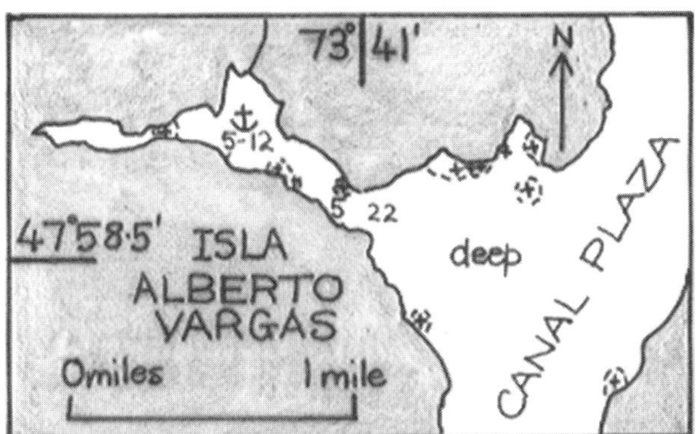

Puerto Contreras. (Charted positions)

5·10 Isla Alberto Vargas – Puerto Contreras

47°58'S 73°42'W

Charts

UK *1287* Chile *901, 919*

General

A very secure anchorage with good holding in 5 to 12m. The inner bay has a bar at its entrance which is too shallow to cross.

5·11 Estero Montenegro

48°S 73°38'·5W

Charts

UK 1287 Chile 901

General

Estero Montenegro is deep with easy access. A well protected anchorage can be found beyond the low tree'd delta, close to the river mouth, in about 4–6m. Approach the delta on a SE heading. There are rocks off the end of the delta and off the opposite shore but the central passage is clear of dangers.

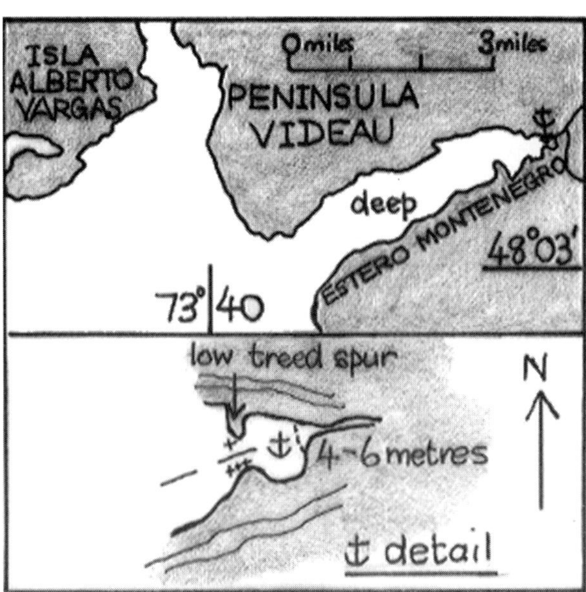

Estero Montenegro. (Charted positions)

5·12 Canal Baker – Puerto Cueri-Cueri

48°01'S 74°15'·5W

Charts

UK *1287* Chile *901, 918*

General

Roughly half-way between Canal Messier and Tortel on the southern shore of Canal Baker. It is popular with those making the passage. The anchorage, which is 1·5M up at the head of the *caleta* in 10–13m, mud, is reputed to be free from squalls but the UK pilot notes heavy overfalls and a strong in-going tide in northerlies of F5 or more. There are three shoal patches inshore along the southwest coast at the head.

Continuation

5·13 Isla Zealous – Caleta Ardevora

47°50'·7S 74°39'·5W

Charts
UK *1287* Chile *901*

Isla Zealous is on the east side of Canal Messier and this *caleta*, which has no official name, is on its east side, off Canal Cronje which leads south from Seno Baker. Kelp marks either side of the channel which has 7m in the middle. Once through the second narrows, depths increase to over 20m. With dramatic high cliffs all around it can be squally but the small *caleta* in the northwest corner remained calm. Good holding. Stream for watering.

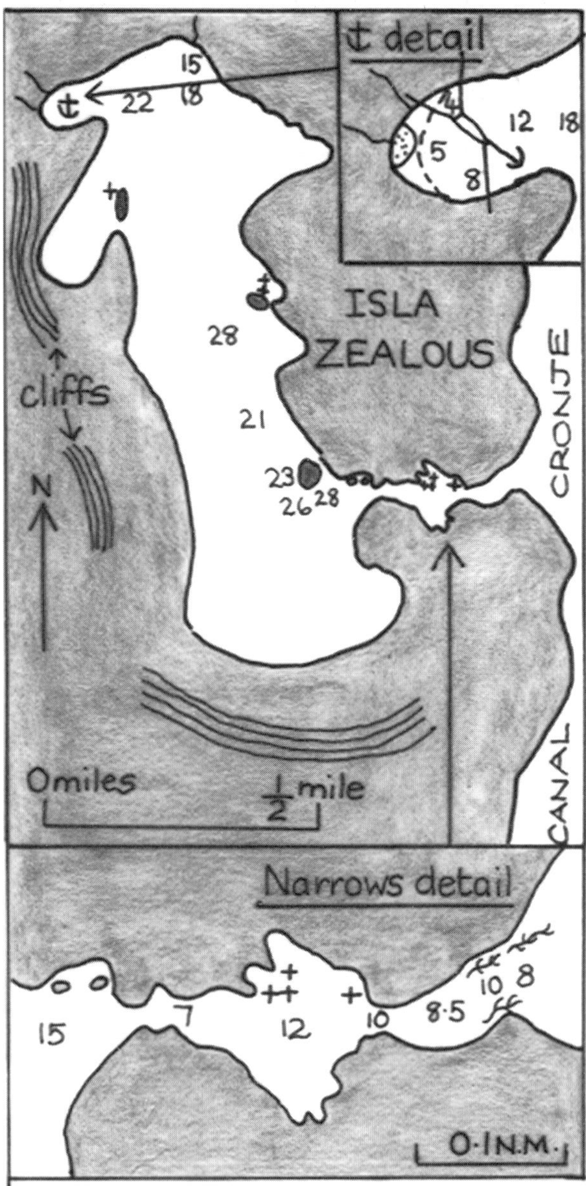

Caleta Ardevora. (GPS 47°50'·7S 74°39'·5W)

5·14 Isla Orlebar – Caleta Hale

47°57'S 74°38'·5W

Charts
UK *1287* Chile *901, 902*

General
The anchorage is in the small bay on the northern side of Caleta Hale. Well sheltered from the north but open to the SSW. There is kelp at the entrance with the depth of about 5m. Water at the beach at low tide. There is a pretty little waterfall about 50m up the stream.

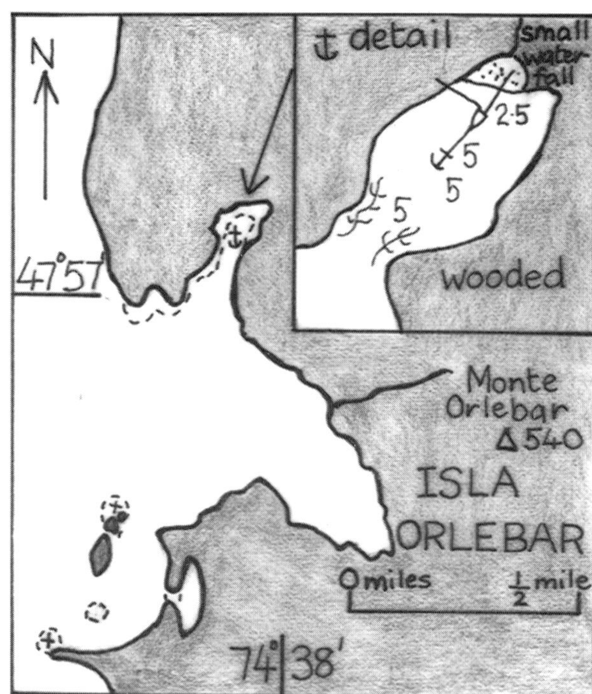

Caleta Hale. (Charted positions)

5·15 Península Swett – Puerto Island

48°04'·5S 74°38'·5W
48°03'S 74°35'W observed on GPS

Charts
UK *1287* Chile *901, 902*

General
Puerto Island is on the eastern side of Canal Messier, 23 miles from San Pedro Lighthouse. The most secure approach is midway between Punta Fleuriais and Isla Phipps. Many of the hazards between this island and the east shore are covered at high water. It has good all-round protection except from strong southwest winds. In these winds the islands and rocks at the entrance to the bay provide

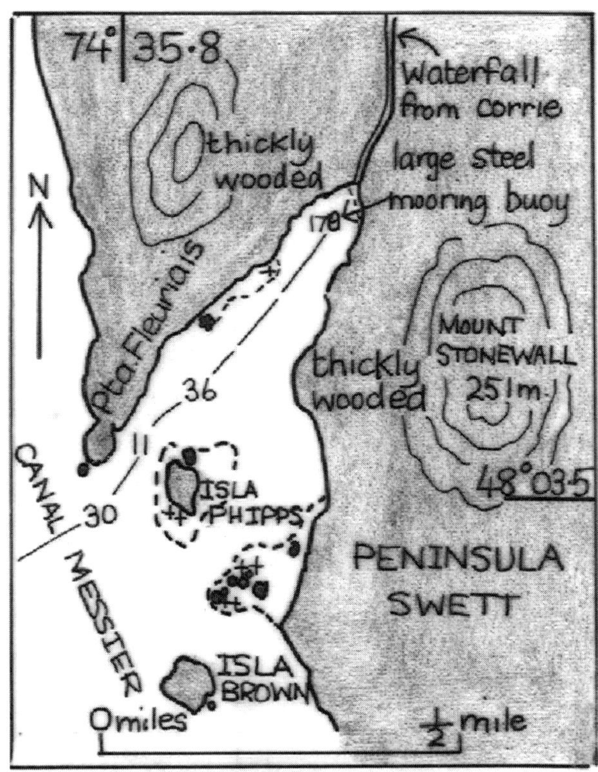

Puerto Island. (GPS positions)

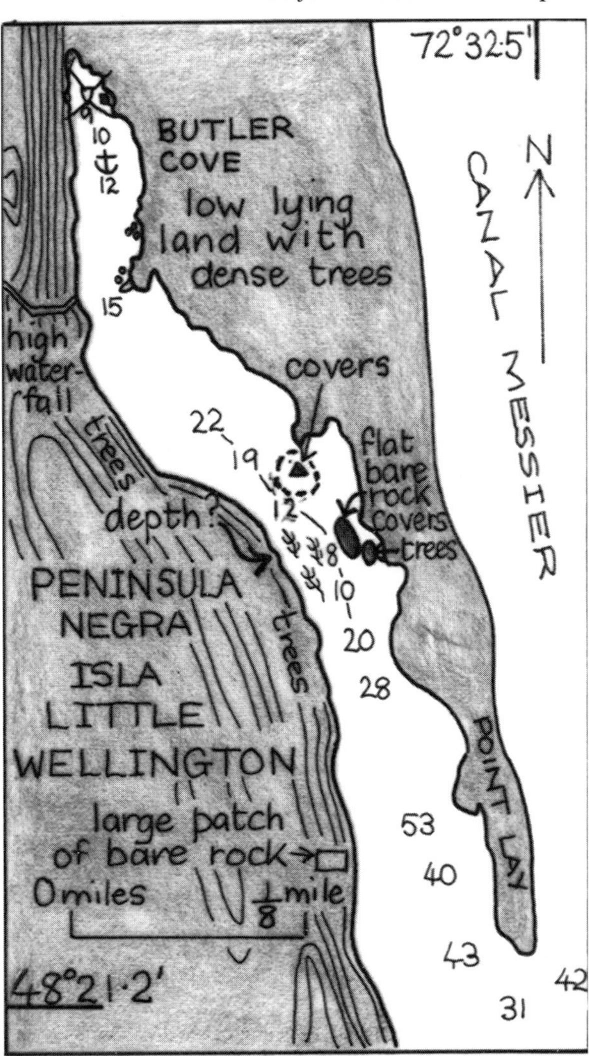

Caleta Point Lay. (GPS positions)

some shelter but a swell enters and the security of the large *Armada* buoy at the head is very welcome. Yachts can anchor nearby but further in, on a mud bottom, 12m. At the very head there is a picturesque waterfall, good for showers and laundry. The shores are thickly wooded.

5·16 Isla Little Wellington – Caleta Point Lay

48°22'S 74°36'W
48°20'·6S 74°33'·4W observed on GPS at the waterfall

Charts
UK *1287* Chile *901*

General
Caleta Point Lay lies behind the long finger of land on the east shore of Peninsula Negra. The first part of the main bay is clear but level with a small island halfway down it is necessary to pass close to a large flat rock on the starboard to avoid shallow water and kelp to port. Once level with this rock turn to port to avoid a large rock that is covered at high water. It is marked by surrounding kelp. Past this dog-leg the *caleta* is clear right to its end. Anchor in about 12m in Butler Cove with good mud holding or moor with shore lines in the small nook at the head of the bay. Punta Wetherall to the south gives initial protection from S–SW winds and the bay is well sheltered. It would be excellent in northerly winds.

5·17 Isla Little Wellington – Abra Cuthbert

48°24'S 74°37'W

Charts
UK *1287* Chile *901*

General
The anchorage is in an unnamed *caleta* on the north side of Abra Cuthbert. Anchor at the head in about 10m. It is an attractive place but it is not a bad weather stop. The terrain is rugged and bare and there is a risk of *rachas*.

5·18 Isla Farquhar – Caleta Connor

48°30'·5S 74°26'·5W

Charts
UK *1287* Chile *901, 902*

General
On the west side of the canal on Isla Farquhar, the entrance to Caleta Connor is wide and clean. The best anchorage is in a small shallow cove in the northeast corner with one or two lines ashore. It is

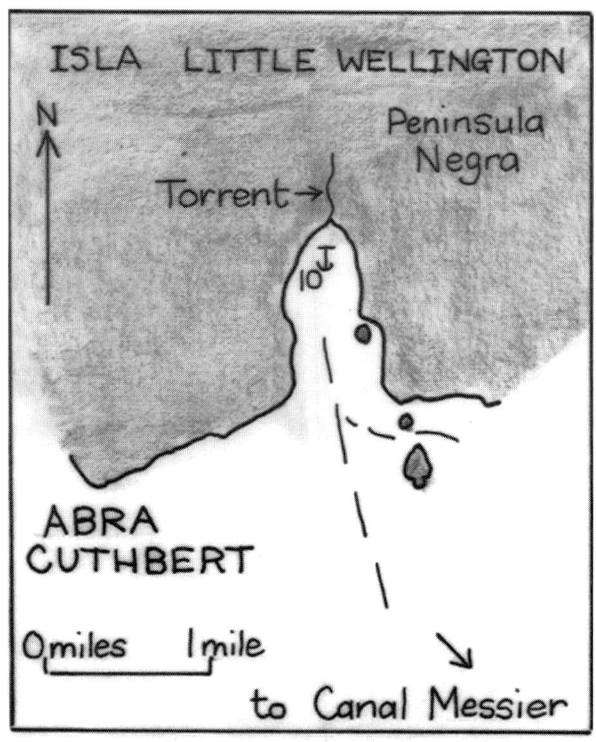

Anchorage in Abra Cuthbert. 48°24'S 74°37'W

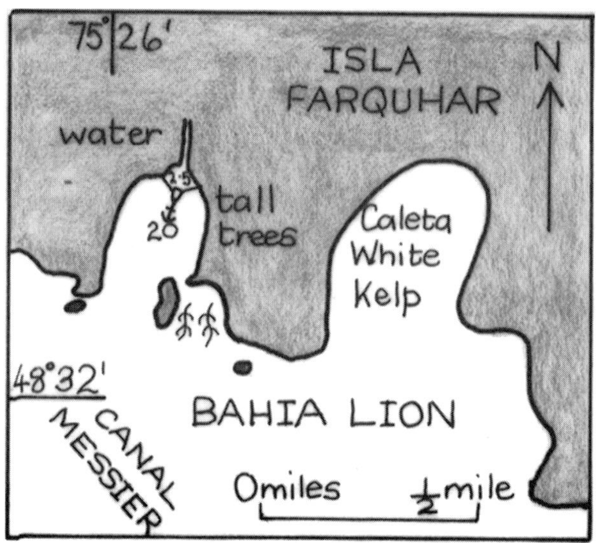

Caleta west of Caleta White Kelp. (Charted positions)

sheltered from all winds, with good holding in strong mud. Beware of the rock off the southern point of the cove. It is also possible to anchor in 18m in mid-channel with good holding in mud, but the river at the head of Caleta Connor runs quite strongly after heavy rainfall which can result in a wind against current situation. On the point south of the cove is a tall tree on which there are a number of name signs of visiting yachts.

5·19 Isla Farquhar – White Kelp Bay

Charts
UK *1287* Chile *901*

General
This is a small bay about half a mile to the west of Caleta White Kelp in Bahía Leon. It provides shelter from winds between west and north. Anchorage is at

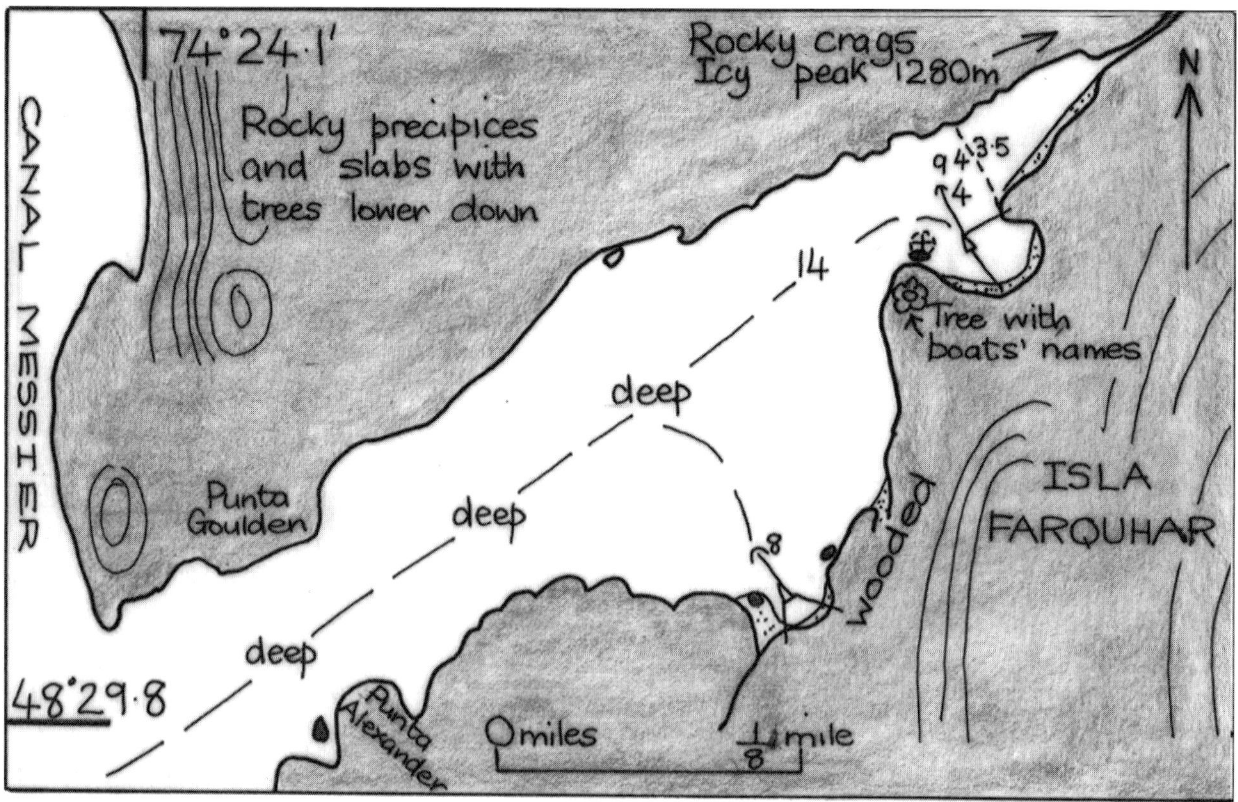

Caleta Connor. (GPS positions)

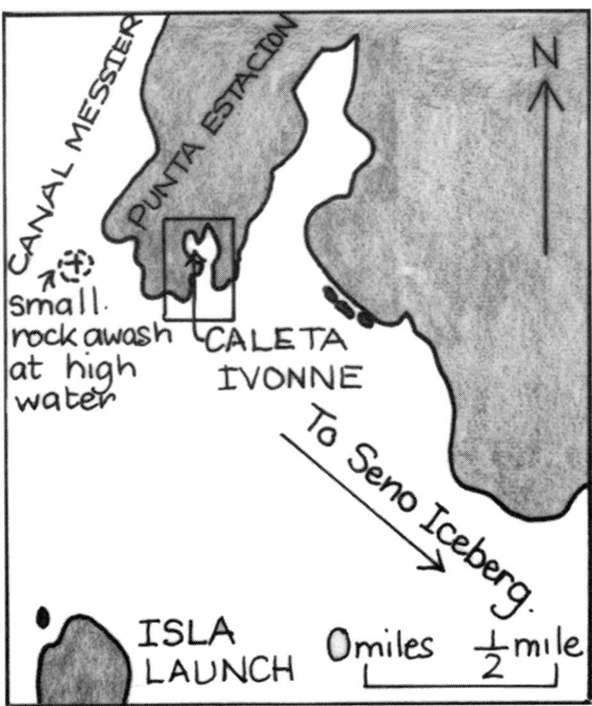

Caleta Ivonne

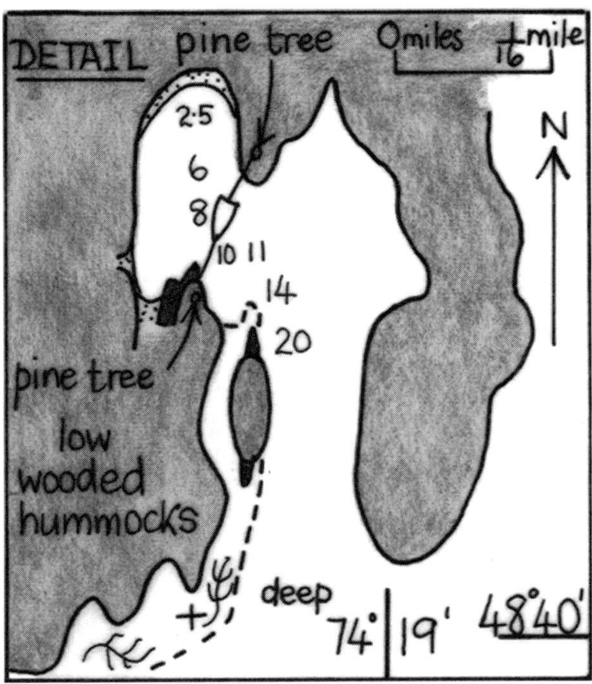

the head of the bay in 18m with two lines ashore, in front of the small waterfall.

5·20 Caleta Ivonne

48°41'S 74°22'W
48°40'S 74°19'W observed on GPS

Charts
UK *1287* Chile *901*

General
Unnamed on the charts, Caleta Ivonne is on the east side of the Canal Messier, north of Isla Launch and under the southern point of Punta Morro Estación. Punta Morro Estación has an unrecorded rock off it, awash at high water. Ivonne has two bays; the anchorage is in the western bay which has a narrow but clean entrance. It is a very well protected and secure anchorage. Anchor in 5–10m, mud, with a line astern or take shore lines straight across the bay. The water is glacial melt water. It is a good stopping place prior to a trip up Seno Iceberg.

Diversion

5·21 Seno Iceberg

48°44'S 74°18'W

Charts
UK *1287* US – Chile *901*

On the east side of the Canal Messier, Seno Iceberg leads to a spectacular glacier which frequently calves, sending bergy bits and brash down the Seno. Calving can cause large waves and it is wise to keep about a mile away from the glacier face. The point on the northwest shore a mile from the glacier face has two rocks about 200m off it. They may be covered at high water and at other times and in certain lights look like bergy bits. They are easily and safely avoided by keeping to the centre line of the Seno.

On both shores, three miles or so to the west of the glacier, there are various nooks where a boat might shelter from bad weather and drifting ice but remaining overnight would be a doubtful proposition. As shown on the sketch plan, there is an anchorage to the north of the glacier in 12m, east of the waterfall, the current from which keeps most of the ice at bay. From the waterfall it is possible to hike to the glacier but depending upon the wind, crew might have to remain on board to cope with a shift in the ice and fend off bergy bits.

Possibly shelter for the night might be found in the *ensenada* on the east side of Punta Yelcho, at the southern entrance to Seno Iceberg. It has not been explored but appears to have good opportunities for tying up to trees. If this proves an illusion, the nearest places are Caleta Ivonne to the north and Bahía Halt to the south.

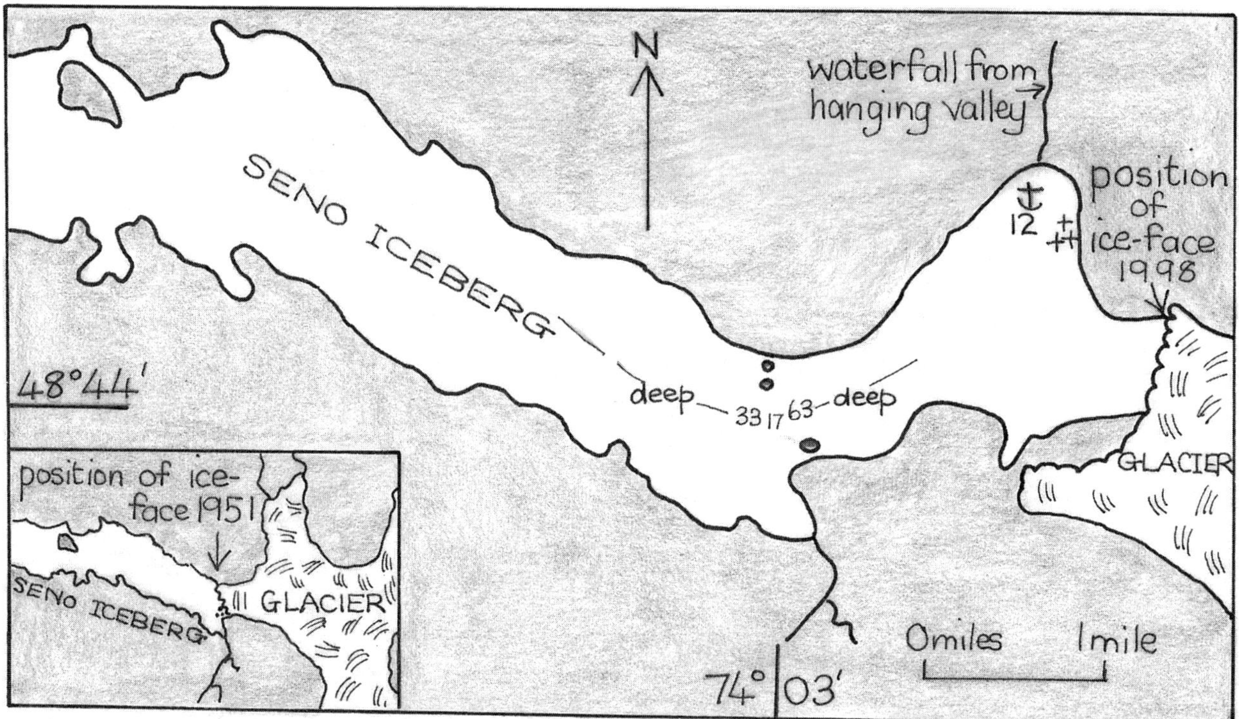

Seno Iceberg (Charted positions)

Continuation

There are three possible anchorages on the east side of Canal Messier in Bahía Liberta, about 5M north of Angostura Inglés. In descending order of merit they are Caleta Vittorio, Bahía Halt and Puerto Gray.

5·22 Isla Vittorio – Caleta Vittorio and Bahía Halt

48°54'S 74°20'W

Charts

UK *1287* Chile *941,908*

General

The two anchorages lie on either side of the passage between Isla Vittorio and the mainland (at a first glance at the chart Isla Vittorio appears to be a peninsula).

On the south side, Caleta Vittorio is a very beautiful anchorage and a good place to wait for a favourable tide. It is protected from all winds. Entrance to the anchorage is around the southeast corner of Isla Victoria. The bottom is mud, 18m. Shallower depths seem to have rocky bottom but it is also possible to moor in the nook at the west end of the *caleta* with a four-point tie off, well sheltered by the large trees. Access is easy and there is all-round protection.

On the north side is Bahía Halt. Approach this anchorage from the north side of Isla Vittorio, favouring the northern shore to stay clear of the shallow areas off the north shore of Isla Vittorio. The anchorage is at the eastern end (see sketch plan) with lines ashore. This anchorage would not be protected in northwest and west winds

5·23 Bahía Liberta – Puerto Gray

48°56'S 74°21'W

Charts

UK *1286* US – Chile *941, 908*

General

Puerto Gray is some 2·5M east of Caleta Vittorio and lies behind an unnamed headland running south to north with a light (listed as 1547Bahía Liberta 48°55'·9S 74°21'·6W Fl.6s27m7M White GRP tower, red band 6m. 024°-vis-334°). There are three basins. The first is shown on chart *908* as the anchorage of Puerto Gray. It lies on the east side of the headland, north of Roca Talisman. It is sheltered but has depths of 20–30m and is not a practical anchorage for a small boat. The second basin, also deep (18–20m), is entered by a narrow passage running southwest behind Talisman, with rocks off the point lying to the south. This is a very difficult entrance. All the rocks on either side of the passage are below water except for an hour or so either side of low water. When covered they are very difficult to see and it would be very easy to run up onto them. The best time to enter the pass is at low water. Beyond that, another narrow but simple passage with a minimum depth of 11m and no kelp leads to a fresh water lagoon with 10–15m, mud, very sheltered. Presumably a boat lying here for a few days would lose its barnacles and weed, if it has any.

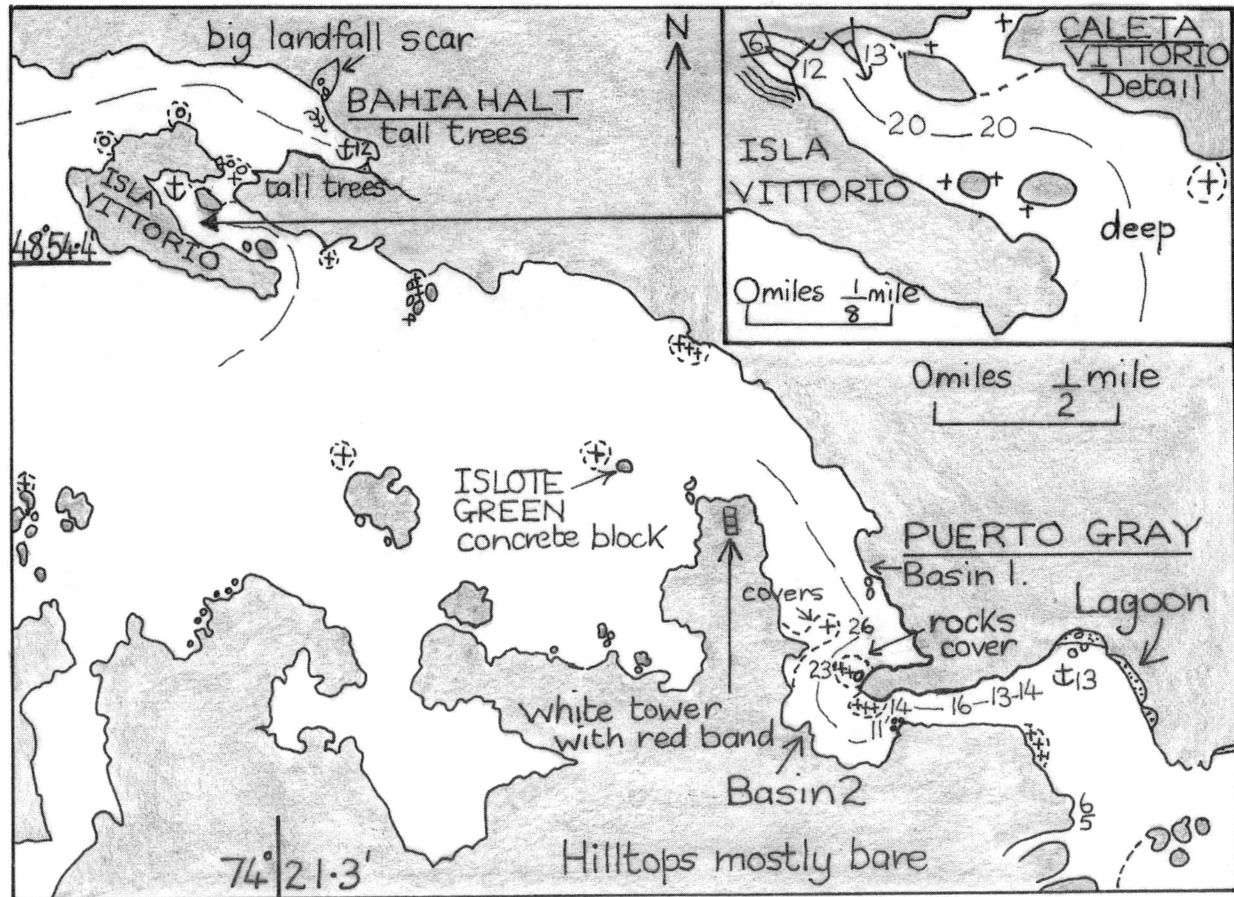

Bahía Halt, Caleta Vittorio and Puerto Gray. (GPS positions)

5·24 Isla Wellington – Caleta Hoskyn

48°57'S 74°27'W

Charts
UK *1287* Chile *941, 910*

General
Caleta Hoskyn is immediately north of Angostura Inglesa, round the south side of Isla Lamarmora and on the west side of the passage. It is recommended as a good waiting place for the tide in the narrows.

5·25 Angostura Inglesa

48°59'S 74°27'W

Charts
UK *1286* Chile *941*

General
According to the Hydrographic Office, the north-going stream begins about HW+45mins, the south-going stream at LW+45mins. However, the timing of slack water may vary by as much as an hour and when northerlies have been blowing, the south-going stream may continue up to two hours after HW, leaving a very short time for the north-going stream to run. In extreme conditions in winter, when the wind has been pushing the tide, the streams may reach 6–8kn. In summer and in reasonable wind conditions the rate rarely exceeds 1–2 knots and at slack water is almost negligible.

It's best to pass at slack water. The narrows are well marked with range markers and port and starboard markers (which look much the same as a light mark). In most parts there is plenty of room for a ship to pass a yacht and if a ship is seen approaching there is adequate space to hold back until it has passed.

Formalities
Regulations for big ships are given below. In practise the full protocol is only followed by cruise liners and large freighters and providing small ships notify Puerto Edén on VHF Ch 16 before entering there should be no problem. Puerto Edén notifies the passage of a large vessel on Ch 16.

a. The International Regulations for Preventing Collisions at Sea obtain, except that north bound traffic has priority.
b. Vessels should give advance notice of passage.
c. From one hour before passage a continuous listening watch should be maintained and a general call made every ten minutes giving the vessels ETA at Isla Medio Canal (48°59'S 74°27'W), her position vis-à-vis a conspicuous feature and current weather.
d. On sighting another vessel, contact should be established on Ch 16.
e. Between Isla Kitt and Islote Entrada two ships are not allowed abeam of each other.

f. If south-bound, a vessel should sound a prolonged blast at Islote Entrada and if a reply is heard wait for the north bound vessel to pass. A second prolonged blast should be sounded at Isla Disraeli.
g. If north-bound, a vessel should sound a prolonged blast at Isla Kitt and at Islote Zealous.

Should you hear gunfire in the vicinity, it may possibly be the Royal Navy giving warning of its approach, following the rules in the *British Admiralty Pilot NP6*. The *Armada* does not follow this custom.

5·26 Caleta Lucas
48°59'S 74°27'W

Charts
UK *1286* Chile *941*

General
On the east side of the channel, entered by a narrow channel with 7m (and kelp) south east of Isla Chinnock. This is another anchorage recommended for those going north as a waiting place for the tide in the Angostura. The bottom is very fine mud, 15m, but good holding after the anchor has settled.

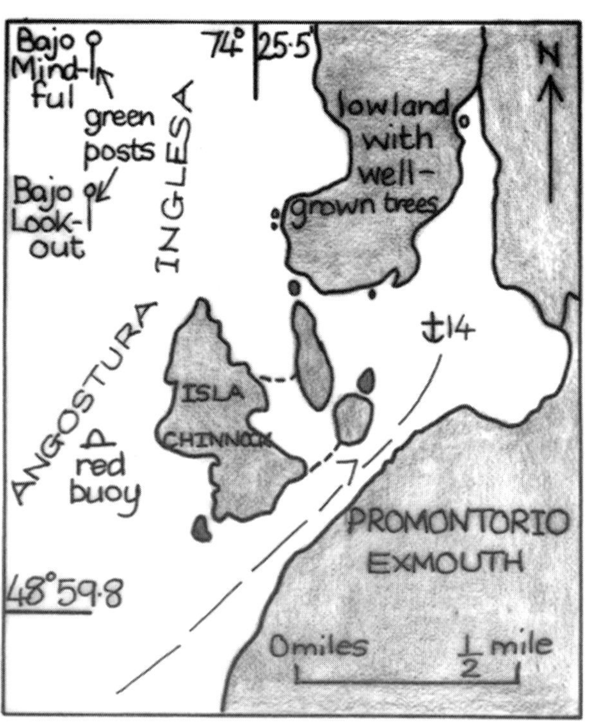

Caleta Lucas. (Charted positions)

5·27 Puerto Simpson
49°02'S 74°32'W

Charts
UK *1286* Chile *910*

General
On the west side of the channel. The north side of the entrance, Punta Roberto, has off-lying rocks. There are various possible anchoring places in 8–10m, mud, good holding. A good place to wait for the tide without going back to Puerto Edén, if going north.

Section 6
Puerto Edén to Canal Sarmiento

Charts
There are no large scale US charts for this section. The small scale charts are *22395* and *22420.*

6·1 Puerto Edén

49°09'S 74°27'W

Charts
UK *1286* Chile *941, 908*

General
Different charts put Puerto Edén in different places but as it is at the north end and on the west side of Paso del Indio, in a bay some two miles from north to south lying behind islands, it is not too difficult to find. Good shelter can be found in the several small bays in the vicinity. The place has wonderful views and friendly and helpful people. There is talk of extending the pier and adding facilities for visitors.

Approach
Call the *capitanía* on the approach. If not stopping at Edén, he should be called anyway.

Anchorage
For formalities, anchor off the *Armada* in the position shown on the sketch chart. It is a prominent blue building with a white roof. If the *Armada* buoy is unoccupied, it might be used but ask first. However, the holding in this area is good and it will probably be less of a hassle to swing to an anchor since if using the buoy it is necessary to use a stern anchor to stop the yacht riding down on the buoy when the wind drops. At the village, holding is moderate, mud, rock and kelp. There is a convenient pier with a least-depth of 1·7m alongside. If staying some days, Caleta Malacca on the north side is well sheltered with excellent holding in silt. The kelp shown at the entrance to Canal Malacca on the Chilean chart is no longer there.

Formalities
The *zarpe* must be checked. In fine weather the *capitanía* (in the *Armada* station) might be reached by dinghy and outboard from the village anchorage.

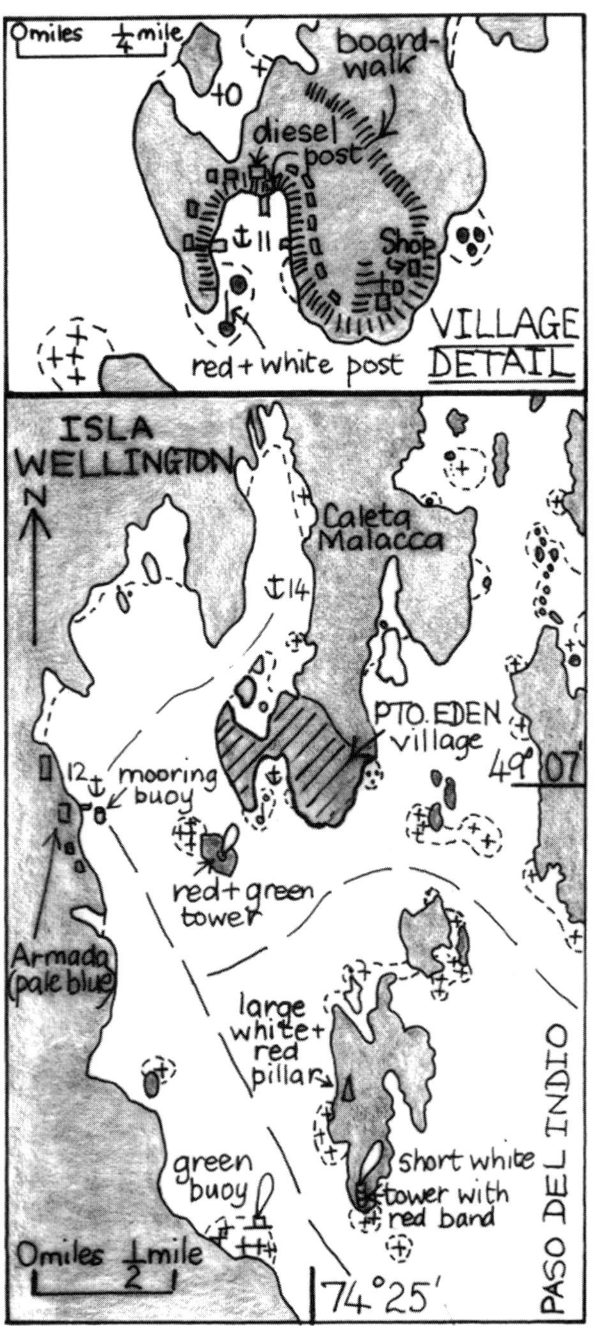

Puerto Eden. (Charted positions)

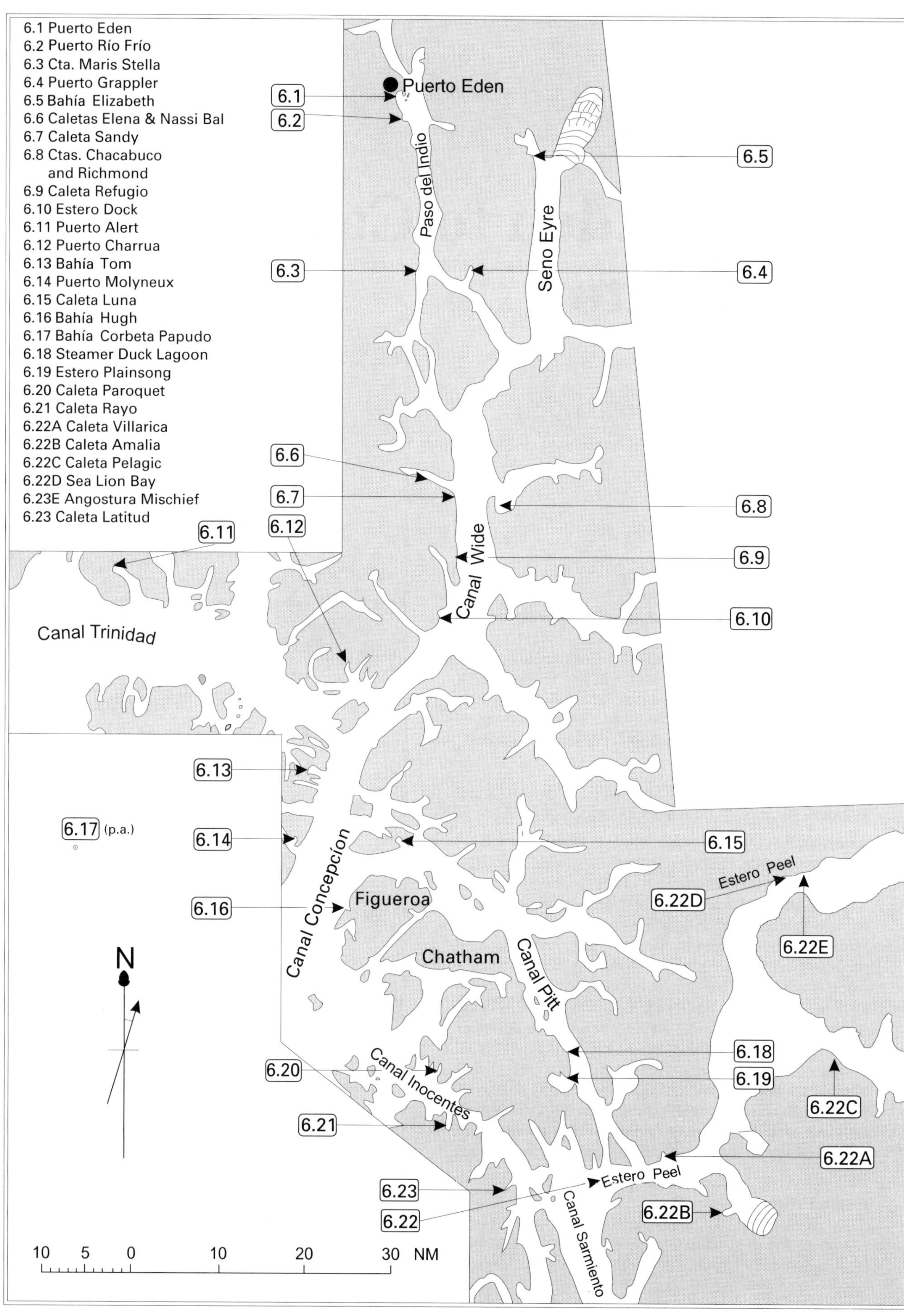

6.1 Puerto Eden
6.2 Puerto Río Frío
6.3 Cta. Maris Stella
6.4 Puerto Grappler
6.5 Bahía Elizabeth
6.6 Caletas Elena & Nassi Bal
6.7 Caleta Sandy
6.8 Ctas. Chacabuco and Richmond
6.9 Caleta Refugio
6.10 Estero Dock
6.11 Puerto Alert
6.12 Puerto Charrua
6.13 Bahía Tom
6.14 Puerto Molyneux
6.15 Caleta Luna
6.16 Bahía Hugh
6.17 Bahía Corbeta Papudo
6.18 Steamer Duck Lagoon
6.19 Estero Plainsong
6.20 Caleta Paroquet
6.21 Caleta Rayo
6.22A Caleta Villarica
6.22B Caleta Amalia
6.22C Caleta Pelagic
6.22D Sea Lion Bay
6.23E Angostura Mischief
6.23 Caleta Latitud
Puerto Eden
Paso del Indio
Seno Eyre
Canal Wide
Canal Trinidad
Canal Concepcíon
Figueroa
Chatham
Canal Pitt
Estero Peel
Canal Inocentes
Canal Sarmiento
6.17 (p.a.)
N
10 5 0 10 20 30 NM

Facilities

Diesel is available through the Empresa Comercial y Agrícola. There has been some doubt about quality; filtering is suggested.

Possibility of showers ashore: ask the *Armada.*

Bread baked on request at the blue house, third left from the Police Station. Fresh *centollas* and sometimes fish. To the east, round a headland and past the Church, is a store with limited supplies and, sometimes, frozen meat. Beyond it, a by-request restaurant *La Barquita.* Fresh supplies are sometimes available after the ferry calls.

If the yacht provides its own stamps letters may be posted at the house of retired Port Captain Jose Navero Leive, to catch the next Navimag ship to Puerto Natales or Puerto Montt. Ask for the house that acts as the post office.

Captain Navero, a source of local knowledge, is planning to board and lodge 'adventure' visitors and may have accommodation.

Communications

The *Navimag* ferry, running between Puerto Montt and Puerto Natales, calls on Wednesdays going south and Saturdays going north.

6·2 Puerto Río Frío

49°12'S 74°24'W

Charts

UK *1286* Chile *941, 908*

General

This bay is easily entered. Anchor in the northern bay in about 5m. The anchorage is very well protected and the holding is good.

6·3 Caleta Maris Stella

49°22'·6S 74°25'W (GPS)

Charts

UK *1286* Chile *941*

General

On the west side of Paso Indio, at the junction of Canales Escape and Grappler, behind Península Broome. It has a clear approach. It is open to the south but otherwise has very good shelter. Anchor in about 14m just south of the kelp-strewn narrows with shore lines to the point of the narrows. A shallow draught yacht could go to the inner bay which is both pretty and tranquil.

Alternative routes

Isla Saumarez can be passed either side. The west side has, from north to south, Canal Escape and Paso del Abismo and its parallel, Paso Piloto Pardo; on the east side is Canal Grappler, with an anchorage at Puerto Grappler, and Canal Icy. Paso Abismo is one-way south and Paso Piloto Pardo is one-way north. Canales Grappler and Icy are two-way.

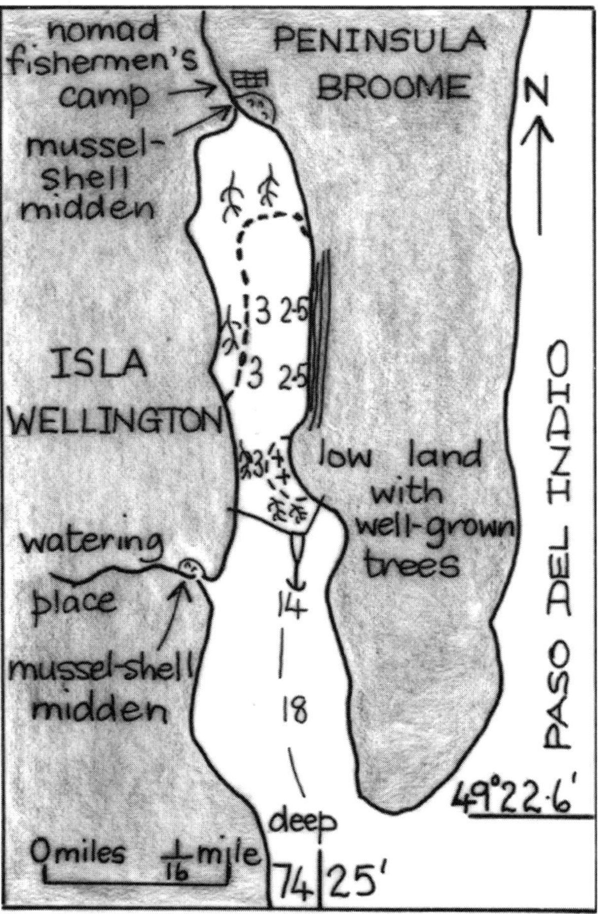

Caleta Maris Stella. (GPS positions)

Pasos Abismo and Piloto Pardo may only be passed in daylight. Many waterfalls come into them and there are coves which may give temporary shelter from the winds which, in unsettled weather, blow either up or down the channel with no half measures. The passage is fairly dramatic and good visibility is advisable.

Canales Grappler and Icy are an easier passage. Canal Grappler has wider views, with a waterfall on either side and if visibility is good, there are grand views of the mountains from Canal Icy.

6·4 Puerto Grappler

49°26'S 74°20'W

49°25'S 74°18'W observed on GPS

Charts

UK *1286* Chile *917, 905*

General

The entrance to Grappler is wide and clean. The anchorage is to the north of Isla Diamante in 6m, mud with good holding. The other recommended anchorage is at the head of the bay in about 3–6m. Although Grappler provides protection from all winds, and is oriented from the south to the northeast, its eastern side is very steep and high and may be prone to *rachas* in strong northwest winds.

Grappler is a good stopping place on the route

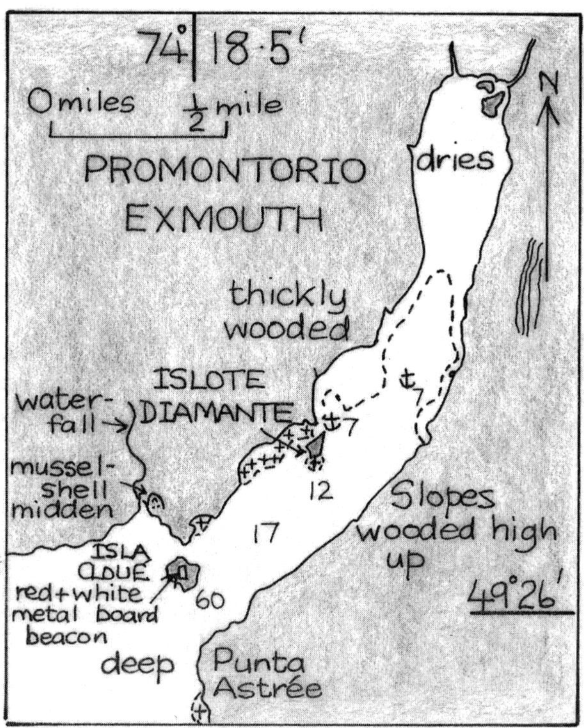

Puerto Grappler. (GPS positions)

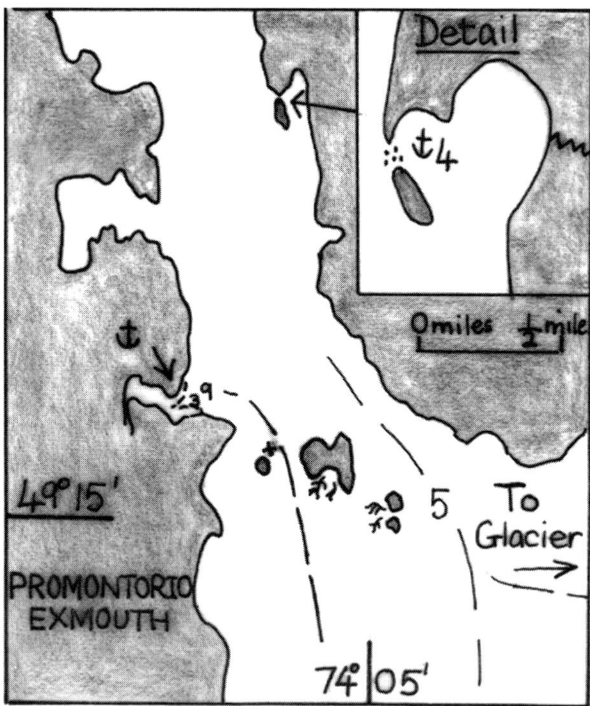

Bahía Elizabeth. (Charted positions)

south and also for those planning a trip up Seno Eyre to view the spectacular Pío XI glacier.

Diversion

6·5 Seno Eyre – Bahía Elizabeth

49°14'·5S 74°05'·9W

Charts
UK *1286* Chile *9510*

General
In settled conditions it is worth making a diversion to the head of Seno Eyre to consider Pío XI, the largest and one of the most spectacular glaciers of the Patagonian Ice Cap. The glacier is advancing and its face is further south than is shown on the charts. There is considerable ice in the Seno. On a clear day the views of Mount Fitzroy and Mount Piramide (3000m+) beyond the glacier are spectacular.

Anchorages
In 1997 ice blocked the entrance to Seno Exmouth which runs off to the southeast and might otherwise provide anchorage. Anchor in Bahía Elizabeth in the bay northwest of Islote Genaro, in about 5m, mud, with excellent holding. A west wind and the flow of water down Bahía Elizabeth keep icebergs out of the anchorage. There is another anchorage on the east side of the bay, 1·5 miles north–northwest of Punta Micalvi, which has good protection from all quarters. It is in a notch with a shingle beach immediately northeast of the islet which closes off the west side of a little *caleta*, 4m, mud and kelp. Waterfall on the east side of the *caleta*. This *caleta* is not immune to ice but the outflow from the waterfall and tucking in well behind the islet as described should minimise the problem except in a strong south wind. The Islotes Mardones can be left to port going north though there is a 5m patch between them and Punta Micalvi.

Another possible anchorage in Seno Eyre is amongst the group of islands about halfway up its western side.

Continuation Canal Wide

6·6 Seno Antrim – Caletas Elena and Nassi Bal

49°46'S 74°24'W

Charts
UK *1286* Chile *906, 910*

General
These *caletas* are in Seno Antrim, on the west side of Canal Wide at 1535Punta Camarón (Fl.15s6m10M white square concrete tower, red bands 187°-vis-032°). Caleta Nassi Bal is a tiny uncharted inlet on the south shore of Antrim about a mile from the entrance. It is about 30m wide. Lie to an anchor at the head of the inlet in 6m, sand, and two stern lines. It is said to be a good alternative to Elena, which may be more easily discovered.

Caleta Elena, on Chile *910*, is deep (30m+ once inside) but the southeast point, Punta Choros, is foul to the northwest up to the middle of the entrance; favour the northern shore. Get stern lines ashore.

6·7 Seno Antrim – Caleta Sandy

49°47'S 74°24'W

Charts
UK *1286* Chile *906, 910*

General
Caleta Sandy is on the west side of Canal Wide, just south of Seno Antrim. The *caleta* has two possible anchorages, with protection from the north on the north shore and from the south, on the south shore. The northern anchorage has a shoal patch (4m) to its south which can be circumnavigated. The southern anchorage has a rock to the northwest which can be observed and avoided. Anchoring depths are in 10m or less, rock and sand, with stern lines ashore.

6·8 Estero Ringdove – Caletas Richmond and Chacabuco

49°47'·3S 74°18'·6W

Charts
UK *1286* Chile *906, 910*

General
There are three anchorages in a very pleasant setting on the eastern side of Punta Hyacinth, at the entrance to Estero Ringdove. All provide good protection from NW and SW winds. The area was important for mussel fishing and there are large piles of shells around the shores but the problem of the *marea roja* has significantly reduced the business. The most secure anchorage is to moor between Isla Rosa and the mainland as shown in the small insert chart. This anchorage is well-protected and with stern and bow shore lines it is very secure. The holding is mud at Caleta Richmond, anchor off the beach in about 14m and two lines off the stern. This anchorage is too deep to anchor in the middle without lines ashore. Caleta Chacabuco, half a mile south of Rosa Island, is also deep and requires lines ashore.

Caution
East winds, especially in autumn, bring much ice down the east-leading Senos Penguin, Europa and Andrés, blocking them and sometimes, even blocking Seno Wide at the narrows with Isla Tópar.

6·9 Isla Wellington – Caleta Refugio

49°52'·8S 74°24'·8W

Charts
UK *1286* Chile *906*

General
1½M north of Punta Camerón, Caleta Refugio is a surprising well-protected anchorage surrounded by

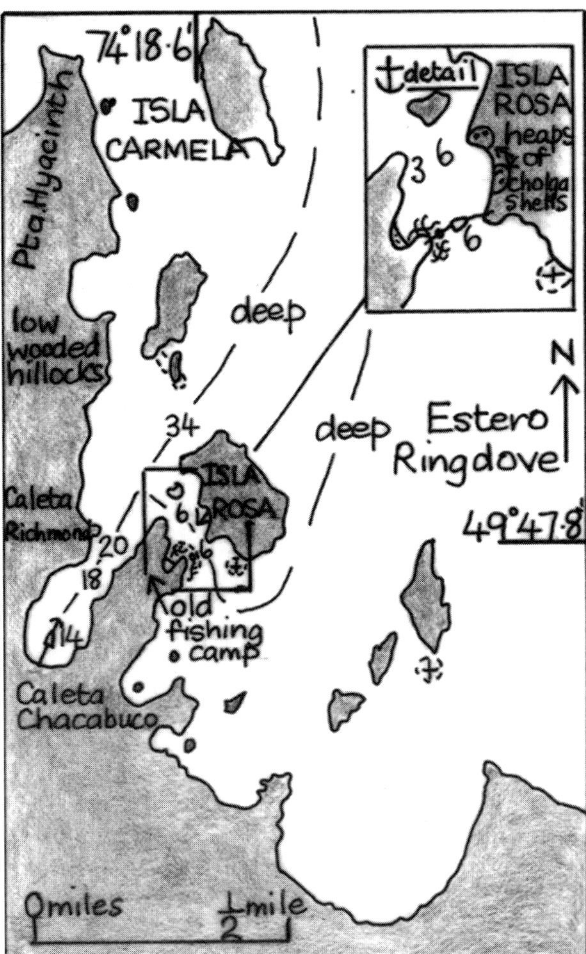

Caletas Richmond and Chacabuco. (GPS positions)

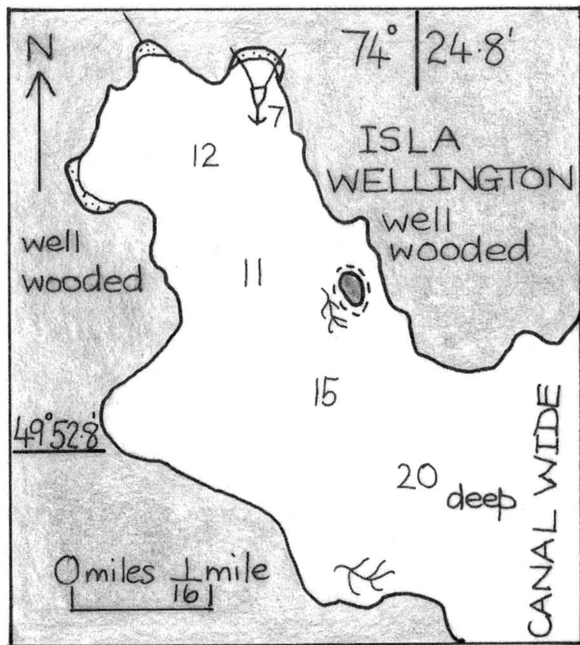

Caleta Refugio. (GPS positions)

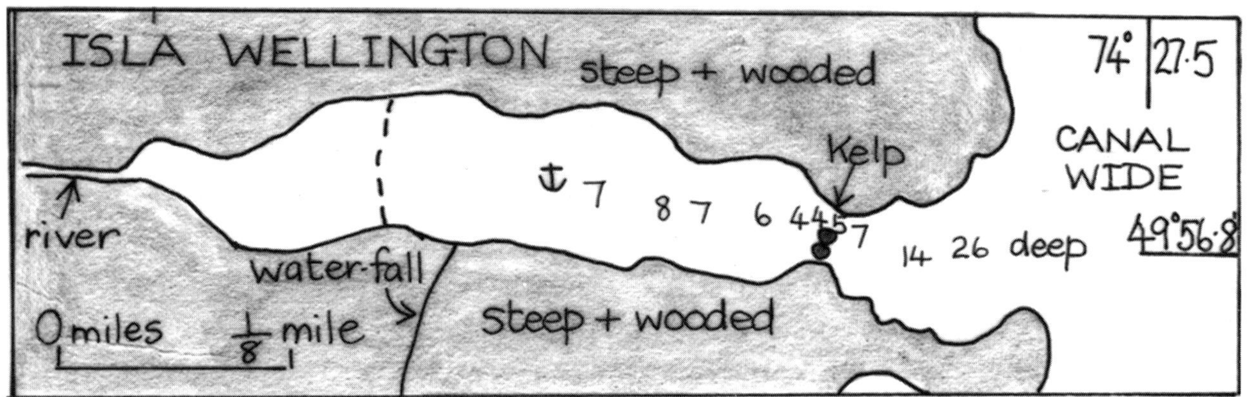

Estero Dock. (GPS positions)

low land and well developed woodland. The approach is easy and a secure anchorage can be taken at the northern end of the bay, in 7m with shorelines.

6·10 Isla Wellington – Estero Dock

49°57'S 74°27'W

Charts
UK *1286* Chile *906*

General
Estero Dock is a pretty anchorage (with otters) on the SE side of Isla Wellington and is easily identified from the east. In strong southerly and northerly winds with white horses in Canal Wide the Estero has been reported calm. The entrance is very narrow but straightforward. At the entrance pass keep to the north side, passing north of the large bare rock in the southern two-thirds of this narrow pass. Depths fall to about 3·5m but the bottom is sandy and the rocks on either side can be seen through the clear water. Once passed the rock depths increase to 7m. Good holding.

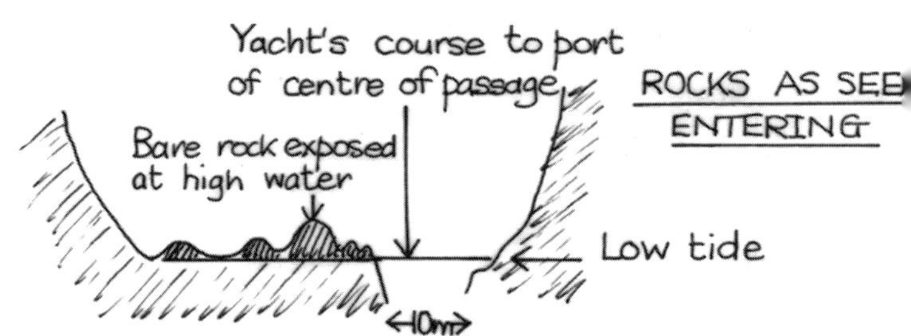

Rocks as seen entering

Golfo Trinidad

6·11 Isla Mornington – Puerto Alert

49°52'S 75°13'W

Charts
UK *1286* Chile *900, 904, 920*

General
If entering or leaving the Pacific through the Golfo Trinidad, there is a very snug and beautiful anchorage at the far northeast corner of Puerto Alert, shown on chart *920* as Fondeadero Mackerel. The anchorage is in 3–5m and is well sheltered by a group of small islands. The stream at the northern end of the bay is good for laundry and fresh water.

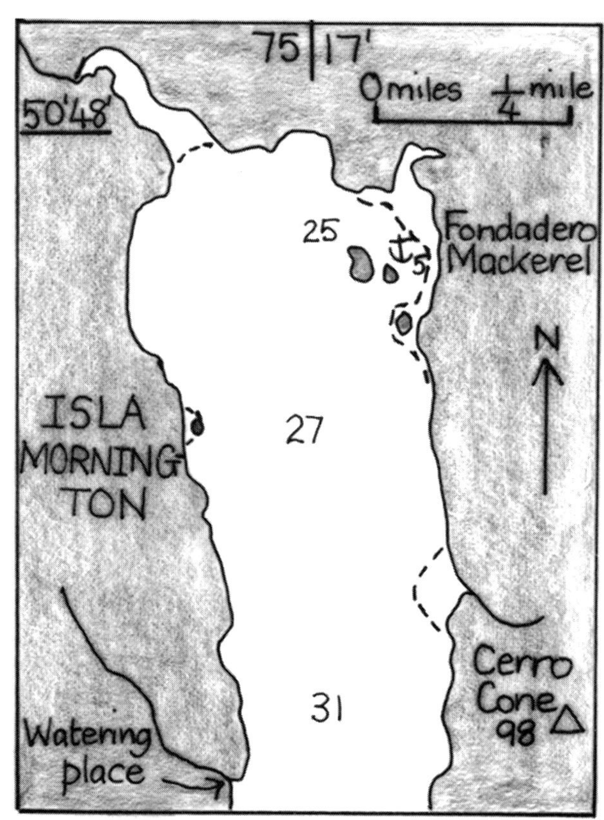

Puerto Alert. (Charted positions)

Paso Brassey

6·12 Puerto Charrúa

50°02'S 74°42'W

Charts
UK *1286* Chile *914*

General
Paso Brassey leads north of Isla Tópar between Canales Wide and Trinidad. Puerto Charrúa is on its north side with precipitous Monte Normanhurst, 625m, on its west shore. Anchorage has been made in 14m or less, close to the 130m waterfall – it is worth a stop if only to see that magnificent waterfall. The high cliffs all around add to the splendour of the anchorage but also produce gusts when the wind is between northwest and northeast. Get lines ashore.

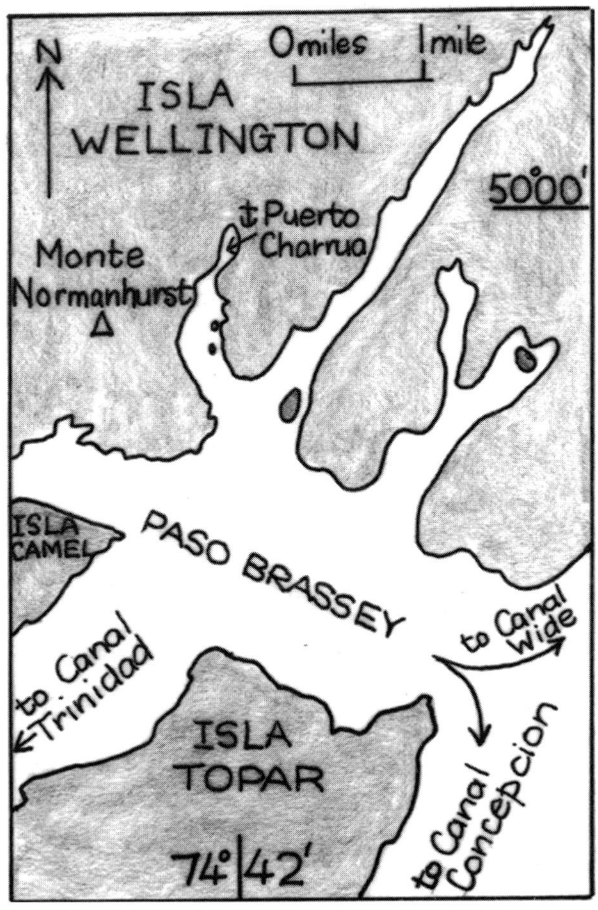

Puerto Charrua. (Charted positions)

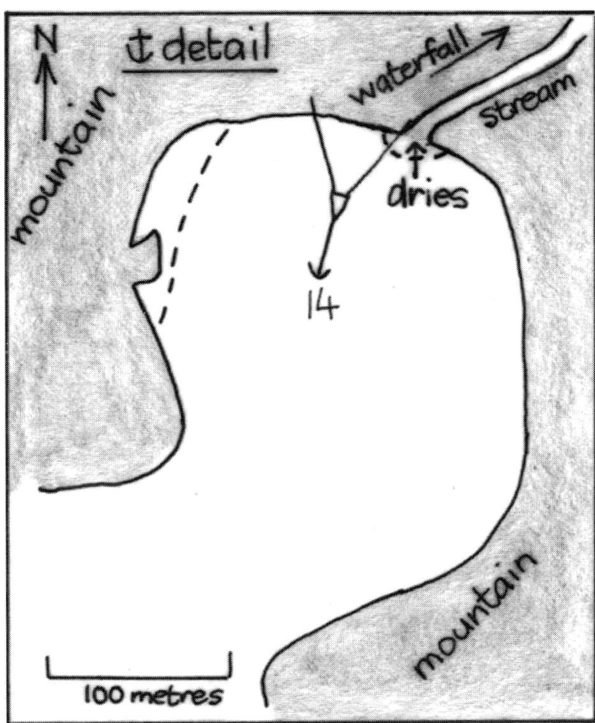

Puerto Charrua. (Charted positions)

Alternatives

Isla Tópar to Estero Peel

The alternatives of Canales Concepción, Inocentes, Angostura Guía and Canal Sarmiento on the one hand and, on the other, Seno San Andrés and Canal Pitt now lie ahead of the south bound vessel. The former is the main route and has some known anchorages. The latter is more liable to ice up; see Isla Chatham. Both connect with Estero Peel which is a suggested diversion.

The usual southwest wind can kick up nasty seas in Canal Concepción for the 30M stretch until well inside the entrance to Canal Inocentes. Canal Pitt offers a much more sheltered route down into Estrecho Peel, at which point there is the choice of Villarica to the east (if going to the Peel Glacier), or Bueno to the west and then south in Canal Sarmiento.

Isla Tópar to Isla Brinkley

Isla Tópar is at the junction of Trinidad and Wide. Isla Brinkley is about 110M south at the junction of Canal Sarmiento and Estrecho de Collingwood.

Concepción, Inocentes, Angostura Guía and Sarmiento

Canal Concepción

6·13 Isla Stratford – Bahía Tom

50°12'·2S 74°48'·7W

Charts
UK *1286* Chile *10000, 914, 915*

General
This is an excellent well-sheltered anchorage protected from all winds. The surrounding countryside is low, and the trees provide protection even in very strong winds. There are a number of possible anchorages in the area. One favoured is at the very head of an indentation between Punta Henry and Punta William. The bearing into the bay is approximately 290°. The GPS co-ordinates of that anchorage are 50°11'·6S 74°49'·4W. The notch itself is about 50m wide. Use a three point mooring, two lines off the stern and one off the bow in about 6m of water. The entrance is clean but favour the centre or the port side of the channel as there are a couple of rocks with kelp at the head. Do not attempt to go in the channel to starboard at the head of the bay as it dries at low tide.

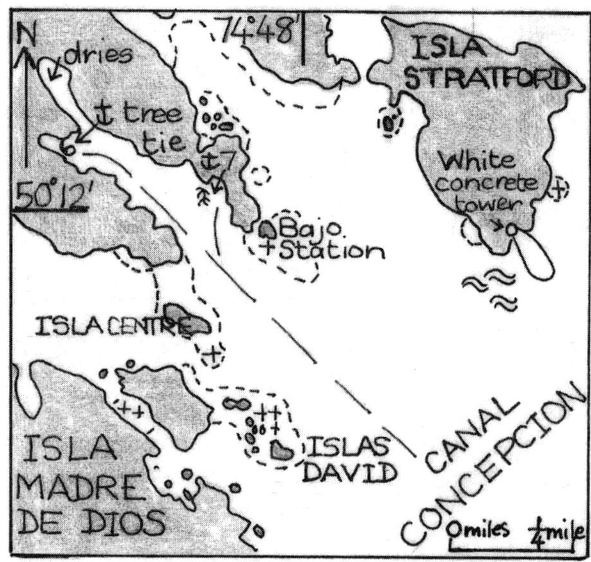

Bahía Tom. (Charted positions)

6·14 Isla Drummond Hay – Puerto Molyneux

50°17'S 74°52'W

Charts
UK *1286* Chile *10000, 911, 912, 914*

General
Going north against a northwest wind in Canal Concepción can be difficult and the anchorage in Seno Molyneux is a useful stopping place if it is not possible to reach Bahía Tom, 10 miles further north. It is half-way along Isla San Miguel, under 1533 Punta San Miguel (Fl.5s5m6M white square concrete tower 3m). Molyneux is not a great anchorage but it is protected from the northwest wind. Anchor in 10m close to an exposed rock on a rocky bottom. Mud has been reported at a depth of 30–35m.

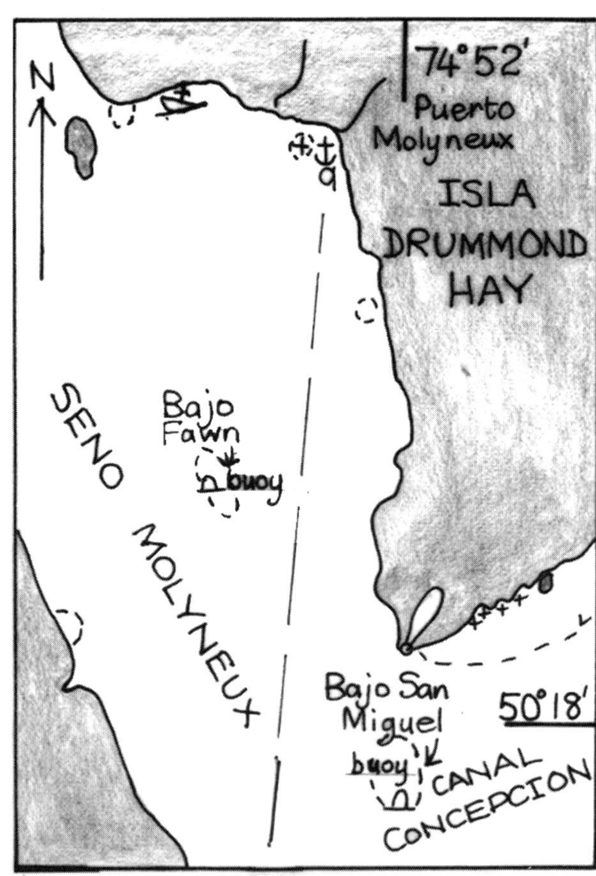

Puerto Molyneux. (Charted positions)

6·15 Isla Canning – Caleta Luna

50°18'S 74°37'W

Charts
UK *1286* Chile *10000, 914*

General
This is a sizeable bay on the SE corner of Isla Canning on Canal Andrés. Because of its size and depth, it probably wouldn't be the best place for bad weather but it is good enough for reasonable conditions. The bay has two arms, one to the W and one to the NW. The NW arm is deep but there are a couple of bays where a yacht could moor close in.

More interestingly, in the S corner of the W arm there is a narrow gut to an inner lagoon which does not appear on chart *914*. The gut is impassable to yachts but is possible in a dinghy, and the lagoon, which is more or less fresh water, is interesting to explore. You can anchor in 7m bow or stern into the flow through the gut with lines ashore. There is a strong outflow from the lagoon on the ebb and a weak inflow on the flood.

There may be other anchorages in the western arm.

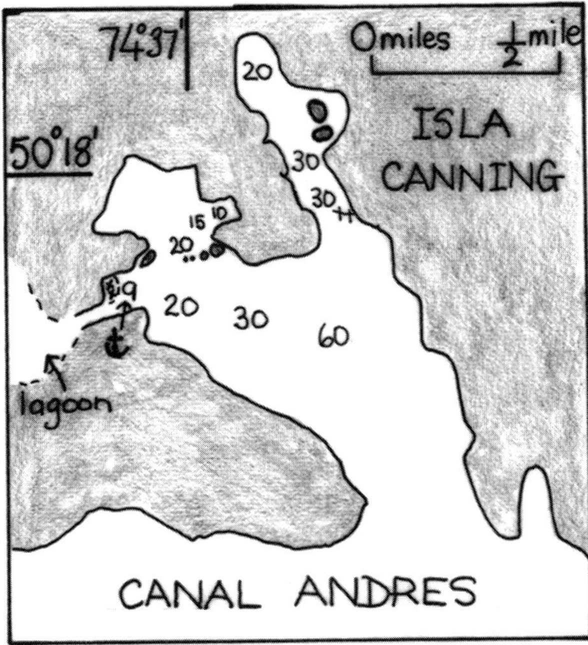

Caleta Luna. (Charted positions)

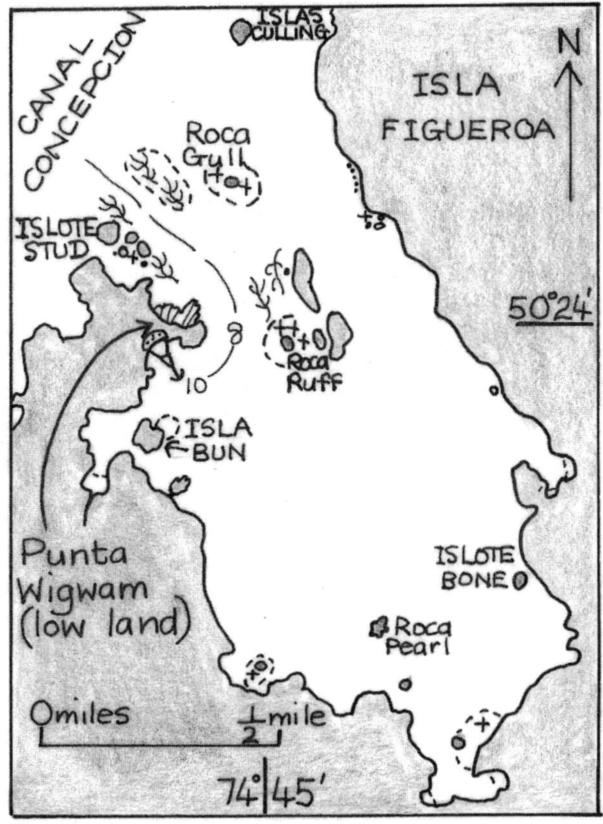

Bahia Hugh. (Charted positions)

6·16 Isla Figueroa – Bahía Hugh

50°24'S 74°45'W

Charts
UK *1286* Chile *10000, 914, 915*

General
Bahía Hugh lies on the northwest coast of Isla Figueroa on the east side of Canal Concepción. The wider entrance is under the northeast shore. Although open to the northwest, even with those winds there is no sea and shelter from the wind might be found in the bay on the west side, 10m or less, mud. Good holding with shore lines. The bottom at the head of the inlet is rocky.

Diversion
Isla Guarello

6·17 Bahía Corbeta Papudo

50°22'S 75°20'W

Chart
UK *1286* Chile *10340*

General
This anchorage is included as it is the only place for miles and miles where a yacht may get assistance if necessary. It is a huge limestone quarry with a resident community of miners. The limestone is shipped to the steel works in Concepción. The mine is at the north end of Isla Guarello which is at the west end of Canal Oeste. Anchor close-to in 10 to 16m. The few yachts that have visited this community have been made very welcome.

Continuation
Canal Pitt

6·18 Isla Chatham – Steamer Duck Lagoon

50°38'S 74°15'W

Charts
UK *1286* Chile *914*

General
Steamer Duck Lagoon has no official name. It is an alternative to Estero Plainsong with a more straightforward entrance though it may be rough in very strong northwesterlies. The entrance is clean and the preferred cove is on the west side (the cove on the E side has inadequate depths). Bow tie-offs as shown are poor but the holding is good and there was perfect shelter with a 30kt wind in Canal Pitt. Abundant wildlife including otters as well as steamer ducks.

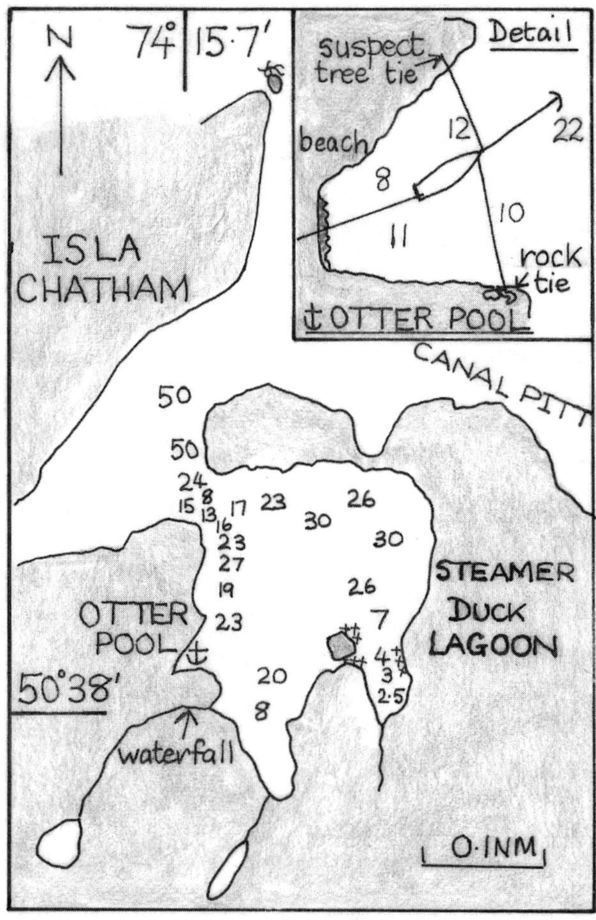

Steamer Duck Lagoon. (Charted positions)

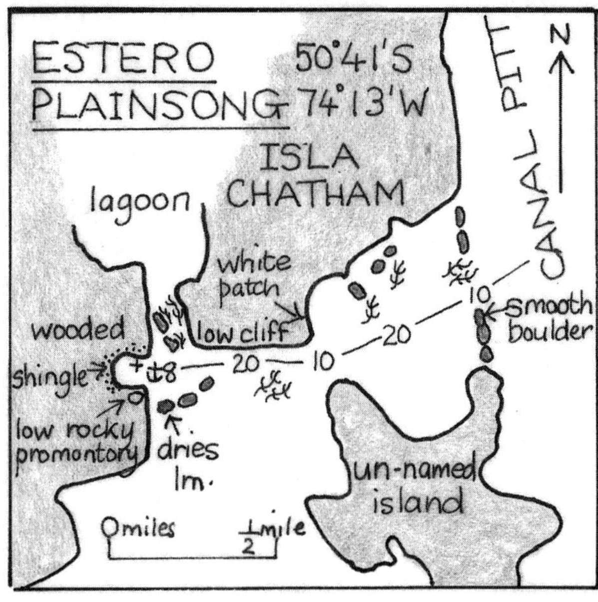

Estero Plainsong

6·19 Isla Chatham – Estero Plainsong

50°41'S 74°13'W

Charts
UK *1286* Chile *10000, 914*

General
This is a useful anchorage half way along the west side of Canal Pitt, at the entrance of an unnamed *estero* running northwest and almost bisecting the island. The *estero* is studded with islands and rocks, and anchorage can be chosen according to conditions.

There are probably several ways of getting into the *estero*. From the north, it can be entered through a passage between Isla Chatham and the next island to the south, keeping closer to the latter. After passing mid-channel between the next two points, turn to starboard holding the shore close on the starboard side. Ahead there is an 8m pool with good shelter.

Canal Pitt – Southern End

The channel between Isla Peel and Isla Chatham is navigable, with depths averaging 40m in mid-channel.

Canal Inocentes

6·20 Isla Chatham – Caleta Paroquet

50°40'S 74°33'W

Charts
UK *1286* Chile *1000, 914, 916*

General
Caleta Paroquet is a really first class anchorage protected from all winds. It is on the west side of Isla Chatham, 3M east of the light on the southwest extremity of Isla Juan, 1528Punta Don (Fl.6s9m7M white GRP tower, red band 6m. 325°-vis-150°) and east of Islotes Long. The land is low and wooded and the entrance has a whitish cliff on the east side of the approach. Half way up the *caleta* there is a peninsula which looks like an island as it is approached from the south. A very secure mooring can be made between this and the main island with bow and stern lines. It is possible to tuck well up into this narrow cut; the overhanging trees on either side provide perfect shelter. A second choice would be to anchor right at the head of the Caleta. It is deep close to the shore but anchoring is possible in 14m, with shore lines.

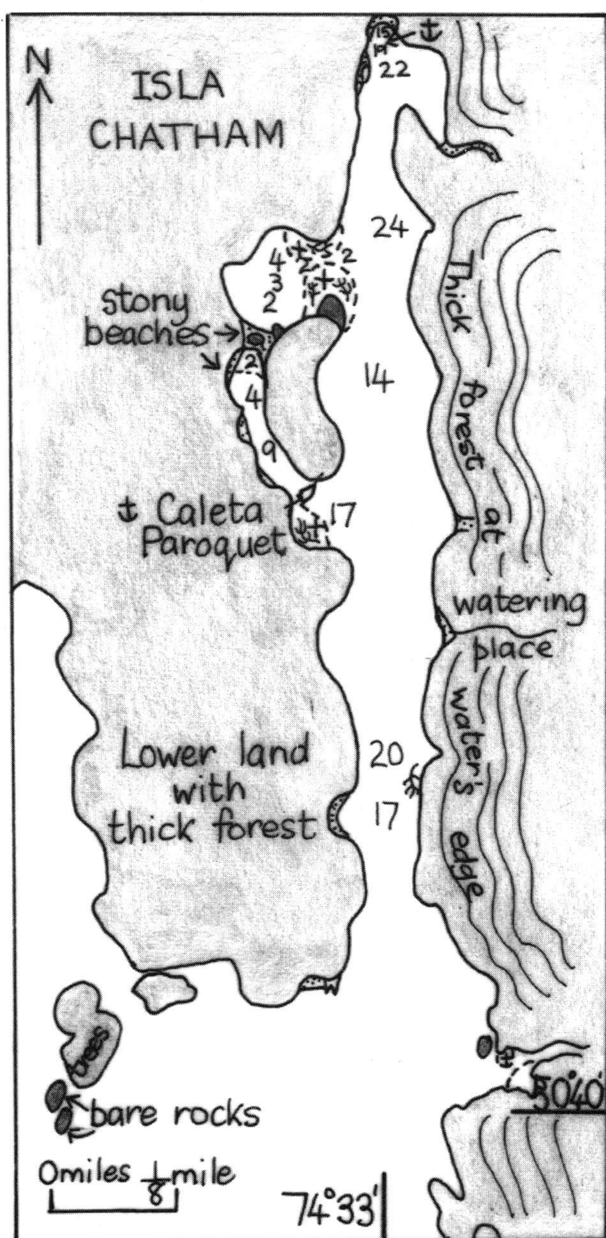

Caleta Paroquet. (GPS positions)

6·21 Isla Hanover – Caleta Rayo

50°45'S 74°32'W

Charts
UK *1286* Chile *914, 916*

General
Caleta Rayo is on Isla Hanover just west of Punta Porpoise. A mooring has been taken between two islands on the western shore in 4·8m (low tide) with three lines ashore; the report expresses disbelief when comparison was made with the chart and adds that it blew hard for 12 hours with the barometer at 986hPa. Large seal colony.

Angostura Guía

Charts
UK *1286, 1282* Chile *10000, 914*

General
Angostura Guía is described by Roth as 'a wonderful mountainous narrows, (with) *cañons*, ravines and domes. It seemed unbelievable to be sailing at sea level with such scenery around us'. It is about 6M long and connects Canal Inocentes with Canal Sarmiento. Estero Peel joins Canal Sarmiento south of Angostura Guía.

Formalities
Commercial vessels have to give one hours notice of passage and whilst on passage call every 10 minutes on 500kHz or Ch 16. Vessels sighting each other should establish contact on Ch 16.

Overtaking or passing a vessel going in the opposite direction is forbidden between Punta Porpoise and Isla Escala light at the south end, a four mile stretch. South-going vessels should wait for those going north. It is fairly easy for a yacht listening out on Ch 16 to be fully aware of the position of vessels in transit through Angostura Guia. Unless visibility is poor a vessel is also easily seen and there is plenty of room to take avoiding action. The Chilean pilots all speak English and will respond to a vessel calling them.

Alternatives

Peel to Tópar

A north bound vessel may care to consider the alternative route between Peel and Tópar mentioned above.

Diversion

6·22 Estero Peel

Charts
UK *1282, 1286* Chile *10000, 914, 10370*
Neither of the two UK charts are adequate.

General
Estero Peel runs east from Canal Sarmiento at 50°52'S for about 15 miles before turning NNE for a further 30 miles. Estero Peel has a number of tide water glaciers running down from the Patagonia ice cap. These include those at the head of Estero Amalia, Estero Asia, Estero Calvo and finally those right at the head of Estero Peel itself. Ventisquero Calvo was the route chosen by Tilman when he crossed the Patagonian ice cap in 1954. A number of anchorages are listed below which have been used with caution by yachts. A fall back plan should be considered in relation to each of these anchorages, should they be blocked or the weather turn foul.

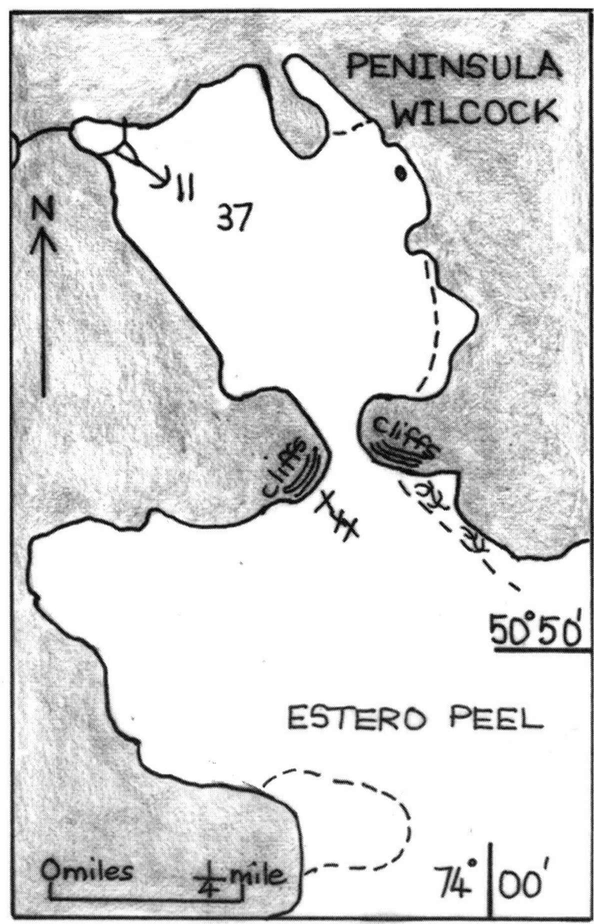

Caleta Villarrica. (Charted positions)

6·22A Península Wilcock – Caleta Villarrica

50°50'S 74°01'W

General

Located on the north side of Estero Peel, this anchorage was recommended by *Andromeda*, a 20m German boat. There is a distinctive cone-shaped hill to the east of the entrance. The entrance to the basin is narrow (25m) but clean. Avoid the rocks and shingle running southeast from the eastern entrance point. Inside is a peaceful, totally protected anchorage. Anchor in the southwestern corner with two stern lines to the shore or in the notch on the northern shore of the bay.

6·22B Estero Amalia – Caleta Amalia

50°56'S 73°51'W

General

Across the *estero* from the glacier is Caleta Amalia. The entrance is clear, but beware of the rock off the southern side of the island as it is covered at high tide. Depths are around 6m between the island and the southern shore. Past the island, the depths increase and are about 30m almost to the head of

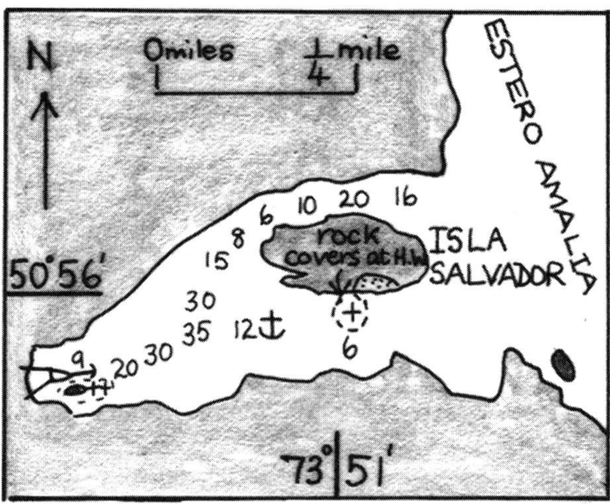

Caleta Amalia. (Charted positions)

the bay. There is an anchorage with good holding in sandy mud in 10m off the notch in the south west end of the island, with a fine view of the glacier over the stern. The face of the glacier is comparatively low so the ice in the immediate area is mostly small bergy bits.

If the entrance to Amalia happens to be blocked by ice, as it was when Tilman was there, there is the indentation he used at 50°54'·76S, 73°50'·45W (by GPS).

6·22C Estero Calvo – Caleta Pelagic

50°38'·23S 73°38'·67W (GPS)

General

Estero Calvo is halfway up the north arm of Peel and is off the east side of UK chart *1286* (which here wrongly labels Estero Peel as Estero Asia). It is about 23M from Isla Peel. The *caleta* is on the south

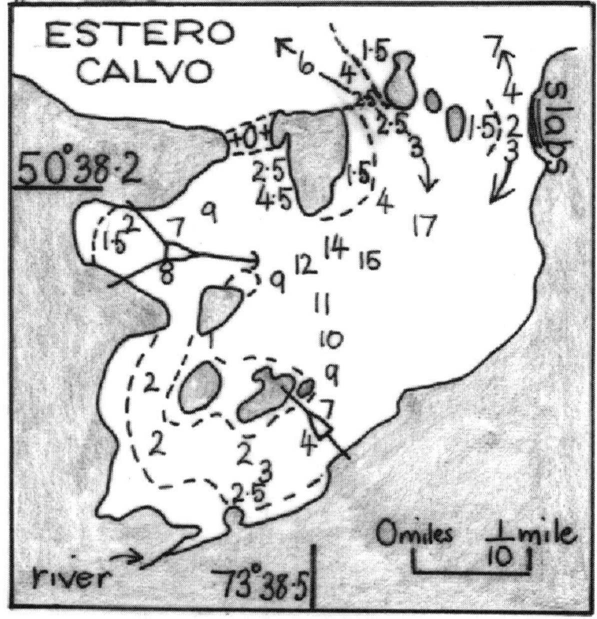

Caleta Pelagic. (Charted positions)

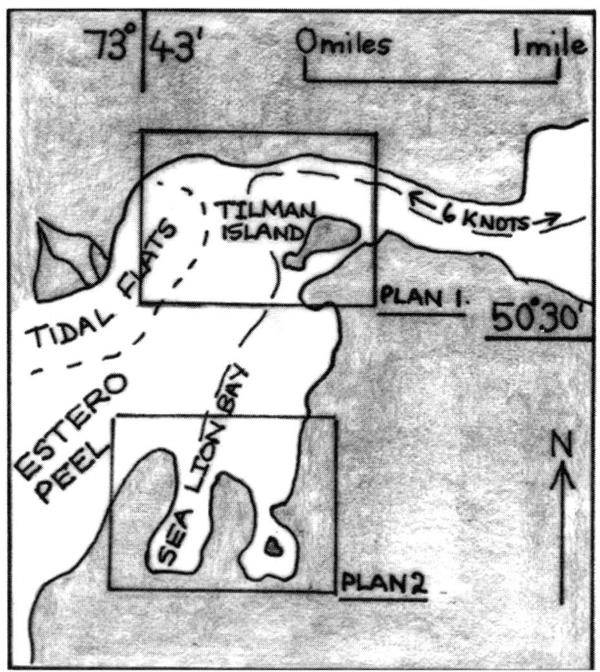

Mischief Narrows

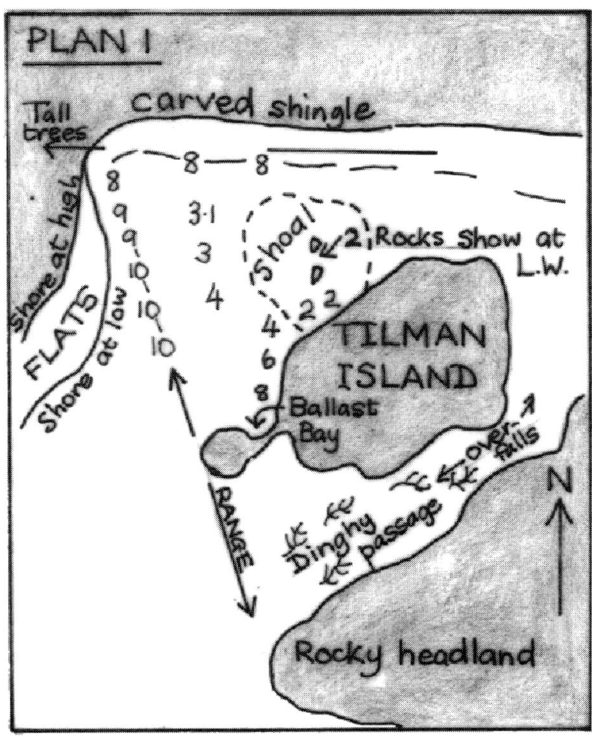

Proctor's Folly – The Narrows

side of the entrance of Estero Calvo. Its entrance is between rocks, is narrow and may be blocked by grounded bergy bits. To enter by the eastern track shown on the plan keep close to the east shore – about 3m from the slab shore. The better entrance is further to the west as shown on the sketch plan. It is worth having a fall-back anchorage in case this *caleta* is blocked by ice.

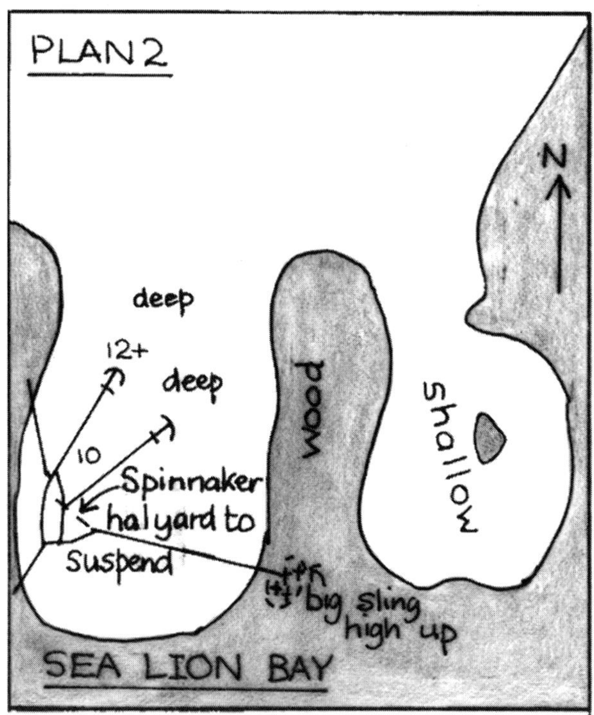

Sea Lion Bay. (Charted positions)

6·22D Sea Lion Bay

50°30'·5S 73°43'W

General

Sea Lion Bay lies just before Mischief Narrows. The plan shows the system used by *Pelagic* to keep their shorelines high up and under tension so that the line stayed clear of the ice. *Pelagic* described this anchorage as 'dodgey'.

It may be possible for a shallow draft, or lifting keel vessel to enter the shallow eastern bay at high water and 'bottom out' at low water. This may be a more secure long term anchorage as it would be less threatened by ice.

6·22E Angostura Mischief

50°29'·5S 73°42'·5W

General

The Chilean chart names this pass Mischief after Tilman's '*Mischief*' which was run aground here while Tilman was busy crossing the icecap. Tilman quotes Procter, who was in charge of the yacht, who having accepted they were firmly aground wrote 'For one thing we had reason to be grateful – the reef kept off the bigger bergs which had been careering down stream, spinning and breaking up with thunderous roars just before reaching us as they grounded on the edge of the reef.'

Pelagic recommends going through the narrows at slack water only as the current runs strongly at 6 knots and to do this at low water so that the shoal area along the shore can be gauged. Bergy bits run aground on the shoal area.

Continuation

6·23 Isla Hanover – Caleta Latitud

50°52'S 74°23'W

Charts

UK *1282, 1286* US Chile *10000, 914, 1002*

General

This *caleta* is on Isla Hanover at the west side of Canal Sarmiento and just north of the entrance to Estero Peel. Although it appears to be a useful place to stop *en route* to the Amalia Glacier, it is not recommended. Winds gust into the bay and NW gusts fan out and make all shores a lee shore. The possible anchorage is in 15m at the head of the bay and very long lines (100m) would be needed to provide a measure of security.

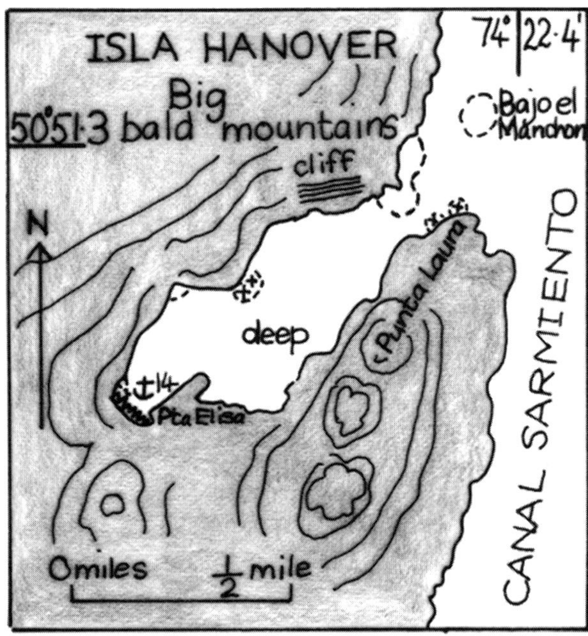

Caleta Latitud. (GPS positions)

Section 7
Canal Sarmiento to Puerto Natales and to Islote Fairway

Canal Sarmiento

Charts
UK charts do not cover the area east of 73°20'W. Large scale US charts only cover the southern part of this section. The small scale chart is *22420*

7·1 Puerto Bueno
50°59'S 74°12'W

Charts
UK *1286, 1282* Chile *10000, 10370, 914, 1002*

General
Puerto Bueno lies on the east side of Canal Sarmiento near the junction with Estero Peel. The entrance is clean and wide to the south of 1518 Islote Pounds (Fl.3s17m6M white GRP tower, red bands 6m, obscured by Isla Hoskins, 144°-vis-156°). The northwestern passage between Islote Pounds and Isla Hoskins Sur has Hecate Rock in the middle and foul ground off Hoskins. Go south about Isla Pounds.

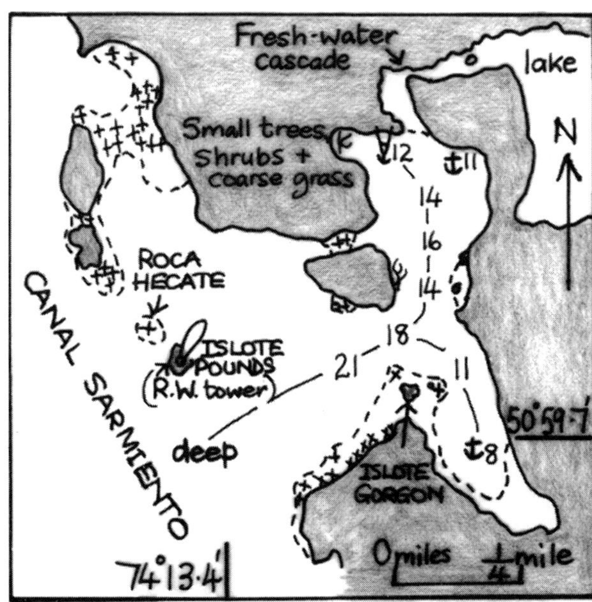

Puerto Bueno. (GPS positions)

Anchorage can be taken close to the shore at either end of the bay, depending on the winds, in 10–15m. At high water it is possible to take the dinghy right up to the base of the waterfall and fill water containers without getting out of the dinghy. From the beach near the waterfall there is an easy walk on small animal trails up to the lake. There are *centollas* in the bay. Puerto Bueno was where Sarmiento spent some time 400 years ago waiting for Drake to pass by – but Drake went into the Pacific through the Straits of Magallan.

7·2 Puerto Mayne
51°19'S 74°04'W

Charts
UK *1282* Chile *10000, 1001, 1002*

General
Puerto Mayne, on Isla Evans, is an impressive bay surrounded with barren hills and edged with trees and shrubs. It has several opportunities for anchoring. The entrance is about 100m wide, but clean. There is good holding at the head of the bay in 10m, mud bottom. Lines ashore are advisable as the bay is subject to gusts and *rachas*. Another well recommended spot is the small bay just before the narrows, in 3m at low tide. This is a four point tree-tie.

7·3 Isla Piazzi – Caleta Moonlight Shadow
51°34'·4S 74°01'·8W

Charts
UK *1282* Chile *10000, 1001*

General
Caleta Moonlight Shadow cuts deep through the low-lying land at the north end of Isla Piazzi. It is a very secure and sheltered anchorage and there is little danger of *rachas*. The entrance is a little hard to find; the co-ordinates noted are for the GPS position at the entrance. The entrance is relatively narrow. Pass to the south of the group of rocks and

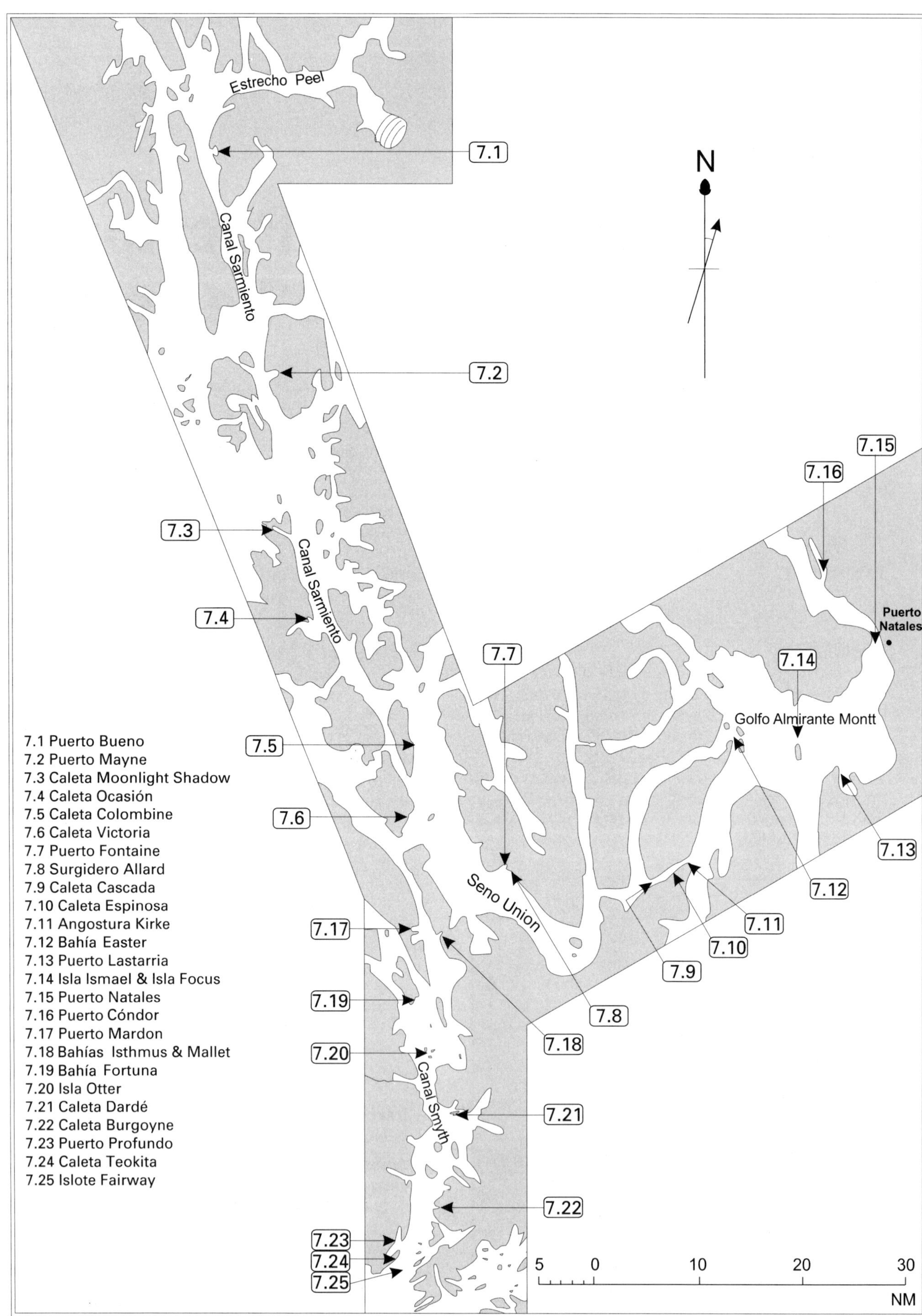
Estrecho Peel
Canal Sarmiento
Canal Sarmiento
Seno Union
Golfo Almirante Montt
Puerto Natales
Canal Smyth
N
5 0 10 20 30
NM
7.1
7.2
7.3
7.4
7.5
7.6
7.7
7.8
7.9
7.10
7.11
7.12
7.13
7.14
7.15
7.16
7.17
7.18
7.19
7.20
7.21
7.22
7.23
7.24
7.25
7.1 Puerto Bueno
7.2 Puerto Mayne
7.3 Caleta Moonlight Shadow
7.4 Caleta Ocasión
7.5 Caleta Colombine
7.6 Caleta Victoria
7.7 Puerto Fontaine
7.8 Surgidero Allard
7.9 Caleta Cascada
7.10 Caleta Espinosa
7.11 Angostura Kirke
7.12 Bahía Easter
7.13 Puerto Lastarria
7.14 Isla Ismael & Isla Focus
7.15 Puerto Natales
7.16 Puerto Cóndor
7.17 Puerto Mardon
7.18 Bahías Isthmus & Mallet
7.19 Bahía Fortuna
7.20 Isla Otter
7.21 Caleta Dardé
7.22 Caleta Burgoyne
7.23 Puerto Profundo
7.24 Caleta Teokita
7.25 Islote Fairway

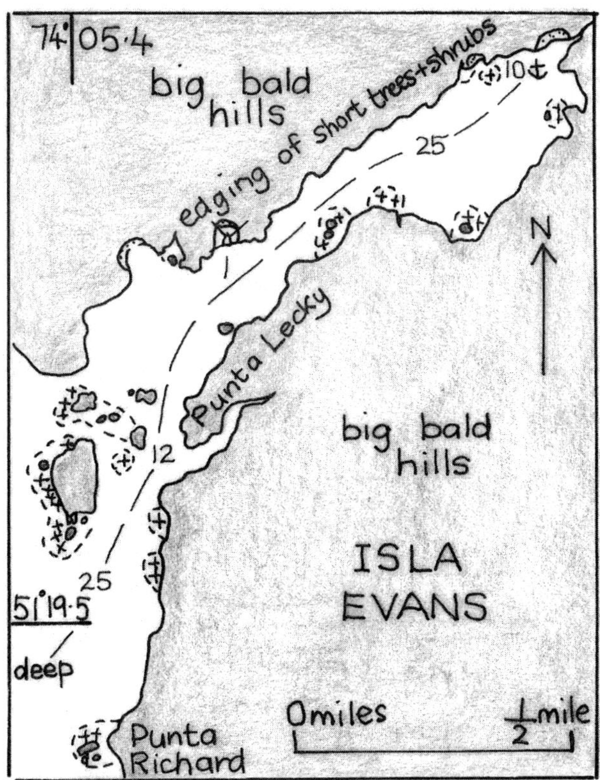

Puerto Mayne. (GPS positions)

small *islotes* on the north side of the entrance. There are long strands of kelp in it but these can be threaded through and the area is soon passed. The depths in the narrows are about 8m and then quickly increase to 15–20m. The *caleta* continues deep with no dangers mid-channel for a mile up to the anchorage (51°33'·7S 74°04'·6W by GPS), a secure nook sheltered by tall trees. Anchor in 7m and take shore lines.

A second choice anchorage is in the next bay, with adequate swinging room in about 12m, soft mud. Access is through a pass about 10m wide with minimum depth of 6m, clear of kelp in its centre.

From either anchorage it is a short distance by dinghy to the head of the Caleta. From there it is a very pleasant walk through the shore-side scrub and out onto moor-like vegetation. When the high point is reached after about half a mile there is a magnificent view over the Pacific

7·4 Isla Piazzi – Caleta Ocasión

51°42'S 74°00'W

Charts

UK *1282* Chile *1001,1002*

General

Travelling south, Caleta Ocasión on Isla Piazzi is a logical stopping place after a 45 mile run from Puerto Bueno or a visit to the Amalia Glacier. It is located on the north shore at the entrance to Abra Lecky's Retreat, itself a bay about 1·5M deep. There are two anchorages, one at the head of Caleta Ocasión itself and the other, the more sheltered, in Caleta Balandra which runs to the west off Caleta Ocasión. There is a lot of kelp and a shallow spot in the entrance to Balandra but it is deeper inside with 4–5m off the northern shore. Anchor in the middle of the bay in 6m, good holding in sand and mud. Put lines ashore.

The *caleta* appears to be used occasionally for shellfish packing.

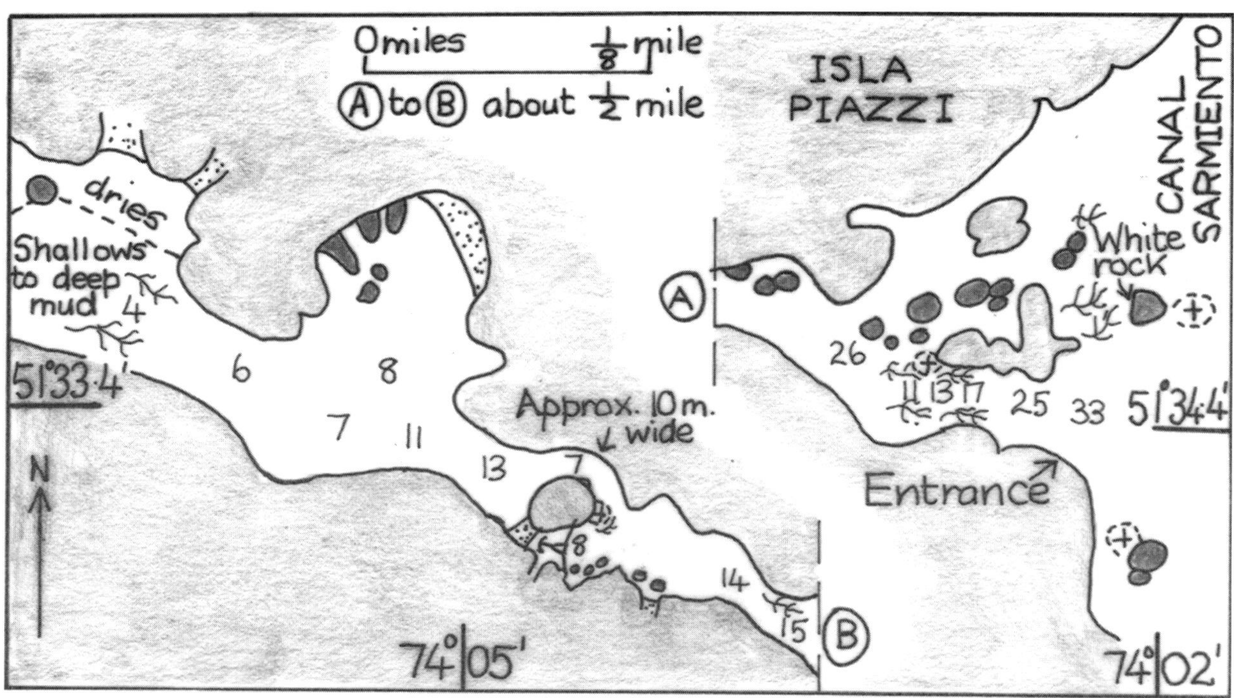

Caleta Moonlight Shadow. (GPS positions)

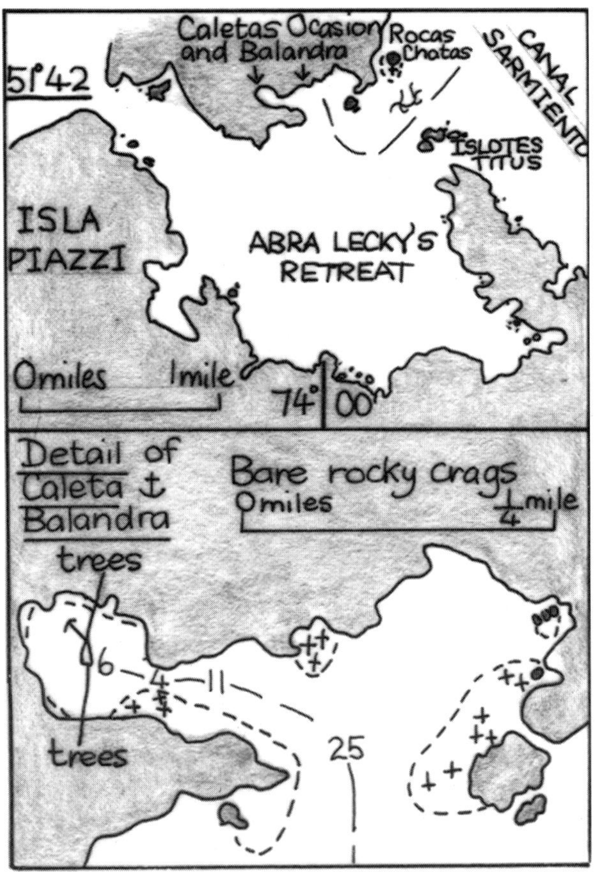

Caleta Balandra. (Charted positions)

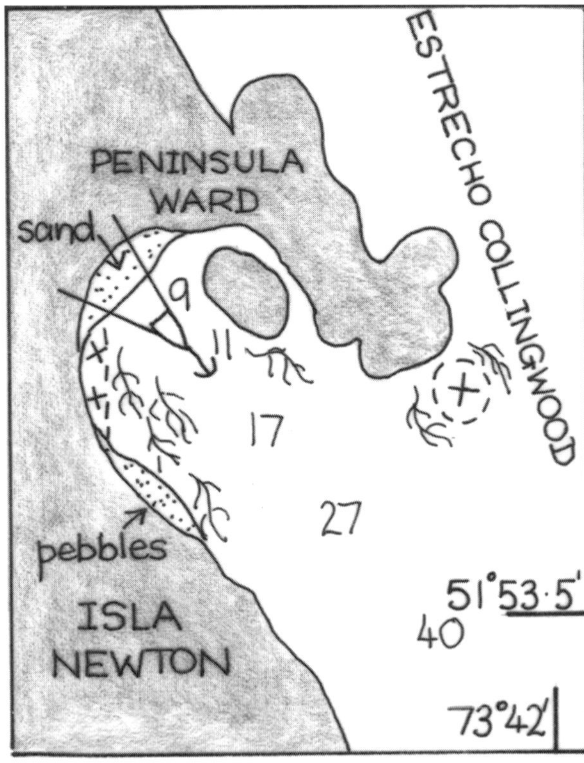

Caleta Columbine (GPS positions)

Estrecho de Collingwood

7·5 Isla Newton – Caleta Colombine

51°52'·4S 73°42'·4W

Charts

UK *1282* Chile *10000, 1007*

General

On Isla Newton, as well as being a tide station Caleta Columbine provides good shelter from north and west winds but is open to southwest winds. The entrance is clean and wide but beware of the rocky shelf that extends out from the eastern point, marked by kelp. Although the entrance to the *caleta* is clean there is considerable kelp as the head of the bay is approached. It is necessary to thread through and anchor among this. The anchorage is off the beach in 6m, sand and mud. There may be some effect from the wake of passing ships.

7·6 Isla Hunter – Caleta Victoria

52°00'S 73°45'W

Charts

UK *1282* Chile *10000, 1007*

General

This *caleta* is not named on the chart, but seems to be known by the name of the Pass on which it is

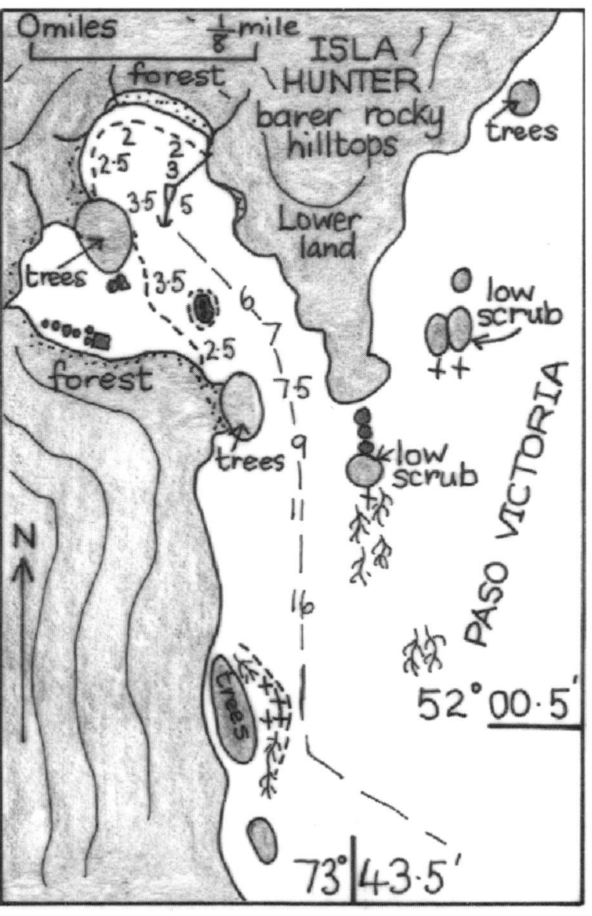

Caleta Victoria. (GPS positions)

located. It provides excellent protection from all winds. Although the entrance is open to the southwest, its not likely that any swell or wind would be a problem in the anchorage. The entrance is clean as long as it is approached on a course around 030°, with care taken to avoid the rocks and kelp that extend a considerable distance out from the islands that are the southern protection to the *caleta*. The entrance is 10m deep and inside it shoals to 4–5m. There is a large rock in the middle, shown on the sketch plan, which may cover at high water. The water is clear and the extent of this rock can be seen under the water. The bottom of the *caleta* is kelp-covered initially but beyond the rock becomes clear. Anchor in silt and take a line ashore. The *caleta* is used by small-boat fishermen from Puerto Natales.

Diversion

Seno Union and Golfo Almirante Montt to Seno Ultima Esperanza via Puerto Natales

General

Puerto Natales is a long detour for yachts *en route* south or north. Before commencing the approach to Puerto Natales, there is a secure anchorage in Caleta Victoria at the southern end of Isla Newton. From there it is about 60 miles to Puerto Natales with no really secure anchorages. Puerto Natales itself is a fairly marginal anchorage. However the passage is spectacular and Puerto Natales is an excellent place for a crew change, to visit the Torres del Paine and to restock.

It is also possible to sail north from Puerto Natales up Seno Ultima Esperanza. The inner parts of this *seno* offer fantastic views of and access to mountains and glaciers. It is a national park and takes the yacht very close to Torres del Paine. Tourism is being developed with 70,000 tourists visiting the Torres del Paine each year.

Charts

UK *1282* Chile *1001*

Leaving Canal Collingwood, the route is through Seno Union, along Canal Morla Vicuña, either through Canal White or Canal Kirke and then across Golfo Almirante Montt passing west of Isla Focus. The route in fact passes through the Andes and is one of the most spectacular waterways in Chile, particularly Estero de las Montañas which runs north for more than 70 miles just prior to the entrance to Canal Morla Vicuña. Although it is possible to reach Natales in one day, the necessity to transit the narrows in Canal Kirke at slack water or the occurrence of strong winds on the eastern side of the Andes often means a two day trip. Canal Kirke is the preferred route as it is shorter and fewer obstacles, but Canal White is more spectacular. In early 1998 Canal Kirke was the only authorised route although the *Armada* state that Canal White will be an approved route in the future.

Some anchorages along the route are described below. Others are

- Puerto Condell at the southern entrance of Canal Santa Maria which leads to Canal White (Charts *1101* and *1104*). It is a bay wide open to the south. The anchorage is close to the beach just west of the south side of Isla Margarita. Anchor in 6m in sand. The anchorage provides protection from the north. A little susceptible to *rachas*.
- Caleta Zorro at the eastern end of Kirke (Charts *1101* and *1062*, sketch at Angostura Kirke below). This bay is clear and deep to its head if entered on a central line. It would be possible to anchor close to the head in about 14m and take shore lines or to tie to the shore near the southern entrance, where fishermen have fixed tyres to make a mooring point. Caleta Zorro is open to the west.
- Caleta Chandler, Canal White. (51°56'·2S 73°00'·7W). This is a good anchorage to use when waiting for a fair tide through Canal White. The entrance to the Caleta is deep and clear. Although not shown on the chart (Chilean *1102*) there is a small indentation about half way up the Caleta on the north shore. It is possible to anchor in 8–15m just outside this indentation and then tie fore-and-aft across it.

Seno Union

7·7 Península Las Montañas – Puerto Fontaine

52°04'S 73°28'W

Charts

UK *1282* Chile *1007, 1101, 10650*

General

Puerto Fontaine is not a good, but a possible, anchorage on the northeast shore of Seno Union, opposite Cabo Año Nuevo. It is sheltered either side of north but poor in south to southeast winds. Río Bermudez comes in at the north shore; anchor outside it in 5–10m but go carefully towards the river mouth as it forms banks. Away from the río, it is deep and very difficult to tie a line ashore.

Laguna Adelaide, fresh water, has depths of 10–12m and it may be possible to get to it up Río Bermudez by keeping to the east shore. It is very narrow and it would be necessary first to explore by dinghy. Waterfall.

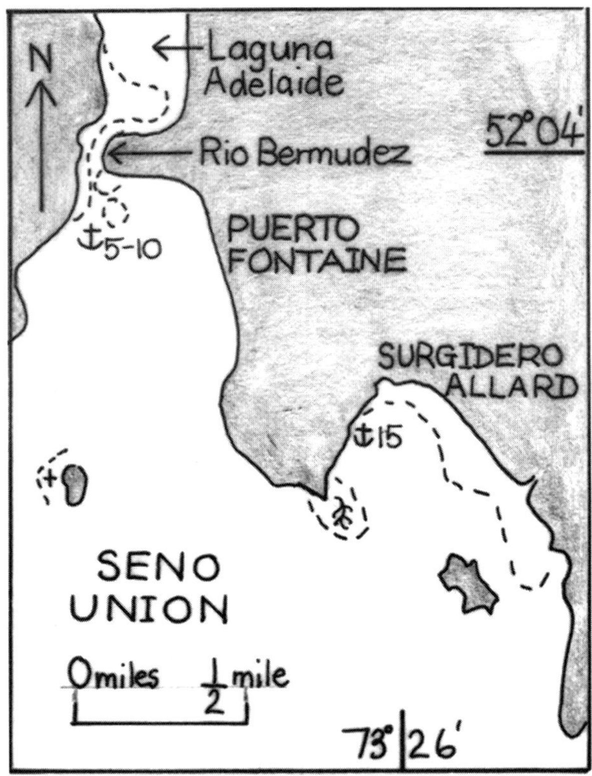

Puerto Fontaine and Surgidero Allard. (Charted positions)

7·8 Península Las Montañas – Surgidero Allard

52°04'S 73°25'W

Charts
UK *1282* Chile *10650, 1101, 1003*

General
Surgidero Allard is on the north side of Seno Union immediately to the southeast of Puerto Fontaine. It provides good shelter from west winds, though it is exposed to southerly winds. The holding is good on a sand bottom

Canal Kirke

7·9 Isla Diego Portales – Caleta Cascada

52°04'·8S 73°05'·1W

Charts
Chile *1101, 10650, 1062*

General
Caleta Cascada is a reasonable anchorage before Canal Kirke. The entrance is easy and clear from the south west. Anchor in about 12m. Good holding. The bay is protected from the west, north and east.

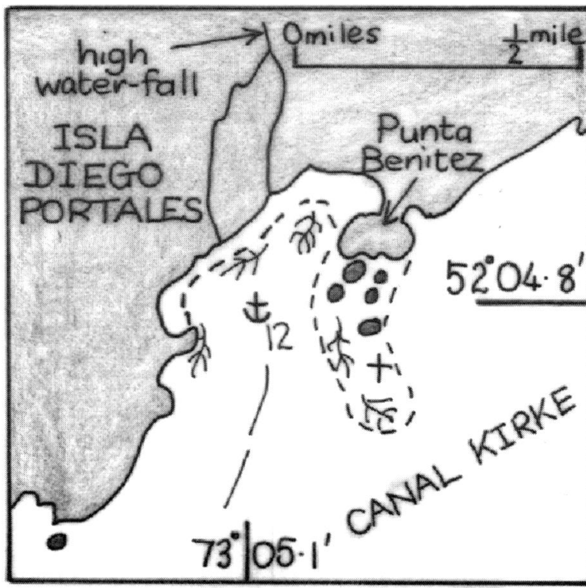

Caleta Cascada. (GPS positions)

7·10 Isla Diego Portales – Caleta Espinosa

52°06'S 73°03'·5W

Charts
Chile *1101, 10650, 1062*

General
Caleta Espinosa is about 1·5M from the southwest end of Canal Kirke and half way to Angostura Kirke. The bays on both sides of the island have been visited; they are both deep (20m plus) and neither were inviting as an anchorage. If waiting some hours for the tide, Caleta Cascada would be better.

7·11 Angostura Kirke

52°03'S 73°00'·7W

Charts
Chile *10650, 1062*

General
Canal Kirke is a narrow pass draining the huge *esteros* that run 30 miles north and south from Puerto Natales. As a result tidal streams can run at 8–10kt in the narrows and at times more than this. Both the *Armada* and local fishermen treat the pass with respect and traverse it at slack water. Times of slack water can vary by as much as an hour. The time of low water is more reliable and the stand is longer than at high water. At slack water in calm conditions the traverse of the pass is straightforward with a 1–2 knot current and little sign of disturbance on the water. It is probably wise to arrive at the pass a short time before slack water and commence the traverse with the current running weakly counter to the yacht direction. This would allow the yacht to hang back if conditions are not right and then go through dead on slack.

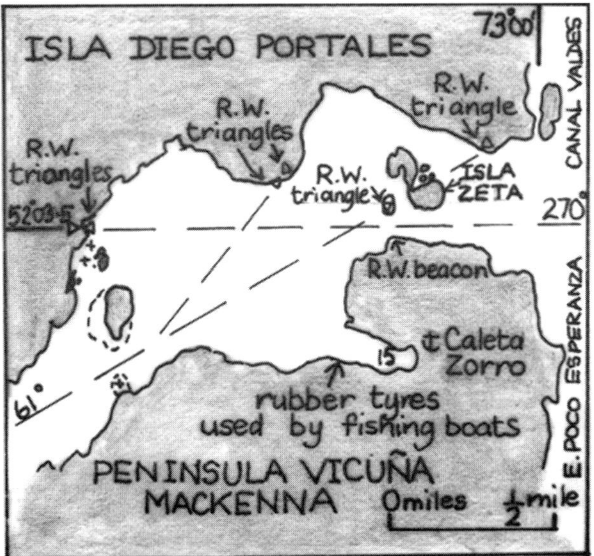

Canal Kirke. (GPS positions)

When moving eastwards, after passing Isla Medio Canal it may be wise to head up towards Punta Escoben, about 039°, in order to identify the leading marks. These are two posts with orange triangles and white borders, on the west shore 400m north of Isla Medio Canal. The line, 090°-vis-270°, leads between Punta Restinga and Isla Merino.

Canal Valdes

7·12 Isla Diego Portales – Bahía Easter

51°55'S 72°54'W

Charts
Chile *1101, 1102*

General
Bahía Easter is at the northeast end of Isla Diego Portales, behind Islas Lavaqui, about 1·5M south of the northern entrance to Canal White. It has good shelter in depths of 11m, sand. There are shallows in the middle of the entrance and round the north edge of the bay.

Golfo Almirante Montt

7·13 Bahía Desengaño – Puerto Lastarria

51°56'S 72°38'W

Charts
Chile *1101, 1104*

General
Located 15 miles south of Puerto Natales, Puerto Lastarria is a large open bay which provides good shelter from west to northwest winds behind the low land on its western side. The holding is very good in heavy clay about 8m, close along the western shore. In strong southerly wind the bay is sufficiently large that the anchorage becomes fairly choppy. In these conditions better shelter may be found at the SE corner of the bay.

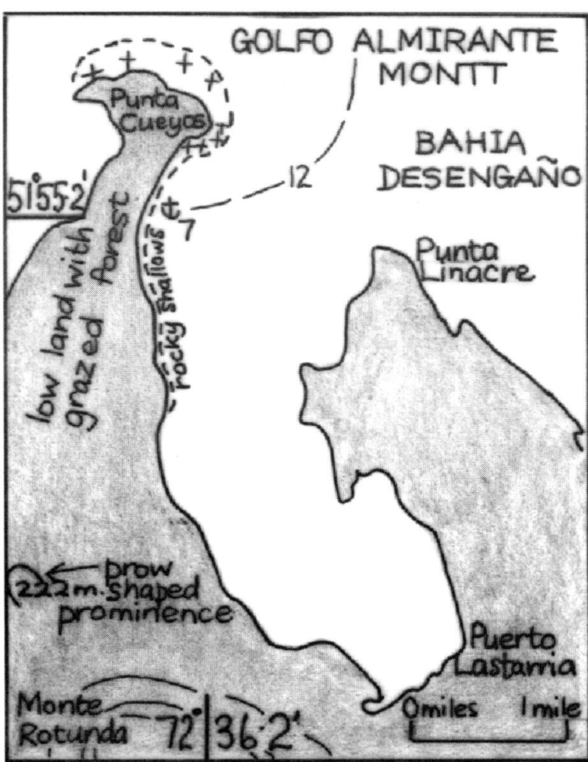

Puerto Lastarria. (Charted positions)

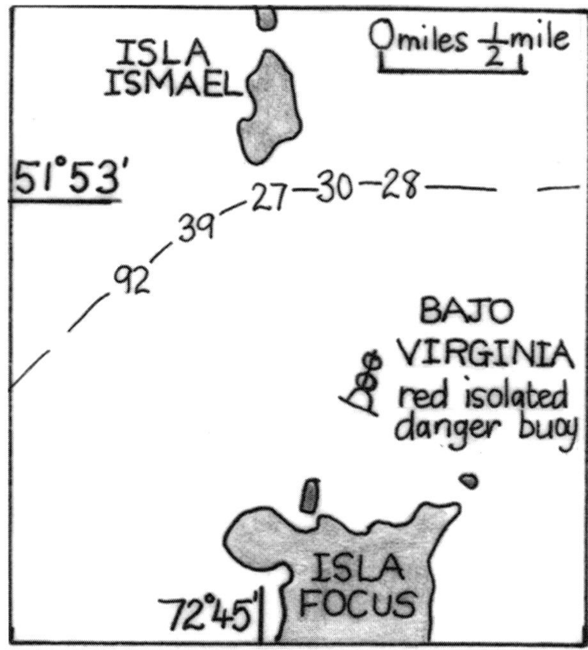

Route between Isla Focus and Isla Ismael. (Charted positions)

7·14 Passage between Isla Ismael and Isla Focus

Charts
Chile *1101*

General
The route between these two islands taken by all fishing boats and the Navimag ferry is to pass about half a mile south of Isla Ismael, as shown on the sketch chart. Depths are much greater than those suggested on the chart with a minimum depth of about 27m if this line is followed.

7·15 Puerto Natales
51°45'S 72°32'W

Charts
Chile *1101, 1135*

Port communications
VHF Ch 16 c/s *PV '21 de Mayo'*

General
Puerto Natales is in fact a very poor place to visit in a yacht as the anchorage in front of the town is totally exposed to the strong northwest and west winds that seem to blow continuously, but particularly in the afternoon. Winds can change from calm to gale force with no warning. Natales is

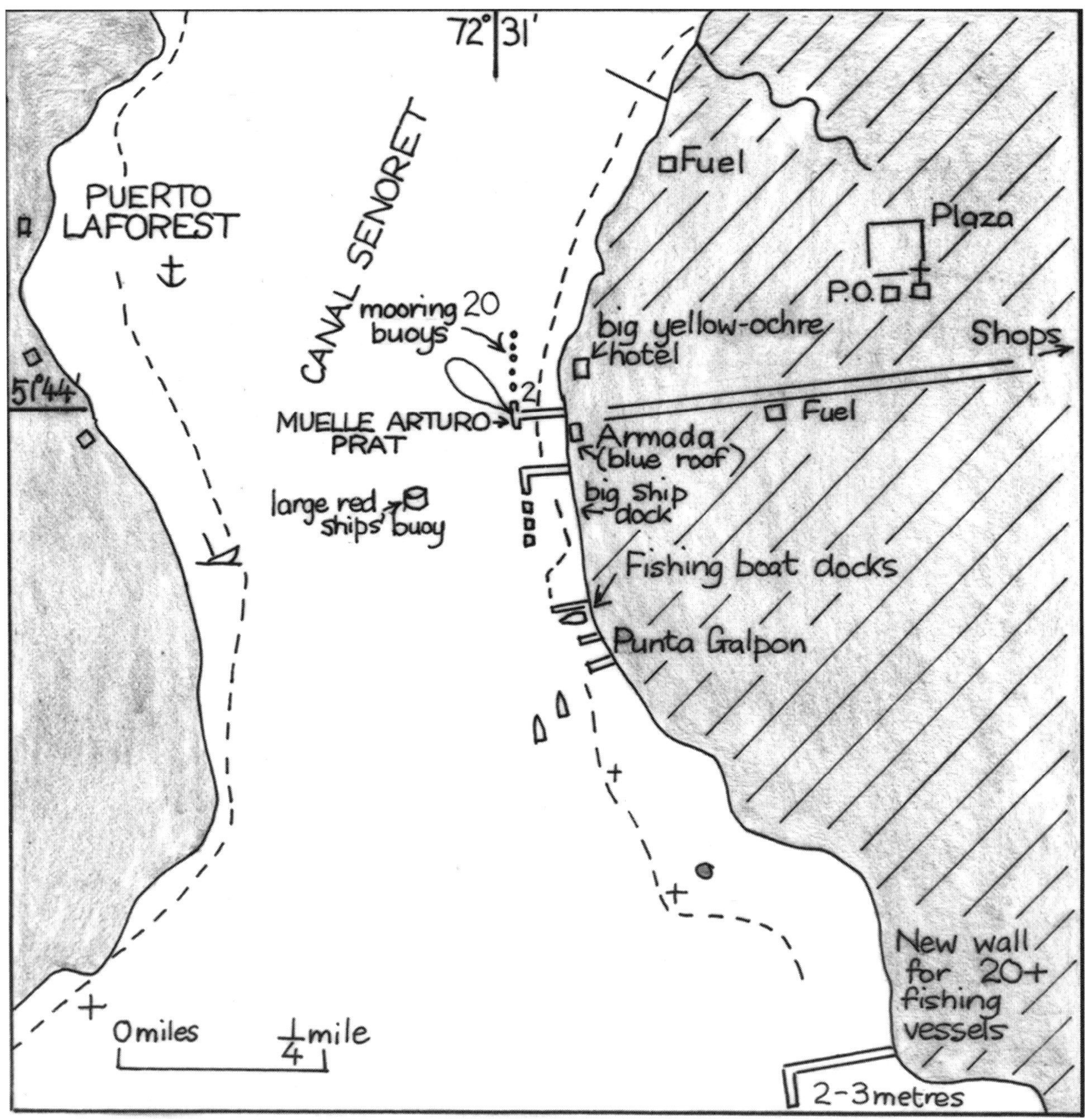

Puerto Natales. (Charted positions)

the principal town of the area serving sheep and cattle farms and the timber industry. Founded in 1912, it has a population of 19,000 and has a strong summer tourist industry, supported by hotels, restaurants and transport facilities; it is the centre for excursions to the glaciers and Parque Nacional Torres del Paine. The money position is uncertain. Banco O'Higgins accepts MasterCard. Travellers cheques attract poor rates. Cambio Stop is said to offer good rates.

Anchorage

Anchorage is off the rock-fringed shore just to the north of a group of local mooring buoys. Anchor in 10m or less, mud and sand, and open to the north. The bottom shelves very quickly. The anchorage is on a shallow shelf that extends less than a tenth of a mile off the shore. The port captain is not happy with yachts staying at anchor without crew on board as yachts have dragged ashore. It may be possible to tie up to one of the buoys. They are owned by two local men, one of whom, Konrado Alvares, owns the gaff rigged schooner, the *Penguin*, built in 1907 in the UK and used until recently as the government launch in the Falklands. Even if permission is given to use a mooring it is wise to set one or two anchors to the northwest as extra security. When the Navimag ferry arrives, it may go beyond the ship terminal dock, turn in Canal Senoret and then, with a line to the large red shipping buoy, go alongside.

The port captain also recommends obtaining permission to tie alongside at the new concrete fishing boat pier at Punta Galpon. There is a small charge for this. The water shelves quickly towards the shore. This pier is very secure from the strongest winds but general security may be a problem as there is a transient population of fishing boats.

It is possible to anchor beside the salmon pens on the shore opposite Puerto Natales at Puerto Laforest to obtain protection from the north and west winds, but the strong winds can make it almost impossible to travel by dinghy across the 3/4 mile stretch between this anchorage and Puerto Natales.

Formalities

The *Capitanía* is a blue-roofed building between the main shipping pier and Muelle Arturo Prat.

There are immigration authorities in Puerto Natales who can authorise a 3 month extension to visa. Alternatively, it is only about 1 hour to the Argentinean border where you can clear back in to Chile.

Facilities

Diesel the nearest pump is on the corner of Bulnes and Militar, two blocks in from the *capitanía.* It is also possible to fill up alongside the fishing boat pier at Punta Galpon. Shell has a mobile truck with diesel; ask at the office on the pier for details.

Water from the pier.

Supermarkets on Bulnes, 3rd and 10th blocks. Other markets and stores – shop around. Excellent fresh fruit and vegetable shops.

Laundry Lavandería Papaguyao, Bulnes 518; Tienda Milodron, Bulnes.

Dentist Dr. Nelson Zuniga, whose clinic is conveniently located on one of the streets surrounding the main square.

Communications

Air Ladeco, Bulnes 530. Buses to Punta Arenas, Puerto Montt, Argentina.

Car hire if renting a car, be sure the spare tyre is in good condition as the road to Torres del Paine is unpaved.

Telephone Area code 61. Office Eberhard 417.

7·16 Estero Ultima Esperanza – Puerto Cóndor

52°40'S 72°41'W

Charts

Chile *1101, 1103*

General

About 8 miles north of Puerto Natales, Puerto Cóndor provides excellent shelter from the prevailing westerly winds and a marvellous place for hiking and viewing the spectacular mountain ranges to the north and west. There are a number of interesting species of birds in the area including flamingos, coots, owls and condors. Estero Eberhardt, which runs north from Puerto Cóndor, is a great spot to explore by dinghy.

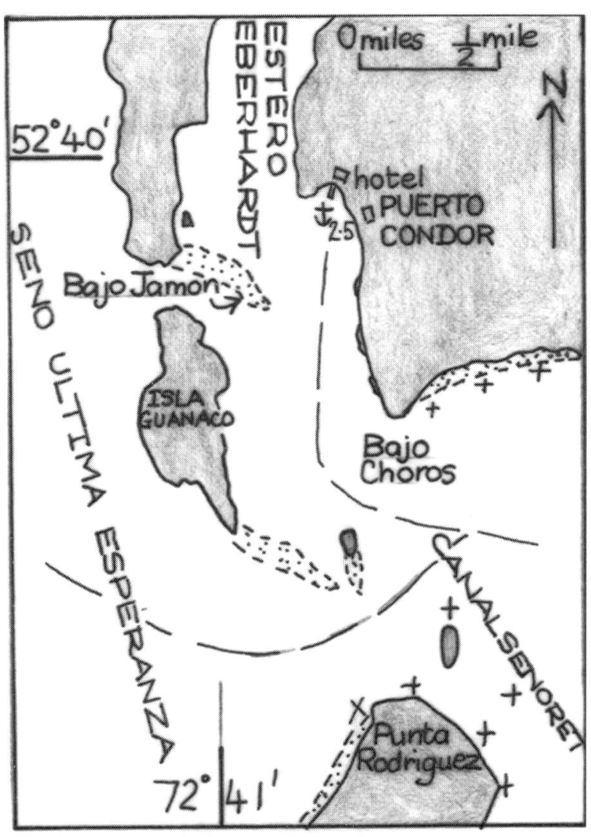

Puerto Condor. (Charted positions)

Seno Ultima Esperanza

General

Chilean chart *1101* shows only part of this area and has no soundings and navigating this area has been described as sailing on the white. The route taken by yacht *Felice* is shown by the sketch plan. Different water temperatures can return deceiving depths on the depth sounder. Chilean chart *1103* and the plan of Puerto Condor give the details of entering the Seno. This is the most difficult part.

The following notes relate to the sketch plan of the Seno:

1. In a small bay by the delta of the mouth of the Rio Serrano a new hostel has been built. The hostel has a good pier but with only 1·7m depth. There is not very good anchoring in the bay with depths falling rapidly from 5 to 20m. Anchor in deep water and take a line to the pier. The bay is open to the south and the south west.
2. A good alternative is to moor to the tourist pier at the west side of the river mouth. The pier is solid with deep water off it. It is only protected to the north and west. In the summer season the tourist boats bring visitors from Puerto Natales here for day trips and use the pier for a short time each day. It would be necessary to leave the pier for the short time that they use it.

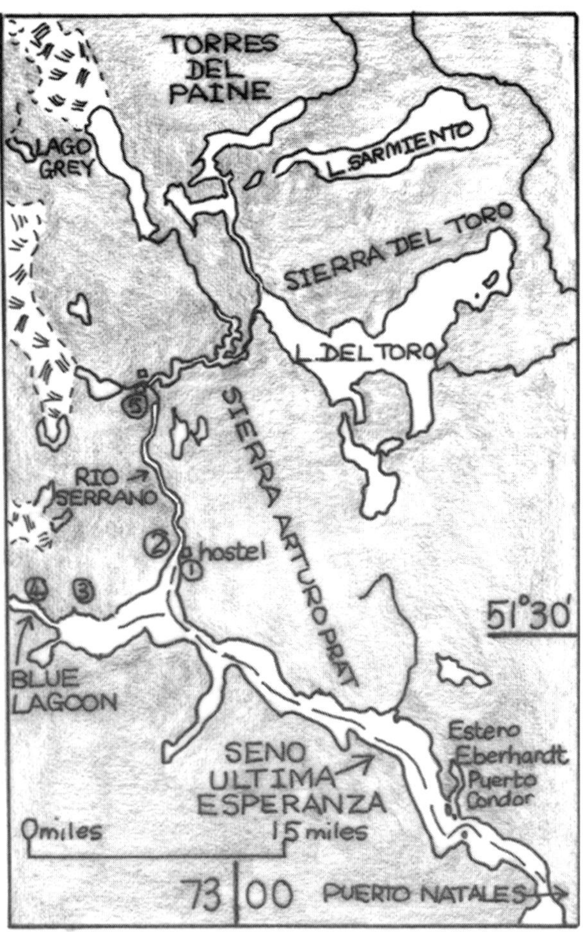

Seno Ultima Esperanza. (Charted positions)

3. An overnight mooring can be found at the west end of the Seno in the third bay east of the river entrance to the Blue Lagoon. Tie alongside the mountain wall on the port side when entering the bay. Tie off to the trees with the yacht tucked in very close to the trees.
4. There is a good dinghy trip into the Blue Lagoon. The quiet river mouth is too shallow for the yacht.
5. It is possible to travel right up the Rio Serrano with a well powered dinghy. The navigation is difficult as the current is strong and the glacier meltwater makes it impossible to see the bottom. Take care of the sand banks in the middle of the river. Branches also add a risk to the inflatable. There is only one necessary portage of about 30m and the dinghy can get right up to Lago del Toro. Tourist companies in Puerto Natales make organised trips in large zodiacs along the full length of this river.

   At position 5 there is an *estancia* about 2 hours up the river, where two big rivers meet. From here it is possible to hire horses to take a very pleasant excursion up into the mountains. The *estancia* offers lodgings.

Continuation
Isla Brinkley to Isla Tamar

The route winds south through Paso Victoria to Canal Smyth merging in to Estrecho Magallanes at Isla Tamar.

Canal Smyth

7·17 Islas Rennell – Puerto Mardon

52°09'·5S 73°42'·6W

Charts

UK *1282* Chile *1007, 1003*

General

On the western side of Canal Smyth, this anchorage within Bahía Welcome is sheltered from all winds. The entrance is narrow, and it is necessary to feel your way through the kelp. Care must be taken to avoid the rock in the centre of the channel. The anchorage is in the centre of the basin in 10m, with good holding. The very high hills that surround the anchorage suggest that it may be prone to *rachas* though none were experienced when it was blowing 30 knots from the northwest. There is a good stream for water at the head of the bay.

Bahía Welcome and Puerto Mardon. (Charted positions)

7·18 Península Zach – Bahías Isthmus and Mallet

52°10'S 73°37'·5W

Charts
UK *1282* Chile *1007, 1003*

General
Coming from the north, it is easy to spot this anchorage at the southern end of Península Zach as there is a tall rusty, red, iron beacon on the northern point. The entrance route is marked with a black and white buoy and further in by a green buoy, both of which should be left to port. Larger ships anchor in this area, but yachts can continue on to Bahía Mallet that is on the east side at the head of Bahía Isthmus. The basin shallows in the southeastern part. The anchorage is in 10m, mud. Boats have experienced *rachas* in this basin. The problem at the head of Bahía Isthmus is that the isthmus itself causes air turbulence which adds to the more normal *rachas* caused by the high ground.

An alternative is to anchor where shown on the plan near the entrance to Bahía Isthmus. The surrounding land is low and less subject to *rachas*. There is a *portage* to Seno Union if anyone feels like a hike and good hiking on the surrounding hills. On a clear day Mount Burney (1760m) can be seen to the southeast.

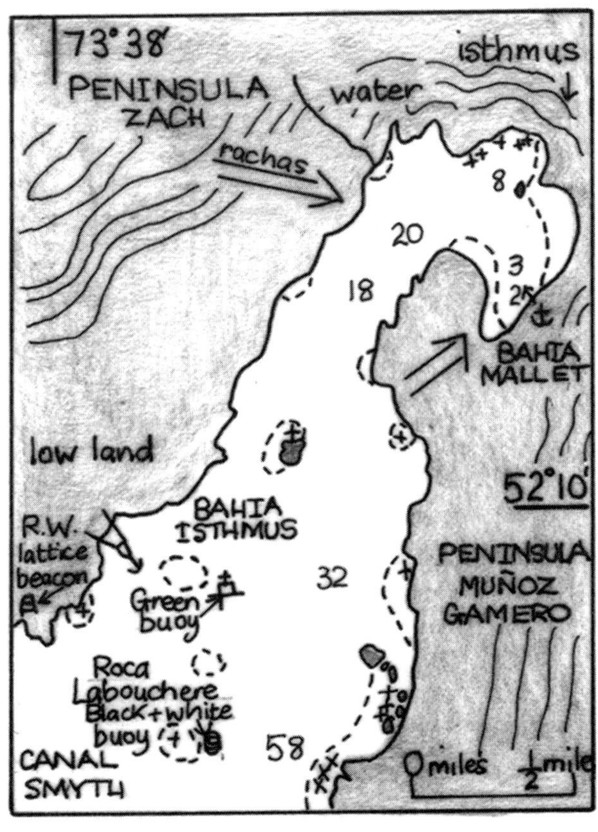

Bahía Isthmus and Bahía Mallet. (Charted positions)

7·19 Isla Baverstock – Bahía Fortuna

52°15'S 73°42'W

Charts
UK *1282, 631* Chile *1007*

General
On the east side of Isla Baverstock and 7M from Bahía Isthmus, it has protection from the north and west. It is not recommended for a night stop but has a waterfall if tanks are low. The entrance has Islote Low on its northeastern side and two other rocks just southeast of Low.

7·20 Islas Otter

52°22'·4S 73°40'W

Charts
UK *1282, 1281, 631* US *22405* Chile *1008*

General
Islas Otter are a group of islands in Canal Smyth between Isla Pedro Montt and Península Muñoz Gamero. On a northbound trip, the shelter amongst

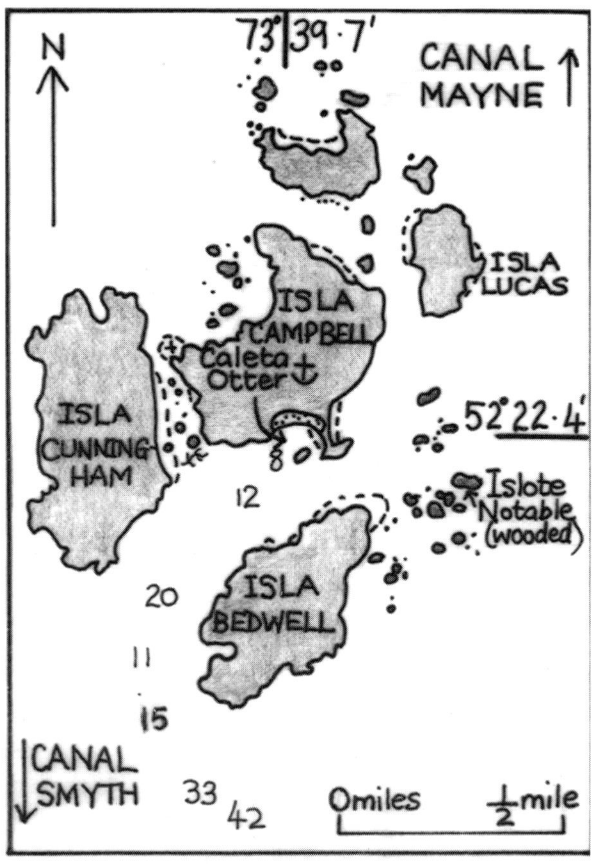

Islas Otter. (Charted positions)

these islands provides good protection from the northwest winds. The bay is open to winds from the southwest. Caleta Otter is on the south side of Isla Campbell and approached from the southwest, between Islas Cunningham and Bedwell. The anchorage is close to the shore underneath Isla Campbell, in mud.

7·21 Isleta Hose – Caleta Dardé

52°28'·5S 73°35'·3W

Charts

UK *1282, 631* US *22405* Chile *1008*

General

Caleta Dardé, named after those who first described it, is on the southwest side of the waist of Isla Hose which is at the waist of Península Muñoz Gamero. The entrance to the *caleta* is obstructed by a small unnamed island. The channel on the northwest side of this small island is not passable. The channel on its southwest side is narrow but with room enough to dodge the kelp-marked rocks if care is taken. Anchor in the *caleta* with lines to a shallow bay the northeast face of the small island, 10m. The bottom comes up quickly and there are two rocks close to the suggested position.

7·22 Caleta Burgoyne

52°37'·5S 73°39'W

Charts

UK *1282, 1281, 631* US *22404* Chile *1009*

General

On the southern part of Península Muñoz Gamero, the entrance to Caleta Burgoyne is immediately south of 1482·5Cabo Walker (Fl(3)9s11m7M White GRP tower, red bands 4m. 035°-vis-188°). The middle of the entrance is clear but within there is a rock marked by a black and white buoy, which should be left to port. Keep in the middle until a small point and two rocks have been passed to port, then make cautiously towards the bay on the north shore; the bottom comes up quickly. Anchor off in 10–15m, mud, with lines ashore. In strong westerly or southwesterly winds the small bay on the west side of the bay would be a good alternative anchorage.

Caleta Burgoyne is a good place to wait for weather in Paso Tamar and is well within range of Islote Fairway on Ch16.

7·23 Isla Manuel Rodrigues – Puerto Profundo

52°41'·05S 73°45'·41W

Charts

UK *1282, 1281, 631* US *22404* Chile *1009*

General

Puerto Profundo, towards the south east end of Isla Manuel Rodrigues, is an excellent stopping place before entering or after leaving the Straits of Magallan. It is an intricate system of waterways amongst low-lying land, and provides excellent

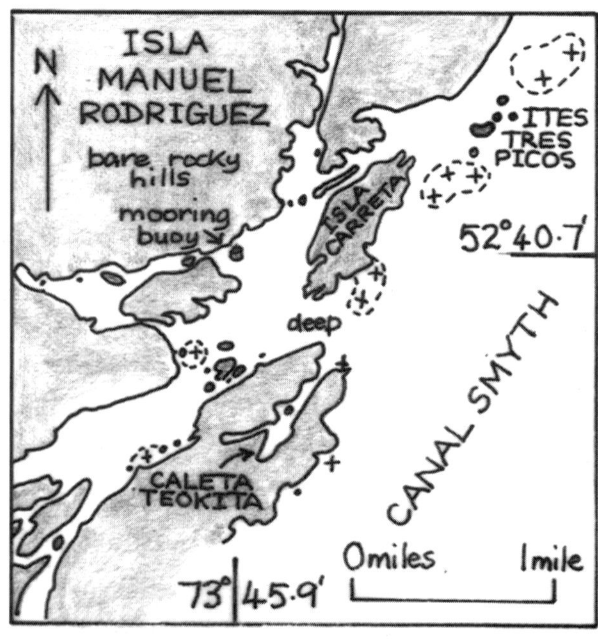

Puerto Profundo. (GPS positions)

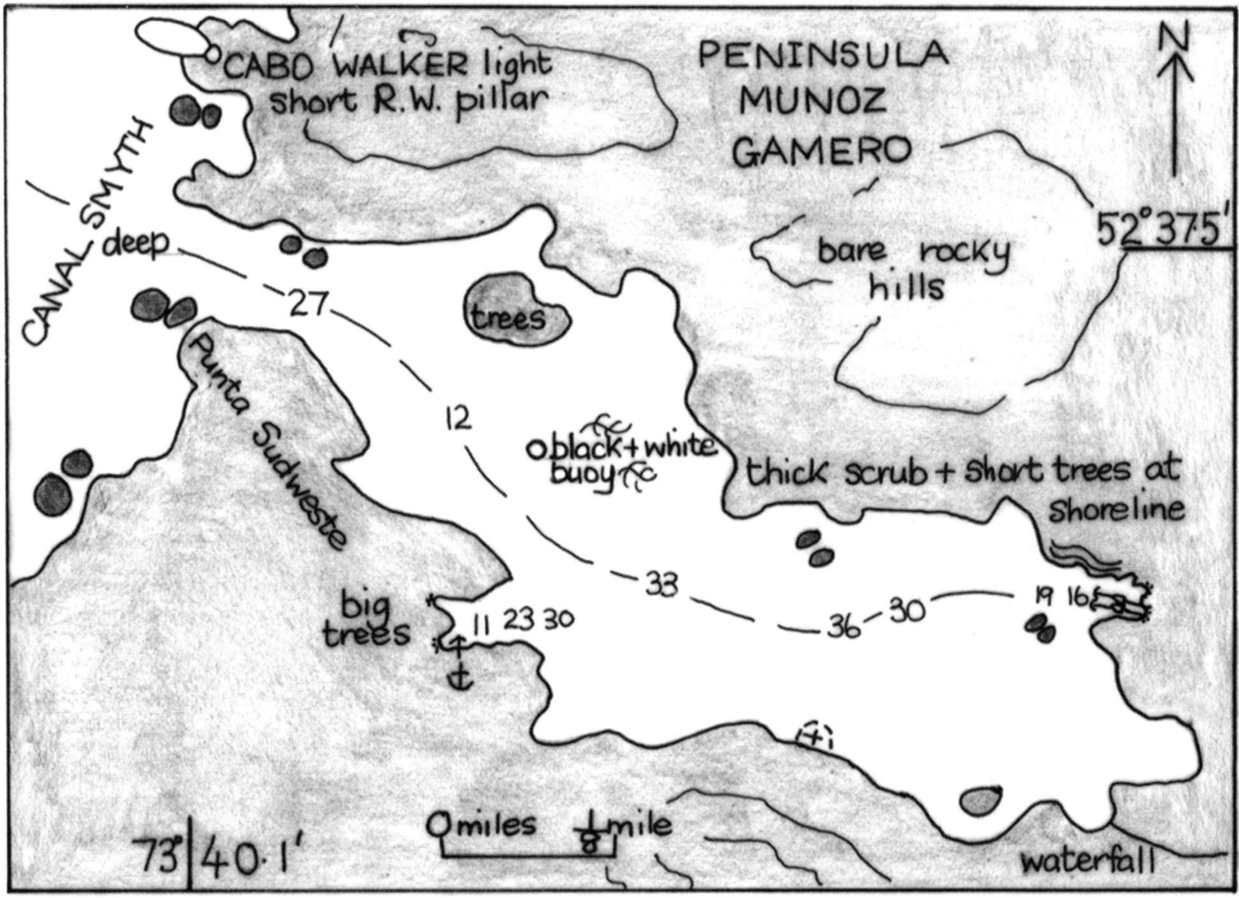

Caleta Burgoyne. (GPS positions)

shelter from all winds. The main harbour is deep, but there is a large *Armada* buoy at 52°40'·7S 73°46'·0W to which a yacht can moor with bow and stern line, or with bow line and a long line to the shore from the stern. From here it is possible to reach Fairway Light on VHF to report your position and obtain a current weather forecast. The entrance to Puerto Profundo is wide and clean, but favour the south side to avoid two rocks to the southeast of Isla Carreta.

7·24 Puerto Profundo – Caleta Teokita

52°41'·2S 73°45'·2W

Charts
UK *1282, 1281, 631* US *22404*, 22412 Chile *1009*

General
The approach to Caleta Teokita, an otherwise unnamed *caleta*, is in the southern arm of the entrance to Puerto Profundo. The entrance is narrow but is easily negotiated. There is kelp either side of the entrance but the route in is clear. The *caleta* is surrounded by low lying hills so that there is little risk of *rachas*. Proceed to the head of the *caleta* as shown on the chart and anchor in mud in about 6m with shore lines. It is possible to anchor very close to the beach at the head of the creek so that the yacht is tucked well under the trees. Caleta Teokita provides better shelter than Puerto Profundo.

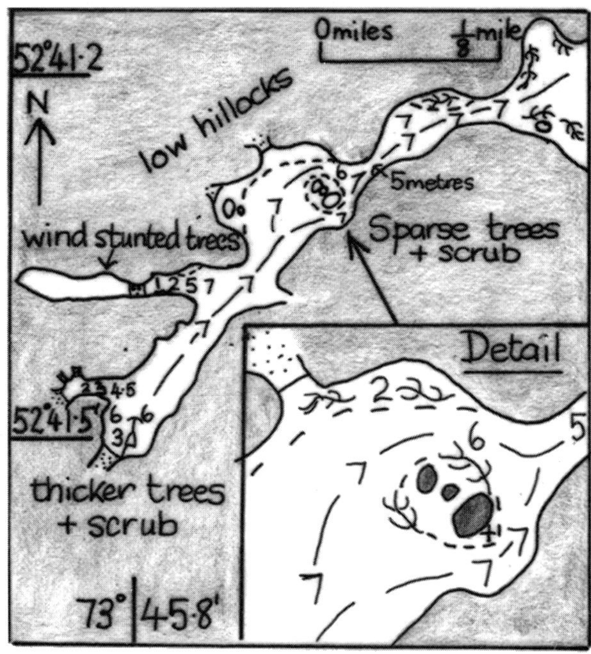

Caleta Teokita. (GPS positions)

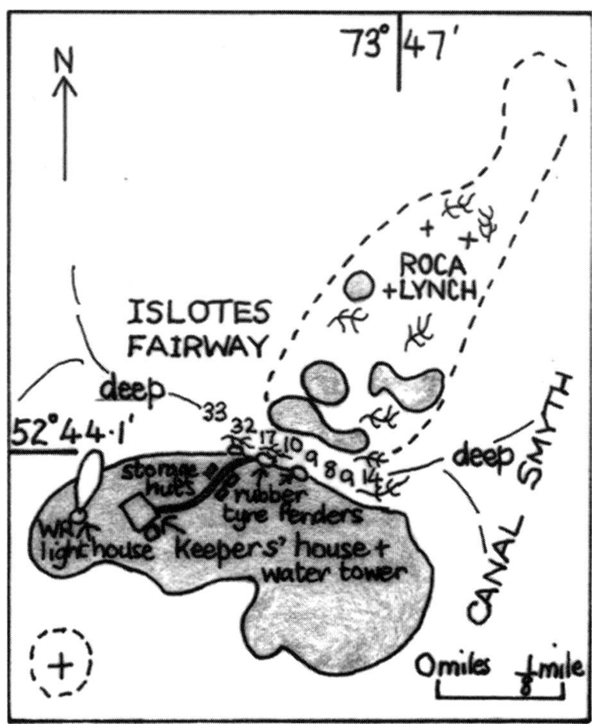

Isla Fairway lighthouse. (Charted positions)

7·25 Islote Fairway

52°43'·9S 73°46'·9W

Charts
UK *1282, 1281, 631* US *22404, 22412* Chile *1009, 11100, 11131*

Light
1480 Islote Fairway Fl.5s38m18M White tower, orange bands 5m 268°-vis-266°. VHF Ch16 c/s *CBM4.*

General
The lighthouse keepers are very hospitable and welcome yachts making a social call at the light. It is possible to moor against large rubber tyres against the north shore of Islote Fairway. Approach either from the west, or via the narrow passage between the *islote* and the small *islote* to its north.

Section 8
The Straits of Magallan, Tamar to Dungeness

8·1 Isla Tamar – Caleta Rachas

52°54'S 73°48'W

Charts
UK *1281, 1282, 631* US *22412* Chile *1114, 11100, 11131*

General
Caleta Rachas is on the east side of Isla Tamar. Reports on the anchorage vary. It has been known to be mirror calm when outside it has been NW F5–6. More often, it has lived up to its name. Be safe and get lines ashore.

Approach
From the north, the approach around the northeast corner of Isla Tamar, Paso Roda, is difficult to identify. The entrance lies between Rochas Izquierdas (the beacon, missing in 1996, was back in place in 1997), and Punta Grup. Great care is needed. Rocks seaward of the Izquierdas need to be

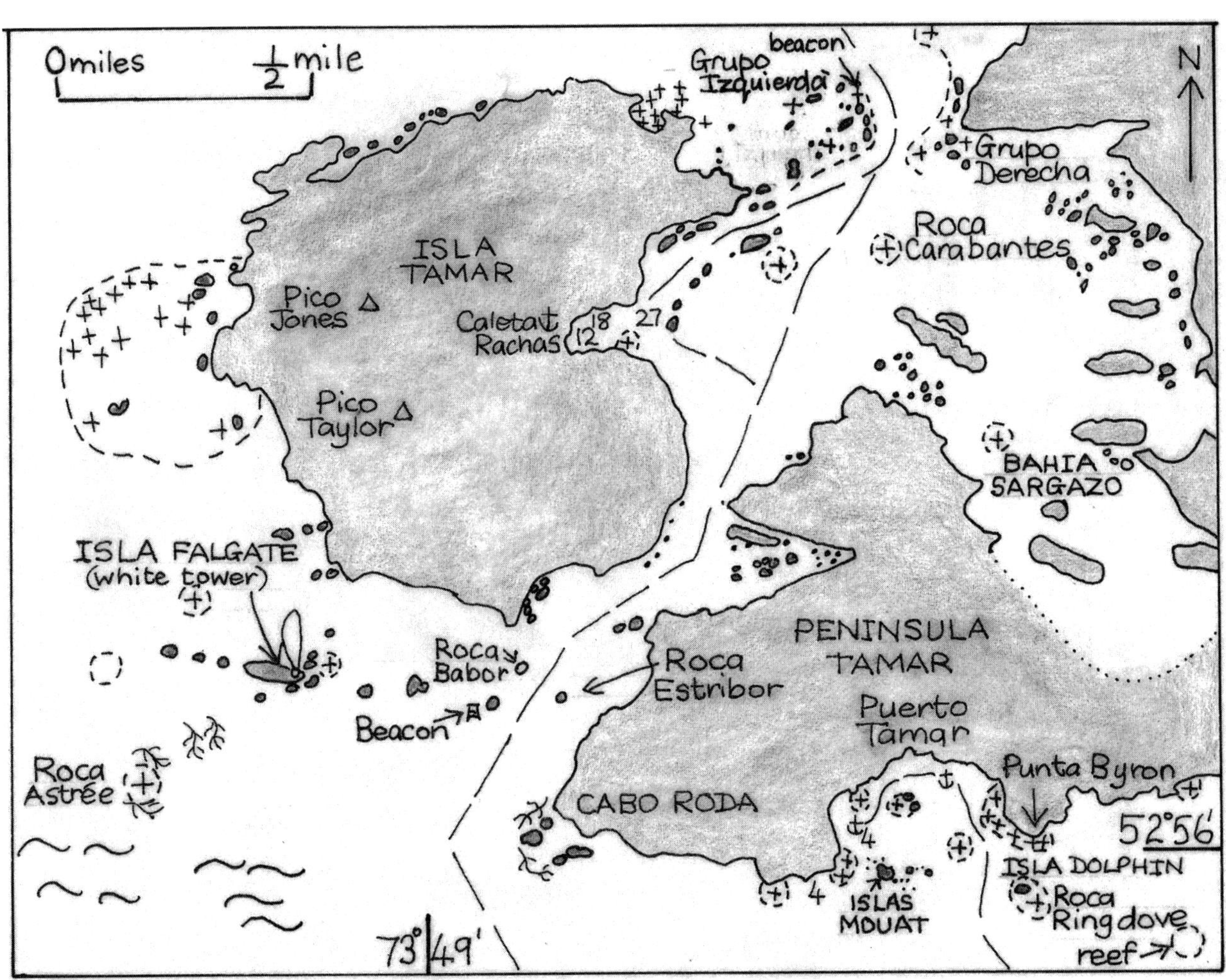

Paso Roda, Caleta Rachas and Puerto Tamar. (Charted positions)

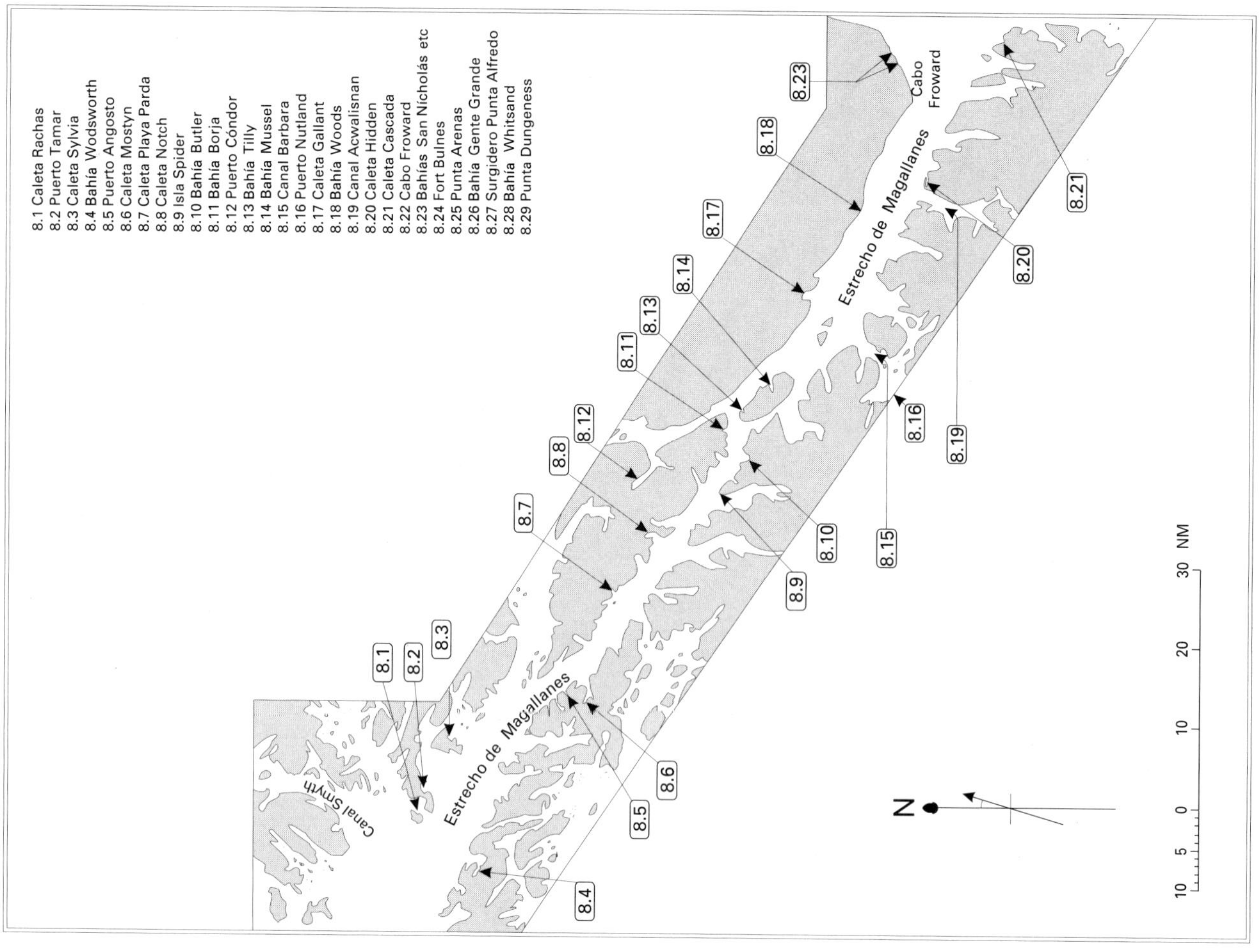
8.1 Caleta Rachas
8.2 Puerto Tamar
8.3 Caleta Sylvia
8.4 Bahía Wodsworth
8.5 Puerto Angosto
8.6 Caleta Mostyn
8.7 Caleta Playa Parda
8.8 Caleta Notch
8.9 Isla Spider
8.10 Bahía Butler
8.11 Bahía Borja
8.12 Puerto Cóndor
8.13 Bahía Tilly
8.14 Bahía Mussel
8.15 Canal Barbara
8.16 Puerto Nutland
8.17 Caleta Gallant
8.18 Bahía Woods
8.19 Canal Acwalisnan
8.20 Caleta Hidden
8.21 Caleta Cascada
8.22 Cabo Froward
8.23 Bahías San Nicholás etc
8.24 Fort Bulnes
8.25 Punta Arenas
8.26 Bahía Gente Grande
8.27 Surgidero Punta Alfredo
8.28 Bahía Whitsand
8.29 Punta Dungeness
Canal Smyth
Estrecho de Magallanes
Estrecho de Magallanes
Cabo Froward
N
10 5 0 10 20 30 NM

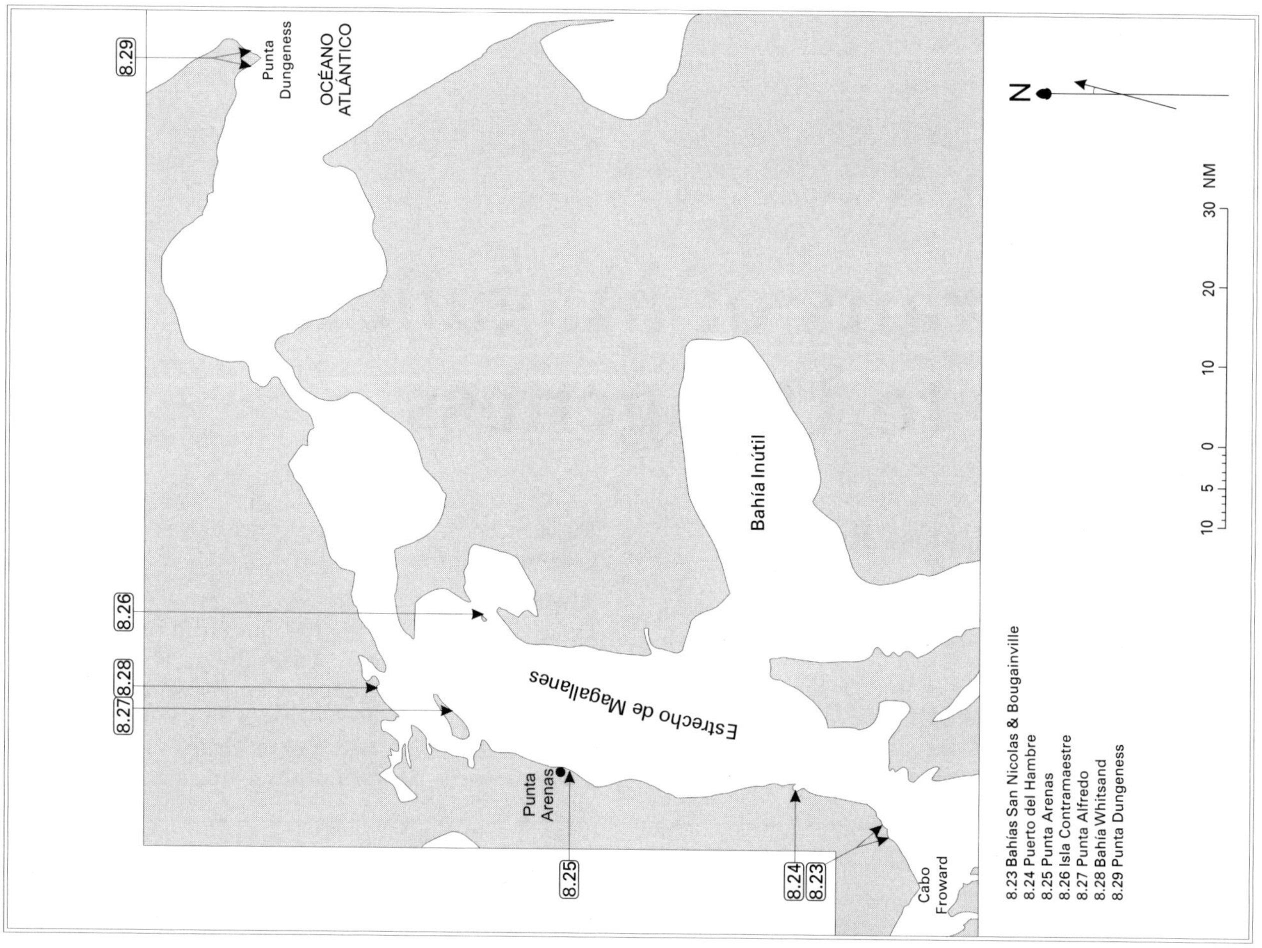
Punta Dungeness
OCÉANO ATLÁNTICO
Bahía Inútil
Estrecho de Magallanes
Punta Arenas
Cabo Froward
8.23 Bahías San Nicolas & Bougainville
8.24 Puerto del Hambre
8.25 Punta Arenas
8.26 Isla Contramaestre
8.27 Punta Alfredo
8.28 Bahía Whitsand
8.29 Punta Dungeness
N
10 5 0 10 20 30 NM

avoided. If coming from the north, hold close to the islet with the marker on it, judging distance off by the kelp. As the island comes abeam there is a barrier of kelp ahead and you should turn sharply to starboard around the marker island in order to leave the kelp and Rocas Derechas, awash, to port. The route is indicted on chart *11131*. From that point in to the anchorage the route then straightforward though the cove has several off-shore islets, the Islotes Cleto. Coming from the northeast, the passage lies between them and Tamar.

The southern entrance is more open.

Anchorage

One anchorage lies at the head of the *caleta*, in about 12m. Alternatively anchor at the head of the bay, in a notch on the N shore with the W end of the most westerly of Islotes Cleto bearing 133°, anchor and lines ashore.

8·2 Península Tamar – Puerto Tamar

52°56'S 73°46'W

Charts

UK *1281 631* US *22412* Chile *1114, 11100, 11200, 11131*

General

On the south side of Península Tamar, it has shelter from the northwest but is subject to *rachas*. Approach Puerto Tamar with the most easterly Islet of Islas Mouat in line with the prominent white mark visible on the shore. When south of the west end of Punta Byron head north to pass west of Isla Dolphin and the east of the shoal patch, which is clearly marked by kelp. Then proceed to anchor east of Isla Spencer off the beach in 5–11m depths.

Paso Largo

8·3 Isla Providencia – Caleta Sylvia

52°58'S 73°32'W

Charts

UK *1281, 631* US *22412* Chile *11200, 1115*

General

Caleta Sylvia is on the southeast side of Isla Providencia and has a hook to the northeast. The gully at the northwest corner funnels the wind and *rachas* can be strong. The rock at the entrance can be passed either side. Go up to the northeast corner and get lines to the trees on the north shore with anchors off, 10m. The tormented vegetation in Caleta Sylvia shows this to be a wild place. It is an anchorage only for use in an emergency.

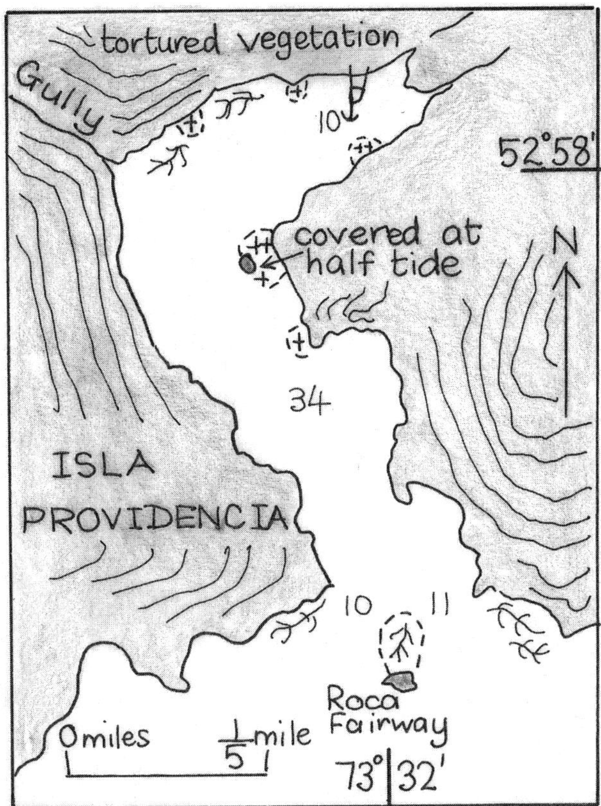

Caleta Sylvia. (Charted positions)

8·4 Isla Desolación – Bahía Wodsworth

52°59'S 74°01'W

Charts

UK *1281, 631* US *22412* Chile *11100, 1107*

General

Wodsworth, on Isla Desalación, is easy to find as the 100m waterfall into the bay is visible from the north side of the Straits 20 miles away. 1478Bahía Felix Light (Fl(2)20s29m18M White round metal tower with red bands and building, 14m) is about a mile to the north. The entrance is wide and clean, and there are no dangers in the bay. There are two possible spots to anchor, in the northwest corner, close west of the waterfall, or at the end of the eastern bay, both with lines ashore.

8·5 Isla Desolación – Puerto Angosto

53°13'S 73°20'W

Charts

UK *1281, 887* US *22412* Chile *11200, 1115*

General

On the southeast part of Isla Desolación (here called Isla Jacques on charts UK *1281* and Chile *1115*), Puerto Angosto is where Joshua Slocum received what he described as a Fuegian autograph, a shower of arrows. The anchorage has strong *rachas* and a rocky bottom. The entrance is wide, but be careful

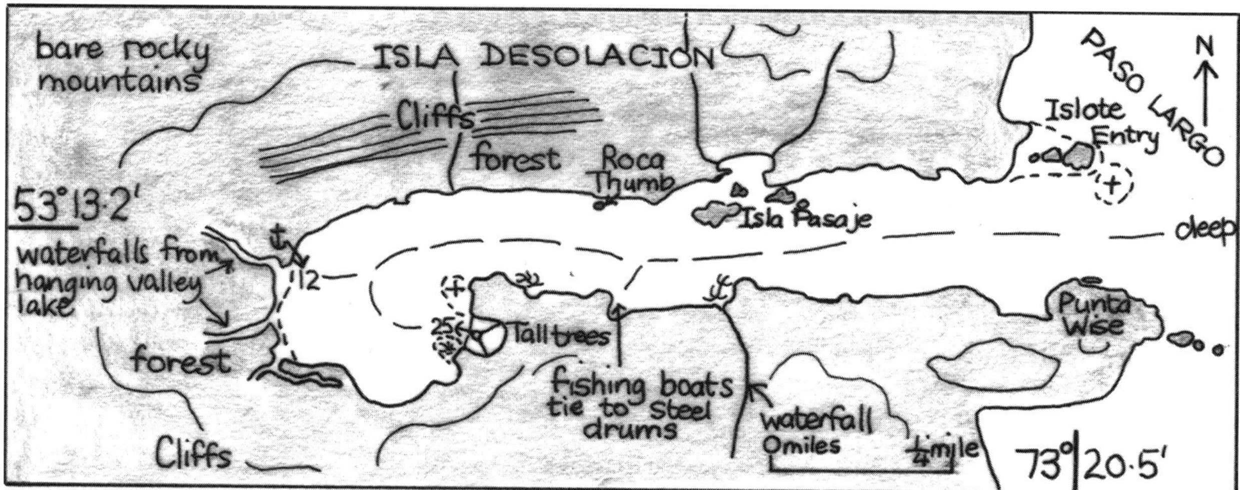

Puerto Angosto. (GPS positions)

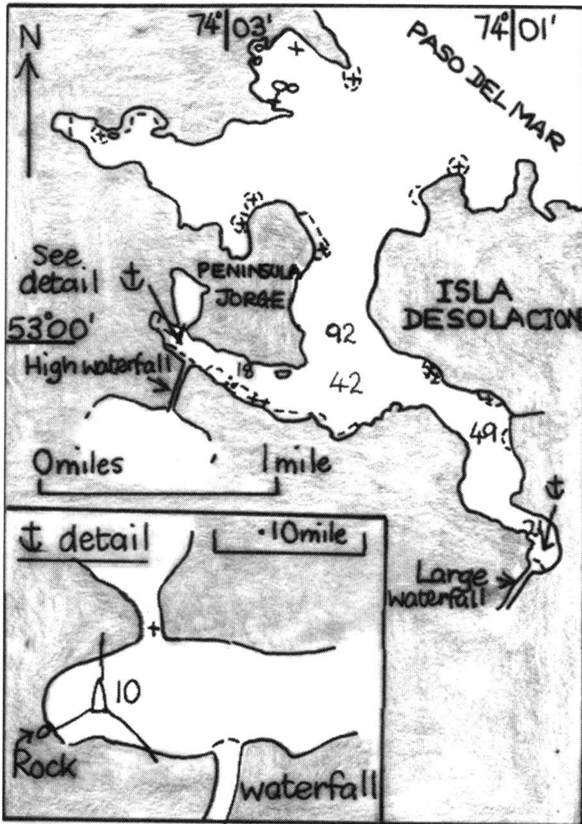

Bahía Wodsworth. (Charted positions)

of the rock off the islands on the northern shore. Once in the entrance there is immediate shelter from strong west winds. There are a number of anchorages.

- Fishermen tie up against the wall as shown on the sketch plan.
- In a notch just inside the bay proper, 6m and lines ashore
- In the small bay south of Punta Hoy. It is possible to take a 4 point line tie-off ashore as well as set anchors. This anchorage is subject to gusts but is secure.
- At the head of the bay near the waterfall with lines ashore.

8·6 Isla Desolación – Caleta Mostyn

53°16'S 73°22'W

Charts

UK *1281, 887* US *22415* Chile *11200*

General

Caleta Mostyn is the northern-most arm at the head

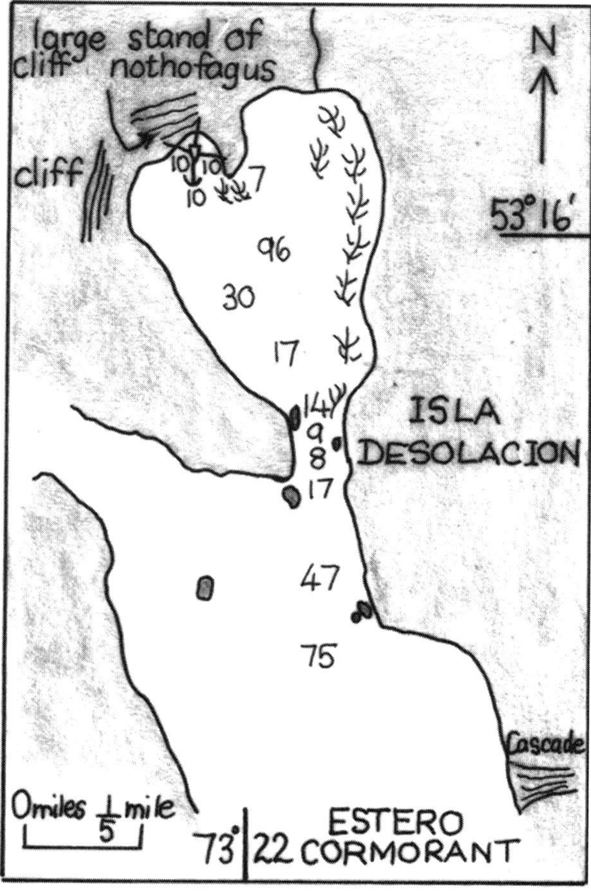

Caleta Mostyn. (Charted positions)

of Estero Cormorant on Isla Desolación. It is a small bay with a narrow entrance marked by two islets on the port side when entering and is to be found by following the northern shore of Cormorant. It has good shelter but may be exposed to south winds. Anchor in the northwest corner in 10m, mud on rock but good holding, and take a line to a good tree. The high surrounding mountains may produce *rachas*.

8·7 Península Córdova – Caleta Playa Parda

53°19'S 73°01'W

Charts
UK *1281, 887* US *22415* Chile *11200, 1118*

General
Caleta Playa Parda is one mile east-northeast of Isla Shelter, at the eastern side of the entrance to Estero Playa Parda. Spectacular scenery, good holding and room to swing. Go into the northern basin (leave Roca Svetland, in the middle of the channel, to port) 10m, mud. Some patches of soft mud but good holding in the centre of the *caleta* with the waterfall bearing 080°. Sheltered from the southwest but said to be subject to *rachas* in northwesterlies, when Caleta Notch, 10M east, may be a better choice of anchorage. Estero Playa Parda, a long inlet about a mile to the west of Caleta Playa Parda, is mentioned in *Mantellero's Guide* as being used by fishermen.

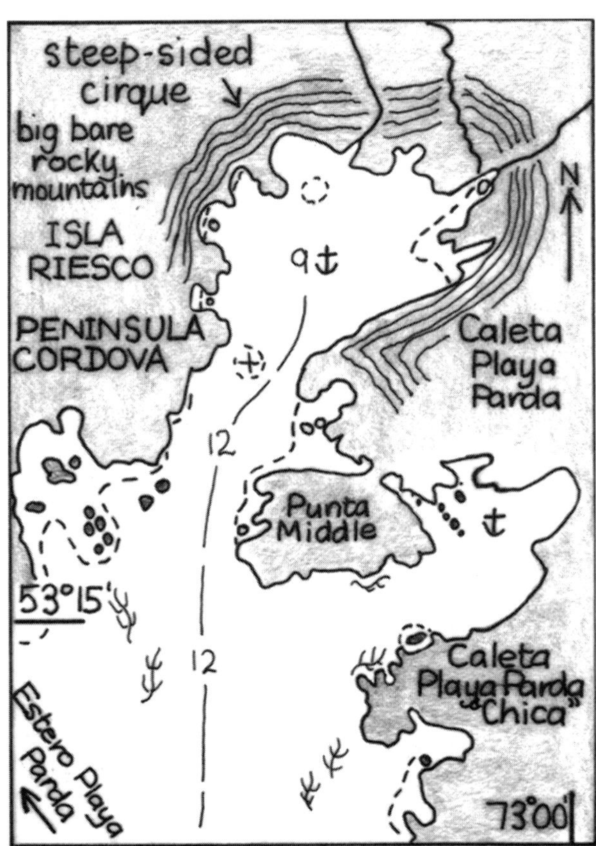

Caleta Playa Parda. (Charted positions)

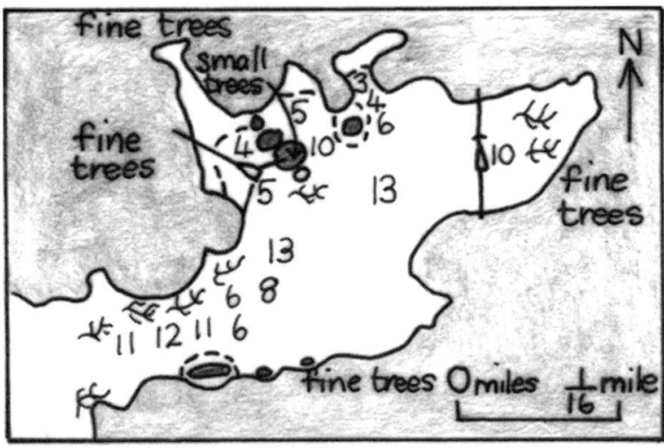

Caleta Playa Parda 'Chica'

A good alternative to Playa Parda is Playa Parda Chica, a small bay well protected from west and northwest winds and with protection from the southwest if tucked into the even smaller bay in the northwest corner. It is possible to take lines ashore and as the surrounding hills are lower than those of Playa Parda and are well wooded, there is less risk of *rachas*. The entrance appears clear and by keeping fairly close to the kelp of the north shore there is a depth of 6–7m.

8·8 Península Córdova – Caleta Notch

53°24'S 72°49'W

Charts
UK *1281, 887* US *22415* Chile 1*1200, 1117*

General
Caleta Notch is about half-way along Península Córdova and is one of the more spectacular anchorages in this area. If you have a copy of the discontinued UK chart *547*, use it. The entrance is narrow but clean, keeping well clear of the rocks on the northern side of the entrance off Isla Collins. It has shelter from all winds, good holding, is well recommended by yachts and coasters alike but it has *rachas* so take lines ashore. Do not try to enter at night. When passing to the east of Isla Westley the rock lying off this island can be avoided by lining up the whitish patch on the shore to the north with the cairn above it. In the inner basin there are several possible anchorages in 3·5 to 11m, hard mud. There is an excellent notch for a small boat just inside the entrance on the port side with a rocky bottom so four lines ashore may be needed. A climb up the hill on the north side gives a good view of the conditions in the Straits.

Paso Tortuoso

Paso Tortuoso has earned its name (see Tilman) and most yachts try to get past as quickly as possible.

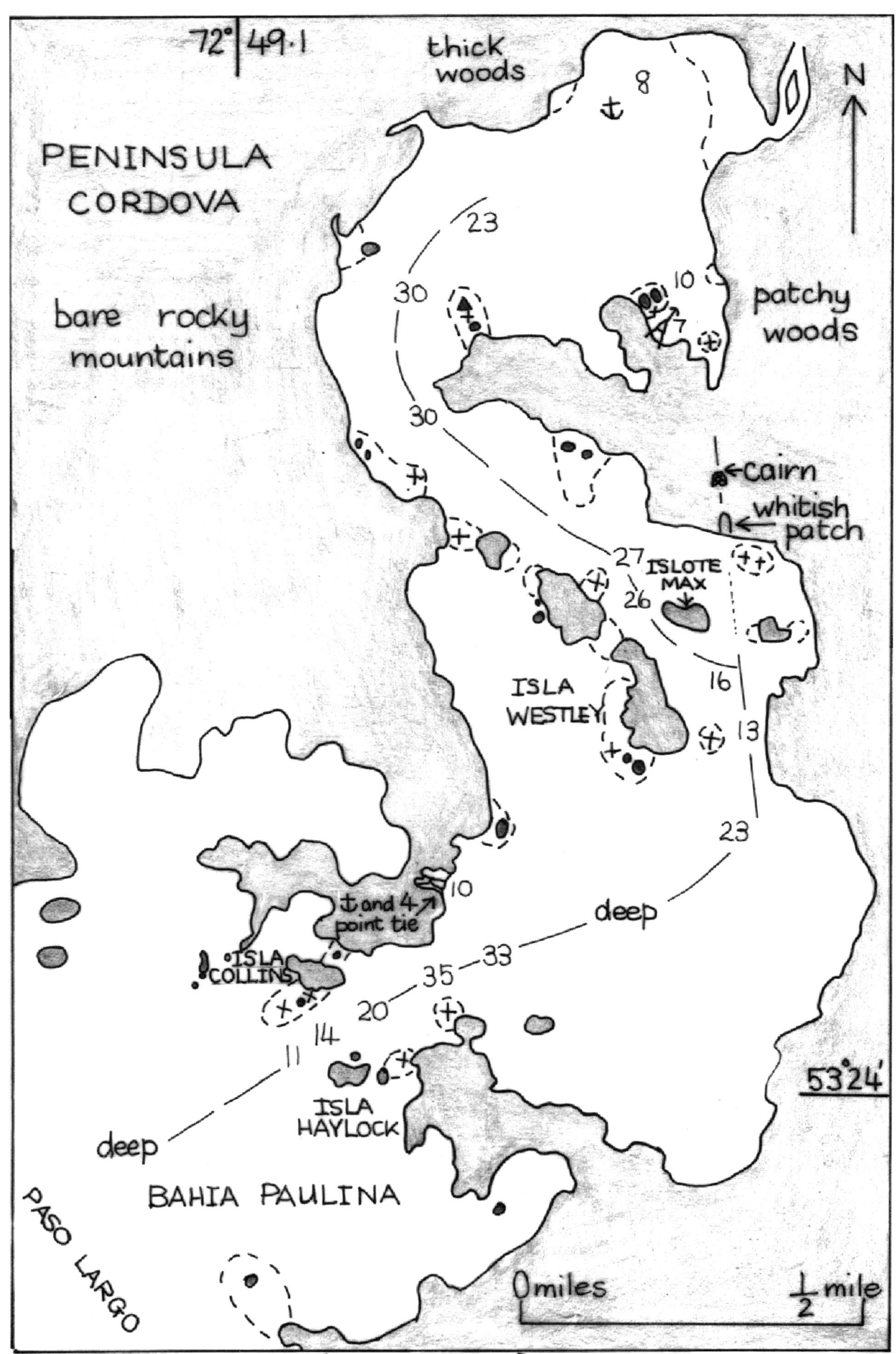

Caleta Notch. (GPS positions)

8·9 Isla Spider

53°31'S 72°40'W

Charts

UK *1281, 554, 887* US *22415* Chile *11230*

General

Isla Spider is at the northwest corner of Península Ulloa. Anchor and moor between the main island and the small island on the east side of Isla Spider. Anchor in about 12m. Very good shelter. Some kelp. Fishing boats use this anchorage and there is evidence of a temporary fishing camp on the shore.

8·10 Península Ulloa – Bahía Butler

53°34'·5S 72°34'W

Charts

UK *1281, 554, 887* US *22415* Chile *11230*

General

Once a yacht on its way west through Paso Tortuoso has passed Cabo Crosstides it is a further 18 miles to Caleta Notch. Tilman used Bahía Butler and found good shelter on the western side anchoring in about 7m some 20m from the shore. Holding mud on rock.

8·11 Península Córdova – Bahía Borja

52°32'S 72°30'W

Charts

UK *1281, 887* US *22415* Chile *11200, 11230, 1117*

General

At the start of Paso Tortuoso on Península Córdova, Bahía Borja faces southeast but is sheltered between southwest and north. The bottom is clay with good holding. It can have strong winds and *rachas* – the UK pilot remarks on very fierce squalls at times – but apparently seas remain low. The best anchorage is on the eastern side at the head of the bay with lines ashore. Names of previous visiting ships are inscribed on the east shore.

Diversion

Canal Jerónimo to Puerto Cóndor

Canal Jerónimo runs northeast from Isla Carlos III. The streams are fairly regular and run up to 8kts northwards and 6kts southwards in the narrows. Slack water lasts about 20 minutes at high water and 10 minutes at low water. Puerto Condor is at 8·12 below.

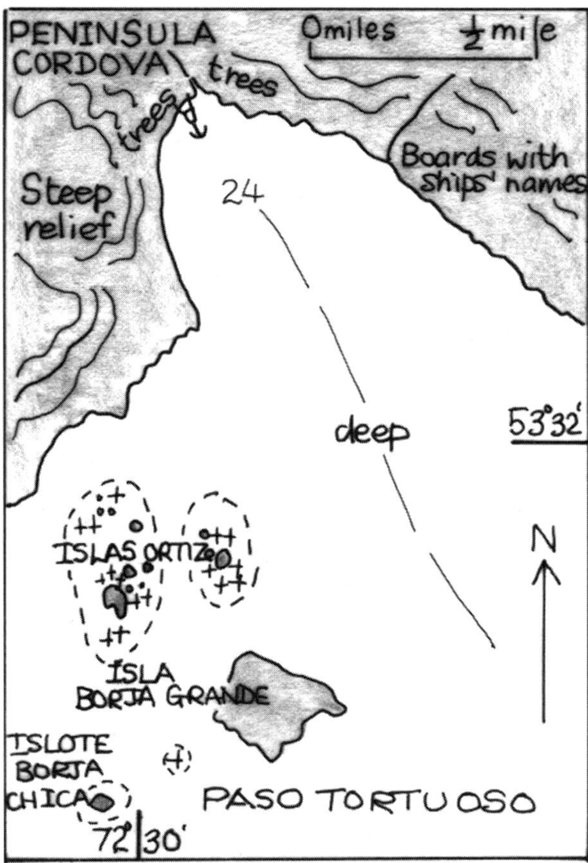

Bahía Borja. (Charted positions)

8·12 Estero Cóndor – Puerto Cóndor

53°21'S 72°38'W

Charts

UK *1281, 887* US *22415* Chile *11200, 11230, 1110*

Puerto Cóndor is at the head of Estero Condor, off Canal Jerónimo. There is no point in going up to it unless you are collecting anchorages. The anchorages are either in the bay north of Isla Dagnino or in Ensenada Llanza. In either place get lines ashore. Lago de la Botella is fresh and accessible by *portage.*

Continuation

Paso Inglés

8·13 Isla Carlos III – Bahía Tilly

53°34'S 72°23'W

Charts

UK *1281, 554, 887* US *22415* Chile *11230, 1117*

General

Bahía Tilly is on the north side of Isla Carlos III. It is subject to squalls but is a fairly sheltered stopping place in Paso Tortuoso. One possibility is to go to the inner basin, passing zig-zag between rocks, and tie up across the narrow end of the bay, lines out ahead and astern to the shores or anchor in 18–20m,

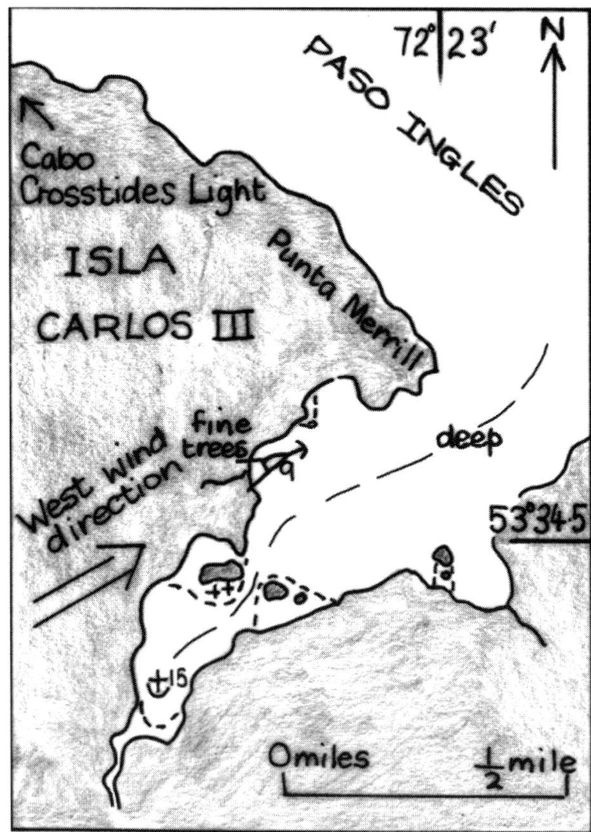

Bahía Tilly. (Charted positions)

mud and kelp, with lines ashore. Several yachts have anchored on the west side of the entrance where shown, an anchorage also used by fishermen. Anchor in about 7m with shorelines or tuck into the cove tying fore-and-aft with shorelines. Good holding. It is the only place with trees that provide good shelter from the west. From this anchorage it is possible to see conditions in Paso Inglés.

8·14 Isla Carlos III – Bahía Mussel

53°36'·4S 72°17'·7W

Charts

UK *1281, 554, 887* US *22415* Chile *11230, 1117*

General

Bahía Mussel is on the NE side of Isla Carlos III and has a view of Paso Inglés. The passage west along Paso Inglés can be difficult and Bahía Mussel is a useful stopping point. The bay is large and there are many anchoring possibilities. The anchorage shown is in 5m with good holding with shorelines. It is reported to be relatively calm in strong winds with *rachas* outside. An attractive spot with woodland of large trees.

Diversion

There are three principal routes connecting Estrecho Magallanes, east of Paso Inglés, and Canal Cockburn. They are:

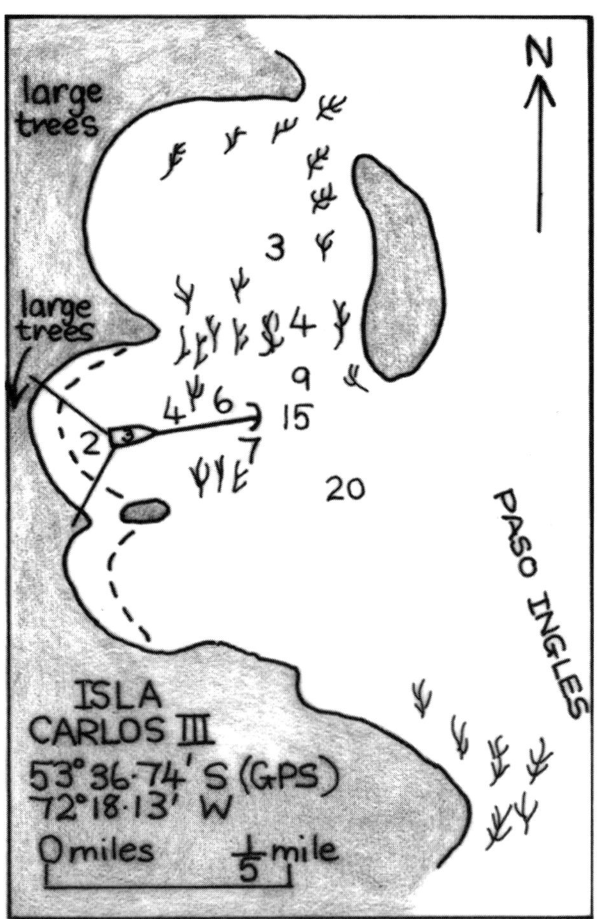

Un-named Caleta. Bahía Mussel

1. **Canal Barbara**. From Cabo Edgworth, at the north entrance to Canal Barbara to Canal Cockburn at 72°W via Canal Barbara is about 40M. Canal Barbara is an impressive Canal and finishes in the north at the most westerly position along Canal Magdalena. However it has several disadvantages. The pilotage is fairly complicated. The Canal is quite open and can be subject to *rachas*, especially if there is north in the wind when it gusts down from Peninsula Bowles. Finally there are very few identifiable anchorages if the weather deteriorates *en route*. Canal Barbara is used regularly by fishing boats.
2. **Seno Pedro and Canal Acwalisnan** From Cabo Edgworth to Canal Cockburn at 72°W via Seno Pedro and Canal Acwalisnan is about 58M. This is much the easiest route of the three. Canal Acwalisnan is well protected and the narrows at Paso O'Ryan are straightforward at slack water. This route is used a lot by local fishing boats. They call Paso O'Ryan 'El corriente de San Pedro'. It is to be hoped that both Canal Barbara and Canal Acwalisnan will become approved routes.
3. **Canal Magdalena – Canal Cockburn** From Cabo Edgworth to Canal Cockburn at 72°W via Canal Magdalena is about 100M. This is currently the only approved route. It is quite tough and keeps the yacht in relatively

unprotected canals for a long way. On the positive side there are well-documented anchorages along the way to break the passage.

The three routes are considered below (Magdalena/Cockburn in section 9).

8·15 Canal Barbara

Charts

UK *554* US *22425* Chile *1201*

General

Canal Barbara is a wide waterway with many islands and shoal areas to complicate the route. The sketch chart shows the route that has been used by yachts and is the one described in UK *Pilot NP6*. The route has been described north to south. Yachts have travelled in both directions through Canal Barbara. However the principal advantage of this route is when travelling south to north as the yacht gains access to Estrecho de Magallanes at the most westerly point. The southern passage may be made in one day. Paso Shag can be transited early in the morning but the northern passage may take two days as it is often necessary to wait for favourable tidal conditions in Paso Shag. The route is as follows:

- Pass east of Cabo Edgeworth, avoiding its off-lying shoals, and head for Isla Wet, staying fairly close to the east coast of Isla Santa Ines after passing the entrance to Ensenada Smyth and take care of an east going set when approaching Isla Wet.
- **Paso Shag** Paso Shag runs between Isla Alcayaga and Isla Santa Ines which is steep-to. At the northeast end the entrance lies between Isla Wet and Isla Santa Ines. The Pass is about 1½ miles long and has a least width of about 200m. The passage throughout lies along the middle of the canal. At the southeast end there may be the odd ice floe coming from the glaciers at the head of Seno Helado.

  At the northern end of Canal Barbara the flood stream runs south from Estrecho de Magallanes. The timing through Paso Shag is important as the current can run at 7 knots with tide rips and eddies. Even near slack water the current still runs quite strongly through the pass but in calm weather this is not problematic. However UK *Pilot NP6* states that the passage 'is not considered safe during southwest winds'. Vessels are recommended to wait for an improvement in the weather. Note that the south-going tidal stream divides at Isla Wet and the north-going stream divides at Isla Alcayaga; in both cases the main stream flows through Paso Shag.

  Slack tide is between 1 hour 15 minutes and 1 hour 50 minutes after slack tide at Punta Arenas. When travelling north it is a good idea to arrive just before high slack water so as to be pushed through the Pass and still have a fair current when travelling north to join Estrecho de Magallanes. At this time the current in the west part of the Paso runs at about 2 knots near spring tide. When exiting, west of Isla Wet the current runs at 4 knots with eddies and tide rips. In calm weather this does not give a problem transiting with the current but it would be difficult to make progress if travelling against it.

  There are numerous shags sitting in the trees on Isla Santa Ines – quite appropriate, considering the name of the pass. In the Canal west of Isla Wet there is a profusion of wild life fishing in the disturbed waters, including families of seals, and much bird life.
- If going north, Puerto Nutland (8·16) makes a good stopping place to wait for slack water to transit Paso Shag. Take care of an east-going set when approaching Isla Alcayaga.
- The passage to east of the headland after passing Puerto Nutland is deep. Make down the west side of Isla Browell, keeping east of the small group of drying rocks shown on the sketch and passing through Angostura Sur between Isla Browell and Isla Santa Ines.
- The northeast coast of Isla Guardian Brito is then followed for 4½ miles. Pass south of the small islands off the southern shore of Peninsula Bowles and east of Isla Commandante. This area can be subject to stronger winds caused by the mountains of Peninsula Bowles and wind funnelling down the large, unnamed *estero* to the northeast.
- Turn southwards and follow a mid-canal course west of the Grupo de los Trece, Islotes Hidrograficos and Islotes Mogotes. Pass between Isla Staines and Isla Stanley and west of Islotes Contramaestre.
- South of Islotes Contramaestre, Canal Barbara can be left via Paso Sur, Paso Aguila or by Paso Adelaide. They are all deep and clear of dangers. Puerto Niemann (9·10) in Canal Adelaide is a good anchorage from which to finish or start the passage through Canal Barbara

Anchorages in Canal Barbara

The documented anchorages are 8·16 Puerto Nutland at the northern end and 9·9 Caleta Louis, 9·10 Puerto Niemann and 9·11 Caleta Tarmac at its southern end. There are no obvious secure anchorages along the main length of the canal and the land is barren and windswept.

The bay (GPS position 54°06'·2S, 72°15'W) on the NE coast of Isla Guardian Brito has been used and found to provide protection from west to southerly winds. It is not recommended. When strong winds blow down the canal from the north, they funnel into this bay making it untenable.

Puerto Dean (53°50'S 72°20'W) is reported to be a good anchorage with better shelter than suggested on the chart. Holding in about 10m in sand.

Seno Helado has also been visited. There is shallow water at the entrance to the Seno where the moraine was deposited but the shallow areas are well marked by kelp. Beyond this area the Seno is deep.

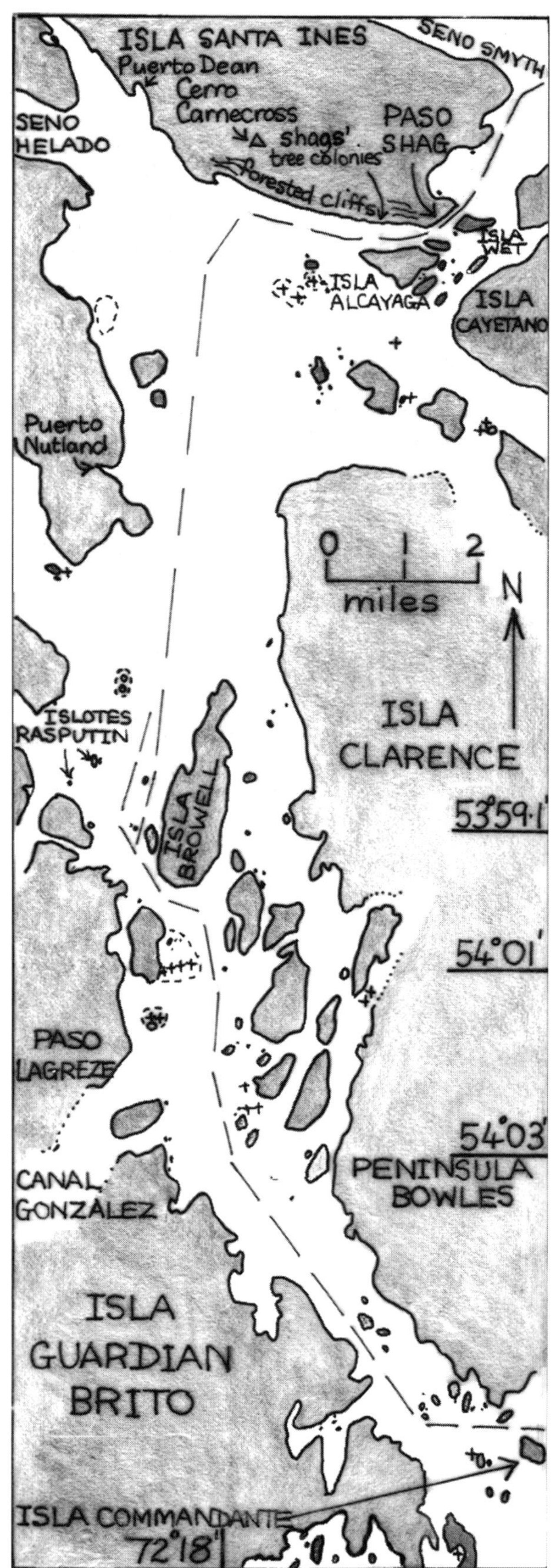

Canal Barbara northern section. (GPS positions)

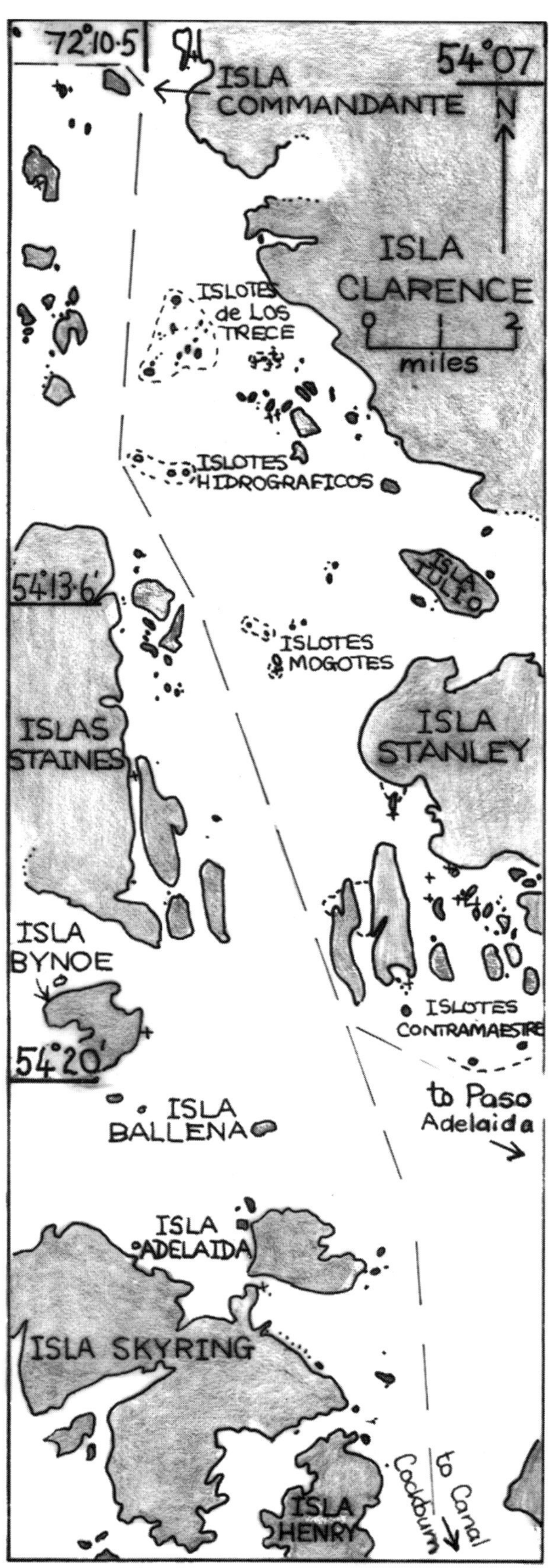

Canal Barbara southern section. (GPS positions)

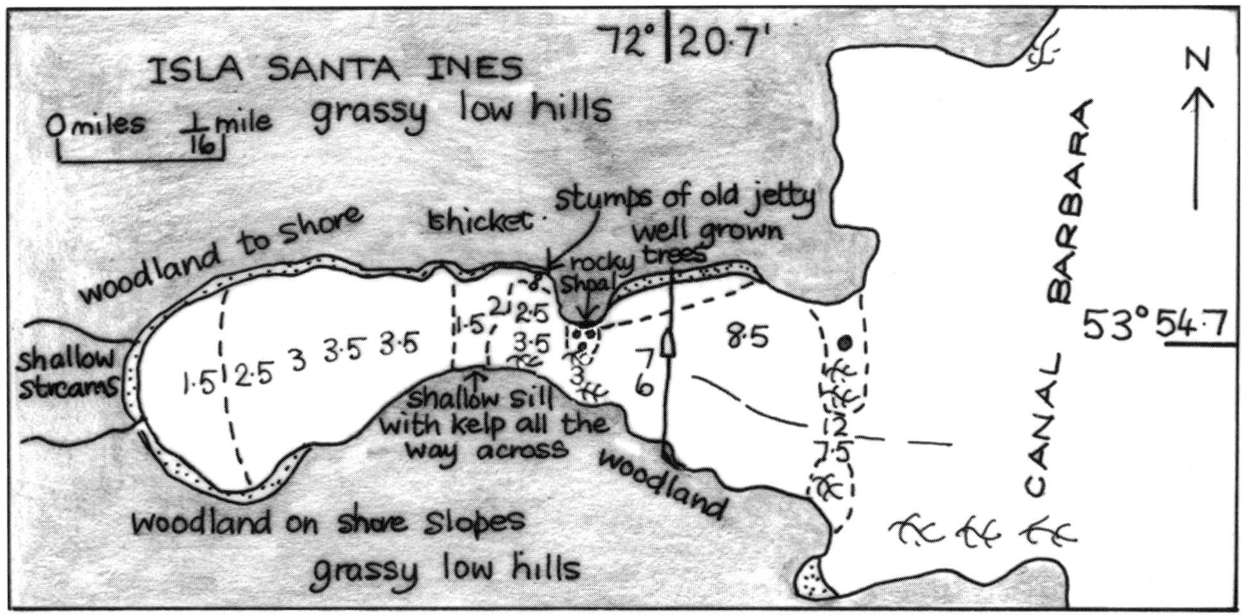

Puerto Nutland. (GPS positions)

A shallow indentation on the south side of the Seno provided a good anchorage with lines ashore. There are extensive glaciers from which ice continually falls and drifts down the Seno.

8·16 Isla Santa Ines – Puerto Nutland

53°54'S 72°20'W

Charts
UK *1201* US *22425* Chile *11300*

General
Puerto Nutland is on Isla Santa Ines about 6 miles southwest of the southern end of Paso Shag. It provides good shelter from all but east winds. The indicated anchorage is in 6m on a mud bottom with shorelines. The anchorage is fairly near the entrance to the bay. It would be possible to anchor beyond the rocky shoal in about 3m just south of the remains of an old jetty but beyond this there is a bar and the depths shoal quickly further into the bay.

Continuation

8·17 Bahía Fortesque – Caleta Gallant

53°42'S 72°00'W

Charts
UK *1281* US *22425* Chile *11300, 1118*

General
Caleta Gallant is the inner part of Bahía Fortescue on Península Brunswick, northeast of Islas Charles. It is behind Isla Wigwam which has shoal water on its east side. From the earliest days, Bahía Fortescue has provided shelter for sailing ships travelling west up the Straits. It is shown on charts from the 1700s.

The entrance to Bahía Fortescue is wide and unencumbered and there is a light on the western shore, 1450Cabo Gallant (Fl(3)9s18m6M White pillar, orange band 5m). The entrance to Caleta Gallant is rather narrow and shallow, with a least depth of around 6m. The best anchorage is as close as possible to the northern side of Isla Wigwam in about 6m on a sand bottom. Winter killed kelp has been a problem on occasion but once the anchor has found a place the holding is good in strong mud. Yachts that have anchored further north than this have experienced *rachas* coming down the valley at the head of the bay. It is also possible to tuck up into

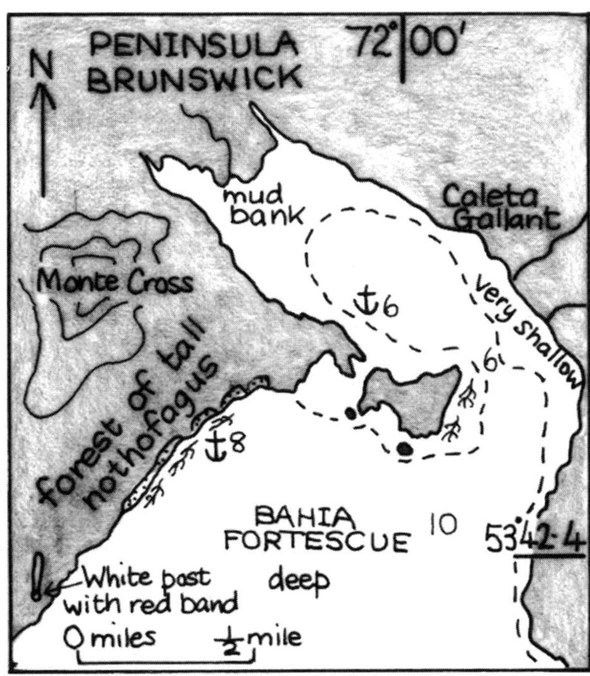

Caleta Gallant. (GPS positions)

the NW corner of Bahía Fortescue under the protection of tall trees on the shore. This is well protected from winds from the west and northwest and is calm even when fresh winds are blowing outside.

Paso Froward

8·18 Península Brunswick – Bahía Woods

53°49'S 71°37'W

Charts
UK *1281* US *22425* Chile *11300, 1120*

General
On Península Brunswick under Cabo Holland, Bahía Woods provides good shelter from winds from the north through to the southwest. Care should be taken to avoid the foul ground extending 200m off the southeast end of Cabo Holland, with Roca Esk awash at its edge. The holding in the bay is good in 4–5m with a bottom of sand and stones. Swell does enter the bay during strong west winds.

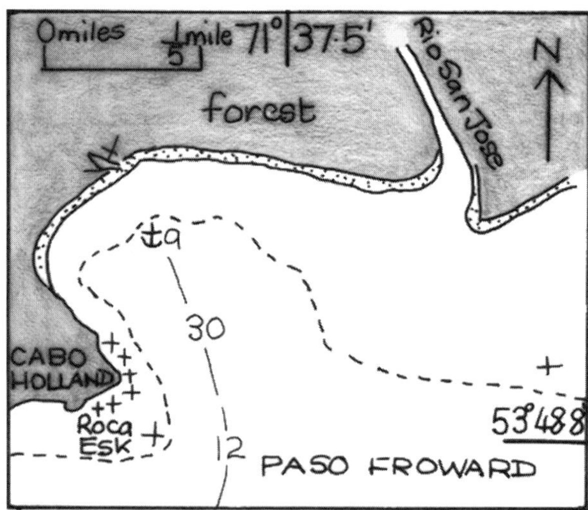

Bahía Woods. (Charted positions)

8·19 Canal Acwalisnan

Charts
UK *554* US *22425* Chile *11300, 1201*

General
Canal Acwalisnan, which leads southwards from Canal Pedro, provides a much shorter route between the Straits of Magallan and the Cockburn Canal than the commercial traffic route using Canal Magdalena. Local fisherman prefer it over Canal Barbara because it can be transited in one day. Acwalisnan is narrow and winding and is therefore more sheltered than Magdalena where strong southwest winds can kick up a nasty head sea. The thick woodland that grows high up the sides of the mountains along Canal Acwalisnan indicate that this is generally sheltered.

There is no good chart of Canales Pedro and Acwalisnan. There are no dangers and depths along the centre track range between 100–120m. Coming from the north, the first obstacle is the pass leading from Canal Pedro into Canal Acwalisnan. There is a wooded island in the middle that should be left to port. This island is not immediately obvious when approaching from the north as it looks part of the hill behind. However as it is approached the continuation of the Canal becomes obvious. The GPS position at the point marked on the exploded view on the sketch plan is 54°05'·50S 71°36'·8W.

The next obstacle is Paso O'Ryan. This pass is narrow and shallow and as a result tidal streams can run up to 8 knots. The flood tide runs south from Estrecho de Magallanes into Seno Pedro and from the south northwards into Canal Acwalisnan at more or less the same time. A passage south timed

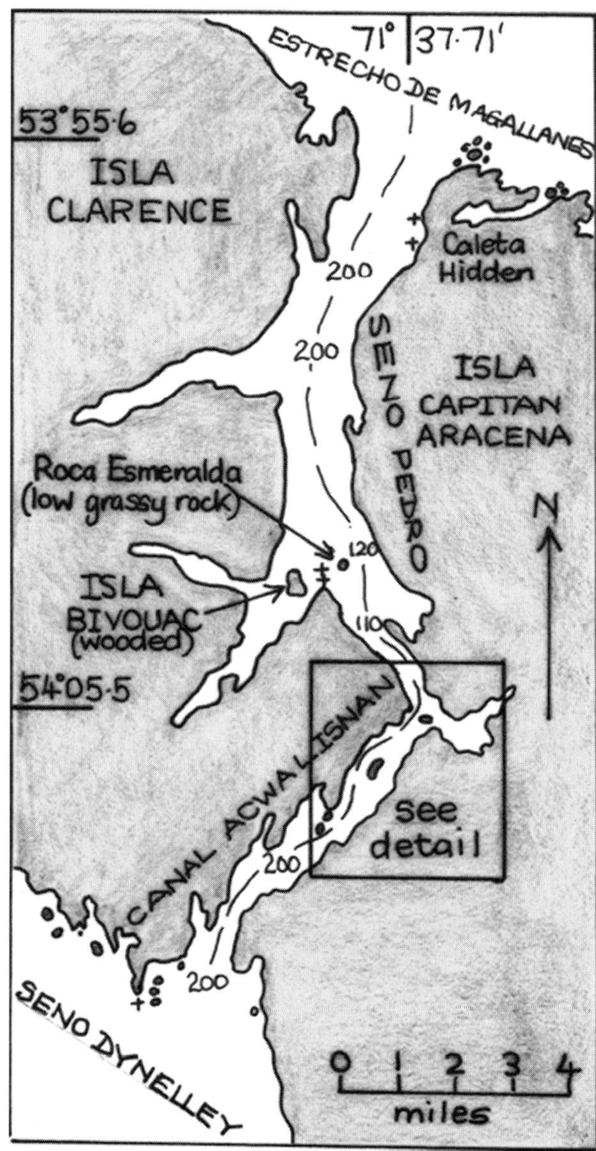

Seno Pedro and Canal Acwalisnan. (GPS positions)

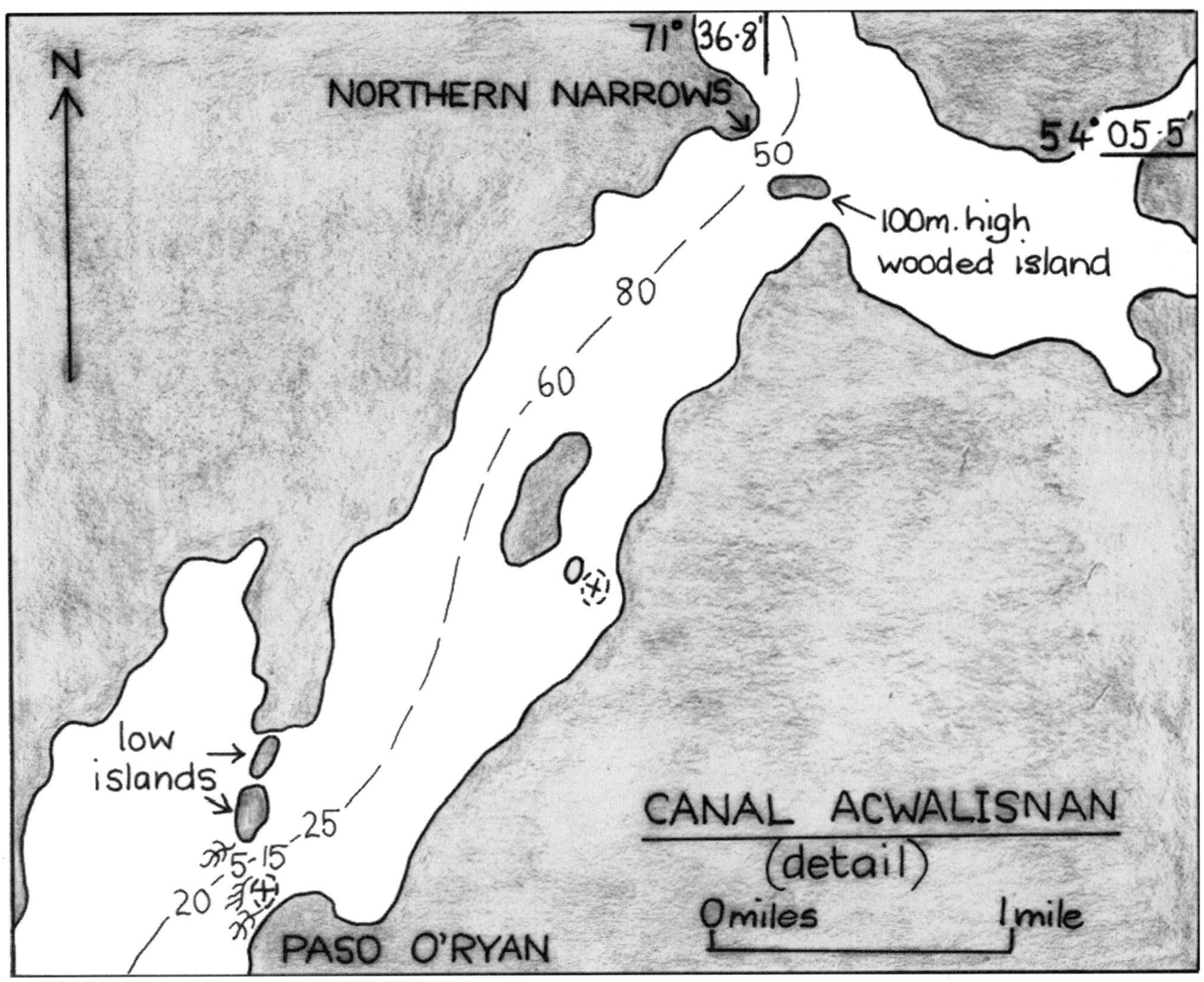

to catch slack high water at Paso O'Ryan will give the yacht a fair tide down Seno Pedro and then on south of Paso O'Ryan. The converse applies and the best time to reach Paso O'Ryan when heading north is to reach there at low water slack. Slack water at Paso O'Bryan is about Bahía Woods +1 hour. Near slack water at springs the current runs at about 2 knots, with some eddies, but the current soon helps push the yacht clear of the narrows.

After exiting Canal Acwalisnan head for the W end of Isla Seebrock and pass between Seebrock and the end of Isla Clarence, keeping along the Isla Clarence shore to avoid the extensive foul ground on the northwest end of Isla Seebrock. Caleta Louis (see 9·9) on the southeast corner of Isla Clarence is a convenient anchorage if it is rough in the Cockburn.

8·20 Isla Capitán Aracena – Caleta Hidden

53°56'·9S 71°34'·2W

Charts

UK *1281* US *22425* Chile *11300, 1201*

General

This anchorage is often used by boats travelling north or south through Canal Acwalisnan. The entrance is about 1·5 miles east of the entrance to Seno Pedro and is marked by a small group of rocky islets east of its entrance. The GPS position of the entrance is 53°56'·6S 71°33'·5W. The Caleta is a ¾-mile long slot with a wider basin at its head. The small notch on the southern side of this passage provides an anchorage protected from all but east winds but it is more secure to continue to the head of the bay, leaving the rock shown to port. Depths fall here but there are no dangers in the centre of this pass and it is clear of kelp. At the head of the bay there are a number of secure anchorages, the best probably being the most westerly bay with good holding and shore lines.

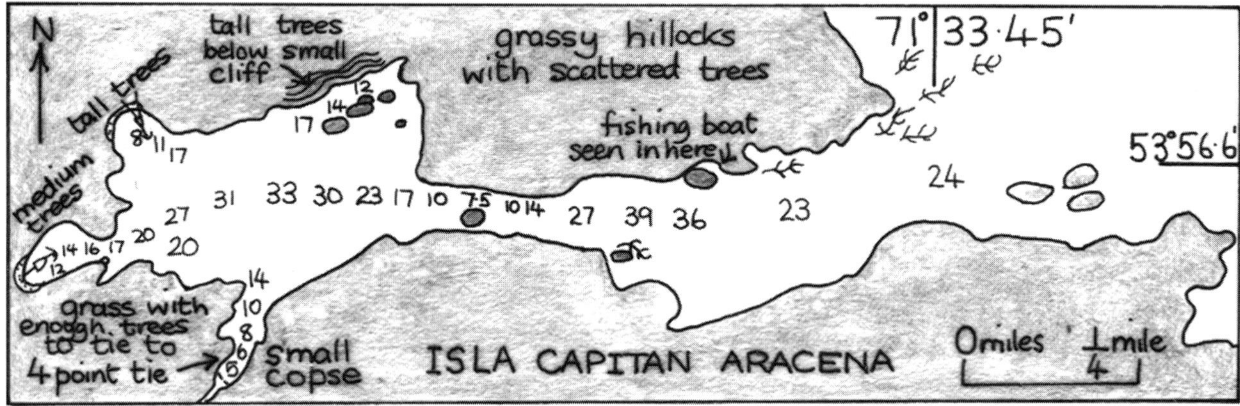

Caleta Hidden. (GPS positions)

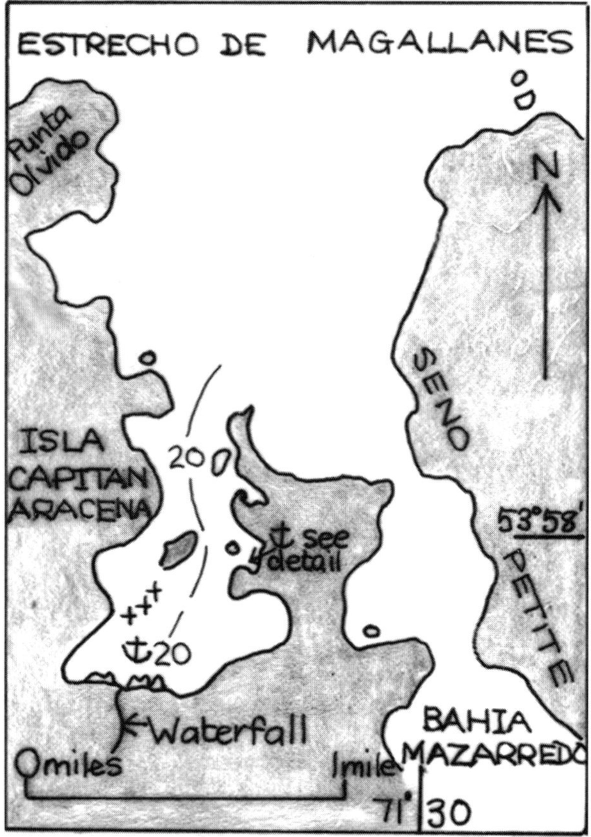

Caleta Cascada. (Charted positions)

8·21 Isla Capitán Aracena – Caleta Cascada

53°58'S 71°31'W

Charts

UK *1281* US *22425* Chile *11300, 1201*

General

The entrance to Cascada is a little narrow but quite clean. The bay is sheltered from all winds. Anchor in 18m at the head of the bay. There is also a small bay on the east side of the entrance with 10m depth in the middle and two stony beaches on the east side. Cormorants nest on the western entrance of the *caleta*. There is good hiking beside the stream leading to the waterfall.

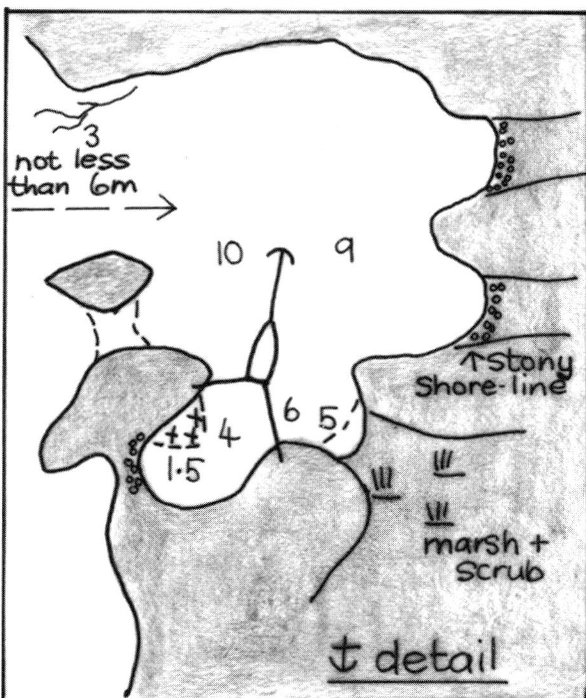

8·22 Cabo Froward

At Cabo Froward, the most southerly point of the mainland, the Magallan Straits turn north via Paso del Hambre and the various narrows to Dungeness and the Atlantic. The main shipping route to Puerto Williams, via Magdalena and the Beagle Channels goes south from this point and is considered below. The characteristics of 1448Cabo Froward light at 53°54'S 71°18'W are Fl.3s20m6M White concrete tower, red band 3m. 276°-vis-126°.

Cabo Froward to Dungeness

Paso del Hambre

General

Between Cabo Froward and Punta Arenas two groups of bays afford some protection if caught by westerlies. There is no protection from east winds

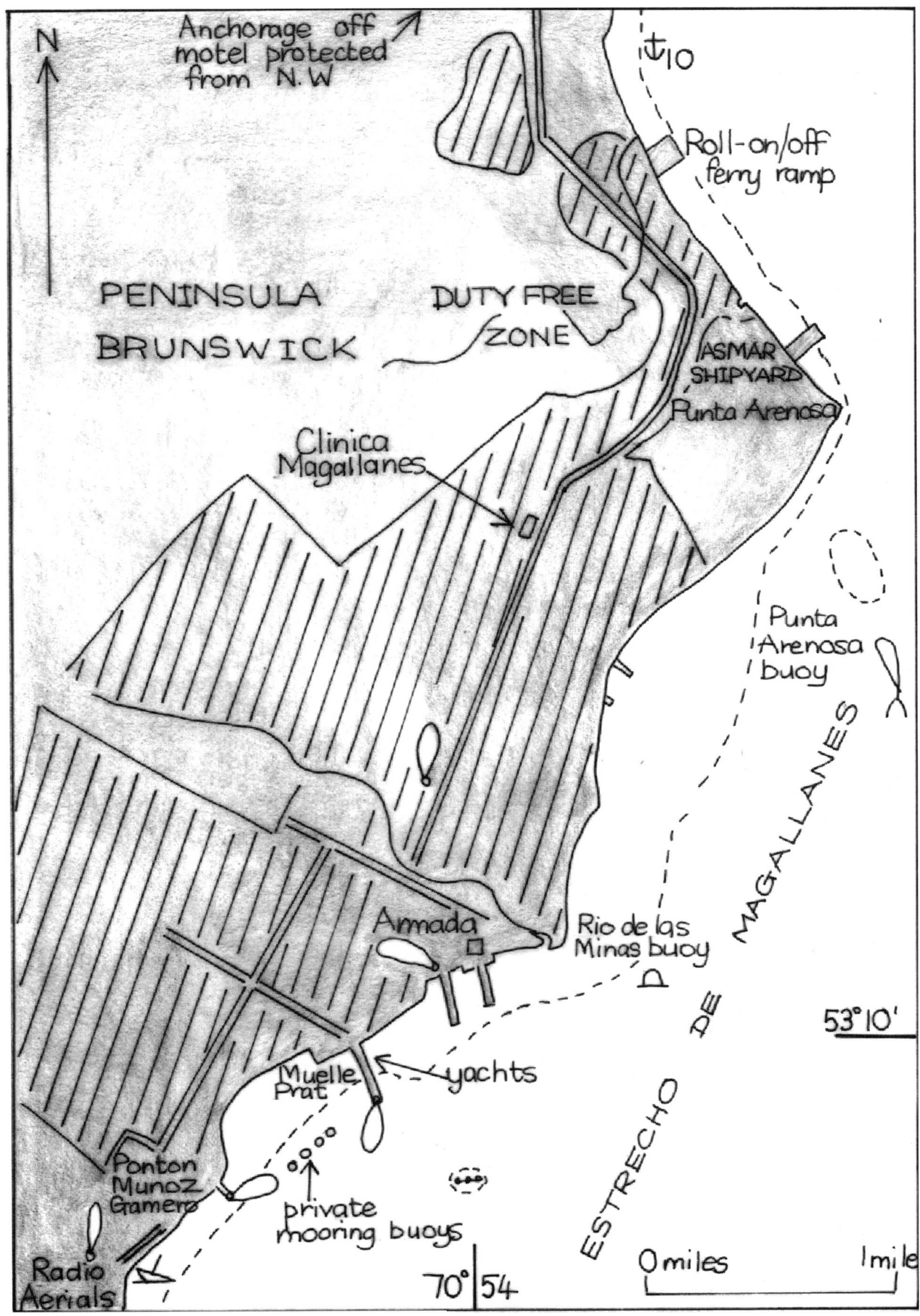

Punta Arenas. (Charted positions)

even at Punta Arenas except at Bahía Porvenir on Tierra del Fuego (chart Chile *1142*). Porvenir has a limiting draft of about 1·7m at low water and a tortuous entrance.

Between Punta Arenas and Punta Dungeness there are two narrows to be negotiated, Segunda Angostura and Primera Angostura. Eastbound vessels are advised to be off the entrance to Segunda Angostura as the east going stream is starting which the UK Pilot states is about 2hrs 30mins before high water at Cabo de Hornos. Westbound vessels are advised to be off the northeast approach of Primera Angostura just before the southwest stream starts, three and a half hours after high water at Cabo de Hornos.

8·23 Península Brunswick – Bahías San Nicolás, Bougainville and del Cañon

Around 53°50'S 73°02'W

Charts

UK *1281* US *22425* Chile *11300, 1121, 1122*

General

Bahía San Nicolás Anchor inside Islote Sanchez and the west point in sand and mud. There is a little pier and a saw mill.

Bahía Bougainville Used by fishermen and sealers. Tuck well in stern to trees. Fresh water rivulet.

Bahía del Cañon Depths of 7–10m within the headlands.

8·24 Península Brunswick – Fort Bulnes

53°38'S 70°55'W

Charts

UK *1281* US – Chile *11300, 1140, 1121*

General

Also known as San Juan de la Posesión and labelled as Puerto del Hambre on Chilean chart *1121*, it is the site of the first colony to be established in Estrecho Magallanes; it did not survive long. The anchorage is a possible day stop to visit the wooden fort on Punta Santa Ana. Anchor on the northeast side of the bay under the fort. Open from East through to South.

Two other possible anchorages are at Puerto del Hambre which Charts *11300* and *1140* have in the correct place, just below the monument considered to be the centre of Chile (the reckoning starts at the south pole). The other, with possibly the best shelter is in Puerto Carreras, the next *caleta* to the north.

8·25 Península Brunswick – Punta Arenas

53°10'S 70°54'W

Charts

UK *554, 1281, 1694* US *22482* Chile *1140, 11410*

Port communications

VHF Ch16, 09, 14 c/s *CBM25* ☎ 22 10 01

General

The capital of the region, the face of Punta Arenas has been being changed under the influence of oil revenues from the Estrecho Magallanes. The population is about 100,000. It still serves the extensive sheep farming industry. Some of the large establishments of former sheep barons have been converted into museums or *monumentos nacionales*.

There are several restaurants and hotels ranging from four stars downwards. There are two museums but diversion for the tourist consists largely of visiting national parks, such as the penguin colony on Isla Magdalena, or the waterways plus very expensive expeditions to Chilean Antarctica.

Berthing

Inquire on Ch16. There is no anchorage as such in Punta Arenas, only an open roadstead. It is possible to shelter by rafting against fishing boats or other vessels tied to the docks but damage during strong winds, particularly from the east, can be substantial. An east wind at Punta Arenas is unlikely but very dangerous when it blows and vessels are advised to leave if one is forecast.

Facilities

Asmar (Astillero y Maestranzas de la Armada) for major repairs.

Fuel, water, electricity at the Muelle Fiscal.

Supermarket Listo, 21 de Mayo by the main square, Plaza Muñoz de Gemero.

Mercado Municipal, Chiloé 600 near Mexicana.

Laundry Autoservicio O'Higgins 969.

British Consulate: Calle Sarmiento 780 (PO Box 237, Punta Arenas) ☎ 24 81 00 and 22 24 75. *Fax* 56 61 22 22 51 Ext 108. There are also Consulates of Argentina and Germany.

Communications

Bus services are quoted as far north as Valdivia and to Argentina (Río Gallegos). Frequent air services provided by four national airlines to Puerto Montt and Santiago, to Puerto Williams every Tuesday (bi-weekly in summer) and to the Falkland Islands.

Car hire Automóvil Club de Chile, Avis, Budget, Hertz and others.

Ferry to Porvenir.

Telephone Area code 61. CTC Plaza Muñoz Gamero, ENTEL Chile, Lautaro Navarro 941.

Canal Nuevo

8·26 Bahía Gente Grande – Isla Contramaestre

52°57'S 70°21'W

Charts
UK *554, 1281, 1694* US *22481* Chile *1140, 1150, 1152*

General
Isla Contramaestre is at the entrance to Bahía Gente Grande on Tierra del Fuego. The anchorage is just round the southwest corner, Punta Baja, strong mud 5m. Shelter from southwest.

8·27 Isla Isabel – Surgidero Punta Alfredo

51°51'·5S 70°38'·5W

Charts
UK *554, 1281,1694* US *22481* Chile *1150*

General
This is an anchorage along the northwest coast of Isla Isabel, about 1·5M from the northeast end of the island. It is opposite a pronounced ravine. Good holding in 14m or less.

8·28 Bahía Whitsand

52°43'S 70°37'W

Charts
UK *554, 1281, 1694* US *22481* Chile *1150*

General
Good shelter from wind if north of southwest. Close up to the shore according to draft.

8·29 Punta Dungeness

52°24'S 68°26'W

Charts
UK *554, 3107* US *22471* Chile *1160*

General
It is possible to anchor either side of Punta Dungeness. The western anchorage is not affected by the tidal stream. Neither side has protection from the south.

Note All vessels passing through Argentine territorial waters are required to report to Cabo Vírgenes Naval Station Ch 16, 67.

Section 9
Cabo Froward to Brazo Noroeste

Canal Magdalena

9·1 Isla Capitán Aracena – Caleta Beaubasin

54°04'·9S 71°03'·3W

Charts
UK *554, 1373* US *22425* Chile *1201*

General
Beaubasin is a very attractive, snug little anchorage on the northwestern entrance to Canal Magdalena. It provides a welcome refuge on a northbound passage if there are strong west winds blowing down the Magallan Straits. There is a sill at the narrows with a least depth of 5m at low water. The anchorage is in 9m, mud and kelp, with lines ashore. There is a little stream on the southern side for fresh water or laundry. There are said to be *centollas* in the bay.

Caleta Beaubasin. (Charted positions)

9·2 Isla Capitán Aracena – Puerto Hope

54°07'·3S 70°59'·9W

Charts
UK *554, 1373* US *22425* Chile *1201, 1121*

General
At the north end of Canal Magdalena, Puerto Hope has a shoal patch with kelp on the north side of the entrance; favour the southern shore. The inner basin is well protected from outside winds but has a reputation for *rachas*. Anchor in 9m in the centre, mud. Good hiking on clean rock in the surrounding hills.

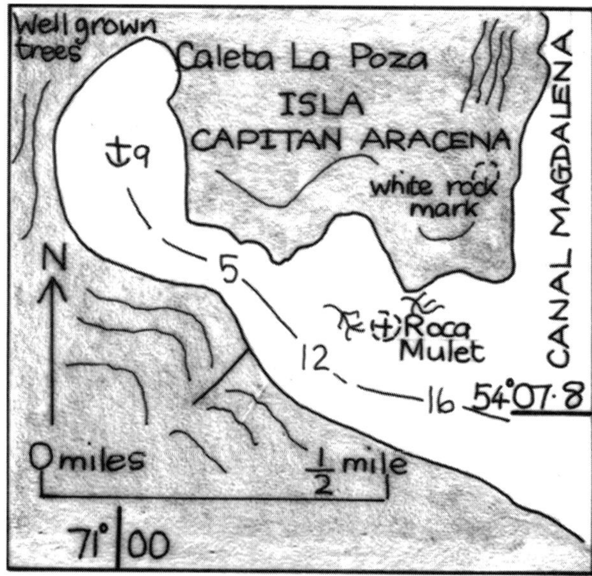

Puerto Hope. (Charted positions)

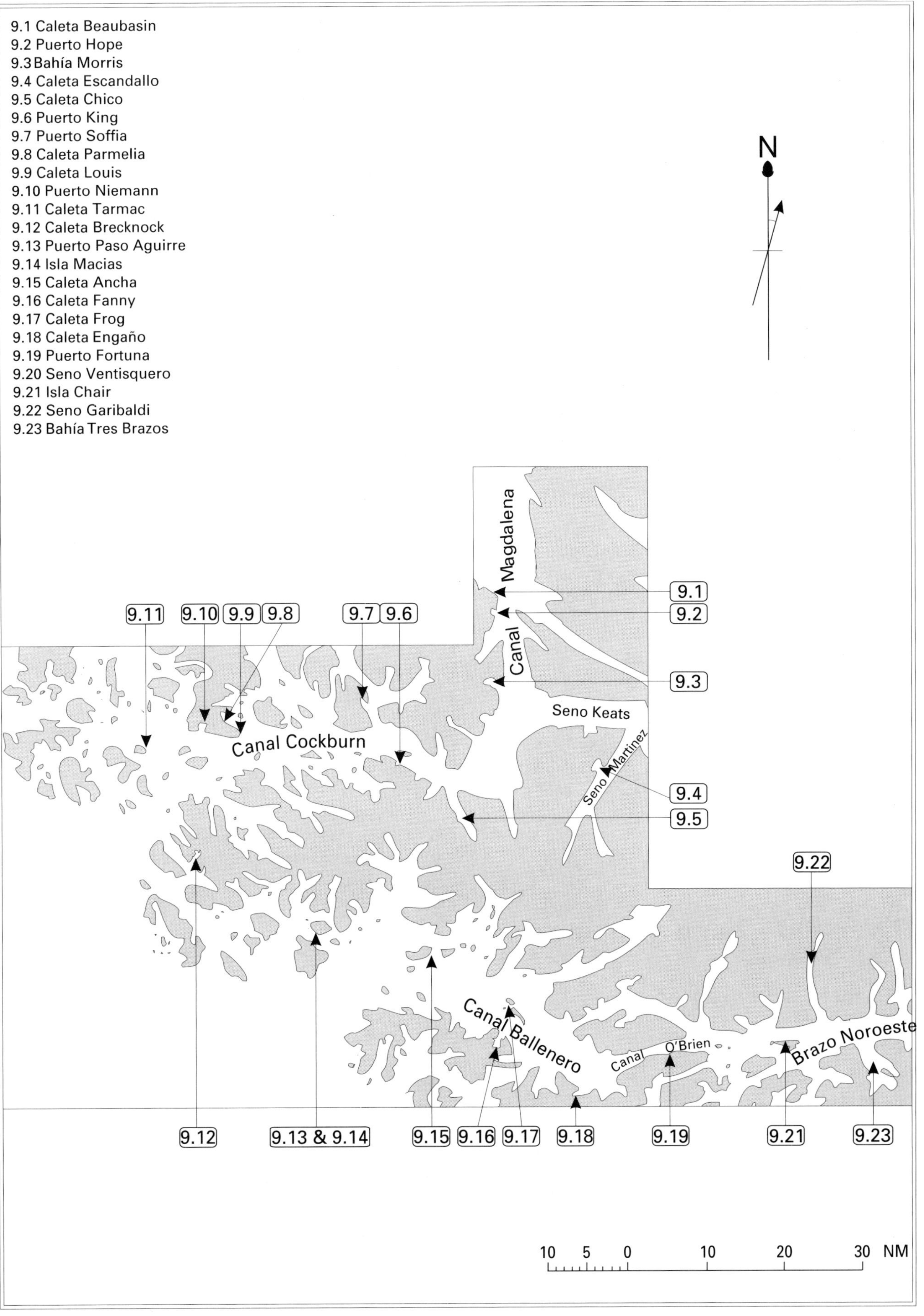
9.1 Caleta Beaubasin
9.2 Puerto Hope
9.3 Bahía Morris
9.4 Caleta Escandallo
9.5 Caleta Chico
9.6 Puerto King
9.7 Puerto Soffia
9.8 Caleta Parmelia
9.9 Caleta Louis
9.10 Puerto Niemann
9.11 Caleta Tarmac
9.12 Caleta Brecknock
9.13 Puerto Paso Aguirre
9.14 Isla Macias
9.15 Caleta Ancha
9.16 Caleta Fanny
9.17 Caleta Frog
9.18 Caleta Engaño
9.19 Puerto Fortuna
9.20 Seno Ventisquero
9.21 Isla Chair
9.22 Seno Garibaldi
9.23 Bahía Tres Brazos
N
Canal Magdalena
Seno Keats
Seno Martinez
Canal Cockburn
Canal Ballenero
Canal O'Brien
Brazo Noroeste
9.1
9.2
9.3
9.4
9.5
9.6
9.7
9.8
9.9
9.10
9.11
9.12
9.13 & 9.14
9.15
9.16
9.17
9.18
9.19
9.21
9.22
9.23
10 5 0 10 20 30 NM

9·3 Isla Capitán Aracena – Bahía Morris

54°15'S 70°53'W

Charts
UK *554, 1373* US *22425* Chile *1201, 1202*

General
Also known as Puerto Sholl, Bahía Morris is half way along the east coast of Isla Capitán Aracena almost opposite Seno Keats. Big ship pilots describe it as the best anchorage in either Canal Magdalena or Canal Cockburn but yachtsmen have labelled it as for emergencies only, probably because the wind blowing up Canal Magdalena comes in to the bay.

There are two anchorages in Bahía Morris. The most obvious is at the very head of the inner bay, with lines ashore. At times of strong west winds, very powerful *rachas* blow down from the surrounding steep mountains. In such conditions, it is better to anchor off the beach and low lying land as shown on the sketch plan. The *rachas* still reached there occasionally but the holding is very good in mud and stones.

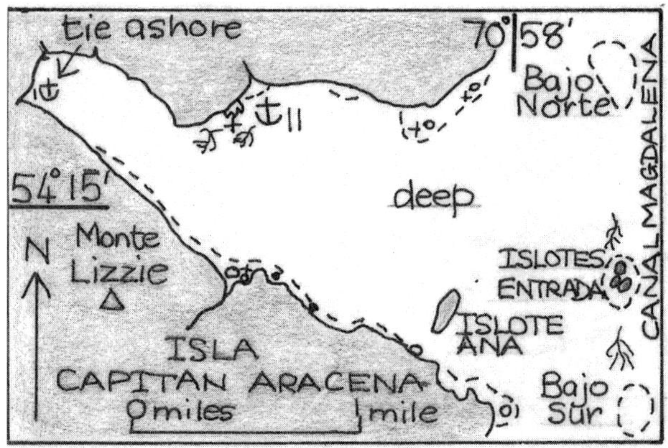

Bahía Morris

Diversion - Seno Martinez

9·4 Tierra del Fuego – Seno Martinez

54°26'S 70°41'W

Charts
UK *554, 1373* US *22425* Chile *1201*

General
Seno Keats leads east off Canal Magdalena and then turns south into Seno Martinez which leads to Caleta Escandallo, about 32M from the entrance of Seno Keats. In Caleta Escandallo there is good shelter from the west and southwest with sandy bays in the two corners. It has a high ridge of mountains surrounding it so *rachas* may be expected.

Continuation
Junction of Canal Magdalena and Canal Cockburn

Canal Cockburn

9·5 Tierra del Fuego – Caleta Chico

54°28'S 71°08'W

Charts
UK *554, 1373* US *22425* Chile *1201*

General
About 4 miles down Seno Chico is an inlet running to the west. At the head of this inlet is a spectacular tidewater glacier that is well worth a visit. About one and a half miles to the north of this inlet there is a small notch, which, with lines ashore is an excellent sheltered anchorage. The sides are very steep, but there are trees to tie off to. There is a fast flowing stream at the head of the bay for an easy supply of fresh water.

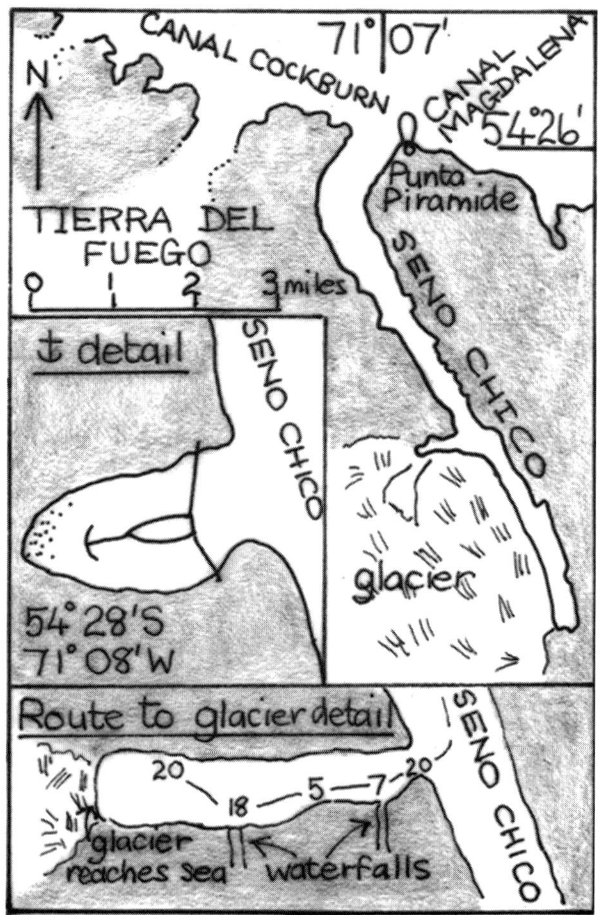

Seno Chico. (Charted positions)

9·6 Isla King – Puerto King

54°24'·7S 71°15'·2W (by chart).

Charts
UK *554, 1373* US *22425* Chile *1201*

General
If you are battling down Canal Cockburn against the prevailing west winds, an anchorage on the western side of Isla King provides excellent shelter but its position cannot be made out from chart *1201*. It is on the northern shore of the island, towards the west end, though the position of 1447.4Isla King light is 54°22'·4S 71°15'·1W. The small notch near the entrance requires three lines ashore. On a clear day there are spectacular views of the glaciers on Mount Sarmiento to the east.

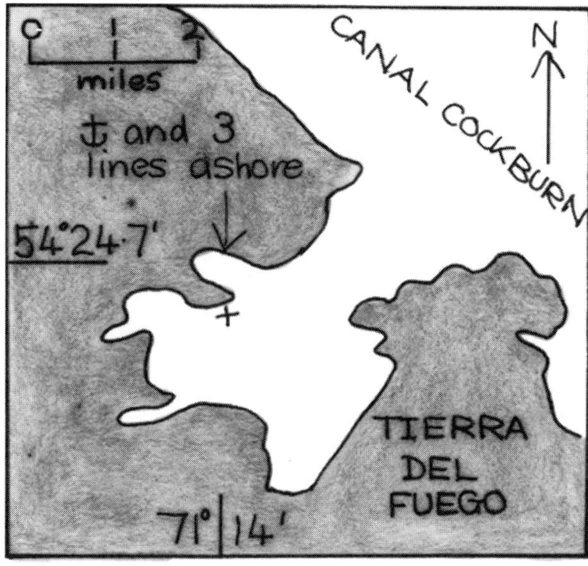

Puerto King. (Charted positions)

9·7 Isla Diego – Puerto Soffia

54°16'S 71°26'W

Charts
UK *554, 1373* US *22425* Chile *1201, 1202*

General
The entrance to this long, deep bay is wide and clean. The anchorage at the head in 9m over a mud, stone and sand bottom provides excellent shelter from all winds. This is classified as a prohibited anchorage, and accordingly it should only be used in the case of bad weather.

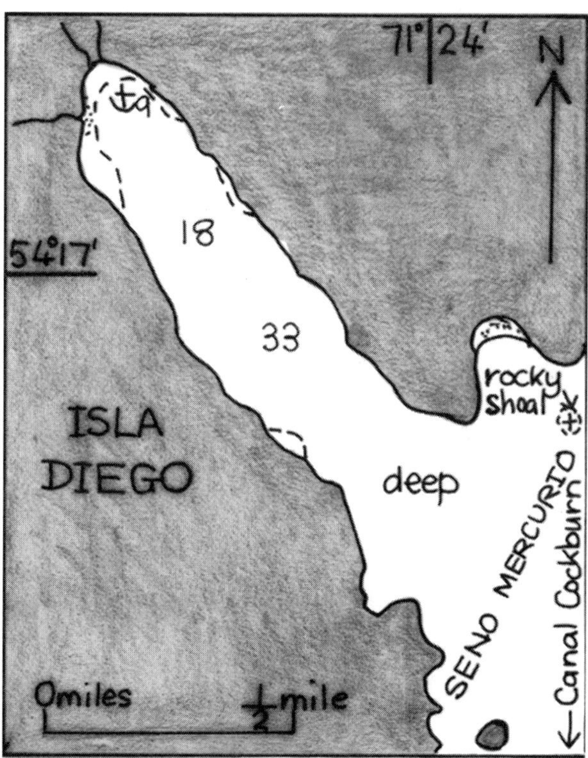

Puerto Soffia. (Charted positions)

9·8 Isla Clarence – Caleta Parmelia

54°18'S 71°51'·4W

Charts
UK *554* US *22425* Chile *1201*

General
This unnamed Caleta was used by yacht Parmelia when they found an uncomfortable swell entering Caleta Louis. On another occasion, in strong westerlies Caleta Louis was tenable whilst the wind howled down Seno Duntze and access to this anchorage would be difficult. There is ample depth all the way up to the anchorage. Once inside the anchorage there is protection from winds from all directions. The Caleta is narrow enough to tie fore and aft across it with plenty of places to secure to. The bottom is mud.

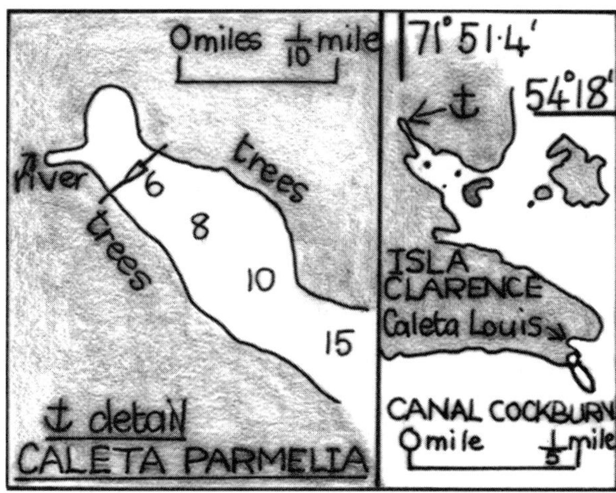

Caleta Parmelia. (Charted positions)

9·9 Isla Clarence – Caleta Louis

54°20'S 71°48'W

Charts
UK *554* US *22425* Chile *1201*

General
This small *caleta* was named by the British yacht *Ayesha*. It is located just north of the light on the south east corner of Isla Clarence in Canal Cockburn (1447·6 Seno Duntze Fl(3)9s7m6M White GRP tower red bands 3m). The anchorage is sometimes used by local fishermen. One user comments that it provides excellent protection from all but east winds; another that it is the most squally and uncomfortable anchorage in the whole of Chile. You pays your money and you takes your choice. The entrance is narrow but clean, with kelp marking the rocks on either side. It is advisable to take a line ashore. Water is available from a stream in the north western corner of the *caleta*. In strong westerlies this *caleta* is subject to quite strong gusts but once anchored and tied up close to the shore under the trees the gusts pass overhead.

9·10 Isla Clarence – Puerto Niemann

54°20'S 71°55'W

Charts
UK *554* US *22425* Chile *1201*

General
Puerto Niemann is a large harbour on the southern side of Isla Clarence. It contains two anchorages, the northern one being bullet proof. The entrance is straightforward, deep with no off-lying hazards. In strong northerly or westerly winds it is a better alternative to Caleta Louis. In northerly winds there is a swell in the entrance to Louis and in strong westerlies it is quite difficult to take lines to the shore.

The northern nook is tucked in below trees, the kelp is fairly close to the shore and does not pose a problem, and once shore lines are fixed it is peaceful. The nook on the western side of the large island in Puerto Niemann is also secure but winds are reported to blow quite strongly between here and the main island.

9·11 Isla Adelaide – Caleta Tarmac

54°22'S 72°05'W

Charts
UK *554* US *22425* Chile *1201*

Located on the northeast side of Isla Adelaide, Tarmac is the north-most of two indentations on the northeastern side of Isla Adelaide. It is well-sheltered form the prevailing west winds and two small islets give some protection from the east. There is considerable kelp in the bay. The holding is poor in 12m on a rocky bottom (hence the name Tarmac). Take lines ashore.

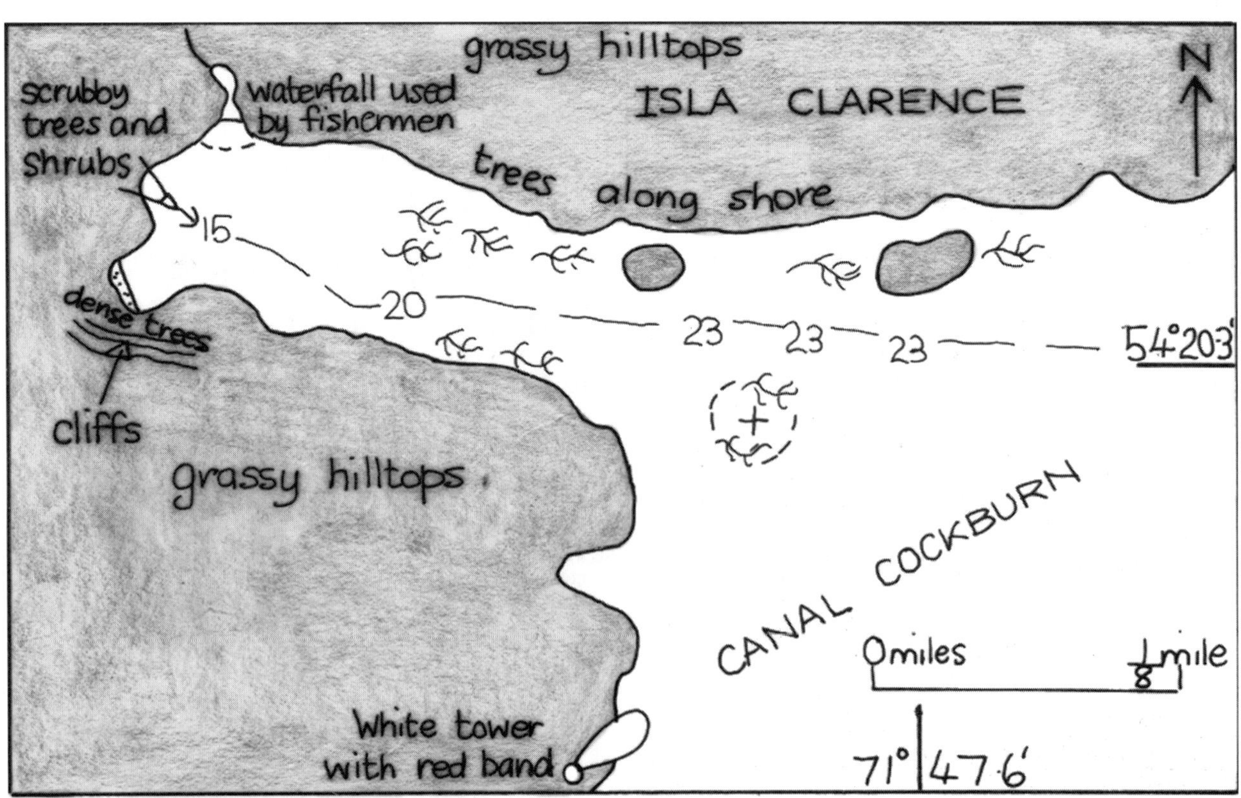

Caleta Louis. (GPS positions)

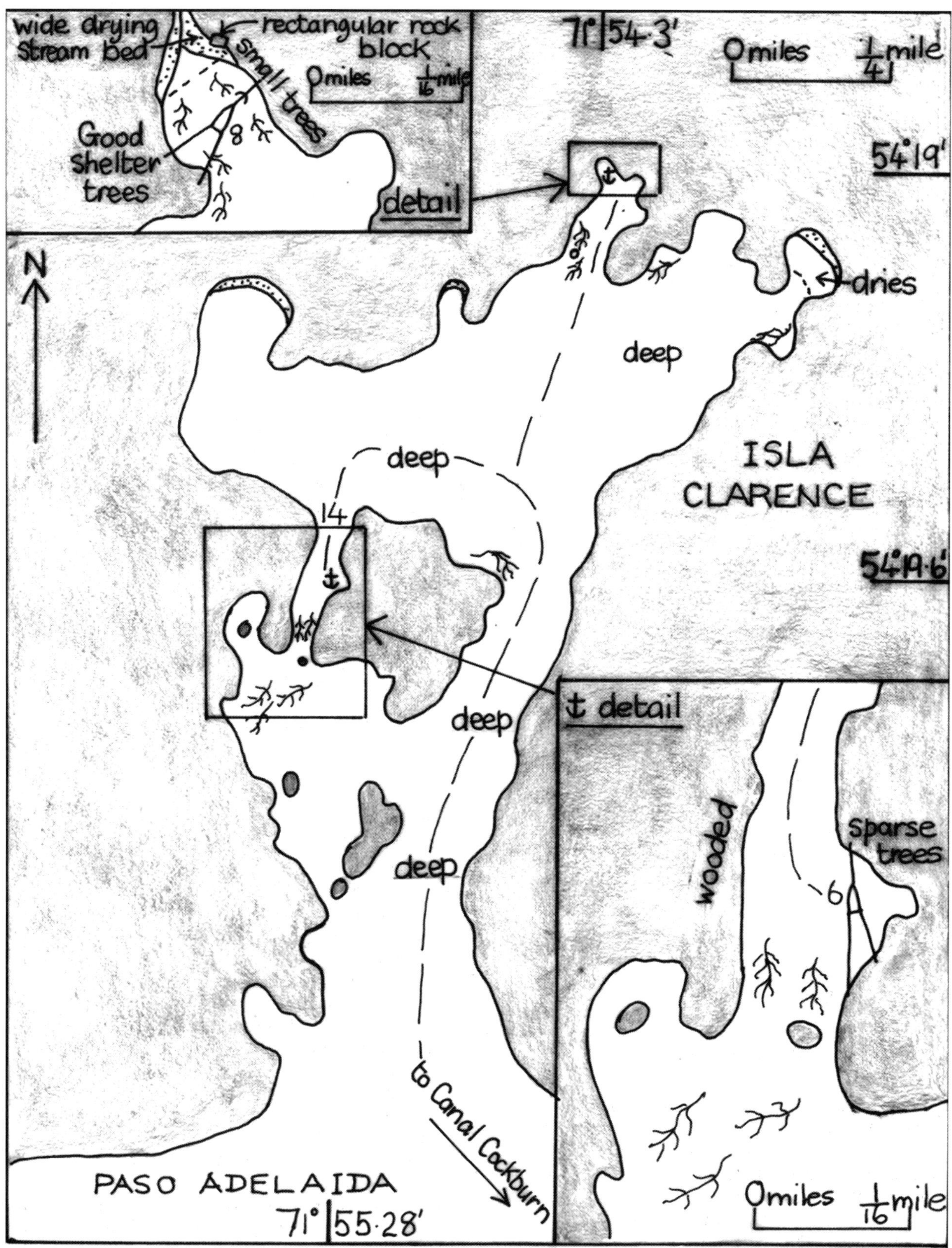

Puerto Niemann. (Charted positions)

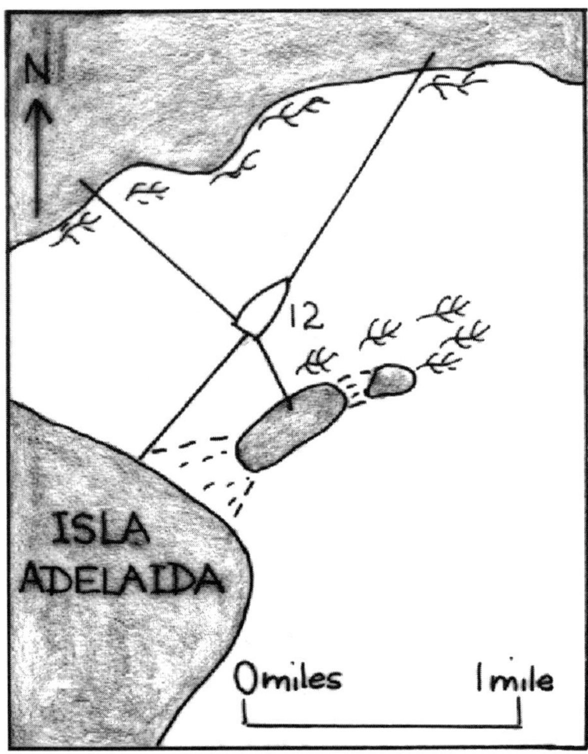

Caleta Tarmac

Canal Ocasión

54°32'·7S 71°54'·5W

Charts
UK *554* US *22425* Chile *1201, 1207, 1221, 1204*

General
Canal Ocasión leads between Canal Cockburn and Canal Brecknock, running north east of Isla Aguirre. If taken, it avoids some of the unpleasantness of the outside world and is the route taken by fishing boats and small ships. Seno Ocasión, leading to Caleta Brecknock, runs off Canal Ocasión.

9·12 Península Brecknock – Caleta Brecknock

54°32'S 71°54'W

Charts
UK *554* US *22425* Chile *1201, 1207, 1221, 1204*

General
Caleta Brecknock is 1½ miles up Seno Ocasión and a justifiably popular anchorage. The surrounding hills and cliffs are spectacular and there is excellent hiking on the exposed glaciated rock. From the head of the small notch anchorage it is possible to scramble to the top of the mountain overlooking the anchorage. There have been reports of boats having trouble with williwaws here whilst anchoring but once tucked back into the notch the yacht should be protected from this problem. The safest anchorage is in a bullet proof notch in the north western corner, with four lines ashore. There are truck tyres along the cliffs to the east of the waterfall and small boats can go alongside but watch out for trees snagging in the rigging.

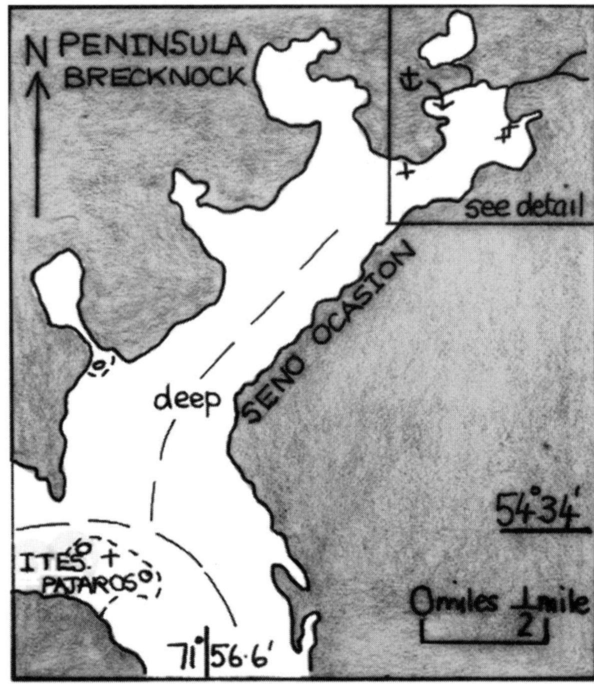

Seno Ocasión. (Charted positions)

Canal Brecknock

9·13 Isla Brecknock – Puerto Paso Aguirre

54°41'·4S 71°32'·7W

Charts
UK *554* US *22425* Chile *1201, 1207, 1221*

General
There are two anchorages shown on the sketch chart, both providing excellent protection, the one to the west being bullet proof. This anchorage is right up in the corner shown on the sketch. The depth falls to about 3m and care needs to be taken as there are rocky areas close in with less water over them. Close in would be very tight for a yacht more than 12–13m long. This anchorage is almost always occupied by fishing boats and it is possible to tie up with them and to take shorelines. The fishermen are very polite and will happily the offer the visitor sea urchins (*erizos*). Delicious but an acquired taste; the eggs are consumed raw with a squeeze of lemon. A box of wine is a good exchange.

The east anchorage has quite a lot of kelp close in but it is possible to anchor clear of the kelp, in about 10m, and to take shorelines.

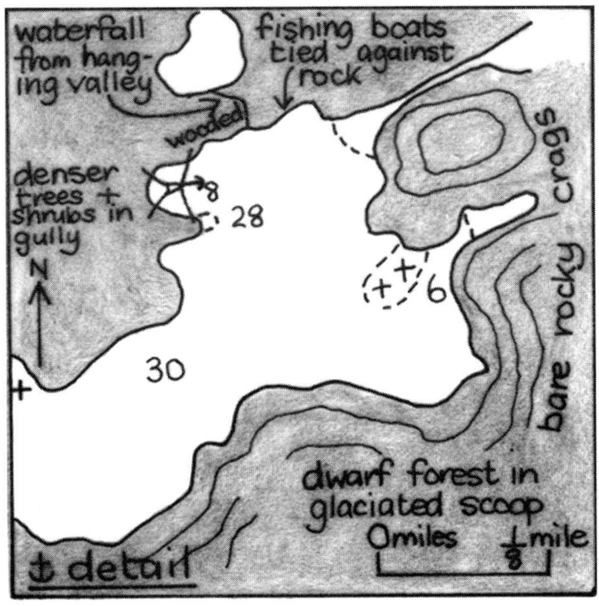

Caleta Brecknock

9·14 Paso Aguirre – Isla Macias

54°42'S 71°32'·2W

Charts
UK *554* US *22425* Chile *1201, 1207, 1221*

General
This is a regularly used anchorage by yachts and by small fishing boats from Punta Arenas. The anchorage lies in the obvious bay on the north side of Isla Macias. Anchor in about 7m and take shore lines. A well protected anchorage.

Puerto Paso Aguirre. (GPS positions)

Islas Macias 54°42'S 71°32'·2W

Canal Ballenero

9·15 Isla Burnt – Caleta Ancha

54°44'S 71°12'W

Charts
UK *554* US *22425, 22418* Chile *1201, 1207, 1221*

General
Caleta Ancha is on the southeast side of Isla Burnt. Anchor near the waterfall with a line astern. The bottom is rock but said to be good holding.

9·16 Isla Stewart – Caleta Fanny

54°53'S 70°58'W

Charts
UK *554, 1373* US *22425*, 22418 Chile *1201, 1203, 1207, 1205*

General
Caleta Fanny is at the northeast end of Isla Stewart. As there is foul ground off Punta Baja it is better to favour the west shore of the approach. The first anchorage is in 15m, rock and kelp, with a three point tie to white painted rocks on the shore in a small cove on the western side of the long indentation. There is considerable kelp along the sides of the cove. It is surrounded by steep hills and subject to strong *rachas* particularly during west winds. The second anchorage is in the SW corner of Puerto Fanny taking a 4 point tie between the small island and the main shore. There is kelp but the depth is 7·5m.

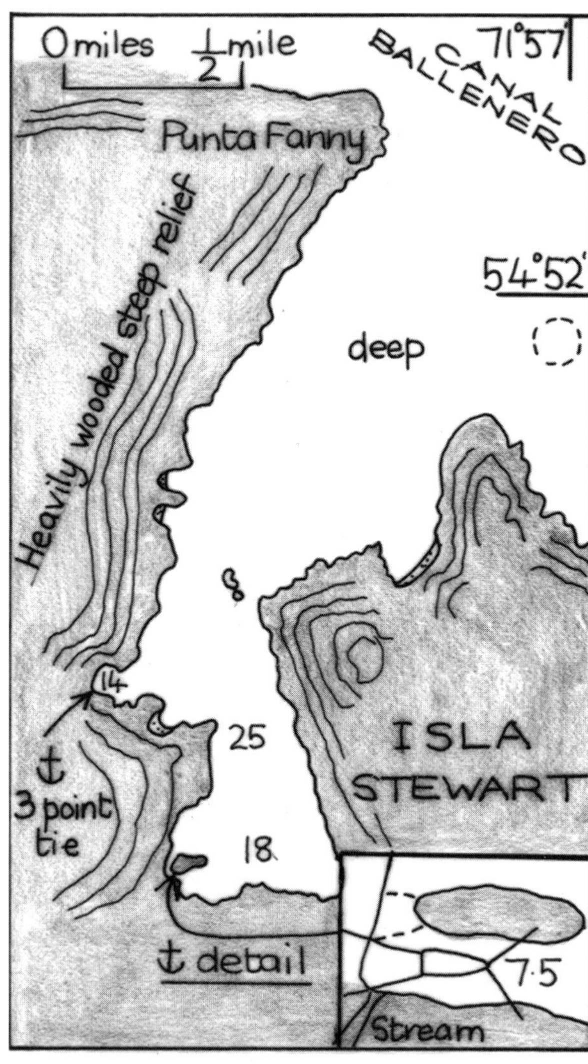

Caleta Fanny. (Charted position)

9·17 Islas del Medio – Caleta Frog

54°49'S 70°57'W

Charts

UK *554, 1373* US *22425, 22418* Chile *1207*

General

This unnamed *caleta* (Caleta Frog) is in the Islas del Medio which lie between Isla Stewart and Isla O'Brien. The anchorage is at the northwest end of the largest island, Isla Grande, off which there is a maze of little islets and shoals. There are two routes into the anchorage. The approach from the north is narrow but is well sheltered from westerly winds. This entrance has considerable kelp fringing it and a least depth of 4·5m. However, especially as it is sheltered, it is fairly straightforward picking a way through this kelp. The approach from the west is wider but has the disadvantage that it is west facing

This anchorage is a good alternative to Puerto Fanny. The surrounding islands are relatively low-lying and it is not subject to the *rachas* that may be found in the latter. It is well protected from winds from all directions. A secure 4 point tie can be made between the islands and holding is good in soft mud.

Although the anchorage does not suffer from *rachas*, in strong west–southwest winds the wind funnels between the islands so that the security of lines is reassuring.

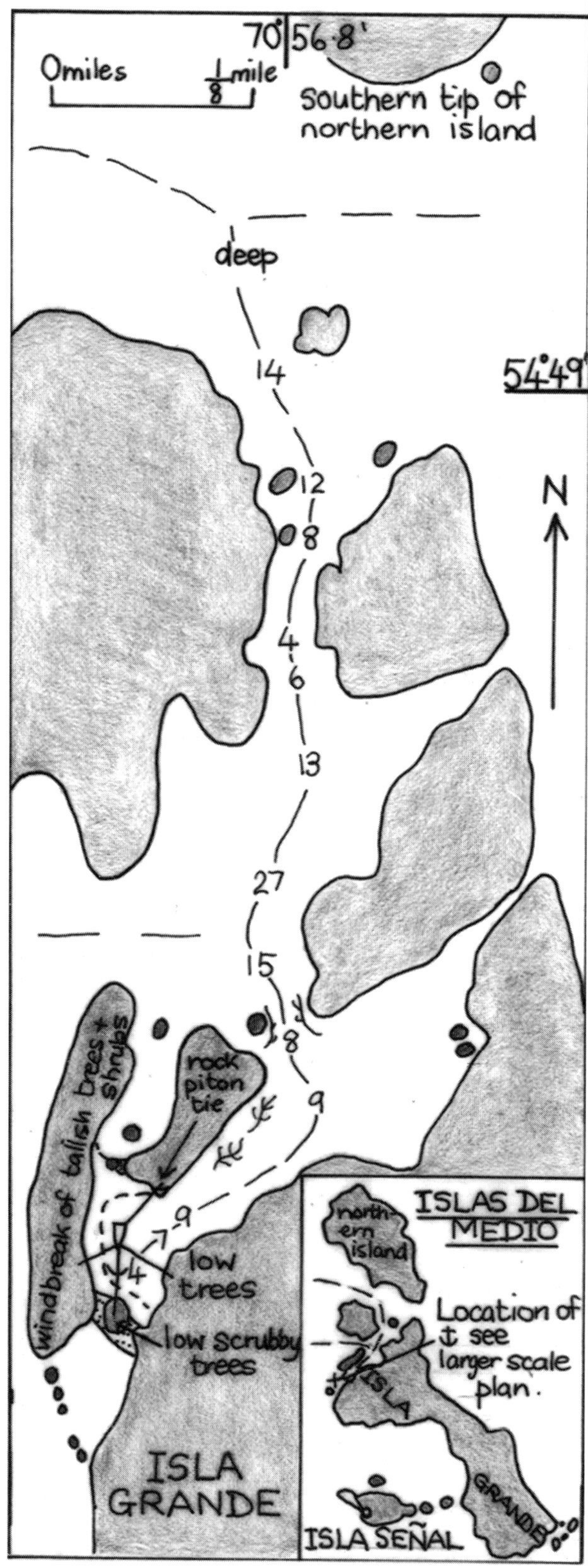

Caleta Frog. (GPS positions)

9·18 Isla Londonderry – Puerto Engaño

54°56'·9S 70°46'·6W

Charts
UK *554,1373* US *22425, 22418* Chile *1203, 1206, 1205*

General
Puerto Engaño is on Isla Londonderry, towards the east end of Canal Ballenero. The anchorage itself is in Caleta Silva in the southwestern corner of Puerto Engaño. The entrance is open. There is a beacon on the northern point of the entrance. The holding is excellent in 8m, sand bottom and there is water available from a stream at the head of the bay. It is also possible to anchor and take shorelines.

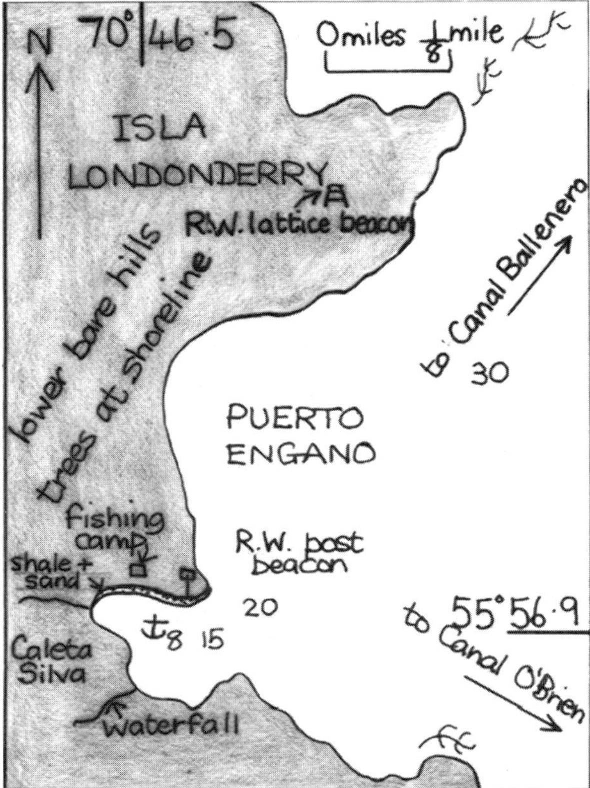

Puerto Egaño. (GPS positions)

Canal O'Brien

9·19 Isla Londonderry – Puerto Fortuna

54°53'S 70°26'W

Charts
UK *554, 1373* US *22418* Chile *1206, 1205*

General
Puerto Fortuna on Canal O'Brien provides good protection from winds from the northwest through to the east. The holding is good in mud, but unfortunately the anchorage is very deep, more than 20m. There is ample swinging room if anchored in the middle of the bay but a more secure position can be found in the southern part of the bay anchoring in about 7m and tying close into the shore. This position gives better protection than the chart suggests.

Puerto Fortuna. (Charted positions)

9·20 Canal Pomar – Seno Ventisquero

54°51'S 70°19'·5W

Charts
UK *554, 1373* US *22418* Chile *1206*

General
This glacier lies at the junction of the west end of Canal Beagle and Canal Pomar. The moraine at the entrance to the Seno is shallow with a depth of 5–7m. At the first narrow shown on insert 1 pass at about 150m from the wooded spur. There is a depth of 5–7m but it is easy to touch! Bergy bits are usually aground on the moraine at this point. The best anchorage is shown in insert 2 but there is an ice threat here.

9·21 Isla Chair

54°52'·5S 70°00'W

Charts
UK *554, 1373* US *22418* Chile *1206*

General
There are two anchorages on Isla Chair, nick-named Cushion and Sur, both of which provide excellent shelter from west winds that are prevalent in the Beagle Canal.

Caleta Cushion is on the eastern end of the island. The approach is from the large bay which is deep and wide. This approach bay provides immediate protection from all but south and east winds. The anchorage is situated in the small bay behind the

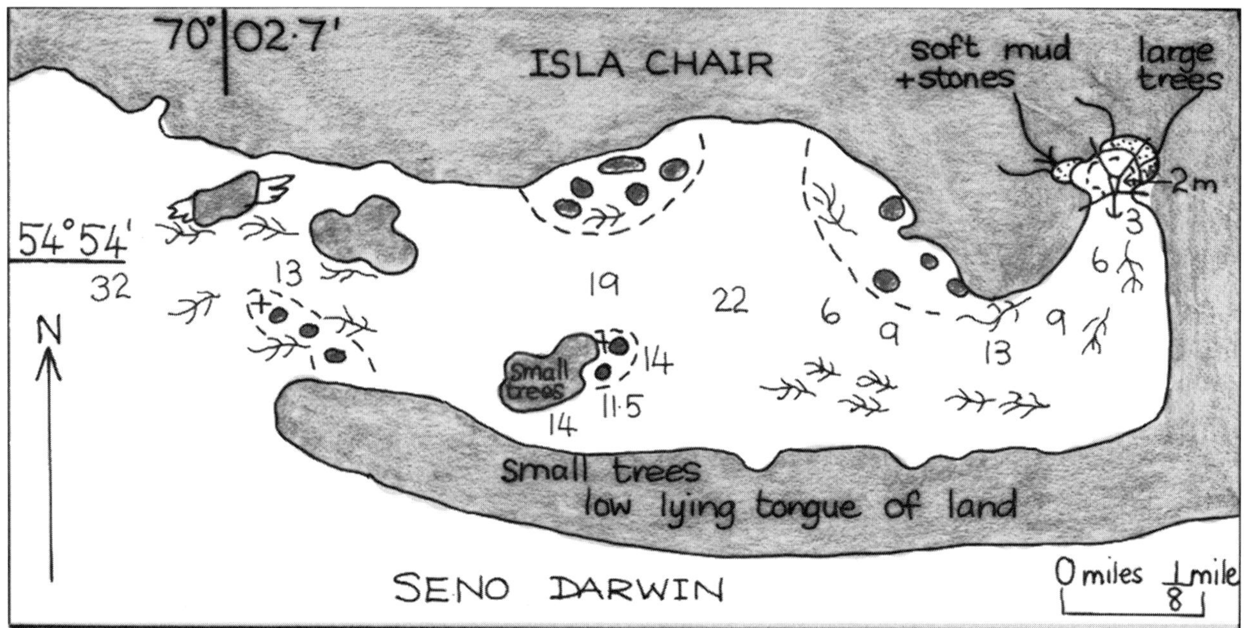

Caleta Sur (GPS positions)

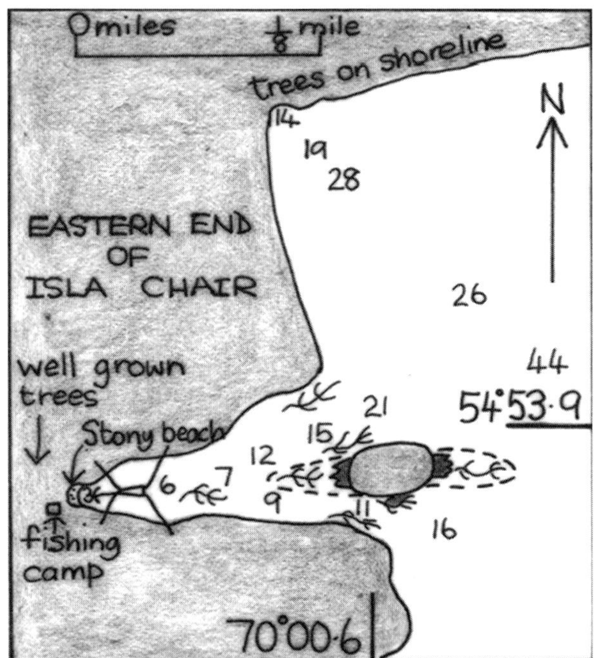

Caleta Cushion

island in the southern part of the bay. The approach leaving the island to port is easy. Holding is good and the bay is surrounded by tall trees, that provide excellent protection and tie-off points for a 4-point mooring. The bay is occasionally used by fishermen.

Caleta Sur is deep into the bay on the southeastern side of the island. The entrance looks difficult, but is actually quite straightforward. There is quite a lot of kelp in the bay which helps mark the safe route clear of rocks. Depths in this inner bay fall from about 7m to 2m near its head. However the bottom is very soft mud and the yacht can sit partly in the mud at low water when snugged up into the

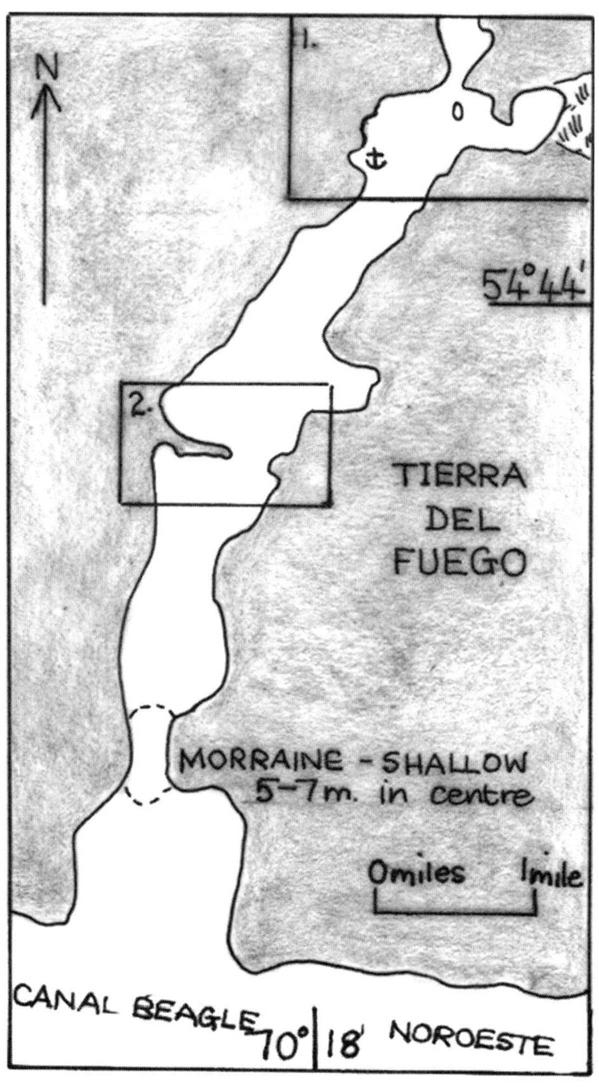

Seno Ventisquero

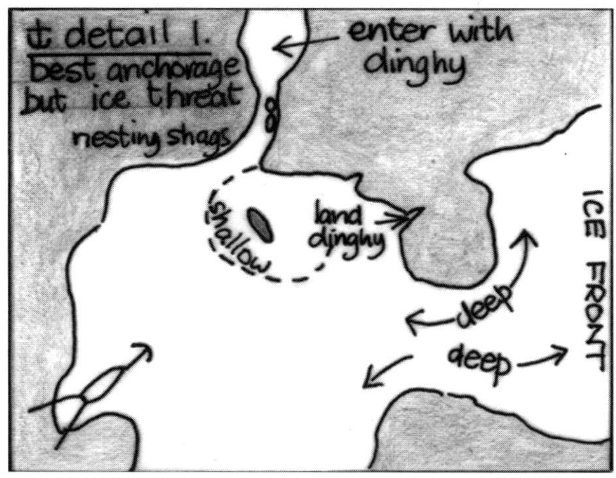

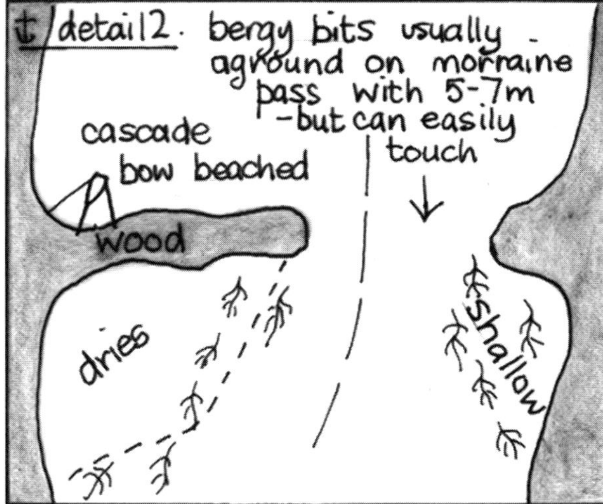

bay. Good holding in very soft mud plus shore lines. The inner basin offers protection from all winds while the outer basin provides protection only from east winds and therefore is of limited value as the prevailing winds are westerlies.

Caleta Cushion is the preferred anchorage as the approach is sheltered from all prevailing winds whilst the approach to Caleta Sur faces these winds and in heavy weather it may be difficult to distinguish the kelp in the outer bay.

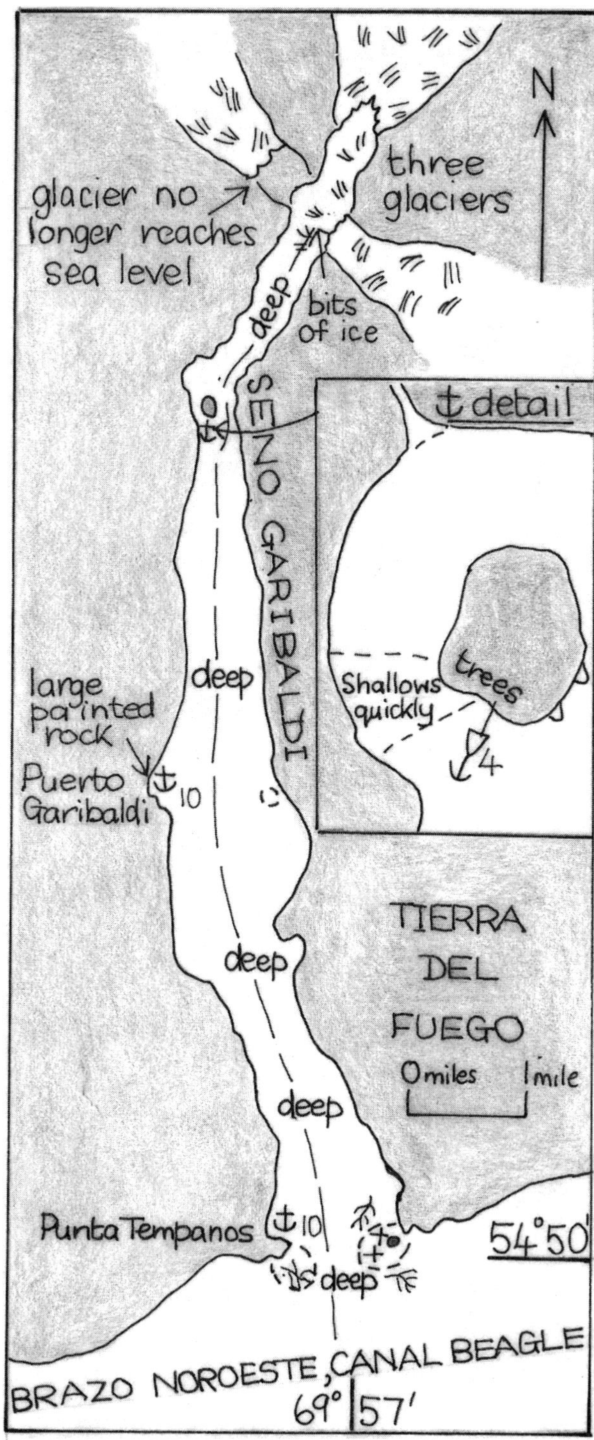

Seno Garibaldi. (Charted positions)

Diversion

9·22 Seno Garibaldi

54°50'S 69°55'W

Charts
UK *554, 1373* US *22418* Chile *1203*

General
The entrance to Seno Garibaldi is at the west end of the Brazo Norte of Canal Beagle. The Seno runs north–south and has three glaciers running into it at the north end. There is an anchorage at the entrance on the west side immediately behind the point, 10m sand and mud, protected from the west. Puerto Garibaldi, about five miles in on the west side, is protected between northwest and southwest. The anchorage is in about 18m, sand and mud. In the north, there is an anchorage south of the island there, with a line ashore. The view of the glaciers from the top of the island is remarkable.

When the wind is fresh, it howls down Seno Garibaldi with *racha* ferocity. The first two anchorages are open and provide negligible protection and although there is some shelter to the south of the island there are far better anchorages within a few miles of the entrance to Seno Garibaldi, for example, at Isla Chair.

Continuation Canal Beagle – Brazo Noroeste

Note In the Beagle channel area several anchorages are prohibited, as are Canal Murray and Paso Goree. Yachts entering Canal Murray will be towed out of the Canal by an *Armada* vessel in an unceremonious way and taken to Puerto Williams. There is no question but that this is a prohibited route.

9·23 Bahía Tres Brazos

54°53'S 69°46'W

Charts

UK *554* US *22418* Chile *1203, 1206*

General

This is a large bay on the S side of Brazo Noroeste, opposite Ventisquero España. Considerable discrepancies have been observed between charts and GPS positions in this area.

The bay has many potential anchorages, the three shown on the plan have been used and found to be secure.

1. This is rated 3 star. It is open to the south west. When mooring pull close into the shore for the maximum protection.
2. Caleta Julia. About 1·5M south of the entrance, behind the first point on the west side. It appears no more than a bay on Chile chart *1206*, but opens up into a sheltered pool where a boat can tie off from shore to shore. The *caleta* is used by fisherman and may be blocked off by lines tied across the entrance. It is rated 5 star and is good for all winds.
3. The third anchorage is at GPS 54°56'·7S 69°46'·1W (on Chile chart *1206*, 54°55'·5S 69°46'·5W), in an unnamed *caleta* about 2·5M further S from Caleta Julia. Once around the point to the S of the entrance, hold to the starboard shore, leave a visible rock to starboard and follow the 'river' round to port. Depths in the narrowest part of the entrance have to be judged by eye. The pool at the head is very well sheltered from all quarters. There is anchorage in 2·5m with lines ashore. Besides excellent shelter and convenient fresh water, the *caleta* is in a lovely setting and has good hiking on the high ground above. It is rated 5 star.

Another *caleta* in the northwest corner of the southwest Brazo has also been suggested but not examined.

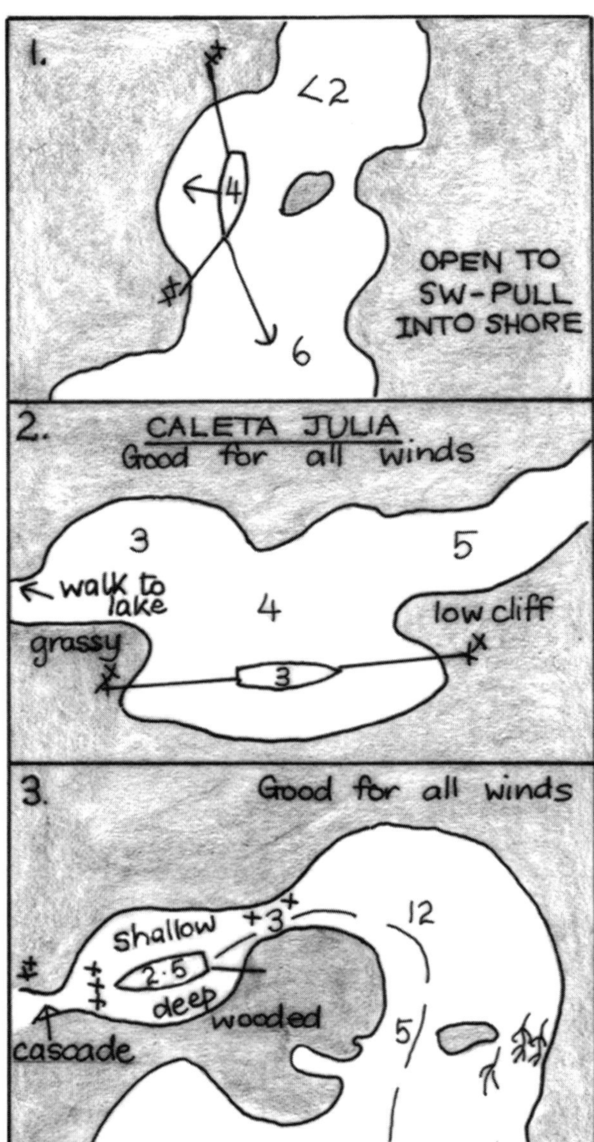

Bahía Tres Brazos – anchorage details

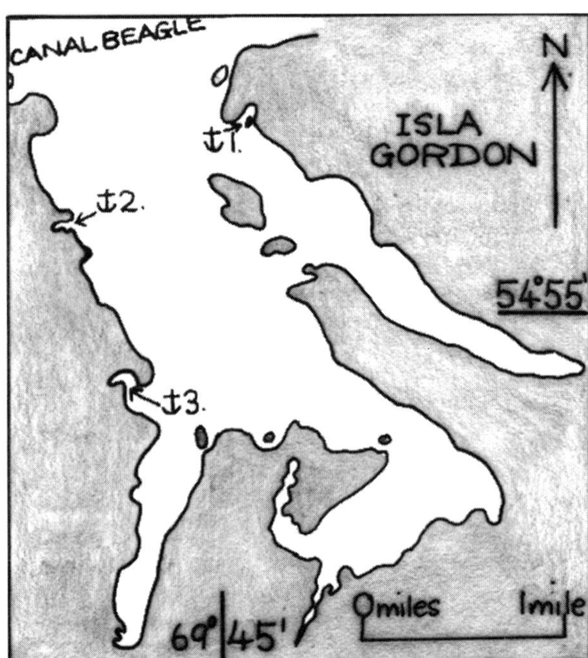

Bahía Tres Brazos. (Charted positions)

Section 10
Brazo Noroeste to Cape Horn

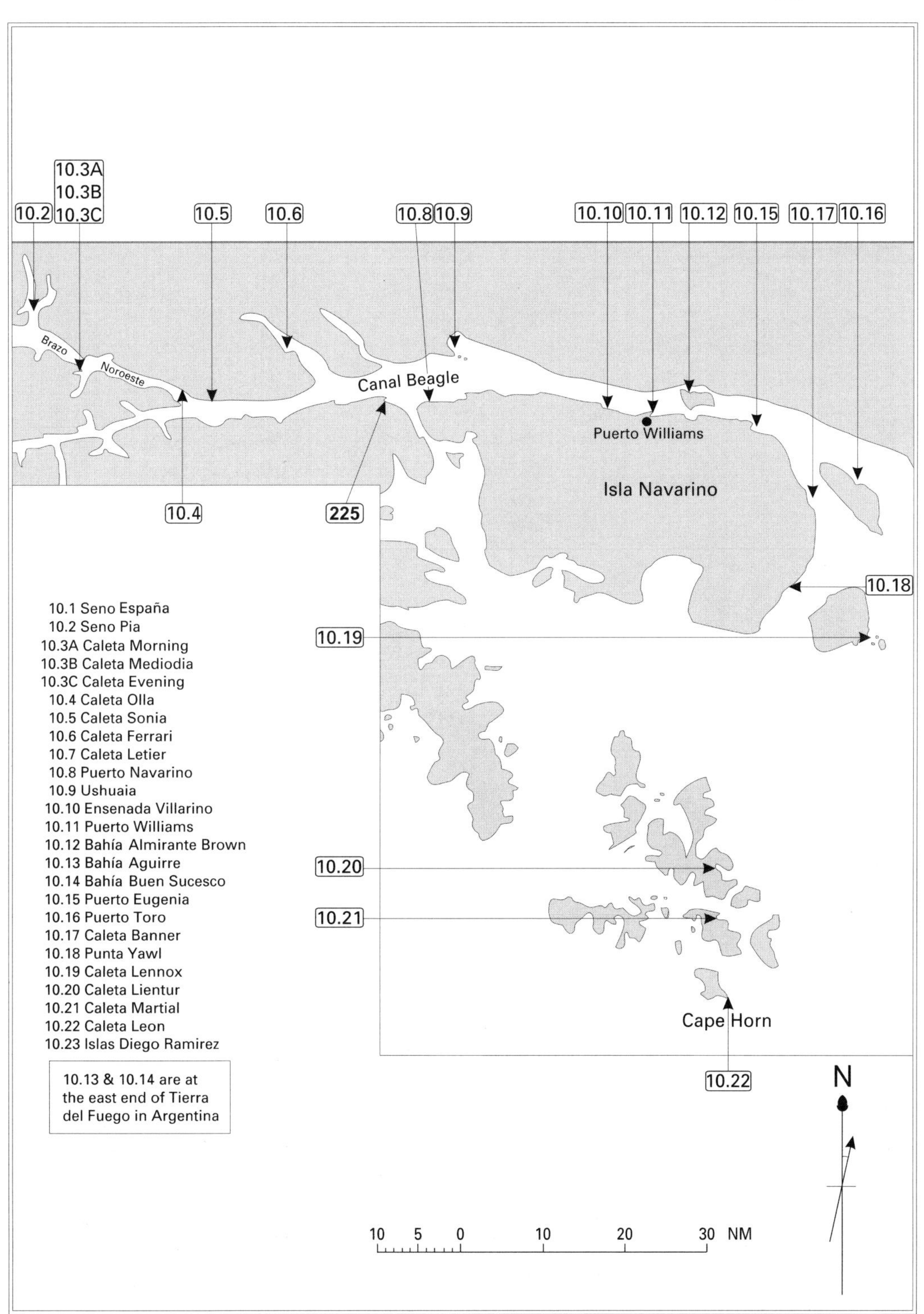

10·1 Seno España

54°49'S 69°46'·5W

Charts
UK *554* US *22418* Chile *1203*

General
This is a difficult Seno with a tricky morraine at the entrance which has plenty of kelp and depths of 2m. Enter centrally, close to HW. Once inside there are a number of anchorages and once through the pass shown there are no dangers through to the glacier.

10·2 Seno Pia

54°48'S 69°40'W

Charts
UK *554* US *22418* Chile *1203*

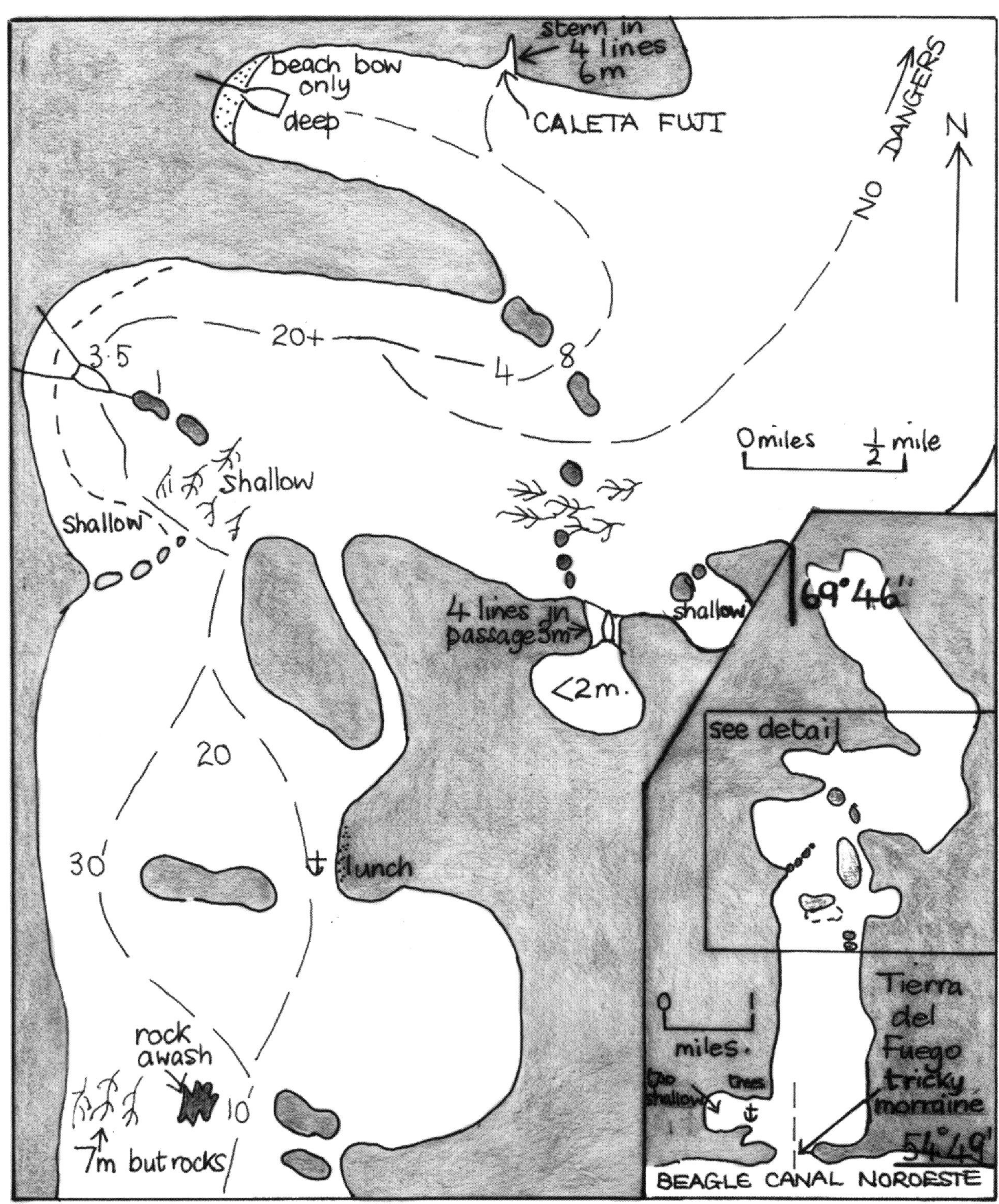

Seno España

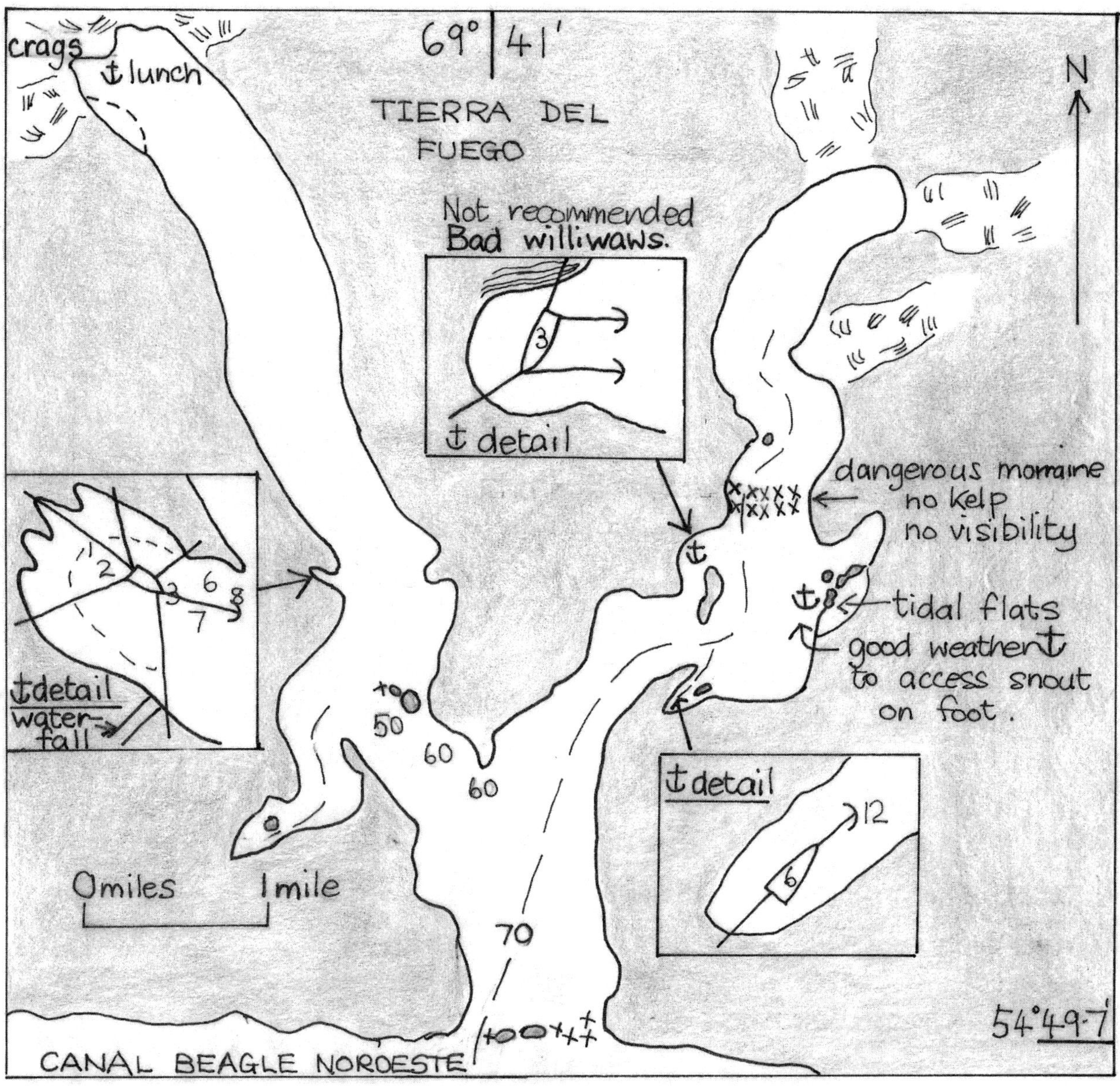

Seno Pia. (Charted positions)

General

A beautiful Seno leading north into Cordillera Darwin from Brazo Norte, 'the avenue of the glaciers'. It is well protected though it would become uncomfortable with a wind blowing up the Seno and the *caletas* can be gusty. In calm conditions it is possible to reach the glacier faces by dinghy (the eastern side of the westernmost glacier is recommended) and yachts have anchored at the head of the Seno. The anchorage shown in the sketch is about two miles up the western arm; a number of other possible anchorages are indicated but have not been explored.

Entrance

There is a 12m bar at the entrance to the Seno and a shoal area off the western shore clearly marked by kelp. A reef extends off the eastern shore to a prominent white rock with two smaller rocks close together further off-shore. Enter about 400m west of these two rocks; the bar has no kelp.

Anchorage

The anchorage shown in the sketch is at GPS 54°46'·3S 69°40'·65W. There is a shoal patch on the south side of the *caleta* where a river comes out and depths are generally greater towards the northern shore. Anchor in 4m, good holding, but put lines ashore as it is squally. Though there is invariably ice in the Seno, it does not seem to come in to the *caleta*.

10·3 Bahía Romanche: Caletas Morning, Mediodía and Evening

54°55'S 69°29'W

Charts

UK *554, 1373* US *22418* Chile *1203, 1206*

General

The entrance to this bay is on the south side of Brazo Nortoeste immediately opposite the spectacular Romanche Glacier. This Glacier is retreating quite rapidly and there is a huge waterfall running from the base of the glacier into tide water. There are three good anchorages in Bahía Romanche. The bay itself is surprisingly well sheltered from the strong westerly winds that can blow down Brazo Norte of Canal Beagle. These anchorages are:

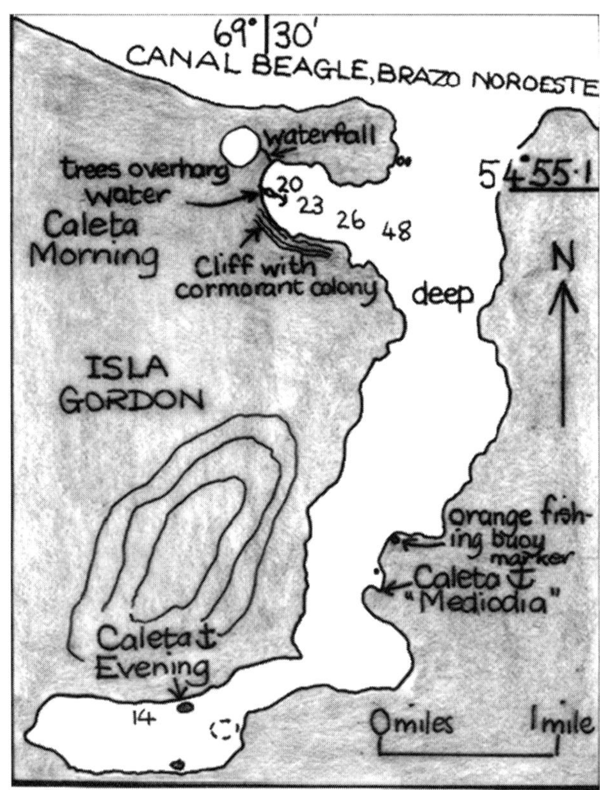

Bahía Romanche (GPS positions)

10·3A Caleta Morning

54°55'S 69°30'W

General

Situated at the entrance and on the west side of Bahía Romanche, Caleta Morning provides all round protection and is generally free from *rachas*. The entrance is wide and clean apart from a rock close to the south shore. The anchorage has good holding in 18m at the head of the bay. There are also rings set into the rocks underneath the cliffs at the southwest corner which could be used for a stern-to tie. These cliffs are the nesting site for blue-eyed cormorants, and condors have also been seen amongst the nests.

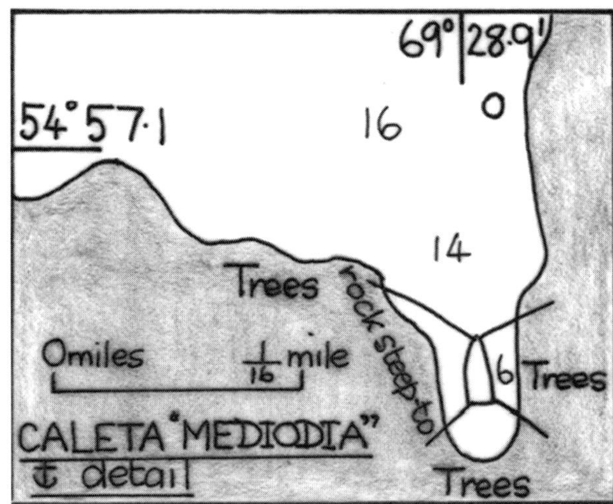

10·3B Caleta Mediodía

54°57'·1S 69°28'·9W

General

This is the most secure anchorage in Bahía Romanche. It is bullet proof. It is used by fishermen and its position has been marked by old orange fishing buoys that have been tied to trees. There is just turning room inside the bay but it would be better to drop anchor and back in before taking 4 shore lines.

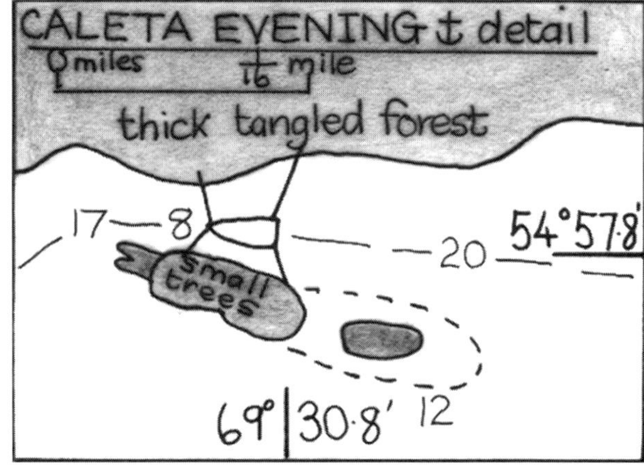

10·3C Caleta Evening

54°57'·8S 69°30'·8W

General

Different charts give the location of Caleta Evening in different positions. However the plan shows a secure anchorage between a small island and thick woodland on the northern shore. This anchorage is better protected than it would appear but could be a little exposed in westerly gale conditions.

10·4 Caleta Olla

54°56'S 69°08'W

Charts

UK *554, 1373* US *22418, 22430* Chile *1203, 1206*

General

Caleta Olla is on the north side of Brazo Norte. It is about 400m in diameter and is sheltered except from the southeast. The British Admiralty Pilot states that, 'A sandbank with 3·4m at its outer end extends half a mile SSE from the east entrance point (of the *caleta*); the bank is sandy and is marked by kelp.' This is not shown on the Chilean chart, nor is it obvious when viewed from above. The bay has perfect protection from the tall trees that grow along its west side. Anchor in 14m and then use shore lines to pull right back close to the beach in about 6m. In this position winds can howl overhead and the anchorage, close in, is windless. Holding is excellent on a sand bottom.

Charter boats often stop here. There is excellent hiking. A trail follows the stream at the northwestern end of the beach, leads through the swamp, goes up beside a large waterfall and on to high ground where there is a wonderful view of both the Italia and Hollandia glaciers – 2 hours plus each way. There is a small Indian *midden* off the beach, and a wide variety of wildflowers. There are many guanaco trails on the shore.

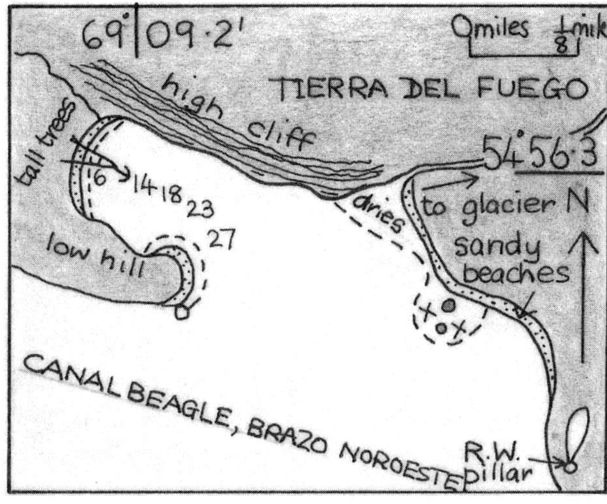

Caleta Olla. (GPS positions)

Canal Beagle – Main Channel

10·5 Caleta Sonia

54°38'S 69°01'W

Charts

UK *554, 1373* US *22430* Chile *1301*

General

Caleta Sonia is just east of 1332Punta Yamana (Fl.12s12m7M white concrete tower, red band 5m 265°-vis-095°). After rounding the headland leave

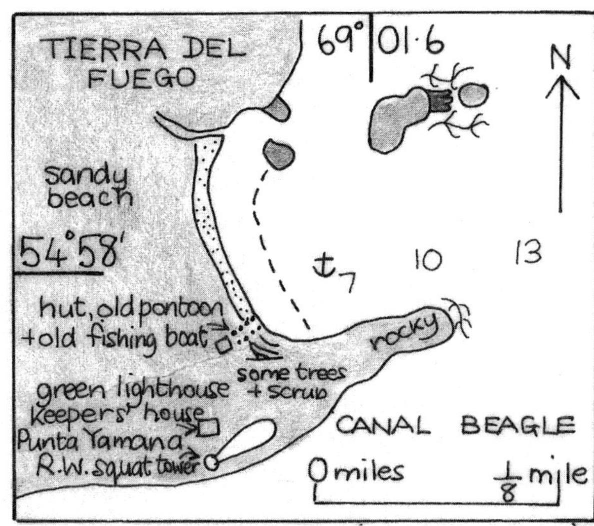

Caleta Sonia. (GPS positions)

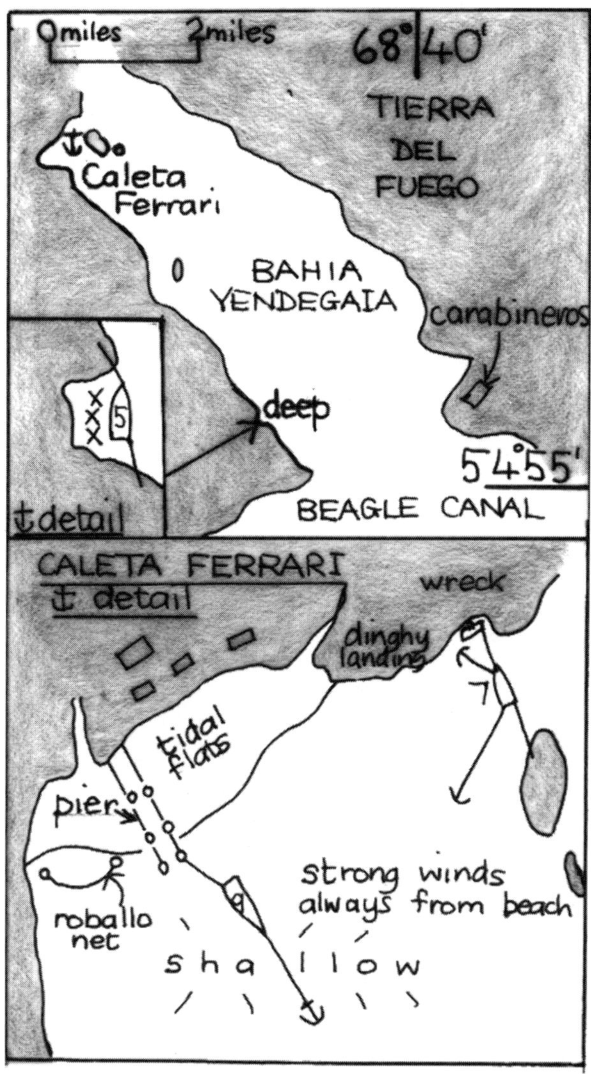

Caleta Ferrari. (Charted positions) 68°48'·8W 54°51'·6S

the small group of islets/rocks to starboard and anchor close to the beach in 15m or less, excellent holding ground in sand and mud. Shore lines can be taken to trees or the remains of an old pier. This anchorage would give good protection from the west but is probably gusty when winds are from the north. In poor conditions Caleta Olla would make a more secure stopping place.

10·6 Caleta Ferrari

54°51'S 68°48'W

Charts

UK *554, 1373* US *22430* Chile *1301*

General

Caleta Ferrari is on the west side of Bahía Yendegaia which is on the north side of Canal Beagle. In general the wind blows strongly from the beach all the time so that for additional security it is possible to set an anchor out from the pier and take bow and stern lines to the southern shore and a further stern line to the pier. Other anchorages are shown on the plan.

Caleta Ferrari is the home of Estancia Yendegaia, owned by Miguel Serka. ☎ (61) 219 285. Horses are for hire and the trail to the glacier (2 hours one way) is very exciting. There is excellent hiking in the surrounding mountains. It is often possible to buy meat from the *estancia*. *Centolla* crab can be caught in the bay behind the islands in 30m of water.

10·7 Peninsula Dumas – Caletas Eugenio and Letier

56°56'S 68°27'W

Charts

UK *554* US *22430* Chile *1307, 1302*

General

These anchorages lie on the northeast corner of Peninsula Dumas (Isla Hoste), at the junction of Canal Beagle and Canal Murray. The access is straightforward and they give good protection from all winds except from the east and south east. Eugenia is better than Letier. Anchor in 5–8m with shore lines.

10·8 Puerto Navarino

54°55'·4S 68°19'·3W

Charts

UK *554, 1373* US *22430* Chile *1301,1307, 1303*

General

Puerto Navarino is 26 miles west of Puerto Williams and almost exactly half way between Puerto Williams and Caleta Olla, the best anchorage at the east end of Brazo Norte, Canal Beagle. It is a good stopping point, especially when travelling west against the prevailing winds. Puerto Navarino has a small *Armada* station that will make the visiting yacht welcome.

Approaches

Paso Weste is more straightforward than Paso Este and is the best route to enter or leave when taking a westerly course.

From the east the approach is via Paso Este. The Chilean chart, *1303*, looks complicated as many rocks and kelp patches are shown. In addition, in March 1998 the buoys were not in the positions shown on the chart. The red buoy shown on the Chilean chart was missing. The position of this buoy is shown on the sketch chart; it may be replaced in time. The second difference was that a red and

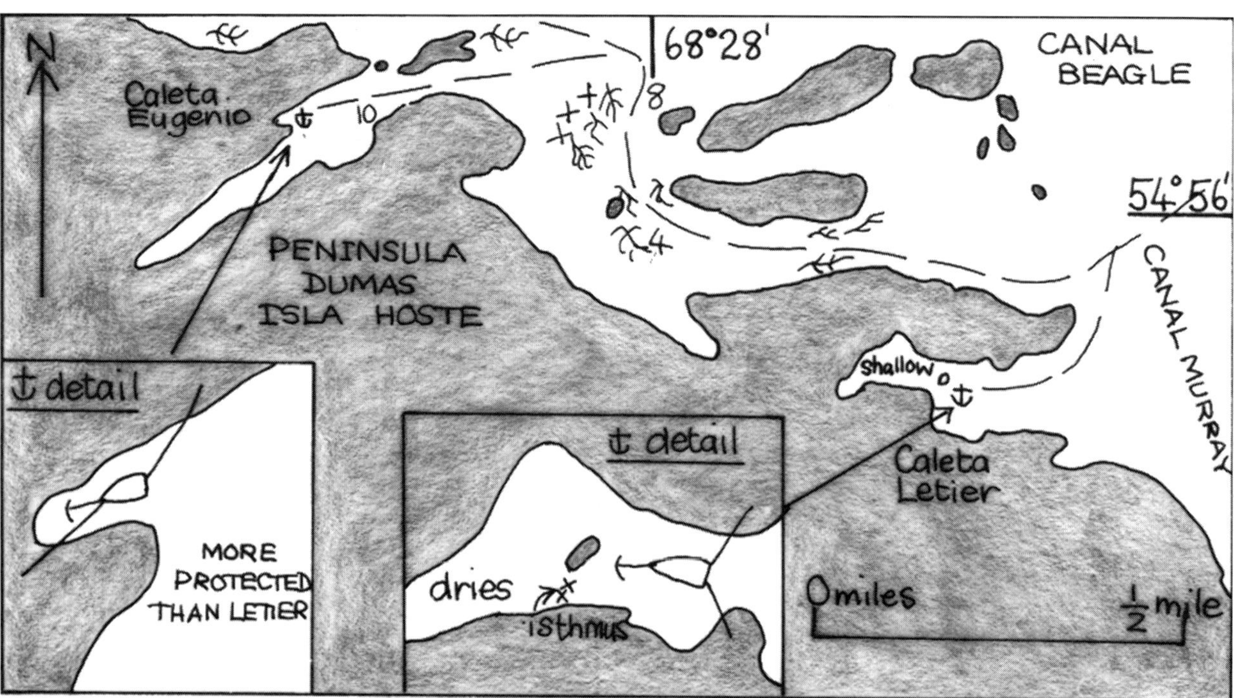

Caletas Eugenio and Letier. (Charted positions)

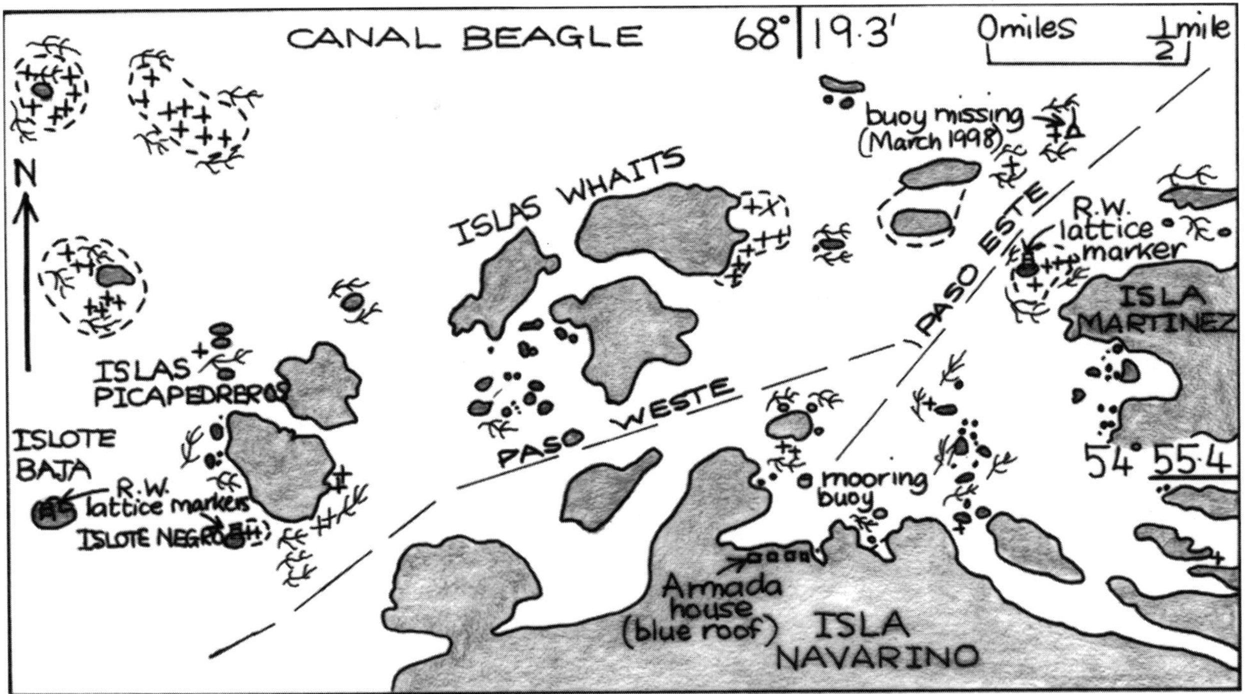

Puerto Navarino. (GPS positions)

white lattice marker sitting on the east end of Rochas Centimolas is not shown on the charts. Once this confusion is sorted out Paso Este is straightforward. Approaching from the northeast, pass the red & white marker on Rochas Centimolas, leaving it to fairly close to port. Once past, the course is direct towards the blue *Armada* building. The entrance to Puerto Navarino is a good example of the rule 'if the yacht avoids kelp patches it is unlikely to hit a rock.'

Anchorage

By calling Navarino radio permission can be obtained to use the *Armada* buoy. Use a stern anchor (in about 20m) to hold the yacht clear of the buoy in case the wind drops. A more sheltered alternative is to anchor in about 7m close to the small jetty in front of the *Armada* building and take a shore-line to this jetty.

Argentina

10·9 Ushuaia

54°49'S 68°19'W

Warning

A yachts should not call at Ushuaia from Chile unless its *zarpe* authorises the visit and all passports have Chilean exit stamps; to do so would be to leave Chile without clearance. Do not depart from Ushuaia bound for the Falklands; first return to Chile. If leaving Argentina, official permission will not be given to anchor anywhere in Argentine waters although it may be agreed verbally that anchoring is permitted for safety reasons (this means that the Argentine anchorages mentioned below and Staten Island may not be visited *en route* to another country). A yacht coming from the Atlantic bound for the *canales* but wishing to stock up in Ushuaia should consider visiting Ushuaia first and then returning to Puerto William for a *zarpe*. In this case, enter along the Argentine shore of Canal Beagle and fly the Argentine courtesy flag. The Chilean *Armada* may call to check your destination.

Charts

UK *554, 1373* US *22430* Chile *1301, 1307*

Lights

1323 Paso Chico Ldg Lts 019·8° *Front* 54°50'·4S 68°15'·9W Fl.6s9m8M
White metal framework tower red band 8m

1323·1 Isla Casco *Rear* 465m from front 54°50'·2S 68°15'·7W Fl.R.3s14m6M
White metal framework tower black bands

Port communications

Call on VHF Ch 16 c/s L3P (and enunciate LIMA TRES PAPA or they won't answer).

General

Ushuaia, population 50,000, is much the best place to stock up before heading through the canals or going to Antarctica. The big charter yachts based here are good sources of information on Antarctica and the Cordillera Darwin area.

The Naval Museum located in the old Jail is excellent and well worth the $5 entrance fee.

Approach

Coming from the west, the entrance to Bahía Ushuaia is through Paso Chico (1323leading marks above). The bay is very shallow and the wind frequently blows very strongly from the west in the afternoon

Formalities

Ushuaia is a port of entry. Call the *Prefectura Naval* on Ch 16 in advance and obtain instructions; immigration formalities may be done aboard. Customs should be cleared at the Customs Office on the main pier as soon as possible during working hours. There may be charges for movements recorded out of hours and at weekends. Details of these procedures change from time to time.

Anchorage

The bay is very shallow and the wind frequently blows very strongly from the west in the afternoon. The holding is not good. The most convenient anchorage is just to the east of the yacht club. Most boats raft to the yacht club which is formed by a grounded old vessel, the *Barracuda*. It is best to tie on the eastern side due to the strong westerly winds. It is very shallow and keel boats can only tie at the extreme southern end; shallower draught yachts can tie further along the ship or to the wharf leading

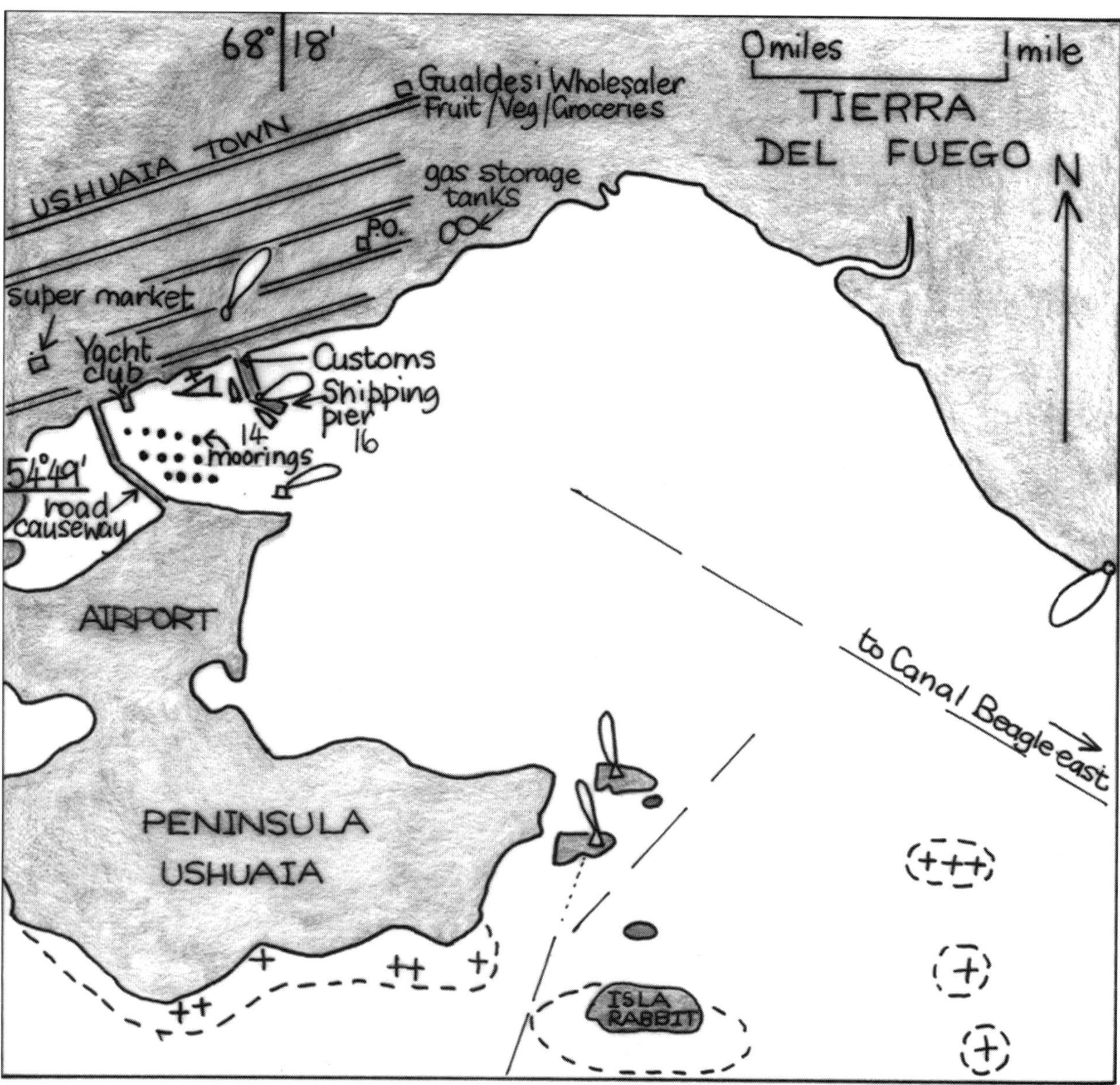

Ushuaia. (Charted positions)

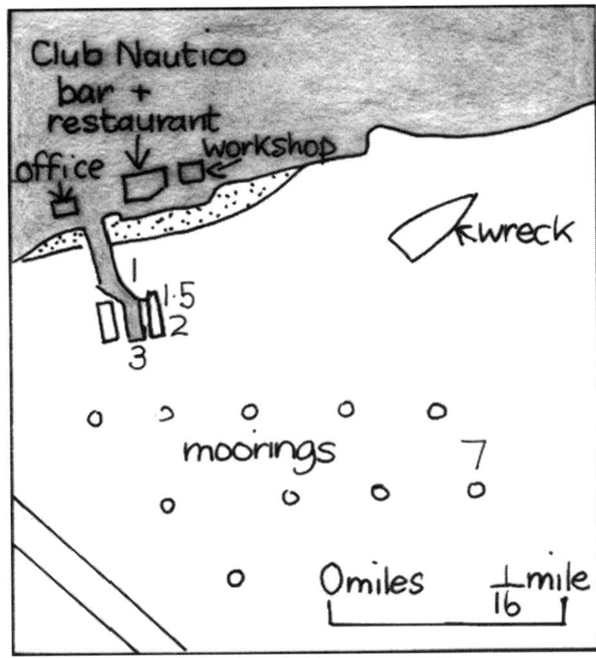

from the *Barracuda* to the land. The alternative is the AFSyN, the sailing and diving club, a $3 taxi run to the west and south of town. There is a jetty, with a water hose. Both clubs may have moorings available if resident yachts are away and both charge $4 a day after a few free days.

Facilities

Diesel and kerosene in cans by dinghy from a YPV gas station about half a mile east of the yacht club. Arrangements can be made to take fuel by bulk (and at a cheaper price) from an outlet further to the east but this source of fuel has a reputation of lower quality than that at the YPV station.

Water hose on the jetty.

There are four supermarkets. The best is Anonima – a $3 taxi ride to the eastern end of the town but they will deliver big loads free. Surty Sur supermarket is a couple of blocks to the west of the yacht club.

Butcher on Belgrano and San Martin. Some yachts purchase a whole or half sheep; they say it keeps, if hung in the rigging.

Good quality vegetables and fruit can be obtained from a wholesaler in case or half-case lots (Gualdesi, 771 Gov. Campo or Allatuni, Godor Godoy 261 and Paz).

Self-service laundrette Los Angeles on J M Rosas – expensive.

Club Náutico has bar, restaurant (pricey) and showers; AFASyN, showers.

Communications

Daily flights to Buenos Aires.

Car hire Taxis. Mail from Europe takes about a week.

Telephone Area Code 901 (calls are cheaper from Puerto Williams).

Chile

10·10 Isla Navarino – Ensenada Villarino

54°55'·2S 67°36'·5W

Charts

UK *554, 1373* US *22430* Chile *1301, 1307*

General

This anchorage is only 6 miles west of Puerto Williams but it is useful if travelling late and an easy stopping place is required. The entrance is straightforward and the bay is well protected from all but easterly winds. There is good holding in about 12m with a shoreline. A peaceful place to stop. When east winds blow in this area they are generally light but a swell does enter this bay if the wind swings to this direction.

10·11 Isla Navarino – Puerto Williams

54°56'S 67°37'W

Charts

UK *554, 1373* US *22430* Chile *1301, 1307, 13150*

Port communications

Ch 16, 09, 14. c/s *CBW* ☎ 62 10 90 *Fax* 62 10 41

General

The town is a naval base and is controlled by the *Armada*. It is also the Chilean administrative centre for the Antarctic. It suffered a serious fire in 1994. The principal civilian occupation is fishing for *centolla* crabs; there is a packing plant 10km west of

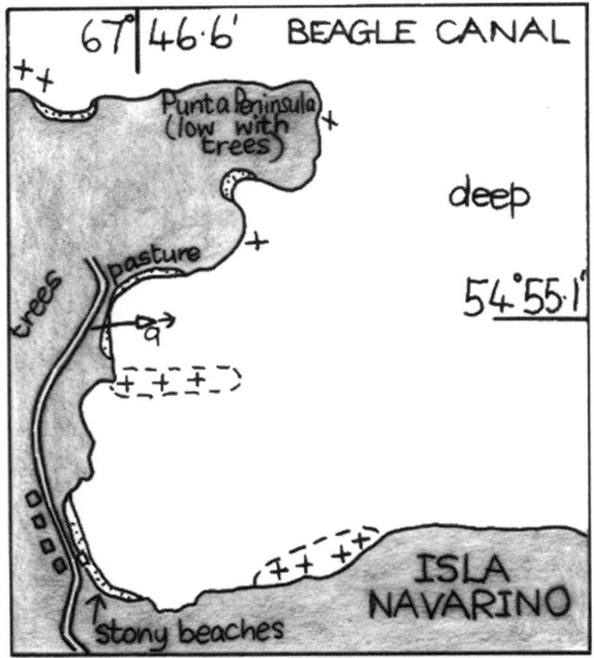

Ensenada Villarino. (GPS positions)

Puerto Williams.

There are several small restaurants, a reasonably priced pension and a hotel a couple of miles west of the town that serves excellent meals. The Museo del fin del Mundo, close to the yacht club, is worth a visit.

Tourism

There is good hiking around Puerto Williams. A trail starts just to the south of the prominent Virgin Mary statute that is reached by following the road winding up the east coast of the inlet and turning left at the first junction and continuing a short distance to a park on the right hand side. It leads to the top of Banner hill with magnificent views up the valley in front of Les Dientes, and also of the Woolastons and Cape Horn. The trail is marked by blue paint splashes on the occasional tree, and there and back takes about 6 hours. From the top of Banner, there is also a 5 day hike which takes you to Les Dientes, the impressive spiked mountain range that can be seen from the Micalvi.

Approach

Call on VHF in advance and give an ETA. The *Armada* and Immigration will visit the yacht when at Micalvi.

Banco Herradura extends 1·2M north of [1316]Punta

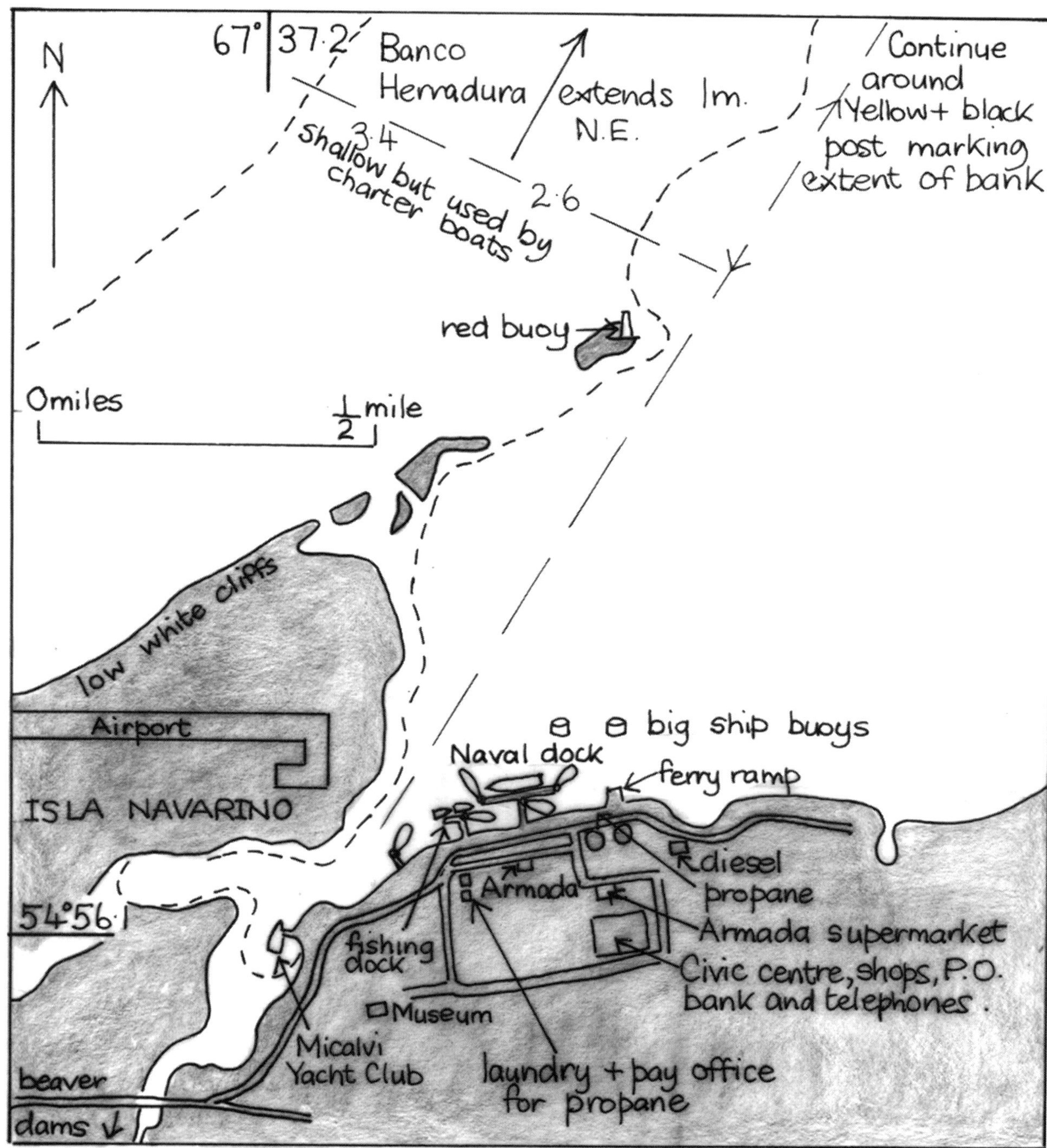

Puerto Williams. (GPS positions)

Gusano (Fl(3)R.9s10m3M red GRP tower 5m) at the end of Península Zañartu which shelters Puerto Williams from the westerlies.

Berthing
Go to the Club de Yates at the Micalvi, a retired munitions carrier, in Seno Lauta. The approach to the Micalvi is a channel with shallow water on either side (5m or less) and there is limited turning room. Charges were US$6 per day in 1997. Alternatively anchor in the river northwest of Micalvi in 4–6m. It is possible to berth alongside at the town but ask the *Capitanía.*

Formalities
The full *zarpe* treatment. Puerto Williams is a port of entry though it has no *Aduana*. If coming from the east with the intention of continuing westward, it may be best to go first to Ushuaia to stock up and then return to Puerto Williams for the *zarpe*. Some yachts arriving from abroad have been told to report to the *Aduana* at Puerto Montt; others have been given no instructions. Either way, check with the *Aduana* at the first opportunity – Punta Arenas, Puerto Chacabuco, Puerto Montt. Yachts heading north through the canales must pay a small buoyage *cum* light fee.

Facilities
Diesel from COPEC in cans or possibly from the *Armada* at their fuel dock.
Propane available through the *Armada.*
Water.
Supermarket run by the *Armada.*
Bank but best to arrive with US dollars, not travellers cheques or credit cards.
Shopping centre – limited and expensive.
Laundry can be taken to the *Armada lavandería* which is on the same street as the Port Captain's office.
Cafetaría at the local bakery.
Hot showers etc on Micalvi.
Bar at Micalvi, lunch on Sundays (excellent *empanandas*) – a very friendly Club. The best restaurant is on top of the hill – ask locals for directions.

Communications
Flights to Punta Arenas, said to be weekly in winter and bi-weekly in summer but check timetables when within Chile; flights are often blocked by bad weather. Advance booking is necessary.
Ferry to Punta Arenas every ten days.
There is no public transport between Puerto Williams and Ushuaia. A passage on a charter yacht may be possible; the going rate in 1998 was US$55. There is a small landing and border post in Argentina at Almanza (c/s L4B Almanza), opposite Puerto Williams, which can be reached by expensive (US$70) taxi from Ushuaia (it is not clear how the reverse journey might be arranged). Checking in and out of Almanza from Puerto Williams can be done by yacht within a day providing the administration at the Chilean end is arranged properly.
Telephone Area code 61. CTC office and also telephone in the shopping centre.

Argentine: East Tierra del Fuego

Gable Island/Harberton Area

To the northeast of Puerto Williams, there are a number of delightful anchorages and winding waterways on the north side of the Beagle Canal. These are mentioned because they are on the Beagle Canal but they can only be visited after entering Argentina and may not be visited after leaving Argentina *en route* to another country.

10·12 Bahía Almirante Brown

54°53'S 67°24'W

Charts
UK *1373* US *22430* Chile *1318*

General
The entrance to Bahía Almirante Brown is a well marked channel around the back of Isla Gable, negotiable in daylight only, giving access to numerous sheltered anchorages amongst the low-lying rural islands. There are range markers to lead one through the narrow canal. The best chart for this area is the Argentinean strip chart for Canal Beagle '*De Isla Becasses A Bahia Lapataia*'. Beyond Isla Gable there are three excellent anchorages, Bahía Relegada, Puerto Harberton and Bahía Cambaceres, with *Armada* buoys in Relegada and Cambaceres. On the north side of Cambaceres there are ruins of an old Yagan Indian house and wild foxes inhabit the area. Harberton is the site of the original settlement in this area by the Bridges family. It is now a large sheep *estancia* and a popular tourist attraction. Catamarans bring visitors each day from Ushuaia. The *estancia* welcomes visiting yachts and the guided tour is well worth the $6. It may be possible to use the pilot boat's mooring; check with the *estancia*. Holding for an anchor is good.

10·13 Bahía Aguirre

54°55'·7S 65°58'·3W

Charts
UK *1373* US *22430* Chile *1340*

General
Travelling from west to east, Bahía Aguirre on the south side of Peninsula Mitre, is the last shelter available before entering the Estrecho de Le Maire. There is an *Armada* buoy in the little bay to the north of Punta Pique. The point itself displays a light. This anchorage provides excellent protection from west and northwest winds but it is subject to swell particularly during strong southwest winds. Another possibility is to anchor further to the north in Puerto Español; holding is reported as good in sand and mud. There is a long reef of rocks and kelp

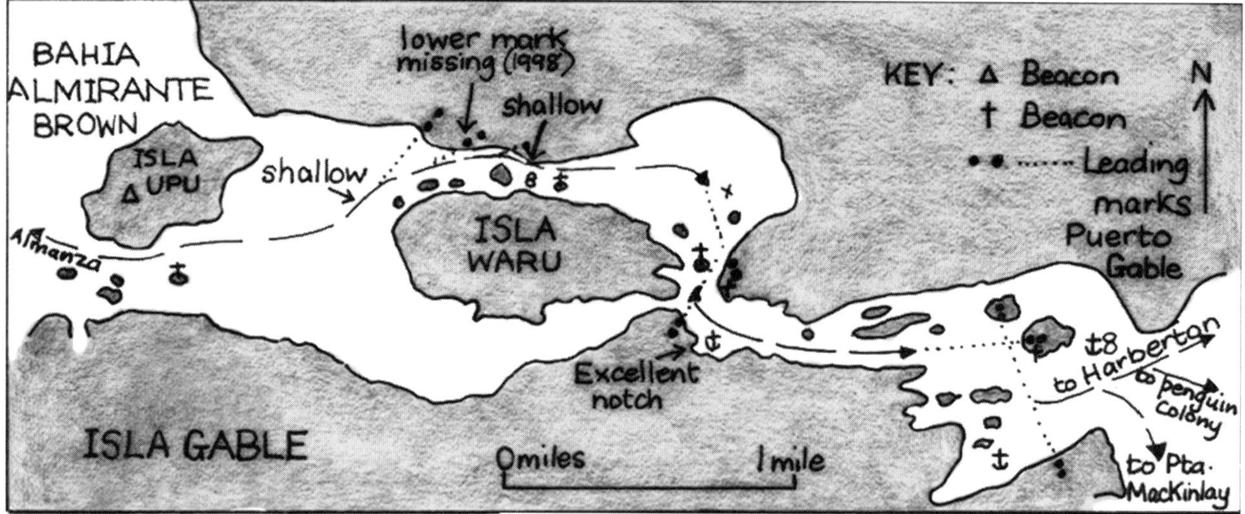

Inside passage north of Isla Gable. Average depth 5–10 metres.
Minimum depth approx 2 metres

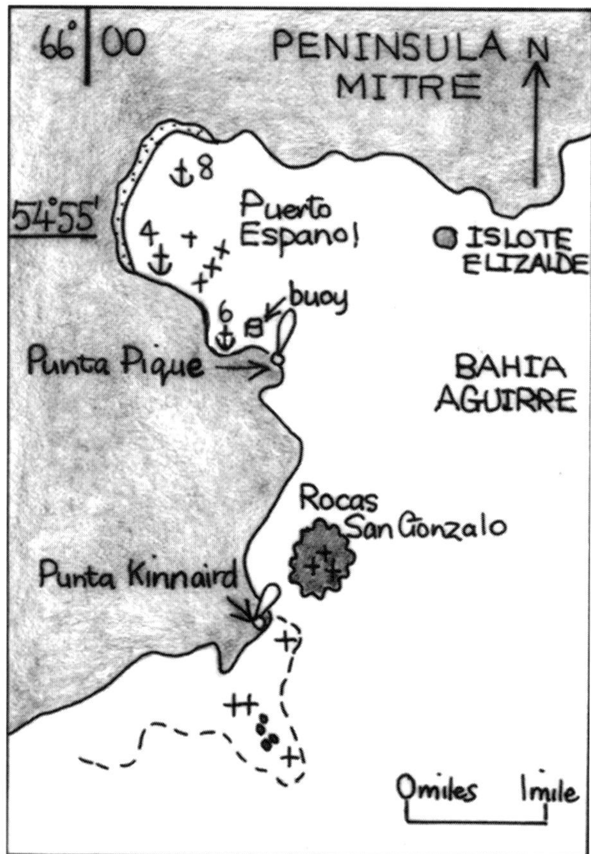

Bahía Aguirre

that extends out from the western entrance to Puerto Español which cuts down on the swell. Neither bay provide shelter from the E or SE. This anchorage would probably be better than the buoy in strong northwest winds as the buoy is exposed to about a one mile fetch from the northwest.

10·14 Bahía Buen Suceso

54°46'S 65°15'W

Charts
UK *1373* US *22430* Chile *1340*

General
This wide-open bay on the east coast of Peninsula Mitre, just south of the narrowest part of the Estrecho de le Maire, provides shelter from north through southwest winds. It is a rolly anchorage but the holding is excellent at the head of the bay, in sand. The large *Armada* buoy in the middle of the bay might be available. There is an Argentinean Naval Station at the head of the bay, and yachts transiting the Straits should report their position on Ch 16.

Estrecho De Le Maire

54°40'S 65°00'W

Charts
UK *1373* US *22430* Chile *1340*

General
The overfalls in the Estrecho de le Maire are notorious, and a transit of the Straits must be made with great respect for the risks involved, particularly going from south to north where a northwest wind against a flood tide can create standing waves of 10 – 12m off Cape San Diego. Yachts should keep to the centre of the Straits where the current is typically three knots. Care should be taken to stay at least eight miles off Cape San Diego and four or five miles off the western end of Staten Island. The current floods north and slack tide in the Straits is at low and high water at the tidal station in Bahía Buen Suceso.

Chile – the Far East and South

Isla Navarino

10·15 Puerto Eugenia

54°56'S 67°17'W

Charts
UK *1373* US *22430* Chile *1301, 1303*

General
At the northeast end of Isla Navarino and between Punta Eugenia and Islote Barlovento, Puerto Eugenia is only ten miles from Puerto Williams and is a good jumping off place for a trip to Cape Horn. It also provides excellent shelter if there is a strong contrary wind in the Beagle when returning from Cape Horn. The entrance is clean and the holding is good in 6–12m.

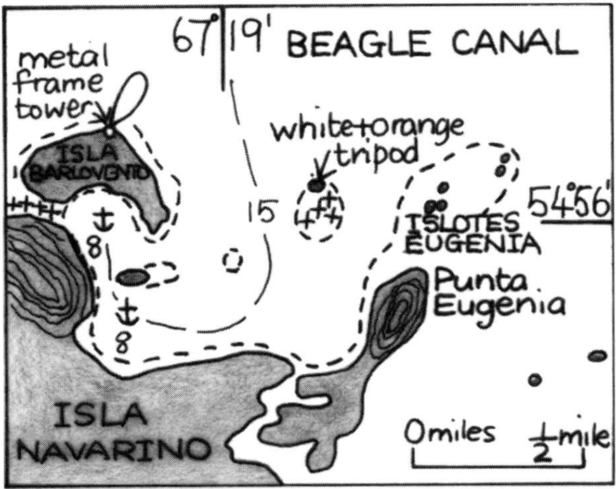

Puerto Eugenia. (Charted positions)

10·16 Puerto Toro

55°04'S 67°04'W

Charts
UK *1373* US *22430* Chile *1301*

General
This was one of the original settlements in Tierra del Fuego and has a small friendly community. The entrance is marked by 1303Puerto Toro light (Fl.5s.6m6M white GRP tower, red band 4m. 150°-vis-301°) and has two drying rocks about 300m northeast of the light. The hills round the bay are high. There is protection from all except NE and E winds. The *caleta* is very deep. It is possible to anchor in about 15m, but the shallow area is quite close to the shore. The other alternatives are to tie to the pier, which by local standards is in reasonable condition, or to anchor off the pier with a line to it.

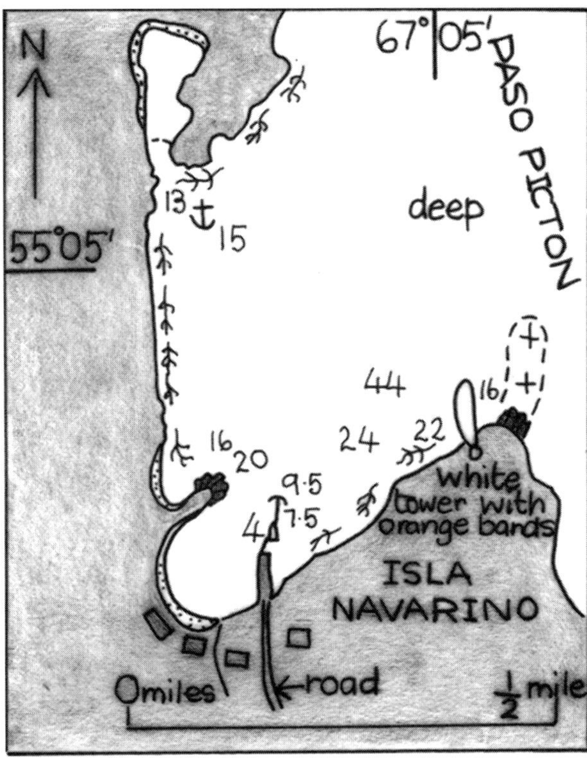

Puerto Toro. (Charted positions)

Isla Picton

10·17 Caleta Banner

55°01'S 66°56'W

Charts
UK *1373* US *22430* Chile *1301, 1303*

General
The *caleta* lies behind Isla Gardiner and is well protected except from the northeast. Anchor according to draft or use the *Armada* buoy in the centre of the bay. There is a boat pier on the east shore and a disused *Armada* base.

10·18 Punta Yawl

55°12'·8S 67°05'·5W

Charts
UK *1373* US *22430* Chile *1301, 1318*

General
This is an emergency anchorage which is not normally included on yachts' *zarpes*. The entrance can be identified by Ite Dingy. Anchor in between Islote Mariotti and Punta Yawl in 7m. Reasonable shelter and good holding though open to the East and best when wind is predominantly north or south. Puerto Toro would be better than Yawl in a westerly.

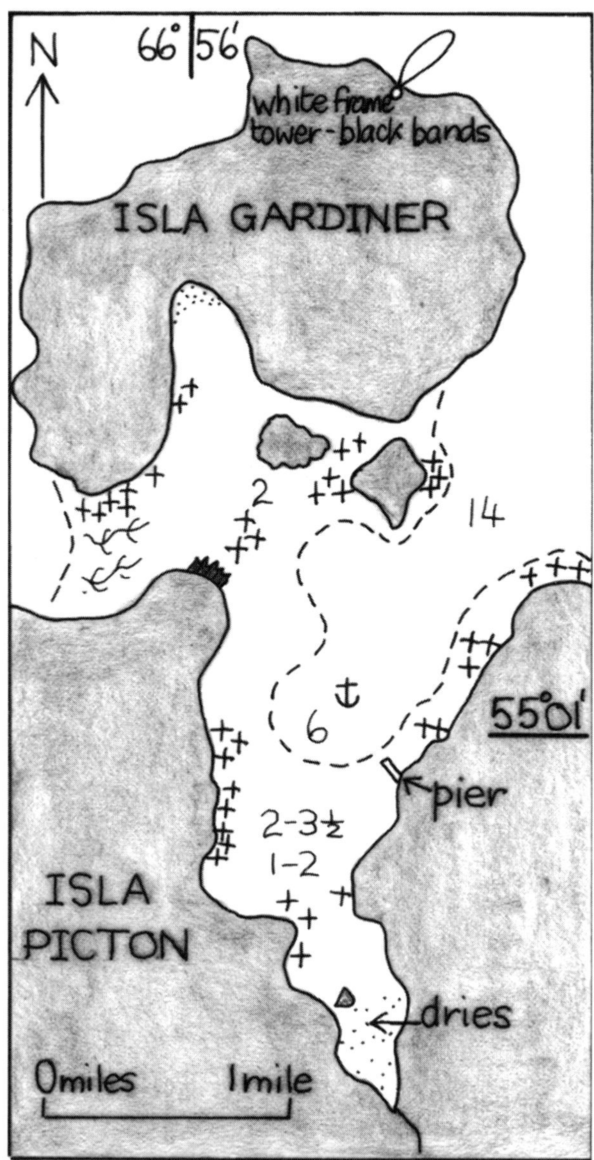

Caleta Banner. (Charted positions)

Isla Lennox

10·19 Caleta Lennox

55°17'S 66°50'W

Charts

UK *1373* US *22430* Chile *1301, 1304*

General

Caleta Lennox provides excellent shelter from winds from the NW through to S and is a pleasant stop *en route* to the Horn, particularly if there are strong southwest winds in Bahía Nassau. It is also a useful anchorage on the way north from the Horn if it is difficult to reach Toro because of fading daylight or strong northwest winds. There is excellent holding in 3–4m over sand.

Formalities

The *Armada* maintains a presence here.

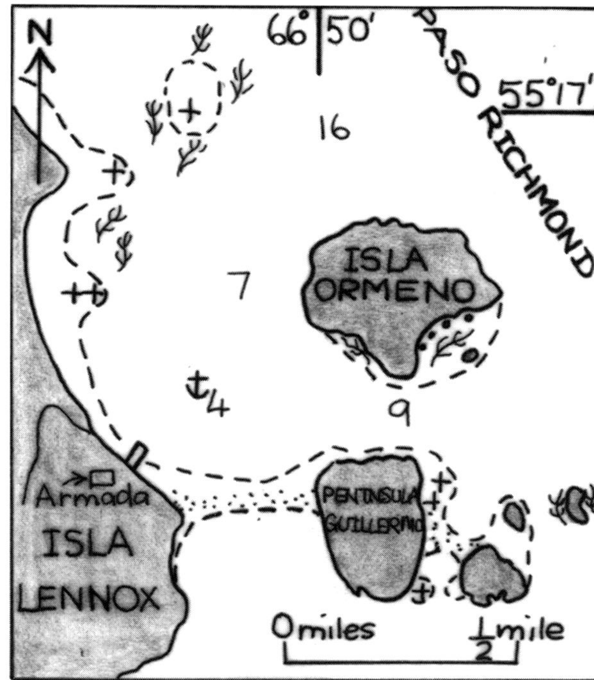

Caleta Lennox. (Charted positions)

The Southern Islands

General

Bahía Nassau has variable and quickly changing weather. The prevailing winds are westerly but easterlies are not uncommon and can be strong, kicking up a nasty sea. It is unwise to cross the bay in any condition of strong wind. There are some *caletas* in Islas Wollaston and Islas Hermite which offer some shelter, none much good in an easterly.

Isla Wollaston

10·20 Caleta Lientur

55°44'S 67°18'W

Charts

UK *1373* US *22430* Chile *1301, 1312*

The scale on *1301* and *1312* is the same and *1301* is easier to read.

General

Caleta Lientur is on the southeast side of Isla Wollaston at the head of Bahía Scourfield. It has shelter to the northeast and southwest but southeast and northwest winds are canalised by the hills. The entrance has a line of kelp across it in 15+m. Anchor close in with lines ashore. Depths from 17m down to zero, sand and mud, good holding. Alternatively, use the *Armada* buoy, if not on the beach as it was in 1998. If the weather is not too windy, a hike up to the nearby lake is worthwhile and gives great views of the Wollaston Islands.

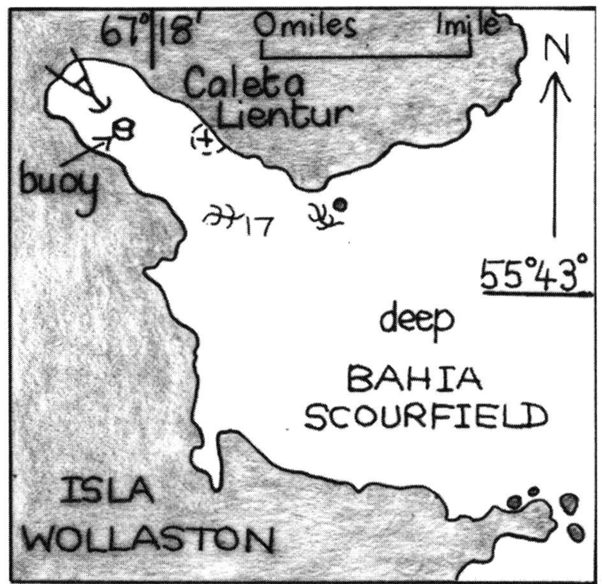

Caleta Lientur. (Charted positions)

Isla Herschel

10·21 Caleta Martial

55°50'·75S 67°17'W

Charts

UK *1373* US *22430* Chile *1301, 1312*
The scale on *1301* and *1312* is the same and *1301* is easier to read.

General

On the northeast coast of Isla Herschel, Caleta Martial is the only anchorage in the Wollaston-Hermite group that the *Armada* will authorise for use on a visit to Cape Horn. It is sheltered from all except east winds, in the event of which you should call Cape Horn or Wollaston Radio and tell them you are moving to Puerto Maxwell on Isla Hermite (preferred by yachts) or Caleta Lientur. In Caleta Martial the northern anchorage is best for N to W winds and the southern anchorage is better in SW winds.

The yellow sand beach at the head of the *caleta* gives easy recognition. The entrance is clean and direct, and the holding is excellent in sand. Heading south through Paso Mar del Sur on the way to Cape Horn, there is a clear safe passage through the islands if you stay close to the SE corner of Isla Herschel.

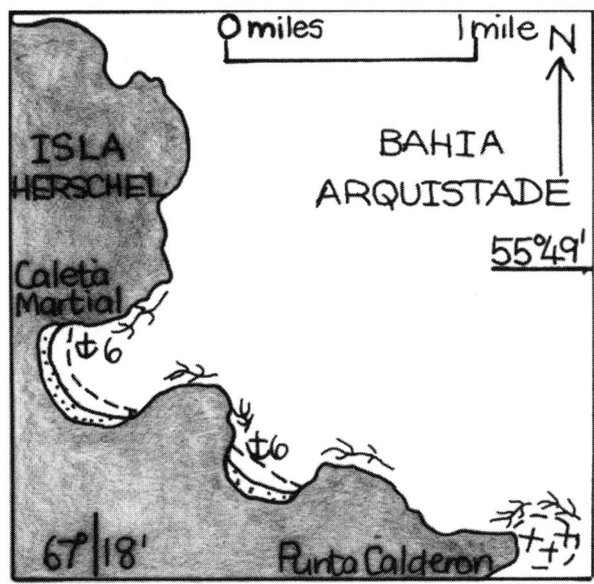

Caleta Martial. (Charted positions)

Isla Hornos

10·22 Caleta León

55°58'·7S 67°16'·3W

Charts

UK *1373* US *22430* Chile *1301, 1312*
The scale on 1301 & 1312 is the same and 1301 is easier to read.

General

Caleta León, 1·5M north west of Punta Espolón (5°58'S 67°13'W), provides only limited protection and is not a good place to stay overnight without

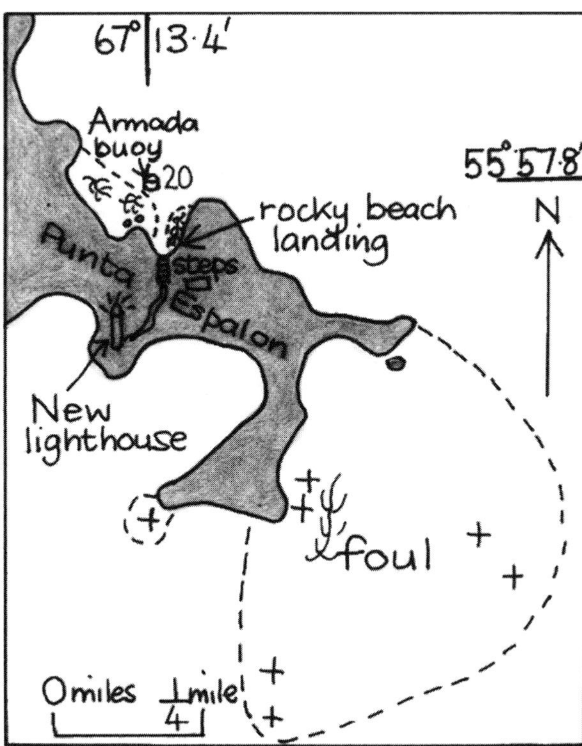

Caleta Leon, Isla Hornos. (GPS positions)

being very sure of the weather. The bottom is very rocky. It is better to use the *Armada* buoy which is very low in the water and you may need a dinghy to get a line to it. The *Armada* have cut a narrow pathway through the kelp to the wooden steps leading up to the lighthouse station. The UK Pilot, NP6, comments that landing is also possible in a cove close east of the Cape.

Wherever the landing, the lighthouse is well worth a visit. The three *Armada* personnel are most welcoming, and would be pleased to stamp mail, log books etc. There is a simple chapel and a number of monuments commemorating the Cape Horners including a stunning sculpture of a Wandering Albatross.

Post Script: It has now been accepted that Drake landed at Cape Horn in 1578, well before Schouten's visit in 1616. There is evidence to show that Drake's discovery was suppressed by the Elizabethan Government for reasons which, in today's terms, might be described as national security.

10·23 Islas Diego Ramirez

56°29'S 68°45'W

Charts

UK *1373* US *29002* Chile *1312, 1315*

General

There are two anchorages, both in the southern group: Fondeadero Oreste (25m, sand) on the east side of Isla Bartolome and Fondeadero Aguila on the northeast side of Isla Gonzalo. They are only tenable after a prolonged period of calm weather. There is a manned *Armada* base on Gonzalo which will give permission to land if requested. The islands, which are bird sanctuaries, were named after the Brothers Nodal who first surveyed Tierra del Fuego in 1618–1619. It was one of the finest of the Spanish expeditions, particularly so as all the crew returned home alive. On which happy note we leave South America.

Section 11
The Pacific Islands

11·1 Isla de Pascua

27°09'S 109°27'W
Also known as Easter Island and Rapa Nui

Approximate Distances

Galápagos–1950–Isla de Pascua–1945–Valdivia
Pitcairn-1100-Isla de Pascua-1620-Juan Fernandez

Charts

UK *1389* Chile 2520 and others listed below. Note that in the *Atlas Hidrográfico de Chile* these charts come immediately before chart *300.*

Lights

1991 Caleta Hanga Piko Ldg Lts *Front* 109° 27°09'·3S 109°26'·4W Fl(4)12s8m6M
White concrete column, orange band 7m 078°-vis-136·5° Radio masts 300m SSW
1991·1 *Rear* 270m from front 27°09'·4S 109°26'·3W LFl.8s40m13M
White concrete column, black band 7m 081°-vis-123° R lights on masts ESE & SSE Runway approach 300m SW
1992 Hang Roa-Otai 27°08'·9S 109°26'·0W Fl.R.5s 6m8M
White GRP tower, red band 3m
1993 Hanga Roa Dir Lt 144° 27°09'·0S 109°26'·0W DirLFl.8s12m12M
White mast, orange band 4m 134°-vis-154° R lights on TV mast 780m ESE

RDF beacons

Easter Island 27°09'·4S 109°25'·6W c/s *IPA* 280kHz

Tides

Standard Port – Pago Pago
Spring Range 0·5m
Neap Range 0·3m

Port communications

VHF Ch 16 c/s *CBY*

General

The island is administered as part of the *región* of Valparaíso. It is largely dependent upon tourism and not much of the original culture remains – what does, is highly visible. The island's hundreds of huge and very famous stone statues, *moais,* are extraordinary, unexplained and well worth visiting. In prosaic terms, the island is not a good stop-over for fuel and stores. Facilities are limited. The anchorages are open. Moreover landing can be difficult; it may be necessary to wait days for conditions to ease before it becomes possible. If landing is possible, always leave enough crew on board to handle the boat when the wind shifts, as it can do both suddenly and dramatically.

Tourism

Apart from paying respects to *moais,* there is a delightful beach at Anakena plus Thor Heyerdahl's restored *moai*; anchor off or drive there.

Approach

Contact the *Armada* on Ch16 for advice and negotiate for clearance. Although there is no clearance charge as such, if officials use a boat to come out there may be a charge by the local boatman (about US$20).

Anchorages

Hanga Roa (500m NE of Punta Roa, 27°08'·6S 109°26'·6W approx., chart *2522*) is the chief anchorage for visitors. Approach the main anchorage, on the direction line 1993Hanga Roa. Anchor in at least 12m, sand and rock, variable holding; inshore are rocks and foul ground.

Hanga Piko, half a mile away to the south of Punta Roa, is closed to yachts though it may possibly be used in emergency, with the permission of the *Armada.* It is impossible to enter in bad weather.

Hanga Anakena on the north coast (27°04'·8S 109°19'·5W chart *2521*) is a beautiful and good anchorage, subject to suitable winds.

Hanga Vinapu on the south coast (27°10'·8S 109°24'W chart *2523*) provides shelter from the SW as well as W winds though subject to swell. Landing, via an oil structure, is difficult and there is nowhere to leave a dinghy. This may be no bad thing as someone will have to stay aboard as taxi-driver as well as ship-minder.

Hanga Hotuiti, south coast, east end, (27°07'·5S 109°16'·5W chart *2523*) is dramatic but not such a good anchorage as the others.

Facilities

Fuel Sunoco (Juan Edmunds), Airport Road.
Water Hose at Hanga Piko.
Change Sunoco fuel station (American Express and possibly other cards). US dollars widely accepted.
Provisions reasonable shops. LanChile fly in supplies twice a week.
Laundry on demand.
General facilities Ask Juan Edmunds; everything from finding a pilot to hiring a horse.

Communications

Air LanChile twice a week en route Santiago – Tahiti & *vice versa*, more frequently in summer when it is heavily booked.
Car (use a 4wd if possible; rain quickly turns tracks to mud), motor-cycle hire: Juan Edmunds, Sunoco; Hertz at airport.
Telephone Area Code 39 Entel office for phone and fax. Coast Radio accepts public correspondence on Ch 16, 09, 10, 14, & 26 24hrs.

11·2 Islas Juan Fernandez

33°38'S 78°51'W

Approximate Distances

Pascua–1620–Fernandez–368–Viña del Mar
Arica –900–Fernandez–454–Valdivia

Charts

UK *1389* US *22492* Chile *509, 510*

Lights

1855 Punta San Carlos 33°37'·0S 78°49'·7W
Fl.12s11m13M
White GRP tower, red band 8m 180°-vis-001° R lts on mast 0·5M ENE
1856 Bahía Cumberland 33°37'·2S 78°49'·5W
Fl.G.5s6m7M
Green framework tower 3m 184°-vis-279°

Tides

Standard Port – Valparaíso
Spring Range: 0·9m
b. Neap Range 0·9
c. HW +00hrs 15mins LW +00hrs 26mins

Port communications

Ch 16 c/s *CBF*

General

The two inhabited islands are Alejandro Selkirk and, 84M to the east, Isla Robinson Crusoe (ex *Juan Bautista*). The two are also called Isla Mas a Fuera and Mas a Tierra for obvious reasons. Both are National Parks.

Alejandro Selkirk is wooded, steep-to and rises to 1645m. About 20 fishing families live on it during the season (September to April) and are visited by boat about once a month for their catch of *langosta*. Be prepared to carry mail to Robinson Crusoe, if going there.

Robinson Crusoe has a population of about 600, living mainly in the village of Juan Batista and occupied with fishing, tourism and some local government. A mainland boat calls every three weeks or so bringing a few visitors but few yachts call though there is an annual race to the island organised by the Club Nautico Oceánico de Chile. The climate is warm and humid and the island, like the Galápagos, has several unique species of flora and fauna.

The office of the Chilean Forestry Organization, CONAF, is worth visiting.

Approach

Straightforward in both cases.

Anchorage

Alejandro Selkirk A visitor will be offered a mooring opposite the former penal colony, midway down the East side.

Robinson Crusoe Anchor in Bahía Cumberland, a beautiful wide bay but subject to strong gusts off the mountains. In strong southerlies yachts have dragged out to sea and conditions are rolly.

Formalities

Contact the *Armada* on Ch 16.

Facilities

On Alejandro Selkirk spring water otherwise nothing except the possibility of trading cigarettes or liquor for *langostas*.
On Robinson Crusoe supplies are very restricted in the few shops. Fish is available and Red Snapper may be caught on a line over the side. Water.

Communications

Robinson Crusoe An airstrip for light aircraft. Post office with telephone.

Appendix

Appendix A
Formalities

Before arrival
Make photocopies of passports, of a crew list with passport details and of the ships papers; the end product is more impressive if stamped with the ship's rubber stamp. You will in due course also be asked for details of fuel and water tankage, how many days food are aboard, the range of the ship (in miles or in days) and of life saving equipment. Details (factory numbers) of the engine (if any), all transceivers and specialist radio equipment (weather and other fax) and possibly of auto-pilots will be required. It is useful to have them listed and copied. It is also useful to copy papers issued to you by the Chilean authorities. This is easily achieved in the towns.

Entry
There are three authorities that must be attended upon: the *Armada* (Navy), the *Aduana* (Customs) and the *Policía Internacional* (International Police). The *Armada* will come to the yacht to check in. The *Aduana* and *Policía* (who handle immigration) may come to the yacht but may have to be visited at their offices. Generally speaking yachts can enter Chile at any major port – Isla de Pascua, Arica, Iquique, Antofagasta, Talcahuano, Valparaíso, Valdivia, Puerto Montt, Castro, Punta Arenas or Puerto Williams. The *Aduana* office for Valdivia is at Osorno, two hours away by bus. There is no *Aduana* at Puerto Williams and yachts are put on trust until they reach a customs post (if entering from the Atlantic and planning to stock up at Ushuaia, go to Ushuaia first and then back to Puerto Williams to avoid entering Chile twice). Chacabuco is technically a port of entry but a yacht using it as such may run into trouble since she will have been in Chilean waters for some time and might have called first at Castro or Puerto Montt.

Immigration
Requirements change but in 1997 situation was as follows:

Citizens of the EU, the USA, Canada and Australia do not need visas; New Zealand citizens and citizens of most Caribbean islands do. All require valid passports. All visitors receive a 90 day entry permit on arrival. This is to be kept securely with the passport. For visitors who did not require a visa, the entry permit may be renewed. This is free for North American citizens but costs EU citizens US$100. The entry permit may be renewed up to 30 days before expiry (don't take no for an answer) and failure to do so before expiry will mean getting involved in a lot of paperwork and perhaps a fine. Sailing in channels is no excuse so far as immigration is concerned. In addition to entry ports, the entry permit can be renewed in Puerto Aysén. If in the south, an alternative is to bus to Argentina (not Peru or Bolivia where border controls are more difficult), stay a night, re-enter Chile the next day and collect another 90 day permit. Sailing to Ushuaia or Puerto Almanzo will achieve the same thing but visitors needing a visa should bear in mind the requirement for a multiple entry a if shuttling between Argentina and Chile in the far south or elsewhere.

Customs
On first arrival a *Declaración de Admision Temporal* must be made to the *Aduana* and a certificate for the yacht obtained. Details of the ship and her equipment – safety, communications, propulsion etc. – will be recorded. The certificate is free and is usually issued for a four month period, renewable for a further four month period up to a total of two years. Allow time for this: renewals during the first year may have to be processed through the customs officer at the original port of entry but one yacht which entered at Isla Pascua had her permit renewed at Chacabuco without fuss. Renewals during the second year must be first processed through the customs headquarters in Valparaíso who issue a clearance to the customs at the port of entry for additional renewals. After two years the yacht is liable for 11% import duty and 18% IVA (*impuesto de valor agregado* – value added tax) on its current estimated value. Renewing a certificate at an office other than the one which issued it incurs administrative delays; start the process in very good time.

Leaving the ship unattended
At some ports, a visiting yacht left unattended whilst the owner or captain is out of the country should be put in bond with the *Aduana*. Yachts are, however, left at Puerto Williams where there is no *Aduana*. Inquire locally wherever you are as views of officials vary.

Importing equipment from abroad
Until recently there were so few visiting yachts in Chile that there was not the customary ability to import parts for a yacht in transit free of duty. This

is often still the case. However, by November 1996 yachts in Valdivia were able to clear shipments through the customs officer in Osorno as parts for a yacht in transit and therefore free of duty. Parts that arrived directly by Fedex with an invoice value of less than US$500 were usually delivered directly to the yacht without payment of duty. Parts coming from Europe by DHL attracted duty which was paid by DHL. Parts arriving by post marked 'for yacht in transit' were duty free.

Ensure the carrier knows in advance that the goods are for a yacht in transit and that you will not pay for any duty they pay on your behalf. Even though the fact that duty has been paid is properly marked on the package, if liable for duty the package will not be released unless duty is paid at the point of delivery. Yachts in transit do not by law have to pay duty but make sure the relevant procedures have been established in advance, if necessary by contacting the customs office. Once a demand for duty has been prepared, it is hard to reverse the situation.

The *Armada* and the *zarpe*

On departing from any Chilean port, you need a *zarpe* or permit, even if going to another Chilean port. This is a document issued by the *Armada* giving ship and crew details and route/destination information. In addition, when clearing out of the country, you will need to contact immigration and customs (through the *Armada*).

Obtaining a *zarpe*

It may take three or four days to get the first *zarpe* for a cruise within Chile; thereafter it will be much easier – a matter of hours, even for a *zarpe* to leave the country. Some ability in Spanish is a real asset in negotiating the document and the effort of speaking in Spanish is appreciated.

The information required is:

1. Boat Information.
2. Crew list and passport information.
3. Water, fuel, stores range. These are listed on the entry papers.
4. Any changes to equipment since entry.
5. General indication of route. These are the ports at which you intend to call, with dates of arrival/departure. Obviously these may only be approximate but even though you know you can not be precise, give a definite plan at this time.
6. Route to be followed, identifying each main canal or pass if appropriate.

The first *zarpe* has to be referred to Valparaíso which may take a few days. It pays to cast your programme as far forward as possible, even though it is not possible to be precise about dates. For instance, it is possible to get a *zarpe* for a passage from Arica to Valparaíso or Valdivia to Ushuaia. Subsequently, unless it has to be referred to Valparaíso again, the *zarpe* is prepared locally for your signature and that of the Port Captain.

On reaching port, intermediate or final, the *Armada,* if present, will examine the *zarpe;* probably details of passports and the yacht will be required again. It is useful to have them ready on a hand-out; once composed, good photo-copying services are available and the end product made even more impressive if stamped with the ship's rubber stamp.

To quote a correspondent, on a lengthy cruise, it is usually a good plan to make it as full as possible without going into detail – make it long on canals and short on ports. A successful application involving a crew change at Puerto Chacabuco was as follows:

'Place and date
Señor
(Gobernador Marítimo de Puerto Montt)
Date
Presente:
Estimado Señor:
Mediante le presente, solicito a Vd. autorización navegación aguas interiores para mi yate *(name):*

(Date of Departure)
(Crew List)
Ruta. Puerto Montt – Seno Reloncaví – Golfo Ancud – Golfo Corcovado – Canal Moraleda – Estero Elefantes – Laguna San Rafael – Seno Aysén – Puerto Chacabuco *(Estimated date of arrival).*

(Estimated date of departure)
(Different crew list)
Ruta. Puerto Chacabuco – Canal Errázuriz – Canal Chacabuco – Canal Pulluche – Boca Wickham – Golf de Penas – Canal Messier – Angostura Inglesa – Canal Wide – Canal Concepción – Canal Sarmiento – Estrecho de Magallanes – Canal Cockburn – Canal Brecknock – Canal Ballenero – Canal Beagle – Ushuaia *(Estimated date of arrival)*

(Estimated date of departure)
(Crew list)
Ruta. Ushuaia – Puerto Williams

Motivo: Fines Turisticas

(Signed)
Capitán'

This allowed scope to pick and choose anchorages *en route.*

Reporting your position

One of the instructions given on each *zarpe* is that all vessels should call the local *Armada* station at 0800 and 2000 each day to report its position (QTH) on HF, known as its PIM – *Posición e Intención de Movimiento.* Trying to get through to the *Armada* at those times can be very difficult if not impossible.

If they do not have HF, yachts are nevertheless expected to report their PIM on VHF which they are obliged to carry. They should also report to lighthouses as they are passed and to ships, whose Pilots will relay the report to the *Armada.* They may be called by *Armada* stations ashore at any time and asked for their PIM.

At 0800 and 2000, the *Armada* station may call vessels known to be in the area, and you may be one in a queue. The shore radio calls the yachts name *por QTH* (pronounced ku tay achay) followed by *cambio* (over). The response is to give the yacht's name and call sign. When recognised, the shore station gives the go ahead which is normally the word *adelante*. The response which should all be in Spanish is '*Navigando de . . a. . ., Latitud. . ., Longitud. . .* , *Romeo Victor* (give true course). . . *grados, Andar* (give speed,). . . *knudos,* Echo Tango Alpha (give your ETA in local time plus day if appropriate). If you are at anchor, the response is *Fondeado en* (place),. . ., *Latitud. . .* , *Longitud. . .* , *Sin novedad* (if you have nothing to report). You may wish to give your ETD and ETA and place of your next planned stop. At the end, when the shore station has acknowledge your message, it will either call the next ship or say '*proximo*' if it wants the next ship to call in.

It may be handy to have the Spanish numerals written out. The other words which tend to vanish from the memory in moments of stress are *grados, minutos, norte, sur, este, oeste, knudos, horas.*

Restrictions and choice of route

There are restrictions in the South which are noted in the appropriate section.

Finale

Be patient. The *Armada* is good humoured, helpful, very well behaved and has a job to do.

Appendix B

Weather Forecasts

Times are UTC unless stated otherwise.

NAVTEX

Navtex transmissions in Chile are in English and Spanish; in Argentina, English only. The area code for Chile is XV and Argentina, VI. Station identities are as follows:

Station	*English*	*Spanish*
Antofagasta	A	H
Valparaíso	B	I
Talcahuano	C	J
Puerto Montt	D	K
Magallanes	E	L
Isla de Pascua	F	M
Ushuaia	A	

VHF

VHF weather forecasts are in Spanish unless otherwise noted:

Station	Channel	Times
Arica	Ch 14 (forecast for area 1)	0215, 1415
Iquique	Ch 14 (forecast for area 1)	0215, 1415
Antofagasta	Ch 10 (local forecast)	0215, 1415
Chañaral	Ch 14 (forecast for area 1)	0215, 1415
Caldera	Ch 14 (forecast for areas 1 & 2)	0215, 1415
Isla de Pascua	Ch 10	0450, 1250, 2050 (in English)
	Ch 10	0500, 0850, 1650 (in Spanish)
Huasco	Ch 14 (forecast for area 1)	0215, 1415
Coquimbo	Ch 14 (forecast for areas 1 & 2)	0215, 1415
Valparaíso	Ch 10 (Synopsis and forecast for areas 1-6)	0135, 1435
Valparaíso	Ch 10 (forecast for Valparaíso Bay)	0215, 1415
San Antonio	Ch 14 (forecast for area 3)	0215, 1415
Juan Fernandez	Ch 14 (situation for Juan Fernandez)	0215, 1415
Talcahuano	Ch 10 (situation for Bahía Concepción)	0210, 1410
Puerto Montt	Ch 10 (situation for Puerto Montt & Canal Chacao)	0145, 1445
San Pedro	Ch 14 (synopsis for areas 5&6)	0210, 1410
Faro Félix	Ch 14 (situation for Bahía Félix)	0150, 1350
Punta Arenas	Ch 10 (forecasts and reports from lighthouses)	0210, 1410
Wollaston	Ch 14 (situation for Islas Wollaston)	0210, 1410
Diego Ramírez	Ch 14 (forecast for Drake Passage)	0210, 1410

Weatherfax Broadcasts

Frequency 4228·2, 8675·2 & 17144·6kHz

Time	*Content*
1115	Surface Analysis
1915	Sea State Analysis
2310	Surface Analysis as at 1800 and forecast as at 1200z the following day

Another useful weatherfax, particularly for an offshore passage or when crossing the Drake passage, is transmitted by New Zealand (ZKLF) at 1030 on 13550·5kHz.

Appendix C
Weather Forecast Areas

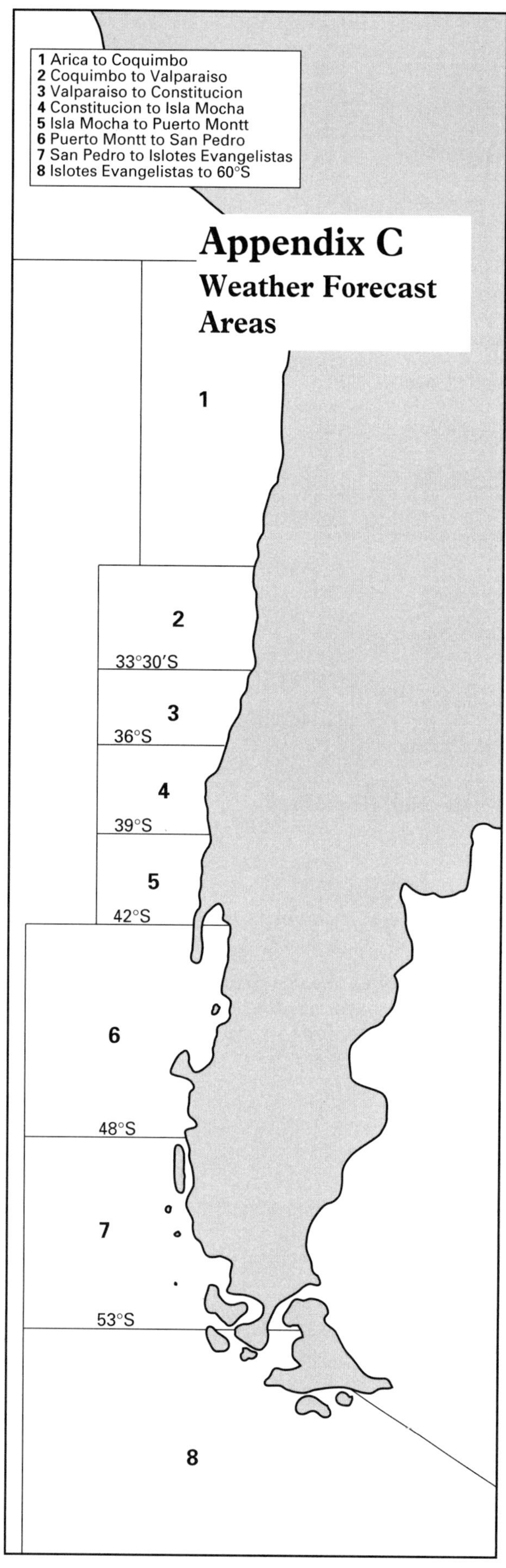

Appendix D
VHF Coast Radio Stations

Coast radio stations which accept public correspondence are shown in **bold type;** those accepting limited public correspondence in *italic type.* All stations accept *zarpe* position reports. Times are UTC.

Chile

VHF is compulsory on yachts and VHF stations and their channels are listed below. Most coast radio stations have both HF and MF which are not listed as operators are expected to have the appropriate manuals aboard.

Note: Faro = Lighthouse

The station call sign is given after its name.

Station	*Position*	*VHF Ch*
Faro Limitrofe Arica CBA70	18°21'S 70°21'W	16, 09, 14 Irregular
Arica CBA2	**18°29'S 60°20'W**	**16, 14, 26 24hrs**
Iquique CBA3	**20°13'S 70°10'W**	**16, 09, 14, 26 24hrs**
Patillos CBA28	20°45'S 70°11'W	16, 09, 14 Irregular
Tocopilla CBA21	22°06'S 70°13'W	16, 09, 14 1200-2200
Mejillones CBA22	23°06'S 70°27'W	16, 09, 14 1200-2200
Antofogasta CBA	**23°40'S 70°25'W**	**16, 09 10, 14, 26 24hrs**[1]
Taltal CBA27	25°24'S 70°29'W	16, 09, 14 1200-2200
Chañaral CBA23	26°21'S 70°38'W	16, 09, 14 24hrs
Caldera CBA5	*27°04'S 70°70'W*	*16, 09, 14 24hrs*
Isla Pascua CBY	**27°09'S 109°23'W**	**16, 09, 10, 14, 26 24hrs**
Hango-Roa CBV3	*27°09'S 109°26'W*	*16, 09, 14 1200-2200*
Huasco CBA24	28°28'S 71°15'W	16, 09, 14 1200-2200
Coquimbo CBA4	**29°57'S 71°21'W**	**16, 09, 14, 26 24hrs**
Los Vilos CBA26	31°54'S 71°31'W	16, 09, 14 1200-2200
Quintero CBV21	32°46'S 71°31'W	16, 09, 14 1200-2200 & on request
Valparaíso CBV	**32°48'S 71°29'W**	**16, 25, 26, 27 24hrs**[1]
Valparaío Capuerto CBV20 24hrs	*33°02'S 71°38'W*	*16, 09, 14*
Faro Curaumilla CBV71	33°06'S 71°45'W	16, 09, 14 Irregular
Faro Panul CBV2	33°34'S 71°37'W	16, 09, 14 1200-2200
San Antonio CBV22	*33°35'S 71°37'W*	*16, 09, 14 24hrs*
Juan Fernandez CBF	*33°37'S 78°50'W*	*16, 09, 14 24hrs*
Rapel CBL26[1]	33°57'S 71°44'W	16, 09, 14 1200-2200
Vichuquén CBT30	34°49'S 72°04'W	16, 09, 14 1200-2200
Constitución CBT21	35°20'S 72°25'W	16, 09, 14 1200-2200
Faro Carranza CBT2	35°33'S 72°37'W	16, 09, 14 24hrs
Isla Quiriquina CBT70	36°36'S 73°03'W	16, 09, 14 Irregular

Station	Position	Channels / Hours
Talcahuano CBT	**36°42'S 73°06'W**	**16, 09, 10, 14, 26 24hrs**[1]
Lirquén CBT22	36°43'S 72°58'W	16, 09, 14 1200-2200
Hualpen CBT71	36°45'S 73°11'W	16, 09, 14 1200-2200
San Vincente CBT23	36°46'S 73°08'W	16, 09, 14 24hrs
Coronel CBT24	37°01'S 73°09'W	16, 09, 14 1200-2200
Lebu CBT25	37°38'S 73°40'W	16, 09, 14 1200-2200
Faro Mocha CBT3	38°25'S 75°53'W	16, 09, 14 24hrs
Lago Villarrica CBL291	39°15'S 72°15'W	16, 09, 14 1200-2200
Valdivia CBT4	39°48'S 73°15'W	16, 09, 14 24hrs
Corral CBT26	39°53'S 72°25'W	16, 09, 14 1200-2200
Puerto Varas CBL202	41°20'S 73°00'W	16, 09, 14 1200-2200
Puerto Montt CBP20	**41°29'S 72°57'W**	**16, 09, 10, 14, 25, 26, 27 24hrs**
Maullín CBP21	41°37'S 73°36'W	16, 09, 14 1200-2200
Calbuco CBP22	41°46'S 73°08'W	16, 09, 14 1200-2200
Faro Corona CBP70	**41°47'S 73°52'W**	**16, 09,14 24hrs**
Pargua CBP44	41°48'S 73°24'W	16, 09, 14 1200-2200
Chacao CBP33	41°50'S 73°31'W	16, 09, 14 1200-2200
Ancud CBP23	41°52'S 73°50'W	16, 09, 14 1200-2200
Quemchi CBP26	42°09'S 73°29'W	16, 09, 14 1200-2200
Achao CBP25	42°28'S 73°30'W	16, 09, 14 1200-2200
Chonchi CBP27	42°37'S 73°47'W	16, 09, 14 1200-2200
Chaitén CBP24	42°55'S 72°43'W	16, 09, 14 1200-2200
Queilén CBP28	43°07'S 73°37'W	16, 09, 14 1200-2200
Castro CBP2	*43°33'S 73°44'W*	*16, 09, 14 24hrs*
Faro Huafo CBP4	*43°34'S 73°45'W*	*16, 09,14 24hrs*
Melinka CBP29	43°54'S 73°45'W	16, 09, 14 1200-2200
Puerto Cisnes CBP30	44°33'S 72°41'W	16, 09, 14 1200-2200
Puerto Aguirre CBP31	45°10'S 73°32'W	16, 09, 14 1200-2200
Puerto Aysén CBP3	45°25'S 72°42'W	16, 09, 14 24hrs
Puerto Chacabuco CBP32	45°28'S 72°49'W	16, 09, 14 1200-2200
Lago Gen. Carrera CBL203	46°40'S 72°25'W	16, 09, 14 1200-2200
Faro Ráper CBM2	*46°49'S 75°37'W*	*16, 09, 14 24hrs*
San Pedro CBS	*47°43'S 74°53'W*	*16, 09, 14 24hrs*
Tortel CBM31	47°51'S 73°36'W	16, 09, 14 1200-2200
Puerto Edén CBM21	49°08'S 72°26'W	16, 09, 14 24hrs
Puerto Natales CBM22	51°45'S 72°32'W	6, 09, 14 1200-2200
Faro Dungeness CBM71	*52°24'S 68°26'W*	*16, 09, 14 24hrs*[2]
Faro Evangelistas CBM3	*52°24'S 75°06'W*	*16, 09, 14 24hrs*
Delgada CBM5	*52°27'S 69°33'W*	*16, 09, 14 24hrs*[2]
Faro Espíritu Santo CBM72	*52°39'S 68°36'W*	*16, 09, 14 24hrs*
Faro Fairway CBM4	*52°44'S 73°47'W*	*16, 09, 14 24hrs*
Bahía Félix CBX	**52°58'S 74°04'W**	**16, 09, 14 24hrs**
Telco CBM9	**53°09'S 70°58'W**	**16, 25 24hrs**
Magallanes CBM	**52°56'S 70°54'W**	**16, 09, 10, 14, 26 24hrs**[1]
Punta Arenas Capuerto CBM25	53°10'S 70°54'W	16, 09, 14 1200-2200
Tierra del Fuego CBM23	53°18'S 70°23'W	16, 09, 14 1200-2200
Puerto Williams CBW	**54°56'S 67°37'W**	**16, 09, 14 24hrs**
Wollaston CBN	*55°37'S 68°18'W*	*16, 09, 14 24hrs*
Diego Ramírez CBM30	56°31'S 68°42'W	16, 09, 14 24hrs

Argentina

Station	Position	Channels / Hours
Ushuaia LPC	54°48'S 68°18'W	16, 09, 24hrs
Ushuaia Prefectura Naval L3P	54°48'S 68°18'W	16, 09, 12, 14 24hrs
Rio Grande Prefectura Naval L4F	53°47'S 67°41'W	16, 09, 12, 14 24hrs

1. Also give medical advice by radio, in Spanish or English. Address 'Medico. . .(name of station)'.
2. Will provide meteorological information and a radar service on request

Appendix E

Direction Finding Stations

Note Ranges for aero beacons are indicated in terms of the power of the transmitter and for marine beacons in nautical miles.

3776 Arica, Chacalluta Airport 18°20'·95S 70°19'·38W c/s *ARI* 340kHz 1·0kW 24hr

3778 Iquique, Chucumata Airport 20°34'·05S 70°10'·90W c/s *UCU* 368kHz 0·4kW 24hr

3780 Mejillones, Aero 23°06'·35S 70°26'·37W c/s *MJL* 240kHz 1·0kW 24hr

3782 Caldera 27°04'·48S 70°49'·89W c/s *CLD* 227kHz 1·0kW 24hr

Note Correction dated 22 Feb 96 to *NP7* lists it as off, 1996 *NP282* lists it as on.

3784 Punta Tortuga 29°55'·94S 71°21'·56W c/s *TUGA* 322·5kHz 160M 24hr

3786 Tongoy 30°5'·74S 71°29'·43W c/s *TOY* 260kHz 3·0kW 24hr

3788 Quintero 32°44'·10S 71°29'·68W c/s ERO *384kHz* 1kW 24hrs

3790 Punta Angeles 33°01'·27S 71°39'·17W c/s *VASO* 300kHz 110M 24hrs

3792 Santo Domingo 33°38'·00S 71°38'·00W c/s *SNO* 355kHz 1kW 24hrs

3794 Constitución 35°18'·22S 72°23'·00W c/s *CTN* 340kHz 1kW 24hrs

3796 Isla Quiriquina, Punta de Faro 36°36'·56S 73°02'·80W c/s *QINA* 315kHz 160M 24hrs

3798 Concepción 36°50'·50S 73°06'·50W c/s *CE* 254kHz 1kW 24hrs
3800 Punta Anegadiza, Isla Mocha 38°22'·93S 73°52'·93W c/s *MOCA* 295kHz 110M 24hrs
3802 Punta Corona, Isla Chiloé 47°47'·10S 73°53'·32W c/s *CONA* 290kHz 110M 24hrs
3804 Chaitén 42°55'·30S 72°43'·05W c/s *TEN* 234kHz 0·4kW Day service only
3806 Isla San Pedro 47°43'·23S 74°53'·43W c/s *ISP* 295kW 1·0kW 1100–0200
3808 Isla Guarello 50°21'·65S 75°20'·10W c/s *IGU* 315kHz 0·5kW 24hrs
3810 Punta Arenas 53°06'·50S 70°54'·02W PA c/s *NAS* 270kHz 3·0kW 24hrs
3812 Punta Dungeness 52°23'·75S 68°25'·92W c/s *GENE* 322·5kHz 110M 24hrs

Appendix F

BBC World Service

General

The following are times and frequencies of the BBC World Service broadcasts to South America. for 1998. Minor variations may occur from month to month, more likely to times than frequencies, but the skeleton is likely to remain stable. Times are UT.

Frequency kHz	*Time*
5970	0000–0800
	2100–2400
6110	2130–2230
6195	1000–1400
7325	0230–0330
9560	2130–2230
9825	2130–2230
9915	0000–0230
	2200–2400
11750	0000–0200
	2000–2400
11765	2130–2230
15190	0900–1130
15220	1100–1400
15390	2130–2215
17790	1100–1130
17840	1400–1700

Appendix G

Cruising in the South

Anchoring

The strong winds and *rachas* found in the canals, particularly the southern portion, require the most secure anchoring techniques. The weather can change very quickly and what was a calm anchorage at 1700hrs can turn into a scene of wind-whipped white water and rain by 0200. There are many tales of boats being literally blown out of what had been a calm, sheltered cove. Even in calm weather it is prudent to anchor in a manner that assumes gales in the middle of the night. The standard procedure in the canals is 2 anchors in tandem and 2 or more lines ashore.

The choice of anchor rests with the owner but for getting through kelp in emergency a Fisherman's anchor has a lot to commend it. Take one as a reserve.

Tandem anchoring

This is far safer and more secure than lying to two separate anchors. With a little practice, tandem anchors are easy to deploy and recover. Two bow rollers, port and starboard bow cleats and a good chain and rope windlass are required. The 'first-down' anchor lies in the port side roller. Its shaft is connected by 6–10m of chain, running around the outside of the pulpit and back to the crown of the main anchor lying in the starboard roller. A retrieval line, 3m longer than the chain, leads from the shackle on the shaft of the first down anchor to the shackle on the shaft of the main anchor. For a Rolls-Royce set-up, the retrieval line should be floating polyprop with snap shackles spliced into both ends but it works fine with regular line.

Prior to anchoring, the 'first down' anchor is held in place on its roller by the retrieval line cleated to the port bow cleat. The main anchor is held in place by the chain from the windlass. With the boat slowly in reverse, let go the 'first-down' anchor by hand using the retrieval line. Then release the windlass and pay out the main anchor. Set it hard with the engine. Place a nylon snubber (5–7m) on the main anchor chain. Take the chain off the windlass and loosely secure it to the starboard cleat. Make sure that the snubber is protected from chafe over the roller.

To retrieve the anchors, haul up the main anchor on the windlass until the shaft reaches the roller. Lock the windlass. Reach around from the port side of the pulpit and bring the retrieval line over the port bow roller. By hand, haul up the 'first-down' anchor. Initially, the only weight is that of the anchor. When the anchor is almost on board the weight will be that of the anchor and half of the chain. Pull the 'first-down' anchor over the roller and secure with the retrieval line to the port cleat. Bring the main anchor all the way home. Disconnect the chain from the crown of the main anchor and store the 'first-down' anchor.

If the 'first-down' anchor is particularly hard to raise, take the chain of the main anchor off the windlass to the starboard bow cleat and use the rope gypsy of the windlass to haul up the retrieval line.

Kelp is prevalent in the canals and a long handled serrated edged knife or machete is often necessary to clear kelp from the anchors.

Lines ashore

Although tandem anchoring is very secure, the strength of the *rachas* and their variable direction dictates that two or three lines ashore are also required. Generally speaking the objective is to anchor as close to the shore as possible and preferably in a notch where the boat can be secured by lines ashore from all four corners or from the two stern quarters and the bow. In some anchorages, e.g. Morris and Soffia it is better to anchor out in the open because there is no notch or because the obvious notch is close to the head of the anchorage and subject to more *rachas* than prevail in the open area to one side.

The best gear seems to be two 100m lines and one or two lengths of 50–60m line. Three or four 4–6m lengths of chain are used to loop around rocks or trees and brought back to be shackled to eye splices on the ends of the lines.

The best type of rope to use for shorelines is probably 3 strand polypropylene. Unlike nylon, it floats, tends to stay above the kelp, tows easily from a dinghy and does not have a life of its own. It is also relatively inexpensive and can be purchased easily in hardware stores *(fereterías)* ashore. If there is space, rope reels on deck are a great asset.

Anchoring and lines ashore often has to be carried out quickly before the boat is blown out of position. There is a fair tide range so it is important to tie the lines ashore at points above high tide. One method is to tie the eye spliced end of the line around the waist, the dinghy painter tied around a leg, row as fast as possible to a pre-selected tree or rock, leap ashore leaving the dinghy to bang around on the rocks, secure as quickly as possible the chain and line and rush back to the boat for the next line. (Sounds easy on paper but wait till you try it). Watch out for rotten trees as they are covered with moss and it is hard to tell good from bad.

Appendix H

Natural History

By John and Fay Garey

Plants

Stretching from the Tropics to Antarctica, from the driest deserts to the wettest rain forest, Chile is home to an astonishing range of plants. About half of the 5,000 or so flowering species are exclusive or endemic to the country, and there are entire families of plants that are found nowhere else but in Chile.

Arriving in Chile, one's first impression is of stepping into a foreign landscape, where the trees, flowers and even the weeds are different. In the central zone, with its Mediterranean-type climate, are trees with unheard-of names *(Peumus boldus, Maytenus boaria, Lithraea cuastica)*, characterised by hard, small, often aromatic leaves designed to withstand the arid conditions. The Chilean palm *(Jubaea chilensis)* grows here, although its numbers have been much reduce by felling for the extraction of 'palm honey', together with bromeliads or pineapple-relatives (*Puya* species), with weird metallic blue or greenish-yellow flowers.

In the northern desert of Atacama are vast tracts of land which are totally devoid of vegetation. However, nearer the coast and in the high altiplano bordering Bolivia, there is sufficient moisture for many types of cactus, shrub and herbaceous plant to exist. These include the giant candelabra cactus, which grows 5mm a year, flowers once a year for 24 hours, and lives to hundreds of years old; and the equally long-lived, slow-growing 'llaretales' or cushion plants, at altitudes over 3500m.

Two of Chile's most distinctive conifers grow in the coastal range and Andes in the south, their populations now shrunk to isolated pockets. The monkey puzzle tree *Araucaria araucana*, with its umbrella-like canopy, reaches heights of 150 feet and more. The alerce *(Fitzroya cupressoides)* has become almost extinct because its wood is so highly prized. It can live to 2,000 years of age.

The richest area is undoubtedly that south of the Río Bio-bio and Concepción, which includes the temperate rain forest of Valdivia and the island of Chiloé. It is a great thrill to see fuchsia, escallonia, berberis, buddleia and other familiar garden shrubs actually growing in the wild. Indeed, Chile has contributed many ornamental plants to our gardens, such as alstroemeria, calceolaria, nasturtium, hippeastrum and schizanthus, and it has also supplied the ancestors of two of our commonest foods, the potato and the strawberry.

Recommended reading

Fora Silvestre de Chile, Palmengarten Sonderheft 19 (1992), translated from German into Spanish

Flora Silvestre de Chile, Zona Araucana (2nd edition, 1991)

Flora Silvestre de Chile, Zona Central (1978)

Cactáceas en la Flora Silvestre de Chile (1989)

all by A Hoffmann (Ediciones Fundación Claudio Gay)

Arboles Nativos de Chile, Claudio Donoso Zegers (Marisa Cuneo Ediciones, 1991), with English and Spanish text.

Birds

One of the great excitements of crossing the Equator and arriving in the Southern Hemisphere is the first sighting of an albatross, the largest of all seabirds. The commonest species are the wandering, the royal and the black-browed albatross, all unmistakable with their huge wingspans and soaring flight. They are often accompanied by pintado petrels, which habitually follow ships and are instantly recognisable from the black and white chequered upper parts. Another ship-follower is the white-chinned petrel, a large, entirely dark brown bird, except for the white chin and pale yellow bill. Much more attractive but very difficult to distinguish are several gadfly petrels that nest in the Juan Fernandez islands and roam the ocean; these small or medium-sized birds are grey and white, with an open 'M' marking across the wings and back. The pink-footed shearwater, a big, rather clumsy-looking bird, also breeds in the archipelago.

As one approaches the mainland, it is a delight to see pelicans – in this case the huge Peruvian or Chilean pelican, the avian equivalent of a giraffe in that it seems to have been designed by a committee, but a master of the air and sea. The silly, open-mouthed, cross-eyed expression of the Peruvian booby similarly belies its expertise; like the pelican, it is found from Arica to Chiloé. More surprising is to encounter penguins, diving and swimming in the clear water and sometimes giving a curious mooing sound exactly like that of a cow. Although their more spectacular kin live in the far south and Antarctica, the Humboldt and closely related Magellanic penguin are much in evidence along the coasts of Chile and Peru. Among the numerous species of tern that inhabit or visit Chile and its off-lying islands, perhaps the most striking is the Inca tern; this is endemic to the Humboldt Current and its dark grey plumage is enlivened by bright red legs and beak.

The colourful red-legged shag shares the inshore waters with the imperial or blue-eyed shag, the rock shag, the guanay cormorant and the olivaceous cormorant, the latter often occurring in rivers and lakes as well. Several types of grebe can be observed in freshwater areas, including the pied-bill grebe, which has a stubby banded beak and lacks the usual crest on the head; and the great grebe – or haula as it is known, possibly because of its poignant miaowing cry – with a long pointed beak and slim, reddish brown neck. Some of the more interesting gulls are the grey gull, of central Chile, which runs across the sand pretending to be a sandpiper; and the kelp gull, the only large, black-backed, white-tailed gull in the southern oceans. A regular summer visitor is the black skimmer, unique in having the lower mandible longer than the upper; at dawn and dusk, flocks of these birds fly low over the water, scooping up food with their extraordinary scissor-like beaks. At the water's edge, snipes, oystercatchers (both the familiar American species and the black oystercatcher), herons and hawks are always busy.

The bird life of Chile is as varied as the country itself and comprises an estimated 439 breeding and migrant species, about 5% of the total world population. One of the most notable natives is the Juan Fernández hummingbird, which makes its presence felt on Robinson Crusoe Island with noisy shrilling from the eucalyptus trees; the male is orange-red, the female bright green and smaller, and for many years they were thought to be different species. The famous condor, depicted in the national coat of arms, is increasingly scarce, but vultures are widespread and it is a strange experience to have one perch on top of the mast. The Andean flamingo, largest of the three endemic species, dwells in the salt lakes and coastal areas of the northern desert. In such barren surroundings, it seems unbelievable to come across this exotic bird, with its pinky-white plumage and long neck, standing motionless by the water on one stilt-like leg, or, when it takes flight, displaying vivid flame-coloured wings edged with black. Equally memorable is the black-necked swan, of coastal lagoons, particularly in Valdivia and Chiloé, which has a pure white body, jet-black neck and crimson beak.

Recommended reading

Seabirds of the World, A Photographic Guide, Peter Harrison (Christopher Helm, 1987)

Guía de Campo de las Aves de Chile, Baulio Aray M, & Guillermo Millie H. (Edvisitorial Universitaria, 1991), with English index

Note Professor Julius Schlatter, of the Universidad Austral de Chile, Valdivia, is a leading ornithologist in the country, who would be pleased to hear of unusual sightings or to help with identification.

Mammals

Sea Lions (*lobos marinos*) are common all along the coast of Chile. Hefty creatures up to 6 feet long, they seem to be equally at home draped over a surf-swept rock, or basking in the calm water of a sheltered harbour, or even swimming far inland up a river. Their curiosity tends to get the better of them when a yacht is at anchor and they will surface just a few yards away, with a loud exhalation of breath; they will also follow a dinghy, diving around playfully and without fear.

The Juan Fernández fur seal is unique to that archipelago and the only mammal native there. When Alexander Selkirk was marooned on Robinson Crusoe Island in 1704, these animals were so numerous that he hunted them for sport. By the beginning of this century, they were on the verge of extinction, but the population has now recovered to about 8,000.

Of dolphins, the sturdy bottlenose and the smaller, more slender spinner dolphin, with a pronounced upright fin, are probably the most likely to be encountered in the open ocean and sometimes even quite close to land. They are always a delight to watch, performing leaps and somersaults apparently for their own benefit, or rushing towards the boat to ride in the bow wave. Much more restricted in distribution are the Chilean or black dolphin, small and black with white underparts, and the similar black porpoise, both inhabiting cold inshore waters south of Valdivia and both considered rare. In these lower latitudes, the piebald dolphin and the blackchin dolphin are reportedly fairly frequent, together with the southern right whale dolphin in deeper waters, all of them variously patterned in black and white.

One of the most widespread whales in the world is the orca or great killer whale, generally seen in coastal areas and estuaries. It is immediately recognisable from the tall dorsal fin, forward-pointing in the male, and the distinctive white markings on the black body.

Sightings of other species of whale are a matter of chance, although yachtsmen venturing as far as Antarctica may be rewarded by the appearance of an enormous blue whale, feeding on krill.

Recommended reading

Whales of the World, A Complete Guide to the World's Living Whales, Dolphins and Porpoises, Lyall Watson (Hutchinson, 1985)

Bibliography

Compiled by Pedro Vergara

It is difficult for a bibliographer to find a happy compromise between listing every book ever published on a subject and being so superficial as not to provide some fascinating gems. The majority of the books mentioned are out of print today but copies can usually be found through book search companies. To limit the bibliography to English titles would be very restrictive so some classic reference books in Spanish have been included. The books often have their own bibliographies and are excellent sources for further research.

Historical and Exploration

The Exploration of the Pacific J C Beaglehole. Published by Black 3rd ed 1966. This is a classic first published in 1934. The book covers, very comprehensively, the early exploration of the route from the Atlantic to the Pacific by Magellan and others.

The Circumnavigators Derek Wilson. Published by M. Evans & Co, New York and Constable & Co. Ltd, UK in 1989.

The Wager Mutiny S W C Pack. Published Alvin Redman, London in 1964.

Byron of the Wager Peter Shankland. Published by Collins, 1975. These books cover the shipwreck of the Wager just south of the Golfo de Penas in 1740. The Wager was part of Anson's fleet sent to attack Valdivia. The books describe the mutiny and how the majority of the crew sailed by open boat back via the canals to Brazil.

In Darwin's Wake John Campbell. Published by Waterline. ISBN 1-85310-755-7.

The Voyage of Charles Darwin. A book linked to the BBC film about the voyage of a replica of the Beagle. Christopher Ralling has selected Darwin's autobiographical writings to form the text of the book.

Three Men of the Beagle R. Lee Marks. Published by Alfred A. Knopf, New York in 1991. The tale of Fitzroy, Darwin and Jeremy Button.

Cruise of the Alert – in Patagonian and Polynesian Waters Dr. R W Coppinger. Published by Swan Sonnenschein & Co, London in 1885. The book describes the cruise of the British ship, the Alert, between 1878 and 1882, on a comprehensive survey trip that included key anchorages in Patagonian waters.

Cap Horn 1882-1883. Rencontre avec les Indiens Yahgan A. Chapman, C Barthe, P Revol and J Dubois. Published by Editos de la Martiniere in Paris in 1995.

The Wilds of Patagonia – A narrative of the Swedish Expedition to Patagonia Carl Skottesberg. Published by Edward Arnold, London in 1911.

Mis Viajes a la Tierra del Fuego published in Milan, 1946;
Andes Patagonicos Viajes de Exploracion a la Cordillera Patagonica Austral published in Buenos Aires, 1945;
Trenta Anos en Tierra del Fuego Published in Buenos Aires in 1956.

These three books were written and published by Alberto M de Agostini. They relate the extraordinary explorations by yacht of this priest who was the first to describe many of the mountains of Patagonia.

Sailing Southward from the Straight of Magellan Rockwell Kent. Published by G P Putnam's Sons in 1924. A classic sailing adventure in the canals, without engine. A book that contains many wonderful woodcuts.

The Eight Sailing Mountain Exploration Books – including *Mischief in Patagonia* H W Tilman. Published by Diadem Books, London in 1987.

Anuario Hidrografico de la Marina de Chile. A series published in 14 volumes by the Servicio Hidrogrfico y Oceanogrfico de Chile. The series covers very comprehensively the exploration and charting of the Canals and has extracts from many authors. It is probably the most comprehensive source of historical information on the canals.

Land of Tempests Eric Shipton. Published by The Travel Book Club in 1963. The travels and climbs of Eric Shipton over the period 1958-62.

The Springs of Enchantment John Earle. Published Hodder and Stoughton, London in 1981. An account of two trips to Patagonia, the first with Eric Shipton.

Two against the Horn by Hal Roth. Published by Stanford Maritime, London in 1979.

The Totore Voyage – an Antarctic Adventure by Gerry Clark. Published by Century Hutchinson, New Zealand in 1988.

By way of Cape Horn and *The War with Cape Horn* A J Villier. Published by Henry Holt and Co, New York in 1930 and Hodder and Stoughton in 1971 respectively.

Cape Horn: The Logical Route Published by William Morrow and Co, New York in 1973; and Cap Horn a la Voile published by Arthaud, Paris in 1995. Two books by Bernard Moitessier.

The Great Days of Cape Horners Yves Le Scal. Published by Souvenir Press, UK in 1966.

Because the Horn is There and *Once is enough* Miles Smeeton and published by Grafton Books, London in 1987 and 1991 respectively.

Sailing Cape Horn- A Maritime History Robin Knox-Johnston. Published by Hodder and Stoughton in 1971.

Then we sailed away – A family adventure by John, Marie, Christine and Rebecca Ridgeway. ISBN 1-85130-775-7.

Chile - General Travel

Full Circle – A south American Journey Luis Sepulveda. ISBN 0-86442-465-5. Published by Lonely Planet Journeys.

Travels in a Thin Country Sara Wheeler. ISBN 0.349-10584-7. Published by Abacus Travel

Chile and Easter Island. A Lonely Planet Travel Survival Kit. ISBN 0-86442-181-8.

Chile and Easter Island. Lonely Planet Atlas. ISBN 0-86442-517-1.

Travel Companion: Chile and Easter Island Gerry Leitner. ISBN 0-646-06042-2. Published by Companion Travel Guide Books, Australia

South American Handbook Ben Box. ISBN 0 900751-74-6. Published by Footprint Handbooks, UK.

The General Travel Books listed above can be obtained through bookshops in the UK such as Edward Stanford Ltd, 12–14 Long Acre, London WC2E 9LP ☎ 0171 836 1321 *Fax* 0171 836 7960.

Chile – A Remote Corner on Earth. Published by Turismo Comunicaciones S.A. This book is the English version of a guide normally printed in Spanish is probably the best guide to the country .

Turistel: Gua Turistica de Chile. Published by Compaia de Telecomunicaciones de Chile S.A, Santiago. The nearest thing to a combined Green and Red Michelin of Chile. In Spanish.

Both the above books are available in bookshops or magazine stalls in Chile.

Chile – Natural History

The Flight of the Condor by Michael Andrew. Published by William Collins & Sons Ltd, in 1983. The story of an excellent BBC natural history series.

Flora Silvestre de Chile – zona Central. Flora Silvestre de Chile – zona Araucana. Flora Silvestre de Chile – zona Austral. Adriana Hoffman J. Published by Fundacion Claudio Gay in 1979,1984 and 1982 respectively.

Flora of Tierra del Fuego David Moore. Published by Anthony Nelson, London in 1983.

Guia de Campo de Las Aves de Chile Braulio Araya M and Guillermo Millie H. Published by Editorial Universtaria, Chile 1996.

Charts

The charts mentioned in this volume are listed below. All three Hydrographic Offices produce charts which are not mentioned in the text.

UK Hydrographic Office

Note All the charts at 1:500,000 have plans of selected ports.

554	Estrecho de Magalanes	550,000
631	Estrecho Magallanes Paso del Mar and Canal Smythe - southern part	100,000
887	Paso Inglés, Tortuoso, Largo and del Mar	100,000
1281	Segunda Angostura to Paso del Mar	300,000
1282	Estrecho de Magallanes to Canal Concepción	300,000
1286	Canal Concepción to Canal del Castillo	300,000
1287	Canal del Castillo to Estero San Esteban	300,000
1288	Seno Cornish to Boca del Guafo	300,000
1289	Islas Guaitecas to Bahía San Pedro	440,000
1313	Channels between Maullin and Montt	152,300
1314	Ports and anchorages on the coast of Chile	Various
1319	Bahía Concepción and Bahía San Vincente	Various
1373	South-eastern part of Tierra del Fuego	550,000
1389	Islands and anchorages in the south-east Pacific Ocean	Various
1694	Segunda Angostura to Punta Arenas	100,000
3070	Bahía Algodonales to Rada de Arica	500,000
3071	Puerto Pan de Azúcar to Bahía Algodonales	500,000
3072	Caleta Totoralillo to Puerto Pan de Azúcar	500,000
3073	Bahía Valparaíso to Caleta Totoralillo	500,000
3074	Golfo Arauco to Bahía Valparaíso	500,000
3075	Bahía San Pedro to Golfo Arauco	500,000
3076	Ports on the coast of Chile	Various
3077	Ports on the coast of Chile	Various
3078	Ports on the coast of Chile	Various
3079	Plans on the coast of Chile	Various
3080	Plans on the coast of Chile	Various
3081	Plans on the coast of Chile	Various
3749	Golfos Corvocado and Ancud	152,300

Defense Mapping Agency, U.S. Department of Commerce

Note although not all are mentioned in the text, this agency produces charts of the whole coast at 1:500,000.

22205	Arica to Mejillones	500,000
22221	Plans on the coast of Chile	Various
22225	Mejillones to Puerto de Caldera	500,000
22250	Puerto de Caldera to Coquimbo	500,000
22259	Bahía de Valparaíso and Puerto Valparaíso	10,000
22261	Plans on the coast of Chile	Various
22262	Puerto Huasco	12,000
22263	Bahía Quintero	15,000
22264	Approaches to Bahías Quintero & Valparaíso	50,000
22281	Punta Porotos to Punta Lengua de Vaca	100,000
22282	Bahías de Coquimbo and Guayacán	36,500
22290	Bahía de Valparaíso to Golfo de Arauco	500,000
22295	Plans on the coast of Chile	Various
22305	Port Talcahuano to Bahía Corral	500,000
22312	Golfo de Arauco	80,000
22335	Bahía Corral to Isla Guafo	500,000
22341	Golfo de Ancud - Northern Part	140,000
22342	Canal de Chacao	60,000
22345	Puerto Montt	20,000
22352	Golfo Corcovado and S.Golfo de Ancud	150,000
22360	Boca del Guafo to Canal Moraleda	200,000
22370	Isla Guafo to Golfo de Penas	500,000
22371	Bahía Darwin to Seno Aisen	200,000
22404	Isla Richards to Islotes Fairway	30,000
22405	Isla Cutter to Isla Richards	30,000
22410	Cabo Deseado to Isla Noir including the Western Part of the Estrecho de Magallanes	276,600
22412	Islote Fairway to Cabo Cooper Key	100,000
22415	Paso Largo, Canal Jerónimo and Paso Tortuoso	Various
22418	Bahía Desolada to Punta Yamana	200,000
22420	Canal Trinidad to Estrecho Magallanes	500,000
22425	Canal Magdalena, Canal Cockburn and Adjacent Channels	165,000
22430	Canal Beagle to Cabo de Hornos	200,000
22471	Primera Angostura to Punta Dungeness	100,000
22481	Bahía Gente Grade to Primera Angostura	100,000
22482	Rada Punta Arenas	20,000
22492	Islands off the coast of Chile Robinson Crusoe Islands	40,000
29002	Antarctic Peninsula	1,500,000

Servicio Hidrográfico y Oceanográfico de la Armada de Chile

Note The Chilean Armada produce about 260 coastal charts plus various instructional charts. A reduced version of the complete collection, which is possible to use for navigation with the aid of a magnifying glass. is available in the *Atlas Hidrográfico de Chile* at a fraction of the cost of the full-scale set.

Many of the small charts have large scale inserts which are not listed.

The logic of the numbering system is sometimes difficult to follow.They are listed as they appear in the Atlas Hidrogáfico.

101	Rada y Puerto Arica	60,610
104	Bahía Iquique	31,250
107	Caleta Patillos	14,490
110	Rada de Arica a Bahía de Iquique	636,360
113	Puertos en la Costa de Chile	46,510
120	Bahía Iquique a Puerto Tocopilla	612,390

1300	Puerto de Tocopilla a Rada de Antofagasta	578,310
131	Puerto Tocopilla	27,030
133	Bahía Mejillones del Sur	105,260
200	Bahía Mejillones del Sur a Puerto de Caldera	1,420,530
206	Caletas en el Litoral de Antofagasta y Atatcama	Various
207	Puertos en la Costa de Chile	Various
212	Rada de Antofagasta	25,970
300	Puerto Caldera a Bahía Coquimbo	1,166,670
303	Puertos en la Costa de Chile	Various
304	Caletas en la Costa de Chile	Various
3210	Puerto Huasco	10,000
311	Puertos Caldera, Calderilla y Bahía Inglesa	59,700
400	Bahía Coquimbo y Bahía de Valparaíso	1,137,720
401	Punta Peroto a Lengua de Vaca	215,520
404	Puertos en la Costa de Chile	Various
411	Bahías de Coquimbo and Guayacán	40,000
412	Bahía Tongoy	75,760
424	Bahía Quintero	25,320
426	Bahía Concón y Club des Yates Viña de Mar	25,000
500	Bahía de Valparaíso a Golfo de Arauco	1,441,360
501	Punta Pite a PuntaTopocalma	523.030
509	Archipiélago de Juan Fernández	Various
510	Bahía Cumberland	11,490
511	Bahía y Puerto Valparaíso	29,150
513	Rada El Algorrobo	21,740
600	Golfo de Arauco a Bahía Corral	1,193,030
611	Bahías Concepción y San Vincente	50,000
612	Puertos Talcahuano, Lirquén y Penco	26,670
623	Bahía y Puerto Corral	50,000
6271	Acceso a Ríos Valdivia y Torna Galeones	32,790
6272	Río Valdivia	32,000
700	Bahía Corral a Isla Guafo	1,356,790
701	Caletas en la Costa de Chile	Various
7210	Canal Chacao	161,290
703	Bahía de Ancud	50,420
704	Puerto Montt a Isla Tac	41,780
705	Puertos en el Golfo de Ancud	Various
706	Isla Malliña al Isla Tabón	85,110
708	Estero Reloncaví	Various
709	Golfo de Ancud	330,580
710	Puertos en Isla de Chiloé	Varioua
711	Canal Dalcahue	27,780
712	Archiépelago de Chiloé	Various
714	Puertos en Chiloe	55,560
715	Isla Tranqui a Isla San Pedro	153,580
716	Islas Desertores y Islas Guaitecas	453,900
717	Peurtos en la Costa de Chile	Various
718	Islas Guiatecas	238,400
721	Caletas en la Costa de Chile	Various
732	Bahía Puerto Montt	29,410
801	Canal Moraleda	706,130
802	Canales Puyuguapi y Jacaf	445,430
803	Canales Pérez Norte y Pérez Sur	341,380
804	Puertos en el Canal Moraleda	Various
807	Croquis de Puertos en el Archiépelago de los Chonos	Various
809	Puerto Lagunas a Punta Pescadores y Seno Aysén	375,880
8290	Seno Aysén	138,890
810	Canal Ferronave	149,250
812	Punta Pescadores a Istmo de Ofqui	345,230
814	Puertos en el Península Tres Montes	Various
9110	Bahía Hoppner y Paso Holloway	143,500
815	Bahía Anna Pink a Canal Messier	700,000
816	Bahía San Quintín	141,500
817	Estero Clemente	15,900
827	Bahía y Puerto Chacabuco	43,500
838	Golfo Elefantes a Laguna San Rafael	143,500
8430	Bahía Anna Pink	160,000
840	Bahías Darwin y Anna Pink	400,000
841	Puertos en las Canales Moraleda y Darwin	Various
842	Canal Darwin	161,000
846	Canales Pulluche, Chacabuco y Adyacentes	160,000
901	Canal Messier y Canal Baker	520,000
902	Puertos y Tenederos en el Canal Messier	Various
904	Canal Trinidad	200,000
905	Puerto Grappler	19,000
906	Angostura Inglesa. Canal Wide	400,000
9510	Senos Exmouth, Eyre y Estero Falcon	130,000
908	Puertos en la Patagonia Occidental	Various
910	Patagonia Occidental. Croquis de Fondeaderos en los Canales	Various
911	Canal Concepción y Canal Oeste	46,500
10340	Canal Oeste	46,500
912	Puertos en el Patagonia Occidental	34,200
914	Canal Wide a Canal Sarmiento	429,200
915	Puertos en el Canal Concepción	Various
916	Puertos en el Canal Inocentes	Various
918	Puertos y Caletas en el Zona de Baker	Various
919	Canal Sierraltа y Puertos en la Zona de Baker	Various
920	Puerto Alert	38,460
941	Angostura Inglesa y Paso de Indio	Various
10000	Canal Trinidad a Estrecho Magallanes	1,080,000
1001	Canal Sarmiento	300,000
1002	Puertos en el Canal Sarmiento	Various
1003	Fondeaderos en el Canal Smyth y Seno Unión	Various
1007	Estrecho Collingwood y Canal Smyth	205,380
1008	Canal Smyth Isla Cutler a Isla Richards	97,400
1009	Canal Smyth Isla Richards a Islotes Fairway	90,000
1101	Seno Última Esperanza y Canales Adyacentes	353.010
1102	Canal White (Seno Última Esperanza)	33,000
1062	Canal y Angostura Kirke	Various
1103	Canal Señoret y Estero Eberhartdt	64,660
1104	Croquis de Puertos en el Seno Última Esperanza	Various
10650	Canal Unión a Canal Kirke	119,470
11131	Estrecho de Magallanes Islote Fairway a Bahía Beaufort	200,510
1107	Bahía Wodsworth	17,300
1110	Puertos en el Canal Jerónimo	Various
1114	Cabo Cooper a Punta Arenas	731,500
1115	Fondeaderos en el Estrecho de Magallanes	Various
1117	Fondeaderos en el Estrecho de Magallanes	Various
1118	Fondeaderos en el Estrecho de Magallanes	Various
1120	Fondeaderos en el Estrecho de Magallanes	Various
1121	Fondeaderos en el Estrecho de Magallanes	Various

1122	Puertos en el Estrecho de Magallanes	Various
1135	Puertos Natales y Bories	27,870
11410	Rada de Punta Arenas	60,710
11100	Estrecho de Magallanes Islotes Evangelistas a Paso del Mar	307,430
11200	Estrecho de Magallanes Paso del Mar a Isla Carlos III	307,020
11230	Canal Jerónimo	153,300
11300	Estrecho de Magallanes Cabo Froward a Paso Tortuoso	314,860
1140	Estrecho de Magallanes Punta Arenas a Cabo Froward	311,420
1150	Estrecho de Magallanes Bahía Gente Grande a Primera Angostura	339,350
1160	Estrecho de Magallanes Primera Angostura a Punta Dungeness	330,800
1201	Canales Magdalena, Cockburn y Adyacentes	480,920
1202	Puertos en el Canal Magdalena y Cockburn	Various
1203	Bahía Desolada a Punta Yamana	542,190
1204	Canal Ocasión, Puertos en la Tierra del Fuego y Paso Pratt	32,250
1205	Puertos en las Canales Ballenero, Pomar y O'Brien	Various
1206	Canal O'Brien a Punta Yamana	305,400
1207	Isla Aguirre a Isla O'Brien	289,090
1221	Canal Ocasión, Caletas Burnt , Ancha y Paso Aguirre	61,870
1301	Canal Beagle a Cabo de Hornos	576,690
1302	Canal Murray	78,190
1303	Puertos en el Canal Beagle	Various
1304	Caletas en las Islas Nueva y Lennox	Various
1307	Canal Beagle de Canal Murray a Puerto Williams	193,800
13150	Canal Beagle, Puerto Willams	24,960
1312	Islas Wollaston a Islas Diego Ramirez	581,740
1315	Islas Diego Ramírez	36,480
1318	Canal Beagle de Puerto Williams a Cabo San Pío e Islas a Sur	237,950
1340	Tierra del FuegoIsla Nueva a Isla de los Estados	630,380
2520	Isla de Pascua (Rapa-Nui)	142,860
2521	Hanga La Perouse y Hanga Anakena	12,990
2522	Hanga Roa y Hanga Pika	16,950
2523	Fondeaderos en Isla de Pascua (Rapa-Nui)	Various

Glossary

The following limited glossary relates to the weather, the abbreviations to be found on charts and some words likely to be useful entering port. For a list containing many words commonly used in connection with sailing, see Webb & Manton, Yachtsman's Ten Language Dictionary (Adlard Coles Nautical).

Aduana, customs
Armada, Navy
bahía, bay
caleta, inlet, bay
canal, strait, canal
estero, sound
morro, headland
puerto, port, bay
seno, sound
surgidero, anchorage, roadstead

Weather

On the radio, if there is a storm warning the forecast starts *aviso temporal.* If, as usual, there is no storm warning, the forecast starts *no hay temporal.* Many words are similar to the English and their meanings guessed. The following may be less familiar.

viento, wind
calma, calm
ventolina, light air
flojito, light breeze
flojo, gentle breeze
bonancible, moderate breeze
fresquito, fresh breeze
fresco, strong breeze
frescachón, near gale
duro, gale
muy duro, strong gale
temporal, storm
borrasca, violent storm
huracán, hurricane
tempestad, *borrasca*, thunderstorm
chubasco, squall
racha, squall
ráfaga, squall
remolino, whirlwind

Note We have not found a qualitative difference between Chubasco, Ráfaga and Racha. Chubasco is a Chilean word; El Diccionario Enciclopédico 'La Fuente' defines racha as ráfaga. All three are commonly translated into English as williwaw, a word which used to be heard only in connection with the Magallanes.

Visibilidad, Visibility
buena, good
regular, moderate
mala, poor
calima, haze
neblina, mist
niebla, fog

Precipitación, Precipitation
aguacero, shower
llovizna, drizzle
lluvia, rain
aguanieve, sleet
nieve, snow
granizada, hail

el cielo, the sky
nube, cloud
nubes altas/bajas, high/low clouds
nubloso, cloudy
cubierto, covered, overcast
claro, despejado, clear
Names of cloud types in Spanish are based on the same Latin words as the names used in English.

Sistemas del tiempo, Weather systems
anticiclón, anticyclone
depresión, depression
vaguada, trough
cresta, dorsal, ridge
cuna, wedge
frente, front
frio, cold
cálido, warm
ocluido, occluded
bajando, falling
subiendo, rising

Lights and charts

Major terms and abbreviations

A	*amarilla*	yellow
Alt	*alternativa*	alternative
Ag Nv	*aguas navegables*	navigable waters
Ang	*angulo*	angle
Ant	*anterior*	anterior, earlier, forward
Apag	*apagado*	extinguished
Arrc	*arrecife*	reef
At	*atenuada*	attenuated
B	*blanca*	white
Ba	*bahía*	bay
	bajamar escorada	chart datum
Bal. E	*baliza elástica*	'elastic' (plastic) buoy
Bco	*banco*	bank
Bo	*bajo*	shoal, under, below, low
Boc	*bocina*	horn, trumpet
Br	*babor*	port (left, not harbour)
C	*campana*	bell
Card	*cardinal*	cardinal
Cañ	*cañon*	canyon
cil	*cilíndrico*	cylindrical
C	*cabo*	cape
Cha	*chimenea*	chimney
Cno	*castillo*	castle
cón	*cónico*	conical
Ct	*centellante*	quick flashing (50-80/min)
CtI	*centellante interrumpida*	interrupted quick flashing
cuad	*cuadrangular*	quadrangular
D	*destello*	flash
Desap	*desaparecida*	disappeared
Dest	*destruida*	destroyed
dique		jetty, quay
Dir	*direccional*	directional
DL	*destello largo*	long flash
E	*este*	east
edif	*edificio*	building
Er	*estribor*	starboard
Est	esférico	spherical
Esp	*especial*	special
Est sñ	*estación de señales*	signal station
ext	*exterior*	exterior
Extr	*extremo*	end, head of pier etc
F	*fija*	fixed
Fca	*fabrica*	factory
FD	*fija y destello*	fixed and flashing
FGpD	*fija y grupo de destellos*	fixed and group flashing
Flot	*flotador*	float
Fondn	*fondeadero*	anchorage
GpCt	*grupo de centellos*	group quick flashing
GpD	*grupo de destellos*	group flashing
GpOc	*grupo de ocultaciones*	group occulting
GpRp	*grupo de centellos rápidos*	group very quick flashing
hel	*helicoidales*	helicoidal
hor	*horizontal*	horizontal
Hund	*hundida*	submerged
I	*interrumpido*	interrupted
Igla	*iglesia*	church
Inf	*inferior*	inferior, lower
Intens	*intensificado*	intensified
Irreg	*irregular*	irregular
Iso	*isofase*	isophase
L	*luz*	light
La	*lateral*	lateral
levante		eastern
M	*millas*	metres
Mte	*monte*	mountain
Mto	*monumento*	monument
N	*norte*	north
Naut	*nautófono*	foghorn
NE	*nordeste*	northeast
No	*número*	number
NW	*noroeste*	northwest
Obst	*obstruction*	obstruction
ocas	*ocasional*	occasional
oct	*octagonal*	octagonal
Pe A	*peligro aislado*	isolated danger
poniente		western
Post	*posterior*	posterior, later
Ppal	*principal*	principal
prohibido		prohibited
Obston	*obstrucción*	obstruction
Prov	*provisional*	provisional
prom	*prominente*	prominent, conspicuous
Pta	*punta*	point
Pto	*puerto*	port1
PTO	*puerto*	port1
R	*roja*	red
Ra	*estación radar*	radar station
Ra+	*radar + suffix*	radar+suffix (Ra Ref etc)
RC	*radiofaro*	circular all-round radio beacon
RD	*radiofaro dirigido*	directional radiobeacon
rect	*rectangular*	rectangular
Ra	*rocas*	rocks
Rp	*centeneallante rápida*	very quick flashing (80-160/min)
RpI	*cent. rápida interrumpida*	interrupted very quick flashing
RW	*radiofaro giratorio*	rotating radiobeacon
s	*sugundos*	seconds
S	*sur*	south
SE	*sudeste*	southeast
sil	*silencio*	silence
Silb	*silbato*	whistle
Sincro	*sincronizda con*	syncronized with
Sir	*sirena*	siren
son	*sonido*	sound, noise, report
Sto/a	*Santo, Santa*	Saint
SW	*sudoetse*	southwest
T	*temporal*	temporarily

Te	*torre*	tower
trans	*transversal*	transversal
triang	*triangular*	triangular
troncoc	*troncocónico*	truncated cone
troncop	*troncopiramidal*	truncated pyramid
TSH	*antena de radio*	radio mast
TV	*antena de TV*	TV mast
U	*centellante ultra-rápida*	ultra quick flashing (+160/min)
UI	*cent. ultra-rápida interrumpido*	interrupted ultra quick flashing
	Ventisquero	Glacier
V	*verde*	green
vivero		shellfish raft or bed
visible		visible
W	*oeste*	west

1. *Note* 'puerto' covers any landing place from a beach to container port.

Ports and Harbours

a popa	stern-to
a proa	bows-to
abrigo	shelter
al costado	alongside
amarrar	to moor
amarradero	mooring
ancho	breadth (see *manga*)
cabo	warp, line (cape)
calado	draught
compuerta	lock, basin
dársena	harbour
dique	dock, jetty
esclusa	lock
escollera	jetty
eslora total	length overall
espigon	spur, spike
fondear	to anchor
fondeadero	anchorage
fondo	depth (bottom, base
knudo	knot
longitud	length (see *eslora*)
lonja	fish market (wholesale)
manga	beam
muelle	mole
noray	bollard, mooring
pantalán	jetty
parar	to stop
pila	pile
práctico	pilot
profundidad	depth
rompeolas	breakwater
varadero	slipway
vertedero (verto)	spoil ground

Direction

barbor	port (left)
estribor	starboard
norte	north
este	east
sur	south
oeste	west

Administration

Aduana	customs
astillero	shipyard
capitán de puerto	harbour master
derechos	dues, rights
dueño	owner
fabrica	factory
ferrocarril	railway
gasoleo	diesel
guarda civil	police (& immigration)
manguera	hosepipe
keroseno	paraffin
patrón	skipper (not owner)
petróleo	petrol (gasoline)
título	certificate

Index

Abismo, Paso del, 101
Abra Cuthbert, 93
Abra Lecky's Retreat, 115
Abtao, Puerto, 33, 34
Acwalisnan, Canal, 85, 134, 138-9
Adelaide, Isla 148, 150
Aduana (Customs), 175
Aguila, Fondeadero, 172
Aguirre, Bahía (Península Mitre), 167-8
Aguirre, Puerto (Isla Las Huichas), 63-4
air transport, 7-8
Alberto Vargas, Isla, 91
Alejandro Selkirk, Isla, 174
Alert, Puerto, 104
algae, see red tide
Algarrobo, 23-4
Allard, Surgidero, 118
Almirantazgo, Seno, 85
Almirante Brown, Bahía, 167
Almirante Montt, Golfo, 119
Amalia, Caleta, 110
Amalia, Estero, 110
Americano, Puerto, 62, 63
Amita, Isla, 55, 56
Ancha, Caleta, 151
anchoring, 180
Ancud, 33
Andrade, Caleta, 38
Angamos, Puerto, 83
Angosto, Puerto, 129-31
Angostura Gu¡a, 105, 109
Angostura Inglesa, 97-8
Angostura Kirke, 118
Angostura Mischief, 111-12
Anihue, Bahía, 54-5
animals, 181-2
Anna Pink, Bahía, 74, 78, 79
Antofagasta, 14-15
Antrim, Seno, 102-3
Apiao, Isla, 44-5
Arboles Espectrales, Estero, 60
Ardevora, Caleta, 92
Arenas, Punta, 87, 88
Argentina, 163-5, 167-8
Arica, 9-11
Armada, 1, 175-7
Atacama desert, 2, 5
Atlantic route, 4
Austral, Caleta, 89, 90
Autin, Isla, 39
Aysén, Seno, 65-9

Bahía Aguirre, 167-8
Bahía Almirante Brown, 167
Bahía Anihue, 54-5
Bahía Anna Pink, 74, 78, 79
Bahía Borja, 133
Bahía Bougainville, 142
Bahía Buen Suceso, 168
Bahía Butler, 133
Bahía Cambaceres, 167
Bahía del Cañon, 142
Bahía Chacabuco, 67
Bahía Coliumo, 24
Bahía de Concepción, 25
Bahía Corbeta Papudo, 107
Bahía Corral, 26
Bahía Cumberland, 174
Bahía Desengaño, 119
Bahía Dorada, 57
Bahía Easter, 119
Bahía Elizabeth, 102
Bahía Exploradores, 71
Bahía Fortescue, 137-8
Bahía Fortuna, 123
Bahía Gente Grande, 143
Bahía Guanaquero, 21
Bahía Halt, 96, 97
Bahía Herradura de Guayacán, 19-20
Bahía Hueihue, 37
Bahía Huellonquen, 48
Bahía Hugh, 107
Bahía Islas, 54-5
Bahía Islotes Ruiz, 72
Bahía Isthmus, 123
Bahía Liberta, 96
Bahía Linao, 37
Bahía Mallet, 123
Bahía Manao, 37
Bahía Morris, 146
Bahía Mussel, 134
Bahía Nassau, 170
Bahía Pisagua, 11-12
Bahía Porvenir, 142
Bahía Quesahuén, 71-2
Bahía Quintero, 21
Bahía Ralún, 37
Bahía Relegada, 167
Bahía Romanche, 160
Bahía San Andres, 81-2
Bahía San Nicolás, 142
Bahía San Pedro, 30
Bahía San Quentín, 83-4
Bahía San Vicente, 25
Bahía Scourfield, 170, 171
Bahía Sotomo, 36
Bahía Tictoc, 49-50
Bahía Tilly, 133-4
Bahía Tom, 106
Bahía Tongoy, 20-21
Bahía Tres Brazos, 156
Bahía Welcome, 122, 123
Bahía Whitsand, 143
Bahía Wodsworth, 129, 130
Bahía Woods, 138
Bahía Yendegaia, 162
Bajo Rappel, 24
Baker, Canal, 90-91
Baker, Río, 90-92
Baker, Seno, 84, 89
Balandra, Caleta, 115, 116
Balladares, Estero, 77, 78
Ballenero, Canal, 151-3
Balmaceda, 67
Banner, Caleta, 169, 170
Bárbara, Canal, 85, 134, 135-7
Bariloche, 27-8
Barrancos, Caleta, 83
Barroso, Puerto, 83
Bartolome, Isla, 172
Baverstock, Isla, 123
BBC World Service, 180
beacons, 179-80
beacons, radio, 6
Beagle, Canal, 153, 155, 156-69
Beaubasin, Caleta, 144
Benjamin, Isla, 60
bibliography, 183-4
birds, 181-2
Blanco Encalada, Caleta, 15-16
Blue Lagoon, 122
Boca Wickham, 74, 79
Bonito, Estero, 38
Bonito, Puerto, 70
Borja, Bahía, 133
Bosque Valdiviano, 2
Bougainville, Bahía, 142
Brassey, Paso, 105
Brazo Noroeste (Canal Beagle), 156, 157-61
Brecknock, Caleta, 150
Brecknock, Canal, 150-51
Brecknock, Isla, 150
Brecknock, Península, 150
Brinkley, Isla, 105, 122
Brunswick, Península, 137-8, 142
Buen Suceso, Bahía, 168
Buena, Puerto, 61
Bueno, Caleta (Estero Slight),83
Bueno, Puerto (Canal Sarmiento), 113
Bueno, Puerto (Isla Florencia), 61
Bulnes, Fort, 142
Burgoyne, Caleta, 124
Burnt, Isla, 151
buses, 8
Buta Chauques, Isla, 39-40
Butler, Bahía, 133
Byron, Laguna, 88

Cabo de Hornos, 171, 172
Cabo Edgeworth, 135
Cabo Froward, 140, 144
Cabo Ráper, 83
Cahuelmo, Estero, 39
Cailin, Isla, 48-9
Calbuco, 34
Caldera, Puerto, 17-18
Caleta Amalia, 110
Caleta Ancha, 151
Caleta Andrade, 38
Caleta Ardevora, 92
Caleta Austral, 89, 90
Caleta Balandra, 115, 116
Caleta Banner, 169, 170
Caleta Barrancos, 83
Caleta Beaubasin, 144
Caleta Blanco Encalada, 15-16
Caleta Brecknock, 150
Caleta Bueno, 83
Caleta Burgoyne, 124
Caleta Calquemán, 60
Caleta Canaveral, 80
Caleta Cascada (Isla Capitán Aracena), 140
Caleta Cascada (Isla Diego Portales), 118
Caleta Chacabuco, 103
Caleta Chandler, 117
Caleta Charlotte, 77
Caleta Chica, 11, 84, 88-9
Caleta Chico, 146
Caleta Christiane, 69
Caleta Cifuncho, 16-17
Caleta Columbine, 116
Caleta Connor, 93-4
Caleta Cushion, 153-5
Caleta Dagny, 67
Caleta Dardé, 124
Caleta Descanso, 70
Caleta El Cobre, 15
Caleta Elena, 102-3
Caleta Equinoccio, 62
Caleta Escandallo, 146
Caleta Espinosa, 118
Caleta Eugenio, 162
Caleta Evening, 160
Caleta Fanny, 151-2
Caleta Feliz, 90
Caleta Ferrari, 162
Caleta Frog, 152
Caleta Gallant, 137
Caleta Galvarino, 74-6
Caleta Gato (Península de Taitao), 81
Caleta Gato (Seno Aysén), 66
Caleta Godoy, 30
Caleta Gualas, 72
Caleta Guayusca, 30
Caleta Hale, 84, 92
Caleta Hidden, 139, 140
Caleta Hoskyn, 97
Caleta Ideal, 84, 88
Caleta Ivonne, 95
Caleta Jacqueline, 77
Caleta Julia, 156
Caleta Lameguapi, 29
Caleta Latitud, 112
Caleta Lennox, 170
Caleta León, 171-2
Caleta Letier, 162
Caleta Lientur, 170, 171
Caleta Linlinao, 43-4
Caleta Lliuco, 30
Caleta Lobato, 80
Caleta Los Baños, 38
Caleta Louis, 135, 139, 147, 148
Caleta Lucas, 98
Caleta Luna, 106-7
Caleta Lynch (Canal Costa), 69
Caleta Lynch (Isla Damas), 18

Caleta Malacca, 99
Caleta Manzano, 37
Caleta Maris Stella, 101
Caleta Martial, 171
Caleta Martin, 36
Caleta Mediodia, 160
Caleta Milagro, 29
Caleta Monono, 82
Caleta Moonlight Shadow, 113-15
Caleta Morgane, 74
Caleta Morning, 160
Caleta Mostyn, 130-31
Caleta Nassi Bal, 102
Caleta Notch, 131, 132
Caleta Ocasión, 115
Caleta Olea, 63
Caleta Olla, 161
Caleta Otter, 124
Caleta Parmelia, 147
Caleta Paroquet, 108
Caleta Patch, 80
Caleta Patillos, 13
Caleta Pelagic, 110-11
Caleta Playa Parda, 131
Caleta Point Lay, 93
Caleta Porcelana, 42-3
Caleta Pozo de Chumildén, 43
Caleta Primera, 71
Caleta Rachas, 127-9
Caleta Rayo, 109
Caleta Refugio, 103-4
Caleta Ricardo, 60, 61
Caleta Richmond, 103
Caleta Rilán, 42
Caleta San Tomás, 83
Caleta Sandy, 103
Caleta Sepulcro, 64-5
Caleta Silva Palma, 49
Caleta Sonia, 161-2
Caleta Suárez, 82
Caleta Sur (Isla Chair), 153-5
Caleta Sylvia, 129
Caleta Tadpole, 56
Caleta Tarmac, 135, 148, 150
Caleta Telele, 39
Caleta Teokita, 125
Caleta Tortel, 90-91
Caleta Totoralillo, 19
Caleta Trana, 26
Caleta Victoria, 116-17
Caleta Villarrica, 110
Caleta Vittorio, 96, 97
Caleta White Kelp, 94-5
Caleta Zorro, 117
Calquemán, Caleta, 60
Calvo, Estero, 110-11
Cambaceres, Bahía, 167
Camello, Punta, 67
Canal, Isla, 61, 62
Canal Acwalisnan, 85, 134, 138-9
Canal Baker, 90-91
Canal Ballenero, 151-3
Canal Bárbara, 85, 134, 135-7
Canal Beagle, 153, 155, 156-69
Canal Brecknock, 150-51
Canal Chacabuco, 74, 77
Canal Chacao, 29, 33
Canal Chidguapi, 34
Canal Chiguo, 48
Canal Cockburn, 134-5, 146-50
Canal Concepcíon, 105-7
Canal Costa, 69, 70
Canal Darwin, 74
Canal Errazuriz, 77
Canal Escape, 101
Canal Gabriel, 85
Canal Grappler, 101
Canal Hornopiren, 38
Canal Icy, 101
Canal Inocentes, 105, 108-9
Canal Jacaf, 56
Canal Jerónimo, 133
Canal Kirke, 117, 118
Canal Laitec, 48
Canal Magdalena, 85, 134-5, 144-6
Canal Malacca, 99
Canal Martinez, 90
Canal Messier, 84, 88-9, 92-7
Canal Moraleda, 55-6
Canal Morla Vicuña, 117
Canal Murray, 156
Canal Nuevo, 143
Canal Ocasión, 150
Canal Perez Norte, 55, 56
Canal Perez Sur, 55, 61
Canal Pitt, 105, 107, 108
Canal Pomar, 153
Canal Pulluche, 74, 77
Canal Puquitín, 51
Canal Queilén, 46
Canal San Pedro, 49
Canal Sarmiento, 105, 109, 112, 113-15
Canal Skorpios, 58
Canal Smyth, 122-5
Canal Valdes, 119
Canal White, 117
Canal Wide, 102-5
Canal de Yal, 44
Canal Yelcho, 48
canales, 2
Canaveral, Caleta, 80
Canning, Isla, 106-7
Cañon, Bahía del, 142
Cape Horn, 171, 172
Capitán Aracena, Isla, 139-40, 144-6
car hire, 8
Carlos III, Isla, 133-4
Carreras, Puerto, 142
Carretera Austral, 90, 91
Carrizal Bajo, Puerto, 18
Cascada, Caleta (Isla Capitán Aracena), 140
Cascada, Caleta (Isla Diego Portales), 118
Castro, 41-2
Chacabuco, Bahía, 67
Chacabuco, Caleta, 103
Chacabuco, Canal, 74, 77
Chacabuco, Puerto, 67-9
Chacao, Canal, 29, 33
Chair, Isla, 153-5
Chaitén, 47
Chandler, Caleta, 117
Charlotte, Caleta, 77
Charrúa, Puerto, 105
charts, 5, 6, 184-6
Chatham, Isla, 107-8
Chaular, Estero, 31
Chaulincc, Isla, 44
Chica, Caleta (Arica), 11
Chica, Caleta (Isla Schröder), 84, 88-9
Chico, Caleta, 146
Chico, Seno, 146
Chiconal, 66
Chidguapi, Canal, 34
Chiguo, Canal, 48
Chiloé, Isla de, 2
Chinnock, Isla, 98
Cholgo, Rada Potreros de, 38
Chonchi, Puerto, 44
Chonos, Archipiélago de, 2
Christiane, Caleta, 69
Chumildén, Caleta Pozo de, 43
Cifuncho, Caleta, 16
Cinco Hermanos, Islas, 66
Clarence, Isla, 147-8
Clemente, Isla, 78
Cobre, Caleta El, 15
Cockburn, Canal, 134-5, 146-50
Coliumo, Bahía, 24
Collingwood, Estrecho de, 116-17
Colocla, Isla, 49, 50
Colonia Grande, Estero, 69
Columbine, Caleta, 116
communications, 7
Concepción, Bahía de, 25
Concepción, Canal, 105-7
Concón, 22-3
Concoto, Isla, 56
Condell, Puerto, 117
Cóndor, Estero, 133
Cóndor, Puerto (Canal Jerónimo), 133
Cóndor, Puerto (Seno Ultima Esperanza), 121
Connor, Caleta, 93-4
Contramaestre, Isla, 142
Contreras, Puerto, 91
Coquimbo, 19-20
Corbeta Papudo, Bahía, 107
Córdova, Península, 131-3
Cormorant, Estero, 131
Corral, Bahía, 26
Corral, Puerto, 26, 28
Costa, Canal, 69, 70
Covadonga, Puerto, 83
cruising season, 5
Cueri-Cueri, Puerto, 91-2
Cumberland, Bahía, 174
Cupquelan, Estero, 71
Cuptana, Isla, 60, 61
Cuptana, Puerto, 60
currency, 6-7
currents, 4
Cushion, Caleta, 153-5
Customs (Aduana), 175-6
Cuthbert, Abra, 93

Dagny, Caleta, 67
Dalcahue, 40-41
Damas, Isla, 18
Dardé, Caleta, 124
Darwin, Canal, 74
Dean, Puerto, 135
Descanso, Caleta, 70
Desengaño, Bahía, 119
Desolación, Isla, 129-31
Desventuradas, Islas, 2
Diego, Isla, 147
Diego Portales, Isla, 118
Diego Ramirez, Islas, 172
Dique, Estero, 33
direction finding stations, 179-80
Dock, Estero, 104
Dorada, Bahía, 57
Drummond Hay, Isla, 106
Dumas, Península, 162
Dungeness, Punta, 140-42, 143

Easter, Bahía, 119
Easter Island, *see* Isla de
Eberhardt, Estero, 121
Edén, Puerto, 87, 88, 99-101
Edgeworth, Cabo, 135
El Cobre, Caleta, 15
El Nino, 4
Elefantes, Estuario, 70
Elefantes, Golfo, 72
Elena, Caleta, 102-3
Elisa, Península, 64
Elizabeth, Bahía, 102
Engaño, Puerto, 153
Ensenada Villarino, 165
Equinoccio, Caleta, 62
Errazuriz, Canal, 77
Escandallo, Caleta, 146
Escape, Canal, 101
Escondido, Puerto (Bahía Tictoc), 50
Escondido, Puerto (Isla Wager), 84, 88
España, Seno, 158
Español, Puerto, 167-8
Espinosa, Caleta, 118
Estero Amalia, 110
Estero Arboles Espectrales, 60
Estero Balladares, 77, 78
Estero Bonito, 38
Estero Cahuelmo, 39
Estero Calvo, 110-11
Estero Chaular, 31
Estero Colonia Grande, 69
Estero Cóndor, 133
Estero Cormorant, 131
Estero Cupquelan, 71
Estero Dique, 33
Estero Dock, 104
Estero Eberhardt, 121
Estero Gori, 74
Estero Huildad, 47
Estero Huito, 34
Estero Ichuac, 44
Estero Leptepu, 42
Estero Mechai, 47
Estero Mitchell, 91
Estero Montenegro, 91
Estero Odger, 70, 71
Estero Pailad, 46
Estero Peel, 105, 109-12, 113
Estero Pellú, 44-5
Estero Picalito, 56-7
Estero Pichicolou, 37
Estero Pillan, 43
Estero Piti-Palena, 53-4
Estero Plainsong, 108
Estero Playa Parda, 131
Estero Quintupeu, 39
Estero Quitralco, 70
Estero Reñihue, 43
Estero Ringdove, 103
Estero Sangra, 65-6
Estero Slight, 83
Estero Sur (Isla Canal), 61
Estero Ultima Esperanza, 121
Estero Yaldad, 48
Estrecho de Collingwood, 116-17
Estrecho de Magallanes, 127-43
Estrecho de la Maire, 168
Estuario Elefantes, 70
Eugenia, Puerto, 169

Eugenio, Caleta, 162
Evans, Isla, 113
Evening, Caleta, 160
Exmouth, Seno, 102
Exploradores, Bahía, 71
Eyre, Seno, 102

Fairway, Islote, 126
Fanny, Caleta, 151-2
Farquhar, Isla, 93-4
Feliz, Caleta, 90
Ferrari, Caleta, 162
festivals, 8
Figueroa, Isla, 107
Filomena, Isla, 59
Florencia, Isla, 61
Focus, Isla, 120
Fondeadero Aguila, 172
Fondeadero Mackerel, 104
Fondeadero Oreste, 172
Fontaine, Puerto, 117, 118
formalities, 5, 175-7
Fort Bulnes, 142
Fortescue, Bahía, 137-8
Fortuna, Bahía (Isla Baverstock), 123
Fortuna, Puerto (Isla Londonderry), 153
Francisco, Puerto, 84, 89
Fresia, Península, 89
Frog, Caleta, 152
Froward, Cabo, 140, 144

Gable Island, 167-8
Gabriel, Canal, 85
Gallant, Caleta, 137
Gallegos, Península, 80
Galvarino, Caleta (Isla Quemada), 74-6
Galverino, Isla (Canal Perez Sur), 62
Garibaldi, Seno, 155-6
Gato, Caleta (Península de Taitao), 81
Gato, Caleta (Seno Aysén), 66
gear and supplies, 6
Gemmel, Isla, 56
Gente Grande, Bahía, 143
geography, 2-3
glossary, 186-8
Godoy, Caleta, 30
Golfo Almirante Montt, 119
Golfo Elefantes, 72
Golfo de Peñas, 84
Golfo de Tres Montes, 83
Golfo Trinidad, 104
Gonzalo, Isla, 172
Goree, Paso, 156
Gori, Estero, 74
Grappler, Canal, 101
Grappler, Puerto, 101-2
Gray, Puerto, 96, 97
Guaitecas, 51
Gualas, Caleta, 72
Guanaquero, Bahía, 21
Guardian Brito, Isla, 135
Guarello, Isla, 107
Guayacán, 19-20
Guayusca, Caleta, 30
Guerrero, Isla, 78
Guía, Angostura, 105, 109

Hale, Caleta, 84, 92
Halt, Bahía, 96, 97
Hambre, Paso del, 140-42
Hambre, Puerto del, 142
Hanga Anakena, 173
Hanga Hotuitu, 173
Hanga Pika, 173
Hanga Roa, 173
Hanga Vinapu, 173
Hanover, Isla, 109, 112
Harberton, Puerto, 167
health, 8
heating, 88
Helado, Seno, 135-7
Hermite, Isla, 170, 171
Herradura de Guayacán, Bahía, 19-20
Hershel, Isla, 171
Hidden, Caleta, 139, 140
Higuerillas, 22-3
holidays, public, 8
Hope, Puerto, 144
Hoppner, Seno, 83
Horn, Cape, 171, 172
Hornopiren, Canal, 38
Hornos, Isla, 171-2
Hose, Isla, 124
Hoskyn, Caleta, 97
Hoste, Isla, 162
Huasco, Puerto, 18, 19
Hueihue, Bahía, 37
Huellonquen, Bahía, 48
Huelmo, Isla, 35
Huequi, Peninsula, 39
Hugh, Bahía, 107
Huichas, Isla Las, 63
Huildad, Estero, 47
Huite, Puerto, 38-9
Huito, Estero, 34
Humos, Isla, 77
Hunter, Isla, 116
hydrographic information, 5-6

Iceberg, Seno, 95-6
Ichuac, Estero, 44
Icy, Canal, 101
Ideal, Caleta, 84, 88
immigration, 175
importing equipment, 175-6
Inchemó, Isla, 79
Inglés, Paso (Straits of Magallan), 133-4
Inglés, Puerto (Isla Chiloé), 31-3
Inglesa, Angostura, 97-8
Inocentes, Canal, 105, 108-9
Iquique, 12-13
Isabel, Isla, 143
Isla Adelaide, 148, 150
Isla Alberto Vargas, 91
Isla Alejandro Selkirk, 174
Isla Amita, 55, 56
Isla Apiao, 44-5
Isla Autin, 39
Isla Bartolome, 172
Isla Baverstock, 123
Isla Benjamin, 60
Isla Brecknock, 150
Isla Brinkley, 105, 122
Isla Burnt, 151
Isla Buta Chauques, 39-40
Isla Cailín, 48-9
Isla Canal, 61, 62
Isla Canning, 106-7
Isla Capitán Aracena, 139-40, 144-6
Isla Carlos III, 133-4
Isla Chair, 153-5
Isla Chatham, 107-8
Isla Chaulinec, 44
Isla Chinnock, 98
Isla Clarence, 147, 148
Isla Clemente, 78
Isla Colocla, 49, 50
Isla Concoto, 56
Isla Contramaestre, 142
Isla Cuptana, 60, 61
Isla Damas, 18
Isla Desolación, 129-31
Isla Diego, 147
Isla Diego Portales, 118
Isla Drummond Hay, 106
Isla Evans, 113
Isla Farquhar, 93-4
Isla Figueroa, 107
Isla Filomena, 59
Isla Florencia, 61
Isla Focus, 120
Isla Gable, 167-8
Isla Galverino, 62
Isla Gemmel, 56
Isla Gonzalo, 172
Isla Guardian Brito, 135
Isla Guarello, 107
Isla Guerrero, 78
Isla Hanover, 109, 112
Isla Hermite, 170, 171
Isla Hershel, 171
Isla Hornos, 171-2
Isla Hose, 124
Isla Hoste, 162
Isla Huelmo, 35
Isla Humos, 77
Isla Hunter, 116
Isla Inchemó, 79
Isla Isabel, 143
Isla Ismael, 120
Isla Jéchica, 58-9
Isla King, 147
Isla Larenas, 63
Isla Larga, 79
Isla Las Huichas, 63
Isla Lennox, 170
Isla Little Wellington, 93
Isla Llancahué, 38
Isla Londonderry, 153
Isla Macias, 151
Isla Magdalena, 57, 60, 62
Isla Malomacun, 38
Isla Mancera, 26, 28
Isla Manuel, 57, 58
Isla Manuel Rodrigues, 124-5
Isla Manzano, 36, 37
Isla Marcacci, 76
Isla Marimeli, 36
Isla Mechuque, 40
Isla Melchor, 64-5
Isla Mornington, 104
Isla Nalcayec, 70
Isla Navarino, 165-7, 169
Isla Newton, 116
Isla Orestes, 63
Isla Orlebar, 84, 92
Isla de Pascua, 2, 3, 173-4
Isla Penguin, 89, 90
Isla Piazzi, 113-15
Isla Picton, 169, 170
Isla Providencia, 129
Isla Quehui, 45, 46
Isla Quemada, 74-6
Isla Rivero, 76-8
Isla Robinson Crusoe, 174
Isla Santa Ines, 135, 137
Isla Schröder, 84, 88-9
Isla Spider, 133
Isla Stewart, 151
Isla Stratford, 106
Isla Tamar, 122, 127-9
Isla Tangbac, 62
Isla Taucolon, 40
Isla Teresa, 62
Isla Tópar, 105
Isla Traiguón, 69
Isla Valverde, 56-7
Isla Vittorio, 96, 97
Isla Wager, 84, 88
Isla Wellington, 97, 103-4
Isla Wet, 135
Isla Zealous, 92
Island, Puerto, 92-3
Islas, Bahía, 54-5
Islas Cinco Hermanos, 66
Islas del Medio, 152
Islas Desventuradas, 2
Islas Diego Ramirez, 172
Islas Otter, 123-4
Islas Rennell, 122
Islas Wollaston, 170, 171
Islote Fairway, 126
Islotes Ruiz, Bahía, 72
Ismael, Isla, 120
Isthmus, Bahía, 123
Ivonne, Caleta, 95

Jacaf, Canal, 56
Jacqueline, Caleta, 77
Jéchica, Isla, 58-9
Jerónimo, Canal, 133
Juan Fernandez, Archipiélago de, 2, 174
Juan Yates, Puerto, 50
Julia, Caleta, 156

kelp, 85
King, Isla, 147
King, Puerto, 147
Kirke, Angostura, 118
Kirke, Canal, 117, 118

La Vega, Surgidero, 34
Laforest, Puerto, 121
Laguna Byron, 88
Laguna San Rafael, 73
Laitec, Canal, 48
Lake District, Chilean, 2, 27, 36
Lameguapi, Caleta, 29
Lampazo, Puerto, 62
languages, 1, 176-7, 186-8
Larenas, Isla, 63
Larga, Isla, 79
Largo, Paso, 129-31
Las Huichas, Isla, 63
Las Montañas, Península, 117-18
Lastarria, Puerto, 119
Latitud, Caleta, 112
Lecky's Retreat, Abra, 115
Lennox, Caleta, 170
Lennox, Isla, 170
León, Caleta, 171-2
Leptepu, Estero, 42
Letier, Caleta, 162
Liberta, Bahía, 96
Lientur, Caleta, 170, 171
lighthouses, 3, 6
lights, 5-6
Linao, Bahía, 37
Linlinao, Caleta, 43-4
Little Wellington, Isla, 93
Llancahué, Isla, 38
Lliuco, Caleta, 30

Lobato, Caleto, 80
Londonderry, Isla, 153
Los Baños, Caleta, 38
Louis, Caleta, 135, 139, 147, 148
Lucas, Caleta, 98
Luna, Caleta, 106-7
Lynch, Caleta (Canal Costa), 69
Lynch, Caleta (Isla Damas), 18

Macias, Isla, 151
Mackerel, Fondeadero, 104
Magallanes, Estrecho de, 127-43
Magdalena, Canal, 85, 134-5, 144-6
Magdalena, Isla, 57, 60, 62
mail, 7
Maire, Estrecho de la, 168
Malacca, Caleta, 99
Mallet, Bahía, 123
Malomacun, Isla, 38
Manao, Bahía, 37
Mancera, Isla, 26, 28
Manuel, Isla, 57, 58
Manuel Rodrigues, Isla, 124-5
Manzano, Caleta, 37
Manzano, Isla, 36, 37
Marcacci, Isla, 76
Mardon, Puerto, 122, 123
marea roja, see red tide
Marimeli, Isla, 36
Marina Jarpa, Puerto, 90
Maris Stella, Caleta, 101
Martial, Caleta, 171
Martin, Caleta, 36
Martinez, Canal, 90
Martinez, Seno, 146
Maullín, River, 70
Maxwell, Puerto, 171
Mayne, Puerto, 113
Mechai, Estero, 47
Mechuque, Isla, 40
Medio, Islas del, 152
Mediodia, Caleta, 160
Mejillones del Sur, 14
Melchor, Isla, 64-5
Melinka, 51-3
Messier, Canal, 84, 88-9, 92-7
Milagro, Caleta, 29
Millabu, Puerto, 78-9
Mischief, Angostura, 111-12
Mitchell, Estero, 91
Molyneux, Puerto, 106
money, 6-7
Monono, Caleta, 82
Montañas, Península Las, 117-18
Montenegro, Estero, 91
Montt, Puerto, 35
Moonlight Shadow, Caleta, 113-15
Moraleda, Canal, 55-6
Morgane, Caleta, 74
Morla Vicuña, Canal, 117
Morning, Caleta, 160
Mornington, Isla, 104
Morris, Bahía, 146
Mostyn, Caleta, 130-31
Muñoz Gamero, Península, 123-4
Murray, Canal, 156
Mussel, Bahía, 134

Nalcayec, Isla, 70
Nassau, Bahía, 170
Nassi Bal, Caleta, 102
Natales, Puerto, 87, 88, 117, 120-21
natural history, 181-2
Navarino, Isla, 165-7, 169
Navarino, Puerto, 162-3
NAVTEX, 177
Navy (Armada), 1, 175-7
Newton, Isla, 116
Niemann, Puerto, 135, 148
Notch, Caleta, 131, 132
Nuevo, Canal, 143
Nutland, Puerto, 135, 137

Ocasión, Caleta (Isla Piazzi), 115
Ocasión, Canal, 150
Ocasión, Seno, 150
Odger, Estero, 70, 71
Olea, Caleta, 63
Olla, Caleta, 161
Omega, Pozo, 83
Oreste, Fondeadero, 172
Orestes, Isla 63
Orlebar, Isla 84, 92
O'Ryan, Paso, 134, 138-9
Otter, Caleta, 124
Otter, Islas, 123-4

Pacific offshore route, 4
Pailad, Estero, 46
Paine, Torres del, 117
Palena, Rada de, 53-4
Pan de Azúcar, Puerto, 17
Papudo, Puerto, 21
Parmelia, Caleta, 147
Paroquet, Caleta, 108
Pascua, Isla de, 2, 3
Paso del Abismo, 101
Paso Aguirre, Puerto, 150-51
Paso Brassey, 105
Paso Goree, 156
Paso del Hambre, 140-42
Paso Inglés, 133-4
Paso Largo, 129-31
Paso O'Ryan, 134, 138-9
Paso Piloto Pardo, 101
Paso Quesahuén, 71
Paso Roda, 127
Paso Shag, 135
Paso Tortuoso, 131
Paso Victoria, 122
Patch, Caleta, 80
Patillos, Caleta, 13
Patos, Río de, 72-3
Pedregoso, Pozo, 58-9
Pedro, Seno, 134, 138, 139
Peel, Estero, 105, 109-12, 113
Pelagic, Caleta, 110-11
Pellú, Estero, 44-5
Peñas, Golfo de, 84
Penguin, Isla, 89, 90
Península Brecknock, 150
Península Brunswick, 137-8, 142
Península Córdova, 131-3
Península Dumas, 162
Península Elisa, 64
Península Fresia, 89
Península Gallegos, 80
Península Huequi, 39
Península Las Montañas, 117-18
Península Muñoz Gamero, 123-4
Península Skyring, 80
Península Swett, 92-3
Península de Taitao, 79, 81-2
Península Tamar, 129
Península Ulloa, 133
Península Wilcock, 110
Península Zach, 123
Perez, Canal, 55, 56
Perez, Puerto, 66
Pia, Seno, 158-9
Piazzi, Isla, 113-15
Picalito, Estero, 56-7
Pichicolou, Estero, 37
Picton, Isla, 169, 170
Pillan, Estero, 43
Piloto Pardo, Paso, 101
pilots and charts, 5, 6
PIM (Posición e Intención de Movimiento), 176-7
Pindo, Puerto, 45, 46
Pisagua, Bahía, 11-12
Piti-Palena, Estero, 53-4
Pitt, Canal, 105, 107, 108
Plainsong, Estero, 108
plants, 181
Playa Parda, Caleta, 131
Playa Parda Chica, 131
Point Lay, Caleta, 93
Policía Internacional, 175
Pomar, Canal, 153
Porcelana, Caleta, 42-3
ports of entry, 175
Porvenir, Bahía (Tierra del Fuego), 142
Porvenir, Punta (Canal Jacaf), 56
Posición e Intención de Movimiento (PIM), 176-7
postal services, 7
Potreros de Cholgo, Rada, 38
Pozo de Chumildén, Caleta, 43
Pozo Omega, 83
Pozo Pedregoso, 58-9
Primera, Caleta, 71
Profundo, Puerto, 124-5
Providencia, Isla, 129
provisions, 7
public holidays, 8
Puerto Abtao, 33, 34
Puerto Aguirre, 63-4
Puerto Alert, 104
Puerto Americano, 62, 63
Puerto Angamos, 83
Puerto Angosto, 129-31
Puerto Barroso, 83
Puerto Bonito, 70
Puerto Buena, 61
Puerto Bueno (Canal Sarmiento), 113
Puerto Bueno (Isla Florencia), 61
Puerto Caldera, 17-18
Puerto Carreras, 142
Puerto Carrizal Bajo, 18
Puerto Chacabuco, 67-9
Puerto Charrúa, 105
Puerto Chonchi, 44
Puerto Condell, 117
Puerto Cóndor (Canal Jerónimo), 133
Puerto Cóndor (Seno Ultima Esperanza), 121
Puerto Contreras, 91
Puerto Corral, 26, 28
Puerto Covadonga, 83
Puerto Cueri-Cueri, 91-2
Puerto Cuptana, 60
Puerto Dean, 135
Puerto Edén, 87, 88, 99-101
Puerto Engaño, 153
Puerto Escondido (Bahía Tictoc), 50
Puerto Escondido (Isla Wager), 84, 88
Puerto Español, 167-8
Puerto Eugenia, 169
Puerto Fontaine, 117, 118
Puerto Fortuna (Isla Londonderry), 153
Puerto Francisco, 84, 89
Puerto Grappler, 101-2
Puerto Gray, 96, 97
Puerto del Hambre, 142
Puerto Harberton, 167
Puerto Hope, 144
Puerto Huasco, 18, 19
Puerto Huite, 38-9
Puerto Inglés, 31-3
Puerto Island, 92-3
Puerto Juan Yates, 50
Puerto King, 147
Puerto Laforest, 121
Puerto Lampazo, 62
Puerto Lastarria, 119
Puerto Mardon, 122, 123
Puerto Marina, Jarpa, 90
Puerto Maxwell, 171
Puerto Mayne, 113
Puerto Melinka, 51-3
Puerto Millabu, 78-9
Puerto Molyneux, 106
Puerto Montt, 35
Puerto Natales, 87, 88, 117, 120-21
Puerto Navarino, 162-3
Puerto Niemann, 135, 148, 149
Puerto Nutland, 135, 137
Puerto Pan de Azúcar, 17
Puerto Papudo, 21
Puerto Paso Aguirre, 150-51
Puerto Perez, 66
Puerto Pindo, 45, 46
Puerto Profundo, 124-5
Puerto Puyuguapi, 57
Puerto Queilén, 46-7
Puerto Quellón, 47-8
Puerto Refugio, 79-80
Puerto Río Frío, 101
Puerto Rosita, 64
Puerto San Antonio, 24
Puerto San Pedro, 49
Puerto Santo Domingo, 55
Puerto Simpson, 98
Puerto Slight, 83
Puerto Soffia, 147
Puerto Taltal, 16
Puerto Tamar, 129
Puerto Tictoc, 49-50
Puerto Tocopilla, 13-14
Puerto Toro, 169
Puerto Voigue, 40
Puerto Williams, 87, 88, 165-7
Puerto Yates, 76
Puerto Yungay, 91
Pulluche, Canal, 74, 77
Punta Alfredo, Surgidero, 143
Punta Arenas, 87, 88, 141, 142
Punta Camello, 67

Punta Dungeness, 140-42, 143
Punta Porvenir, 56
Punta Rouse, 63
Punta Yal, 46
Punta Yawl, 169
Puquitín, Canal, 51
Puyuguapi, Puerto, 57

QTH, 176-7
Quehui, Isla, 45, 46
Queilén, Canal, 46
Queilén, Puerto, 46-7
Quellón, Puerto, 47-8
Quemada, Isla, 74-6
Quemchi, 39
Quesahuén, Bahía, 71-2
Quesahuén, Paso, 71
Quintero, Bahía, 21
Quintupeu, Estero, 39
Quitralco, Estero, 70

Rachas, Caleta, 127-9
Rada de Palena, 53-4
Rada Potreros de Cholgo, 38
radio, 7, 178-9
BBC World Service, 180
rail transport, 8
rain, 3
Ralún, Bahía, 37
Rapa Nui, *see* Isla de Pascua
Ráper, Cabo, 83
Rappel, Bajo, 24
Rayo, Caleta, 109
RDF beacons, 6
red tide (marea roja), 7, 59
Refugio, Caleta (Isla Wellington), 103-4
Refugio, Puerto (Bahía Anna Pink), 79-80
Relegada, Bahía, 167
Reloncaví, Seno, 36
Reñihue, Estero, 43
Rennell, Islas, 122
rescue services, 6
Ricardo, Caleta, 60, 61
Richmond, Caleta, 103
Rilán, Caleta, 42
Ringdove, Estero, 103
Río Baker, 90-92
Río Frío, Puerto, 101
Río de Patos, 72-3
Río Serrano, 122
Río Témpanos, 72-3
Rivero, Isla, 76-8
Robinson Crusoe, Isla, 174
Roda, Paso, 127
Romanche, Bahía, 160
Rosita, Puerto, 64
Rouse, Punta, 63
routes, 4-5

safety, 6
salmon farms, 31
San Andrés, Bahía, 81-2
San Andrés, Seno, 105
San Antonio, Puerto, 24
San Juan de la Posesión (Fort Bulnes), 142
San Nicolás, Bahía, 142
San Pedro, Bahía (S of Valdivia), 30
San Pedro, Canal (Isla Chiloé), 49
San Pedro, Puerto (Isla Chiloé), 49
San Quentín, Bahía, 83-4
San Rafael, Laguna, 73
San Tomás, Caleta, 83
San Vicente, Bahía, 25
Sandy, Caleta, 103
Sangra, Estero, 65-6
Santa Ines, Isla, 135, 137
Santo Domingo, Puerto, 55
Sarmiento, Canal, 105, 109, 112, 113-15
Schröder, Isla, 84, 88-9
Scourfield, Bahía, 170, 171
sea, 4
Sea Lion Bay, 111
sea mammals, 182
search and rescue, 6
season, cruising, 5
security, 6
Seno Almirantazgo, 85
Seno Antrim, 102-3
Seno Aysén, 65-9
Seno Baker, 84, 89
Seno Chico, 146
Seno España, 158
Seno Exmouth, 102
Seno Eyre, 102
Seno Garibaldi, 155-6
Seno Helado, 135-7
Seno Hoppner, 83
Seno Iceberg, 95-6
Seno Martinez, 146
Seno Ocasión, 150
Seno Pedro, 134, 138, 139
Seno Pia, 158-9
Seno Reloncaví, 36
Seno San Andrés, 105
Seno Ultima Esperanza, 117, 122
Seno Union, 117-18
Seno Ventisquero (Canal Pomar), 153
Seno Ventisquero, (Puerto Puyuguapi), 57
Sepulcro, Caleta, 64-5
Serrano, Río, 122
Shag, Paso, 135
shellfish, 7, 59
ship's stores, 7
shorelines, 180-81
Silva Palma, Caleta, 49
Simpson, Puerto, 98
Skorpios, Canal, 58
Skyring, Península, 80
Slight, Estero, 83
Slight, Puerto, 83
Smyth, Canal, 122-5
Soffia, Puerto, 147
Sonia, Caleta, 161-2
Sotomo, Bahía, 36
Spider, Isla, 133
Steamer Duck Lagoon, 107, 108
Stewart, Isla, 151
Straits of Magallan, 127-43
Stratford, Isla, 106
Suárez, Caleta, 82
supplies and gear, 7
Sur, Caleta (Isla Chair), 153-5
Sur, Estero (Isla Canal), 61
Surgidero Allard, 118
Surgidero La Vega, 34
Surgidero Punta Alfredo, 143
Swett, Península, 92-3
Sylvia, Caleta, 129

Tadpole, Caleta, 56
Taitao, Península de, 79, 81-2
Talcahuano, 25
Taltal, Puerto, 16
Tamar, Isla, 122, 127-9
Tamar, Península, 129
Tamar, Puerto, 129
Tangbac, Isla, 62
Tarmac, Caleta, 135, 148, 150
Taucolon, Isla, 40
taxis, 8
Telele, Caleta, 39
telephones, 7
Témpanos, Río, 72-3
temperatures, 3
Teokita, Caleta, 125
Teresa, Isla, 62
Tictoc, Bahía, 49-50
Tictoc, Puerto, 49-50
tides, 4
Tierra del Fuego, 142, 143, 146, 163-5, 167-8
Tilly, Bahía, 133-4
time (standard/summer), 7
timing (cruising season), 5
Tocopilla, Puerto, 13-14
Tom, Bahía, 106
Tongoy, Bahía, 20-21
Tópar, Isla, 105
Toro, Puerto, 169
Torres del Paine, 117, 121
Tortel, Caleta, 90-91
Tortuoso, Paso, 131
Totoralillo, Caleta, 19
Traiguén, Isla, 69
Trana, Caleta, 26
transport, 7-8
Tres Brazos, Bahía, 156
Tres Montes, Golfo de, 83
Trinidad, Golfo, 104
tsunamis, 4

Ulloa, Península, 133
Ultima Esperanza, Estero, 121
Ultima Esperanza, Seno, 122
Union, Seno, 117-18
Ushuaia, 87, 88, 163-5

Valdes, Canal, 119
Valdivia, 2, 26-9
Valparaíso, 23
Valverde, Isla, 56-7
Vega, Surgidero La, 34
Ventisquero, Seno (Canal Pomar), 153
Ventisquero, Seno (Puerto Puyuguapi), 57
VHF, coast radio stations, 7, 178-9
VHF, weather forecasts, 3, 177
Victoria, Caleta, 116-17
Victoria, Paso, 122
Villarica, 27
Villarino, Ensenada, 165
Villarrica, Caleta, 110
Viña del Mar, 22-3
Vittorio, Caleta, 96, 97
Vittorio, Isla, 96, 97
Voigue, Puerto, 40

Wager, Isla, 84, 88
weather, 3
weather, forecasts, 3, 177-8
Weatherfax broadcasts, 177
Welcome, Bahía, 122, 123
Wellington, Isla, 97, 103-4
Wet, Isla, 135
White, Canal, 117
White Kelp Bay, 94-5
Whitsand, Bahía, 143
Wickham, Boca, 74, 79
Wide, Canal, 102-5
Wilcock, Península, 110
Williams, Puerto, 165-7
winds, 3, 4
Wodsworth, Bahía, 129, 130
Wollaston, Isla, 170, 171
Woods, Bahía, 138

Yal, Canal de, 44
Yal, Punta, 46
Yaldad, Estero, 48
Yates, Puerto, 76
Yawl, Punta, 169
Yelcho, Canal, 48
Yendegaia, Bahía, 162
Yungay, Puerto, 91

Zach, Península, 123
zarpe, 5, 176
Zealous, Isla, 92
Zorro, Caleta, 117